Cooperation, Environment, and Sustainability in Border Regions

edited by

Paul Ganster

San Diego State University Press
Institute for Regional Studies of the Californias

2001

Contents

iv

List of Maps

Acknowledgments

Many individuals deserve recognition for their assistance on the production of this volume. Bronle Crosby, Alison McNee, and Bertha Hernández provided the copy editing, often made more challenging by issues of translation. The many maps and illustrations were created or redrawn by Sophia Habl, Harry Johnson, David Lindsay, and Paul Ganster. Alan Sweedler provided valuable suggestions in the organization of the book.

Many individuals and institutions assisted with the organization of the postconference field trip for the BRIT group. Charlotte Ochiqui, then Border Projects Coordinator at the Institute for Regional Studies of the Californias, helped develop the agenda for the field trip and coordinated local arrangements. Alison McNee and Bertha Hernández, also of the IRSC staff, provided assistance with the field trip. Rector Víctor Abel Beltrán Corona of the Autonomous University of Baja California provided significant support for the field trip following the conference, including briefings in Mexicali and Ensenada as well as transportation for the BRIT group. The dean of the UABC Ensenada campus, Ernesto Campos González, was helpful by arranging meetings with his faculty and co-sponsoring a public forum in Ensenada. Agustín Sández, Director of the Institute for Social Research of UABC in Mexicali organized and hosted a briefing on regional issues with researchers and private sector representatives. Dr. Jorge Santibáñez, President of El Colegio de la Frontera Norte, hosted a session and a reception at his campus in San Antonio de los Buenos. The mayor of Ensenada, Dr. Daniel Quintero, kindly organized a public forum that included members of the local private sector and local and state elected officials. Mike Wilken, director of the CUNA Foundation, arranged the meeting with members of the Pai Pai community of Santa Catarina. Finally, members of the Campo Band of Kumeyaay Indians and the Viejas Band of Mission Indians kindly met with participants during the field trip. Dr. Ricardo Félix, of the Viejas Casino, arranged a briefing and tour of the facilities at the Viejas reservation. The conference was supported by a generous grant from the William and Flora Hewlett Foundation and other assistance from the Southwest Center for Environmental Research and Policy.

I
Introduction

Cooperation, Environment, and Sustainability in Border Regions: Introduction and Overview

Paul Ganster[*]

This volume of essays is based on a selection of papers presented at the Border Regions in Transition (BRIT) III conference held in San Diego, California, in January 1999. The core of participants were members of an international network of border specialists known as the Border Regions in Transition group. Their first meeting was in Berlin in 1994 (Ganster et al. 1997) and the second meeting was held in Joensuu, Finland, on the Russian-Finnish border in 1997 (Eskelinen, Liikanen, and Oksa 1999). The third meeting was in 1999 in San Diego, California, and the fourth was held in northern India, hosted by Panjab University in Chandigarh, India, in 2000. The fifth meeting of the network was in 2001 in Tartu, Estonia.

Each of the meetings of the Border Regions in Transition network includes a multidisciplinary academic conference, presentations and interactions with local government officials and nongovernmental organizations, and a field trip for participants to a nearby border region. In this fashion, the academic researchers have sought to enrich their scientific perspectives through the combination of different disciplines and methodological perspectives, interaction with local experts, and research in the field. Not only have the participants been able to convey their research results to regional practitioners, but they have gained important insight from the regions that has strengthened future research efforts.

The meetings that produced the material for the present volume were held in San Diego and included a trip to Tijuana, Baja California, Mexico, for a session at El Colegio de la Frontera Norte, a research and graduate institute, and a tour through urban Tijuana. The post conference field trip took the participants across

* Ganster is director of the Institute for Regional Studies of the Californias at San Diego State University, San Diego, California, USA. The author wishes to thank Alan Sweedler for providing useful comments on a draft of this essay.

northern Baja California and the border areas of Southern California. The itinerary began with a visit to the Baja California port city of Ensenada, located some one hundred kilometers south of the border. There, researchers from the Autonomous University of Baja California (UABC), Ensenada, briefed the BRIT participants on regional issues and ongoing research activities. At Ensenada, the BRIT contingent also participated in a public forum on "Ensenada within the Framework of Border Cooperation" that was organized by UABC, local government, and the local private sector. This forum enabled BRIT members to hear about regional development issues from local business leaders, Ensenada mayor Dr. Daniel Quintero, university researchers, and members of the Baja California state legislature. At the same time, BRIT members Norris Clement (San Diego State University) and Heikki Eskelinen (University of Joensuu, Finland) made presentations on experiences in transborder cooperation from Europe and North America and how these might be relevant to Baja California.

Many border areas around the world have cultural and ethnic populations that have been separated from each other by the international boundary. BRIT field trip participants visited Native American groups, both in Baja California, Mexico, and California, USA. These groups have been isolated from each other since the establishment of the international boundary in 1848 through the middle of their traditional territories. In Baja California, the BRIT group piled into an old bus for a short trip off the paved highway to the Pai Pai Indian community at Santa Catarina, located in the mountains in the middle of the Baja California peninsula. At Santa Catarina, the group was briefed on local issues by the traditional cultural leader of the Pai Pai as well as by the elected political leader, Juan Albañez. Mike Wilken, of the Institute for Native Cultures (CUNA) in Ensenada, provided a background on the history of indigenous peoples in the Baja California-California border region. Later in the field trip, on the north side of the international boundary, the BRIT group met with representatives of the Campo Band of Kumeyaay Indians for a discussion of Native American issues led by personnel from the Campo Environmental Protection Agency and by traditional cultural leader Fidel Hyde. They also toured a wetlands restoration project in a high mountain valley using traditional land management techniques and technology. At the Viejas Band reservation, tribal leaders and managers provided a discussion of economic development activities of the group. These now include a gambling casino, a large outlet mall, and a recently purchased bank.

Through the field trip, then, the BRIT group was able to meet with related Native Americans from Baja California and Southern California. These groups ranged from those at Santa Catarina that are still practicing many traditional cultural and economic activities, including language, arts and crafts, and use of native plant foods to their more affluent relatives in the United States that are running large economic enterprises, yet have lost much of their traditional culture and language. For the past few years, the California and Baja California groups have been addressing the many issues related to physical separation from relatives caused by the international border. These include the political issue of obtaining the ability to move freely back and forth across the international boundary, economic development for the poorer Baja California groups, and re-introduction of native language and cultural features to Native Americans north of the border.

The field trip also stopped at San Felipe, a small tourist and fishing center on the Gulf of California to the south of Mexicali, the state capital of Baja California. In Mexicali, the BRIT researchers visited the Kenworth-Kenmex manufac-turing plant where heavy duty diesel trucks are assembled. Also in the state capital, the Autonomous University of Baja California, Mexicali campus, and the Industrial Development Commission of Mexicali organized a briefing forum on regional issues, including the regional economy, regional agricultural charac-teristics, migration, and industrial policy of Mexicali. Across the international boundary, in the Imperial Valley of California, the tour stopped at the Calexico campus of San Diego State University for a briefing on Imperial Valley issues by Dean Khosrow Fatemi, development officer John Rennison, and Andy Horne, one of the directors of the Imperial Irrigation District that manages one of the largest and most productive irrigation districts in the world.

These field tours have become an integral part of the BRIT periodic confer-ences. Participants have learned that interactions with practitioners help inform their research and also provide an important method for learning about other bor-der regions of the world. The field trips, in combination with the conferences, produce important synergies, enhancing the value of the events to the partici-pants.

The key themes of the San Diego BRIT meetings were transborder coopera-tion, border environmental concerns, and issues of sustainable development in border zones and these topics are reflected in the essays presented in the present volume. The first section of the book is this introductory essay that summarizes the essays and discusses central concepts and topics. The second section includes two articles on methodological and theoretical approaches to border research. Sections three through seven have essays grouped together by region, including the U.S.-Mexican border region, European borders, the Baltic region, Rus-sian-Finnish border regions, and Asian border regions.

Section two of the book, "Transboundary Collaboration: Conceptualization and Theoretical Considerations," has two essays. Norris Clement's "Interna-tional Transboundary Collaboration: A Policy-Oriented Conceptual Frame-work," develops a framework for helping practitioners and researchers better understand the changing functions of international boundaries and the basic ra-tionale behind the concept of transboundary collaboration. Using the concepts of cross-border linkages and asymmetries, he shows how these will lead to en-hanced interdependence within the context of open borders. Clement concludes with a suggestion for a common approach to analyzing borders in a comparative context. The second essay is Joachim Blatter's "Cross-Border Regions: A Step toward Sustainable Development? Experiences and Considerations from Exam-ples in Europe and North America." Blatter discusses the role of territorial integration and cooperation across political boundaries as facilitating or hindering efforts toward sustainable development based on experiences in the European Lake Constance and North American Cascadia regions.

The next section includes six essays that address issues of environment, quality of life, region building, and labor in the U.S.-Mexican border region. Francisco Lara, in "Cross-Border Partnerships for Environmental Management: The U.S.-Mexican Border Experience," notes that the building of cross-border partnerships is a strategy used by local organizational along the U.S.-Mexican border to cope with regional environmental problems. With increased prominence due to issues associated with the North American Free Trade Agreement (NAFTA), these partnerships now constitute collaborative arrangements that can be conceptualized as networks of interactions. Lara's study concentrates on these new cross-border alignments in the San Diego-Tijuana area of the U.S.-Mexican border. Samuel Schmidt also looks at cross-border partnerships, but for the El Paso-Ciudad Juárez area, in his essay "The Challenges of Region Building: The Paso del Norte Region." Schmidt notes the asymmetries inherent in this region and reviews their impact on cooperative ventures. He concludes with a call for binational integration from the bottom up to solve problems facing both sides of the border. Basilio Verduzco Chávez also addresses the issue of solving regional environmental problems, but from the perspective of the relationship between civil society and policies designed to solve borderlands environmental problems. Based on an analysis of border environmental conflicts, Verduzco Chávez explores the link between activism of civil society and outcomes of environmental diplomacy and policy.

Whereas the first three essays of this section dealing with the U.S.-Mexican border address themes related to environmental issues, the last three analyze social and labor issues. Joan B. Anderson, in "Trends in Quality-of-Life Indicators in U.S. and Mexican Border Regions, 1950–1990," examines census data for Mexican border municipalities and U.S. counties to present trends in population, income, poverty, and quality-of-life variables. She observes that after showing improvement during the 1970s, both sides of the border experienced an increase in poverty during the 1980s. In contrast, other indicators showed steady improvement from 1950 to 1990, although improvement slowed during the 1980s. Her essay suggests the central role that empirical indicators play in measuring the quality of human life and progress toward sustainable economies. The next essay provides a detailed analysis of some of the factors that comprise quality of life for one region of the U.S.-Mexican border. Arturo Ranfla G., Djamel Toudert, Guillermo Álvarez de la T., and Guadalupe Ortega V., in "An Exploratory Study of Urban Marginality in Baja California," explore the issue of social inequality in the face of the globalization process. The authors use urban basic geostatistic areas (AGEBs) to identify patterns of inequality within Baja California cities to understand the role that the border plays in the development of neighboring Mexican cities. They also compare these results to other Mexican border states and the nation as a whole. They consider their border-adjacent location and high rates of migration to be determinants of varying levels of marginalization. Their research results are quite significant since in the Mexican national context the northern border is widely viewed as affluent but they clearly document significant pockets of poverty within a relatively well off Mexican border region. Edward J. Williams and Joel Stillerman, in their article on unionization of the *maquiladora* (assembly plant) industry, examine the potential of the labor side accord to the North American Free Trade Agreement to become an effective tool in cross-border efforts to unionize this largely nonunion industry. They conclude that the labor side agreement may play an indirect role in promoting international alliances to support labor rights in Mexico.

Part four contains six papers that address issues of cooperation on environmental and health issues and on development policies and practices in a number of European border regions. "Social Movements and the Transborder Chloride Pollution of the Rhine River," by Emmanuelle Mühlenhöver, reconsiders the role of social actors, borders, and environmental rationales in the context of transborder environmental issues, using the case of the Rhine River. She concludes that the importance of these actors is often underestimated in setting the agenda for addressing transborder pollution issues. However, she cautions that environmental arguments often serve as covers for other rationales, whether economic, political, or strategic. Mühlenhöver's work also demonstrates how issues of transborder cooperation and environment become intimately bound up with social and political concerns. The next two essays focus on the Hungarian border regions. Imre Nagy looks at the environmental problems that face Hungary's seven border regions and the cross-border nature of pollutants in "Environmental Problems in the Seven Hungarian Border Regions." Nagy then discusses how these problems are being dealt with by different levels of government and across borders. He notes that in most cases, cross-border cooperation to improve the environment is being handled through international agreements and organizations, but local efforts are lacking. Ágnes Pál, in "Socioeconomic Processes in the Hungarian-Yugoslavian-Romanian Border Zone: Approaches to the Danube-Tizsa-Maros-Körös (DKMT) Euroregion," deals specifically with this Euroregion on the triple Hungarian-Yugoslavian-Romanian border. She points to the difficulties in constructing a successful region and conducting cooperative efforts due to economic, political, and social differences across borders. Pál also outlines how the three countries are attempting to overcome these difficulties to make the region prosper. Both Pál and Nagy reveal the difficulties that the formerly highly centralized nation encounters when attempting to develop local efforts to cooperate across the international border.

The last two essays of part four of the volume explore aspects of the Irish border. Derek Bond, Tom Frawley, and Charles Ferguson, in their essay "Cross-Border Development in Northern Ireland: A Focus on the Future," study the efforts of border peoples in Ireland to work together to find regional solutions to their historically and geographically different needs. Specifically, they examine the Cooperation and Working Together (CAWT) forum created for cross-border collaboration between health boards and how this experience might aid the further development of effective tools for the Irish border. They note the complexities of cross-border initiatives, even on such obvious areas as health, yet affirm the value of demonstrations such as CAWT. Adrian Moore and Gerard Parr also address the Irish border area, which, as they point out, has suffered particularly severe economic and social deprivation where peripherality and politically motivated violence have combined to retard economic growth. They analyze the development of Project BORDER, a telecommunications infrastructure project funded by the International Regions (INTERREG) II program of the European Union and designed to promote economic development by bringing information to individuals and companies, enabling them to become competitive in a wider European and world market. Based on response from the initial release of Project BORDER, the authors conclude that the system great promise for overcoming the data and information barrier that is problematic for the Irish border and other border regions around the world.

Part five of this volume brings together three essays that examine topics of the borders of Estonia and Karelia. Eiki Berg, in "Frontiers and Lines on Estonian Mental Maps," analyzes how Estonians perceive geographical space and international boundaries. He points out how the model of Estonia as a Western-oriented ethnic state housing a divided society is a product of overlapping constructed and real boundaries—a conflicting and contradictory vision. Berg also observes that people living within the Estonian border region with Russia do not necessarily perceive the official state boundary as a separation line nor in terms of the official definition of the border. Nonetheless, he concludes that there are still more barriers than gateways on Estonian mental maps. Ilkka Liikanen, in his essay on "Environmental Campaigns and Political Mobilization in the Northwestern Border Areas of the Former Soviet Union," studies the foundations of the concept of econationalism and presents brief case studies of environmental campaigns in the northwestern border areas of the former Soviet Union—the Union Republic of Estonia and the Autonomous Republic of Karelia. He looks at the effect of environmental movements on mobilization of political opposition and also comments on the relevance of these movements to the debate on mental and political boundaries. Liikanen concludes that in both the Estonian and Karelian cases, the environmental movements played different, but significant, roles in the emergence of political culture and institutions. Gulnara Roll and Robben Romano, in their essay "Challenges to and Opportunities for Development of an Effective Transboundary Water Management Regime in the Lake Peipus Basin—the Estonian-Russian Border Area," also examine the issue of constructing institutions in a border region. The Lake Peipus Basin lies on the border between Estonia and Russia, a border that was created in the early 1990s, destroying the existing environmental management systems for this important ecosystem and region. This paper discusses the formation of a new transboundary environmental management system in the region along with the challenges and opportunities to its implementation. They underline the key role that the region's strong network of experts, nongovernmental organizations, and local government representatives are playing in the process.

Part six deals specifically with the situation of Kaliningrad, a Russian oblast physically separate from the Russian Federation. In "A Russian Enclave within the European Union? Kaliningrad Reconsidered," Lyndelle Fairlie examines the political implications of the oblast's separation from Russia and the policies that affect it by comparing it to the experiences of other Russian oblasts. She also looks at its future place within the European Union as the EU enlarges to include Lithuania and Poland and makes policy recommendations to both Moscow and Brussels. Pertti Joenniemi furthers the discussion of this oblast in "Kaliningrad as a Discursive Battlefield." He calls attention to the many conceptualizations of Kaliningrad and its position with regard to Russia and the European Union. He analyzes tendencies both toward isolation and territorialism (raising borders) as well as greater opportunities for development and integration (breaking borders). Joenniemi concludes that Kaliningrad is in a prime position to spearhead change in the region and determine its own future if it takes advantage of its relationships with the European Union and the Russian Federation.

Part seven of this volume looks at relationships across the Finnish-Russian border and the process of Russian regionalization. In "Across the Northern Divide: Initiatives of Transborder Cooperation along the Finnish-Russian Border," Heikki Eskelinen investigates the primary steps toward cross-border cooperation across the only border between the Russian Federation and the European Union since 1995. He examines the roles that actors play to build or break barriers at different levels and the programs that have been instituted in the same vein. Pirjo Jukarainen takes a more social approach to the study of Finnish borders in "National Divisions and Borderland Youth." She uses interviews conducted with adolescents on both the Finnish-Russian and Finnish-Swedish borders to characterize feelings that borderland youth hold about the "other side" of the Finnish border. Jukarainen points to the everlasting significance of national boundaries in these two border regions and the extent of nationalism despite efforts to break borders down. Alexander Sergounin tracks the process of regionalization in Russia since the breakup of the Soviet Union in "Russia's Regionalization in the Context of the Financial/Political Crisis." He focuses on the financial and political crises in particular and their effect on the relationships between members of the Russian Federation. According to Sergounin, regionalism will either lead to successful reforms or further disintegration, thus determining the future of the Russian Federation.

In part eight, cross-border developments and conflicts on the Asian continent are examined. In "Developing the Transborder Region: Planned or Spontaneous? Cases from Asia," Chung-Tong Wu utilizes several examples of cross-border development in Asia to compare those that have been government funded and those that have not. Wu looks at the Tumen River Development Zone (China-Russia-North Korea), Nong Khai on the Thai-Laos border, the China-Vietnam border, Hong Kong and Shenzhen, and the Thai-Malaysian border. He then uses those cases to identify the factors that promote varying degrees of development across borders. Finally, Sanjay Chaturvedi looks at the hostile nature of the border region between Indian and Pakistan in "Common Pasts and Dividing Futures: A Critical Geopolitics of Indo-Pak Border(s)." He discusses the physical, social, and cultural significance of the barrier in the region's history and attempts to analyze the political discourse that contributes to such enmity. The Indo-Pak border is an example of a border as a barrier, dividing families and villages.

The central themes of the San Diego BRIT conference and the present volume were transborder cooperation, environment, and development. These themes are particularly relevant in the U.S.-Mexican border region with its high rates of population growth, urbanization, and industrialization that have raised significant concerns about the long-term viability of the region.[1] All of these themes are treated in this volume, although some themes are more prominent, as indicated in Table 1.

The relevance of almost all these papers to the issue of tranboundary cooperation is striking. Clearly, the issue of working across international boundaries is important in most border regions of the world. These essays collectively provide new information and insights regarding cooperation in border regions. The topic of transborder cooperation is addressed from a number of different perspectives for different regions. Pál and Nagy, for the Hungarian borders, stress the importance of international support and assistance in developing transborder cooperation, noting that local, indigenous efforts are weak. Perhaps this is the inevitable result of highly centralized political systems where border regions historically have had few options for working with adjacent regions across an international boundary and there is little tradition of public participation in the policy process on the local level. Mexico is another centralized state that has been undergoing a process of decentralization, a process accelerated by the North American Free Trade Agreement and the adoption of U.S.-Mexican environmental accords and institutions that require public participation and encourage local transboundary cooperation.

Williams and Stillerman, writing about the North American Agreement on Labor Cooperation, conclude that this binational body created in conjunction with the North American Free Trade Agreement is weak and its greatest impact might be encouragement of cross-border cooperation of U.S. and Mexican labor movements. Other researchers underline the importance of a bottom-up approach. Schmidt, writing about the El Paso, Texas-Ciudad Juárez, Chihuahua, case on the U.S.-Mexican border, emphasizes the critical nature of developing broad, grassroots support to facilitate cross-border integration and promote region building. Wu, in his analysis of Asian borders contrasts local, spontaneous efforts toward transborder cooperation with those brought by national and international agencies.

Basilio Verduzco Chávez, also addressing the U.S.-Mexican border, emphasizes the critical role of civil society in policy development in the environmental

Table 1. Subject, Region, and Theme of Essays			Theme		
Author	**Title/Subject**	**Region**	Cooperation	Environment	Development
Clement	International Transboundary Collaboration: Conceptual Framework	International	X		X
Blatter	Cross-Border Regions	North America, Europe	X	X	X
Lara	Cross-Border Partnerships for Environmental Management	U.S.-Mexican border	X	X	
Schmidt	Challenges for Region Building	U.S.-Mexican border	X		
Verduzco	Civil Society and Regions in Environmental Policy	U.S.-Mexican border	X	X	
Anderson	Quality of Life Indicators	U.S.-Mexican border	X		X
Ranfla et al.	Urban Marginality	Mexican-U.S. border			X
Williams & Stillerman	Unionization of the *Maquiladora* Industry	U.S.-Mexican border	X		X
Mühlenhöver	Transborder Chloride Pollution of the Rhine River	Europe	X	X	
Nagy	Environmental Problems in the Seven Hungarian Border Regions	Hungarian borders	X	X	
Pál	Approaches to the Danube-Tisza-Maros-Körös Euroregion	Hungarian-Yugoslavian-Romanian borders	X	X	
Bond et al.	Cross-Border Development in Northern Ireland	Ireland	X		X
Moore, Parr & Cook	Regional Development and Economic Regeneration	Ireland	X		X
Berg	Estonian Mental Maps	Estonia-Russia	X		
Liikanen	Environmental Campaigns and Political Mobilization in the Northwestern Border Areas of the Former Soviet Union	Russian-Estonian-Finnish (Karelia) border	X	X	
Roll and Romano	Transboundary Water Management Regime in the Lake Peipus Basin	Estonian-Russian border	X	X	
Fairlie	Kaliningrad Reconsidered	Kaliningrad	X		X
Joenniemi	Kaliningrad	Kaliningrad	X		
Eskelinen	Transborder Cooperation along the Finnish-Russian Border	Finnish-Russian border	X		X
Jukarainen	Borderland Youth	Russian-Finnish; Finnish-Swedish	X		
Sergounin	Russia's Regionalization	Russia	X		
Wu	Developing the Transborder Region: Planned or Spontaneous? Cases from Asia	China-Russia-North Korea; Thai-Laos; China-Vietnam; Hong Kong- Shenzhen; Thai-Malaysian borders	X		X
Chaturvedi	A Critical Geopolitics of Indo-Pak Border(s)	India-Pakistan borders	X		

arena. Francisco Lara, researching the San Diego-Tijuana region within the context of the U.S.-Mexican border, demonstrates how local organizations have forged cross-border alliances to address regional environmental issues. Emmanuelle Mühlenhöver also reviews the role of social actors, but with respect to the case of transborder chloride pollution in the Rhine River. She documents how environmental causes often become enmeshed with a range of other agendas, including economic, social, or political. She suggests that the environmental concern is often a convenient vehicle for other interests. Ilkka Liikanen also writes about environmental campaigns and links this to broader political mobilization in the case of the northwestern border areas of the former Soviet Union. All of these cases demonstrate that local and regional movements for transborder cooperation on the environment usually embrace other activities and agendas. Perhaps the lesson here is that issues such as environment or development are complex interwoven phenomena. Since environmental protection and conservation are directly related to development policies and standards of living, and must involve public policy formulation, grassroots and local movements often embrace diverse issues that are ultimately linked in the arena of human welfare.

The cases presented in this volume provide examples of borders with different degrees of openness and different levels of cooperation. At one end of the spectrum are borders such as the India-Pakistan border, where two neighboring states have largely closed the common border with physical barriers and also have constructed of social and cultural barriers to transborder cooperation and integration. While this situation serves the geopolitical whims of the two national states, local border populations suffer. At the other end of the spectrum are the internal borders of the European Union, where integration and cooperation are moving rapidly and where major barriers to additional cross-border interaction are largely psychological and matters of perception. An excellent example is the Finnish-Swedish border that has a long history of openness and cooperation, even achieving local integration of public administration for urban management in the Tornio-Haparanda area. Despite this high degree of integration and absence of conflict, the youth of the region evidence strong feelings of "us versus them," reflecting long traditions of nationalism and separatism at the national level (Jukarainen). Thus, cooperation in border regions involves more than reducing physical and administrative barriers and addressing economic asymmetries. Mental barriers are often important and quite difficult to address.

The essays of this volume demonstrate the increasing maturity of border studies. Scholars have begun to describe process and to develop a theory of borders and border regions, as seen in the essays of Joachim Blatter, Norris Clement, and Chung-Tong Wu.[2] But Clement also notes the need for additional descriptive studies that are multidisciplinary in nature in order to get beyond "analyzing transboundary relationships in a fragmented, discipline-centered way ... [that] is likely to ignore the multifaceted nature of such relationships and the contradictions that can arise" (Clement). The monodisciplinary approach to the study of border regions is often produced by barriers (or borders) between one academic discipline and others. As academic researchers interact more with the policy community, with nongovernmental organizations, and with the private sector, their research tends to become more multidisciplinary. People in the "real world" tend not to be interested in the types of methodological questions and approaches that distinguish one academic discipline from another. These practitioners tend to deal with real problems that are inherently multidisciplinary and they want research results that are likewise multidisciplinary.

In border regions, narrow studies are necessitated because of the lack of empirical data for the region of study, requiring researchers to develop data through survey research or painstaking manipulation of existing information. Since border regions traditionally have been marginalized, statistical information typically is of poorer quality and quantity than for central regions or the nation as a whole. Moreover, the data available in one part of a border region are collected in different ways and at different scales than the equivalent on the other side of the border. As a result, the researcher faces the daunting task of harmonizing data across the international boundary.[3] This, of course, is precisely the same difficulty that practitioners in border regions face on a daily basis; thus, better cross-border data and information can contribute to the processes of cooperation and integration. Moore, Parr, and Cook address this need in their essay about developing a computer-based system to provide economic, social, and environmental information for the Irish border region as a requirement for economic development.

Endnotes

1. See Ganster, ed. 2000a for a review of demographic, economic, and environmental conditions in the region.

2. For discussion of the field of border studies that examines European and North American approaches, see van der Velde 2000.

3. A recent, and successful, effort to harmonize geospatial data across the U.S.-Mexican international boundary is Ganster, ed. 2000b.

References

Eskelinen, Heikki, Ilkka Liikanen, and Jukka Oksa, eds. 1999. *Curtains of Iron and Gold. Reconstructing Borders and Scales of Interaction.* Aldershot: Ashgate.

Ganster, Paul, ed. 2000a. *The U.S.-Mexican Border Environment: A Road Map to a Sustainable 2020.* San Diego: San Diego State University Press. SCERP Monograph Series, No. 1.

Ganster, Paul, ed. 2000b. *San Diego-Tijuana International Border Area Planning Atlas.* San Diego: Institute for Regional Studies of the Californias and San Diego State University Press.

Ganster, Paul, Alan Sweedler, James Scott, and Wolf-Dieter Eberwein, eds. 1997. *Borders and Border Regions in Europe and North America.* San Diego: Institute for Regional Studies of the Californias and San Diego State University Press.

Van der Velde, Martin. 2000. "On the Value of a Transatlantic Dialogue on Border Research." Pp. 281–90 in *European Perspectives on Borderlands*, Joachim Blatter and Norris Clement, eds. Special Number of the *Journal of Borderlands Studies*, Vol. XV, No. 1 (Spring 2000). San Diego: San Diego State University Press.

II
Transborder Collaboration: Conceptualization and Theoretical Considerations

International Transboundary Collaboration: A Policy-Oriented Conceptual Framework

Norris Clement[*]

Abstract

This article develops a framework for helping both practitioners and researchers to better understand the changing functions of international boundaries and the basic rationale behind the concept of (international) transboundary collaboration (TBC). Building on the concepts of cross-border linkages and asymmetries, the author shows how these will lead to heightened interdependence in the context of relatively open borders. Such interdependence presents both opportunities and challenges that, if properly addressed through transboundary collaboration, can result in higher levels of prosperity and quality of life, while diminishing conflict in the region. These outcomes are presented as the major objectives of TBC. In order to better understand how this framework plays out in different border situations, the author also suggests that relatively standardized multidisciplinary border studies be carried out utilizing a template that is briefly presented and discussed. Finally, possible limitations and applications of the framework and the template are considered.

Introduction

In recent years, the function of international boundaries has changed dramatically. In general, they have become more open and present fewer barriers to cross-boundary activity and the development of border regions. The development of adjoining border regions partially depends on their ability to successfully regionalize decision-making processes across international boundaries.

* Clement is Director of International Projects at the Institue for Regional Studies of the Californias, San Diego State University. The author is indebted to many colleagues, including Joachim Blatter, Paul Ganster, and Alan Sweedler, for their help in developing this article.

Analyzing transboundary relationships in a fragmented, discipline-centered way, however, is likely to ignore the multifaceted nature of such relationships and the contradictions that can arise. Therefore, an interdisciplinary approach to border studies is necessary to understand this complex and often perplexing phenomenon (Clement, Ganster, and Sweedler 1998).

As the number of international boundaries and border regions[1] multiply or are transformed by changing local and international political and economic circumstances, the need to understand them in the context of public policy grows. Nevertheless, despite recent widening interest in borderlands and a corresponding outpour of literature, most academic work has been directed toward specific geographic regions (such as the U.S.-Mexican border region) or specific aspects of a region (for example, transboundary environmental collaboration). Very little attention has been focused on a theory of transboundary collaboration, particularly one that can be helpful to those charged with managing practical projects in transboundary settings.[2]

The primary objective of this paper is to present a framework for practitioners and researchers to understand the changing functions of international boundaries and the rationale behind the concept of (international) transboundary collaboration (TBC). This endeavor grew out of the frustration experienced when trying to condense the enormous amount of information available about the U.S.-Mexican border region into 20-minute briefings for legislators and decision makers who lacked firsthand knowledge. The goal here is to synthesize the essence of the transboundary relationship, help organize the vast amounts of information that can be used to describe and analyze that relationship, and promote better understanding of the need for and nature of transboundary collaboration.

A secondary objective is to outline a template for the standardized study of border regions so that borderlands scholars can begin to answer some frequently asked questions, including: What conditions seem to be most conducive to successful transboundary collaboration? What kinds of policies have been effective around the world in contributing to successful transboundary collaboration?

This essay is divided into three sections. The first section contains the major elements of a conceptual framework for analyzing and understanding the changing functions of international boundaries and transboundary collaborative relationships. The second section is a template for organizing collaborative studies in border regions. This approach is multidisciplinary and can be of assistance in identifying those factors likely to stimulate or hinder transboundary collaboration in specific regions. Such studies, if carried out in large enough numbers, could generate interesting hypotheses worthy of in-depth research and might eventually engender empirically based policy recommendations. The third section presents some of the limitations, applications, and extensions of this approach.

Characteristics of International Boundaries and Border Regions

Borders serve as legal, economic, and administrative dividing lines between national jurisdictions. As such, they set both the territorial and jurisdictional limits of nation-states and, hence, of national sovereignty. Borders may serve as "barriers" or as "points of contact and integration" between the people and systems of two (or more) adjacent countries, depending on the degree of openness between neighbors. Along relatively closed international boundaries, the border will serve as a barrier; along relatively open boundaries, it will spark integration (Hansen 1996).

Boundaries can be either internal or external. Internal boundaries refer to those between member countries within an economic union in which formal barriers of all kinds are virtually nonexistent. External boundaries refer to those boundaries between member and nonmember countries in which barriers to entry and exit are significant. External boundaries serve as (imperfect) filters for the control and regulation of flow from one jurisdiction to another (linkages). Thus, the interests of border regions can differ markedly from that of nation-states. While nations tend to view international boundaries as delineating the geographical limits of national sovereignty, border regions tend to view them as barriers to all types of intercourse with neighbors on the "other side."

Boundaries can be settled and defined or disputed and undefined.[3] They arbitrarily assign the limits of national jurisdiction for a vast array of transborder public policy issues that "spill over" from one side to the other, including air basins, underground aquifers, ocean waters, resources, public health, police and fire protection, and natural disasters such as earthquakes and floods.

Human boundaries seldom coincide with natural boundaries (such as mountain ranges or bodies of water). Thus, from the economic, geographic, environmental, historical, or ethnical perspectives, they artificially divide natural regions. International boundaries often disrupt social and economic transactions and create extrapolitical jurisdictions, exacerbating the fragmentation of governance (Martínez 1994; Friedmann 1996; Zuñiga 1998).

The emerging new economy is characterized by increased openness, lower tariffs, fewer barriers to commerce, and rapid technological innovations that lead to greater globalization.[4] It has diminished, but not totally eliminated, the barrier quality of economic borders; however, political borders remain that often impede regional decision making. The new economy, based on conservative ideology emphasizing market-oriented, supply-side economics, has resulted in central governments' diminished involvement in attaining full employment and economic growth. This devolution of power means that local and regional governments are forced to accept more responsibility for economic development in their own jurisdictions. In the hope of reducing conflict and improving prosperity and quality of life, transboundary collaboration between local governments, businesses, and nongovernmental organizations (NGOs) has expanded in many areas of the world in an attempt to regionalize decision making across international (and intranational) boundaries.

Despite this general tendency toward more open borders, some borders have become more closed in the post-Cold War era—especially those between the former Soviet Bloc countries—due primarily to ethnic and nationalist conflicts.

Defining Transboundary Regions: Two Options

Regions adjoining international boundaries may consist of two or more subregions and can be defined in two ways: (1) by including the administrative jurisdictions adjacent to an international boundary (the states or counties closest to the boundary); or (2) by measuring the volume of transborder interaction (linkages and flows). While the former is certainly the most convenient, as demographic and economic data scaled to county or municipal jurisdiction is usually available, the latter is more desirable for understanding the true nature of cross-boundary relationships.

Characteristics of Regions Partitioned by International Boundaries

Subregions adjacent to international boundaries, particularly those on external boundaries, are likely to be asymmetrical in one or more of the following areas:

- Geography: resources, topography, built environment
- Demography: age structure, growth rate, size, ethnicity, density per unit of land
- Economy: factor endowment (available input) and output structure, long-term growth rate, development
- Political system: centralization or decentralization, organization of government functions, legal systems, common practice
- Culture: history, ethnicity, language, customs

Geographic and economic asymmetries can give rise to transboundary commerce in the form of formal and informal networks for exploiting potentially profitable business opportunities. Political and cultural asymmetries, by contrast, can serve as obstacles to transboundary collaboration. The economies of neighboring subregions are frequently complementary in the structure and cost of both inputs (characteristics of the labor force, natural resources, capital, entrepreneurship) and outputs (final goods and services).

Adjoining border regions characterized by openness are usually interdependent and generate a variety of linkages and cross-boundary flows. Linkages and flows can be either legal or illegal and their volume and nature are influenced by prevailing market conditions and government-imposed regulations. These can be identified as:

- Tangible goods flows: including raw materials as well as intermediate, capital, and final goods (usually in response to market conditions)

- Human flows: including (1) those who wish to buy or sell goods and services in response to market conditions; (2) those involved in formal or informal networks;[5] and (3) those responding to nonmarket needs (such as tourism)
- Resource and environmental flows: including issues of water supply and quality, air pollution, bioresources, and hazardous and industrial waste. Embedded in these flows is an ongoing and sometimes invisible diffusion and adaptation of culture and technology.

Obstacles to transborder cooperation can limit cross-border interdependence. These obstacles can be defined as structural characteristics that impede or block cross-border activity and cooperation. Such obstacles can be identified as cultural, linguistic, or historical differences that impede interaction, or as institutional or systemic differences that make communication and collaborative decision making difficult due to: (1) the absence of a cross-boundary counterpart institution due to differences in function or organization; (2) differences in decision-making processes; (3) security measures that limit or delay cross-border exchanges; and/or (4) national restrictions on the entry and exit of persons and tangible goods.

Implications for Border Region Development: Transboundary Collaboration

Transborder relationships are usually characterized by *asymmetries*, *complementaries*, *linkages*, and *obstacles*. Collectively, they present both *opportunities* (situations that, if properly acted on, could raise prosperity and/or quality of life or reduce border conflict) and *challenges* (situations that, if not properly acted on, could lower prosperity and/or quality of life or increase borderland conflict).

Figure 1. Regional Transboundary Relationships

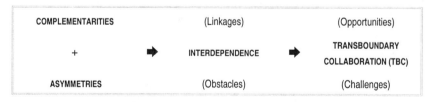

To properly manage both kinds of situations, some form of transboundary collaboration is usually required. The main goals of TBC are to raise the level of international competitiveness, prosperity, and quality of life, and to reduce or eliminate cross-boundary conflicts. TBC has (at least) two main features: (1) physical infrastructure (from border crossing facilities, highways and bridges to facilities for private and public transportation), and (2) a management structure or the potential (based on formal or informal relationships) to take advantage of opportunities and confront challenges.

One challenge is to adequately regionalize decision making in the subregions divided by an international boundary. Not only must border regions regionalize their decision-making processes, but they must do so in collaboration with a host of organizations on the "other side" that are likely to be organized very differently in many aspects—economically, politically, legally, and/or culturally. This increases the number of decision makers, the heterogeneity of the decision-making body, and the complexity of the decision-making process.

There are three basic economic concepts that necessitate transborder cooperation: economies of scale, externalities (both positive and negative), and transaction costs. Economies of scale in a border region usually consist of joint involvement in the creation of infrastructure needed for development. The construction of bridges, highways, and port facilities may be feasible only if financed by all parties that enjoy their benefits (positive externalities). Even if only one side were able to finance construction of, for example, a regional airport, some benefits would accrue automatically to the "other side" in increased access and lower travel costs. This is also true of social infrastructure (education and health services, police and fire protection). Even marketing efforts to promote a region's exports, investments, and tourism in the transborder region and extol the region's virtues can frequently be done cheaper and more effectively in concert. Lobbying efforts in the involved nations' capitals or before transnational governmental bodies (such as the European Union) are often more effective if done collaboratively.

Negative externalities must also be taken into account and managed by all parties. For example, transmittable diseases or air or water pollution on one side of a boundary can easily spill over to the other, raising regional health costs and lowering quality of life. Transborder collaboration can result in improved management of such problems.

Transaction costs are those over and above the normal production and distribution costs associated with buying and selling, including gathering information on market conditions and negotiating, writing, and enforcing agreements. In cross-border situations, such costs are likely to be high compared to expected profits, and thus discourage economic activity. For example, entrepreneurs who lack information about market conditions, legal constraints, common business practices, language, or culture on the "other side" may be reluctant to do business there, even though it is regarded as part of the local or regional market area. By limiting the size of the market, high transaction costs can also inhibit the realization of economies of scale in the private production of goods.

It follows, then, that transborder consultation and coordination must exist in order to realize potential economies of scale, manage spillover effects, and lower transaction costs. Decision making must be regionalized, even in those areas divided by an international boundary.

The Dynamics of Transboundary Collaboration

It is widely recognized that successful transboundary collaboration can be a rather static outgrowth of a myriad of factors, including demographic characteristics (ranging from culture and language to population growth rates and density), levels of economic development, national economic and political decision-making patterns, legal and administrative systems and competency, and cross-border communication and infrastructure. A historic legacy of transborder conflict may also play an important role in conditioning transboundary collaborative efforts. Another important determinant is the nature of transnational institutions. This may vary significantly from economic and political union (as in contemporary Europe) or a free trade area (as in North America) to simple membership in the global economy, subject only to the rules of the World Trade Organization.

As transborder relationships evolve, dynamic patterns may also be observed and predicted. One such pattern could be progression from local "informal, non-binding transborder relationships to formal, non-binding" relationships or to formal, binding relationships enforced by transborder institutions and established under international treaty. Many other patterns may become common and new studies will engender a better understanding of them (Blatter 1997). The existence of such mechanisms does not imply anything a priori about the nature of transborder relationships. They may range from "peaceful coexistence" to "partners in development." It must be accepted and noted, however, that from the outset there will be a strong element of competition between border regions in addition to cooperation.[6]

In areas where collaboration has begun to flourish, each region seems to have adopted its own approach to transborder endeavors based on its history, culture, resources, capacities, and its national and international niche. Some approaches to TBC have been more successful than others, though it is difficult to measure success in such matters.[7]

Benefits and Costs of Transboundary Collaboration

There will inevitably be both benefits and costs to implementing transborder collaboration and only when the benefits are perceived as greater than the costs will subregions be willing to participate. The nature and division of costs and benefits depends on circumstances inherent in each region, but a few observations can be made here at the conceptual level.

First, TBC implies an increase in economic, political, and social integration between participating subregions. Integration across an international boundary usually results in some loss of national sovereignty (security), the need to associate with foreigners (possibly perceived as undesirable), and the risks associated with any new venture (that is, the risks involved in investing resources in a process that could fail at any time).

Second, there are always winners and losers in integration, and the benefits and losses are not likely to be distributed evenly. By pursuing the objectives of

TBC (conflict reduction and increased international competitiveness, prosperity, and quality of life), each subregion opens itself to new social, political, and economic forces. These are likely to benefit one side of the boundary more than the other(s) and some sectors of each subregional community are likely to benefit, while others may be hurt.

Third, the complexity of transborder relationships implies that regardless of the outcome of TBC, the process itself will result in a loss of hegemony by central governments to subnational actors. This consequence can be viewed from a variety of perspectives as either negative or positive, but probably always with some anxiety. The omnipresent danger, of course, is that the process of TBC can, under certain circumstances, result in fragmentation of the nation-state.

A Template for Organizing Border Region Studies

Existing studies of border regions differ widely in objectives, methods, and scope. Therefore, existing literature on border regions is a set of heterogeneous studies designed to achieve a wide variety of objectives. This section outlines an approach to border studies that will: (1) systematically identify factors that contribute to specific border regions' problems as well as those that describe their main characteristics. The template can then be utilized to identify and analyze the main characteristics of border regions within the conceptual framework sketched out in the first section of this paper; and (2) provide a systematic, multidisciplinary approach to the study of border regions that is useful to academics and practitioners. If such relatively standardized comparative studies are carried out in sufficient numbers, they can be used to generate hypotheses and, eventually, policy-relevant theories about transboundary collaboration and the development of border regions.

Defining Relevant Regions to be Studied: Macro- and Micro-Border Regions

Macro-border regions differ significantly in size and geographic space. For example, the U.S.-Mexican border region is large, covering some 2,062 miles (3,326 kilometers) from east to west, whereas the Hungarian-Slovenian border region is relatively small, with an international boundary of 63 miles (102 kilometers). Furthermore, micro-border regions exist along many boundaries and characterized by their relatively high degree of (actual or potential) interaction. Along the U.S.-Mexican boundary, for instance, there are about twenty micro-border regions (referred to as "twin cities"), ranging from Brownsville-Matamoros in the East to San Diego-Tijuana in the West. The case can be made that in the U.S.-Mexican border region, despite many similarities between urban areas and their respective hinterlands, so much heterogeneity exists that lumping them all into a single region for study would likely conceal more than it would reveal. The relevant unit for the study of border regions (though difficult to determine) should be the local (micro) region, characterized by a relatively high degree of transborder interaction, actual or potential. An alternative unit for study—for data collection purposes—would be those administrative units adjacent to an international boundary that exhibit intensive cross-boundary activity. Thus, in the case of the U.S.-Mexican border region, the relevant unit of study could be twin cities, urban zones, and their hinterlands (such as the County of San Diego and the Municipality of Tijuana) or the region defined by the 10 counties of Southern California and the five municipalities of Baja California that exhibit a relatively integrated region in terms of economic activity, infrastructure, environment, and cultural interaction.

A Collaborative Multidisciplinary Approach to the Study of Border Regions

This section presents a three-part template for collaborative micro-border region studies: (1) a suggested process for organizing a study; (2) a detailed overview of topics to be included in a study; and (3) a brief discussion of how to interpret findings. These studies are collaborative because academics from each subregion of the border in question carry out parallel studies, detail prevalent conditions on their side of the border, and use objectives, methods, and scopes that are as similar as possible.

The Process for Organizing a Study

Although there are many ways to organize such a study, the following can be helpful in simultaneously advancing both the study and transboundary collaboration.[8] From the outset, organizers should establish two working groups (one from each side of the border), each comprising of academic specialists and practitioners familiar with both public policy and the border region. If this is not possible, then one working group with representatives from both sides of the border will suffice. Representatives from each side of the border should be designated to organize the working group(s), edit the final report, write an introduction and final summary section about the main findings, and offer recommendations for future study and public policy.

Workshops should be employed for homogenizing the objectives, scope, and nature of each section of the study as well as possible by comparing outlines and, eventually, drafts of each section. They should also present final section reports to other members of the multinational team for feedback to its authors. Workshops involving both academics and practitioners can be very helpful for discussing data sources and ideas, developing additional transboundary collaborative works, and developing ongoing discourse.[9]

Upon completion of the study, its main findings must be presented to regional policymakers, leaders of the private sector, and concerned nongovernmental organizations at conferences scheduled (ideally) on both sides of the border. Such conferences can be important events that lead to new phases of collaboration among participating agencies. Press conferences are also useful for publicizing the study's publication to the media on both sides of the boundary.

Contents of the Study

Studies of micro-border regions might consist of sections organized by the subjects listed below. Each section should include an essay (with appropriate maps, tables, and graphs) written for concerned lay people. The first and final sections should be written by project organizers, and the rest by individuals, subject to feedback provided by workshop participants. All participants should be familiar with the study's conceptual framework, and should be urged to organize their essays according to that framework.

Expository section introductions are helpful. The final section should clearly summarize major findings (including challenges and opportunities), note gaps in available data, and identify any areas where further study is needed. In most countries, required information is available from secondary sources, so there is usually little need for surveys or interviews.[10]

The approximate number of pages for each section is indicated in parenthesis next to the section heading. It is estimated that the entire study should not exceed 100–150 pages (35,000–50,000 words, depending on font size, line spacing, and format).

Section Headings and Guidelines

Introduction to the Study and Macro-Border Region (3–4 pages)

An overview of the entire border region with the most important elements detailed in the categories listed below. Its objective is to establish the context of the micro-region under study.

Geography, Climate, Resources, and Infrastructure (5–6 pages)

- Maps of both sides of the boundary in their national context
- Available Geographic Information Systems (GIS) and applications
- Overview of main geographic characteristics of the border region in its national context, including topography, climate, natural resources, natural barriers, land use, population density, rural land tenure, and urbanization patterns
- Level of physical infrastructure development, including transportation links and corridors, water supplies, energy generation and importation, and major infrastructure gaps

Demography, Culture, and Language (4–5 pages)

- Population size, as well as rates of growth and sources of growth (indigenous and immigrant)
- Main ethnic/cultural groups, including numbers and rates of growth
- Age structure
- Labor force participation rates (overall as well as male and female)
- Health and education statistics

History, Sovereignty, and Security (5–7 pages)

- Brief overview of national and regional history with special emphasis on shifting boundaries, ethnic and national regional conflicts, and conflicts between regional and national groups in neighboring countries

- Changing locations and functions of the international boundary in recent times
- Overview of the current situation with respect to intraregional conflicts and rivalries (one country only), conflicts and rivalries between each region and its larger nation, and cross-boundary conflicts and rivalries

Economics (6–8 pages)

- Gross regional product (size, per capita, distribution, rates of growth) (1980-present)
- Employment and output by sector (two digit, for region and country) (1980-present)
- Unemployment and underemployment rates, regional and national (1990s by year)
- Inflation rates (1990s by year)
- 10 leading exports and imports (current)
- Major trading partners (by exports and imports, current)
- Foreign investment in region (value, in which sectors)
- Five main countries investing in region
- Estimates of local, informal transboundary transactions (informal wholesale and retail expenditures not included in export/import figures)
- Estimated size of informal sector in border region (qualitative/quantitative illegal flows of aliens, arms, drugs, wildlife, and so on)
- Estimates of numbers and earnings of commuter workers
- Existence of regional models (input/output or other economic development plans)

Environment and Quality of Life (4–6 pages)

- Water quality and supply problems
- Hazardous waste and industrial problems
- Air pollution
- Bioresource issues
- National and transboundary environmental management practices

Governance and Planning Systems (4–6 pages)

- Brief overview of transnational governance (such as the European or North American Free Trade Agreement) including treaties, institutions and their competencies, region/border-oriented policy instruments and programs
- Brief overview of the nation's governmental structure and systems including its constitution (unitary state or federation); revenue distribution, structure and political power of municipalities;

public-private relationship (for example, statist in France, corporativist in Austria, or pluralistic in the United States)

Transboundary Collaboration (6–8 pages)

* Brief overview of regional history of transboundary cooperation (informal and formal)
* Main institutions and current areas of collaboration
* Major accomplishments and problems

Summary of Findings and Policy Recommendations (10–15 pages)

* Summary of main findings of each essay on each side
* Synthesis of main findings and discrepancies between them, if any interpretation of findings and implications for understanding the *problematique* of the border region (see below)

Interpreting the Findings

The primary reason for presenting the conceptual framework in the first section of this paper is to provide a means for interpreting studies generated using this template. The main logic of that framework rests on the assumption that asymmetries and complementaries between the two or more subregions on any given boundary give rise to actual and potential transboundary links that are often impeded or blocked by common obstacles. These links and obstacles constitute opportunities and challenges that, if properly managed, can lead to increased prosperity, better quality of life, reduction of regional conflict, and fulfillment of the basic goals of transboundary collaboration.

One study cannot be expected to treat all extant issues in a region exhaustively; however, most can be identified, as can the need for further studies. Workshops carried out in conjunction with individual studies can stimulate discussion between participants, both academics and practitioners, which can be extremely useful in identifying trouble spots, framing policy responses, and stimulating collaboration. The new economic environment requires partnerships of all kinds (public-private, public-academic, private-academic, and public-private-academic) to fully mobilize a region's resources in concert.

Conclusions and Recommendations

The conceptual framework and template presented here represent only one of many possible approaches to understanding and studying border regions. Perhaps this presentation will stimulate the development of other approaches that can capture the essence of the issues that academics and practitioners attempt to understand and deal with using public policy.

Limitations of the Framework and Template

This conceptual framework does lack a precise definition for the studied region. This deficiency, however, seems endemic in regional science in general, not just in this approach. Also, the terms used here are not commonly employed when discussing border region development. More familiar terms might resonate better with those viewing the framework for the first time.

The classification system in the template has limitations. First, there are many different ways of classifying the information utilized by academics and practitioners associated with border region development. Again, this is only one way of arranging such information. This exercise may evoke discussion and the development of this classification system (or wholly new ones) to better serve this purpose. Second, many topics could have fit into two or more sections in the template. Decisions were made by the consideration of which discipline studies this sort of phenomenon most. Given the author's lack of knowledge of the domain of all relevant disciplines, it is likely that mistakes were made. Perhaps fuller discussion of the template will correct these deficiencies. Finally, given the fact that this approach to border region studies is in its infancy, there are (unfortunately) no practical models for those who would employ this template in specific border regions. It is hoped that financing can be obtained for two or three studies to test the feasibility of this classification system in a variety of border regions, which in turn, could be models for further studies.

Expected Uses and Applications

This approach to the study of border regions, if adopted by a number of research institutions, could yield a sample of border studies that could fulfill a number of objectives, including:

- Creation of categories of international boundaries and border regions based on a variety of factors (such as open versus closed boundaries or urban, high density cross-boundary regions versus rural, low density cross-boundary regions)
- Generation and/or testing of hypotheses about: (1) the changing functions of international boundaries; (2) conditions and policies that contribute to successful transboundary collaboration; and/or (3) conditions that lead to the development of border regions (increasing competitiveness, prosperity, and quality of life, and decreasing cross-border conflict)
- A basis for more detailed studies of particular aspects of border regions problems (such as in-depth studies of transboundary collaboration in environmental or public health areas)
- Development of texts for both practitioners and university students in worldwide border region studies courses

International border region studies is an emerging, multidisciplinary academic specialization with strong ties to public policy analysis. To earn the respect of their colleagues and establish links with practitioners already working in the field, academics must begin to generate the type of studies suggested here. This essay is an invitation to borderlands scholars to enter the discussion about the methodological and empirical foundations of their work.

Endnotes

1. The terms "boundary" and "border" can be used interchangeably. In practice, border is more commonly used, at least in English. In order to avoid confusion, boundary is used here to mean a line that fixes the limits of a nation's territory, referring exclusively to its international character. The region adjoining a boundary will be referred to here as a border region consisting of two or more subregions—one on each side of the boundary. Macroborder regions designate the entire border region abutting the length of an international boundary (such as the U.S.-Mexican border region), whereas microborder regions refer to a particular section of a macroborder region (such as San Diego-Tijuana).

2. One major exception to this is the work by Ratti and Reichman (1993). Another contribution in this area was produced by the Linkage Assistance and Cooperation for the European Border Regions (LACE) Project (Association of European Border Regions 1997), which relates almost entirely to cross-boundary institutions developed within the European Union. See their website at: http://www.lace.aebr-ageg.de.

3. For an organization that specializes in this area, see the International Boundaries Research Unit's website at: http://www-ibru.dur.ac.uk/.

4. As it is used here, globalization means "... the widening and deepening of international flows of trade, finance and information in a single, integrated global market" (United Nations Development Programme 1997: 82). This process is generally recognized as having developed after World War II, although its roots can be traced back much farther, and there is evidence that elementary forms of globalization were present in earlier centuries.

5. The term "network economy" covers a lot of conceptual territory and transcends the traditional spheres of economic transactions where goods and services are traded only for money. Complex modern economies are held together by many kinds of collaborative networks, including those that involve transportation, communications, and information, and whose successful operation is essential to national and regional development. The main question pursued here is whether the recent trend toward the eradication of old borders implies the elimination of all related impediments.

6. Some competition can be minimized if complementaries are identified and operated by a "cross-border industrial strategy." Such a strategy, based on the comparative advantages of each region, could increase economic activity on both sides of a boundary. The aim is to attract investment to a region, ideally with part of production on one side of the border based on its comparative advantages and the rest on the other side, based on its advantages. This has been attempted along the U.S.-Mexican border, notably between San Diego, California, and Tijuana, Baja California.

7. Two possible measures of TBC success come to mind: (1) to measure input (number and quality of ongoing transborder actions initiated); or (2) to measure output (an index of economic prosperity and quality of life or specific transborder actions carried out). A combination of the two could also be used.

8. The study was based on an earlier version of this approach (Clement and Zepeda 1993).

9. The workshops started in 1992 at the outset of the "San Diego-Tijuana in Transition" study and were continued through 1998. These seminars, publicized through electronic mail and printed announcements, were called "The Californias in Transition." Participants included academics, private and public sector officials, and researchers from both sides of the California-Baja California boundary.

10. In addition to this study, which is based on secondary data, another type of study, based on the opinions of public and private sector leaders, could be carried out to better determine and comprehend the perceptions of local decision makers on both sides of an international boundary.

References

Association of European Border Regions (AEBR). 1997. *Practical Guide to Cross-Border Cooperation*. Gronau: AEBR.

Clement, Norris, Paul Ganster, and Alan Sweedler. 1998. "Development, Environment, and Security in Asymmetrical Border Regions: European and North American Perspectives." Pp. 243–81. In *Curtains of Iron and Gold: Reconstructing Borders and Scales of Interaction*, Heikki Eskelinen, Ilkka Liikanen, and Jukka Oksa, eds. Aldershot: Ashgate.

Clement, Norris, and Eduardo Zepeda, eds. 1993. *San Diego-Tijuana in Transition*. San Diego: Institute for Regional Studies of the Californias, San Diego State University.

Friedmann, John. 1996. "Introduction to Borders, Margins and Frontiers: Myth and Metaphor." In *Frontiers in Regional Development*, Yehuda Gradus and Harvey Lithwick, eds. Lanham: Rowman and Littlefield.

Hansen, Niles. 1996. "Barrier Effects in the U.S.-Mexico Border Area." In *New Borders and Old Barriers in Spatial Development*, Peter Nijkamp, ed. Brookfield: Avebury.

Martínez, Oscar. 1994. *Border People: Life and Society in the U.S.-Mexico Borderlands*. Tucson: University of Arizona Press.

Ratti, Remigio, and Shalom Reichman, eds. 1993. *The Theory and Practice of Transborder Cooperation*. Basel and Franfurt: Verlag Helning Lichenhahn.

U.N. Development Programme. 1997. *Human Development Report*. New York and Oxford: Oxford University Press.

Zuñiga, Victor. 1998. "Nations and Borders: Romantic Nationalism and the Project of Modernity." In *The U.S.-Mexico Border: Transcending Divisions, Contesting Identities*, David Spener and Kathleen Staudt, eds. Boulder: Lynne Rienner Publishers.

Cross-Border Regions: A Step toward Sustainable Development? Experiences and Considerations from Examples in Europe and North America

Joachim Blatter[*]

Abstract

This paper discusses the role of territorial integration (cooperation across territorially defined borders) as facilitating or hindering efforts toward sustainable development based on experiences of cross-border region building in Europe and North America. The conceptual core of sustainable development is seen here as intersectoral integration, or coordination across sectorally or functionally defined boundaries. The creation of cross-border institutions and participation in cross-border activities gained momentum both in Europe and North America in the 1990s. Four important functions of cross-border cooperation are derived from the observation of this activity, including establishment of a regulatory regime, function as a transfer hinge, creation of an innovation pole, and facilitation of cross-border coalition building. Examples show the usefulness of cross-border cooperation to aid in the progress of environmental policies. They also demonstrate possible negative side effects and a deepening of the sectoral cleavages between various "advocacy-coalitions." The paper concludes with a vision and some empirical evidence of cross-border regions as fertile grounds for

---

* Blatter is Assistant Professor at the University of Constance, Germany. The author would like to thank Suzanne Cornwell and Helen Ingram for their help, as well as the Studienstiftung des Deutschen Volkes, Bonn, and the Gottfried Daimler und Karl Benz Stiftung, Ladenburg, for their financial support of this research on cross-border cooperation in Europe and North America.

multilayered integration processes that are necessary to achieve more sustainable ways of living.

Introduction and Overview

Much has been written about whether free trade provides more economic opportunities or risks to the environment. This essay argues that the discussion is too narrowly focused, providing neither an adequate description of the observable transformation processes toward continental and regional integration nor a clear definition of good policy. The question is therefore expanded in this study to a more comprehensive discussion, asking: Does the evolving territorial integration process facilitate or hinder the search for sustainable development?

The political level or territorial span from which empirical material is drawn to address this question is reduced here to cross-border regions, but the conceptual basis is expanded from the free flow of goods to reduction of boundaries between territorial units, and from environmental policies to sustainable development. Instead of looking at the continental or global level, subnational cross-border regions will be examined. Although cross-border region building has gained momentum since the late 1980s, it is still almost totally neglected in mainstream social science discourses.

To answer the postulated question, this article first presents cooperative activities in two cross-border regions—one in Europe and one in North America. Through the description of institutions and the provision of some examples of policy accomplishments, it becomes clear that cross-border activities extend far beyond free trade policies and encompass almost all policy areas. Therefore, the observed activities can be labeled as either "cross-border region building" or "territorial integration" processes.

After showing that territorial integration occurs on a regional level, the essay turns to what this means in the search for better policies. Opportunities opened up by cross-border cooperation are highlighted and examples from the field of environmental policy are drawn upon, identifying four functional goals/tasks that can be furthered by transboundary cooperation.

The essay then turns to the downside of territorial integration in the search for sustainable development. Based on the insight that sustainable development as a "holistic approach" is a reaction to the problems created by functional and sectoral differentiation in modern societies, organizations, and administrations, "sustainable development" is defined as the integration of environmental, social, and economic goals. Implementation of sustainable development, then, depends on institutions that coordinate and integrate different sectoral goals and interests and bring together the many actors. This paper reevaluates cross-border linkages against this expanded concept of the preconditions necessary to formulate good policies. It shows that cross-border or interterritorial cooperation fosters antagonistic communities and makes the bridging of intersectoral boundaries more difficult. Territorial integration is thus seen as inimical to sustainable development. Nevertheless, the essay concludes with a vision (and empirical evidence) of cross-border regions as potential testing grounds for the kind of multilayered integration necessary to more peaceful and sustainable ways of living.

The Neglected Layer of Regional Integration: Emerging Subnational Cross-Border Regions

Until recently, major social science discourses paid little attention to subnational cross-border cooperation. In the early 1990s, however, scholars of federalism and regional science began to trace the increasing number of international activities of subnational political units in Europe and North America (Michelmann and Soldatos 1990; Brown and Fry 1993; Hocking 1993a; Groen 1994, 1995). Although much attention was given to the "para-diplomatic" (Soldatos 1990, 1993) or "interregional" (Raich 1995) activities of provinces, states, *Länder*, cantons, and cities, their "microdiplomatic" (or cross-border) activities have more tradition and are more notable (Cohn and Smith 1996; Martínez 1986; Swanson 1976). In some border regions, such developments have advanced to the point that the older notion of microdiplomacy should be replaced by that of "cross-border institution building," even though most cross-border institutions are little more than informal networks.

Many reasons are offered to explain this phenomenon. Global economic, technological, ecological, and social developments all contribute to a rapid increase in interdependence across territorial boundaries and to a political process that Brian Hocking (1993b) calls "localizing foreign policy." Factors within political systems, including trends toward decentralization in most Western countries and, more importantly, the political move toward continental integration, have created opportunities that are being pursued by increasingly professional subnational organizations. In Europe, the Single European Act (1987) initiated the European Internal Market, and the Maastricht Treaty (1992) set the framework for Monetary Union. In North America, similar initiatives were fostered by the Free Trade Agreement (FTA) between Canada and the United States in 1988 and by the 1994 North American Free Trade Agreement (NAFTA) between the United States, Canada, and Mexico. These highly visible signs of political integration can be seen as catalysts that have stimulated and facilitated new subnational cross-border activities over the last decade.

Cross-border region building in both Europe and North America has mushroomed since the late 1980s. The new momentum of continental integration spilled over into the borderlands, causing new motivations for "micro-integration" (Haefliger 1996). Older cross-border links were reinvigorated and, for the first time received enough political and financial support to fulfill some longstanding goals. Even more significantly, new initiatives sprang up in almost every border region. Even in areas with no history of cross-border cooperation (and where there was limited socioeconomic [1] or environmental interdependence), the "idea" [2] of a common region became a salient topic in the late 1980s and early 1990s, changing perceptions about both borders and neighbors.

Two regional examples—one from Europe and one from North America—will demonstrate this in greater detail.

A European Example: The Lake Constance Region

Lake Constance is the second largest lake in Central Europe and forms part of the border between Germany, Switzerland, and Austria. Cross-border cooperation in the Lake Constance region (*Bodensee*) involves a variety of geographic definitions. An evolving consensus purports that this "Euroregion," called Euregio Bodensee, has about two million inhabitants and includes the German counties of Constance, Singen, Sigmaringen, and Bodensee in the *Land* (German state level) of Baden-Württemberg and Lindau County in the *Land* of Bavaria; the Austrian *Land* of Vorarlberg; the Swiss cantons of Saint Gall, Thurgau, Appenzell Inner Rhodes, Appenzell Outer Rhodes, and Schaffhausen; and Liechtenstein (see Figure 1) (Leuenberger and Walker 1992).

Cross-border cooperation has a long tradition in this region. A first, extensive wave of institution building, which focused mainly on water and environmental issues, emerged in the 1960s and early 1970s. Since then, environmental groups around the lake have worked together closely. In fact, the beginning of the environmental movement in Germany was closely tied to the (unsuccessful) cross-border undertaking to turn the Rhine River into a navigable waterway from Basel to Lake Constance (Drexler 1980; Scherer and Müller 1994).

Until the 1960s, the fisheries commission (Internationale Bevollmächtigten-konferenz für die Bodenseefischerei–IBKF), created in 1893, was the only inter-governmental institution in the region (Müller-Schnegg 1994: 122–23). In 1960, the International Commission for the Protection of Lake Constance (Internationale Gewaesserschutzkommission für den Bodensee–IGKB) was established as the result of an international agreement between the German *Länder* of Baden-Württemberg and Bavaria, the Swiss Confederation, the Swiss cantons of Saint Gall and Thurgau, and the Republic of Austria. This international agreement has provided a strong legal basis for a common environmental regime and has institutionalized cross-border cooperation through the creation of a commission and a variety of working groups and boards (Blatter 1994a).

During the late 1960s and early 1970s, two additional cross-border commissions were created: a regulatory body for shipping on the lake (Internationale Schiffahrts kommission für den Bodensee–ISKB); and a commission for spatial planning (Deutsch-Schweizerische Raumordnungs kommission–DSRK). The DSRK produced a comprehensive spatial development plan (*Leitbild*) for the Lake Constance area in the early 1980s (Leuenberger and Walker 1992).

In the early 1970s, a German *Landrat* (county-level chief executive) encouraged by similar initiatives in other regions and by proposals in the European Council tried to initiate a cross-border regional institution comprising municipalities on the eastern end of Lake Constance called Euregio Bodamica. In response, the government of Baden-Württemberg called a meeting of the political leaders of the *Länder* and cantons in Constance in 1972. Without any formal

Figure 1. Euregio Bodensee

agreement or parliamentary ratification, they founded the International Confer-ence of Government Leaders (Internationale Konferenz der Regierungschefs der Bodenseeländer–IBK) (Bullinger 1977).

In addition to such political and administrative linkages, many private cross-border contacts emerged after World War II that were often institutional-ized over time. One study of cross-border linkages in the Lake Constance region identified over two hundred cooperative associations that held regular meetings (Müller-Schnegg 1994). The union of the region's Chambers of Commerce, the association of water utilities, and the association of municipal tourist offices are especially important. Annual meetings and other events are hosted by political parties and professional organizations, in addition to regular cultural, religious, and sports activities (Müller-Schnegg 1994).

The second wave of cross-border activity and institution building began in the late 1980s. The Lake Constance Council (*Bodenseerat*)—a private association of regional political, economic, and scientific leaders—was founded in 1991 in the wake of two conferences on cross-border cooperation at the University of Constance. Spurred by European integration, this group proclaimed itself the voice of the cross-border region and has lobbied both within the region itself and in the state capitals. Several working groups have been created to focus on economics, science, culture, the environment, and politics (Müller-Schnegg 1994: 216).

As a reaction to the founding of the *Bodenseerat*, the IBK enhanced the scale and scope of its own activities. Having formerly dealt almost exclusively with water concerns, the IBK broadened its agenda to include major political issues, augmented its organizational structure, and introduced an annual budget. It produced a new regional *Leitbild* and marketed it widely.[3] It also set up an office that provides information about the Euregio Bodensee to people living both within and outside the region and sponsor a regionwide news service (Informationswissenschaft 1998). As a result of this new public awareness, several area newspapers now carry special sections dedicated to the "other side" of the border. In 1995, the Electronic Mall Bodensee began service on the Internet, serving as a platform for all initiatives and organizations in the cross-border region.[4] It is financed primarily by the IBK and is managed by three universities around the lake.

Environmental groups were also stimulated by the activities of the Lake Constance Council and by the new awareness and public discussions of Euroregions. They focused their cooperative efforts on a new, more formal structure called the Environmental Council of Lake Constance (Umweltrat Bodensee) (Scherer and Müller 1994).

All of these activities began in the late 1980s, but were given new impetus when the EU launched the INTERREG initiative for border regions in 1990. From 1991 to 1993, ECU900 million (US$772.1 million) were made available to border regions in Western Europe to promote transboundary cooperation. Border regions apply for funds by submitting operational programs. New regional steering committees then decide which projects will be funded and implemented. The INTERREG steering committees consist mainly of regional officials, although federal governments and the EU commission also participate.[5]

The most recent development in this region was the formation of a cross-border association of municipalities around Lake Constance (*Arbeitsgemeinschaft Bodensee UferGemeinden*) in 1995. Smaller binational groupings, such as the Borderland Conference (*Grenzlandkonferenz*) between the neighboring municipalities of Constance, Kreuzlingen, and Tägerwilen, as well as larger cross-border groupings have also been formed, such as the Working Community of the Alpine Countries (ARGE ALP) (Müller-Schnegg 1994: 221–22).

This broad variety of cross-border institutions and connections shows how far integration has already gone in this region. The following section outlines just a few examples of the many policies and accomplishments that have been realized in this cross-border region.

Accomplishments

During its first 20 years, the International Commission for the Protection of Lake Constance (IGKB) concentrated its efforts on the lake's organic contamination. Its remarkable endeavors, involving a DM6.7 billion (US$2.9 billion) expenditure from 1960 to 1995 for sewage treatment facilities around the lake, have resulted in a significant reduction of phosphorous in the lake. The collective activities to protect Lake Constance's water quality have created one of the most successful environmental regimes in the world in terms of real results. They have also been the wellspring of an innovative environmental strategy now commonly referred to as the "ecosystem approach." In 1986, the ecosystem approach was presented for the first time in a European cross-border region in a *Denkschrift* (think piece) published by the commission.[6] Therein, both the identification of ecological problems and the range of their causes were given a wider scope and water quality was no longer put forth as the only problem. Habitat preservation and the ecological importance of coastal areas (*Flachwasserzone*) were also recognized as major concerns. In 1987, the IGKB formulated new guidelines (*Richtlinien*) based on this new, comprehensive approach that would be implemented in the communities around the lake in the following years (IGKB 1987).

Within a very short period (1993–1994), a new convenient, efficient, and direct, 43.4-mile (70-kilometer) railway link was planned and installed over existing tracks from the German town of Engen to the Swiss town of Wil, which straddles the border at Constance-Kreuzlingen. This was possible due to growing cross-border awareness fostered by increased discourse on regional and transborder cooperation, making it evident that the small Swiss railway corporation (Mittelthurgau-Bahn) and the German county of Constance had synergetic needs and means (Schnell 1994). In addition, a new translake ferry was financed by subnational governments and began operations in the summer of 1997.

A North American Example: Cascadia

"Cascadia" is a young and dynamic cross-border region in North America on the western edge of the U.S.-Canadian border. Different groups define the boundaries of Cascadia in many ways, depending on their interests and agendas. Such definitions range from one view that includes only the watershed of the Georgia Basin and Puget Sound, to one called "Main Street Cascadia" (the Vancouver, Seattle, Portland corridor), to one that includes Washington, British Columbia, and sometimes even Oregon. The broadest approach sees the cross-border entity as a "Pacific Northwest Economic Region" that encompasses five U.S. states (Washington, Oregon, Idaho, Montana, and Alaska) and two Canadian provinces (British Columbia and Alberta) (see Figure 2).

Until the 1980s, border matters in the Pacific Northwest were dealt with primarily by the International Joint Commission (IJC), which was established by the federal governments in 1909 to deal with border-related problems along the entire U.S.-Canadian border. Since then, however, local governments have taken on an increasingly important role. In the famous Trail Smelter Case (1926–1934), subnational regions were not involved and Canada acted independently of London in international affairs for the first time (Murray 1972). British Columbia's Premier Bennett was a major player in the 1961 Columbia River Treaty, but cross-border negotiations and the signing of the actual treaty remained a federal matter (Swainson 1979). Since then, subnational groups have dominated water-related cross-border activities (Quinn 1991; Alper and Monahan 1986). In general, subnational cross-border groups have undertaken political and nontechnical activities much later in the Pacific Northwest than in other areas along the U.S.-Canadian border,[7] but have gained strong momentum recently.[8]

When cross-border links were first being set up in Europe, British Columbia rejected attempts from Washington state legislatures to establish formal cross-border contacts (Rutan 1981, 1985). Because of the region's limited socioeconomic interdependence and pervasive natural resources, cross-border relations have historically been distant and characterized by economic competition; however, a drastic change occurred in the last quarter of the 1980s to break this trend. In 1988, the year the U.S.-Canada Free Trade Agreement was signed, British Columbia signed an agreement with Washington called the "Pacific Northwest Economic Partnership" to encourage communication among private-sector business people (Goddard and Smith 1993: 10). The governments of British Columbia and Oregon, and California and Alaska have signed similar, although less successful, agreements as well. The Energy Cooperation Agreement between British Columbia and Washington also followed in 1989 (Alper 1996; Sparke 1999).

In December 1988, a tanker accident off the Washington coast caused an oil spill that affected the Olympic Peninsula and Vancouver Island. Expressing its strong dissatisfaction with the response of federal authorities and in spite of federal resistance, the British Columbian government initiated the International Oil Spill Task Force, comprising representatives from British Columbia, Washington, Oregon, Alaska, and California (Groen 1991: 218–46).

A group of the region's legislators initiated the Pacific Northwest Legislative Leadership Forum in October 1989 and founded the Pacific Northwest Economic Region (PNWER) in 1991. With the subnational legislatures' ratification of cooperative agreements, the inclusion of governors and premiers, and the support and participation of many private companies, the PNWER has become a comprehensive political institution that promotes economic development and trade both within its border region and abroad. It has a sophisticated organiza-

Figure 2. Cascadia

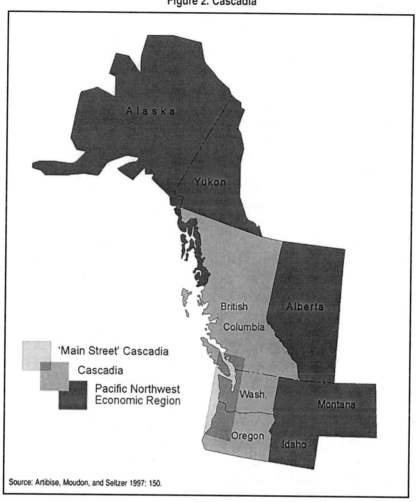

Source: Artibise, Moudon, and Seltzer 1997: 150.

tional structure comprising of an executive director, an executive committee, a delegate council, and several working groups (for agriculture, environmental technology, exports, forest products, government procurement, recycling, telecommunications, and tourism). In 1994, the PNWER also formally established a Private Sector Council.

An ecological vision of the Pacific Northwest boasts a longer history of collaboration. In his novel, *Ecotopia*, Ernest Callenbach (1975) envisioned an independent ecological state in the Pacific Northwest. *Washington Post* journalist Joel Garreau (1981) drew the boundaries of another nation called "Ecotopia" in his book, *The Nine Nations of North America*, stretching along the West Coast from Northern California to Alaska, encompassing the western parts of Oregon, Washington, and British Columbia. It was not until recently that this vision started to gain real momentum, established a deeper ideological foundation, and produced some institutional influence. Among ecologists, an emerging model based on "bioregions" defines regions by watersheds. One of the intellectual designers of this idea is David McCloskey, Professor of Sociology at Seattle University and founder of the Cascadia Institute. His map of Cascadia, based on watersheds, turned out to be very similar to Garreau's delineation of Ecotopia. *The Cascadia Times*, an independent monthly newspaper for the Pacific Northwest that is published in Portland, Oregon, appeared on the Internet in 1996. It covers the bioregion defined by the range of the pacific salmon (Cascadia Times 1998).

Real cross-border institution building among environmental nongovernmental organizations (NGOs) started in the early 1990s. The Seattle-based People for Puget Sound and the British Columbian Georgia Strait Alliance signed the Sound and Straits '92 Agreement and significantly increased their interaction (Alper 1996).

In 1991, Canadian Member of Parliament Robert L. Wenman (Conservative Party, British Columbia) and U.S. Congressman John Miller (Republican, Washington) prepared a proposal that envisioned a "metro corridor" from Vancouver, B.C., to Portland, Oregon, as an urban demonstration project to be showcased at the Earth Summit in Rio de Janeiro in 1992 (Alper 1996). Their Cascadia Corridor Commission was to be an advisory body with the authority to establish a forum to coordinate the consideration of regional issues by local, state, provincial, regional, and national governments. It was also to develop a strategic plan for environmentally sound economic development in the Cascadia region. The concept of a Cascadia Corridor Commission gained immediate support in the Pacific Northwest and Washington, D.C. a bill that laid the legal and financial foundation for such a commission passed in both the U.S. House and Senate; however, Washington state and new provincial officials feared heavy federal involvement, backed out, and the initiative failed (Alley 1998). The New Democratic Party that was elected to the British Columbian government opposed free trade agreements and was suspicious of the Cascadia idea, which they saw as an attempt to make British Columbia part of the United States (Harcourt 1996). Nonetheless, the Cascadia idea continued to be promoted on both sides of the border in more modest forms. In the United States, then-retired Senator John Miller brought the idea to the Discovery Institute, a conservative think tank in Seattle, where he started the Cascadia Program focused on "the four Ts" (Transportation, Trade, Tourism, and Technology) throughout the corridor (Schell and Hamer 1995: 154). Furthermore, the mayors of the major cities along "Main Street Cascadia" created the Cascadia Task Force and the Cascadia Economic Council, which also includes leading private corporations.

Discussion of a Cascadia Corridor Commission resulted in an Environmental Cooperation Agreement between Washington state and British Columbia in May 1992 and in the development of a sophisticated structure for regular and comprehensive cooperation on environmental issues. The agreement established the Environmental Cooperation Council, whose members include British Columbia's Deputy Minister of the Environment, Lands and Parks and the Director of the Washington Department of Ecology (Alley 1998). The signing of the Growth Management Agreement and the Transportation Cooperation Agreement between British Columbia and Washington state in September 1994 furthered transgovernmental cooperation, although both agreements functioned merely as legal frameworks for activities already underway.

As in the Lake Constance region, more formal and comprehensive links between municipalities are the latest developments in Cascadia. Major cities in the region were already active participants in the Cascadia Project. Since March 1994, representatives of the three metropolitan areas of Portland, Seattle, and Vancouver have met as the Cascadia Metropolitan Caucus to develop a cooperative agenda on environmental issues, land use, and transportation planning. Smaller cities along the border have always enjoyed many informal contacts, but have recently focused and formalized their connections by founding the Association of Border Communities (Artibise 1996).

Accomplishments

The 1988 oil spill did not result in cross-border conflict, which it well might have, given that the U.S. reaction was to protect its own coastline by towing the leaking tanker out to sea, resulting in the spill being carried to the coast of Canada's Vancouver Island. Instead, subnational groups reacted immediately to coordinate and strengthen protection efforts. The Oil Spill Task Force provided comprehensive recommendations that ranged from risk prevention to developing joint infrastructure (Groen 1991: 228–35).

Under the auspices of the British Columbia-Washington State Environmental Cooperation Council, an International Marine Science Panel composed of U.S. and Canadian scientists was appointed in July 1993. The Marine Science Panel produced a report that contained high priority recommendations. A detailed action plan was then formulated, which now must be implemented by the Puget Sound-Georgia Basin International Task Force (Puget Sound/Georgia Basin Initiative 1998). The activities of the council and its subgroups have resulted in cross-border interagency Memorandums of Understanding (MOUs) in which cross-border information and participation in permit processes are assured. Such an MOU has already been signed for air pollution permits and another is being prepared for water pollution permits and environmental assessment procedures. Several of of the Marine Science Panel's recommendations are now being implemented on both sides of the border (Okrainetz 1996; Schneider Ross 1996).

The restoration of a Seattle-Vancouver train link that had ceased operation 13 years previously was an early success for Cascadia activists. Amtrak revived the connection in May 1995 with one round-trip train daily (Kelly 1995). In addition, rail services in Washington and Oregon were extended. These successes are remarkable because they occurred at a time when Amtrak was forced by budget cuts from the new Republican-dominated U.S. Congress to reduce services in most other parts of the United States (Seattle Post Intelligencer 1995). This newly restored Seattle-Vancouver connection is seen as the first step toward a high-speed train corridor from Oregon to Vancouver (Alper 1996: 7; Mazza 1995a).

The tourism industry has started to promote Cascadia as well. "Cascadia—The Two Nation Vacation" is the cooperative marketing effort of Alaska, Alberta, British Columbia, Idaho, Oregon and Washington and is coordinated by the Discovery Institute (Cascadia 1998).[9]

The Lake Constance and Cascadia cross-border regions represent a general trend toward cross-border region building using a broad variety of cross-border links. In these cases, such region building is primariy achieved through informal interorganizational networks and "soft institutions" that are not based on formal legal treaties (Lang 1989).

Better Policies through Cross-Border Cooperation

The following analytical description will focus first on opportunities opened up by cross-border institutions. Four important functions of cross-border cooperation are to: (1) establish a *regulatory regime*; (2) function as a *transfer hinge*; (3) create an *innovation pole*; and (4) facilitate cross-border *coalition building*. These four functions often overlap and, although their differences are merely analytical, they are useful for highlighting various elements. Each originates from different disciplines: the first stems from the dominant legalistic and normative approach toward international and cross-border cooperation, the next two from economic considerations, and the last is based on a typical political science approach. The following examples are drawn from environmental policy, but the functions can be applied to all policy areas and goals.

Establishing a Regulatory Regime

In the absence of an authority to deal with negative externalities across the border, one way to reduce problems is to build an environmental "regime." Krasner (1983: 2) defines a regime as "a set of implicit or explicit principles, norms, rules and decision-making procedures around which actors' expectations converge in a given arena of international relations." The main goals of a regime are to reduce uncertainty, harmonize standards and policies, and monitor activities to ensure compliance. Environmental regimes first started in border regions such as Lake Constance (Prittwitz 1984) and the North American Great Lakes. In the 1980s, several continental and global environmental regimes emerged to confront various problems. The British Columbia-Washington Environmental Cooperation Council is a recent and dynamic example of such a regime. There is much literature on the characteristics and functions of such regimes (Haas, Keohane, and Levy 1995). Less attention, however, has been given to the last three functions since they may emerge within regimes but do not demand a regulatory regime framework because they are not based on potentially restricting norms for the participants.

Functioning as a Transfer Hinge

Many examples of useful cross-border learning exist. One notable example is an effort first implemented in Basel, Switzerland, to integrate all regional public transportation systems through a simple and reasonably priced monthly pass, or "ecoticket," called an *Umweltkarte*. It was introduced by a high profile public awareness campaign and proved to be a great success. Basel shared its *Umweltkarte* concept with its cross-border partner, the German city of Freiburg, which later spread from Freiburg throughout Germany (Blatter 1995).

Creating an Innovation Pole

The rapid installation of a new cross-border rail link is an example of cross-border cooperation based on an effective use of synergy. The small Swiss railway corporation, Mittelthurgau-Bahn, and the German county of Constance had complementary needs and means, and cooperated in a very personal and nonbureaucratic manner to make swift solutions possible to satisfy their needs. The results were impressive; there was a 40 percent increase in the number of passengers on the German side in the first year of service. This new alliance for public transportation became a highly recognized model in Germany and Switzerland because both countries' railway systems are in the process of restructuring (Schnell 1994). Because of its cross-border success, the Mittelthurgau-Bahn made a successful bid for the takeover of another railway connection on the Swiss side of the lake that had formerly been provided by the national railway company.

In these instances, the border regions served as "contact zones " (Ratti 1993a, 1993b). In the previous example, cross-border cooperation became a transfer hinge as an innovative concept was transferred from one country to another through the contact of border towns. In the latter example, cross-border cooperation acted as an innovation pole, as both countries gained innovative answers to their needs from their cooperative efforts.

Facilitating Cross-Border Coalition Building

The way to progress has been discussed here in the context of interterritorial coordination or the creation and transfer of innovations. These paths may be adequate for many projects and measures, but shifts toward better policies often counter the routines and agendas of interested groups and political actors. Conflict and competition thus arise between "advocacy coalitions" (Sabatier 1991, 1993) or between sectoral departments or agencies. International and cross-border political pressure can help to overcome resistance or to settle a contested policy. Such external pressure is often problematic, however, because it can result in adverse reactions and makes it easy to discredit foreign demand for change as imperialist behavior. In 1992, for example, British Columbia's forestry minister stated that from his point of view, "Vice-President-elect Gore has nothing to say in any kind of administrative sense about what happens in B.C." (Smith 1992/93: 8). Thus, it is more effective when domestic actors use transborder connections to strengthen their positions in cross-sectoral disputes.

Joint statements, proclaimed goals, and ratified plans provide normative obligations for governments to use in interdepartmental conflicts or when implementing programs. Keohane and Nye (1976: 10) introduced the concept of "coalition building" to the theory of transnational and transgovernmental relations. They define coalition building as in the effort "to improve their chances of policy success, governmental sub-units may attempt to bring actors from other governments into their own decision-making processes as allies." Central to this concept is its recognition of the many layers of political interrelations and arenas (Cascadia 1998).[10] Keohane and Nye, however, focus on the relationship between international activities of subnational actors and intergovernmental relations within a federation. Coalition building should include not only the whole range of political actors (politicians, bureaucrats, NGOs) and potentially connected political arenas (especially the intersectoral arena), but also the whole spectrum of "political resources" (such as knowledge, binding or nonbinding normative proclamations, reputation, or money). These can be gained from cross-border cooperation and applied to various political processes. The following are four examples that illustrate the wide range of situations made possible by cross-border coalition building.

In 1988, following the oil spill off the coast of Washington state, British Columbia's minister for the environment used cross-border linkages to stop the developmental aspirations of a cabinet colleague. By using both the Oil Spill Task Force and cross-border public awareness, he levied pressure against the minister for energy's attempt to sign an offshore drilling accord with the U.S. federal government. The Minister of the Environment announced a five-year drilling moratorium "in order to complement the work of the B.C.-Washington-Alaska Task Force on Oil Spills." Energy Minister Davis noted glumly, "While the province and the federal government jointly carried out some very extensive studies ... I don't think either Ottawa or Victoria wants to parade this one forward for final resolution right now" (Groen 1991: 237). Groen stressed that "the search for an accord, a twenty-five year old federal-provincial issue, has been delayed out of concern for trans-border sensitivities" (1991: 237–38). Even more important than the provincial-federal dimension was the intersectoral arena, in which cross-border linkage was put to use.

An example from the Lake Constance region reveals the mechanism that an established cross-border advocacy coalition could use against controversial projects in border regions. In the early 1990s, plans were brought forth to build new hydroelectric power plants along the Alpine Rhine River in Switzerland. The Alpine Rhine River is the main inflow into Lake Constance, which raised concerns about its possible negative effects on the lake. The IGKB used an already well-established mechanism to handle the problem. The scientific board prepared a report on possible consequences, the commission passed a resolution against the plans, and delegations from Baden-Württemberg and Bavaria drew up official submissions to the Swiss federal agency responsible for permissions.

The water protection agencies of the Swiss cantons used their domestic contacts to prevent the construction of these hydropower plants (Blatter 1994a).

Other examples show the limitations of cross-border coalition building. In 1993, environmental groups in the Georgia Basin-Puget Sound region developed the idea to establish a cooperative International Biosphere Reserve, comprising the Northwest Straits Sanctuary in northern Puget Sound on the Washington side and the British Columbian Strait of Juan de Fuca (Georgia Strait Alliance 1995a). When resistance emerged, the coalition tried to use cross-border coalition-building strategies to overcome the hurdles and meetings "brought together the most active players in marine conservation from government (at provincial, state and federal levels) and non-governmental organizations from BC and Washington State, and provided fertile ground for information sharing, brainstorming and a heightened sense of inspiration" (Georgia Strait Alliance 1995b). In August 1995, *Sans Boundary News* reported that Canadian federal and provincial agencies had signed a Memorandum of Understanding with substantial commitments to a National Marine Conservation Area adjoining the U.S. border. "An important point was made in the MOU to propose to the United States to create similar areas on Washington's side of the border." The British Columbia-Washington Environmental Cooperation Council, fearing that losing a first attempt would discredit the council, refused to endorse a commitment to the proposed Common Conservation Area. Today, chances for the project look poor (Georgia Strait Alliance 1996).

The regulation of motor boats on Lake Constance is another example of cross-border coalition building. The number of motor boats on Lake Constance had rapidly increased since the 1950s, sparking a battle over international regulations that lasted from the late 1960s until the early 1990s. Attempts around the lake to implement restrictions on motor boats by the environmental advocacy coalition resulted in the creation and fostering of an equivalent boat-user oriented advocacy coalition. Caught between these advocacy coalitions were the transgovernmental commissions—the water commission (IGKB) on one side and the shipping commission (ISKB) on the other. In the 1970s, a confrontational round of public squabbles and unsuccessful negotiations led the Conference of Government Leaders (IBK) to establish a subcommission in which members of all interested groups participated. This integrated subcommission then successfully mediated the conflict. The most remarkable result was the introduction of a unique and binding new standard for motor boat exhaust (Blatter 1994a).

The last example clearly demonstrates that a distinction between the functions of cross-border cooperation is strictly analytical. In the case of the motor boats, cross-border cooperation fulfilled three functions: it created a regulatory regime; produced a new, innovative standard; and demonstrated the extended use of coalition-building strategies.

Consequences of the Search for Sustainability

While cross-boundary cooperation is valuable to further policy goals, it does not necessarily help promote solutions based on sustainable development. Included among the preconditions that promote sustainable development is the existence of institutions that help to overcome intersectoral cleavage. This section will demonstrate that cross-border linkage makes such preconditions more difficult to establish.

Current debates on sustainable development center on the declaration signed at the "Earth Summit" in Rio de Janeiro in 1992. The official definition of sustainable development is: "Development that meets the needs of the present without compromising the ability of future generations to meet their own needs" (World Commission on Environment and Development 1987).

Achieving cross-sectoral integration is key to any attempt to carry out plans that work toward sustainability. As Thierstein and Walser (1997) stated, "The strengths lie in its cross sectional character which integrates economics, ecology and social aspects." Principle 25 of the Rio Declaration states that peace, development, and environmental protection are interdependent and indivisible (Thierstein and Walser 1997). Elizabeth Dowdeswell, Executive Director of the United Nations Environmental Program (UNEP) also noted, "As we focus on sustainable development, a more holistic approach is needed ... " (1995: 5). For scholars of international environmental law, the "principle of integration" is one of four legal principles that sustainable development entails (Sands 1995: 61). Others have also stressed that "the most essential principle of international law for sustainable development is the principle, be it legal or otherwise, of integration" (Mann 1995: 71).

The need for integrated economic, ecological, and social goals is reflected not only in international law, but also in regional planning, resulting in the evolution of integrated development plans. One example is a report by the British Columbia Commission on Resources and Environment (1994: 11) called *Finding Common Ground: A Shared Vision for Land Use in British Columbia*. Its authors state that "land use planning and management shall be cross-sectoral, comprehensive and integrated. The processes will address the full range of environmental, social and economic concerns and values."

The institutional reaction to the Rio Declaration was that many countries created integrative round tables, commissions, or interagency task forces at national and regional levels (Thierstein and Walser 1997). It is this institutional layer or institutional precondition for sustainable development that must be focused on. Although there are other meaningful definitions and indicators for sustainable development (Pezzoli 1997a, 1997b), there are good reasons to focus on this institutional definition.

Among political scientists, the "New Institutionalism" (March and Olsen 1989; DiMaggio and Powell 1991; Keck 1991; Lownds 1996; Scharpf 1997) brought attention to the fact that policy and politics are strongly influenced by institutional involvement since institutions are not restricted to organizations and

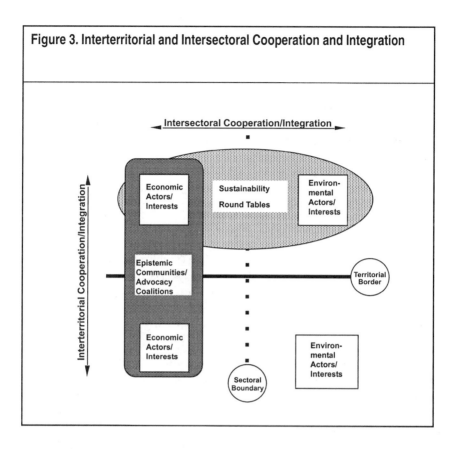

Figure 3. Interterritorial and Intersectoral Cooperation and Integration

formal rules. The sociological branch of the new institutionalism includes routines, symbols, and leitmotifs as important aspects of institutional settings (Göhler 1994; Immergut 1997).

An institutional criterion for sustainable development reflects new approaches to urban and regional planning. The most important element of successful planning is not the development of comprehensive plans with detailed indicators, but a planning process embedded in institutional settings. Intersectoral communication and cooperation, round tables, and forums are deemed crucial elements to moving toward innovative and sustainable development (Sinning 1995; Kräft 1995; Knieling 1994).[11]

The next step is to apply this definition of sustainability to the emerging cross-border regions. A striking characteristic of cross-border regions is that linkages across the border are almost always centered around sectoral focal points. Sectoral differentiation in the process of cross-border region building occurs at different levels:

- Formation of selective "policy networks" (Marin and Mayntz 1991)

- The existence and importance of antagonistic "epistemic communities" (Haas 1989)
- Antagonistic "visions" of what a cross-border region is intended to accomplish

That two different cross-border sectoral policy networks exist in the Lake Constance region became very obvious in light of events that occurred at the University of Constance in April 1995. An international meeting called "Environmental Policy in Border Regions: Lake Constance—A Model for Europe?" was financed by the environmental subcommission of the Conference of Government Leaders (IBK) and attended by scientists, politicians, bureaucrats, consultants, and members of nongovernmental organizations involved in environmental policies from communities all around the lake. Two weeks later, a book presentation also brought together a broad variety of politicians, bureaucrats, and business people from the Euregio Bodensee. A guide to all private companies in the bordering communities was published in a collaborative cross-border effort. No one attended both meetings. The network links of the environmental actors are clearly emerging along the same lines as the business group links; however, although both groups are investing more time and resources into better communication across the border, the same cannot be said for their efforts to communicate with each other.[12]

Not only are time and resources redirected by cross-border activities, but sectoral and antagonistic world views and beliefs become reinforced by communication with like-minded people from across the border. Peter M. Haas' (1989) notion of "epistemic communities"[13] draws attention to situations in which experts from various countries share beliefs and try to influence the policies of their national governments as a group. He points to the positive effects that epistemic communities have had on international cooperation. It is important to note, however, that what is helpful for interterritorial coordination and integration appears to negatively affect cross-sectoral coordination. The ripple effect caused by epistemic communities is clearly illustrated by the disputed motor boat regulations on Lake Constance discussed previously. The two advocacy coalitions[14] (environmentalists on one side and boaters on the other), along with their respective transgovernmental commissions, perceived the problem quite differently. The negative effects of the boats was obvious to the environmentalists; as such, their argument relied heavily on the large number of boats on the lake (over 50,000). Conversely, boat users denied that the boats were a serious threat; they perceived the circumstance to be an artificial statistical problem created by (German) boat permit regulations that force boat owners to register their boats even if they use them only once a year. The cross-border links and communications that existed among like-minded people reinforced these different perceptions and made it very difficult to compromise (Blatter 1994a).

Opposing advocacy coalitions and epistemic communities in border regions are not limited to specific controversies. Indeed, antagonism is a central characteristic of emerging cross-border regions underpinned by ideas that become stimulating visions for the different actors within such groups.

Environmentalists and business groups are generally the two dominant coalitions or communities in any area. The cleavage between these vision-based[15] communities is pronounced in the Pacific Northwest. Here, the differing visions of cross-border regions are clearly defined. Senator Bluechel, founder of the PNWER, made his view clear in an article entitled, "Reaping Profit from the New World Order" (Bluechel 1991). Another pronouncement made by the PNWER also cements this idea, "PNWER's objective is to put together the necessary critical mass for the region to become a major player in the new global economy" (PNWER 1997). This view is again present in the Discovery Institute's publication, *International Seattle: Creating a Globally Competitive Community.* This work was the starting point of the business community's engagement in the Cascadia Project (Hamer and Chapman 1993). Their vision refers to "'region states' in a borderless world" (Ohmae 1993).[16]

Environmentalists from the Pacific Northwest refer to a common cross-border "bioregion." In their view, natural flows (such as a common watershed), not economic exchanges, are the essential bonds between people in a community (Henkel 1993; McCloskey 1995). "The coming Cascadia may even prefigure a form of biologically rooted, ecological self-governance that transcends and essentially replaces the reign of nation-states" (Mazza 1995c: 1). Even though both the business and environmental communities downplay the future importance of the nation-state, their visions for Cascadia are diametrically opposed. Belief in the need for adaptation to a placeless and borderless global economy is pitted against a vision of self-governance in accordance with inherent biological and cultural characteristics (Mazza 1995b; Henkel 1993).

A few examples will illustrate just how important symbols and names can be in these struggles toward building cross-border regions. Environmental groups established a foundation for Lake Constance (*Bodenseestiftung*) in 1995 primarily because they feared that the *Bodenseerat* would get the same idea and coin the name first (Pfrommer 1994). When the business-oriented *Bodenseerat* came up with a logo for the common cross-border region, the IBK reacted by promoting its own official logo for the Euregio Bodensee. In the Pacific Northwest, McCloskey of Seattle and Artibise of Vancouver have disputed the use of and rights to the name "Cascadia Institute." The two creators of the different concepts about Cascadia are found at the center of the rivalrous epistemic communities in this cross-border region.

There is almost no communication across the boundary between these communities. Greater cross-border communication aggravates this problem as actors rely on their own sectoral philosophical and professional views and visions to bridge cross-border institutional and cultural differences. Investing time in interterritorial understanding and cooperation reduces the possibilities for cross-sectoral communication and coordination.

In summary, territorial integration fosters antagonistic communities and networks that make the difficulties more complicated to overcome. As such, it seems that cross-border institution building actually constrains the search for sustainability. For metropolitan areas, Bollens (1997) has shown that the fragmentation and compartmentalization of regional governance is the price that must be paid when cities coordinate and cooperate on a regional level. One of the central characteristics of governance in the EU is strong sectoral fragmentation (Eising and Kohler-Koch 1994: 187). Environmental regimes are not only a scientific concept, but "sectoral legal systems" (Gehring 1991) as well that are almost always limited to sectoral policy goals.

Dialectic Innovation: An Avenue toward Integration on All Levels?

There is some evidence that fragmentation is not an inevitable outcome of territorial integration. Cross-border regions also have the potential to fulfill the necessary next step in the differentiation-integration dialectic. After increased sectoral differentiation and fragmentation as a result of intensified cooperation across territorial borders, some intersectoral reintegration is possible. In both cross-border regions described in this paper, the bigger country delivers most of the essentials of cross-border integration.

Conceptual framework: It is no coincidence that the ideas that facilitate interterritorial cooperation (both the idea of a bioregion and the idea of an economic region) were generated in the United States, while similar concepts were also generated in Germany.

Finance: A U.S. foundation provides British Columbia's Georgia Strait Alliance with the funding for its cross-border activities. Most of the money for PNWER and the Cascadia Project came from the U.S. side. At Lake Constance, the resource-rich and powerful German ENGOs (environmental nongovernmental organizations) are the motors that drive cross-border environmental cooperation.

Administrative and scientific capacity: In the Lake Constance area, the much larger German *Länder* administration was the driving force in initiating and institutionalizing cross-border linkages. Baden-Württemberg's Institute for Marine Biology is the principal scientific institution involved in ecological discussions around the lake (Blatter 1994a: 26–27). In the economic realm, it is no accident that the Euregio-Bureau is located in and sponsored mainly by the county administration of Constance. In Cascadia, the institutions most actively pursuing economic cooperation are located in Seattle.

In contrast, the smaller and more consensus-oriented countries in these two regions have a greater potential for bridging intersectoral boundaries.

- In the case of the Lake Constance motor boat controversy, after the advocacy coalitions promoted their antagonistic positions by consulting German institutes, it was the Swiss members of the water and shipping commission who found common ground and smoothed the way for final compromise (Blatter 1994a).

- In contrast to the polarized concepts held by the U.S. factions, the main Canadian approaches (formulated by the Georgia Basin Initiative, the British Columbian Institute for Sustainable Cities, and the Cascadia Institute) are not very different. Ironically, one reason that there has been no successful synthesis in this region may be the cultural similarities of the West. British Columbia has a rather populist and polarized political culture, making it more similar to the United States than to the rest of Canada (Morley 1990). This could be one reason that, until now, British Columbian actors have been unable to bridge the different cross-border coalitions. British Columbian political culture does not provide the necessary degree of intersectoral consensus to complement U.S. ideas for interterritorial cooperation and integration.

Hope still remains that this dialectic may lead to sustainability, the necessary third step toward region building. After thesis (cross-border economic region) and antithesis (cross-border bioregion), there may be synthesis (sustainable region). The examples of Lake Constance and Cascadia offer some support for the proposition that the key to successful integration at all levels is not the imposition of similarity or homogeneity, but the encouragement of complementary factors. Cross-border regions could be ideal places for the power and dynamics of different systems to come together to find the ways and means needed for compromise and integration.

Endnotes

1. There is limited economic interdependence between subregions in both examples. The proponents of cross-border cooperation contend that the border inhibits interdependence and is therefore a reason for cooperation (Goldberg and Levi 1992/1993). However, recent research has shown that even in cross-border regions with a long tradition of cooperation—such as the German-Dutch border, with 30 years of cross-border political cooperation—substantial economic cooperation has not been created (Hamm 1996).

2. Note that the word "idea" is used here in a constructivist sense. Ideas are independent factors that shape the identities and preferences of political actors. In this case, new awareness of continental integration and enhanced competition has changed the identities of border regions from "national peripheries" to "European heartlands." Furthermore, political actors in border areas have shifted their perceptions of their cross-border counterparts from indifferent neighbors to potentially cooperative partners and allies. This change has occurred simply because new options have been discovered through integration discourse. The spillover of integration dynamics from the continental level to border regions should be seen as "idea-driven" since initiatives in the border regions often begin well before the allocation of policy programs and funds to the border regions, as will be demonstrated in the following examples.

3. See <http://www.bitcom.ch/lokal/euro/erklaerung.gif>.

4. See <http://www-iwi.unisg.ch/iwi4/cc/emb/index.html>.

5. Geschäftsordnung des Begleitenden Ausschusses zum INTERREG II Programm "Bodensee-Hochrhein" (Standing Orders of the Committee for the INTERREG II Program "Bodensee-Hochrhein").

6. It took about ten years longer to introduce an ecosystem approach on the Rhine River (de Villeneuve 1996); however, the ecosystem approach was officially adopted at the Great Lakes in 1978 (Dworsky 1993).

7. For descriptions of developments in other U.S.-Canadian border regions, see Feldman and Gardner 1984; Feldman and Gardner 1990; Alper 1986; Fanjoy 1990.

8. It remains to be seen whether the momentum of cooperation survives the hostilities of the "fishery war" of the summer of 1997.

9. For activities coordinated by the Discovery Institute, see <http://www.discovery.org/cascadia.html>.

10. For example, the relation between the different levels of government (the executive and the legislative branches), the public, and the private sector. For a comprehensive discussion, see Blatter 1997.

11. Since the focus of this essay is on the institutions of cross-border or interterritorial integration, the need for coherence dictates that sustainability is defined in institutional terms as well.

12. Note that the generalization of this event is not based on a solid network analysis, but on the author's impressions during the six years he spent observing cross-border activities in his home region.

13. Haas (1989: 384) defines "epistemic communities" as "a specific community of experts sharing a belief in a common set of cause-and-effect relationships as well as common values to which policies governing these relationships will be applied."

14. Advocacy coalitions and epistemic communities are used here interchangeably since the core of both concepts is that the members of these groups share a belief system of cognitive convergence (Scharpf 1997: 42). Haas' concept of epistemic communities applies here because it focuses on cognitive factors in international relations (Haas 1989). Sabatier's (1993) concept of advocacy coalitions is even more accurate in two aspects: (1) there are not one but two rivalrous communities, and (2) these groups are not only bound by normative and causal beliefs, but also by material interests.

15. The word "vision" occurs often in these actor's statements and writings. Visions should be seen as a mixture of ideology and mission. They are almost as fundamental and deep as ideologies, but not as encompassing since they are bound only to one project and not to politics in general. "Mission" is a word from management literature that stresses the stimulating aspect of a common endeavor. Visions for cross-border regions embody three aspects: a label (region-state versus bioregion); a point of reference (global market place versus natural carrying capacity); and an ontological basis (anarchic competition versus holistic harmony).

16. Kenichi Ohmae was Chief Executive of McKinsey in North America.

References

Alley, Jaime. 1998. "The British Columbia/Washington Environmental Cooperation Council: An Evolving Model of Canada/U.S. Interjurisdictional Cooperation." In *Environmental Management on North America's Borders,* Richard Kiy and John D. Wirth, eds. College Station: Texas A&M University Press.

Alper, Donald K. 1986. "Recent Trends in U.S.-Canada Regional Diplomacy." Pp. 118–153 in *Across Boundaries. Transborder Interaction in Comparative Perspective,* Oscar J. Martínez, ed. El Paso: Texas Western Press.

Alper, Donald K. 1996. "The Idea of Cascadia: Emergent Transborder Regionalism in the Pacific Northwest-Western Canada." *Journal of Borderlands Studies* 11 (2): 1–22.

Alper, Donald K., and R.L. Monahan. 1986. "Regional Transboundary Negotiations Leading to the Skagit River Treaty: Analysis and Future Application." *Canadian Public Policy* 7 (1): 163–74.

Artibise, A.F.J. 1996. *Redefining B.C.'s Place in Canada: The Emergence of Cascadia as a Strategic Alliance.* Vancouver.

Artibise, Alan, Anne Vernez Moudon, and Ethan Seltzer. 1997. "Cascadia: An Emerging Regional Model." Pp. 149–74 in *Cities in Our Future*, Robert Geddes, ed. Washington, D.C.: Island Press.

Blatter, Joachim. 1994a. *Erfolgsbedingungen grenzüberschreitender Zusammenarbeit im Umweltschutz. Das Beispiel Gewässerschutz am Bodensee.* EURES discussion paper No. 37. Freiburg: EURES.

Blatter, Joachim. 1994b. *Erfolgsbedingungen grenzüberschreitender Zusammenarbeit im Umweltschutz. Das Beispiel Gewässer—und Auenschutz am Oberrhein.* EURES discussion paper No. 43. Freiburg: EURES.

Blatter, Joachim. 1995. *Möglichkeiten und Restriktionen für umweltorientierte Maßnahmen im Personennahverkehr. Eine Analyse der Freiburger Verkehrspolitik unter besonderer Berücksichtigung der Parkraumpolitik und der regionalen Zusammenarbeit im ÖPNV.* EURES discussion paper No. 47. Freiburg: EURES.

Blatter, Joachim. 1997. "Explaining Cross-Border Cooperation: A Border-Focused and Border-External Approach." *Journal of Borderlands Studies* 12 (1 & 2): 151–74.

Bluechel, Alan. 1991. "Reaping Profit from a New World Order." *The Journal of State Government* 64 (1): 18–21.

Blyth, Mark M. 1997. "Any More Bright Ideas? The Ideational Turn of Comparative Political Economy." *Comparative Politics* 29 (2): 229–50.

Bollens, Scott A. 1997. "Fragments of Regionalism: The Limits of Southern California Governance." *Journal of Urban Affairs* 19 (1): 105–22.

British Columbia Commission on Resources and Environment, ed. 1994. *Finding Common Ground: A Shared Vision for Land Use in British Columbia.* Victoria: British Columbia Commission on Resources and Environment.

Brown, D.M., and E.H. Fry, eds. 1993. *States and Provinces in the International Economy.* Berkeley: Institute of Governmental Studies Press.

Bullinger, D. 1977. "Grenzüberschreitende Zusammenarbeit in der Regionalpolitik. Theoretische Ansätze und ihre Bedeutung für das Bodensee-gebiet." Master's thesis, University of Constance, Constance, Germany.

Callenbach, Ernest. 1975. *Ecotopia: The Notebooks and Reports of William Weston.* Berkeley: Banyan Tree Books.

Cascadia. 1998. http://www.youra.com/cascadia/index.htm.

Cascadia Times. 1998. http://cascadia.times.org.

Cohn, T.H., and P.J. Smith. 1996. "Subnational Governments as International Actors: Constituent Diplomacy in British Columbia and the Pacific Northwest." *BC Studies* 110 (Summer): 29–44.

Daly, Herman E. 1996. *Beyond Growth: The Economics of Sustainable Development.* Boston: Beacon.

De Villeneuve, Carel H.V. 1996. "Western Europe's Artery: The Rhine." *Natural Resources Journal* 36 (3): 441–54.

DiMaggio, Paul J., and Walter W. Powell. 1991. "Introduction." Pp. 1–38 in *The New Institutionalism in Organizational Analysis*, Walter W. Powell and Paul J. DiMaggio, eds. Chicago and London: University of Chicago Press.

Dowdeswell, E. 1995. "Sustainable Development: The Contribution of International Law." Pp. 3–6 in *Sustainable Development and International Law*, Winfried Lang, ed. London, Dordrecht, and Boston: Graham and Trotman/Martinus Nijhoff.

Drexler, A.M. 1980. *Umweltpolitik am Bodensee Baden-Württemberg.* Constance: Dr. Neinhaus Verlag.

Dworsky, Leonard B. 1993. "Ecosystem Management: Great Lakes Perspectives." *Natural Resources Journal* 33 (2): 347–62.

Eising, Rainer, and Beate Kohler-Koch, eds. 1994. "Inflation und Zerfaserung: Trends der Interessenvermittlung in der Europäischen Gemeinschaft." In *Staat und Verbände*, Wolfgang Streek, ed. Opladen: Westdeutscher Verlag.

Fanjoy, E. 1990. "A View from the Inside: The Conference of New England Governors and Eastern Canadian Premiers." *Canadian Parliamentary Review* (Fall): 20–25.

Feldman, E.J., and L. Gardner. 1984. "The Impact of Federalism on the Organization of Canadian Foreign Policy." *Publius* 14 (4): 33–60.

Feldman, E.J., and L. Gardner. 1990. "Canada." Pp. 176–210 in *Federalism and International Relations. The Role of Subnational Units,* H. J. Michelmann and P. Soldatos, eds. Oxford: Clarendon Press.

Garreau, Joel. 1981. *The Nine Nations of America.* Boston: Houghton Mifflin.

Garrett, G., and B.R. Weingast. 1993. "Ideas, Interests, and Institutions: Constructing the European Community's Internal Market." Pp. 173–206 in *Ideas in Foreign Policy. Beliefs, Institutions, and Political Change,* J. Goldstein and R.O. Keohane, eds. Ithaca and London: Cornell University Press.

Gehring, Thomas. 1991. "International Environmental Regimes: Dynamic Sectoral Legal Systems." Pp. 35–56 in *Yearbook of International Environmental Law* (1990). London and Norwell: Graham and Trotman.

Georgia Strait Alliance. 1995a. *Saving Georgia Strait Newsletter* (June). Gabriola Island: Georgia Strait Alliance.

Georgia Strait Alliance. 1995b. *Saving Georgia Strait Newsletter* (August-October). Gabriola Island: Georgia Strait Alliance.

Georgia Strait Alliance. 1996. *Saving Georgia Strait Newsletter* (Spring). Gabriola Island: Georgia Strait Alliance.

Goddard, A.M., and P.J. Smith. 1993. *The Development of Subnational Relations: The Case of the Pacific Northwest and Western Canada.* Vancouver.

Göhler, Gerhard, ed. 1994. *Die Eigenart der Institutionen. Zum Profil politischer Institutionentheorie.* Baden-Baden: Nomos.

Goldberg, M.A., and M.D. Levi. 1992/1993. "The Evolving Experience along the Pacific Northwest Corridor Called Cascadia." *The New Pacific* 7 (Winter): 28–32.

Goldstein, J., and Robert. O. Keohane, eds. 1993. *Ideas in Foreign Policy. Beliefs, Institutions, and Political Change.* Ithaca and London: Cornell University Press.

Groen, J.P. 1991. "Provincial International Activity: Case Studies of the Barret and Vander Zalm Administrations in British Columbia." Master's thesis, Simon Fraser University, British Columbia, Canada.

Groen, J.P. 1994. "British Columbia's International Relations: Consolidating a Coalition Building Strategy." *BC Studies* 102: 54–82.

Groen, J.P. 1995. "Intergovernmental Relations and the International Activities of Ontario and Alberta." Ph.D. diss., Queen's University, Kingston, Ontario.

Haas, Peter M. 1989. "Do Regimes Matter? Epistemic Communities and Mediterranean Pollution Control." *International Organisation* 43: 377–403.

Haas, Peter. M., Robert O. Keohane, and Marc. A. Levy, eds. 1995. *Institutions for the Earth. Sources of Effective International Environmental Protection.* Cambridge and London: MIT Press.

Haefliger, Christian J. 1996. "Mikrointegration: Sechs Mal die 'Aussen-Schweiz.'" *Regio-Inform* 1: 2–4.

Hamer, J., and B. Chapman. 1993. *International Seattle: Creating a Globally Competitive Community.* Seattle: Discovery Institute Press.

Hamm, Rüdiger. 1996. "European Border Regions—Driving Force of European Integration?" Paper presented at the 36th European Congress of the European Regional Science Association, 26–30 August, Zürich, Switzerland.

Harcourt, Mike (former Premier of British Columbia). 1996. Interview with author. 11 August.

Henkel, W.B. 1993. "Cascadia: A State of (Various) Mind(s)." *Chicago Review* 39: 110–18.

Hocking, Brian, ed. 1993a. *Foreign Relations and Federal States*. London and New York: Leicester University Press.

Hocking, Brian. 1993b. *Localizing Foreign Policy: Non-Central Governments and Multilayered Diplomacy*. London and New York: MacMillan.

Immergut, E.M. 1997. "The Normative Roots of the New Institutionalism: Historical Institutionalism and Comparative Policy Studies." In *Beiträge zur Theorieentwicklung in der Politik—und Verwaltungswissenschaft*, A. Benz and W. Seibel, eds. Baden-Baden: Nomos.

Informationswissenschaft. 1998. http://www/inf-wiss.uni-konstanz.de/emb/region.

Internationale Gewässerschutzkommission für den Bodensee (IGKB). 1987. *Richtlinien für die Reinhaltung des Bodensees vom 27 Mai 1987* (mit Kommentierungen). Langenargen: IGKB.

Keck, Otto. 1991. "Der neue Institutionalismus in der Theorie der Internationalen Politik." *Politische Vierteljahresschrift* 4: 635–53.

Kelly, E. 1995. "Northwest Amtrak Train on Fast Track in State." *Gannett News Service* (27 April).

Keohane, Robert O., Peter M. Haas, and Marc A. Levy. 1995. "The Effectiveness of International Environmental Institutions." Pp. 3–24 in *Institutions for the Earth. Sources of Effective International Environmental Protection*, Robert O. Keohane, Peter M. Haas, and Marc A. Levy, eds. Cambridge and London: MIT Press.

Keohane, Robert O., and J.S. Nye. 1976. "Introduction." Pp. 3–17 in *Canada and the United States: Transnational and Transgovernmental Relations*, A. Baker Fox, A.O. Hero, and Joseph S. Nye, eds. New York and London: Columbia University Press.

Knieling, Jörg. 1994. "Intermediäre Organisationen und kooperative Regionalentwicklung." *Raumordnung und Raumforschung* 2: 116–26.

Kräft, Ralf. 1995. "Die Postmoderne und kooperative Planung." *Raumplanung* 71: 249–52.

Krasner, S.D., ed. 1983. *International Regimes*. Ithaca and London: Cornell University Press.

Lang, Winfried. 1989. "Die normative Qualität grenzüberschreitender Regionen. Zum Begriff der 'soft institution.'" *Archiv des Völkerrechts* 27: 253–85.

Leuenberger, T., and D. Walker. 1992. *Euroregion Bodensee—Grundlagen für ein grenzüberschreitendes Impulsprogramm. Gutachten im Auftrag der deutschen, österreichischen und schweizerischen Bundesländer und Kantone der Bodenseeregion*. Saint Gall: Hochschule St. Gallen.

Lownds, Vivien. 1996. "Varieties of New Institutionalism: A Critical Appraisal." *Public Administration* 74 (Summer): 181–97.

Mann, H. 1995. "Comments on a Paper by Philippe Sands." Pp. 67–71 in *Sustainable Development and International Law*, W. Lang, ed. London, Dordrecht, and Boston: Graham and Trotman/Martinus Nijhoff.

March, James G., and Johan P. Olsen. 1989. *Rediscovering Institutions. The Organizational Basis of Politics*. New York and London: Free Press.

Marin, Bernd, and Renate Mayntz, eds. 1991. *Policy Networks*. Frankfurt: Campus.

Martínez, O.J. 1986. *Across Boundaries: Transborder Interactions in Comparative Perspective*. El Paso: University of Texas Press.

Mazza, P. 1995a. "Amtrak Rechristens Northwest line "The Cascadia"—High-Speed Rail Coming?" (July) http://www.tnews.com/text/the_cascadia.html.

Mazza, P. 1995b. "Cascadia Emerging: The End and Beginning of the World." (July) http://www.tnews.com:80/text/emerge.html.

Mazza, P. 1995c. "Lifeplace or Marketplace? Bioregions, Region States and the Contested Turf of Regionalism." (July) http://www.tnews.com/text/lifeplace_marketplace.html.

McCloskey, D.D. 1995. "Cascadia: A Great Green Land on the Northeast Pacific Rim." (July) http://www.tnews.com:80/text/mccloskey.html.

Michelmann, H.J., and P. Soldatos, eds. 1990. *Federalism and International Relations. The Role of Subnational Units*. Oxford: Clarendon Press

Morley, T. 1990. "Politics as Theater: Paradox and Complexity in British Columbia." *Journal of Canadian Studies* 25 (3): 19–37.

Müller-Schnegg, H. 1994. "Bestandsaufnahme der grenzueberschreitenden Kooperation in der Bodenseeregion." Ph.D. diss., University of Saint Gall, Saint Gall, Switzerland.

Murray, K.A. 1972. "The Trail Smelter Case: International Air Pollution in the Columbia Valley." *BC Studies* 15: 68–85.

Ohmae, Keniche. 1993. "The Rise of the Region State." *Foreign Affairs* 72: 78–87.

Okrainetz, Glen (Ministry of Environment, Lands and Parks, Province of British Columbia). 1996. Interview with author. Victoria, British Columbia, Canada (30 July).

Pacific Northwest Economic Region (PNWER). 1997. http://www.ei.gov.bc.ca/~PNWER/Default.htm.

Pezzoli, Keith. 1997a. "Sustainable Development: A Transdisciplinary Overview of the Literature." *Journal of Environmental Planning and Management* 40 (5): 549–74.

Pezzoli, Keith. 1997b. "Sustainable Development Literature: A Transdisciplinary Bibliography." *Journal of Environmental Planning and Management* 40 (5): 575–601.

Pfrommer, Wolfgang (Bund für Umwelt und Naturschutz Deutschland). 1994. Interview with author. Constance, Germany (26 November).

Prittwitz, V. 1984. *Umweltaussenpolitik. Grenzueberschreitende Luftverschmutzung in Europa.* Frankfurt: Campus.

Puget Sound/Georgia Basin Initiative. 1998. http://www.epa.gov/region10/www/pugsnd/html.

Quinn, F. 1991. "Canada-United States Relations along the Waterfront." *Zeitschrift für Kanada-Studien* 11: 79–93.

Raich, S. 1995. *Grenzüberschreitende und interregionale Zusammenarbeit in einem "Europa der Regionen." Dargestellt anhand der Fallbeispiele Großregion Saar-Lor-Lux, EUREGIO und "Vier Motoren für Europa"—Ein Beitrag zum Europäischen Integrationsprozeß.* Schriftenreihe des Europäischen Zentrums für Föderalismus-Forschung, Band 3. Baden-Baden: Nomos.

Ratti, Remigio. 1993a. "How Can Existing Barriers and Border Effects be Overcome? A Theoretical Approach." Pp. 60–69 in *Regional Networks, Border Regions and European Integration*, R. Cappelin and P.W.J. Batey, eds. European Research in Regional Science Series, No. 3. London: Pion Limited.

Ratti, Remigio. 1993b. "Strategies to Overcome Barriers: From Theory to Practice." Pp. 241–68 in *Theory and Practice of Transborder Cooperation*, R. Ratti and S. Reichman, eds. Basel, Frankfurt on the Main: Helbing und Lichtenhahn.

Rutan, G.F. 1981. "Legislative Interaction of a Canadian Province and an American State—Thoughts upon Sub-National Cross-Border Relations." *American Review of Canadian Studies* 6 (2): 67–79.

Rutan, G.F. 1985. "British Columbia-Washington State Governmental Interrelations: Some Findings upon the Failure of Structure." *American Review of Canadian Studies* 15 (1): 97–110.

Sabatier, Paul A. 1991. "Toward Better Theories of the Policy Process." *Political Science and Politics* 24 (2) (June): 147–156.

Sabatier, Paul A. 1993. "Advocacy-Koalitionen, Policy-Wandel und Policy-Lernen: Eine Alternative zur Phasenheuristik." Pp. 116–48 in *Policy-Analyse; Kritik und Neuorientierung*, A. Héritier, ed. Opladen: Westdeutscher Verlag.

Sands, P. 1995. "International Law in the Field of Sustainable Development: Emerging Legal Principles." Pp. 53–66 in *Sustainable Development and International Law*, Winfried Lang, ed. London, Dordrecht, and Boston: Graham and Trotman/Martinus Nijhoff.

Scharpf, Fritz W. 1997. *Games Real Actors Play. Actor-Centered Institutionalism in Policy Research.* Boulder: Westview Press.

Schell, P., and J. Hamer. 1995. "Cascadia: The New Binationalism of Western Canada and the U.S. Pacific Northwest." Pp. 140–56 in *Identities in North America: The Search for Community*, R.L. Earle and J.D. Wirth, eds. Stanford: Stanford University Press.

Scherer, R., and H. Müller. 1994. *Erfolgsbedingungen grenzüberschreitender Zusammenarbeit im Umweltschutz. Das Beispiel Bodenseeregion.* EURES discussion paper No. 34. Freiburg: EURES.

Schimank, U. 1996. *Theorien gesellschaftlicher Differenzierung.* Opladen: Leske und Budrich.

Schneider Ross, Holly (Puget Sound-Georgia Strait Liaison, Puget Sound Water Quality Authority). 1996. Interview with author (24 July).

Schnell, K.D. 1994. *Erfolgsbedinungen grenzüberschreitender Zusammenarbeit im Umweltschutz. Das Beispiel ÖPNV in der Bodenseeregion.* EURES discussion paper No. 36. Freiburg: EURES.

Sinning, Heidi. 1995. "Verfahrensinnivationen kooperativer Stadt—und Regionalentwicklung." *Raumordnung und Raumforschung* 3: 169–76.

Smith, C. 1992/1993. "Olé." *The New Pacific* 7: 8–9.

Soldatos, P. 1990. "An Explanatory Framework for the Study of Federated States as Foreign-Policy Actors." Pp. 34–53 in *Federalism and International Relations. The Role of Subnational Units*, H. J. Michelmann and P. Soldatos, eds. Oxford: Clarendon Press.

Soldatos, P. 1993. "Cascading Subnational Paradiplomacy in an Interdependent and Transnational World." Pp. 65–92 in *States and Provinces in the International Economy*, D.M. Brown and E.H. Fry, eds. Berkeley: Institute of Governmental Studies Press.

Sparke, Matthew. 1999. "Free Trade, Transborder Boosterism and the Reinvention of Cascadia." *BC Studies.*

Swainson, N.A. 1979. *Conflict over the Columbia. The Canadian Background to an Historic Treaty.* Montreal: McGill-Queen's University Press.

Swanson, R.F. 1976. "The Range of Direct Relations between States and Provinces." *International Perspectives* (March/April): 18–27.

Thierstein, A., and U. Egger. 1994. *Integrative Regionalpolitik.* Zürich: Ruegger Verlag.

Thierstein, A., and M. Walser. 1997. "Sustainable Regional Development: The Squaring of the Circle or a Gimmick?" *Entrepreneurship & Regional Development* 9: 159–73.

World Commission on Environment and Development. 1987. *Our Common Future.* Oxford: Oxford University Press.

III
Environment, Region, and Society in the U.S.-Mexican Border Region

Cross-Border Partnerships for Environmental Management: The U.S.-Mexican Border Experience

Francisco Lara Valencia[*]

Abstract

The building of cross-border partnerships is a strategy traditionally used by local organizations along the U.S.-Mexican border to cope with regional environmental problems. However, the prominence of these partnerships has grown recently as a consequence of the institutional innovations introduced by the environmental side agreement of the North America Free Trade Agreement (NAFTA). Cross-border partnerships constitute collaborative arrangements among autonomous organizations and can be conceptualized as networks of interactions. The goals of this study are to describe and analyze the configuration, content, and strength of the interactions among environmental organizations in the Tijuana-San Diego area, and to determine how different they are from traditional interorganizational partnerships along the U.S.-Mexican border.

Introduction

The increasing intricacy and severity of environmental problems along the U.S.-Mexican border, combined with very important institutional developments during the last decade, have necessarily resulted in a proliferation of innovative and complex interorganizational arrangements in the region. These arrangements, which fit into what have been called "social partnerships" (Waddock

* Lara is a lecturer and researcher at the School of Economics at the Autonomous University of Baja California in Tijuana, Mexico. He is pursuing a doctorate in Urban and Environmental Planning at the University of Michigan at Ann Arbor with the support of the Fulbright Scholarship Program and the Mexican Council of Science and Technology (CONACYT). This research was supported by the University of Michigan's Rackham School of Graduate Studies.

1989), "inter-organizational cooperative initiatives" (Nunn and Rosentraub 1997), or simply "organizational networks" (Mizruchi and Galaskiewicz 1994) are cross-border partnerships among otherwise independent organizations, aimed at some common goals. Such associations are not necessarily new, but they have gained prominence since the launch of NAFTA, and particularly after the creation of the Border Environment Cooperation Commission (BECC) and the North American Development Bank (NADBank), two institutional innovations intended to strengthen public participation and local involvement in borderlands environmental policy making and planning.

These cross-border partnerships embody different forms and levels of cooperation among private, public, and community organizations, as they satisfy their own organizational objectives while establishing relationships across national jurisdictions. Many advocates of transboundary cooperation believe that the "success of cross-border environmental policy is greatly influenced by the general interaction system that is present in a border region" (Scherer and Blatter 1994). It follows that cross-border partnerships and the ways in which transboundary cooperation is developed and sustained are critical components of any strategy to correct longstanding environmental problems along the border. The recognized potential for transboundary cooperation underscores the logic of investigating how local environmental organizations can elicit and sustain collaborative arrangements across the international border.

Nonetheless, few studies have explored the many facets of transboundary cooperation along the U.S.-Mexican border, and the worthiness of the research that has been done has been questioned. The argument that transboundary cooperation is neither practically feasible nor politically viable considering the history and deep asymmetry that characterizes U.S.-Mexican relations has been posed repeatedly (Friedmann and Morales 1984; Herzog 1991). Despite this argument, there is no shortage of calls for more communication between local authorities, more involvement of local communities, and more cross-border coordination and planning. In the San Diego-Tijuana area, such calls for more systematic efforts of transboundary cooperation are commonly heard, and actually undertaken. However, most of what is known about such undertakings in the region is based on anecdotal reports; there is no real data on particular transboundary actions that have promoted cooperation, nor any serious analysis of how and why such arrangements evolve. And yet, this is exactly the information that planners, administrators, and community advocates need in order to form transboundary ties and evaluate the results of their cross-border efforts.

In response to this need, this paper attempts to provide answers to three specific research questions about cross-border partnerships in the San Diego-Tijuana region:

1. What types of organizations are involved directly or indirectly in cross-border partnerships, and what sectors do these organizations represent?

2. What are the dominant patterns of interaction among local environmental organizations, and how different are these patterns from traditional interorganizational interactions along the U.S.-Mexican border?

3. What specific types of transboundary cooperation are now being undertaken in the region, and what is their significance in terms of institutional capacity building?

As a preamble to the core analysis, this paper introduces a set of ideas intended as an analytical framework and to set up a methodological approach cogent to the objectives of this study.

The Context of Cross-Border Partnerships

Partnership building in international border regions can be defined as a political process that relies on mutual interests and includes activities that bring equivalent benefits to the participants (Blatter 1995). Thus, participation in transboundary arrangements occurs only after incentives have been carefully weighed and the participants are sure of obtaining certain benefits, or at least perceive a reasonable potential for benefit. These benefits range from tangible gains (such as access to infrastructure or improved air quality) to intangible benefits (gaining an ally or avoiding conflict with a neighboring country).

In general, supporters of these partnerships tend to justify their development by emphasizing the advantages of reducing the threshold of uncertainty that affects long-term planning, and stressing the potential of the economies of scale that could result from joint construction and management of regional facilities (Capellini 1993; Anderson 1983; OECD 1979; Hansen 1986). Cross-border partnerships are also said to have the potential to reduce the misuse of shared natural resources and to control the negative effects on the environment from urban and industrial growth. From a policy-making perspective, then, transboundary cooperation has been touted as the best available mechanism to implement ecosystem management and environmental sustainability programs in border contexts (Scherer and Blatter 1994).

Although transboundary cooperation seems to be the most rational tool for handling border issues, developing such collaboration is complex and difficulties render it the exception rather than the rule. This is caused primarily by the fact that international borders are simultaneously areas of conflict and collaboration; indeed, two opposing dimensions coexist and interact continually, shaping the nature and depth of transboundary relations (OECD 1979).

Therefore, under what conditions does partnership building become the means preferred by border communities for settling differences or planning development? The answers to this critical question tend to emphasize the role of structural variables or to stress the importance of organizational factors.

From a structural standpoint, cross-border partnerships depend largely on local actors' receptiveness to cooperation, which is determined by those factors within their social and political environment that support the development of interorganizational links across the border (Mumme 1987; Hansen 1986; Scott

1988b). There are five such factors: (1) a certain level of decentralization and the allocation of certain responsibilities to local or regional authorities; (2) the existence of institutional structures that facilitate participation in transboundary issues; (3) the willingness to accept binational solutions to shared problems; (4) community optimism that embraces a shared vision of the future; and (5) the existence of situations in which cooperation is a feasible and viable way to obtain tangible, equitable benefits for the participants.

Proponents of the organizational perspective (Martinos and Humphreys 1992; Scherer and Blatter 1994) identify four specific factors that contribute to developing transboundary cooperation: (1) the commitment that an organization shows to cross-border arrangements as the preferred strategy for handling regional problems; (2) resources allocated to cross-border endeavors; (3) the ability to overcome language and other idiosyncratic cultural differences; and (4) the ability to identify appropriate counterparts on each side of the border.

Although these two perspectives are commonly held separately in the literature, their edges are blurred. Rather than being alternatives, these approaches are complementary and together provide the basis for responding to the why, when, where, and who of cooperative networks within borderlands.

Cross-Border Partnerships along the U.S.-Mexican Border

Until recently, the most prevalent cross-border partnerships in the U.S.-Mexican border region were dyadic arrangements in which two organizations in the same sector and sharing common interests came together to collaborate. Such affiliations were distinguished by their reactive, problem-oriented nature. They were usually stimulated by an opportunity created by a change in policy or by the rise of a specific situation perceived as a problem by participants. Examples of such arrangements are joint corporate ventures, joint or special commissions formed by public agencies, and the various partnerships formed by nongovernmental organizations.

More recently, cross-border arrangements in the region have grown more sophisticated, often involving many organizations and cross-sectoral alliances, and playing a very active role in setting the border policy agenda. Although these second-generation arrangements are still committed to solving particular problems, their focus transcends short-term, reactive approaches. Many of these partnerships focus on developing opportunities for more intensive transboundary interaction that could lead to synergies in environmental planning and cooperation. As a result, second generation partnerships are proactive arrangements whose medium- and long-term commitments force them to embrace wide-spectrum strategies and form interorganizational networks. To testify to the vitality of this type of partnership along the U.S.-Mexican border,[1] there are many examples of such transboundary networks, regional development alliances, or binational coalitions that bridge sectoral differences and share a common vision. Thus, cross-border partnerships in the border region currently range from those in which a single organization interacts with another single organization in the same sector, to those in which multiple organizations from different sectors are represented in some ongoing enterprise. It is important to observe, however, that the development of these partnerships is not necessarily an evolutionary process in which organizations gradually advance from less to more complex alliances. They exist side-by-side, and many of them are far from recent partnerships. Lately, these coalitions have been created and recreated as collective responses to societal problems. As such, they adopt modalities conditioned by the dominant values, interests, and resources of their members, and by the problems they are intended to solve.

Some very important differences are evident in the extremes of this spectrum of cross-border partnerships. Their contribution to the formation of social capital in the form of problem-solving capabilities is vastly different. Large interorganizational networks can mobilize and combine many resources, thereby amplifying the societal impact of individual organizations. Interaction within a network implies coordination and usually involves routines that, once implemented, augment the organizational capabilities of individual participants and give rise to social reciprocation.[2] Accordingly, multilayered partnerships undertake more complex enterprises—a quality particularly valuable in the social context of receding governmental involvement.

Furthermore, these contrasting types of arrangements have different life cycles. Certainly the multisectoral, multiorganizational partnerships are complex and necessarily slower to act than their smaller brethren. Nevertheless, once consensus has been reached, multilayered partnerships tend to show greater resilience and adaptability to change. Dyadic associations tend to be more vulnerable and short lived.

Another important difference is that ventures undertaken by less complex affiliations are inextricably linked to the partner organizations. Complex partnerships tend to set up and develop projects that are detached from individual participant organizations. Although these may not necessarily be tangible entities, the outcome of these detached programs may be a collaborative atmosphere that induces growing interactions among organizations. As emphasized by Scott (1995), the main force in the creation of this kind of milieu is synergy, a process that implies mutual benefit and efficiency, consequently reinforcing the importance and desirability of participation in collaborative arrangements.

Ultimately, multiorganizational, transboundary partnerships crystallize in interorganizational networks that function as systems of complex interactions. To the extent that these interactions lead to maximum organizational performance or to the reduction of harm generated by noncooperative actions, networks then become the channel for routine transfer or exchange of different resources (Mizruchi and Galaskiewicz 1994: 231). Such resources generally consist of information, support, material resources, and so on. Once such a network has been established, it may constrain its participants' behavior, leading to give-and-take, and eventually to systemic exchanges based on reciprocity and trust. Depending upon the frequency, direction, content, and density of these relationships, networks may be clear indicators of potential for a collaborative milieu within a region.

An Analytical Framework

Cross-border partnerships adopt distinct modalities and have different degrees of coalescence; these reflect capacity, degree of autonomy of cooperating bodies, as well as specific interests and priorities. The three levels of coalescence are convergence, collaboration, and comanagement.[3] Figure 1 shows these levels as a pyramid of cross-border interaction.

The convergence level represents the lowest degree of coalescence. Convergence actions are the spontaneous outcome of the day-to-day interplay of communities that occupy contiguous territories. Interaction takes place through frequent but informal contact, direct conduits, and personal meetings between representatives of organizations on both sides of the border. One main purpose of partnerships at this level is to keep communities on the "other side" of the border aware of actions that, if undertaken, might have cross-border implications. Thus, one of the main features of convergence-level collaboration is the exchange of information and data. Because associations at this level are so informal, there are no legal obligations; but these interactions may lead to identifying difficulties and the discussion of possible solutions. Eventually, convergence-level partnerships can lead to synchronized actions, a feature of most advanced levels of cooperation.

At the collaboration level, flexible partnerships form as binational committees or task forces. They are based on the willingness of participants to act concurrently to address border problems according to specific joint agreements. Although these actions are usually parallel activities (that is, each party accomplishes its tasks using its own means and is subject to the institutional and social constraints imposed upon it by its own national circumstances), collaboration usually involves the exchange of funding and information, and access to infrastructure and services. Although such alliances are fairly informal, regular mutual consultation is expected and rewarded.

Comanagement is the highest level of coalescence. It implies a determination by involved parties to act by pooling their institutional, human, and financial resources to carry out certain tasks that are commonly performed through binational bodies. At this level of partnership, arrangements are formalized. Thus, if the parties are public sector organizations, comanagement usually implies agreements endorsed by political authorities. In the case of private or civic organizations, agreements may be less formal. The most important outcome of partnerships at this level is the formulation of binational policies and programs that are undertaken through binational commissions, consortiums, or cross-border coalitions.

Although for the purposes of this particular analysis this three-level system is sufficient, it should be noted that Figure 1 implicitly recognizes that

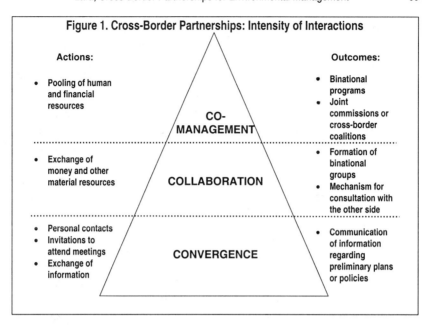

Figure 1. Cross-Border Partnerships: Intensity of Interactions

Actions:

- Pooling of human and financial resources

CO-MANAGEMENT

- Exchange of money and other material resources

COLLABORATION

- Personal contacts
- Invitations to attend meetings
- Exchange of information

CONVERGENCE

Outcomes:

- Binational programs
- Joint commissions or cross-border coalitions

- Formation of binational groups
- Mechanism for consultation with the other side

- Communication of information regarding preliminary plans or policies

noncooperation and open conflict are likely alternatives. Noncooperation implies no interaction at all and the dismissal by at least one of the parties of those potential benefits that could yield the development of cross-border partnerships. Conflict is the opposite of cooperation since it entails the willingness of one the participants to monopolize particular resources and their potential benefits. If they were represented in Figure 1, both of these circumstances would be shown below the convergence level as the negative extreme of the continuum.

A Network Approach to Cross-Border Partnerships

Cross-border partnerships are an outgrowth of network building and comprise a variety of actions and different levels of complexity. Partnership building crystallizes and operates because of contacts made according to the involved parties' perceptions, knowledge, and priorities. Social network analysis is a conceptual and methodological tool that provides a useful framework for exploring cross-border partnerships. Such framework describes social interactions as networks of relations, and identifies patterns of interaction, traces flows of information and other resources, and explores the effects of these relations on the entities that form a network (Wasserman and Faust 1994).

From a network perspective, the relations among social actors are usually described as having content, direction, and strength. The content of relations refers to the resource exchanged in which the exchange may be directed or undirected. In an interorganizational network, two organizations may exchange information about funding opportunities or policy matters that affect the whole network or only a part of it. Furthermore, relations also differ in strength and may operate in a number of ways. For example, pairs of organizations may exchange information and/or large or small amounts of resources such as money, goods, or services. Thus, the dimensions of the content of interaction reflect relational strength.

The web of relations within a social network defines its structure. Network density is one of the most widely used measures of social network structure. Densely knit networks have high numbers of direct interactions, while in sparsely knit networks, interactions are less frequent and tend to create longer paths. Similarities in the kinds of interactions undertaken by network actors suggest a network role. Actors with similar interaction patterns within the network occupy equivalent positions (Wasserman and Faust 1994). Those who share equivalent positions are likely to share similar access to network resources. For example, some central positions have greater access to diverse sources of information, while other less central positions may have a limited pool of new ideas or information on which to draw. Centrality is another word for social influence and power (Knoke and Kuklinsky 1982).

Thus, when studying interorganizational networks, it is also important to examine which organizations are central to or isolated from the network. Social network analysis has developed measures of centrality that can be used to identify those network members with the most connections (high nodal degree) and those whose departure would cause the network to fall apart (cut-points).

Empirical Analysis Data

The objective of this study is to describe the configuration, content, and strength of the interaction between environmental organizations in the Tijuana-San Diego area and to determine how different they are from traditional interorganizational partnerships along the U.S.-Mexican border. The first step of the study was to identify the main organizational actors on both sides of the border. An initial list was created with the information provided by the Public Outreach Office of the Border Environment Cooperation Commission (BECC).[4] That information was supplemented with archival materials and direct consultation with local analysts and environmentalists. Important municipal organizations (such as planning departments and environmental agencies on both sides of the border) were also included in the network. A total of 35 organizations were identified, including academic institutions, government agencies, and groups of volunteers (see Appendix 1 for a complete listing). All of these organizations were surveyed during the spring of 1998 by mail and/or convenience survey.[5] Ultimately, the analysis was based on a 15 by 15 matrix in which the cells corresponded to the relations between the organizations that responded and returned the questionnaire. For confidentiality, the names of the organizations were omitted. Instead, a code was used to identify organizations as academic, government, or volunteer, and whether they are based in Tijuana or San Diego.

The questionnaire used to gather data for this analysis was designed to obtain information about the entire interorganizational network. In a whole network study, informants are given a roster of all the actors in the network and asked to identify any connection between their own organization and the remaining groups with regard to specific content (Knoke and Kuklinski 1982). Every organization in the network is asked about every other organization, to give an overall picture of the structure of relations, and to reveal disenfranchisement as well as connection. For this study, respondents were asked to indicate organizations with which they routinely and directly conduct projects, or exchange information, political levering, money, or other material resources. This information was intended to provide mainly relational data, but also revealed information that qualified the nature of the links. The actual analysis was done using UCINET, a statistical computer program specially designed for the quantitative analysis of network data (Borgatti, Everett, and Freeman 1992: 85).

Empirical Analysis

Cross-Border Activity: Actors and Types of Interaction

Two indicators of network activity are the density and strength of interaction between one organization and the other organizations in its network. Density can be calculated as the number of ties divided by the total number of possible ties within a binary matrix of interorganizational links (Borgatti, Everett, and Freeman 1992). Strength can be interpreted as a function of the type of resources exchanged between pairs of actors in the network. For instance, a weaker interaction might be merely the exchange of information, while stronger ties would be the exchange or pooling of financial and human resources. This approach is consistent with the three-level scheme presented in Figure 1.

The 15 organizations included in this study constitute a relatively dense network (Figure 2). The estimated density for the entire network is 0.56, which means that at the time of the survey, almost six out of 10 potential interorganizational links had been made. When the network is divided into three subnetworks—San Diego, Tijuana, and their cross-border interactions—a pattern of relations emerges. Figure 2 presents these subnetworks as segments of the density matrix: upper left triangle (San Diego), lower left rectangle (cross-border network), and lower right triangle (Tijuana). Network density for the San Diego portion was estimated at 0.93, and for Tijuana the measure was approximately 0.52. The density of cross-border interactions was estimated at 0.48.

An important caveat is that these density estimates do not take into account the strengths of the links. Figure 2 shows that networking in San Diego is dominated by connections at the comanagement (code 3 in Figure 2) and collaboration (code 2) levels. Links reported by organizations in San Diego rarely remained at the convergence (code 1) level. Conversely, Tijuana's subnetwork connections are primarily at the collaboration level, followed by comanagement interactions. Convergence-level interactions represented 21 percent of total links reported by organizations in Tijuana. The cross-border subnetwork is very similar to Tijuana in density and strength. In fact, half of transboundary interactions were at the collaboration level, and the remaining half were distributed almost evenly between the convergence and comanagement levels.

Figure 2. Cross-Border Partnerships, Matrix of Densities, and Levels of Intensity

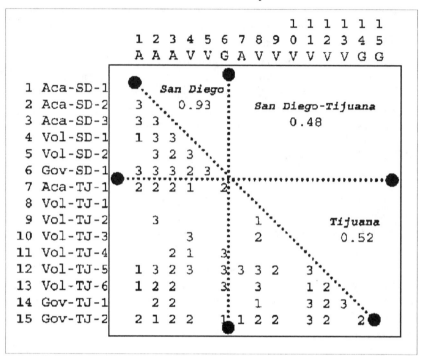

To have a complete picture it is necessary to see which type of organizations are leading the activity within each subnetwork. Figure 2 shows that in San Diego, partnership building is undertaken equally by academic, volunteer, and government organizations, while in Tijuana, the most prominent partnership builders are volunteer organizations and a government agency. In fact, the highest nodal degree (11) in San Diego belongs to two academic institutions, followed by a volunteer organization (Vol-SD-2) and a government agency (Gov-SD-1).[6] In Tijuana, network primacy was held by one volunteer organization (Vol-TJ-5) with a nodal degree of 12, followed by a government agency. The data in Figure 2 also show that networks in San Diego are strong partnerships without sectoral distinction. In other words, whether the organization is public or private seems to have no bearing on whether its partnerships are at the collaboration or comanagement level. By contrast, Mexican organizations seem to be more selective in establishing partnerships, and academic and government agency links are mostly at the convergence and collaboration level.

Cross-border interactions are more complex. On the one hand, volunteer organizations have a greater propensity to form transborder alliances at the highest level of cooperation than academic or governmental organizations. Indeed, all of the comanagement cross-border partnerships identified involved volunteer organizations in Tijuana. On the other hand, the only two organizations in the survey that did not participate in cross-border arrangements were volunteer organizations, both of which were well connected in their respective countries.

Network Structure

One approach to studying the structure of interorganizational networks is to use the concept of "position." An organization's position can be defined as its set of relationships with the other organizations in its network. If this set of links is similar to that of other organizations, then the two groups occupy "structurally equivalent" positions within the network.[7] "Substitutability" is another term for equivalence, since it assumes that actors who occupy a similar position will relate and behave in a similar manner vis-à-vis groups that occupy other positions within the network.[8] Structural equivalence is a useful tool for studying actors that are likely to play the same role within the network.

The dendrogram in Figure 3 shows the result of applying a hierarchical clustering based on the Johnson's connectedness method (Knoke and Kuklinski 1982). In this example, clustering was done using a matrix of dissimilarities based on Euclidean distances, meaning that the smaller the dissimilarities between two organizations, the greater the chance that they will be clustered together.[9] After a cluster is formed, it is treated as a new unit, and its distance from other units is utilized to fuse it at the next step, based always on the shortest distance between clusters (Borgatti, Everett, and Freeman 1992: 169). As shown in Figure 3, this procedure resulted in four clusters and one isolate for the San Diego-Tijuana data.

The first cluster of interest (Cluster IV) is an agglomeration made up of Gov-TJ-2, Vol-TJ-5, and Vol-TJ-6. At the time of the survey, the organizations

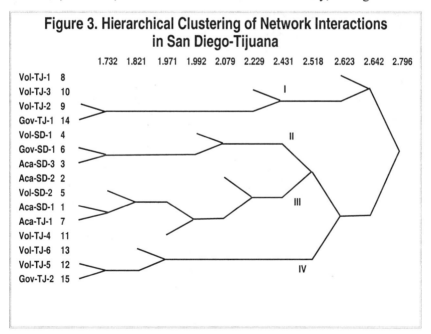

Figure 3. Hierarchical Clustering of Network Interactions in San Diego-Tijuana

in this entirely Mexican cluster were among the most active participants in their network. Consequently, all of them showed high rates of connectedness and diversity in their partnerships. All of these organizations had above-average nodal degrees, and one of them had the highest in the whole network.[10] With the exception of Vol-TJ-6, these organizations sustained varied partnerships with government, academic, and volunteer organizations on both sides of the border. The binational balance of these organizations' partnerships is notable, as the number of their cross-border connections roughly matched the number of their connections with other Mexican organizations.

Cluster II is a U.S. agglomerate made up of Aca-SD-3, Gov-SD-1, and Vol-SD-1. Connectedness and heterogeneity of partnerships for all of the organizations in this cluster are among the highest in the network. Aca-SD-3 formed 80 percent of all its potential links within the network, and the other two cluster members formed at least 70 percent of theirs. As a result, these organizations sustain partnerships in other sectors as well as their own. All of the organizations in Cluster II were equally active in both the national and cross-border arenas, allowing for a binational balance like that of Cluster IV.

Three U.S. and two Mexican organizations form Cluster III, the most complex and largest cluster within the network. Two academic players, Aca-TJ-1 and Aca-SD-1, joined to create the initial aggregate in this cluster. Both organizations have an intermediate level of connectedness and show very similar patterns of partnership. In fact, the only difference between them was that the Mexican university reported one less link than the U.S. university. Next, two volunteer organizations with intermediate connectedness were added to the cluster. Vol-SD-2 was the only organization in San Diego that reported no cross-border partnerships, although it was well connected on its side of the border. The last addition to the cluster is Aca-SD-2, a very well connected academic institution with a well-balanced array of partnerships on both sides of the border. Aside from their interconnectedness, criteria for clustering such heterogeneous organizations are not easy to determine. The groups' own selectivity, sectoral dominance, and nationality play important roles in how and why they form their partnerships.

Cluster I comprises Vol-TJ-2, Gov-TJ-1 and Vol-TJ-3. This is another nationally based cluster with all of its organizations in Tijuana. The three components all have a below-average level of interorganizational connectedness, even though two of them (except Vol-TJ-3) show a propensity to become primarily involved with other Mexican organizations. This tendency is the reason that this cluster is later grouped with Vol-TJ-1, the only isolate within the network.

Vol-TJ-1 is unique because, even though it rates an intermediate level of connectedness, all its partnerships are exclusively with other Mexican organizations. Furthermore, most of the links reported by this organization were with other volunteer organizations, a pattern based not only on national consideration, but also on sectoral affinity. Such selectivity may be presumed an attribute of old, established volunteer organizations with a traditional vision of partnership building.

Conclusion

Despite the lack of previous analysis for comparison, there is no doubt that the density of interorganizational links detected in this study of the Tijuana-San Diego area reflects a very active network. As indicated by John Scott (1988: 115), when assessing network density, the analyst must take into account the nature of both social relationships and existing circumstances since these affect the logical limits to an organization's ability to sustain multiple contacts within a network. Clearly, the greater the stakes entailed in an exchange, the more careful an organization will be in establishing a partnership. In addition, the greater an organization's available social and organizational capital, the greater its ability to overcome barriers to networking and the greater the likelihood that it will become involved in collaborative arrangements.

Patterns of interaction in San Diego reflect a less hierarchical and more open institutional system than in Tijuana. According to the data gathered for this study, there is no sector that is clearly dominant, nor is there a detectable pattern of sectoral exclusion. Compared to Tijuana, the San Diego subnetwork has a broader range of interorganizational links that include virtually all kinds of sectoral partnerships. It is evident that networking in Tijuana is more selective, as inferred from the lower density of interactions and the intermediate strength of the partnerships there. The relatively low level of activity in the transboundary network reflects the constraints faced by organizations that attempt to participate in cross-border arrangements. Certainly, the ability of two organizations to collaborate effectively is greater when both belong to the same social and institutional system. However, the reduced discrepancy in densities between subnetworks shows that the obstacles that preclude the development of interorganizational links between San Diego and Tijuana are of similar magnitude to the obstacles faced by Mexican organizations when they attempt to interact among themselves.

The degree to which San Diego and Tijuana organizations have overcome the barriers inherent in an international border is remarkable. They have developed not only a relatively dense transboundary network, but also a web of collaborative and comanagement partnerships. It is also notable that neither side appears to monopolize transboundary interactions. Both U.S. and Mexican organizations reported a number of transborder interactions involving diverse players.

This study shows that although universities still play a key role in cross-border networks, volunteer organizations from both sides are also major players, even challenging the predominance of Tijuana's academic institutions. Transboundary environmental cooperation is a domain in which government organizations do not yet play a leading role, although the analysis shows that some public agencies are actively involved.

Cluster analysis suggests that both factors associated with nationality and organizational attributes heavily influence the structure of the San Diego-Tijuana interorganizational network. These findings are not unexpected, as the international border acts as both barrier and filter to environmental networking. Sectoral boundaries have a much smaller, but similar effect within each national domain. Jurisdictional or credential-based criteria can also deflect attempts at cross-sector affiliations. Future studies may shed additional light on the circumstances that have allowed organizations to overcome constraints, develop connections, and occupy positions of influence within the network.

Endnotes

1. Examples of these cross-border partnerships along the U.S.-Mexican border include the San Diego Dialogue, a partnership between San Diego and Tijuana that includes academicians, business people, public officers, the media, education, and the arts; the Border Network for Public Health and the Environment, which includes volunteer organizations and universities; and the Great Vision Project, an alliance among local and state governments, business organizations, and universities in the Sonora-Arizona region.

2. Routines provide the basis for reciprocation, the foundation for cooperation. This process is called "tit-for-tat" in game theory analysis (Ridley and Low 1996: 201).

3. This is a reformulation of the OECD scheme of cross-border cooperation. Changes were introduced to adjust to the inclusion of nongovernmental actors and a more visual display (OECD 1979).

4. The information consisted of attendance lists at public meetings organized to inform and discuss projects to improve wastewater management capabilities in the City of Tijuana. Most of these meetings were held between December 1996 and May 1997.

5. Most selected informants responded to the questionnaires during the "Encuentro sobre Medio Ambiente Fronterizo," organized in Ciudad Juárez, Mexico, on March 24, 1998, by the Latin American Studies Center at the University of Arizona.

6. Nodal degree is the total number of direct links that a particular organization has with the others in a network.

7. Two actors, x and y, are structurally equivalent if for any given relation R and any actor z in the same network, xRz if and only if yRz, and zRx if and only if zRy (Knoke and Kuklinski 1982)

8. There are two ways to explain the source of this similar behavior. One is based on the argument of competing roles that lead to a sort of organizational mimicking, and the other maintains that common sources of influence produce similar behavior (Mizruchi 1994: 333).

9. Distance here is understood as social proximity and is related to structural equivalence. If a pair of actors have identical relations with others, their distance is zero. If they have increasingly different patterns of ties, they are increasingly distant from each other (see Knoke and Kuklinsky 1982: 60).

10. The mean nodal degree for the whole network was 7.87 and the standard deviation was 2.90.

References

Anderson, Malcolm. 1983. "The Political Problems of Frontier Regions." Pp. 1–17 in *Frontier Regions in Western Europe*, Malcolm Anderson, ed. London: F. Cass.

Blatter, Joachim. 1995. "Political Cooperation in Cross-Border Regions: Two Explanatory Approaches." Paper presented at the 36th Congress of the European Regional Science Association, 26–30 August, Zurich, Switzerland.

Borgatti, S., M. Everett, and L. Freeman. 1992. *UCINET IV, Network Analysis Software.* Reference Manual. Harvard, Analytic Technologies.

Capellini, R. 1993. "Interregional Cooperation and Internationalization of Regional Economies in Alps-Adria." Pp. 17–45 in *Development Strategies in the Alpine-Adriatic Region*, Gyula Horváth, ed. Pécs: Centre for Regional Studies, Hungarian Academy of Sciences.

Friedmann, John, and Rebecca Morales. 1984. "Transborder Planning: A Case of Sophisticated Provocation." Paper presented at the Conference of the Association of Borderlands Studies, Tijuana, Mexico.

Hansen, Niles. 1986. "Conflict Resolution and the Evolution of Cooperation in the U.S.-Mexico Borderlands." *Journal of Borderlands Studies* 1 (1): 34–38.

Herzog, Lawrence. 1991. "International Boundary Cities: The Debate on Transfrontier Planning in Two Border Regions." *Natural Resources Journal* 31 (Winter): 587–608.

Knoke, David, and James H. Kuklinski. 1982. *Network Analysis.* University Papers 28. Newbury Park: Sage Publications.

Martinos, H., and E. Humphreys. 1992. "Transnational Networks: Evolution and Future Issues." *Ekistics* 353: 13–20.

Mizruchi, Mark S. 1994. "Social Network Analysis: Recent Achievements and Current Controversies." *Acta Sociologica* 37: 329–43.

Mizruchi, Mark S., and Joseph Galaskiewicz. 1994. "Networks of Interoganizational Relations." Pp. 230–53 in *Advances in Social Network Analysis: Research in the Social and Behavioral Sciences*, Stanley Wasserman and Joseph Galaskiewicz, eds. Thousand Oaks: Sage Publications.

Mumme, Stephen. 1987. "State and Local Influence in Transboundary Environmental Policy Making Along the U.S.-Mexico Border: The Case of Air Quality Management." *Journal of Borderlands Studies* 2 (1): 1–16.

Nunn, Samuel, and Mark S. Rosentraub. 1997. "Dimensions of Interjurisdictional Cooperation." *Journal of the American Planning Association* 63 (2): 205–19.

Organization for Economic Co-operation and Development (OECD). 1979. *Environmental Protection in Frontier Regions.* Paris: OECD.

Ridley, M., and B.S. Low. 1996. "Can Selfishness Save the Environment?" Pp. 198–212 in *Readings in Planning Theory*, Scott Campbell and Susan Fainsten, eds. Cambridge: Blackwell Publishers.

Scott, James. 1988. "Transborder Cooperation, Regional Initiatives and Sovereignty Conflicts in Western Europe: The Case of the Upper Rhine Valley." *Publius* 19: 139–56.

Scott, James. 1995. "Dutch-German Euroregions: A Model for Transboundary Cooperation?" Paper presented at the Western Social Science Association/Association of Borderlands Scholars Conference, 26–29 April, Oakland, California, USA.

Scott, John. 1988. "Social Network Analysis." *Sociology* 22 (1): 109–27.

Scherer, R., and Joachim Blatter. 1994. "Preconditions for a Successful Cross-Border Cooperation on Environmental Issues. Research Results and Recommendations for a Better Practice." http://www.unisg.ch/~siasr/public/cbla5b.html.

United States-Mexico Border Health Association. 1994. *Sister Communities Health Profiles. United States-Mexico Border 1989–1991.* El Paso: United States-Mexico Border Health Association.

U.S. Environmental Protection Agency. 1996. *U.S.-Mexico Border XXI Program: Framework Document.* Washington, D.C.: U.S. Environmental Protection Agency.

Waddock, S.A. 1989. "Understanding Social Partnerships, an Evolutionary Model." *Administration and Society* 21 (1): 78–100.

Wasserman, Stanley, and Katherine Faust. 1994. *Social Network Analysis: Methods and Applications.* New York: Cambridge University Press.

Appendix 1. Environmental Organizations Surveyed in the San Diego-Tijuana Region

#	Name	Sector	Location
1	AIRESANO	Volunteer	Tijuana
2	Amas de Casa de Playas de Tijuana	Volunteer	Tijuana
3	Asociación de Ecología de Rosarito	Volunteer	Tijuana
4	Center for U.S.-Mexican Studies, University of California, San Diego (UCSD)	Academic	San Diego
5	Centro de Enseñanza Técnica y Superior (CETYS)	Academic	Tijuana
6	Citizens Against Recreational Eviction	Volunteer	San Diego
7	Citizens Revolting Against Pollution	Volunteer	San Diego
8	City of Imperial Beach	Governmental	San Diego
9	Comisión Estatal de Servicios Públicos de Tijuana (CESPT)	Governmental	Tijuana
10	Comité de Planeación para el Desarrollo Municipal (COPLADEM)	Governmental	Tijuana
11	Consejo Estatal de Ecología	Governmental	Tijuana
12	County of San Diego, Environmental Services Department	Governmental	San Diego
13	County of San Diego, Department of Environmental Health	Governmental	San Diego
14	Dirección de Planeación Urbana y Ecología	Governmental	Tijuana
15	Ecological Life System Institute	Volunteer	San Diego
16	Eco-Sol Educación y Cultura Ecológica	Volunteer	Tijuana
17	El Colegio de la Frontera Norte (COLEF)	Academic	Tijuana
18	Environmental Health Coalition	Academic	San Diego
19	Grupo Comunitario "El Florido"	Volunteer	Tijuana
20	Grupo Ecologista Gaviotas, A.C.	Volunteer	Tijuana
21	Institute for Regional Studies of the Californias, San Diego State University (SDSU)	Academic	San Diego
22	Instituto Tecnológico de Tijuana	Academic	Tijuana
23	Movimiento Ecologista de Baja California, A.C.	Volunteer	Tijuana
24	Proyecto Fronterizo de Educación Ambiental, A.C.	Volunteer	Tijuana
25	San Diego Audobon Society	Volunteer	San Diego
26	San Diego BayKeeper	Volunteer	San Diego
27	San Diego-Tijuana Environmental Committee	Volunteer	San Diego

#	Name	Sector	Location
28	San Diego Association of Governments (SANDAG)	Governmental	San Diego
29	School of International Relations and Pacific Studies, University of California, San Diego (UCSD)	Academic	San Diego
30	Sierra Club	Volunteer	San Diego
31	Southwest Network for Environmental and Economic Justice	Volunteer	San Diego
32	Southwest Wetlands Interpretative Association	Volunteer	San Diego
33	Surfrider Foundation	Volunteer	San Diego
34	Tijuana River National Estuarine Research Reserve	Governmental	San Diego
35	Universidad Autónoma de Baja California	Academic	Tijuana

The Challenges of Region Building: The Paso del Norte Region

Samuel Schmidt[*]

Abstract

This paper addresses the challenges and opportunities of region building, using the Paso del Norte region as a case in point. The region's binational nature and multiple jurisdictions have been perceived as hindrances to regional cooperation, making it unable to harmonize policies across boundaries. Such disregard has left many issues unresolved and has created new problems for the region. This study discusses the asymmetries inherent in this region and their impact on cooperative ventures. A region-building project is proposed for the Paso del Norte region, calling for binational integration from the bottom up to solve problems facing both sides of the border.

Region Building

Region building has become an important subject in the international relations and development literature (Anderson 1997). Borderlines have become obsolete and an increase in regional thinking, transactions, and cross-border organizational connections has been witnessed (Evans 1997). Both the processes of region building and globalization challenge existing political paradigms and notions of the role of the state. According to some scholars, the state is disappearing entirely (Evans 1997), while others claim that the role of the state to act alone is becoming obsolete (Dror 1996). The debate also addresses the state's capacity to handle problems with outdated models and new sets of political actors and political pressures. In the global age, international asymmetries have also become a relevant factor concerning region building.

The evolution of the global economy has introduced important challenges to the concept and perception of sovereignty and, thus, the role of borders (Anderson 1997). While European countries have implemented adaptations in the ex-

---

* Schmidt is Professor of Social Sciences at the Autonomous University of Ciudad Juárez, Chihuahua, Mexico.

change of both goods and people, not all countries are willing to accept such changes. The United States, for example, has approved more restrictive immigration laws and other policies that foster barriers with Mexico (Schmidt 1996; Woodford Bray 1998) and have criminalized labor (Schmidt and Spector 1998).

The Euroregion

Transborder cooperation has been a reality within the European Community for the last 30 years (Scott 1997). Its developments have now reached a point where political borders interfere with regional development. The experience of integration in Europe can serve as a guide for developing new cooperative attitudes, policy ideas, and relationships among countries. A precise motivation for European states to develop such intense cross-border collaboration is unclear. Was European coalescence driven by the need to improve international cooperation? Or was it due to the governments' willingness to recognize a regional drive for collaboration and the resolution of problems created largely by borders themselves? Or, has regional cooperation simply become a trend impossible for governments to ignore? Postwar animosities produced a distance that was reversed by European reconstruction requiring a new type of policy that has helped to deconstruct borders.

The European experience has not been duplicated elsewhere. Along the U.S.-Mexican border, both countries have agreed to cooperate binationally, but have not developed practical means to do so. While Europe embarks on a comprehensive cooperative effort, the United States and Mexico make partial decisions to cope with single issues, neither approaching the border as part of their binational relationship nor as an entity in itself.

In Europe, political borders have lost their role as security enforcers. In the case of Mexico and the United States, old and new challenges (such as drug trafficking) reinforce the idea that the border should continue to be used as an instrument to control the flows of goods and people—to the extent of militarizing the borderlands (Dunn 1996). There are both costs and benefits in maintaining these border controls. The costs include social and political tensions, while the benefits relate to controls on drug trafficking. People expect immediate advantages, such as quicker border crossings, better opportunities for transborder collaboration, and increased security, while governments may be working toward a long-term agenda. In the end, what might be perceived as a local cost could be contributing to a national political benefit and vice versa.[1]

The U.S.-Mexican Border

The U.S.-Mexican borderland is a region of paradox, encounter, and detachment; it is full of discrepancies. Even the units of measure differ: inches and centimeters, gallons and liters, dollars and pesos. For Mexicans, the borderline represents the beginning of their nation[2] and the daily challenge to defend their nationalism. *Fronterizos* (borderlanders) feel that they are protecting the motherland every day, with a painful reminder always in front of them—those U.S.

territories that once were Mexico's.[3] For those on the other side of the border, the borderline is an indisputable limit (dubbed by many an insurmountable barrier[4]); intruders are to be prosecuted with the full force of the law if they dare to enter without permission (Schmidt 1996). Stereotyping and mutual prejudice define the limited friendship (Castañeda and Pastor 1988) between these "distant neighbors" (Riding 1985).

Few cooperative efforts along the U.S.-Mexican border have been attempted. The International Boundary and Water Commission (IBWC) (Bustamante 1999a), which provides water services to the U.S.-Mexican border region, has been considered a model institution, but it has not been duplicated in other areas. The commission's limited and well-defined scope is probably the key to its success. However, it has recently been forced to enter other arenas, such as environmental management, which may cause problems for the commission (Bustamante 1999). In the post-NAFTA era, other new institutions—such as the Border Environment Cooperation Commission (BECC) and the North American Development Bank (NADBank)—have had limited influence.

Bilateral governmental and nongovernmental cooperation between the United States and Mexico has been limited. Private enterprises now benefit from such collaboration, generating jobs and production. However, if regionalism is left to entrepreneurs, it will continue to lack a framework for development. For Ciudad Juárez and El Paso, internationalization has not resulted in solutions for social or economic problems. Paradoxically, although they form one of the most integrated international areas, both Ciudad Juárez and El Paso are poor: El Paso has almost double the average national unemployment rate, and a high percentage of its population depends on food stamps (Schmidt, Gil, and Castro 1995). As in many other border regions, economic growth has led to high immigration rates, resulting in shortages of resources, poverty (Ranfla et al. 1999), and poor quality of life. Both cities suffer from serious health problems, such as hepatitis and tuberculosis (Ortega 1991), and extreme pollution levels (Baker 1991; Barry and Sims 1993). The region faces tremendous challenges to sustainable development (Schmidt 1998). Government support to the region is meager at best, in part because both nations mistrust each other and their priorities differ. For a region to collaborate, it must eliminate both national and local rivalries and sidestep the obstacles to unity.

Traditionally, borders have played a controlling role and, with the current international policies, they will continue to fulfill this function. It could, however, be a stabilizing factor. For example, if it were flexible, it would be able to contain migration. If migrants were to settle only on the Mexican side, they would create instabilities (such as labor shortages on the U.S. side and labor surpluses on the Mexican side) that would affect both the United States and Mexico. If the region can manage to jointly accommodate the huge influx of workers, it could create a larger market and create new local economic opportunities for sustained growth, including an unfettered labor flow.

Defining the Paso del Norte Region

El Paso del Norte is the convergence point of two countries (Mexico and the United States), three states (Chihuahua, Texas, and New Mexico), several counties (among them El Paso, Ciudad Juárez, and Doña Ana), and several small cities. There are many asymmetries in the region. Ciudad Juárez, with over one million inhabitants, is among the 10 most important cities in Mexico in terms of size and industry (due mostly to *maquiladoras*). El Paso is located at the extreme western end of Texas. It has a population of almost seven hundred thousand, and is one of the poorest cities of its size in the United States. It lacks economic and political clout, but plays an important role for New Mexico since a segment of El Paso's population buys and rents houses and cars in New Mexico to avoid high taxes in Texas. It also represents employment opportunities for New Mexicans. The role of Sunland Park—one of the poorest cities in southern New Mexico—in the region could be significant when specific issues such as water are addressed. The city has rights to the Mesilla Bolson, which crosses the border with Ciudad Juárez. Las Cruces is the most important city in southern New Mexico in terms of size, as well as economic, social, and educational relevance. It has limited influence in El Paso and Ciudad Juárez, although in recent years its role in higher education has increased since New Mexico State University began offering in-state tuition to students from El Paso and Ciudad Juárez. Also, Las Cruces could play a prominent role with regard to the water issue.

There is little collaboration between Ciudad Juárez and El Paso due to the lack of a regional culture and the obstacles imposed by the political border. In 1991, the mayors of the two cities began joint city council meetings—an endeavor that ended as soon as both left office (there is no immediate re-election in Mexico). Some time later, the Environmental Defense Fund (a nongovernmental organization) created an "air quality district," an effort that required several years to deal with two federal bureaucracies. When the district was finally recognized by both federal governments, it received neither budgetary nor political support; thus, its influence remains very limited.

In a survey conducted by the author in 1998 in Ciudad Juárez, Mexican agencies were asked about levels of cooperation with their U.S. counterparts. Their answers were as follows:

1. Asociación de Maquiladoras, A.C. (AMAQ): The Maquiladora Plants Association has no institutional collaboration; each corporation takes care of itself.

2. Cámara Nacional de Comercio (CANACO): The chamber of commerce works with the New Mexico Chamber of Commerce in Las Cruces to advise customs administrators about bridge crossing issues, tourism, and the "Hermanos a través de la frontera" (brothers across the border) program.

3. Cámara Nacional de la Industria de Transformación (CANACINTRA): The industrial chamber does not engage in foreign activities.

4. Instituto Municipal de Investigación y Planeación (IMIP): The municipal planning institute has cooperative agreements with El Paso and New Mexico re-

garding border crossings; they also work with the transportation industry in Austin, Texas.

5. Asociación de Transportistas de Ciudad Juárez, A.C. (ATC): The transportation industry association does not collaborate with any U.S. agency.

6. Cámera de Agentes Aduanales de la República Mexicana (CAAAREM): The customs agents association does not work with anyone in the United States. It updates its own membership in the face of international legal changes. The customs agents have their own warehouses in El Paso from which they process imports.

7. Asociación Mexicana de Agencias de Viajes (AMAV): The travel agents association does not cooperate with anyone on the other side of the border.

8. Asociación de Restaurantes Similares y Conexos (ARESCO): Its activities in El Paso relate to food handling.

9. Labor unions do not work together. The American Federation of Labor and Congress of Industrial Organizations (AFL-CIO) has a *maquiladora* project, but no formal collaboration with border unions.

10. Nongovernmental organizations (NGOs): Some informal contacts exist between NGOs, particularly those that deal with women's rights. Education foundations, such as the Margarita Miranda de Mascareñas and the health-oriented Mexican Federation of Private Health Associations and Community Development (FEMAP) from Ciudad Juárez, work and raise funds on both sides of the border, but their cooperation with other foundations is limited.

When professional associations, such as the Engineers and Architects Association were questioned, they simply acknowledged that binational cooperation does not exist. Many such associations play an important role in Mexican politics, and in some cases in policy making. This is not necessarily the case in the United States, where influence is exercised via boards, committees, or Congress. The lack of cooperation at this level shows how difficult it is to design a region-building agenda from the bottom up.

The development of the U.S-Mexican border lacks order, has unresolved challenges, and has created new problems which, regardless of their importance, have not changed governmental perceptions and understanding. It is important to jointly decide how to deal with old problems (water, border crossings) and new ones (drug trafficking). Both governments seem to be prisoners of tradition and unable to change their way of thinking to generate an innovative decision-making process.

The region lacks a strong and diversified economic infrastructure, and so depends on external support. For example, demographic pressures are difficult to relieve due to the lack of fiscal support. Both border areas compete for scarce resources; they attempt to attract investment by lowering salaries and providing fiscal incentives. These policies have debilitated the regional economy. Although NAFTA has produced new binational institutions focused on the environment and labor affairs, after four years they have yet to prove their efficacy.

Moreover, NAFTA was never intended to function as an integration process, but merely as a trade agreement.

Border Asymmetry

Asymmetry can be the most serious obstacle to region building. In order to integrate a region, such obstacles must first be identified. Since both sides compete, it can be difficult to combine resources. Regardless of their specific differences, both El Paso and Ciudad Juárez lack basics. In the early 1990s, 60 percent of Ciudad Juárez's housing (Arreola and Curtis 1993) made up about three hundred *colonias* (neighborhoods—these were irregular settlements characterized by poor infrastructure and services), while almost 15 percent of the population of El Paso lacked basic services such as water and sewage (Schmidt and Lorey 1994).

Mexico can be defined as a centralized system; its cities are dependent on funding and political decisions made at both the state and federal levels. Although the U.S. system is more decentralized and U.S. border cities have more opportunities to tax their populations and issue bonds to support city level projects, they too require support from the state and federal governments. Mexican cities are restricted because, by law, they cannot issue bonds. It is common at border-related meetings to hear people from both sides complain because of their distance from Mexico City and Washington, D.C. The border population feels that it has been relegated to the political fringes; some feel there is no border development plan at all.

Border residents deal with two languages, but they are not necessarily bilingual; thus, prejudice abounds. Measurements are different: Mexico uses the metric system, while the United States uses the old English system. The measurement of water in both liters and gallons complicates border dialogue and understanding. Mexico is struggling to leave the Third World, while the United States dominates global economics and politics. These asymmetries are reflected at the border. Vila's findings (1997, 1996) show that "otherness" marks borderlanders, creating a cultural and ideological boundary that is very difficult to cross.

The economic and social gaps between the countries are wide. Even though U.S. border cities (with the exception of San Diego) are considered poor, many of their Mexican sister cities (Tijuana and Ciudad Juárez in particular, important both within their states and nationally) are poorer still.

Another obstacle to unity is the difference in legal systems and multijurisdictional authority. This is illustrated by the two countries' approaches to water issues. In Mexico, all water belongs to the nation and major decisions are made in Mexico City. In Texas, water belongs to landowners; in New Mexico, different systems are used, including old indigenous law, Spanish law, and Anglo-Saxon law. Generally, water rights are awarded to the first users.[5] Each aquifer has its own rules, but all come under common state principles. For example, the State Engineer has the power to rescind future drilling rights. These rules are based on the principle of protecting the common well-being—a rather subjective concept. In the lands between Elephant Butte and the Rio Grande, many people had no drilling rights, but drilled their property anyway to satisfy their needs. The Mendenhall Doctrine protects those who have made clear their intention to establish water rights by drilling and installing a pump. In addition, city planning authorities, state and federal water authorities, and the International Boundary and Water Commission (IBWC) must be considered.

A Region-Building Project

Undoubtedly, Ciudad Juárez and El Paso are a long way from forming an integrated region. A region-building project will require a combination of conventional and unconventional ideas, supported by area strengths. The following introduces some ideas for assembling a region-building agenda in the Paso del Norte region:

- Create a university consortium. Usually, dialogue among scholars already exists, or is easier to initiate than among politicians. Although many universities exist in the region, the number of border scholars is limited. The border studies experiment in Las Cruces has had problems in the past. Although the University of Texas at El Paso (UTEP) has had a border studies center for over twenty years, it has been a center for controversy and political conflict, as its directors have been frequently removed by the administration and its budget constantly cut. The University of Ciudad Juárez just began a border studies program in 1998.

- Start a university-based region-building project with an advisory board that includes prominent people in business, government, and NGOs. This project should identify complementary factors and partners. A major challenge would be to get support from the media.

- Focus on a relevant issue. Once the project is created, it must center on a key platform. In the Paso del Norte region, this is water. It is a very contentious issue, and many failed attempts have been made to get key players to talk. Nonetheless, despite all of the scientific data that exist on the seriousness of this issue, politicians are not easily convinced that a new set of decisions must be made.

- Create a regional council. It is recommended that a council similar to the one at the Dutch-German border be created (Scott 1997). A positive basis for such a council would come from successful experiences at the project level.

- Start an educational project to create a regional culture. With assistance from local universities, the council could launch a program to create regional identity, promote understanding to alleviate bias and prejudice, and facilitate collaboration on different levels.

Conclusion

One of the key questions that border studies examine is: How can border people work to improve their quality of life, employment opportunities, and competitiveness with other regions? Their relationship with their neighboring country is important, but perhaps even more so is the extent of their binational cooperation.

The European case provides a good example of the move toward continental integration, although North America does not appear to be looking to it as a model. The United States, Canada, and Mexico are making progress toward creating a large market, but integration is not yet an objective. The creation of markets may induce new perceptions of the role of borders, but in the context of free markets, the traditional need for control persists and blocks cooperative efforts to solve local problems that, because of their international nature, often become national problems.

True cooperation between neighboring nations may require new thinking and such a process of region building. An initiative that integrates organizations from the bottom up will mobilize new resources, bring new actors into the policy-making arena, and may force people to adopt fresh approaches to regional problems.

Endnotes

1. This can be exemplified by traffic control at the border: border commuters may wait in line up to one hour, suffering pollution and the cost of wasted time. At the federal level, however, the goals of this policy are to reduce smuggling and drug traffic.

2. Tijuana's seal reads *Aquí Empieza la Patria* (Here Begins the Motherland).

3. Laura Durazo, NGO representative at the conference "Transborder Cooperation and Sustainable Development in a Comparative Context," began her presentation with a map showing the historical developments of the U.S.-Mexican border to demonstrate the causes of what she termed "present wounds."

4. Vila's analysis of identity construction at the U.S.-Mexican border shows the many obstacles faced by *fronterizos*.

5. Some Native Americans claim that archeological excavations on mountaintops prove that their ancestors used water at the river's source long before the Spaniards did, and thus the water belongs to them. Current regulations give water rights to those who use irrigation channels *(acequias)*.

References

Anderson, Malcolm. 1997. "The Political Science of Frontiers." In *Borders and Border Regions in Europe and North America*, Paul Ganster, Alan Sweedler, James Scott, and Wolf-Dieter Eberwein, eds. San Diego: Institute for Regional Studies of the Californias and San Diego State University Press.

Arreola, Daniel. D., and J.R. Curtis. 1993. *The Mexican Border Cities: Landscape Anatomy and Place Personality*. Tucson: University of Arizona Press.

Baker, George. 1991. "Mexican Labor is Not Cheap." *Río Bravo* 1 (Fall): 7–26.

Barry, Tom, and Beth Sims. 1993. *The Challenge of Cross-Border Environmentalism: The U.S.-Mexico Case*. Albuquerque: Resource Center Press.

Bray, Donald, and Marjorie Woodford. 1998. "North America without Walls." *Mesquite Review* (September-October): 11–27

Bustamante Redondo, Joaquín. 1999a. *La Comisión Internacional de Límites y Aguas entre México y los Estados Unidos*. Ciudad Juárez: Universidad Autónoma de Ciudad Juárez.

Bustamante Redondo, Joaquín 1999b. Personal communication with author.

Castañeda, Jorge, and Robert A. Pastor. 1988. *Limits to Friendship: The United States and Mexico*. New York: Knopf.

Dror, Yehezkel. 1996. *La capacidad de gobernar*. México, D.F.: Fondo de Cultura Económica.

Dunn, Timothy J. 1996. *The Militarization of the U.S.-Mexico Border, 1978–1992: Low-Intensity Conflict Doctrine Comes Home*. Austin: CMAS Books, University of Texas at Austin.

Evans, Peter. 1997. "The Eclipse of the State? Reflections on Stateness in an Era of Globalization." *World Politics* 50 (October): 62–87.

Ortega, Herbert H. 1991. *U.S.-Mexico Border Health Statistics*. Washington, D.C.: Pan American Health Organization (PAHO).

Ranfla, Arturo, Djamel Toudert, Guillermo Alvarez de la Torre, and Guadalupe Ortega. 1999. "Estudio exploratorio de la marginalidad urbana en la frontera de Baja California." Paper presented at the Transborder Cooperation and Sustainable Development in a Comparative Context conference, 9–12 January, San Diego, California, USA.

Riding, Alan. 1985. *Vecinos distantes*. México, D.F.: Joaquín Mortiz.

Schmidt, Samuel. 1995. "Planning a Bi-National Metropolis at the U.S.-Mexico Border: The Case of El Paso-Ciudad Juárez." In *North American Cities and the Global Economy*, Peter Karl Kresl and Gary Gappert, eds. Thousand Oaks: Sage Urban Affairs Annual Review Series.

Schmidt, Samuel. 1996. "Detentions et deportation a la frontiere entre le Mexique et les Etats-Unis." *Cultures & Conflicts: Circuler, Enfermer, Eloigner; Zones díattente et centres de rétention des démocraties occidentale* 23: 155–85

Schmidt, Samuel. 1998. "Desarrollo sustentable en la frontera México-Estados Unidos. ¿Quimera o propósito factible?" *Revista mexicana de comercio exterior* 48 (5): 360–67.

Schmidt, Samuel, Jorge Gil, and Jorge Castro. 1995. "El desarrollo urbano en la frontera México-Estados Unidos. Estudio delphi en ocho ciudades fronterizas." *Frontera norte* 7 (January-June): 13.

Schmidt, Samuel, and David Lorey. 1994. *Policy Recommendations for Managing the El Paso-Ciudad Juárez Metropolitan Area*. El Paso: El Paso Community Foundation, Center for Inter-American and Border Studies, University of Texas at El Paso.

Schmidt, Samuel, and Carlos Spector. 1998. "EU: aborrecimiento anti-mexicano." *La crisis* 147 (October): 17–23.

Scott, James. 1997. "Dutch-German Euroregions: A Model for Transboundary Cooperation?" In *Borders and Border Regions in Europe and North America*, Paul Ganster, Alan Sweedler, James Scott, and Wolf-Dieter Eberwein, eds. San Diego: Institute for Regional Studies of the Californias and San Diego State University Press.

Secretaría de Desarrollo Urbano y Ecología (SEDUE), and U.S. Environmental Protection Agency (EPA). 1992. *Plan integral ambiental fronterizo. Primera etapa (1992–1994)*. México, D.F.: SEDUE.

Vila, Pablo. 1996. "Catolicismo y mexicanidad: una narrativa desde la frontera." *Frontera norte* 8 (15): 57–89.

Vila, Pablo. 1997. "Narrative Identities: The Emplotment of the Mexican on the U.S.-Mexico Border." *The Sociological Quarterly* 38 (1): 147–83.

Civil Society and the Definition of Regions in Environmental Policy[*]

Basilio Verduzco Chávez[*]

Abstract

This paper examines the relationship between civil society and the policies designed to solve environmental problems in borderlands. From an empirical perspective, this relationship is problematic. Citizen mobilization must be considered as it relates to institutional responses and as it contributes to the development of civil society and the democratization of political and civil institutions. Drawing on the findings of a study of environmental conflicts in the U.S.-Mexican border region (see Verduzco 1977), this essay explores the links between various observed patterns of activism and the outcomes of environmental diplomacy and other policies aimed at resolving the region's environmental problems.

Introduction

Since the 1970s, it has been common practice within the field of international relations to include groups that represent civil society in discussions of environmental policies, agreements, and protocols. Many scholars have studied civil society's contributions to assessing levels of environmental damage and pushing national governments to make stronger commitments to protect the environment (Caldwell 1990; Chaterjee and Finger 1994; Stairs and Taylor 1992). Questions remain unanswered as to whether environmental activism by certain groups is related to the ideal of a modern civil society based on free association of citizens, defense of the private realm, or the pursuit of universal rather than particularistic values and interests, and whether actions taken by civil society have regional implications within a nation-state.

Exploring what the regional implications of civil society's participation in environmental policy are makes sense for three reasons. First, along with other

* Verduzco Chávez is Professor in the Department of Regional Studies (INESR) at the University of Guadalajara, Mexico.

social movements, environmentalism is a contemporary movement that has been linked to the idea of civil society (Cohen and Arato 1992). However, the category of "civil society" is broader than the notion of "social movement," raising questions of how the two are connected.[1] According to Cohen and Arato (1992), civil society is a category that encompasses elements of legality, publicity, civil associations, mass culture, and family. Environmentalism, by contrast, refers to the aggregation of a diverse array of demands posed by groups with different perspectives on society and its relationship to nature. Environmental work does not always move toward the democratization of political life or decentralization. Dryzek and Lester (1989) posit that the perspectives of some environmentalists follow conservative lines and maintain a Hobbesian view that favors centralized forms of decision making. One problem in linking an ever-changing civil society to policy design is that it is not clear how civil society relates to contemporary social movements, such as environmentalism, and whether demands made by activists should be considered as contributions to the democratization of civil society and the decentralization of political institutions.

Second, representatives of civil society bring critical assessments to international forums that are often restricted to analyses of regional situations or events limited to a small portion of a nation's territory. Their proposals stem from discourse developed in dynamic regions and urban centers where civil society's most active speakers dwell. The third reason to explore this topic regards the specific territorial targets of policies conducted by countries trying to fulfill promises they made during international negotiations.

Variables in the relationship between environmental activism and the democratization of society and decision making have been explored at a macroregional level. Bomberg (1998) analyzed the influence of green activism, and green parties in particular, on both policy outcomes and development. Nelson (1996) mentions environmental activism's relation to the rise of civil society in Central Europe. One study of transnational environmental activism on the U.S.-Mexican border advanced some hypotheses that linked local conditions to patterns of environmental conflict and policies designed to solve the border region's environmental problems (Verduzco 1997).

This study analyzed levels of environmental activism measured in terms of rates of environmental conflict. These rates were defined as the number of protests presented by citizens to federal environmental agencies per ten thousand inhabitants in a municipality. Levels of activism were then associated with elements that conform to the dynamics of civil society: the existence of organizations, access to and dissemination of information, and local political practices reflecting the democratic ideal.[2] The elements considered in the study included sources of diffusion of activism or those elements that could help to explain the extent to which environmental activism was moving from centers of activism to less experienced areas. Centers of activism include places with a tradition of citizens who speak out against influences on their private lives from the economy and state institutions. In other words, mobilization against public or private decisions or projects that threaten their lifestyles and well-being. The study looked at large, well-developed urban centers in both Mexico and the United States since regional public policies are influenced by experienced activists in such places. The study concludes that the rise in activism and the observable differences in the character of the groups involved do affect institutional responses to some forms of citizen participation. This essay seeks to expand this argument to suggest that civil society plays an important role in designing regional environmental policies that determine who will receive the benefits of such policies and who will pay the financial costs and environmental burdens associated with them.

Thus, two questions demand attention: (1) To what extent does environmental activism influence the design of both national and international policies that determine which regions or areas will be protected or unprotected by domestic law or international agreements? And (2) How does such activism contribute to the democratization of society, the evolution of political institutions, and the elimination of regional disparities or the achievement of environmental justice.

Diffusion of Activism and the Organization of Civil Society

This essay regards civil society as both the individual actions and collective efforts of groups in a society as well as individual interests, practices, and relationships. New theories about civil society regard it as "self-limiting democratizing movements seeking to expand and protect spaces for both negative liberty and positive freedom and to recreate egalitarian forms of solidarity" (Cohen and Arato 1992). Thus, civil society is the territory of purposeful agents whose activities are intended to influence the decision-making procedures that shape public and private life. Two common characteristics of involved social groups are the defense of private interests and work toward the democratization of society. Because gaining influence is an important goal of active citizens, the relationship between environmental activism and the types of policies it targets in a region should be explored.

Does the transformation of civil society's institutions result from the participation of interest groups in the dissemination of resources and information? Does civil society emerge where citizen participation is not a key feature of social life? Some scholars regard the role of civil society in the design of public policy as positive because it may help to achieve justice in the context of a liberal democracy. They argue that civil society contributes to the shape of designs that determine the allocation of benefits and their costs by influencing policy making. For example, Schneider and Ingram (1997) argue that such designs are part of every policy instrument and can be found in the different stages of policy implementation, such as statutes and administrative guidelines. They suggest that public policies should be regarded as instruments for intervention in public life and shaping private decisions. Public policies are therefore like any other instrument designed to serve a purpose and yield an outcome, defining costs and benefits and how they are distributed among different groups and places.

Schneider and Ingram indicate that the policy designs of international environmental treaties or protocols and some domestic policies contain such elements as target populations, specified goals, and problems to be solved, in addition to rules, rationales, and assumptions.[3] These policy instruments are created in a historical context in which regions within a nation-state are not only part of the polity, but are also individually influenced by social processes.

Since the early 1980s, civil society in the U.S.-Mexican border region has consistently shaped the design of environmental policies in the region. Such policies not only distinguish the binational region from the rest of the two countries, but also provide the tools and opportunities for policymakers to delineate both deserving and undeserving groups along the lines of power, transnational interests, and income distribution. Borderland dwellers are defined as the target population in various policies, although structural goals such as economic development and industrialization greatly influence policy design. When a treaty is signed to prevent the illegal transport of toxic wastes across the border, for example, the policy's target is not only of regional public interest; those who generate or handle such wastes are also considered, making the relocation of facilities a possible secondary target.

The effect of civil society in the U.S.-Mexican border region on area policy is hardly unique. There is general agreement among scholars that citizen participation expands as a result of increased social awareness. Societies change and learn in part due to the various efforts and levels of activism of social groups. Less-experienced activists learn the repertoire of activism by looking at the ways that other groups frame and handle problems, and may even borrow resources from successful activists. This has happened before in different industrial societies (Tarrow 1994; Snow and Benford 1992). In his book on social movements, Tarrow (1994) provides examples of nineteenth-century revolutionary movements in Europe, student mobilizations in the late 1960s in Europe and the United States, and civic protests against state socialism during the 1980s. He argues that "cycles of protest have some traceable paths of diffusion from large cities to the rural periphery, or—as is often the case—from the periphery to center. They often spread from heavily industrial areas to adjacent areas of light industry and farming, along river valleys, or through other major routes of communication" (Tarrow 1994: 155–56).

Nongovernmental organizations (NGOs) are recognized as important contributors to the negotiation and implementation of international treaties and protocols. Susskind (1994: 130–31) cites three reasons for NGOs to become active participants in treaty making: (1) NGOs can force national governments to consider various domestic views; (2) by voicing different interests, NGOs can enhance the implementation of new international treaties aimed to protect the environment and to enhance international cooperation; and (3) NGOs can assure that national governments are accountable for the promises they make.

An examination of networks of international cooperation is key to assessing civil society's role in shaping regional public policies. Although efforts remain on a microregional level, international cooperation networks have become increasingly important in the U.S.-Mexican border region. Some well-known networks include: the Coalition for Environmental Justice, an organization that has tried to connect grassroots groups to more structured organizations; the Border Network for Health and Environment, established with the support of the Border Ecology Project and activists from Sonora, Baja California, Arizona, and Southern California; and the Binational Network, fostered by the Texas Center for Policy Studies and the Monterrey (Nuevo León)-based Bioconservación, A.C. (Verduzco 1997).

Scholars who have analyzed social, economic, cultural, and political processes in border regions agree that given transnational integration and its manifestation in the borderlands, the study of such subjects cannot be defined by the limits imposed by international boundaries. Any notion of borderland civil society needs to include the transnational aspects of elements that define civil society in general, such as concerned citizens, families, and organizations. The composition and scope of the interests of borderland activists, along with the resources they use and their repertoire of actions, help to explain what policies are targeted for a border region and when they are put in place.

There is evidence of growing cooperation between organized groups on both sides of international borders worldwide and even at multinational levels (Keck and Sikkink 1998). The work of scholars and policy analysts such as Durazo, Kamp, and Land (1993), Barry and Sims (1994), Barba (1993), and Zabin and Brown (1996) show how activists are learning to communicate, exchange information, and link the work of well-organized groups with that of grassroots groups and other community activists who may have had little or no experience in dealing with environmental issues. A large part of the work is aimed at increasing cooperation among groups from both sides of the border, indicating that the notion of a transnational civil society in the U.S.-Mexican border region has progressed in the last decade. One study on environmental conflicts in the border region (Verduzco 1997) provides strong evidence that the international diffusion of activism and the internationalization of environmental conflicts do not occur randomly along the U.S.-Mexican border. In the six Mexican border states where the study was conducted (Baja California, Coahuila, Chihuahua, Nuevo León, Sonora, and Tamaulipas), growing levels of environmental activism have led to a process of regional differentiation in which mobilized and organized groups focus on particular areas that thereby tend to be protected by environmental policies, while other areas are implicitly left out.

The spread of activism influences the organization of civil society in regions or localities where citizens publicly organize against conditions of exclusion, the invasion of privacy, and practices that attempt to constrain individual rights. Such influences can be seen in the issues that are brought to light and how they are framed, and in the causal stories that are presented to determine public policies. The following is a summary of some of the patterns of activism observed in northern Mexico during the early 1990s to illustrate this point (Verduzco 1997).

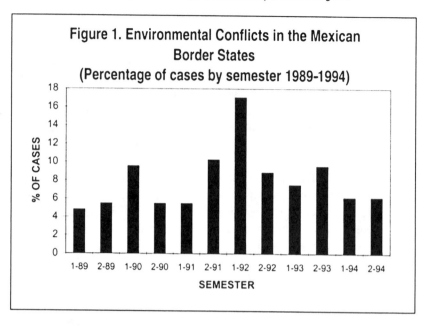

Figure 1. Environmental Conflicts in the Mexican Border States (Percentage of cases by semester 1989-1994)

The most evident trend in activism in northern Mexico is the ability of experienced organized groups that claim to represent the interests of civil society to seize any opportunity to expand their agendas. Mexico underwent some of the most drastic political and economic changes between 1994 and 1998, including the decline of the political monopoly held for more than six decades by one party and the negotiation of a free trade agreement with the United States and Canada. Using the emergence of conflicts as an indicator of the level of environmental mobilization in northern Mexico during these years, a pattern emerges surrounding the dates when the trade agreement was still being debated in the U.S. Congress. Figure 1 shows that 24 percent of all conflicts that emerged during that six-year period did so in 1992. Levels of activism were especially high during the first semester of that year, when 17 percent of conflicts occurred.[4]

A second pattern is distinguished in variations in the interest expressed by activists about different environmental issues. Toxic waste and air pollution were major concerns; however, interest in air pollution was more pronounced farther away from the border, while interest in toxic waste was higher closer to the border. This suggests that activists living closer to the border tend to worry more about the hazardous elements of industrialization. This may be interpreted as successful fallout from experienced groups in the United States that have expanded their agendas south of the border. Groups that have succeeded in this respect include the Coalition for Environmental Justice, which has crossed the border and repeatedly raised concerns about working conditions and safety in the *maquiladoras*; the Environmental Health Coalition, which has forged an alliance with activists in Baja California; and the Texas Center for Policy Studies, which has targeted legal aspects of pollution prevention and stressed the need to expand the principle of "right to know" on both sides of the border (see Table 1).

Table 1. Environmental Conflicts by Problem Type and Border Corridor

Problem	Border	Border Corridor* 100 km.	100 + km.	Total
	Cases / %	Cases / %	Cases / %	Cases / %
Noise	4 / 7.0	1 / 14.3	19 / 22.9	24 / 16.3
Hazardous Materials	25 / 43.8	1 / 14.3	20 / 24.1	46 / 31.3
Water Pollution	22 / 38.5	4 / 57.1	24 / 27.9	50 / 34.0
Toxic Waste	36 / 63.1	4 / 57.1	32 / 38.5	72 / 48.9
Air Pollution	19 / 33.3	3 / 42.8	46 / 55.4	68 / 46.2

* Municipalities were grouped into three border corridors assuming different levels of exposure to international interaction and considering their inclusion on different diplomatic agreements. "Border" refers to municipalities on the international border; 100km refers to municipalities located within the 100-kilometer (62-mile) corridor protected by the La Paz Agreement; and 100+km refers to municipalities located beyond the 100-kilometer corridor. Note: Percentages refer to the total number of cases observed in that corridor. A 100 percent total is not obtained because one case may refer to different problems.
Source: Verduzco 1997.

The number of complaints presented to regional offices of the Federal Attorney for Environmental Protection (Procuraduría Federal de Protección al Ambiente–PROFEPA) by environmental groups shows that such groups have an important strategic function in voicing the concerns of society, increasing environmental awareness, and exposing the negative effects of contamination to less-mobilized sectors of society. There were, however, differences in how these groups handled problems in different parts of the border region. In cities on the border and in the corridor where most state capitals are located, environmental groups voiced less than 15 percent of complaints. In the more rural corridor, within 100 kilometers of the border, such groups voiced 20 percent.

These patterns do not fully reveal regional differences in levels of social mobilization that may exist across the region. They do, however, show that activists stress different themes in different regions to demand that citizen participation be incorporated in policy-making processes.

The Borderlands as Protected Areas

One of the controversies surrounding these increasing levels of environmental activism is that such activism does shape policy designs that define places or social groups as target populations and recipients of different levels of environmental protection. A movement for environmental justice has emerged as minorities and the poor complain about unfair distribution of the costs and benefits of development (di Chiro 1992; Bryant 1995). One topic that needs further exploration is the role that movements included in the category of civil society have played in setting borderlands apart in terms of environmental protection.

From the U.S. perspective, Barry and Sims (1994) claim that little or no attention was given to the border region until activists brought pressure to bear. They call the region "the other America" because of the conditions of poverty and environmental degradation observed there and suggest that attention to borderland problems has increased only recently as environmental activists have pointed to patterns of degradation and poor quality of life. On the Mexican side, the situation is quite different. Mexico as a whole has moved very slowly to consider the environment in its development policies. However, the many policy instruments targeted to the border region reveal that the borderland is gaining importance and receiving more attention than other parts of Mexico.

Mexico and the United States have signed several treaties to address serious environmental problems that constitute a threat to future development in the two countries.[5] The observable policy design of these agreements clearly reveals interests and values that define the border as a region deserving of more attention than other parts of the two countries. This includes the formation of task groups to work on environmental issues and foster cooperation, the definition of a specific area as the target for the policies, and the allocation of resources directed to solving specific problems such as water pollution or toxic waste disposal.

In 1983, Mexico and the United States signed an agreement for environmental protection of the border region that was a landmark both in terms of its goals and its explicit definition of a target area. This agreement's unprecedented spatial dimension responded to the challenges of environmental interdependence as well as the concerns of social groups in the United States regarding the rapid growth rates in terms of population and manufacturing jobs in Mexico's border cities while environmental protection was being ignored. Whether or not particular decisions conform to this agreement is a constant source of debate and criticism from environmental groups. The well-known debate concerning a waste site in Sierra Blanca, Texas, is one example, but violations to the agreement are frequently denounced by activists concerned about the effects of hazards from other facilities.

Other responses also show that the federal governments of both countries, and particularly Mexico, are quite interested in creating an image of strong environmental protectionism. Examples of state agencies' responses to citizens' demands in a specific region include various borderland environmental programs and the Border Environment Cooperation Commission (BECC), a binational agency that deals with concerns raised by citizens on both sides of the border. According to Johnson and Beaulieu (1996), NGOs from both countries have played an important role in raising concerns about the effects of trade on the environment and in shaping institutions created to deal with transboundary environmental issues.

Environmental activists who represent the interests of civil society have played a crucial role in putting pressure on both national governments to sign agreements and develop programs and policies to attend to the concerns of the borderland citizenry. They may, however, be helping to legitimize policy instruments and political institutions that work against the larger goals of democratization and social justice. Their support of actions targeted to a specific problem, program, or geographic area may be used by decision makers to postpone further transformations of decision-making procedures that could expand opportunities for civic participation elsewhere.

Framing Problems and the Protection of Regions

The segregation of people in different regions in such a way that some parts of a country may be defined as the target for environmental protection while others are left behind is not a direct outcome of a dynamic civil society. This lack of environmental justice could, however, be a by-product of the lack of development and democratization of the institutions of civil society—that is, the existence of an active and responsible citizenry and the organizations that may channel its participation to attain social goals. In a society in transition, environmental conflicts reveal political and economic power practices that leave citizens no alternatives to contentious actions, including civil disobedience. The ways that activists frame problems influence policy design and the ways that decisionmakers deal with problems.

A review of how conflicts on one side of the border become international and the different responses such conflicts receive from institutions of the state shows the relationship between problem-framing efforts and policy outcomes.[6] State institutions tend to favor territorial solutions to environmental conflicts, but regional policy instruments are designed to take the potential for internationalization of controversies into account. Not all problems with transboundary effects lead to strong binational coalitions. On both sides of the border, experienced activists and their ability to develop a common agenda determine which problems generate international controversy. Internationalization generally means that problems are put forth as threats to communities on both sides of the border. Activists give varying emphasis to issues of public health, social justice, lack of rules, and authoritarian decision making.

Community activists along the border have raised the point that environmental concerns are not always the actual motive for citizen participation. Access to privileged political positions, financial gain, and publicity are sometimes the true motives of the most dynamic actors, claiming to represent the interests of civil society. These hidden agendas influence how problems are framed and what policies are recommended. A group leader whose real interest is to gain notoriety and access to political positions will tend to work through existing power networks rather than challenge them or build new ones. Hidden agendas that are not oriented to the democratization of society have various consequences. Among the most common negative consequences are formation of single-issue movements, short-lived groups and organizations, corruption of activists, and manipulation of community demands for political reasons.

When the border region *is* slated to receive benefits from environmental protection policies, the whole population of the region may not be targeted. Rather, a specific group—such as industrial workers, inhabitants of a particular neighborhood, entrepreneurs, or a limited age group—may be focused on. In such cases, the democratization of civil society does not advance.

In the long run, the evolution of society to a level that encourages citizens to participate is key to developing civil society. Until that point is reached, group efforts are catalysts for change in policy making. Such groups keep civil society active, but cannot be expected to give the structural transformation of society precedence over striving for solutions to the problems that are their main concerns. One clear advantage to the variety of problem-solving efforts in the border region is that they help to create the conditions for institutional arrangements that are open to public participation.

Conclusion

The pattern of citizen participation on the U.S.-Mexican border and the institutional response to it suggest that the debate about environmental policies needs to move beyond its current focus on specific problems in the border region. Giving priority to the study of environmentalism in specific areas will not contribute much. Rather, focus needs to shift to trends and movement toward the transformation of civil society. Group activism may then be assessed in terms of its contribution to the broader process of democratization and to the establishment of decentralized responses to environmental problems.

The extent to which activism is translated into policies that protect the borderland is determined by how economic and political power are distributed in the region. By looking at regional environmental protests and using them as an indicator of an area's likelihood of receiving environmental protection policies, two views of the border emerge. The first points to different levels of opportunity for corridors that lie at different distances from the border; the second suggests that opportunities exist for creating pollution-free paradises within the region. These different views are the result of different policy designs. One has been laid out in binational agreements negotiated under the influence of civil society in its international role. The other is used in domestic policies forged with the aid of civil society in its national role. (Dividing the role of civil society allows for analytical focus on the larger process of transition toward a democratic society.) Research suggesting that policies created under the influence of an active citizenry lead to social and regional differences should not lead analysts to conclude that environmental activism is not making important achievements toward preventing the penetration of the state and the economy into social life.

To the extent that environmental activism keeps the ideal of active political participation among citizens alive, it also contributes to the construction of civil society. Some may argue that policies targeted to a specific region contribute to decentralization and diversity, thus conforming to interests defended by modern civil societies. This does not happen, however, if institutional reforms that tend toward democratization and reduction of the role of central government bureaucracies are also promoted. This entails a change in the policy-making process, including international treaty negotiation and the implementation of developmental policies aimed at fostering regional economic growth and trade.

In theorizing about civil society, it is not that the state has responded to citizen demands in the borderlands or the state's institutional transformation to encourage active citizen participation that is problematic; it is that policies are created as a manifestation of state power. The signing of treaties and the creation of specific programs and commissions may actually be misleading. As Cohen and Arato (1992) have correctly pointed out, the success of social movements at the level of civil society should be assessed in terms of the democratization of values, norms, and institutions rooted in a political culture, not in terms of particular goals.

Endnotes

1. For a review of the origins of the civil society category and its current association with the idea of democracy, see Seligman 1992: 139–61.

2. The concept of environmental conflict analyzed in the study referred to situations that involved some form of citizen activism against specific facilities. Two databases were developed, one on controversies reported by newspapers and another for complaints to environmental protection agencies from concerned individuals and groups.

3. Target populations are the recipients of policy benefits or burdens, goals or problems are the values to be distributed, rules are the elements that guide or constrain action, rationales are the elements that explain or legitimate policy, and assumptions are the logical connections that tie the other elements together (Schneider and Ingram 1997: 2).

4. This information is derived from an extensive survey of newspapers and interviews with government officials and activists in border states. The survey's goal was to identify controversies surrounding environmental problems at specific facilities. At least one major newspaper was reviewed for each state. The emergence date for a conflict was estimated using event-data methodology, setting the beginning date of a conflict as the time the first event is reported. The database on which this report is based comprised a total of 147 cases.

5. See, for example: the Cooperative Agreement on Marine Pollution by Hydrocarbon or Other Noxious Substance Spills / *Acuerdo de Cooperación sobre la Contaminación del Medio Marino por Derrames de Hidrocarburos y Otras Sustancias Nocivas*, signed in Mexico City on July 24, 1980; the Agreement for the Protection and Improvement of the Environment in the Border Zone / *Convenio para la Protección y Mejoramiento del Medio Ambiente en la Zona Fronteriza*, signed in La Paz on August 14, 1983; the Cooperative Agreement for the Solution of Drainage Problems in San Diego, California/ Tijuana, Baja California / *Acuerdo de Cooperación para la Solución de los Problemas de Saneamiento en San Diego, California/Tijuana, Baja California,* signed in San Diego on July 18, 1985; the Cooperative Agreement on Transborder Movements of Hazardous Wastes and Dangerous Substances / *Acuerdo de Cooperación sobre Movimientos Transfronterizos de Desechos Peligrosos y Sustancias Peligrosas*, signed in Washington, D.C., on November 12, 1986; and more recently, the North American Agreement on Environmental Cooperation / *Acuerdo de Cooperación Ambiental de América del Norte,* signed in Ottawa, Washington, D.C., and Mexico City on September 14, 1993.

6. The internationalization of a conflict is a process in which activists from both sides of the border are involved in targeted actions to change the policy or decision that led, or may lead to, an environmental problem.

References

Barba Pirez, Regina. 1993. "La unión de grupos ambientalistas en el proceso de negociaciones del Tratado de Libre Comercio." *Frontera Norte* 5: 10.

Barry, Tom, and Beth Sims. 1994. *The Challenge of Cross-Border Environmentalism: The U.S.-Mexico Case*. Albuquerque: Resource Center Press.

Bomberg, Elizabeth. 1998. *Green Parties and Politics in the European Union*. London: Routledge.

Bryant, Bunyan, ed. 1995. *Environmental Justice: Issues, Policies and Solutions*. Washington, D.C.: Island Press.

Caldwell, Lynton K. 1990. *International Environmental Policy: Emergence and Dimensions*. Durham: Duke University Press.

Chatterjee, Pratap, and Mathias Finger. 1994. *The Earth Brokers: Power Politics and World Development*. London: Routledge.

Cohen, Jean L., and Andrew Arato. 1992. *Civil Society and Political Theory*. Cambridge: MIT Press.

Di Chiro, Giovanna. 1992. "Defining Environmental Justice: Women's Voices and Grassroots Politics." *Socialist Review* 22: 4.

Dryzek, John S., and James P. Lester. 1989. "Alternative Views of the Environmental Problematic." Pp. 314–30 in *Environmental Politics and Policy*, James P. Lester, ed. Durham: Duke University Press.

Durazo, Laura, Dick Kamp, and Geof Land. 1993. *Environmental and Health Issues in the Interior of Mexico: Options for Transnational Safeguards*. Tijuana and Bisbee: Proyecto Fronterizo de Educación Ambiental and Border Ecology Project.

Johnson, Pierre Marc, and André Beaulieu. 1996. *The Environment and NAFTA: Understanding and Implementing the New Continental Law*. Washington, D.C.: Island Press.

Keck, Margaret E., and Kathryn Sikkink. 1998. *Activists beyond Borders: Advocacy Networks in International Politics*. Ithaca: Cornell University Press.

Nelson, Daniel N. 1996. "Civil Society and the Endangered." *Social Research* 63 (2): 344–68.

Schneider, Anne L., and Helen Ingram. 1997. *Policy Design for Democracy*. Lawrence: University Press of Kansas.

Seligman, Adam B. 1992. "The Fragile Ethical Vision of Civil Society." Pp. 139–61 in *Citizenship and Social Theory*, Bryan S. Turner, ed. London: Sage Publications.

Snow, David, and Robert Benford. 1992. "Master Frames and Cycles of Protest." In *Frontiers in Social Movement Theory*, Aldon D. Morris and Carol McClurg Mueller, eds. New Haven: Yale University Press.

Stairs, Kevin, and Peter Taylor. 1992. "Non-Governmental Organizations and the Legal Protection of the Oceans: A Case Study." Pp. 110–41 in *The International Politics of the Environment*, Andrew Hurrel and Benedict Kingsbury, eds. Oxford: Oxford University Press.

Susskind, Lawrence. 1994. *Environmental Diplomacy: Negotiating More Effective Global Agreements*. New York: Oxford University Press.

Tarrow, Sydney. 1994. *Power in Movement: Social Movements, Collective Action, and Politics*. Cambridge: Cambridge University Press.

Verduzco, Basilio. 1997. *Transnational Activism and Environmental Conflicts in the United States-Mexico Border Region*. Ph.D. diss., Rutgers University, New Brunswick, New Jersey, USA.

Zabin, Carol, and Andrea Brown. 1996. "Community and Improving Quality of Life in the Mexican Border Region: An Analysis of NGOs and Grassroots Organizations." NAID homepage (March 1999), http://naid.sppsr.ucla.edu.

Trends in Quality-of-Life Indicators in U.S. and Mexican Border Regions, 1950–1990

Joan B. Anderson[*]

Abstract

This study uses data from the U.S. and Mexican censuses for 1950 through 1990 to present trends in population, income, poverty, and quality-of-life variables for the four U.S. and six Mexican border states, as well as for 25 U.S. border counties and 36 Mexican border *municipios* (municipalities). Evidence suggests that after decreasing somewhat during the 1970s, both sides of the border experienced an overall increase in poverty during the 1980s. In contrast, most quality-of-life indicators have showed steady improvement from 1950 to 1990, although such improvement slowed during the 1980s. Decreasing poverty in the border region would require a focused antipoverty policy in addition to economic expansion and freer trade. A discussion of some potentially effective policies is included.

Introduction

The post-World War II era has been a period of growth for both sides of the U.S.-Mexican border in terms of population and economy. In 1950, the U.S.-Mexican border region was sparsely populated, primarily rural, and poor. Between 1950 and 1990, both sides of the border attracted masses of migrants. On the U.S. side, this was attributed to a national "snowbelt" to "sunbelt" migration pattern. On the Mexican side, it was a manifestation of rural to urban and interior to northern border migration patterns. The latter was stimulated by U.S. demand for low-cost, unskilled agricultural and industrial labor. The overall trend toward the globalization of production that occurred during this

---

* Anderson is Professor in the School of Business Administration at the University of San Diego.

40-year period contributed to the rapid industrial and urban growth in the binational region, including the emergence of a series of twin cities.

As these changes have occurred, what has happened to the well-being of border area residents? How have migration, urbanization, and industrialization affected poverty levels and quality of life? This study focuses on poverty and quality-of-life indicators on both sides of the border, and how the inter-relatedness of the two diverse economies affect them. More importantly, it is concerned with the ways that economic policies might be altered to help diminish poverty.

The fact that the U.S.-Mexican border bears the world's largest economic disparity has an important influence on the dynamics of the region. The area's poverty level and strategies for coping with it are affected by the border. Two studies, one by Anderson, Clement, and Shellhammer (1980) based on 1970 U.S. census data, and the other by Stoddard and Hedderson (1989) using 1970 and 1980 U.S. census data, found that poverty rates tend to be lower in the Mexican border region than for Mexico as a whole and higher in the U.S. border region than for the United States as a whole. Pick, Butler, and Jones (1990) concur with regard to Mexico; however, their findings show that by 1980, the U.S. border states were *not* statistically more impoverished than the rest of the United States. The 1994 study by Betts and Slottje stresses that people are better off at the western end of the border and increasingly poorer toward the eastern end. In the Mexican border region, an economy based on U.S. discards gives the poor access to an abundant supply of secondhand materials and, for some, a better education for their children on the U.S. side (Anderson and de la Rosa 1991). Organized labor in the United States and others have charged that the availability of Mexican labor on the U.S. side may depress wages and increase unemployment for U.S. citizens while providing low-cost labor for agriculture and industry.

This paper presents trends in poverty and quality-of-life variables on both the U.S. and Mexican sides of the border. It examines U.S. data for the four border states (California, Arizona, New Mexico, and Texas) and 25 border counties: two in California, four in Arizona, four in New Mexico, and 15 in Texas. It also includes data on the six Mexican border states (Baja California, Sonora, Chihuahua, Coahuila, Nuevo León, and Tamaulipas) and 36 border *municipios*: four in Baja California, 10 in Sonora, seven in Chihuahua, five in Coahuila, one in Nuevo León, and nine in Tamaulipas (see Figure 1). Data are derived from U.S. and Mexican censuses for 1950 through 1990.

Trends in Poverty

The term "poverty" is used here to refer to income levels that are insufficient to cover a family's basic needs. The gauge used to measure poverty in Mexico is the percentage of wage earners earning less than one minimum wage. In the United States, poverty levels are determined by the percentage of families living below the established U.S. poverty line (see Table 1).[1] According to Article 123 of the Mexican Constitution of 1917, minimum wages are to be set at a level

Figure 1. U.S.-Mexican Border Twin Cities

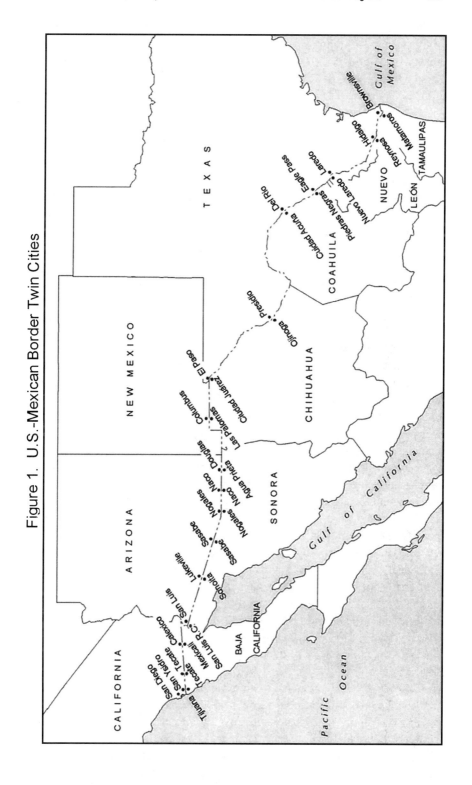

sufficient to satisfy the basic needs of a family and educate its children. With this as the standard, a family with an income below one minimum wage would not be able to meet its basic needs, and would be considered to be living in poverty. A study by the Centro de Estudios del Trabajo (Center of Labor Studies) (1986) detailed the basic basket of necessities for Mexican families. According to this gauge, 40 percent of minimum annual income was needed to supply basic nutritional requirements in 1983. By 1985, 100 percent was needed, mainly due to inflation. This same study estimated that in 1985, 2.5 minimum wages would be required to meet basic needs. Since the purchasing power of the Mexican minimum wage in 1990 was about half of what it had been in 1980, the data recorded here also report the percentage of wage earners receiving less than two minimum wages. By 1990, two minimum wages were probably a more accurate measure of the poverty line for Mexico. At the same time, this measure could also apply to the United States. In 1980, the U.S. minimum wage of $3.10 per hour for a full-time worker (40 hours per week, 50 weeks per year) yielded an annual income that was 74 percent of the poverty level set for a family of four. By 1990, the $3.80 per hour minimum wage for a full-time worker yielded an annual income that was just 59 percent of the poverty level set for a family of four. In other words, it would have taken almost two U.S. minimum wages to even reach the poverty line by 1990.

Although available data are unable to provide information that is as exact as is desired, they are able to indicate trends. The Mexican census reported that for all but twelve (excepting Santa Cruz, P.G. Guerrero, Agua Prieta, Janos, Ojinaga, Ocampo, Jiménez, Guerrero, Hidalgo, Anáhuac, Río Bravo, and Valle Hermoso) borderland *municipios*, the percentage of workers earning less than one minimum wage has decreased for each census year since 1970. However, since it took slightly more than two minimum wages in 1990 to yield the same purchasing power as one 1980 minimum wage, comparing the percentage of workers with less than two minimum wages in 1990 to those with less than one 1980 minimum wage suggests a significant increase in Mexican borderland poverty during the 1980s. This fall in purchasing power may help to explain the increase in labor force participation. As presented in the Mexican census, individual wage data give only a rough approximation of poverty trends because they do not take all of the wage earners in a family into account. González de la Rocha's (1986) study of poor families' survival strategies in Guadalajara indicates that as real wages fall, more members of a family tend to join the labor force to make ends meet. Such an increase in participation would prevent family income from falling as far below the poverty line as the reported trend seems to indicate.

Family income statistics are more readily available on the U.S. Side of the border. The predominant trend between 1970 and 1980 was a decrease in the number of families living below the poverty line; this number then increased between 1980 and 1990, in many areas to a higher rate than in 1970. In San Diego, Jeff Davis, and Kinney counties, the percentage of families living below

Table 1. Mexican Workers and Families below the Poverty Level

State and Municipality	% of Economically Active Population Earning Less than Minimum Wage		1990 Wage Earners	
	1970	1980	% Less than Minimum Wage	% Less than 2 Minimum Wages
Mexico	64.3	55.6	26.5	63.2
Baja California	55.3	52.0	9.4	40.0
Ensenada	40.4	21.4	11.5	47.2
Tijuana	44.5	24.6	10.9	43.8
Tecate	43.9	23.8	9.2	42.7
Mexicali	36.9	21.8	7.6	34.4
Sonora	56.2	47.8	11.9	52.7
San Luis Río Colorado	20.0	15.5	9.3	43.2
Puerto Peñasco	22.6	11.2	11.1	47.0
Caborca	26.6	10.6	9.8	57.7
Altar	13.0	10.4	6.8	54.8
Saric	23.6	19.8	13.9	46.4
Nogales	33.9	8.3	8.8	51.1
Santa Cruz	15.6	17.4	13.2	71.9
Cananea	29.5	12.6	8.4	36.5
Naco	36.6	21.2	10.5	59.3
Agua Prieta	39.7	11.5	12.7	52.4
Chihuahua	62.1	55.7	14.8	52.8
Janos	13.5	10.2	38.7	71.5
Asención	23.9	16.9	12.6	50.0
Juárez	46.3	15.7	6.4	44.9
Guadalupe	14.7	12.0	9.2	54.4
P.G. Guerrero	13.5	20.5	11.4	66.3
Ojinaga	23.9	17.5	22.6	61.7
Ocampo	9.7	18.4	40.6	70.0
Coahuila	66.3	53.5	18.3	60.9
Acuña	46.4	24.1	8.1	62.6
Jiménez	10.7	18.6	31.8	78.5
Piedras Negras	45.4	20.8	14.0	55.3
Guerrero	10.2	19.5	25.3	72.4
Hidalgo	11.7	20.0	24.3	77.2
Nuevo León	55.5	44.9	15.6	58.7
Anáhuac	14.6	22.9	25.8	67.9
Tamaulipas	61.9	52.9	23.1	61.1
Nuevo Laredo	47.0	24.7	17.8	58.6
Guerrero	22.3	21.5	19.6	52.0
Mier	34.9	30.8	26.4	62.6
Miguel Alemán	35.7	23.1	20.7	58.4
Camargo	28.4	26.8	24.7	65.4
Reynosa	37.3	18.8	16.1	58.0
Río Bravo	30.2	19.7	21.5	67.2
Valle Hermosa	31.5	23.8	27.5	65.8
Matamoros	41.2	17.3	11.7	51.1

Source: Secretaría de Programación y Presupuesto 1981; 1990 Mexican Census.

Table 2. U.S. Families below the Poverty Level

	% Families below Poverty Line				% Families below Poverty Line		
	1970	1980	1990		1970	1980	1990
United States	10.7	9.6	10.0	**Texas**	14.7	11.1	14.1
California	8.4	8.7	9.3	El Paso	17.4	18.0	22.4
San Diego	8.6	8.4	8.1	Hudspeth	28.2	25.7	32.4
Imperial	16.2	12.7	20.8	Culberson	18.6	17.3	26.2
Arizona	11.5	9.5	11.4	Jeff Davis	26.5	19.6	15.0
Yuma	13.6	12.3	15.4	Presidio	40.9	34.6	40.2
Pima	10.8	9.1	12.0	Brewster	27.1	14.8	22.4
Santa Cruz	20.0	13.4	22.0	Terrell	23.6	16.1	20.6
Cochise	13.4	11.8	15.8	Val Verde	24.5	24.3	29.4
New Mexico	18.6	14.0	16.5	Kinney	45.7	29.0	22.0
Hidalgo	22.1	14.7	18.1	Maverick	44.1	34.4	45.6
Grant	11.8	12.4	17.7	Webb	38.5	29.0	33.1
Luna	20.5	19.2	24.9	Zapata	50.6	23.8	36.0
Doña Ana	20.7	18.3	20.7	Starr	52.3	45.0	56.5
				Hidalgo	42.2	29.0	36.3
				Cameron	38.6	26.0	33.7

Source: 1990 U.S. Census.

the poverty level has decreased over time. In Grant and El Paso counties, and in the state of California as a whole, however, poverty has increased. Some of the Texas border counties are exceptionally poor. Eleven had 25 percent or more families living below the poverty level, with a high of 45 percent in Starr County. Evidence suggests that after easing somewhat during the 1970s, poverty increased on both sides of the border during the 1980s.

When comparing the poverty levels of border states to national averages for the census years 1970, 1980, and 1990, California proves to have had lower levels than the United States as a whole, while Texas and New Mexico had higher levels. Arizona also had a higher poverty rate than the nation in 1970 and 1990, but was roughly equal to the national average in 1980. At the same time, the poverty rates in all six Mexican border states were substantially lower than the Mexican national average. In both countries, the rate of poverty was generally higher farther east along the border.

Quality-of-Life Indicators

Poverty means both economic and sociological losses to society. Poverty limits market size as well as the development of human resources, decreasing both demand and supply. Trends in quality-of-life indicators must be examined to understand the effects of poverty, especially in light of imperfect income measurements. Life expectancy and infant mortality are indicators that help to quantitatively measure the status of health and sanitation. Adequate housing is measured here by access to piped water and plumbing. Educational attainment is another quality-of-life indicator used in this study, which is evaluated by student/teacher ratios in primary education (a visible sign of private and public priorities for education), the percentage of the population with basic literacy, and the percentage that achieves a designated level of education.

Figure 2 shows life expectancy in the U.S.-Mexican border states. On average, life expectancy is about five years longer on the U.S. side. Both the United States and Mexico have experienced a steady increase in life expectancy, with the Mexican border states following that trend. Life expectancy in the U.S. border states remained relatively constant between 1980 and 1990, although it fell from slightly above the national average to slightly below it.

Infant deaths per 1,000 live births (see Figure 3 and Table 3) are significantly less than the national average in all of the Mexican border states except Chihuahua. The infant death rate in the Mexican border states is still over twice that of their U.S. counterparts, but infant mortality has generally decreased in all of the border states. Those rates in the U.S. border states are very close to the national average. Improvement in the United States has been slower than in Mexico, but consistent.[2] Improved medical techniques, medicines, access to medical care, and sanitation all contribute to the progress of these two indicators.

Tables 4 and 5 present data on plumbing facilities. During the period of this study, all of the Mexican border states, along with California and Arizona (and Texas in 1980), had higher proportions of housing with plumbing than their respective national averages. Only Texas (except in 1980) and New Mexico had fewer dwellings with complete plumbing than the national average. In 1990, all Texas border counties, Grant and Luna counties in New Mexico, Yuma County in Arizona, and Imperial County in California, had less than the national average. Eight of the 15 Texas border counties had more than 5 percent of housing without plumbing, with a high of 10 percent in Maverick County. These data may reflect conditions in the *colonias* (neighborhoods) that line the Texas border. In these areas, land is sold cheaply without water or sewage facilities and without provisions for development of infrastructure to provide them.

On the Mexican side, almost all border counties had higher percentages of housing with sewer and water than the national average. Only Tamaulipas had a smaller percentage with sewers than Mexico as a whole. The *municipio* with the lowest rates was Ocampo, Chihuahua, where only 8.9 percent of houses were connected to a sewer system, 42.8 percent had a toilet, and 5.5 percent were connected to water. Cananea, Sonora, had the highest rate, with 90.7 percent connected a sewer system, 94 percent with a toilet, and 86.4 percent connected to water.

Illiteracy rates, shown in Table 6, decreased steadily between 1950 and 1970 in the Mexican border region, leveling off between 1970 and 1990. The Mexican

Figure 2. Mexican and U.S. Life Expectancy at Birth

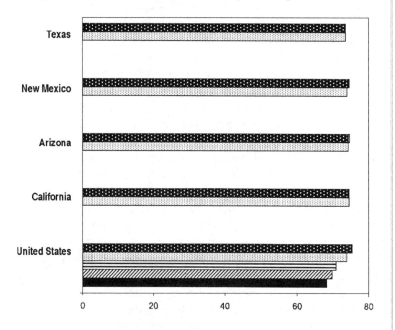

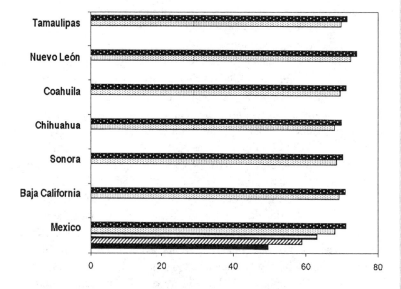

Source: Instituto Nacional de Estadística, Geografía e Informática and U.S. Census Bureau.

Figure 3. Infant Mortality Rates in U.S. and Mexican Border States

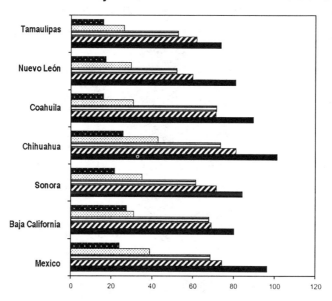

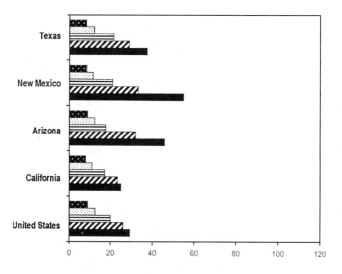

Number of deaths per 1,000 live births

■ 1950 ▨ 1960 ≡ 1970 ⊡ 1980 ▨ 1990

Source: Instituto Nacional de Estadística, Geografía e Informática and U.S. Census Bureau.

Table 3. Infant Deaths per Thousand Live Births in Mexican and U.S. Border States and U.S. Border Counties

	Infant Deaths per Thousand Live Births				
	1950	1960	1970	1980	1990*
Mexico	96.2	74.2	68.5	38.8	23.9
Baja California	80.1	69	67.8	31.0	27.5
Sonora	84.0	71.5	61.3	35.0	21.6
Chihuahua	101.1	81.1	73.5	42.8	25.8
Coahuila	89.6	71.3	71.6	30.8	16.2
Nuevo León	80.9	59.8	52.0	29.7	17.3
Tamaulipas	73.8	61.8	52.7	26.3	16.2
United States	29.3	26.0	20.0	12.6	9.0
California	25.0	23.3	17.2	11.1	8.0
San Diego	27.3	23.4	17.7	11.3	7.4
Imperial	40.8	35.4	15.8	5.3	6.4
Arizona	45.8	31.9	17.7	12.4	8.9
Yuma	51.2	38.3	18.1	13.7	7.9
Pima	29.9	27.7	17.7	8.0	8.0
Santa Cruz	38.2	28.8	15.2	6.2	9.3
Cochise	34.2	27.5	13.7	12.5	8.2
New Mexico	54.8	33.2	21.0	11.5	8.5
Hidalgo	22.6	29.9	18.5	16.1	6.9
Grant	54.4	35.9	21.7	24.0	6.2
Luna	34.1	17.9	25.6	7.3	6.3
Doña Ana	43.2	24.5	19.7	10.6	7.8
Texas	37.4	28.9	21.4	12.2	8.3
El Paso	43.4	25.8	18.0	10.3	7.1
Hudspeth	41.5	40.8	62.5	0.0	0.0
Culberson	45.5	54.1	12.2	10.4	5.5
Jeff Davis	17.9	33.3	90.9	0.0	17.2
Presidio	29.3	0.0	15.4	0.0	11.3
Brewster	37.2	28.4	27.4	14.0	18.0
Terrell	52.6	38.5	31.3	0.0	0.0
Val Verde	85.5	30.2	18.3	8.0	6.8
Kinney	46.0	35.7	31.3	0.0	8.1
Maverick	55.8	30.7	16.3	3.6	6.2
Webb	55.0	21.7	18.3	12.5	7.4
Zapata	7.7	17.5	27.0	19.5	8.5
Starr	28.0	16.1	12.9	16.8	4.4
Hidalgo	78.5	30.4	20.7	9.4	5.6
Cameron	70.8	35.2	18.8	8.9	6.8

* 1990 U.S. County figures are 1989–1991 average.
Source: Mexican Census; INEGI 1994; Lorey 1993: 64; U.S. Census Data.

Table 4. Percent of Mexican Dwellings Lacking Water and Sewage Services

State and Municipality	% Without Sewer	% Without Sewer	% Without Toilet	% Not Connected to Water
	1980	1990	1990	1990
Mexico	42.8	36.4	25.2	51.9
Baja California	34.1	33.2	8.1	41.1
Ensenada		34.4	10.3	42.5
Tijuana		34.9	8.7	44.1
Tecate		37.5	12.7	46.6
Mexicali		30.2	5.9	36.3
Sonora	46.2	34.2	10.3	43.0
San Luis Río Colorado		30.8	8.2	39.3
Puerto Peñasco		30.8	6.9	42.1
Caborca		44.1	15.7	51.8
Altar		53.0	25.7	59.1
Saric		38.0	18.2	52.6
Nogales		20.0	9.1	31.8
Santa Cruz		32.1	12.3	40.8
Cananea		9.3	6.0	13.6
Naco		23.0	7.8	30.1
Agua Prieta		24.6	6.5	33.5
Chihuahua	42.8	33.5	17.5	41.1
Janos		66.6	15.1	78.4
Asención		52.1	18.2	57.0
Juárez		22.4	9.0	31.7
Guadalupe		66.1	16.0	74.0
P.G. Guerrero		65.7	10.5	73.5
Ojinaga		28.0	17.1	37.4
Ocampo		91.1	57.2	94.5
Coahuila	40.9	31.8	13.3	40.6
Acuña		45.0	10.1	54.7
Jiménez		87.3	17.2	91.4
Piedras Negras		26.9	5.5	35.6
Guerrero		75.3	11.1	80.3
Hidalgo		86.8	11.1	88.2
Nuevo León	30.9	19.1	6.2	27.8
Anáhuac		52.6	13.1	60.8
Tamaulipas	43.5	40.2	9.5	48.9
Nuevo Laredo		19.1	5.7	27.3
Guerrero		38.5	17.2	48.0
Mier		42.1	4.0	45.9
Miguel Alemán		26.0	9.9	34.4
Camargo		45.1	12.4	54.5
Reynosa		35.6	7.6	43.3
Río Bravo		53.5	7.4	59.7
Valle Hermosa		54.6	6.0	59.6
Matamoros		39.6	6.5	49.4

Source: 1990 Mexican Census.

Table 5. U.S. Dwellings Lacking Some or All Plumbing Facilities

	% Dwellings Lacking Some or All Plumbing Facilities				
	1950	1960	1970	1980	1990
United States	36.9	26.0	5.5	2.2	1.1
California	14.0	13.4	1.5	1.2	0.6
San Diego	11.2	11.1	1.5	1.1	0.5
Imperial	48.2	41.7	5.5	2.7	1.7
Arizona	37.5	23.8	4.3	2.1	1.9
Yuma	45.6	29.4	5.4	1.2	1.3
Pima	28.8	15.9	2.5	1.2	0.6
Santa Cruz	49.2	45.7	9.0	2.5	0.8
Cochise	42.9	29.0	3.1	1.3	0.9
New Mexico	49.0	31.3	8.3	3.6	3.2
Hidalgo	45.5	30.5	4.1	0.9	0.4
Grant	50.4	42.7	7.9	1.9	2.1
Luna	47.7	41.6	6.5	1.5	1.7
Doña Ana	58.2	38.3	6.2	2.8	0.8
Texas	46.8	31.2	6.0	1.9	1.2
El Paso	44.1	26.4	7.9	2.9	1.7
Hudspeth	73.6	43.2	7.6	5.0	8.6
Culberson	44.0	34.3	7.8	1.6	2.7
Jeff Davis	52.6	30.4	13.0	4.9	7.9
Presidio	64.4	48.6	25.3	9.5	5.7
Brewster	50.7	35.5	7.9	3.2	6.4
Terrell	55.3	49.0	3.6	3.0	2.3
Val Verde	59.0	34.7	7.3	2.4	2.0
Kinney	73.2	47.3	25.6	7.4	6.1
Maverick	71.1	55.8	25.5	10.3	10.0
Webb	67.7	56.4	16.7	5.5	4.0
Zapata	94.1	71.2	37.0	9.1	3.5
Starr	78.1	65.0	46.4	14.7	9.9
Hidalgo	66.3	55.3	25.1	9.6	6.2
Cameron	59.4	49.0	21.3	8.0	3.8

Source: U.S. Department of Commerce, Economics and Statistics Administration, Bureau of the Census 1993: Table 6.

debt crisis of the 1980s contributed to the tendency to allocate fewer resources to education—an investment in human capital and the future—in favor of alleviating immediate pressures. The further erosion of education levels may have been due to the response along the border to falling real wages and the high demand for laborers (especially female) in the *maquiladora* (assembly plant) industry—both encouraging young people to leave school.[3] U.S. illiteracy also leveled off in the 1970s. Due to the assumption that illiteracy was less than 5 percent in the United States, such data were not collected in the 1980 and 1990 censuses.

Given the lack of literacy data for the United States after 1970 and the need for a measure of educational attainment beyond literacy, this study examined the proportion of the Mexican border population that had received more than a primary education, and that of the U.S. border population that received at least a high school education. Tables 8 and 9 show that almost all of the counties and *municipios* studied experienced a steady improvement in educational attainment. In 1990, the portion of the Mexican population that received more than a primary education was still very low. However, all of the border states, with the exception of Chihuahua, were above the national average. All border *municipios* in Baja California and most of those in Sonora were also above the national average. In the rest of the Mexican border states, most *municipios* were below the national average, particularly rural ones. The more urbanized *municipios* of Juárez, Piedras Negras, Nuevo Laredo, Reynoso, and Matamoros had much higher rates of educational achievement. On the U.S. side, the number of high school graduates was below the national average in all border counties except San Diego, Pima, and Cochise. In six Texas counties, less than half of the population had graduated from high school.

The ratio of students to teachers in primary school (see Figure 4) can be used as a gauge of educational effort. The Mexican data from 1950 to 1990 show a slow, but steady, decrease in the primary school student/teacher ratio. By 1990, no Mexican border state had a higher ratio than the national average (about 30 pupils per teacher). The U.S. national average remained 23 students per teacher between 1980 and 1990. Of the U.S. border states, only Arizona consistently maintained a lower ratio than the national average, reaching 20 pupils per teacher in 1980 and 1990. California had the highest student/teacher ratio in 1950 and was still above the national average for each census year except 1970. By 1990, California (the most affluent U.S. border state) was the only border state with a student/teacher ratio higher than the national average. New Mexico and Texas both lowered their student/teacher ratios during the 1980s from above to below the national average.

Despite these indications that poverty increased in the U.S.-Mexican border region on both sides in the 1980s, there was some improvement in life expectancy, infant mortality, and education. Even so, improvement slowed and, in some cases, was reversed during the 1980s. The Mexican border region continues to be somewhat better off than the national average and the U.S. border

Table 6. Mexican Illiteracy

	Percent Illiterate				
	1950	1960	1970	1980	1990
Mexico	44.2	44.5	23.7	17.0	7.6
Baja California	15.2	14.8	7.9	6.6	3.0
Ensenada	14.3	12.7	8.0	6.9	3.8
Tijuana	11.4	12.0	7.6	7.9	2.7
Tecate	12.8	13.7	8.6	8.8	3.3
Mexicali	17.5	16.9	8.0	8.0	3.0
Sonora	22.1	18.9	9.2	9.5	3.6
San Luis Río Colorado	18.5	18.5	7.3	9.6	3.3
Puerto Peñasco		13.3	8.7	9.4	2.4
Caborca	14.7	18.0	9.8	11.7	4.3
Altar	15.2	11.7	7.2	13.4	4.6
Saric	25.9	19.6	10.9	13.9	4.4
Nogales	11.2	12.3	6.0	6.2	1.7
Santa Cruz	13.9	26.9	6.9	8.4	2.4
Cananea	10.4	13.0	3.0	4.1	1.2
Naco	14.5	13.2	3.7	8.4	2.2
Agua Prieta	16.8	14.1	7.2	8.3	2.2
Chihuahua	21.9	20.0	8.6	10.0	3.9
Janos	20.6	18.9	6.1	11.4	2.6
Asención	15.1	15.7	7.3	9.5	6.7
Juárez	13.0	13.4	6.6	7.4	2.2
Guadalupe	21.7	38.8	9.5	14.5	4.6
P.G. Guerrero	19.4	18.5	8.3	11.5	4.2
Ojinaga	24.3	19.9	7.2	10.4	4.1
Ocampo	41.5	43.0	21.6	21.1	12.2
Coahuila	20.8	15.7	8.4	8.8	3.5
Acuña	15.6	13.7	6.3	8.5	3.1
Jiménez	19.7	17.1	9.5	10.0	4.3
Piedras Negras	12.9	13.9	6.8	7.1	2.8
Guerrero	17.3	14.5	11.7	12.1	6.3
Hidalgo	17.2	30.4	14.2	16.9	6.1
Nuevo León	17.6	15.6	7.2	7.4	3.0
Anáhuac	20.0	20.8	9.0	10.5	4.7
Tamaulipas	21.0	18.2	9.7	9.7	4.4
Nuevo Laredo	12.6	11.9	8.0	8.0	3.1
Guerrero	9.8	14.9	8.3	9.3	3.9
Mier	11.7	10.8	4.5	7.0	3.3
Miguel Alemán		13.7	4.6	7.1	3.4
Camargo	21.4	16.8	6.7	9.7	5.6
Reynosa	23.5	17.3	9.4	8.1	3.8
Río Bravo			9.7	10.3	5.3
Valle Hermosa		17.9	9.0	9.2	4.7
Matamoros	20.7	16.9	8.8	8.7	3.7

Source: Mexican Census data.

Table 7. U.S. Illiteracy

	% Illiterate		
	1950	1960	1970
United States	3.3	2.4	1.2
California	2.2	1.8	1.1
Arizona	6.2	3.8	1.8
New Mexico	6.6	4.0	2.2
Texas	5.4	4.1	2.2

Note: Illiteracy data are unavailable at the state level after 1970.
Source: U.S. Census data.

region continues to be somewhat worse off than its national average. The data indicate that poverty and its effects on quality of life remain significant in the border region, but could be improved by different approaches to policy.

Policy and the Prospects for Alleviation of Poverty

Trends in poverty depend in part on economic trends, but are more affected by specific policies. Toward the end of the 1980s and the early 1990s—until the peso devaluation in December 1994—the Mexican economy began to show positive growth rates, a boom in the *maquiladora* industry, and a slowing of inflation. After a long period of expansion during the 1980s, the United States experienced a period of recession from 1991 to 1992, followed by a period of slow, but steady, growth and low inflation. The initiation of the North American Free Trade Agreement (NAFTA) provided a stimulus to both economies. Increased trade and new investment in the border region benefited both sides. The increased competition that accompanies increased trade helped open up the Mexican market to imported goods by lowering the prices of goods once protected by monopoly. The additional trade, however, has put pressure on border infrastructure, increasing the need for highways, bridges, and border crossings to accommodate the high flows of traffic and goods. In the short-run, much of NAFTA's potential benefit to Mexico was undercut by the 1994 peso devaluation. The devaluation and subsequent period of inflation caused real wages in Mexico to plummet, adding to economic pressures on poor working-class families. In addition, the provisions of the NAFTA agreement and the neoliberal economic policies put in place under President Carlos Salinas de Gortari (1988–1994), and especially the rapid decrease in the real minimum wage and decreased support for public education, tended to increase income inequalities, with a disproportionate amount of the gains from economic growth going to upper income groups.

A focused antipoverty policy is needed for the border region, along with economic expansion and freer trade. Growth helps a society when it can be

Table 8. Mexican Educational Attainment

	% of Population 15 Years and Older with More than Primary School Education				
	1950	1960	1970	1980	1990
Mexico	5.3	7.70	12.69	18.80	25.60
Border Region	1.72	10.43	15.10	17.34	28.36
Baja California					
Ensenada	10.06		19.64	18.75	32.70
Tijuana	12.99		17.85	20.35	29.63
Tecate	11.97		15.89	18.69	27.93
Mexicali	7.71		16.88	20.64	34.08
Sonora					
San Luis Río Colorado	4.52	6.86	13.29	12.44	25.64
Puerto Peñasco		8.05	11.94	11.62	24.34
Caborca	5.87	10.10	13.51	17.18	25.69
Altar	4.71	9.16	12.26	7.97	17.93
Saric	2.43	1.93	5.90	10.69	11.47
Nogales	11.68	16.43	19.79	13.21	28.88
Santa Cruz	3.78	3.26	3.83	1.09	8.00
Cananea	10.97	16.83	24.60	9.97	34.52
Naco	8.85	3.66	14.34	6.90	26.12
Agua Prieta	6.64	7.10	15.01	10.12	23.65
Chihuahua					
Janos	2.92	1.60	4.85	13.00	4.70
Asención	3.14	2.34	7.53	20.06	10.86
Juárez	10.76	11.74	14.70	16.89	26.80
Guadalupe	1.84	1.54	6.03	6.43	8.14
P.G. Guerrero	2.45	2.57	3.88	14.77	8.97
Ojinaga	3.14	3.89	8.68	17.49	17.71
Ocampo	1.70	0.30	1.34	14.48	5.27
Coahuila					
Acuña	3.59	8.51	10.24	14.01	21.42
Jiménez	1.33	0.93	1.85	14.46	5.58
Piedras Negras	9.10	15.58	16.49	7.52	28.09
Guerrero	1.84	0.58	3.12	13.45	7.45
Hidalgo	1.42	1.67	1.55	16.28	6.19
Nuevo León					
Anáhuac	3.68	8.14	11.14	12.62	16.55
Tamaulipas					
Nuevo Laredo	10.26	15.49	15.71	16.49	29.23
Guerrero	2.18	7.42	13.10	2.43	20.11
Mier	3.21	11.28	18.99	6.55	21.86
Miguel Alemán		7.09	12.65	9.89	22.48
Camargo	2.73	6.14	8.85	7.99	16.87
Reynosa	4.58	8.52	12.40	16.93	28.09
Río Bravo			7.76	16.81	20.25
Valle Hermosa		6.40	9.08	10.65	22.32
Matamoros	5.61	10.25	14.16	16.69	27.74

Source: Calculated from Mexican Census data.

Table 9. U.S. Educational Attainment

	% of Population 25 Years or Older with High School Diploma				
	1952	1962	1972	1983	1990
United States	34.3	41.1	52.3	66.5	75.2
California	47.6	51.5	62.6	73.5	76.2
San Diego	50.6	54.6	65.3	78.0	81.9
Imperial	29.9	33.8	43.1	50.9	53.2
Arizona	38.8	45.7	58.1	72.4	78.7
Yuma	32.7	39.7	50.3	61.6	64.9
Pima	45.6	51.7	63.1	74.6	80.5
Santa Cruz	32.1	39.7	43.5	54.0	57.2
Cochise	34.7	44.5	55.9	68.8	78.7
New Mexico	35.4	45.5	55.2	68.9	75.1
Hidalgo	27.8	35.8	39.0	59.9	71.6
Grant	33.6	37.5	48.5	63.2	70.5
Luna	30.2	38.6	40.1	57.0	58.8
Doña Ana	30.1	41.7	54.2	65.1	70.4
Texas	30.6	39.5	47.4	62.6	72.1
El Paso	37.2	45.6	51.1	59.5	63.7
Hudspeth	19.8	38.8	38.4	46.3	48.1
Culberson	30.8	35.1	43.2	44.3	53.3
Jeff Davis	27.8	33.0	43.4	55.0	69.5
Presidio	22.6	37.6	28.6	41.1	43.9
Brewster	36.0	45.3	49.7	67.5	73.2
Terrell	26.2	31.2	39.7	59.9	66.3
Val Verde	20.6	38.2	42.9	51.1	56.1
Kinney	15.2	30.2	23.2	40.1	56.2
Maverick	12.8	20.9	24.2	32.2	35.7
Webb	17.3	25.3	32.1	41.5	47.8
Zapata	8.3	13.2	21.6	41.3	50.1
Starr	11.4	18.5	21.9	26.6	31.6
Hidalgo	21.4	25.8	30.3	41.1	46.6
Cameron	24.8	31.2	34.9	43.8	50.0

Source: City and County Data Books.

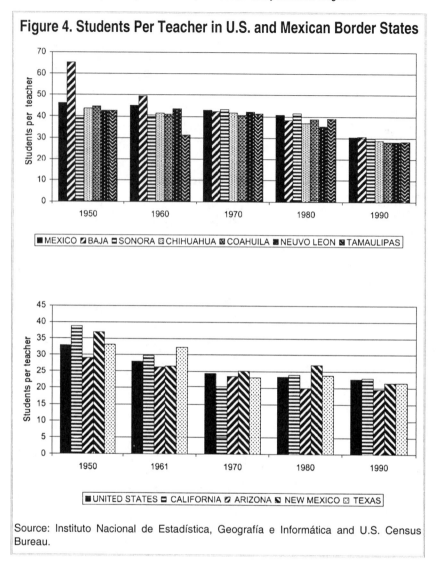

Figure 4. Students Per Teacher in U.S. and Mexican Border States

■MEXICO ◪BAJA ☐SONORA ⊞CHIHUAHUA ▨COAHUILA ▩NEUVO LEON ▨TAMAULIPAS

■UNITED STATES ☐ CALIFORNIA ◪ ARIZONA ◩ NEW MEXICO ⊡ TEXAS

Source: Instituto Nacional de Estadística, Geografía e Informática and U.S. Census Bureau.

sustained and when it is not structured to favor solely upper income groups, but even then its effects are limited. Reduction of structural poverty requires well-targeted and well-administered policies.

The allocation of more resources to education could make a big difference in both the United States and Mexico as an investment in human capital. The payoff period is long, but has a high return. Both countries have decreased funding for education for different reasons. Mexico's federal expenditures on education fell from 16.4 percent of total federal spending in 1972 to 13.9 percent in 1990. U.S. education expenditures fell from 3.2 percent of federal spending in 1972 to 1.7 percent in 1990 (World Bank 1992). Not only does the education budget need to be augmented, but allocation within that budget needs to shift toward the education of low-income families, with more schools being constructed and staffed in poor and rural neighborhoods. Other policies needed in both countries include providing adequate pay to ensure high quality teachers, financing support materials and programs (like the U.S. Head Start program) to help compensate for children's roots in poverty, implementing programs to slow the school dropout rate, and job training to increase opportunities for the working poor. The funding of such activities will be difficult for Mexico since it is burdened by debt services. In the United States, funding would require a major shift in policy priorities.

Two other key policy changes could make major contributions to alleviating poverty in the Mexican border region. The first is a change in Mexican wage policy. Mexico's tradition of linking wages to the legal minimum wage has given the government the power to strongly influence wage changes, at least for unskilled and semi-skilled workers. During the 1980s, this policy was one cause of drastic decreases in the real wage. The rationale for this policy has been to combat inflation and to attract foreign investment, especially in the *maquiladora* industry. However, econometric studies suggest that the decrease in real wages is not effective in combating inflation and may actually increase it (Kosak 1991; Anderson 1995)—a phenomenon that can be explained by two factors. One is that Mexican wage income is a much smaller proportion of national income than in the United States (about 30 percent in Mexico compared to about 75 percent in the United States). It therefore has a proportionately smaller inflationary effect. The decline in wage income lowers demand, which in turn lowers production—one explanation for the slump in Mexico's economic performance throughout much of the 1980s. According to Morrison's (1991) econometric study, lower wages were effective in increasing *maquiladora* employment. While they caused a shift from domestic employment to the *maquiladoras*, they did not increase overall employment in the Mexican border region. The Morrison study suggests that an increased wage would not have an adverse effect on the level of employment. Allowing real minimum wages to rise, thereby increasing the real earnings of semi-skilled and unskilled labor, would stimulate both demand and the economy. This would be especially effective in boosting the incomes of poor families, thus helping to equalize the distribution of income.

The second key policy would be for Mexico to restructure its mechanisms for obtaining credit so that it could become available to small producers. A special and sizable fund for making loans (even in small amounts) to small enterprises, especially those in poor neighborhoods, could produce a high return in increased productivity and decreased poverty. Working capital is in short supply in the informal sector, often preventing increased levels of production. In his study of the Peruvian informal sector, DeSoto (1986) suggested that issuing formal land and housing titles that could be used as collateral for borrowing could alleviate the problem of capital shortage. In 1989, Mexico began the *Solidaridad* (Solidarity) program, one component of which was awarding property titles.

There is, however, no evidence that this effectively channeled credit to the poor. Lack of credit to small enterprises remains a critical issue.

In the United States, welfare payments and unemployment compensation puts poverty on a somewhat higher plane. Even so, the political climate that has resulted in significant cuts in welfare spending (under the guise of "welfare reform") and the rapid increase in housing costs, especially in California, has caused a rise in the number of poor and homeless families. To attack the problems related to poverty, welfare reform must include job/skill training, drug counseling, and other rehabilitation programs. A concerted effort toward developing more truly low-cost housing and the provision of more facilities for those homeless who are mentally ill are other much-needed policies.

The United States needs to revise its federal and state policies that create work disincentives for the poor. One of the most notable of these disincentives is access to medical care. Welfare recipients are entitled to medical benefits, but when they obtain low paying jobs, those benefits are lost after a set period of time. With low skill levels, these people, and especially those with children, are unlikely to find jobs that provide adequate medical benefits. They need access to medical care or some type of national medical insurance. In addition, subsidized childcare, literacy, and job-training programs would further enable people to enter the job market.

In both the United States and Mexico, high employment taxes raise the cost of labor and tend to encourage the substitution of capital for labor. While social security is important (it has successfully eased poverty among the elderly in the United States), its method of financing discourages employment. Raising those funds through either a general income tax or a value-added tax would lower the cost of labor and tend to increase the labor/output ratio.

In Mexico, poverty alleviation policies are especially important since the economy has historically been hampered by inequities. Income distribution figures show that the poorest 40 percent of the population earn 9.9 percent of the total national income, while the richest 10 percent of the population receive 40.6 percent. In the United States, the poorest 40 percent earn 16.7 percent of the national income, and the richest 10 percent receive 25 percent (World Bank 1990). This huge inequity in Mexico signifies that a large portion of the population is disenfranchised from the economic system. Their potential labor resources are thus wasted and their low income levels retard the growth of demand that is needed to stimulate production and overall economic growth. For a free market system to function efficiently, a reasonable amount of income equality is required. Unfortunately, unequal distribution is political as well as economic, and is maintained by the sociopolitical sectors that gain from it.

Conclusions

Improving living standards for the poor on both sides of the border will require significant policy changes in both the United States and Mexico. The policy trends of the 1980s were negative in this respect. In the United States, the regressivity of taxes (including payroll taxes) increased, while transfer payments to the poor decreased. The free market rhetoric of the 1980s too often translated into a license for big business to engage in anticompetitive behavior. Mexico, dealing with its debt crisis, eliminated subsidies on many basic goods bought by the poor, decreased special loan funds for the poor, and decreased real wages for unskilled and semi-skilled workers. Both countries decreased spending on education and infrastructure investment.

Poverty in the Mexican border region appears to be less than the national average, suggesting a positive influence from the U.S. economy. Most border counties on the U.S. side, however, are poorer than the national average. This study indicates that during the 1980s, poverty increased in most U.S. border counties and Mexican border *municipios*, and especially in those that are predominately rural.

Lessening poverty in the border region is possible. Opening up the border and encouraging freer trade could certainly contribute to this goal. At the same time, only significant changes in policy and concerted efforts by both governments can effectively lower the number of working poor. Since some of the needed policy changes work against vested national interests, making such changes will be difficult. Even more difficult will be the allocation of resources to sustain such policies. Poverty alleviation programs compete for resources with what are often louder, more powerful constituencies than the poor. Ultimately, the cure for poverty is money, and that is hard to come by.

Endnotes

1. These are not exactly equivalent, but are the best available measures given the available data.

2. Except in Imperial, Santa Cruz, Luna, Jeff Davis, Presidio, Brewster, Kinney, and Maverick counties.

3. A random sampling of 459 Tijuana households in 1991 showed that 13.1 percent of girls between the ages of 13 and 18 were employed in the *maquiladora,* manufacturing, or commercial industries (Anderson and Dimon 1991).

References

Anderson, Joan B. 1995. "Direct Foreign Investment, Economic Cycles, and Mexican Wage Policy." Paper presented at the International Symposium of Economic and Financial Cycles and NAFTA, June, Mexico City, Mexico.

Anderson, Joan B., Norris Clement, and Kenneth Shellhammer. 1980. *Economic Importance of the U.S. Southwest Border Region.* San Diego: California Border Area Resource Center, San Diego State University.

Anderson, Joan B., and Martín de la Rosa. 1991. "Economic Survival Strategies of Poor Families in the U.S.-Mexico Border Region." *Journal of Borderlands Studies* 6 (1): 51–68.

Anderson, Joan B., and Denise Dimon. 1991. "Determinants of Mexican Women's Work Decisions." Paper presented at the 16th International Congress of the Latin American Studies Association, 4–6 April, Washington, D.C., USA.

Banco de México. *Indicadores Económicos.* México, D.F.: Banco de México.

Betts, Dianne C., and Daniel J. Slottje. 1994. *Crisis on the Rio Grande: Poverty, Unemployment, and Economic Development on the Texas-Mexico Border*. Boulder: Westview Press.

Brook, Kathleen. 1986. "Patterns of Labor Force Participation in the U.S.-Mexico Border Region, 1970–1980." *Journal of Borderlands Studies* 1 (1): 109–32.

Centro de Estudios del Trabajo, A.C. 1986. *Salario mínimo y canasta básica*. México, D.F.: Centro de Estudios del Trabajo.

DeSoto, Hernando. 1986. *El otro sendero*. Lima: Instituto Libertad y Democracia.

González de la Rocha, Mercedes. 1986. *Los recursos de la pobreza: familias de bajos ingresos de Guadalajara*. Guadalajara: El Colegio de Jalisco, A.C.

Instituto Nacional de Estadística, Geografía e Informática (INEGI). 1994. *Estadísticas históricas de México*. Aguascalientes: INEGI.

Kosak, Eric. 1991. *A Simultaneous Regression Model for Growth and Inflation in Mexico*. San Diego: University of San Diego.

Lorey, David E. 1993. *United States-Mexico Border Statistics since 1900: 1990 Update*. Los Angeles: UCLA Latin American Center Publications.

Morrison, Jane. 1991. *U.S.-Mexican Wage Differentials and Employment in Maquiladoras*. Irvine: University of California at Irvine.

Pick, James B., Edgar W. Butler, and Glenda L. Jones. 1990. *Socio-Economic Inequality in the U.S.-Mexico Borderlands*. Riverside: University of California at Riverside.

Secretaría de Programación y Presupuesto, Coordinación General de los Servicios Nacionales de Estadística, Geografía e Informática. 1981. *X censo general de población y vivienda, 1980*. México, D.F.: Secretaría de Programación y Presupuesto, Coordinación General de los Servicios Nacionales de Estadística, Geografía e Informática.

Stoddard, Ellwyn R., and John Hedderson. 1989. "Patterns of Poverty along the U.S.-Mexico Border." *Borderlands Research Monograph Series*, No. 3. Las Cruces: Joint Border Research Institute, New Mexico State University.

U.S. Department of Commerce, Economics and Statistics Administration, Bureau of the Census. 1993. *1990 Census of Population and Housing: Summary of Social, Economic, and Housing Characteristics*. Washington, D.C.: U.S. Department of Commerce, Economics and Statistics Administration, Bureau of the Census.

World Bank. 1990. *World Development Report*. New York: Oxford University Press.

World Bank. 1992. *World Development Report*. New York: Oxford University Press.

An Exploratory Study of Urban Marginality in Baja California

Arturo Ranfla G., Djamel Toudert, Guillermo
Álvarez de la T., Guadalupe Ortega V.[*]

Abstract

This essay explores the issue of social inequality in the face of economic restructuring an globalization, focusing specifically on the cities of Baja California and comparing them to other Mexican border states and Mexico as a whole. The study uses urban basic geostatistic areas (AGEBs) to identify patterns of inequality and considers their location near the border and migratory patterns as additional determinants contributing to varying levels of marginalization. The study was conducted in an effort to understand the role that the border plays in the development of border cities.

Introduction

In the last two decades, globalization and the process of regional and national restructuring in most national economies have been identified as deteriorating factors in human living conditions (Astorga and Moguel 1996; World Bank 1987). Within this framework, interest has recently intensified on studies that research the issue of social inequality in terms of well-being.

It is pertinent, therefore, to move forward in the study of inequalities, a topic that is approached here from the perspective of marginalization (or marginality) in its most extensive meaning: lack of participation or exclusion (Germani 1973). The focus is on inequalities in the allocation of the benefits of public investment in infrastructure (piped water, sewage collector system, electricity) and in services (education). It also deals with the inequalities associated with the availability of private resources as indicated by income and other characteristics of housing.

---

[*] The authors are researchers at the Institute for Social Research of the Autonomous University of Baja California in Mexicali, Baja California, Mexico.

This study explores the intra- and interurban inequality that exists with regard to marginalization in the main cities of Baja California, a state along Mexico's northern border that is characterized as having one of the highest levels of well-being in the country. It is also a state with low marginalization, which is characteristic of states on Mexico's northern border. Although the border states are relatively well-off in terms of the nation as a whole and urban areas are better off than rural areas (Coplamar 1983; Estrella V. 1984), it does noe mean that inequalities are nonexistent—the issue of urban marginality is important to residents and policymakers in the region. The inequalities in the main cities of Baja California are precisely the focus of this paper.

This study of the socioeconomic and territorial inequalities at the urban level includes the cities of Mexicali, Tecate, and Tijuana, located on the border, and of the port of Ensenada, about 86 miles (138 kilometers) south of the border. Some 398 urban basic geostatistic areas (AGEBs—acronym in Spanish for *áreas geoestadísticas básicas*, equivalent to a census tract) were used, which facilitated the maintenance of a regional comparison framework and the identification of inequalities in terms of marginalization and distribution patterns. The objectives of this study are to identify the marginalized areas in the interior of these urban centers on a smaller scale than those traditionally used in studies of national coverage—federal entities and municipalities (Conapo-Conagua 1993; Coplamar 1983; INEGI 1993b). They are also to emphasize the role that the border location plays in the growth of each of these urban centers. From the results obtained, hypotheses were established about the importance of other variables for the regional and local marginalization that have not been considered in national studies. In the cities analyzed, due to the population mobility and the urban expansion dynamics, these variables could help understand the determinant role played by the border in the development of these cities.

Marginalization along Mexico's Northern Border in the National Context

The study carried out by the Consejo Nacional de Población (Conapo) (National Population Council) and the Comisión Nacional del Agua (Conagua) (National Water Commission), with data from the 1990 Census for the states and municipalities of Mexico (Conapo-Conagua 1993), classified federal entities according to their marginalization levels into five categories (see Table 1). Two features stand out from this information. First, all entities in the northern border of Mexico fall within the categories of low or very low marginalization; four were classified as low marginalization (Tamaulipas, Sonora, Chihuahua, and Coahuila). Second, two of the three federal entities within the category of very low marginalization are located in the border (Baja California and Nuevo León), surpassed only by Mexico's Federal District, an entity that because it is the capital and seat of federal power has traditionally been favored not only with infrastructure, but also with a series of subsidies and other advantage for its population.

Table 1. Classification of Mexican Federal Entities According to Marginalization Level, 1990

Marginalization Level	Number of Federal Entities	Federal Entities
Very High	6	1. Chiapas, 2. Oaxaca, 3. Guerrero, 4. Hidalgo, 5. Veracruz, 6. Puebla
High	9	7. San Luis Potosí, 8. Zacatecas, 9. Tabasco, 10. Campeche, 11. Yucatán, 12. Michoacán, 13. Guanajuato, 14. Querétaro, 15. Durango
Medium	4	16. Tlaxcala, 17. Nayarit, 18. Sinaloa, 19. Quintana Roo
Low	10	20. Morelos, 21. State of Mexico, 22. Tamaulipas, 23. Colima, 24. Jalisco, 25. Sonora, 26. Chihuahua, 27. Aguascalientes, 28. Baja California Sur, 29. Coahuila
Very Low	3	30. Baja California, 31. Nuevo León, 32. Federal District

Source: Conapo-Conagua 1993: 41, Table 2.

The fact that the six states that constitute Mexico's northern border present better living conditions than most of the other states in the country places this region in an advantageous position in comparative terms. The positions of Baja California and Nuevo León stand out in particular. The latter state is characterized by its strong industrial development, while the former has received important public investments, particularly in hydraulic works and urban infrastructure. Baja California was also favored with a tax and customs system that has allowed its population to import goods from the United States duty free.

The aforementioned Conapo-Conagua study (1993), in addition to analyzing the federal entities, also conducted an exercise to determine the degree of marginalization of the then 2,403 municipalities of Mexico. This allowed the identification of municipal differences within each state. Table 2 shows the position of the 273 municipalities that comprise the six states in the northern border of Mexico. It also shows the 39 municipalities within these states that are adjacent to the international border.

The data in Table 2 show that the situation of the municipalities adjacent to the United States is better, in general terms, than the rest of the municipalities in the northern border states, since no border municipality is placed in the categories of high or very high marginalization. Consequently, except for the three border municipalities in Coahuila, the rest were classified in the low or very low marginalization level. This, however, is not the case with Mexico's northern border states' municipalities as a whole; these show 27 cases of high

Table 2. Distribution of Municipalities in States along the Northern Border According to Degree of Marginalization, 1990

State	# of Municipal-ities	Number of Municipalities according to Marginalization Level				
		Very Low	Low	Medium	High	Very High
Total border state municipalities	273	57	149	36	27	4
% Border state municipalities	100.0	20.9	54.5	13.2	9.9	1.5
Baja California	4	4				
Sonora	70	15	50	5		
Chihuahua	67	9	35	8	11	4
Coahuila	38	9	21	8		
Nuevo León	51	12	31	3	5	
Tamaulipas	43	8	12	12	11	
Total border municipalities	39	15	21	3		
% Border municipalities	100.0	38.5	53.8	7.7		
Baja California	3	3				
Sonora	11	5	6			
Chihuahua	7	1	6			
Coahuila	7	1	3	3		
Nuevo León	1		1			
Tamaulipas	10	5	5			

Source: Conapo-Conagua 1993: 45–101, Table 3.

marginalization (including four in Nuevo León) and four cases of very high marginalization in Chihuahua. In other words, three out of four municipalities in Mexico's northern border states were classified as having low or very low levels of marginalization (75.4%), while nine out of 10 municipalities adjacent to the international border were placed within these same categories (92.3%).

Overall, Tables 1 and 2 indicate that, on the one hand, within the context of the Mexican federal entities, Mexico's northern border states present better living conditions than the national average and, on the other hand, that within these border states, the municipalities adjacent to the United States register better living conditions than the rest of the municipalities of the border states. In other words, the further north the states or municipalities are located, the better living condition levels are expected.

Some Characteristics of Baja California

The position of Baja California in the national context, as well as in Mexico's northern border states as a whole, is quite clear. Even though at the federal entity level it is surpassed by the state of Nuevo León, when municipalities are the units of analysis, it is the only northern border state whose municipalities were all classified as having very low marginalization. However, it is evident that when the scale of observation units are changed, different results are obtained. Even Nuevo León reported municipalities with high marginalization, despite its occupance of a better position than Baja California at the federal state level, surpassed only by the Federal District.

Baja California's situation is the result of its history. As part of Mexico's process of territorial integration of the mid-twentieth century, Baja California benefitted from investments in infrastructure and amenities carried out in Mexico that also responded to migratory and economic dynamics. Since the first decade of the twentieth century, these dynamics were already oriented toward the neighboring country to the north. This put Baja California in an important position in the regional context of the country because of the number of public works projects and amount of invested funds. Paul Lamartine Yates emphasizes this process because it places the state within the group of entities with greater investments accumulated in hydraulic works, generation of electricity, urban infrastructure, and for trade during the 1946–1955 period (1965: 65–88).

Baja California has several special economic characteristics. First, in terms of its relative importance in the Mexican economy, its participation oscillates between two or three percentage points[1] of the total. Second, it has attracted a significant amount of foreign investment during recent years (Mercado and Fernández 1996: 666). In 1997, Baja California had 33.1 percent of the total *maquiladora* (assembly plant) industry in Mexico, 22.3 percent of employed personnel, and 22.3 percent of value added generated by these industries (INEGI 1998). This highlights how Baja California's economy is marginal in terms of its representation with respect to the Mexican economy as a whole, but is leading because of its behavior and dynamics with the interdependent and global market model, in which the exporting *maquiladora* industry has great importance.

Baja California's "privileged" position is associated with the rapid process of urbanization supported by important public investments in amenities and infrastructure in irrigation, potable water, communications, electric power, as well as the location of three of its four main cities (Mexicali, Tecate, and Tijuana), adjacent to the United States. These cities, particularly Mexicali and Tijuana, have been receiving a significant number of migrants. In 1995, a total of 83.5 percent of the state population was urban, residing in districts of 15,000 or more inhabitants, while the percentage at the national level was 59.9. Another indicator of the level of urbanization in this state is that, in 1995, a total of 78.8 percent of the population lived in districts of 100,000 or more inhabitants, whereas the national average was 59.9 percent (INEGI 1997).

According to the most recent studies conducted for Mexico as a whole, Baja California has levels of well-being that are above the national average—surpassed only by the Federal District and Nuevo León (Conapo-Conagua 1993; INEGI 1993b). The state's population registers percentages that are above the national average with regard to some of the indicators measured by the census, particularly education and housing. Above average income and employment indicators for Baja California also demonstrate the well-being of the region's population. However, two characteristics stand out in these studies. First, the level of smallest aggregation is the municipality that is treated as a homogeneous unit and no differences can be identified internally, such as urban-rural or interurban contrasts. Second, because the studies are for the country as a whole, the averages with which such analytical units are compared are affected by the extreme values of municipalities with strong deficiencies in the indicators used. Thus, the same indicators for Baja California are diluted and appear, in the best case, minimal.[2]

In order to eliminate the extreme cases that are present in Mexico and to be able to compare the marginality within Baja California cities, the smallest units of analysis reported in the census for urban areas, the basic geostatistic areas (AGEBs), were used. This approach makes the interregional and intraurban inequalities noticeable and also identifies the most depressed areas in the urban footprint. It is well known that some areas that are better off than others exist within each city, not only in terms of infrastructure, but also with regard to its population's characteristics. The urban space is not homogeneous and, to the degree that the units of analysis are smaller, the differences can be observed with greater clarity.

Work Method

The final results of the 1990 census (INEGI 1993a) were used to evaluate the characteristics and the conditions of development at an intraurban scale for the cities of Ensenada, Mexicali, Tecate, and Tijuana. These were published at the level of urban basic geostatistic areas (AGEBs), which is the smallest spatial unit for which information is available. With the census data, nine indicators were built for each of the urban basic geostatistic areas in order to construct an index of marginalization. It should be mentioned that the indicators were worked in percentages in order to standardize the information and for its values to be in direct relation to marginalization. Thus, a high value in the indicator represents high marginalization. The indicators used are as follows:[3]

1. Percentage of private homes without piped water inside the home
2. Percentage of homes not connected to a sewage collector system

3. Percentage of homes without cement floors
4. Percentage of homes without electricity
5. Percentage of homes that are not built with bricks nor blocks (durable material)
6. Percentage of private homes with one room (one room only)
7. Percentage of employed population with maximum income of two times the minimum salary
8. Percentage of illiterate population 15 years of age or older
9. Percentage of population 15 years of age or older without basic middle schooling

Once the values of the nine indicators were estimated for each of the 398 basic geostatistic areas of the four cities,[4] a synthetic indicator for marginality was built and calculated for each of the AGEBs through the technique of principal components. The result of this process generated a standardized index (centered on averages) for the first five factorial axes resulting from the nine variables used. These five axes represent or explain 90.70 percent of the total variance. However, in order to present the results and facilitate their reading without substantially modifying them, only the first two factorial axes were used. These explain the 65.18 percent of the total variance. The construction of three complementary ordinal variables followed, which allowed the establishment of relationships between the observed characteristics.

For the construction of these ordinal variables, three of the nine indicators were selected. These had to be representative of the general housing conditions, income, and education. The following indicators were, therefore, selected:

1. Percentage of private homes with one room
2. Percentage of employed population with income of up to 2.0 times the minimum salary
3. Percentage of illiterate population 15 years of age or older

Since the original values of each of these indicators are continuous data, these were transformed into ordinal variables with the three categories of high, medium, and low, depending on the intensity with which the indicator is presented in each AGEB.

The statistical typology obtained from the set of urban basic geostatistic areas of Baja California allowed its classification in each of the cities, which facilitated the analysis in several ways:

• in relation to the variables and their qualitative expression vis-a-vis the marginality represented by the resulting index for each AGEB
• through the territorial representation of the different profiles of marginalization in the maps of the results for each of the cities

Figure 1. Position of Variables Used on the Factorial Axes

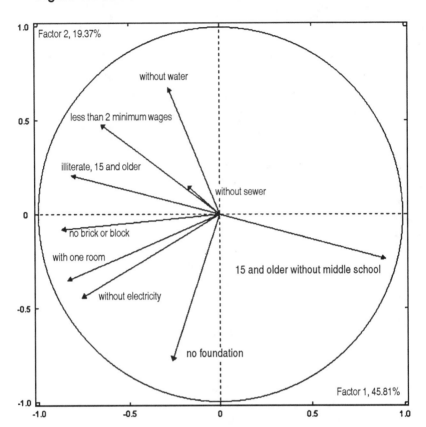

Characterization of Urban Marginalization in Baja California

For the purpose of presenting the research results, the inequalities in terms of marginalization in the four cities covered were approached at the AGEB level in two stages. First, in a general way, it consists in an interurban comparison of the four Baja California cities with respect to the marginalization profile of each. Second, it is an intraurban comparison to identify the distribution of the nucleus of marginalization within each of them.

Toward a Typology of Urban Marginalization

As mentioned earlier, the analytical approach was developed using the first two factorial axes. The multidimensional distribution of the universe of the variables and their adjustment with respect to these axes show a first typology of the marginalization variables used for the four sites. As a result, Figure 1 shows a first group of variables that is more or less defined by Axis 1 (horizontal axis) due to the proximity of the variables to the axis. The variables that make up this

Figure 2. Position of AGEBs of the Cities Studied on the Two Factorial Axes

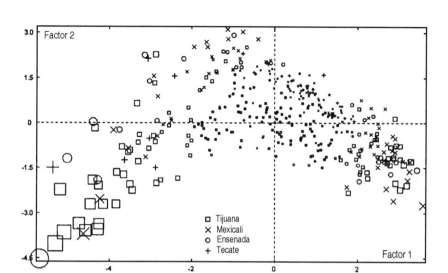

first group are: homes without electricity; homes that are not made of durable material; homes with one room only; income; illiterate population; and population without basic middle schooling. The second group of variables is defined by Axis 2 (vertical axis), comprised of homes without piped water; homes without sewage collector system; and homes without cement floors. This grouping emphasizes Axis 1 as an expression of the socioeconomic and housing variables, particularly those referring to the construction characteristics. By contrast, Axis 2 is definitely configured by variables that predominantly express deficiencies in the housing infrastructure.

Figure 2 shows the dispersion diagram of the AGEBs around the factorial axes 1 and 2, in which the origin (intersection of both axes) corresponds to the central profile of the total spatial units used; that is, it represents the medium conditions of the AGEBs as a whole. From this distribution, some aspects are identified and should be emphasized: the number of AGEBs distributed over Axis 1 is greater than over Axis 2. This means that the marginalization profile for most of these analytical units responds more to the socioeconomic and housing construction (size and materials) characteristic variables than to those of housing related to infrastructure.

The distance of each point with respect to origin reflects the distance of that AGEB with respect to the average profile or conditions. Figure 2 shows that the number of units in the atypical profiles is arranged in a decreasing pattern with the sequence Tijuana, Tecate, Ensenada, and Mexicali. Tijuana presents the greater number of atypical AGEBs, while Mexicali is the opposite. This is be-

Figure 3. Position of Ordinal Variables on Two Axes at the Level of All Urban AGEBs

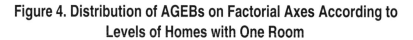

cause Tijuana is the largest city, with a continuous inflow of population and with the strongest and most dynamic economy of the state.[5]

The previous observations help identify the profiles and their factorial distribution; however, these are not enough to explain the nature and magnitude of each. As a result, Figure 3 includes the ordinal variables of the two axes in order to establish the relationships between the profiles and the numeric and ordinal variables. Therefore, Figure 3 shows the distribution of the three ordinal variables used: homes with one room (V6), individual income (V7), and illiterate

Figure 4. Distribution of AGEBs on Factorial Axes According to Levels of Homes with One Room

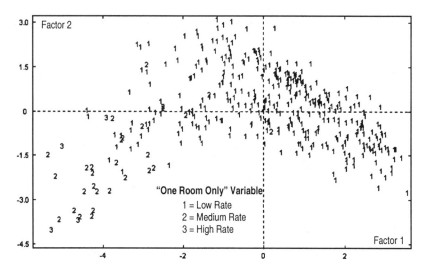

Figure 5. Distribution of AGEBs on Factorial Axes According to Levels of Income Less or Equal to Two Times the Minimum Salary

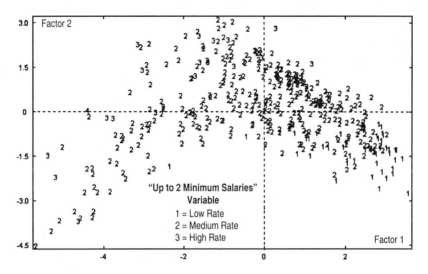

Figure 6. Distribution of AGEBs According to Levels of Education

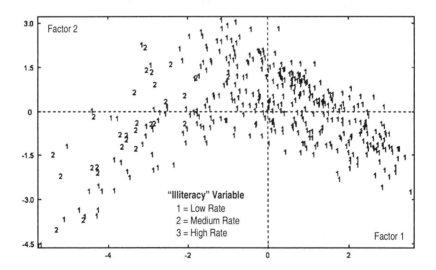

population (V8). The variables are defined as follows: (1) low indicator value, (2) medium value, and (3) high indicator value.

According to the results, the typical marginalization profile in Baja California's cities discussed in this document is configured by a presence at the median population level with income that is less than two times the minimum salary. The most atypical profile of marginalization is found on the left side of Figure 3,

Figure 7. Relationship between AGEB Classes with Marginalization Level and Ordinal Variables of Housing, Education, and Income

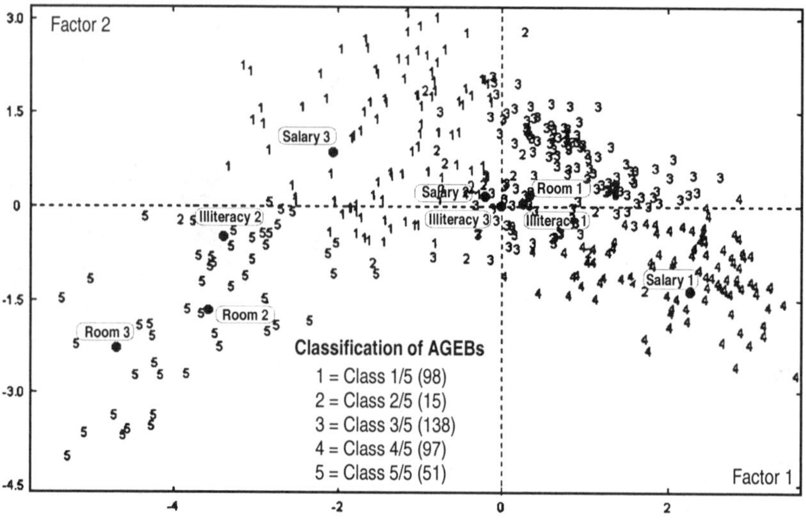

whose characteristic mainly related to a medium to high presence of homes with one room and of illiteracy at a medium level. This difference causes the distribution of spatial units in Figure 3 to present, in a general way, a marginalization gradient that moves from right to left; the representative units of greater urban marginality in Baja California can be found in the extreme left. This observation is corroborated in detail in Figures 4, 5, and 6.

The marginalization indices were ordered into five groups or profiles. For practical reasons, the description is placed only over three profiles. With this structure, the AGEB group is characterized by a hierarchy in terms of the numeric variables and the ordinal ones used in this analysis, which are described in Figure 7. Therefore, Group 3 represents the profile-type of the composition of the nine variables used. Class 4 can be found in the extremes; it does not have a profile or marginal spaces. It corresponds to the AGEBs whose population registers the lowest percentages in each of the variables used (better living conditions due to the low presence of the considered variables). Class 5 can be found at the other extreme; its characteristic is a high number of homes with one room and a medium level of illiteracy and, therefore, it has the highest marginalization indices.

The analysis indicates that there are a series of aspects of the variables used that are worth reflecting upon regarding urban marginalization in Baja California. The first is that income of less than two minimum salaries does not seem to be a determinant factor with respect to marginalization. The second, illiteracy, also does not have a very defined behavior in relation to marginalization. Instead, the degree of urban marginalization in the estimated standard for Baja Cal-

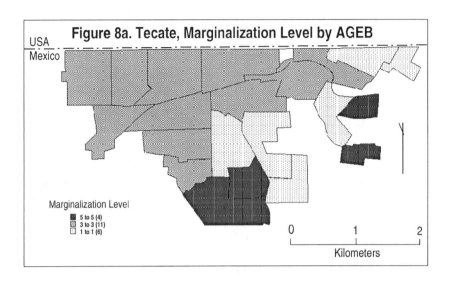

Figure 8a. Tecate, Marginalization Level by AGEB

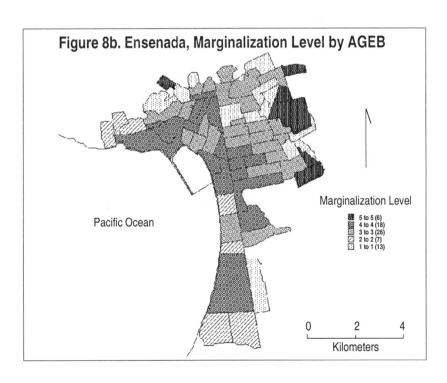

Figure 8b. Ensenada, Marginalization Level by AGEB

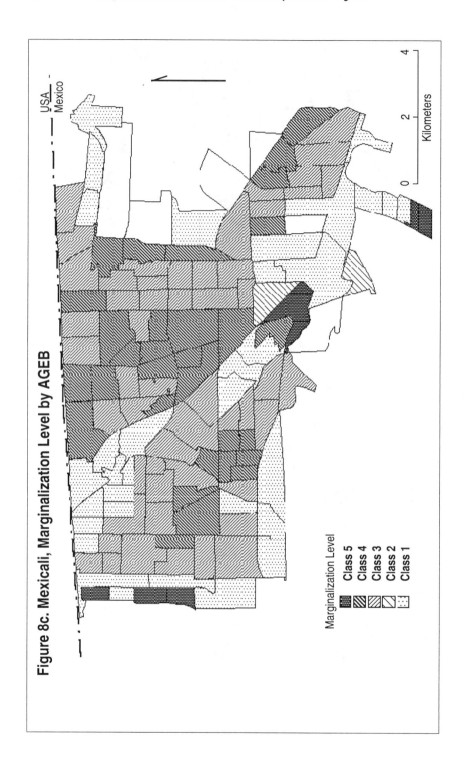

Figure 8c. Mexicali, Marginalization Level by AGEB

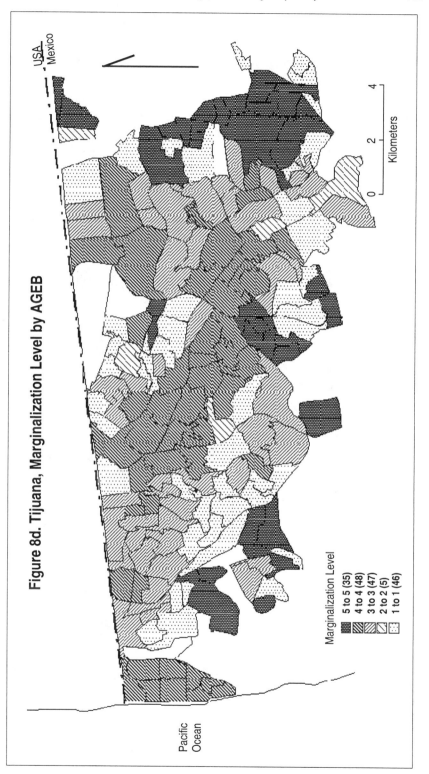

Figure 8d. Tijuana, Marginalization Level by AGEB

Marginalization Level

5 to 5 (35)
4 to 4 (48)
3 to 3 (47)
2 to 2 (5)
1 to 1 (46)

ifornia seems to be more related to housing characteristics—infrastructure as well as its reduced size.

Inter- and Intraurban Dimension of Marginalization in Baja California

Before proceeding with the description of inter- and intraurban marginalization, some of the characteristics of the cities being studied should be mentioned. All four cities present limitations to their physical growth (see Figure 8). The expansion northward in three of the cities—Mexicali, Tecate, and Tijuana—is impossible because of their border location adjacent to the international boundary. With regard to the city of Ensenada, such limitations are presented eastward, since it is a port in the Pacific coastline.

Tijuana is the largest city in terms of population. Slightly more than half of the total inhabitants of the four cities analyzed reside there (51.9%). It is followed by Mexicali with 32.5 percent, while the smallest city is Tecate. Overall, Tijuana and Mexicali have about 70 percent of the total population for Baja California and 83 percent of the state's urban population of those who live in localities of 15,000 or more inhabitants (INEGI 1997).

The historical origins, as well as the subsequent physical expansion of Ensenada, Mexicali, and Tijuana have been linked to the aforementioned barriers. The initial settlement and subsequent growth of Mexicali and Tijuana resulted from the location of the international border and as point of entrance and exit of population, goods, and services from one country to the other. Ensenada's growth, in contrast, was due to its location on the ocean and its fishing industry.

Finally, is should be emphasized that three of these border cities (Mexicali, Tecate, and Tijuana) are relatively young settlements,[6] that date from the early twentieth century (Ranfla and Álvarez 1998; Ranfla, Álvarez, and Ortega 1989). Ensenada was founded in the eighteenth century during the peninsula's mission period, but its economic development and population took place at the same time as Mexicali and Tijuana.

These features provide the context within which to place the characteristics of marginalization. From the spatial perspective, the maps in Figure 8 show the AGEBs classification according to the marginalization levels as well as the location of each one of the cities under study. It should be kept in mind that the numeration of the classes do not indicate a hierarchical order of marginalization levels.[7] As a result, the real hierarchy is shown in the maps according to shading; the darkest is for the AGEBs with greater marginalization and the lightest is for the lesser ones.

A first general aspect that stands out is that in the four cities the marginalized areas are located mainly in the periphery or outskirts of the city (see Figure 8). It seems, however, that Ensenada and Mexicali are similar in terms of marginalization since the areas of low and very low marginalization predominate (lightest shades). In contrast, in Tecate and Tijuana a lesser presence of the areas of low marginalization is observed, since the three dark shades predominate.

At the level of each of the cities, Figure 8 shows that in Ensenada the coastal portion of the city presents the levels of lowest marginalization that extend slightly northward of the bay and eastward from the coast toward the middle part of the city.

Mexicali is the city that presents the lowest number of AGEBs with the highest levels of marginalization that, without exception, are located in the periphery (see Figure 8). The areas that follow in descending order of marginalization (Class 1) are also peripheral in their majority and are adjacent to the previous ones. The exceptions are the AGEBs that appear near the international border and extend toward the southeast. This phenomenon is associated to the history of the city and its land use, since this AGEB group belongs to the oldest part of Mexicali. The areas with the least marginalization are located in different areas of the city; of these, the area of greatest size belongs to the geographical center of the city that extends northward until it runs into the international border.

One aspect that stands out in the city of Tecate is that its AGEBs are distributed in three of the five classes of marginalization (see Figure 8), with a predominance in the middle levels of marginalization (Class 3). However, the rest of the AGEBs are found in a situation of greater marginalization, with the presence of areas corresponding to the highest levels of marginalization (Class 5) in the city's east and southeast peripheries (Classes 1 and 5), with the absence of areas with classifications of very low marginalization (Class 4 with the lightest color).

Finally, Tijuana presents a pattern of marginalization distribution that is clearly defined and that could be considered concentric. The majority of AGEBs with the lowest levels of marginalization (lightest color) are concentrated in the geographic center of the urban area, in a diagonal strip with a northeast, southeast direction (see Figure 8). Marginalization increases gradually around this strip until it reaches the periphery where the areas of greater marginalization are located. One aspect that calls attention to Tijuana is that, even though it is the largest city, it has fewer areas of very low marginalization when compared to Mexicali, and a greater number of areas of very high marginalization.

A Reflection with Regard to Marginalization in Baja California

A first conclusion of the work presented here is that, within the national context, the states in the northern border of Mexico present lower levels of marginalization than the national average, particularly Nuevo León and Baja California. Second, when the municipalities of the northern border states are considered as the universe of the study, those that present the lowest levels of marginalization are those located adjacent to the international border with the United States. Additionally, as the size of the observation units (from states to municipalities) are reduced, there are noticeable differences within each of the border states. Also evident is the heterogeneity of space in terms of marginalization.

From the analysis of marginalization at the municipal level, Baja California stands out as the only northern border state whose municipalities have the same classification of marginalization as the state overall. However, this does not mean that depressed or marginalized areas do not exist in the state. The favorable position of the state refers to its national comparison, not that marginalization does not exist in the state. Therefore, when the analysis of Baja California goes beyond the statewide level and focuses on the main cities, the picture changes. Significant differences emerge and a differentiated space is obvious in terms of marginalization that shows not only the intensity with which the phenomenon is present, but also its location within these cities.

Since the end of the nineteenth century, border cities have demonstrated a pattern of continuous physical expansion that resulted from the arrival of migrants and the dynamism of their economies. Thus, income levels are generally not low, as the results for Baja California show. However, the continuous transformation of space generates precarious housing and infrastructure conditions, a temporary result of the process of the city's consolidation in its different sectors and neighborhoods. The population and income growth is faster than the capability to provide quality infrastructure and housing.

Intra- and Interurban Marginalization in the Cities of Baja California

One limitation of what has been discussed here, with respect to the intra- and interurban analysis, is that census information was used for the estimates of the marginalization indices. These reflect to a greater extent those inequality aspects associated with public investment (especially in infrastructure and education) and manifest, to a lesser extent, the marginalization arising from private resources whose use here was captured through housing characteristics (floor and wall materials and home size). These indicators exclude many aspects related to marginalization, particularly to poverty. Also excluded are those associated with personal wealth and the consumption of basic goods that were only captured indirectly through the indicator of personal income.

Despite these limitations, the variables considered in this study permitted the first estimates of urban marginalization in Baja California in which two modalities of marginalization were identified. One is considered typical and was manifested by the presence of the illiterate population and with income less than two minimum salaries. The second, denominated here as atypical marginalization, was characterized by a medium and high presence of homes with one room and illiteracy at mid level. However, when a hierarchical (ordinal) version of three of the selected variables (income, homes with one room, and illiteracy) is added to the analysis, the result is that urban marginalization in Baja California seems to be more associated with the housing characteristics (construction materials, size, and infrastructure) than with the population's income and literacy.

The fact that income and illiteracy do not appear as important variables of urban marginalization in Baja California is due to the minimal presence of illiterate populations in its cities. This phenomenon of less illiteracy is not only a result of the urban character of the study—considering that the majority of the illiterate population is rural—but it is also a manifestation of the educational profile of the migrant population that arrives in these cities. In other words, despite the fact that people constantly arrive in border cities (particularly Tijuana and to a lesser degree, Mexicali), they usually arrive at least knowing how to read and write and, thus, are classified as literate. The urban space in Baja California is, thus, almost homogenous in terms of illiteracy.

Something similar occurs with income since including the population with income of less than two minimum salaries leads to the homogenization of the analytical units (AGEBs). The population that earns the highest income in Mexico lives in Baja California, particularly in its urban centers, and only a few people earn incomes of that magnitude.

In every case, what resulted irrelevant as a differentiating criterion for marginalization was income, but not the variable itself, since other indicators associated with income did play an important role in the marginalization of the cities. These indicators included the size of the home and types of materials used in the construction of the walls and floors.

A good-size home, built of durable materials can be related to two factors: (1) the amount of income—greater salaries allow the enlargement or improvement of the home in the short term, while at the same time taking care of the regular home expenses—and (2) the length of residency in the city or time that the home has been constituted as such, considering that for the middle or low income population the possibility of investing in home improvements comes with time. This is because, first, there has to be a major investment in the acquisition of a lot, in the construction of the home (or its equivalent of paying rent), and in the purchase of durable goods that are necessary for the home at the same time that the expenses related to children and family are borne.

A fact that stands out is that the areas of greater marginalization and, consequently, with substandard homes are found in the periphery of the cities. These are areas of recent creation and the place of settlements of recently formed homes and/or migrant populations.

In this sense, the migratory dynamics of the state should be kept in mind, since the cities of Tecate and Tijuana are the ones with the fastest industrial growth and receive the greatest numbers of migrants proportionally. This leads to the hypothesis—rather than the statement—that the greater presence of areas of high marginalization in these cities, as well as their peripheral position, results from the rapid physical expansion of the city. This expansion causes the public infrastructure investments to be overdrawn by the population growth itself and, consequently, of the city. Another element that also restricts the allocation of adequate infrastructure in these cities is the rough topography, as opposed to Mexicali, located in a flat valley floor.

There seem to be two patterns of marginalization. One corresponds to Mexicali and Ensenada, with a greater presence of areas with low or very low marginalization. The other is comprised of Tecate and Tijuana with a greater presence of areas with high marginalization. However, the four cities have in common that the location of the areas of high marginalization is predominantly on the periphery or outskirts.

The aspects of urban marginalization of Baja California described in this study suggest consideration of a number of other points for future analysis. These include:

1. Migration dynamics, including location and composition
2. Typography and its effects in terms of engineering and costs in the allocation and access to infrastructure for improvement of living conditions
3. Intraurban mobility in terms of time and cost of transportation systems, including public and private transportation as well as number of vehicles and roads, are critical for urban integration
4. Some variables linked to the explanation of accumulation of material wealth of the household that are associated with the border context of Baja California, which facilitates the access to imported new and used goods
5. The nature and quantification of the patterns of economic dependency in families

The gradual inclusion of the aforementioned elements in future research studies would be of great use to enrich a regionalized analysis of marginalization. These would build on the initial conclusions of the present work.

Endnotes

1. In 1995, the participation of Baja California in the national gross domestic product (GDP) was 2.3 percent of the total, while in 1990, the participation of its population in the national total was 2.5 percent.

2. The limitations of the studies conducted for the country as a whole have already been documented in other works. Zenteno Quintero and Cruz Peñeiro (1998) approach the case of the work carried out by Coplamar during the early 1980s, while Ortega (2000) reviews the same case and the work conducted by Conapo-Conagua (1993) and INEGI (1993b) for the case of Baja California.

3. Originally, more than these nine variables were included; however, those that were redundant with these nine variables were eliminated. The elimination of the variables was carried out at the correlation matrix. Those that registered high correlations with one or more variables were eliminated. As a result, the "most representative" were identified, the same percentage of explained variants was maintained, and the presentation of the results was simplified.

4. For purpose of the analysis, 398 AGEBs were considered; those without population, as well as those that registered less than eight homes per km^2, were eliminated.

5. For example, in 1998, personnel employed in nonagricultural activities in Tijuana was double, in absolute terms, than that in Mexicali.

6. In general, these three settlements originated in the early twentieth century, even though historians state that Tijuana was founded in 1889.

7. The class that represents greater marginalization indices is number 5, while the one that represents the AGEBs of less marginalization is number 4.

References

Astorga, E., and J. Moguel. 1996. "Neoliberalismo y pobreza en América Latina. Los casos de Chile y México." *Economía informa* 256.

Consejo Nacional de Población-Comisión Nacional del Agua (Conapo-Conagua). 1993. *Indicadores socioeconómicos e índice de marginación municipal 1990.* México, D.F.: Conapo-Conagua.

Coordinación General del Plan Nacional de Zonas Deprimidas y Grupos Marginados (Coplamar). 1983. *Necesidades esenciales en México. Situación actual y perspectivas al año 2000. Vol. 5. Geografía de la marginación.* 2nd ed. México, D.F.: Siglo XXI Editores.

Estrella V., Gabriel. 1984. "Los niveles mínimos de bienestar en el Estado de Baja California, 1983." Final report for IIS-UABC research program, Mexicali.

Germani, Gino. 1973. *El concepto de marginalidad. Significado, raíces históricas y cuestiones teóricas, con particular referencia a la marginalidad urbana.* Buenos Aires: Ediciones Nueva Visión, Colección Fichas.

Instituto Nacional de Estadística, Geografía e Informática (INEGI). 1993a. SCINCE (compact disk). Aguascalientes: INEGI.

Instituto Nacional de Estadística, Geografía e Informática (INEGI). 1993b. *Niveles de bienestar en México.* Aguascalientes: INEGI.

Instituto Nacional de Estadística, Geografía e Informática (INEGI). 1997. *Conteo '95. Resultados definitivos. Tabulados básicos. Estados Unidos Mexicanos.* Aguascalientes: INEGI.

Instituto Nacional de Estadística, Geografía e Informática (INEGI). 1998. *Estadísticas de la industria maquiladora de exportación.* Aguascalientes: INEGI

Mercado, A., and O. Fernández. 1996. "La estrategia de la inversión japonesa en el marco del TLCN." *Revista de Comercio Exterior* 46.

Ortega V., Guadalupe. 2000. "Satisfacción de necesidades básicas en Baja California: mitos y realidades." *Estudios fronterizos* 1 (1).

Ranfla, A., and Guillermo Álvarez de la T. 1988. "Migración y formas urbanas en el crecimiento de Tijuana 1900–1984." *Revista Mexicana de Sociología* 50 (4).

Ranfla, A., Guillermo Álvarez, and Guadalupe Ortega. 1989. "Expansión física y desarrollo urbano de Tijuana." In *Historia de Tijuana 1889–1989.* Tijuana: UABC-Gobierno del Estado de Baja California-XII Ayuntamiento de Tijuana.

World Bank. 1987. *La pobreza en América Latina.* Washington, D.C.: World Bank.

Yates, Paul Lamartine. 1965. *El desarrollo regional de México.* México, D.F.: Banco de México.

Zenteno Quintero, René M., and Rodolfo Cruz Piñeiro. 1988. "Un contexto geográfico para la investigación demográfica de la frontera norte." *Estudios demográficos y urbanos* 3 (3).

The Unionization of the *Maquiladora* Industry and the North American Agreement on Labor Cooperation: Strategies Conceived and Frustrated

Edward J. Williams and Joel Stillerman[*]

Abstract

Many scholars have examined the North American Free Trade Agreement's (NAFTA) effects on the Mexican economy, yet few have studied the potential of the treaty's labor side accord—the North American Agreement on Labor Cooperation (NAALC)—to become an effective tool in cross-border efforts to unionize the *maquiladora* (assembly plant) industry. Through an analysis of the NAALC's provisions and its structure, the political context for labor organization in the United States and Mexico, and labor activists' complaints under the NAALC, the authors seek to assess the side accord's potential utility for redressing worker's grievances in northern Mexico's assembly industry. The authors found that due to its weak enforcement provisions, the NAALC will unlikely help Mexican activists in the face of joint efforts by pro-government union, arbitration boards, local governments, and employers to prevent the emergence of independent unions. However, since the NAALC does encourage cross-border collaboration between labor activists, it may play an indirect role in promoting international alliances regarding labor rights and providing negative publicity regarding the Mexican government's nonenforcement of its own labor laws.

---

* Williams is Professor of Political Science at the University of Arizona; Stillerman is Lecturer in Latin American Studies and Sociology at the University of Arizona.

Introduction

The effects of the North American Free Trade Agreement (NAFTA) on the economies of its member nations have sparked significant controversy among social scientists and policymakers. However, few observers have systematically examined the potential effectiveness of the treaty's labor side accord for promoting worker rights in the three signatory countries. This paper looks at the potential of the North American Agreement on Labor Cooperation (NAALC) to become a tool for cross-border efforts to unionize the *maquiladora* industry. Through an analysis of the accord, an understanding of the political context for union activism in the United States and Mexico, and a look at the cases brought before the NAALC to date, this study argues that the agreement can only indirectly help such organizing efforts. The NAALC has weak enforcement powers that are unlikely to counteract entrenched political actors who oppose independent unionism in *maquiladoras*. Rather than compelling its member countries to enforce their own labor laws, the accord can potentially play a positive role for workers by promoting cross-border alliances and by providing negative publicity for anti-labor policies and employers. The NAALC is neither a panacea nor an obstacle to cross-border organizing; it is a modest tool in labor's uphill battle to organize the *maquiladora* sector.

Several unions and nongovernmental organizations (NGOs) have tried to use the NAALC's provisions to defend labor rights in the member countries. Efforts to support independent unions in the *maquiladora* industry have been most notable (Compa 1997). Indeed, the *maquiladora* industry has been a thorn in the side of organized labor since its inception in the mid-1960s. Over the years, U.S. labor groups have initiated a series of strategies to counter the *maquiladora* industry's growth. Since the 1980s, NGOs and lawyers have entered the fray to support unionization in Mexico's northern border region. Campaigns designed to condemn the industry and catalyze political opposition have damned the *maquila* industry as a magnet for "runaway shops" (factories that close and move to lower wage areas), a contributor to undocumented migration, a plague of "sweatshops" that exploit Mexican workers, and a polluter of borderlands air and water that threatens the health and well-being of people on both sides of the international boundary. While each of these charges has some validity, none has formed the basis of a successful campaign to stem the industry's growth. The Mexican *maquiladora* industry continues to flourish.[1]

By facilitating the organization of borderlands assembly plants, the NAALC seemed to offer an opportunity for U.S. unions and labor activists. Organizing Mexican workers represented an end in itself, but it would also increase labor costs on the Mexican side, thereby both diminishing the comparative advantage of the Mexican location and saving U.S. jobs. Almost immediately, some U.S. and Mexican labor activists attempted to utilize the accord to further unionization of the *maquiladora* industry. By November 1999, labor activists had brought 22 cases before the National Administrative Offices (NAOs) of the three countries; seven of these cases focused on *maquiladoras* (U.S. NAO 1999).[2] At least some groups within the two labor movements saw the NAALC as an opportunity to defend labor rights. After testing the accord, many activists believe their initial concerns about its cumbersome procedures and weak enforcement mechanisms may be correct.

Activists' criticisms of the NAALC's flawed design may be just, but the potential for cross-border labor collaboration between U.S. and Mexican activists is influenced by several other factors. During the Cold War, U.S. unions collaborated with their government in its foreign policy objectives. To pursue the government's geopolitical goals, U.S. unions often attempted to manipulate labor activists in Latin America. Mexican activists can therefore legitimately question the motives of U.S. activists who now profess this newfound desire to collaborate with them. In contrast, successful grassroots efforts at cross-border organization began in the 1980s, before the NAALC was established. The side accord must therefore be considered within this longer and contradictory historical frame. Another factor relates to the state-led assault on trade unionism in both countries, today an apparently global trend. Then-President Ronald Reagan sparked efforts to undermine the labor movement, while Mexican administrations since the early 1980s have weakened the historic alliance of the Institutional Revolutionary Party (Partido Revolucionario Institucional–PRI) with the Confederation of Mexican Workers (Confederación de Trabajadores de México–CTM), a labor organization long favored by the government. Moreover, neoliberal policies in the United States and Mexico have battered union strongholds through privatization, downsizing, runaway shops, and so on.

Bureaucratization and corruption in the leadership of both labor movements compound this negative scenario. U.S. union leaders watched unionization levels decline after their wartime expansion under the Congress of Industrial Organizations (CIO); they often focused on the anti-communist crusade at home and abroad, "bread-and-butter" demands, and personal gain within the union bureaucracy, rather than mobilization for social change. Likewise, Mexico's official unions suppressed independent unions, often forming an unholy alliance with employers, venal labor inspectors, and local government officials to the detriment of their putative constituents.

Events leading to favorable changes—such as John Sweeney's election as president of the American Federation of Labor and Congress of Industrial Organizations (AFL-CIO), the death of CTM leader Fidel Velázquez, incipient democratization in Mexico, and a growing sector of U.S. and Mexican unions and nonprofit organizations that promote independent unionism and genuine international collaboration—offer hope, but do not augur fundamental changes in either country's labor movement.

In the United States, cross-border organization is only one of organized labor's many priorities, and is unlikely to gain full-scale commitment by the AFL-CIO. By contrast, independent unions and NGOs in Mexico need to fight official labor and public authorities every step of the way. Small victories may be outweighed by a trend toward the weakening of genuine trade unions in Mexico, particularly in the *maquiladora* sector.

Based on a review of complaints brought before the U.S. National Administrative Office (NAO) under the NAALC regarding violations of labor rights in the *maquiladora* sector, this paper argues that while cross-border labor activist coalitions have attempted to exploit the agreement to its fullest extent, the NAALC's lack of enforcement mechanisms means that it will have little, if any, concrete positive effects on Mexico's *maquiladora* workers. Even though the U.S. NAO can call for ministerial consultations and educational initiatives if it finds that labor laws regarding the right to organize are not enforced in Mexico, these exchanges will not compel the Mexican government to enforce its own laws. Indeed, the efforts of independent labor activists in Mexico's *maquilas* are thwarted at every turn by the business, judicial, and trade union setting.

However, by fostering cross-border collaboration between labor activists, the agreement may enhance the effectiveness of what Maria Lorena Cook (1997) calls the "transnational political arena," wherein citizens of one country use the political institutions and actors of another to gain political clout at home. NAO public hearings permit aggrieved Mexican workers to testify in the United States regarding labor rights violations in Mexico, thereby increasing their political power at home through the negative publicity that damns Mexico's political system and labor courts. By the same token, U.S. labor and human rights activists can provide their Mexican counterparts with resources and prestige that increase their own standing at home. Mexico's officials may respond to grievances if they believe negative publicity from NAALC proceedings could hurt the country's political and economic standing. In short, the NAALC may be more useful to union activists as a publicity device and institutional resource than as a supranational adjudication body.

Some might argue that this essay's focus on the *maquiladora* industry as a potential sector for activists' use of the NAALC is misplaced. The accord is not restricted to assembly plants; the NAALC covers labor conditions in all work places, and fewer than half its cases have involved *maquiladora* workers. However, *maquiladoras* do provide a crucial test case for the accord. The industry is the fastest growing employer in Mexico, a traditional target of U.S. labor, and a setting in which workers are particularly vulnerable to employers. Insights from this discussion may also be applied more broadly to the whole issue of cross-border activism in the NAFTA era.

This paper is divided into several parts. The first section sets out the policy and political context, featuring discussions of the NAALC and the *maquiladora* industry. The second part describes and analyzes the influence of the political actors involved in the conflict, offering special attention to the Mexican government and Mexican organized labor. The third section details the utilization of the NAALC in seven labor disputes that involved attempts to unionize *maquiladoras* in Mexican border states. The conclusion contains two sections. It first examines the influence of political forces in the United States and Mexico that oppose unions and the organization of *maquiladora* workers. It then examines characteristics of the NAALC that may be developed in the future to help empower unions in the United States, Canada, and Mexico.

Policy and Political Context

The North American Agreement on Labor Cooperation and the *maquiladora* industry form the two major components of the policy and political context of this study. The NAALC may provide labor activists in Mexico and the United States an additional tool for forming alliances confronting new challenges created by the NAFTA treaty, but its three-tiered structure, lengthy review process, and weak enforcement mechanisms invite skepticism. The NAALC may only indirectly nurture organizing efforts by shining the public spotlight on labor law violations and by encouraging labor activists across borders to develop ties.

The *maquiladora* industry is an ideal setting for cross-border organization. Given its proximity to the United States, low labor and environmental standards, and weak traditions of militant unionism, the sector represents an opportunity for labor activists on both sides of the border. Due to its reputation for labor abuses and the threat it offers to union shops in North America, the industry is an excellent target for international organizing campaigns. The NAALC could serve a broad campaign to defend worker rights in the assembly plants. It is thus important to highlight the provisions of the accord that inspired cross-border unionization efforts in the *maquiladora* sector in the 1990s.

The North American Agreement on Labor Cooperation (NAALC)

The NAALC's objectives and obligations suggest that it may serve as a tool for cross-border organization. The accord seeks to improve working conditions, promote a set of 11 labor principles, encourage information exchanges and cooperation, promote compliance with and enforcement of national labor laws, and foster transparent administration of the law (U.S. NAO 1993: 2–3). The 11 labor principles under the NAALC are: freedom of association and the right to organize; collective bargaining rights; the right to strike; the prohibition of forced labor; protection of child labor; minimum employment standards; nondiscrimination; equal pay for men and women; prevention of occupational injuries and illnesses; compensation for workplace injury and illness; and protection of migrant workers (U.S. NAO 1993: Annex 1, 33–35).

The NAALC includes a council comprising labor ministers of the member countries; an international secretariat to offer technical assistance to the council; National Administrative Offices (NAOs) based in each country that are responsible for implementing the agreement; and national advisory committees composed of representatives from labor, business, academia, and the public-at-large (U.S. NAO 1998b). The agreement has a complex, multitiered structure for evaluating complaints. Activists submit complaints of alleged violations of any of the 11 principles to the NAO of another country. One or more parties may file a petition with their own NAO regarding violations in another member country.

The NAALC mandates cross-border collaboration between labor advocates by requiring individuals or groups to file complaints regarding violations in another country—a process that only functions if advocates in more than one country work together (Compa 1997: 10). The petitioned NAO may call a public hearing if it determines that the issue falls under the 11 labor principles. If the hearing suggests that labor laws have not been enforced, the NAO may call for a second level of review consisting of ministerial consultations in the three countries on the issues raised. Under the accord, the process, from submission of the complaint to the NAO's issue of its final report, may take as long as 240 days, or almost eight months (U.S. NAO 1998b: Appendix 2).

The third tier for review is an Evaluation Committee of Experts (ECE). If the matter involves a company that trades with a NAFTA partner and refers to an issue governed by analogous laws in both countries, the matter may go to an ECE made up of independent experts. However, the first three principles (the rights to organize, collectively bargain, and strike) cannot be brought before an ECE. The issue must also reflect a pattern of practice rather than a one-time violation, and be focused specifically on enforcement. The ECE review and responses from governments can last at least another 240 days (Compa 1997: 11–12; U.S. NAO 1993: 15–17).

Further consultation may be requested if, after the ECE report, a party finds a persistent pattern of nonenforcement of minimum wage, occupational safety, or child labor laws. If the issue is not resolved in additional ministerial consultations within 60 days (the fourth tier of review), one or more of the parties may request dispute resolution from the Ministerial Council, the fifth level. If after 20 days the council meets and fails to resolve the dispute within an additional 60 days, a party may request arbitration, the sixth tier. The process of arbitration can ultimately lead to a fine or suspension of NAFTA benefits (the seventh level), and could take several years (U.S. NAO 1993: 17–27).

The following discusses how labor activists may be able to use these NAALC institutions and complex process of complaint review as an effective tool for creating independent unions in the *maquiladoras*.

The Maquiladora *Industry*

Several characteristics of the *maquiladora* industry invite unions and labor rights advocates to utilize it as the test case for the NAALC: proximity, its relative familiarity, and its affront to organized labor (particularly in the United States). In addition, the industry pays relatively low wages, suggesting a milieu conducive to organizational efforts.

At the most basic level of influence, geographic proximity to the United States recommends the industry as a test case. Organizers find literally thousands of target plants within a mile or so of the international boundary. They can fly to El Paso or to San Diego, cross the line to Ciudad Juárez or Tijuana, and within an hour launch organizational efforts. The industry's scale underscores its social and economic importance; by 1999, the more than three thousand assembly plants employed over one million Mexican workers (CJM 1999: 12).

The logic of U.S. organizers targeting borderlands assembly plants to test the competence of the NAALC also comes, in part, from familiarity with the territory and the industry. A number of labor union activists and worker rights advocates have been working the borderlands for years (Williams and Passé-Smith 1992; Cook 1997). Even U.S. newcomers find the border area more familiar than other parts of Mexico. English is widely used in Mexican border cities, their spatial patterns and grids approximate U.S. urban areas, and even architectural designs tend to be less "foreign" (Arreola and Curtis 1993).

Familiarity with U.S.-owned companies in the *maquiladora* industry is also an incentive for U.S. activists to promote unionization of the assembly plants. Union organizers know and work with the Fortune 500 companies that own and operate assembly plants in the Mexican border region. Organizing General Dynamics, General Electric, or General Motors in Matamoros or Nogales is, assuredly, rather different than bargaining with those companies in Indiana or Michigan, but many accoutrements of the larger scenario are quite similar. The plants look the same, work organization is familiar, and English is spoken by top management (Cook 1997).

Moreover, U.S. labor bears a special antipathy for the *maquiladora* industry. Beginning with the establishment of Mexico's Border Industrialization Program in 1965, assembly plants in Mexico were the first example of significant job movement away from the United States to Mexico. As labor union analysts see it, the several "runaway plants" of the 1960s presaged massive job losses during the 1980s (EPI et al. 1997). Indeed, the significant periods of expansion in the *maquiladora* sector (in the early 1980s and after 1994) followed peso devaluations that translated into significant wage declines. "Every available indicator of wage performance declined from 1983–1988" (Middlebrook 1995; see also EPI et al. 1997) and "from 1982 until the present ... the ongoing decline in the peso's value has greatly accelerated the tempo of *maquiladora* investment" (Tiano 1994: 20). During the 1980s and 1990s, U.S. labor activists witnessed the intertwined processes of job decline at home, declining wages in Mexico, and the expansion of the *maquila* industry—all pointing to the need to promote unionization in the assembly plants.

In sum, the apparent opportunities presented by the NAALC, combined with special characteristics of the *maquiladora* industry, sparked U.S. and Mexican unions and labor rights advocates to launch initiatives in the mid-1990s to organize the assembly plants in the U.S.-Mexican borderlands. Several provisions of the NAALC appeared to facilitate unionization initiatives, while several features of the *maquiladora* industry recommended it as the logical focus for their organizational efforts.

The Political Actors

In addition to the NAALC's formal provisions and the peculiarities of the *maquiladora* sector, one must weigh the larger political context to infer the relative influence of the several political actors and the value they accord the *maquiladora* industry. In both Mexico and the United States, the rise of neoliberalism means that the influence of the labor movement wanes and the prestige and value of the *maquiladora* program waxes. Moreover, government favors the industry and seeks to undermine organized labor. Additionally, in recent decades, complacent labor leaders have abdicated their role as promoters of a dynamic and militant labor movement, while the largest Mexican union confederation, the Confederation of Mexican Workers (CTM), supports the *maquila* industry. A survey of the political actors in the two nations illustrates these observations.

Mexico

In Mexico, the labor movement is in decline, the *maquiladora* program is increasingly valued, and most labor chieftains support the government's line against independent organization of the assembly plants. Analyzing these three facts leads inexorably to the conclusion that organizing the *maquiladora* industry is extraordinarily difficult, if not impossible.

The analysis begins with the declining political influence of Mexican organized labor. The causes of the decline began with the rise of neoliberalism, evident in a series of post-1982 and post-1994 policies and programs that responded to Mexico's economic crises and were designed to "modernize" the economy and polity. These policies included wage freezes; a series of privatizations, liquidations, and restructurings; and the negative economic fallout of trade liberalization.

Wage freezes began with the austerity programs initiated immediately after Miguel de la Madrid's accession to power in 1982. Real income for Mexico's workers ranked 50 percent lower in 1990 than in 1982. Workers' economic plight probably improved a trifle in the 1990–1994 period, but even then, the data were in dispute. Furthermore, the government reduced subsidies that benefited lower income workers (*Mexico Update* 1990; *Review of the Economic Situation of Mexico* 1990; *Mexico Business Monthly* 1993; de Palma 1994; *Latin American Weekly Report* 1995; Tierney 1994; Tiano 1994; Middlebrook 1995; Cook 1995; LaBotz 1992). The economic crisis of 1994–1995 signified more misery for Mexico's workers, as the screws tightened on the austerity program and workers made more sacrifices (EPI et al. 1997).

Mexico's liquidations, restructurings, and privatizations meant more negative outcomes for workers and organized labor. Initiated under de la Madrid, the measures continued into the 1990s, when privatization emerged as the most celebrated dimension of President Carlos Salinas's economic blueprint (1988–1994). The measures also figured prominently in President Ernesto Zedillo's policies (1994–2000), designed to respond to the mid-1990s economic crisis (Williams 1990; Lajous 1989; Mexican Investment Board 1995: 4; *New York Times* 1993; *Review of the Economic Situation in Mexico* 1994; *Latin American Weekly Report* 1994; Cook 1995; EPI et al. 1997).

Trade liberalization policies also militate against organized labor and Mexico's workers. As tariffs diminished after Mexico's 1986 affiliation with the General Agreement on Tariffs and Trade (GATT) and the NAFTA of 1994, the country's protected industries felt the sting of competition, as layoffs and downsizings continued.

The economic logic of the affair is straightforward. The government seeks to create an environment conducive to expanding private foreign investment. In pursuit of that goal, Mexico City has enacted policies that impoverished workers, subjugated the unions and disciplined their leaders, and alienated the union movement from its long-lived association with the government and the PRI.[3]

As Mexico's ruling elites withdraw their support of the nation's union movement, they increasingly embrace the assembly industry. From the national level to local *municipios* (municipalities), the *maquiladora* industry's prestige expands. From its inception through the mid-1980s, Mexican policymakers depicted the assembly plant industry as a necessary evil designed to assist Mexico's economy on the margins, but not as an integral element of a long-term economic strategy. That perspective has been replaced by a sympathetic posture for several reasons. Economic crises have dragged on or been replaced by new emergencies. Certain Asian nations—notably South Korea and Taiwan—have had well-advertised success utilizing assembly plants for their own industrial takeoffs. Furthermore, the ideology of Mexico's decision-making elites evolved to a posture more in tune with private sector initiatives. Hence, the *maquiladora* industry is now a "priority sector" of the economy.

Three special characteristics of the Mexican labor movement define the final influence that militates against a successful strategy to utilize the NAALC to unionize the *maquiladora* industry. The movement is: (1) government dominated, (2) nationalistic, and (3) supportive of Mexico's developmental policies. Mexico's labor union leaders operate in a semi-authoritarian system, in which the heavy hand of governmental power comes quite close to dictating the policies and programs of Mexico's union movement. Mexico's governing elites mandate the formulation and implementation of policies and programs formally promulgated by Mexican organized labor. The role of government grew even more assertive during the 1980s and 1990s. Government purged a number of Mexican labor leaders and imprisoned others. Mexico's labor leaders fell into line, pledging their support to the "modernization" of the Mexican economy (Williams and Passé-Smith 1992; Cook 1995; Quintero 1998; LaBotz 1992).

More than simply supporting government policy, official union leaders have historically played an instrumental role in suppressing democratic trade unions, a goal often achieved in part through collaboration with employers. *Charro* (pro-government) union leaders helped the government purge independent movements in the railroad and auto unions from the 1940s until the 1970s. In fact, automobile transnationals moved their plants from traditional industrial areas to central and northern Mexico during the 1970s and 1980s to evade independent movements. Many specifically requested CTM representation at the new plants to ensure labor peace and exclude independent union movements (Middlebrook 1995; Roxborough 1984).

Government-aligned labor leaders have been notorious for setting up "protection" contracts with *maquila* owners in which a given plant is "unionized," but none of the workers are aware of the fact, nor have any ever seen the contract. When workers attempt to set up an independent union, labor Conciliation and Arbitration Boards (CABs), allied with official unions and local employers, invariably deny the union its registration because the plant is "already unionized." This practice provides union dues to corrupt labor leaders, satisfies employer desires for labor peace, and keeps effective unionism at bay. Thus, above and beyond government fiat, Mexico's official unions are guilty of blocking genuine unionism at the source, particularly in the northern assembly plants (Quintero 1998; de la Garza 1994; LaBotz 1992).

In addition to such efforts to suppress independent unions, Mexico's government-aligned labor leaders are also nationalists who promote Mexico's development. As early as 1954, the dominant CTM officially pronounced its obligation to the nation over its duty to support class struggles (Ryan et al. 1970). As nationalists, Mexico's official labor leaders share a deeply ingrained anti-Americanism, especially the older cadre of leaders who have experienced the humiliation of U.S. imperialistic muscle flexing. U.S. citizens, even if they are blue-collar workers, are not to be trusted. Thus, Mexican unionists shrink back from joining U.S. unionists to organize the *maquiladora* industry under the aegis of the NAALC (Williams 1997; Cook 1995).

Developmentalism also forms part of the analytical scenario. Official labor leaders strive to contribute to the nation's economic growth, which translates into jobs for Mexico's massive number of unemployed and underemployed workers. Mexican organized labor correctly observes that the expansion of the *maquiladora* industry represents the most dynamic source of jobs in Mexico today. Mexico's official unions therefore count several reasons to support the industry and refuse to cooperate with U.S. unions bent on organizing it. Prudent self-interest in an authoritarian system counsels the wisdom of supporting the government on important issues. Official unions also have vested interests in preventing independent unions from entering the *maquiladora* sector. Additionally, a history of binational interaction teaches that U.S. citizens should not be trusted. Finally, the growing *maquiladora* industry creates jobs for Mexicans, a goal embraced by Mexico's official unions in light of the collapse of its traditional industrial base during the 1980s and 1990s.

Obviously, then, the balance of political forces in Mexico appears quite unfavorable to a strategy that utilizes the NAALC to organize the *maquiladora* industry. The government is extremely favorable to the *maquiladora* industry and decreasingly sympathetic to organized labor. Just as significantly, for reasons clear and understandable, most components of organized labor in Mexico toe the governmental line against unionization of the industry.

The United States

The influence and policy proclivities of political actors in the United States weigh less in the balance of forces than their Mexican counterparts, but they form a part of the larger whole. U.S. organized labor's political punch and the U.S. government's commitment to the NAALC and/or the *maquiladora* industry define relevant components of the analysis. The NAALC would clearly be more salient if U.S. labor wielded mighty political influence and U.S. federal, state, and local governments disdained the *maquiladora* industry. But exactly the opposite is true, so the NAALC becomes less important in strategies to organize the *maquiladora* industry.

As in Mexico, neoliberalism exercises enormous influence in the United States, as pro-business and anti-labor attitudes pervade the system. In addition, both Mexican and U.S. governmental and private interests have been reorganizing the economy in a spree of downsizing, privatizing, liquidating, and restructuring, and have diminished the strength and influence of U.S. organized labor. The U.S. labor movement's own sins also contributed to its waning influence. Since the labor movement's apogee immediately after World War II, its top leadership abdicated the movement's erstwhile goals to prioritize labor organizing. Unions focused on servicing their existing members, neither expanding their base in large manufacturing or the public sector, nor venturing out to organize low-skilled services, light industry, or private sector white-collar professionals. Hence, although the economy expanded until the early 1970s, organized labor declined. Labor leadership also capitulated to successive administrations' Cold War domestic and foreign policy goals, participating in internal purges of some of the most dynamic activists at home, and pressing anti-communist objectives abroad—to the detriment of labor movements in many other countries (Bronfenbrenner et al. 1998; Nissen 1999; Sims 1992; Goldfield 1993).

Table 1 provides data on the decline of U.S. organized labor. Absolute membership increased from 1945 to 1975, with marginal increases continuing through 1980. After that year, the absolute numbers of union members declined. Data on membership as a percentage of the overall workforce tell a more important tale. After a peak relative membership in 1945, the percentage figure dropped 10 percent over 30 years (1975), and another 10 percent over the next 23 years (1998).

Federal, state, and local governmental policies and postures on the *maquiladora* industry in the United States define the second half of the NAALC's applicability to the assembly plants in Mexico. Washington is substantially less concerned with the *maquiladora* industry than Mexico City, but the issue has some relevance nonetheless. Traditionally, the issue turned on attempts to amend or abrogate tariff provisions that promoted the *maquiladora* industry; later discussions focused on approval of NAFTA. From the perspective

Table 1. U.S. Union Membership, Selected Years

Year	Union Membership*	Membership as % of Workforce
1945	14,300,000	35.5
1975	19,600,000	25.5
1998	16,200,000	13.9

* Rounded to the nearest 100,000.
Sources: Famighetti 1996: 157; Bureau of Labor Statistics 1999.

of Washington, any measurable threat to the *maquiladora* program faded in the late 1970s, diminished further in the 1980s, and definitively passed from the realm of possibility in 1994—the year NAFTA took effect and the Republican Party took over the U.S. Congress.

State and local governments in the United States are much more concerned with and supportive of the *maquiladora* industry than Washington. They evince conscious opposition to any measures that jeopardize the industry, including its unionization and/or intrusion from Washington or any international bureaucracy that attempts to apply the NAALC.

In the U.S. borderlands, traditional local business elites have coalesced with a newly evolved "transnational capitalist class" to support the *maquiladora* industry (Sklair 1992). Traditional merchants grow prosperous as the Mexican borderlands expand their populations. Large numbers of Mexicans cross the border to shop, many of whom are *maquiladora* workers who spend significant shares of their wages in U.S. border cities. An early study by Mexico's Banco Nacional de Comercio Exterior (National Foreign Trade Bank) estimated that *maquila* workers spent 60 to 75 percent of their wages on the U.S. side (Williams 1987). The borderlands "transnational capitalist class" is a product of the *maquiladora* industry. The group comprises an assortment of entrepreneurs, developers, executives, managers, bankers, and brokers who work in the industry or service it. These men and women owe their livelihoods to the assembly plants, and they doggedly support the *maquiladora* industry.

Traditional commercial groups and the newer interests affiliated with the *maquiladora* industry have comparatively few members, but they exercise significant political influence in the border states, especially in communities located along the boundary. They are relatively rich, well-educated, and politically sophisticated in a milieu characterized by poverty, inadequate public education, and low levels of political mobilization.

In sum, the political equation in Mexico and the United States offers little succor for a strategy designed to test the efficacy of the NAALC to facilitate unionization in the *maquiladora* industry. In both countries, federal and local governments support the industry, while organized labor wanes in political influence. In Mexico, even the mainstream of the union movement supports the *maquiladora* industry and eschews efforts to organize it. The NAALC in itself cannot compensate for this inhospitable setting, as a review of the several cases pursued under the agreement will demonstrate.

The NAALC and Organizational Initiatives

Initial complaints under the agreement offer little reason to believe that the NAALC will directly contribute to a campaign to organize the *maquiladoras* in the Mexican borderlands, or, for that matter, any Mexican industry elsewhere in the nation. Submissions to the U.S. NAO regarding Mexican *maquiladoras* point to a persistent and unholy alliance between official unions, Conciliation and Arbitration Boards (CABs), local governments, and employers that has thus far effectively crushed several efforts to establish independent unions in the *maquila* sector. Growing participation in cross-border organization by a broader spectrum of unions and NGOs is a positive sign, but can only be seen as an indirect result of the treaty.

To date, there have been 22 submissions to NAOs under the NAALC, 12 of which involve cases in Mexico. Of these 12, seven involved the *maquiladora* industry, and two of the seven complaints were withdrawn. In the following discussion the focus is placed on the latter cases (U.S. NAO 1999).[4] The complaints examined revolved around U.S. and Mexican labor activists' collaborative attempts to organize *maquiladoras* in the cities of Chihuahua, Ciudad Juárez, Nuevo Laredo, Cananea, and Tijuana, as well as a complaint regarding pregnancy testing in plants throughout the border region. Except for the latter case, all of the complaints raise the issue of the right to organize, pointing to the NAALC's lack of adequate enforcement mechanisms in this area.

After failing to win the CTM's cooperation in 1994, the United Electrical, Radio, and Machine Workers of America (UE) and the International Brotherhood of Teamsters (IBT) recruited Mexico's small Authentic Labor Front (Frente Auténtico del Trabajo–FAT), an independent union federation, to launch organizing efforts in two assembly plants owned by Honeywell and General Electric in Chihuahua (U.S. NAO 1994; Myerson 1994a, 1994b, 1994c). In the Honeywell case, activists sought to affiliate with an independent Mexican steel union—the Union of Metal, Steel, Iron, and Allied Workers (Sindicato de Trabajadores de la Industria Metálica, Acero, Hierro, Conexos y Similares–STIMAHCS)—that later participated in several other complaints under the NAALC. During organizing efforts, employers fired workers who were active in the campaign and pressured them to accept severance payments, thereby causing them to lose their right to seek legal redress through the CABs for their unjust dismissals.

In the General Electric (GE) case, the company tried to prevent independent union activists from distributing campaign literature. In February 1994, the activists appealed the case to the U.S. NAO, arguing that the Mexican government colluded with management in frustrating the organizing efforts because it did not apply its own labor code that protects the right to organize unions without employer or government interference. The U.S. NAO ruled that U.S. petitioners' evidence did not prove that the Mexican government was in violation of its own labor code. Since the fired workers did not pursue their case through the Mexican CABs, there was no evidence that the law had not been enforced. The NAO argued that it was not within its jurisdiction to scrutinize company behavior; rather, it was charged with verifying that governments enforce their own laws. For this reason, the NAO did not call for ministerial consultations.

The third case under consideration appeared to signify qualified success for Mexican and U.S. petitioners, although their gains may have been only symbolic. Filed in August 1994, it dealt with Mexican workers in a Sony *maquiladora* in Nuevo Laredo, Tamaulipas. In this case, four U.S. and Mexican human/worker rights groups filed the petition with the U.S. NAO: the International Labor Rights Fund (ILRF), the American Friends Service Committee (AFSC), the Coalition for Justice in the Maquiladoras (CJM), and Mexico's National Association of Democratic Lawyers (Asociación Nacional de Abogados Democráticos–ANAD).

Sony workers attempted to replace their CTM union, but management responded with layoffs and intimidation, police repressed a work stoppage (apparently requested by management) following the representation election, and based on both technicalities and the CTM's preexisting representation of the workers, the CAB denied the independent unions' request for legal recognition. The U.S. NAO found the Mexican CAB in violation of Mexican laws and called for ministerial consultations between Mexico and the United States. The consultations called for remedial measures, including three seminars to educate interested parties on proper union registration procedures. The decision clearly censured the Nuevo Laredo CAB for failing to register the aspiring Mexican unionists (U.S. NAO 1995a; Compa 1997; EPI et al. 1997).

In late 1996, indications surfaced that the complainants in the Sony dispute might return to the U.S. NAO with another petition. They contended that the CAB continued to obstruct the dissidents' challenge to the official union. Hence, Mexico remained in violation of its own labor code and therefore stood in violation of the NAALC. Then-Secretary Robert Reich requested a follow-up report on the issue, lending some hope to the dissidents' ongoing complaint. However, to date, no concrete measures in the workers' favor have been enacted (U.S. NAO 1997: 2).

If these initial submissions indicate that the NAALC has little direct influence on the fate of unionization drives in the *maquilas*, two withdrawn cases suggest that, in some cases, the submission process itself may nudge employers and local officials to recognize independent unions. The United Electrical, Radio, and Machine Workers of America (UE) filed a petition against a GE plant, but withdrew the complaint in January 1995 before the review process was completed. They made this decision in response to the release of an

NAO-commissioned report regarding the labor law issues at stake in the case (U.S. NAO 1995b).

On October 11, 1996, the Communications Workers of America (CWA), the Mexican Telephone Workers Union (Sindicato de Telefonistas de la República Mexicana–STRM), and the Mexican Federation of Unions of Goods and Services Employers (Federación de Sindicatos de Empresas de Bienes y Servicios–FESEBES) filed the fifth petition, a complaint regarding Maxi-Switch, a computer switchboard producer in Cananea, Sonora. Like the Sony case, the unions accused the company and an official union of signing a protection contract to prevent formation of an independent union. Although the NAO review was pending, the CWA withdrew the petition after the Mexican government agreed to recognize the STRM union. In this case, it appears that the threat of an unfavorable NAO review nudged the Mexican government into action. However, the CWA believes that the strikers' just demands, not the NAALC, led to government intervention. Although these cases suggest that the threat of an NAO review may improve conditions for Mexican workers, their success should not be overestimated. Even though the STRM was registered, workers who were fired for organizing the union were never reinstated (Compa 1997; AFL-CIO 1996; CWA 1998).

Human Rights Watch (HRW), ILRF, and ANAD submitted the sixth complaint on May 16, 1997. They protested *maquiladoras'* common use of pregnancy testing. In a study of assembly plants in several border cities, HRW found that officials in 38 of the 43 factories studied routinely administered pregnancy tests to applicants, asked them intrusive questions about sexual activity and contraception, refused to hire pregnant applicants, and intimidated or dismissed employees who became pregnant. The women offered testimony that their union representatives ignored this legal and human rights violation. The NAO found that while the Mexican NAO denied that these practices were either widespread or illegal, Mexico City's Human Rights Commission was aware of the problem and was working to end the practice. The NAO recommended ministerial consultations, and informational seminars will be pursued (U.S. NAO 1998d).

The seventh and final submission referred to the most highly publicized case of any discussed here. It concerns the Han Young subsidiary of Hyundai in Tijuana, Baja California. On October 30, 1997, ANAD, ILRF, the Support Committee for Maquiladora Workers (SCMW), and STIMACHS petitioned the U.S. NAO on behalf of the workers in the plant. Later, Work Safe Southern California, the United Steelworkers (USWA), and the U.S. and Canadian autoworkers unions joined the case.

In the petition, the groups argued that the local CAB actively conspired with the CTM and the Confederation of Revolutionary Workers and Peasants (Confederación Revolucionaria de Obreros y Campesinos–CROC) to block formation of an independent union to replace the CROC's protection contract. In this case, the CAB illegally called for two separate representation elections in order to ensure a CROC or CTM victory. Both were plagued by irregularities, but the independent union, affiliated with STIMACHS, prevailed in each. In an addendum, the NAO found serious health and safety violations that were penalized by the Mexican government, although there is no evidence that fines were assessed. The NAO called for ministerial consultations and, subsequently, the independent union held a strike that was initially ruled illegal, although later successfully appealed in the Mexican courts. The Han Young workers' fragile victories were due, in part, to pressure the Teamsters brought to bear on President Clinton to raise the issue with President Zedillo. Despite this success, the union faces ongoing intimidation from management (U.S. NAO 1998e; CLR 1999; ILRF 1998).[5]

Conclusions

The petitions and hearings to date under the NAALC suggest several tentative conclusions about both the NAOs' official activities in the United States and Mexico, and the union and labor rights advocates in the two countries. First, despite a Democratic administration in Washington, the decisions of the U.S. NAO reflect no conspicuous partisanship in favor of unions or labor rights advocates. The U.S. NAO found in favor of labor in several of the cases, but due to the NAALC's design, the only result was ministerial consultations. The Clinton administration did not take a particularly activist stance on labor's behalf (with the exception of the Han Young case). This outcome is unsurprising given the president's emphasis on free trade and efforts to reduce the Democratic Party's traditional support for unions and the welfare state.

As for labor activism and strategies, the petitions thus far brim with implications for the NAALC and efforts to organize the *maquiladora* industry. In Mexico, the dominant government-aligned unions eschewed participation in initiatives to unionize assembly plants. The local CTM and CROC affiliates, in league with the municipality and CAB authorities, opposed binational organization in the Sony, Maxi-Switch, and Han Young cases. In the Mexican borderlands, the FAT has been the most active participant in binational efforts. The FAT is small and fairly radical; it is a loose federation rather than an established union. Most important for this analysis, the FAT is one of Mexico's few independent labor organizations—it does not toe the governmental line. Labor rights groups active on the Mexican side also boast an independent posture. Although the FAT's work is promising, it is still a marginal actor within Mexico's still largely state-controlled union movement.

Mainstream labor unions in the United States proved rather more forthcoming than their Mexican counterparts in the petitions, but their ranks were incomplete and their enthusiasm for the NAALC clearly limited. An increasing number of unions became involved in the complaints over time. The Teamsters' and UE's initial participation later extended to the CWA, UAW, CAW and USWA, suggesting that a broader coalition of U.S. and Canadian unions may emerge around these issues in the future. The labor and human rights nongovernmental organizations (NGOs) on the U.S. side rallied to the initiative more energetically, but, like the Mexican FAT, they are far less significant than organized labor in the overall panoply of political forces.

Evidence from the petitions suggests a set of problems that the NAALC, in its current form, cannot overcome. Independent union organization in the *maquiladoras* faces a powerful Mexican alliance of government-aligned unions, CABs, local authorities, and employers. The Mexican government intervenes in cases of flagrant labor rights violations in a weak and ephemeral fashion, engaging in temporary "damage control" until negative publicity brought about by the complaints fades from the public eye. Independent organizing efforts and cross-border ties are widespread, but the opponents to genuine labor activists are overwhelmingly powerful. Because the NAALC does not offer mechanisms to enforce rights to organize, collectively bargain, and strike, it can provide no concrete support in resolving this negative scenario. Indirectly, the NAALC has created a forum and a set of institutions that promote the expansion of preexisting cross-border organization initiatives, and has publicized the hurdles independent unions face in Mexico. In the balance, however, the cards are clearly stacked against organizing the *maquilas*.

These broader economic, political, and legal impediments will no doubt remain in place for the foreseeable future; there are, however, a number of modest but hopeful signs worth noting. Positive changes among U.S. and Mexican labor activists, as well as potential indirect effects the NAALC may have on labor organization represent modest countertrends to the general picture. Since 1994, a growing number of unions and labor rights groups in the United States have participated in the NAALC submission process, creating a ripple of cross-border collaboration and activism in conjunction with the NAO public hearing process (Compa 1997; Cook 1997). Many of these groups responded to the U.S. NAO's 1997 request for comments on the NAALC's effectiveness. Specifically, the UAW, IAM, AFL-CIO, ILRF, CWA, and Jerome Levinson (lead lawyer for the Sony-Nuevo Laredo case) all sent detailed comments to the NAO.

The fact that these groups agreed to comment on the NAALC reflects their sustained concern about the issues at stake. More importantly, their analyses identify significant flaws in the NAALC's design and function, and include alternative proposals that could form the platform for a campaign to redesign the agreement or press for the renegotiation of NAFTA. First, activists argue that during NAFTA's negotiation, many unions called for the inclusion of a clause defending core labor standards in the treaty itself, thereby permitting sanctions of labor rights violations that were as strong as those penalizing trade violations. In this regard, the NAALC not only has weak enforcement powers, but the trade benefits member countries gain from the treaty would not be jeopardized in any way by an individual country's violation of or withdrawal from the NAALC. Thus, apart from the flaws in its design, the NAALC can have little influence on the workings of NAFTA as a side accord.

Second, activists argue that the agreement respects each country's sovereignty, and thereby does not challenge existing labor laws in member countries.

For example, the downward spiral of wages in Mexico after the 1995 peso crisis, and U.S. employers' threats to close factories in order to cow union activists are not sanctioned in either country. NAALC institutions can do nothing to reverse these affronts to workers' rights and living conditions, and propose no absolute minimum of internationally recognized labor rights.

Third, because the side agreement is charged with promoting the enforcement of existing laws, it cannot directly sanction those who most often violate workers' rights—companies. In the first two submissions to the U.S. NAO, there was substantial evidence that employers had vitiated workers' rights to free association and to choose their collective bargaining representative without interference. However, the NAO is charged with scrutinizing governments' adherence to and enforcement of their laws. Since the companies successfully pressured workers not to pursue their cases in the CABs, there was no record that Mexico's legal institutions had operated incorrectly. Thus, the NAO ruled that the complaint was outside its jurisdiction, even though there was evidence that the companies violated Mexico's laws. The problem with focusing exclusively on state-level compliance with and enforcement of laws is that it does not hold corporations accountable for their actions.

Fourth, activists argued that the NAOs and the international secretariat have not taken adequate advantage of the opportunities presented by the public hearings and studies commissioned under the accord. Specifically, except for the Han Young case, companies involved in the disputes did not appear at the public hearings, and there is no evidence that the U.S. NAO made a special effort to ensure their attendance. The NAO also placed strict time limits on Mexican activists' testimony. Additionally, in the first two cases, the media was denied access to the public hearings and cabinet-level officials have been conspicuously absent at seminars organized by the NAO as part of ministerial consultation. Finally, after commissioning a report on U.S. employers' threats to close their factories in order to prevent unionization, the international secretariat delayed its release for nine months and only devoted one and a half pages of an official publication to the 110-page report. In short, the U.S. NAO and Dallas secretariat have not used the NAALC's limited institutions to gain the maximum possible results for aggrieved labor activists.

In response to the NAALC's flawed design and implementation, activists suggest a number of alternatives. Ideally, they call for the renegotiation of NAFTA with the inclusion of core labor principles in the treaty, permitting trade sanctions against companies and countries that violate these labor standards. They also call for a number of additional ambitious changes, including: the creation of a code of conduct for U.S. multinationals, modeled after the existing code adopted by the Organization for Economic Cooperation and Development (OECD) and International Labor Organization (ILO); annual audits of the labor practices of companies operating in two or more NAFTA countries; and a provision in the NAALC that would permit workers to take legal action against corporations and permit sanctions for violation of any of the 11 labor principles. On a more modest level, activists call for opening up NAO review hearings to the public and granting them greater publicity, making the submission process less costly and cumbersome, and compelling companies involved in complaints to attend public hearings.[6]

Both criticisms and recommendations reflect U.S. labor activists' growing sophistication in thinking about labor rights in this international context. The comments do not recall U.S. unions' Cold War era paternalism toward workers in the developing world, nor do they reflect protectionist sympathies. Rather, these comments are similar in tenor and concept to recent U.S. labor and student activists' platforms regarding codes of conduct and monitoring for sweatshops in the developing world that are subcontracted by U.S. apparel manufacturers. They call for international enforcement of fundamental labor rights rather than protection of U.S. jobs. This greater maturity, though evident in only a handful of unions and NGOs, could form the rationale for more ambitious international organization campaigns—to which reforming the NAALC could be a start.

While Mexican activists face greater hurdles, recent events give rise to cautious optimism. The passing of the CTM's 97-year-old chief, Fidel Velázquez, and/or a split within Mexico's union movement might increase the influence of the independent (and generally more democratic) unions (Working Together 1996). Specifically, the FAT and other independent labor organizations may be less restrained in their attempts to organize the assembly plants. There is evidence of this in the NAALC submissions. For example, STIMACHS, which collaborates with the FAT, was consistently involved in NAALC submissions throughout the border area, suggesting that independent unionism is not merely an isolated local phenomenon. The democratic lawyers' association's involvement in several submissions also suggests that independent unions are finding allies within civil society that may strengthen their political clout.

Mexican activists have also used favorable outcomes of NAALC submissions to call for broader organizing campaigns. After the Mexican government intervened on behalf of Maxi-Switch workers, "the 'Forista' movement of independent unions in Mexico announced a plan to launch large-scale organizing drives in the *maquiladora* manufacturing areas"(Compa 1997: 18). Likewise, after winning legal recognition of their strike, Han Young workers called a *consulta* (similar to a citizens' referendum) for May 30, 1999, in Baja California to ask *maquiladora* workers their opinions about wages, benefits, the right to organize, and economic policy. Although these groups are still marginal in the Mexican labor movement and the Mexican government still opposes their efforts at every turn, the geographic expansion of their efforts and the extension of their concerns to broader policy questions are encouraging.

Much of this discussion focuses on political impediments to activists' effective use of the NAALC, as well as the agreement's flaws, but the accord can have indirect positive results. Specifically, the NAO review process can shine light on egregious legal violations, mobilize cross-border activists, and promote studies and exchanges that activists may use to their own advantage. In the second GE case and the Maxi-Switch case, for example, activists withdrew their complaints after the threat of an NAO proceeding or the release of an NAO report that brought them favorable outcomes. Likewise, international publicity and the Teamsters' political advocacy for Han Young workers led President Clinton to raise their concerns with President Zedillo, leading to the Mexican government's intervention on the workers' behalf. Finally, the submission process itself requires more intensive coordination and communication between labor activists on both sides of the border than might otherwise occur, potentially leading to more durable ties between U.S. and Mexican activists (Compa 1997; Cook 1997).

Stephen Herzenberg (1996) argues that the cooperative activities mandated under the agreement may also contribute to organizational initiatives in the future. In hierarchical order of potential effectiveness, they include: (1) cooperative programs and special studies launched by the several NAOs and the Dallas international secretariat; (2) public seminars designated by the labor ministers as a means to rectify complaints certified by the NAOs; and (3) initiatives by Evaluation Committees of Experts (ECE), called into existence to assist the several labor ministers to resolve issues. Although to date, the U.S. NAO has not vigorously exploited these resources, activists may learn to use them to their greater advantage.

Since the NAALC's formation in 1994, the three NAOs have organized cooperative programs. They usually involve informational seminars and workshops on topics like industrial safety and hygiene, worker training, quality and productivity, and so on. The programs never consciously focus upon industrial relations and have practically nothing to do with union organization, per se. However, they do tangentially touch on issues of representation and organization in an educational setting. More importantly, they bring together unionists from all three NAALC member nations who may be interested in more than merely cooperating to further safety and hygiene. Like the complaint process, they provide a vehicle for cross-border fertilization and collaboration.

The international secretariat's special studies, which first appeared in 1996, also imply potential for organizational efforts. They provided excellent statistical data on North American labor markets, but had little influence on organization on the ground. A second report, issued in 1997, about the effects sudden plant closings have on freedom of association and workers' rights to organize in the three countries, packs more political punch. The Mexican NAO's censure of Sprint's plant closing in California prompted the Mexican and U.S. labor ministers to commission the study. Although the secretariat delayed the study's release and gave it scant publicity, it may serve activists in the future (AFL-CIO 1996).

In reviewing the first several years of the NAALC's influence, a public seminar in Mexico City in September 1995 stands out as the best example of how the agreement's procedures might catalyze effective organizational efforts that have real significance for unionizing either the *maquiladora* industry or other industries in the three member nations. Then-secretaries Santiago Oñate and Robert Reich ordered the seminar in response to their finding that the Mexican CAB in Nuevo Laredo had unlawfully prohibited Mexican dissident *sindicalistas* from registering their union. Sparked by the presentation and discussion of "Union Registration and Certification: Current Law and Practice in Mexico," and probably emboldened by the attendance of U.S. and Canadian sympathizers, Mexican critics and dissidents roundly and vociferously condemned Mexican law and practice in a rare demonstration of open defiance.[7]

Finally, the Evaluation Committee of Experts (ECE) may have potential for invigorating the NAALC in the future. The committees have not yet been employed, though they may be called upon to analyze the issues raised in Case #9701 regarding pregnancy testing in the *maquilas* (AFL-CIO 1996). The labor ministers may appoint the ECEs to assist in dispute resolution. On the positive side, they may be appointed at the request of any one country. Although the ECEs cannot undertake explicit studies and reports on freedom of association, collective bargaining, and the right to strike, their competence is quite broad. Even more than the cooperative programs, their studies possess the potential for criticism, advocating remedial action, and rallying the faithful to the cause.

While not quite designed to resolve all issues, the skillful exploitation of those several provisions of the NAALC and simultaneous efforts to mobilize the accord's critics on both sides of the border might promise a more vigorous agreement in the future. Used in combination with effective political strategies and Mexico's incipient democratic transformation, friends of the NAALC argue that the agreement may yet contribute to the unionization of the *maquiladora* industry and to other initiatives in the coming years.

The optimists may be correct, but present trends and currents give pause. The political milieu in Mexico and the United States remains hostile to organized labor, to unionization of the *maquiladora* industry, and to vigorous application of the North American Agreement on Labor Cooperation. All of the complaints reviewed to date offer troubling indications that the NAALC is essentially impotent. Despite several favorable decisions at the U.S. NAO level and at the binational level of ministerial consultations including Mexico's labor minister, it appears that the situation on the ground remains unchanged. Local government and CAB officials, employers, and government-allied union leaders operate with little interference from the Mexican state or NAALC institutions, and continue to block dissident unionists' organizational initiatives.

Endnotes

1. For elements of the ongoing critique, see NACLA 1975; Seligson and Williams 1981; Williams and Passé-Smith 1992; Cook 1997; Williams 1996.

2. An eighth case regarding a subsidiary of a Connecticut paper manufacturer may also refer to a *maquiladora* plant; available information on the case does not specify the type of plant involved.

3. On the erosion of the corporatist pact between labor and the state during the 1980s and 1990s, see Williams and Passé-Smith 1992; Middlebrook 1995; Cook 1995; LaBotz 1992.

4. For discussions of the cases that do not involve the *maquila* industry, see Compa 1997; EPI et al. 1997; Cook 1997; Williams 1997; U.S. Department of Labor 1995.

5. A more recent submission to the U.S. NAO involved the independent union at ITAPSA (a subsidiary of Echlin, a Connecticut paper manufacturer located outside Mexico City). Because the available information is unclear about whether this plant is a *maquiladora* or not, it is excluded from this discussion. Like most of the other cases reviewed, it concerns CABs' and official unions' efforts to block independent unions' right to organize and collectively bargain. The U.S. NAO's review recommended ministerial consultations on the case (see U.S. NAO 1998a).

6. This discussion is based on comments sent to the Commision for Labor Cooperation by the AFL-CIO (January 30, 1998), International Association of Machinists (January 29, 1998), UAW (December 22, 1997), Jerome Levinson (December 18, 1997), CWA (January 30, 1998), and ILRF (January 30, 1998).

7. From an interview conducted by Edward J. Williams with a person (who wishes to remain anonymous) who was present at the First Seminar on Registration Procedures for Labor Unions, Mexico City, 13–14 September, 1995.

References

AFL-CIO. 1996. "Upcoming Studies from the Labor Secretariat. Comment to the Secretariat on Review of NAALC by AFL-CIO." *Labor Bulletin of the Commission for Labor Cooperation* 1 (August 10): 2.

Arreola, Daniel D., and James R. Curtis. 1993. *The Mexican Border Cities: Landscape Anatomy and Place Personality*. Tucson: University of Arizona Press.

Bronfenbrenner, Kate, Sheldon Friedman, Richard W. Hurd, Rudolph A. Oswald, and Ronald L. Seeber, eds. 1998. *Organizing to Win: New Research on Organizing Strategies*. Ithaca: Cornell University ILR Press.

Bureau of Labor Statistics. 1999. "Labor Force Statistics from the Current Population Survey." (cited 15 May) http://stats.bls.gov/newsrels.htm.

Center for Labor Rights (CLR). 1999. News alert from the October 6 union of the Han Young *maquiladora*. E-mail communication to author. (3 May).

Coalition for Justice in the Maquiladoras (CJM). 1999. *Annual Report 1998*. San Antonio: CJM.

Communications Workers of America (CWA). 1998. *Review of the North American Agreement on Labor Cooperation: Comments of the CWA*. (30 January).

Compa, Lance. 1997. "NAFTA's Labor Side Accord: A Three-Year Accounting." *NAFTA: Law and Business Review of the Americas* 3 (3): 6–23.

Cook, Maria Lorena. 1995. "Mexican State-Labor Relations and the Political Implications of Free Trade." *Latin American Perspectives* 84 (22): 79.

Cook, Maria Lorena. 1997. "Regional Integration and Transnational Politics: Popular Sector Strategies in the NAFTA Era." Pp. 516–40 in *The New Politics of Inequality in Latin America: Rethinking Participation and Representation*, Douglas Chalmers, Carlos Vilas, Katherine Hite, Scott B. Martin, Kerianne Piester, and Monique Segarra, eds. New York: Oxford University Press.

De la Garza, Enrique. 1994. "Sindicalismo y restructuración productiva en México." *Revista Mexicana de Sociología* 56 (1): 3–28.

De Palma, Anthony. 1995. "Figures Confirm a Million Job Losses." *Latin American Weekly Report* (3 August): 340.

Economic Policy Institute (EPI), Institute for Policy Studies, International Labor Rights Fund, Public Citizen's Global Trade Watch, Sierra Club, and U.S. Business and Industrial

Council on Higher Education. 1997. *The Failed Experiment: NAFTA at Three Years.* Washington, D.C.: EPI.

Famighetti, Robert, ed. 1996. "U.S. Union Membership, 1930–1994." P. 157 in *The World Book Almanac and Book of Facts.* Mahwah: World Almanac Books.

El Financiero Internacional. 1994. "Unions Pressure U.S. on NAFTA Labor." (19–25 September): 3.

Goldfield, Michael. 1993. "Race and the CIO: The Possibilities for Racial Egalitarianism during the 1930s and 1940s." *International Labor and Working-Class History* 44 (Fall): 1–32.

Herzenberg, Stephen. 1996. *Switching Tracks: Using NAFTA's Labor Agreement to Move toward the High Road.* Border Briefing no. 2. Albuquerque: Interhemispheric Resource Center.

International Labor Rights Fund (ILRF). 1998. *Comments for NAALC Review.* (30 January).

LaBotz, Dan. 1992. *Mask of Democracy: Labor Suppression in Mexico Today.* Boston: South End Press.

Lajous, Adrian. 1989. "Teléfonos de México." *El Informador* (Guadalajara) (11 July): A4.

Latin American Weekly Report. 1994. "Rural Alert." (21 July): 316.

Mexican Investment Board. 1995. "Mexico's National Railroad System." *Mexico Investment Update.* Mexico City: Mexican Investment Board.

Mexico Business Monthly. 1993. "Mexico: Economic Indicators." (November): 22.

Mexico Update. 1990. "New Phase of the Pact." 1 (June): 2

Middlebrook, Kevin. 1995. *The Paradox of Revolution: Labor, the State, and Authoritarianism in Mexico.* Baltimore: Johns Hopkins University Press.

Myerson, Allen R. 1994a. "Big Labor's Strategic Raid in Mexico." *New York Times* (12 September): C1.

Myerson, Allen R. 1994b. "Reich Supports Mexico on Union Organizing." *New York Times* (13 October): C7.

New York Times. 1993. "Mexico Sells Off State Companies." (27 October): A1.

New York Times. 1994. "Mexico's Pact for Stability in the Economy." (27 September): C1.

Nissen, Bruce, ed. 1999. *Which Direction for Organized Labor? Essays on Organizing, Outreach, and Internal Transformations.* Detroit: Wayne State University Press.

North American Congress on Latin America (NACLA). 1975. "Hit and Run: U.S. Runaway Shops on the Mexican Border." *Latin America and Empire Report* 9 (5): 1–32.

Quintero, Cirila. 1998. "Sindicalismo en las maquiladoras fronterizas. Balance y perspectivas." *Estudios Sociológicos* 16 (46): 89–116.

Review of the Economic Situation of Mexico. 1990. "Development Bank Subsidies." 66 (774): 232–37.

Review of the Economic Situation in Mexico. 1994. (August): 360.

Roxborough, Ian. 1984. *Unions and Politics in Mexico: The Case of the Automobile Iindustry.* Cambridge: Cambridge University Press.

Ryan, John Morris, Donald A. Allison, Jr., Thomas G. Squire, Gary D. Suttle, Kay B. Warren, Harry R. Bradley, Robert B. Johnson, Gerald F. Croteau, Cathy C. Council. 1970. *Area Handbook for Mexico.* Washington, D.C.: Superintendent of Documents.

Seligson, Mitchell A., and Edward J. Williams. 1981. *Maquiladoras and Migration: Workers in the Mexican-United States Border Industrialization Program.* Austin: Mexican-United States Border Research Program, University of Texas.

Sims, Beth. 1992. *Workers of the World Undermined: American Labor's Role in U.S. Foreign Policy.* Boston: South End Press.

Sklair, Leslie. 1992. "The Maquila Industry and the Creation of a Transnational Class in the U.S.-Mexico Border Region." Pp. 69–88 in *Changing Boundaries in the Americas*, Lawrence A. Herzog, ed. San Diego: Center for U.S.-Mexican Studies, University of California at San Diego.

Tiano, Susan. 1994. *Patriarchy on the Line: Labor, Gender, and Ideology in the Mexican Maquila Industry.* Philadelphia: Temple University Press.

Tierney, Jennifer. 1994. "New Wage, Price Pact Signed." *El Financiero Internacional* (3–9 October).

U.S. Department of Labor. 1995. *Foreign Labor Trends: Mexico, 1994–1995.* Mexico City: U.S. Embassy.

U.S. National Administrative Office (NAO). 1993. *North American Agreement on Labor Cooperation between the Government of the United States of America, the Government of Canada, and the Government of the United Mexican States.* Washington, D.C.: Bureau of International Labor Affairs, U.S. Department of Labor.

U.S. National Administrative Office (NAO). 1994. *North American Agreement on Labor Cooperation; Public Report of Review of NAO Submission, no. 940001 and NAO Submission no. 940002* (12 October). Washington, D.C.: Bureau of International Labor Affairs, U.S. Department of Labor.

U.S. National Administrative Office (NAO). 1995a. *Public Report of Review of NAO Submission, no. 90003* (11 April). Washington, D.C.: Bureau of International Labor Affairs, U.S. Department of Labor.

U.S. National Administrative Office (NAO). 1995b. *Status of Submissions; Public Report of Review of NAO Submission, no. 940003* (11 April). Washington, D.C.: Bureau of International Labor Affairs, U.S. Department of Labor.

U.S. National Administrative Office (NAO). 1997. *Work Plan for July 1996-February 1997.* Washington, D.C.: Bureau of International Labor Affairs, U.S. Department of Labor.

U.S. National Administrative Office (NAO). 1998a. *Public Report of Review of NAO Submission, no. 9703* (21 August). Washington, D.C.: Bureau of International Labor Affairs, U.S. Department of Labor.

U.S. National Administrative Office (NAO). 1998b. *North American Agreement on Labor Cooperation: A Guide* (April). Washington, D.C.: Bureau of International Labor Affairs, U.S. Department of Labor.

U.S. National Administrative Office (NAO). 1998c. *Status of Submissions under the North American Agreement on Labor Cooperation (NAALC)* (21 December). Washington, D.C.: Bureau of International Labor Affairs, U.S. Department of Labor.

U.S. National Administrative Office (NAO). 1998d. *Public Report of Review of NAO Submission, no. 9701* (12 January). Washington, D.C.: Bureau of International Labor Affairs, U.S. Department of Labor.

U.S. National Administrative Office (NAO). 1998e. *Public Report of Review of NAO Submission, no. 9702* (28 April). Washington, D.C.: Bureau of International Labor Affairs, U.S. Department of Labor.

U.S. National Administrative Office (NAO). 1999. *Status of Submissions under the North America Agreement on Labor Cooperation (NAALC)* (16 September). Washington, D.C.: Bureau of International Labor Affairs, U.S. Department of Labor.

Williams, Edward J. 1987. "The Maquiladora Program: Mexican and U.S. Perspectives." Pp. 47–64 in *Arizona's Relations with Northern Mexico*, Michael C. Meyer and John A. Garcia, eds. Phoenix: Arizona Town Hall.

Williams, Edward J. 1990. Interview with a Cananea worker-activist. Tucson, Arizona (7 August).

Williams, Edward J. 1996. "The Maquiladora Industry and Environmental Degradation in the United States-Mexican Borderlands." *St. Mary's Law Journal* 27 (4): 765–815.

Williams, Edward J. 1997. "Discord in U.S.-Mexico Labor Relations and the North American Agreement on Labor Cooperation." Pp. 161–79 in *Bridging the Border: Transforming Mexico-U.S. Relations,* Rodolfo de la Garza and Jesús Velasco, eds. Lanham: Rowman and Littlefield.

Williams, Edward J., and John T. Passé-Smith. 1992. *The Unionization of the Maquiladora Industry: The Tamaulipan Case in National Context.* San Diego: Institute for Regional Studies of the Californias, San Diego State University.

Working Together. 1996. "May Day Marks Growing Rift in Mexico's Official Unions." 18 (May–June): 1.

IV
European Borders:
Environmental Issues and
Development Cooperation

Social Movements and the Transborder Chloride Pollution of the Rhine River

Emmanuelle Mühlenhöver[*]

Abstract

Drawing on the insights regarding the international pollution of the Rhine River, this paper reconsiders the role of social actors, borders, and environmental rationales in the context of transborder environmental issues. It first focuses on the potential importance of social movements in transborder conflicts. Although their role is generally underestimated, these complex actors may be of particular importance in setting the agenda for transborder pollution issues. The paper then reconsiders the role of borders, arguing that they often serve as strategic assets for social actors, who use them to achieve their goals. Thus, in addition to contributing to the emergence of transborder pollution problems and impeding their settling, borders might also endorse a strategic dimension in these issues. Finally, the actors' goals in transborder pollution conflicts are reexamined. Although they always sound "green enough," their rationales are not necessarily as environmentally friendly as they appear. Indeed, environmental arguments often serve as covers for other rationales, be they economic, strategic, or political.

Introduction

In the growing literature on cross-national and transborder environmental problems, three phenomena stand out. First, those actors that play crucial roles in the political process leading from agenda setting to resolution of transborder environmental problems are mostly institutionalized. Second, borders are viewed as having merely structural impacts on either the emergence or the development of these pollution problems. Third, the actors' apparent environmental rationales are systematically considered to be authentic. All three of these analytical patterns are certainly helpful in understanding the various issues related to transborder pollution cases, from the emergence of the problem at stake to the

---

* Mühlenhöver is Visiting Fellow at Harvard University and Ph.D. candidate at Sciences-Po, Paris, France.

formal or informal collaboration instated to solve it. However, given their dominance and popularity, these patterns may leave the reader with the mistaken impression that there are no other types of actors involved, no other possible roles for borders, and no alternative underlying reasons for environmental arguments.

This paper aims to provide a different approach from a different perspective to all three of these factors: analyzing actors, borders, and the environment. The first section of this paper argues that in addition to institutional entities, some informal, nonstructured political actors—such as social movements—may play an important part in transborder environmental issues. The question is then to determine what role they play, at what stage they intervene, and how they achieve their goals. The second section, which focuses on borders, argues that these actors may increase their effectiveness by consciously using the political and symbolic aspects of borders as part of their strategies. This highlights the fact that borders might not merely have a structural impact upon the emergence of transfrontier environmental problems, but they might also endorse a strategic dimension. Finally, the third section assumes that in some cases, actors' apparent environmental concerns may not be consistent with their real objectives. This calls into question the true nature and purpose of the rationales underlying formal environmental arguments, and stresses the general fragility of environmental rhetoric.

To illustrate these alternative perspectives, this paper uses the case of the chloride pollution of the Rhine, one of the most studied cases of transborder river pollution. To keep it simple, this case study is hereafter referred to as "the chloride case." In a nutshell, for several decades salt residue discharges, dumped into the Rhine River mainly by French potash mines, polluted Holland's main source of drinking and irrigation water. This foreign chloride pollution caused severe economic losses in the Netherlands, against which opposition gradually emerged in several segments of the Dutch population. After years of suffering from the effects of this pollution, a strong social movement emerged in Holland in the early 1970s to protest French salt dumping. As a result, the Dutch government asked its French counterpart to inject the unwanted salt into the subsoil, and in the mid-1970s, the French government agreed to do so to settle the emerging diplomatic conflict. French public opinion, however, opposed this international agreement, as the injections were considered potentially hazardous to the local environment and it was feared that the injections could contaminate groundwater sources located nearby. Soon after, a second "environmental" social movement emerged in France, opposing the injections. The opposition between the two movements became so strong that in 1979, the two governments put a hold on their diplomatic relations. This unprecedented diplomatic crisis within the European Community explains why the environmental conflict became a major political concern for both countries into the 1990s.

It is important to point out the methodological and epistemological limitations of this study. The following is a narrative and interpretive history of the role played by social movements in the events that led up to the 1979 Holland-France crisis and its aftermath. The study draws heavily upon the Dutch and French protagonists' personal observations and perceptions. Two decades after the events occurred, some of their recollections might be inaccurate or distorted by historical reconstruction, which would reduce the epistemological reliability of the data. Moreover, findings from a single case study do not allow for much generalization. Therefore, the aim of this paper is not to propose new theoretical perspectives. It is rather to induce some new ideas about social actors working collectively and, as such, playing a crucial role in transborder pollution issues and using symbolic dimensions of borders in their strategies, whether or not these are used to defend environmental causes. Further case studies would be needed to confirm these findings and develop a theoretical framework from them.

Reconsidering Actors

As far as actors are concerned, most literature that focuses on transborder pollution issues follows common patterns. To begin with, most studies traditionally consider institutionalized entities to be the key actors. For instance, the objective of most analyses is to understand how local, regional, and/or national administrations and international organizations deal with the transborder issue at stake. Those scholars who stress the importance of nonstate actors focus on clearly defined and institutionalized entities as well, such as nongovernmental organization (NGOs). While this is extremely helpful in understanding the social actors' strategies, most such analyses choose not to examine more informal, broader-based actors—such as social movements. This is perhaps due to the fact that most of the literature focuses on "downstream" processes, as scholars concentrate on the management and problem-solving phases of the problem. By doing so, they sometimes neglect to examine "upstream" events, that may have occurred during the development and agenda-setting phases. By focusing on these "upstream" events, this section aims to provide a different perspective on the actors involved in transborder environmental issues.

To begin with, the role and importance of structured entities, especially state-related ones, should be reconsidered. Many scholars[1] actually concur that transborder environmental problems are best solved by direct dialogue between states, dialogues at the regional level, or, increasingly, by cooperation "based on agreements among associations of local governments" (Scott 1997: 111). Subnational groups are increasingly perceived as crucial actors in the management of transborder issues (Atkey 1970; Hocking 1993; Cooper 1986; Duchacek 1988, 1990; Dymant 1990).

> In these days of rapid economic and political change on a global scale ... subnational actors, such as states, provinces, regions, and cities, are playing an increasingly vital role in international relations—a trend that shows every indication of continuing and, indeed, accelerating ... [As a result,] border regions permeate the sovereignty of the nation-state as they respond to the exigencies of transboundary problem solving—largely through informal cooperation and tacit

agreements among local authorities. Understandably, much discussion has taken place about the increasing importance of subnational diplomacy and border regions in the international system (Ganster et al. 1997: 4).

The gradual emergence and institutionalization of this type of subnational diplomacy seems to be particularly dominant in Western Europe, where regional and (increasingly) local actors are involved in problem solving. Scott, for instance, stresses that "the slow evolution of transboundary interaction in Western Europe from informal encounters among local officials to more structured and institutionalized forms of policy making has been widely documented and assessed" (1997: 107). One tangible example of such cooperative mechanisms would be the emerging "Euroregions," which have a significant ability to structure and organize regional transborder cooperation in environmental matters (Scott 1997). Although generally private law organizations, these Euroregions are mainly composed of official institutions and administrations, including local governments. At any rate, entities described as intervening in the transborder problem-solving procedure are all well defined and structured, as well as state related (whether their level of jurisdiction is central, regional, or local).

In the specific domain of transboundary water pollution issues, the conclusions found in the literature on role distribution are very similar. Many scholars believe that "purity of water … is a matter for cooperation between neighboring states" (Anderson 1997: 39), explaining why most macrolevel studies on transborder water issues focus on bi- or multinational institutions. Well-known examples of such institutions include the U.S.-Canadian International Joint Commission (Lemarquand 1993; Becker 1993) and the International Commission for the Protection of the Rhine (ICPR), particularly relevant in the chloride case study (Bernauer 1995, 1997; Bernauer and Moser 1996). Similarly, at the microlevel, other authors stress the capacity of local authorities to conclude international agreements to solve parochial transborder pollution problems (Iglesias 1995).

Most scholars writing on the Rhine's chloride pollution follow this trend and tend to assume that the main actors involved in the management of the pollution issue are state-related entities. Some authors, for instance, generically refer to the actors involved in the case as "France," "the Netherlands," or "Germany" (Bernauer 1995, 1997). Others insist on "institutionalized" procedures "among national government agencies" (Bernauer and Moser 1996: 399), or on the role that smaller, state-related entities, such as municipalities, may play (Bernauer and Moser 1996: 393).[2] Given the general agreement that these state-related entities dominate the political management of virtually any transborder pollution problem, it is only natural that the analyses attempting to explain the actors' negotiation strategies point at typical state-related behaviors. In the chloride case, the listed management strategies are typically "cooperation within international institutions," "financial compensation," "coercion," or "issue linkage." All of these strategies belong to the states' classical bargaining methods.

The field observations made in preparation for this study, however, indicate two major points of dissent with these analyses. For one, it is not apparent that well-structured, "state-related" actors are solely predominant in the management of transborder environmental issues. In the chloride case, for instance, many nonstate actors appeared and disappeared throughout the process and played a major role throughout the conflict. It was the opposition between two national social movements that placed the issue on the international agenda and spurred the diplomatic turmoil. It follows from there that the actors' strategies instigated to solve the problem did not solely belong to the domain of classic, realist, "public" diplomatic strategies. Even if diplomatic interplay between the French and Dutch governments was intense in the chloride case and obliterated more subtle strategies, other nonstate, nonstructured actors were involved, using strategies of their own that were sometimes as decisive as those of the state-related entities. This leads to this study's first hypothesis: social actors, formal or informal, may have an impact upon transborder pollution issues, especially if several social entities (such as NGOs, unions, public opinion, and so on) work together (or at least pursue the same goal at the same time) to create and manage a transborder environmental issue.

Before developing this hypothesis any further, it seems necessary to recall the role traditionally conferred to social actors within the context of transborder environmental issues. Several scholars have actually acknowledged that "influential international nongovernmental organizations and transfrontier political coalitions ... apply pressure on both governments and international organizations" (Anderson 1997: 39). The importance of NGOs has actually been quite widely acknowledged. Manno, for instance, underlined the capacity of NGOs to influence bilateral negotiations between the United States and Canada on the Great Lakes water quality agreement (1994: 69). Other authors have claimed that NGOs have the capacity to create a "diplomatic niche" that allows them to fill in gaps in official negotiations, whether they are multilateral or bilateral (Princen and Finger 1994). Some authors have also pointed to the strategies used by interest groups (Hocking 1993; Duchacek 1990), or have focused on network strategies (Hocking 1993). Most of these studies, however, remain quite limited in two respects: they often consider social actors independently from each other, neglecting to analyze the impact of their joint actions; and they often focus on nonstate actors that are, again, quite structured and monolithic, such as NGOs or firms.

These limitations are particularly evident with regard to the chloride case analysis. Bernauer and Moser stress that some "nonstate actors, such as firms" (1996: 401) are involved in management, and that "information networks have also developed at the nongovernmental level, such as the IAWR (International Association of Waterworks in the Rhine basin)" (1996: 393). However, their listing of the nonstate actors involved is incomplete; under the heading "nongovernmental actors," they only list a few companies, one company network, one municipality, and one NGO (Bernauer and Moser 1996; Bernauer

1995). It certainly provides an excellent basis for analyzing civil society's role in transborder issues, especially since most other studies do not even mention these societal actors. Yet, the mere analysis of these monolithic and independent entities is insufficient to explain all the dynamics at work in this complex transborder pollution issue. Indeed, in this case, the interactions between various structured nonstate actors—such as NGOs and firms—and between them and less structured actors—such as protesters or public opinion in general—actually explain the emergence and evolution of the transborder pollution issue.

It is argued here that these types of multifaceted and complex interactions between formal and informal social actors, and the way they work, correspond to and can best be comprehended by the concept of "social movements." Social movements are difficult to define because they are a constantly changing informal actor, or "actor nebula," whose existence is equivocal and whose structure, if there is one, is elusive. In spite of their confusing appearance though, it is the central hypothesis of this paper that two conflicting national social movements (NSM)—that is, social movements that emerged in a national context and valuing this context—have surfaced in the chloride issue, one in France, the other in the Netherlands. It is further argued that the opposition between the two movements is responsible for setting the agenda of the transborder pollution issue. Although these NSMs have gone unmentioned in the literature so far, they should be considered as potential actors in cross-national environmental issues.

So far, the theoretical background that would help examine this topic is poorly developed. Indeed, almost none of the literature on social movements examines the role of "national" social movements in cross-national contexts. There is abundant literature on the internal role of national social movements (Touraine and Wieworka 1984; Tilly 1999; Klandermans and Jenkins 1995), but it does not study their potential international or transfrontier influence. Studies on transnational social movements, however, have been done (see Nerfin's "third system theory" [1986]). In these studies, the national dimension of the movements is lacking, as only transnational movements are analyzed.[3] Since this paper is concerned with the *transborder* role that *national* social movements might play, the only theoretical background that aids the discussion is Walker's work on social movements and world politics (1994). Nonetheless, the analytical instruments proposed by Walker remain insufficient for this particular analysis.

Before explaining the NSMs' role in the chloride case, it is essential to define what is precisely meant by this concept since "social movements" are defined in many different ways by different scholars. All of the meanings have some common traits, however, allowing the following definition to be agreed upon.

> A social movement exists in a process whereby several different actors, be they individuals, informal groups and/or organizations, come to elaborate, through their joint action and/or communication, a shared definition of themselves as being part of the same side in a social conflict. By doing so, they provide a meaning to otherwise unconnected protest events or symbolic antagonistic

practices, and make explicit the emergence of specific conflicts and issues (Melucci [1989] in Diani 1992).

Social movements usually share four common features:

1. They consist of informal interaction networks. Social movements may encompass structured actors such as NGOs, interest groups, and so forth, but they also include other less definable entities, such as public opinion and protest groups and/or protest events. The nature of the relationship between their different components, also called "segments," may vary. It is clear that whatever form and shape these relationships may take, the dynamics of the global entity (the social movement) that result from the aggregation of small entities (the segments) are different than the mere sum of the individual components' dynamics. What this means is that communication between the segments and their occasional joint action reinforces their combined strength, in part because it reinforces their mutual image. That, in turn, reinforces their influence potential. Therefore, the actions and strategies of NSMs should be studied individually (that is, each segment's strategy should be looked at separately), but their effect on issues should also be considered as resulting from a group dynamic.

2. Social movements share common beliefs and a common definition of problems; however, they may have different motivations for tackling each problem.

3. The actions of social movements are often based on protest, emerging to denounce events that seem unfair or with which they disagree. Their purpose is not to repair, but to draw attention to a problem and to get it on the political agenda.

4. The actions of social movements occur largely outside institutions. Their denunciation of institutional decisions are often actions of public protest that occur outside of administrative arenas, in some cases even illegally.

In the chloride case, two "national" social movements were involved, each of which adhered to these four defining criteria. In the beginning of the conflict, a Dutch Social Movement (DSM) emerged to protest the saline pollution of the Rhine, for which the French were held responsible. In response, a social movement arose in France to protest Dutch demands for reparation (injections) that were deemed environmentally unacceptable. The opposition between these two movements became so intense that it caused a diplomatic clash between France and the Netherlands and put the chloride issue on the international agenda. To understand why these two social movements emerged and opposed each other so strongly, it is necessary to go back to the causes of the initial chloride pollution. Following the chronology of events, the reader will see how first the Dutch and then the French NSM emerged, what their respective social components were, and what the group dynamic that resulted from the aggregation of these individual segments provoked.

The Dutch Social Movement emerged in direct response to the saline pollution of the Rhine. The river has been polluted for decades, if not centuries. Chemical discharges from innumerable plants located next to the Rhine have made it "the biggest sewer of Europe," as the press has denounced. It contains more than fifteen hundred toxic substances (cadmium, lead, arsenic, and so on). Although these pollutants have been responsible for several major environmental crises (such as the famous Sandoz spill), the cause of the Rhine's biggest environmental and political crisis seems harmless by comparison to these heavy metals. Twenty to thirty million tons of sodium chloride, also known as simple table salt, were discharged into the river each year for decades. These massive discharges were extremely harmful from an environmental point of view, as excessive salinity causes two main types of damage: corrosion of water pipes, which leaches harmful agents into drinking water, and agricultural damage, as salt concentrations higher than 150 chloride ions per liter considerably reduce plant growth (at least by 25%).

The Dutch were far more vulnerable to saline pollution than other Rhine-dependent countries for three primary reasons. First, the Netherlands is located downstream, at the very end of the Rhine, meaning that they receive the chlorides discharged by all upstream riparian countries and, therefore, the highest concentrations of salt pollution. Second, the Dutch rely on the Rhine for 70 percent of their drinking water, whereas other riparian states do not rely on it for that purpose at all. Hence, its salinity provoked massive and recurrent salt-related corrosion of the Dutch water pipe system, requiring very costly renewal programs. Third, agriculture and horticulture are two of Holland's largest production and income resources, drawing about 70 percent of their irrigation water from the Rhine. This explains why the saline pollution of the river had such a great impact on the country's environment and economy.

As far as the origin of the pollution is concerned, dozens of nonpoint sources discharge salt into the river. The main point sources, however, are easily identified: 70 to 80 percent of the salt is dumped into the river by mines in Germany and France. Of these, the main single polluter is the Mines de Potasses d'Alsace (MDPA), a state-owned French potash mine located in Alsace. Because the pro-

Table 1. Types of Water Consumption by Rhine Riparian States

	Switzerland	France	Germany	Netherlands
Drinking Water				X
Industrial Processes	X	X	X	X
Energy Production				X
Leisure	X	X	X	X
Wastewater	X	X	X	X
Navigation	X	X	X	X
Irrigation				X

Source: Bernauer 1997: 161.

duction of potash yields a high amount of chloride by-products, the MDPA chose to dispose of this waste by dumping it into the "free" sewage facility (the Rhine River) at a high discharge rate (about 353 pounds [160 kilograms] per second[4]). This explains why Dutch protest focused on the MDPA, although it was only responsible for as much as 40 percent of the Rhine's chloride pollution.

Given the Netherlands' heavy reliance on the Rhine for both irrigation and drinking water, the environmental and economic costs borne by the Dutch due to excessive salinity, and the responsibility of the MDPA for that salinity, it is quite natural that the Dutch requested that the MDPA change its chloride discharge policy. Requests from Dutch farmers and waterworks became particularly compelling from 1972 onward. Indeed, a severe drought caused the Rhine's chloride concentration to reach 350 milligrams per liter in 1971, considerably reducing both the quantity and quality of Dutch agricultural output. Farmers lost an average of 40 percent of their yearly income, and up to 9 percent of the Dutch GNP was lost.

The protests voiced by farmers and the resulting public outcry were the basis for the Dutch Social Movement (DSM), which developed incrementally from then on. Because of their tremendous losses, Dutch farmers were the first to request that their government convince the French government to force the MDPA to stop, or at least to reduce, their salt discharges. They were soon joined by the Dutch waterworks, united in the International Association of Waterworks in the Rhine basin (IAWR), a powerful lobbying entity with many connections to the Dutch government. Ecologists then joined the protest movement as the Reinwater Foundation (literally, the "Pure Water Foundation"). This organization was very efficient in raising public interest in the chloride issue. It launched boycotts against French (specifically Alsacian) products, and created a symbolic and spectacular International Water Court to judge the polluters. The Reinwater Foundation was the main interlocutor of Dutch and international press and television coverage.[5] Their effectiveness in the media was reinforced by Reinwater's ability to orient international cultural events to its cause. For instance, the 1983 Biennial Environmental Film Festival held in Rotterdam was "captured" by the organization to draw attention to the salinity problem. As one witness stated, "[during the festival] all attentions were focused on transborder environmental issues, be they about water, air or wastes, which are, as we see now, the new sources for international conflict" (L'Express 1983). Lobbying political parties and targeting influential politicians were other strategies used by Reinwater to draw attention and supporters. The organization was eventually able to gather support from all political parties, partly because the Dutch population so massively supported their claims.[6] The Dutch population indeed joined the movement as spontaneous protest events emerged all over the country with concerned citizens participating in sit-ins and demonstrations. Broad public sympathy and support were actually partly encouraged by the media, another segment to support the social movement.

The incremental development and accumulation of these protest strategies finally resulted in the Dutch government voicing its citizens' demands and asking the French government to become involved. At the request of the Hague, several interministerial conferences were held to find alternatives to dumping salt in the river. The first of these conferences was held at the Hague in 1972. It resulted in the signing of the Bonn Convention in 1976, in which the French government agreed that MDPA salt discharges would be reduced to 265 pounds (120 kilograms) per second. The remaining salt (88 pounds [40 kilograms] per second) would be disposed of by either subsoil injections or topsoil stacking in Alsace. Neither of these solutions were enacted, however, as the French perceived these alternatives as harmful to the French environment, and opposed the agreement. This opposition gave birth to the French Social Movement (FSM).

To understand the development of the FSM, one must look at the French perspective. Although the French government agreed to injecting or stacking the excessive salt, the population of Alsace claimed that none of the alternatives to dumping were environmentally acceptable, as they carried risks to the Alsatian subsoil. Both stacking and injecting the salt were indeed thought to have the potential to contaminate the Grande Oolithe, supposedly the largest European underground freshwater layer. The link between saline pollution, the MDPA, and groundwater quality was easy to make as the company had already fouled groundwater so severely in the 1930s that the water supply from the Rhine had to be interrupted for several months in the entire region. Fears that a similar catastrophe would recur were strong, particularly among older citizens. Communities near the potential injection sites were the first to oppose the dumping alternatives. They started to defend their interests with the creation of "NIMBY" (Not In My Back Yard) structures. This local opposition soon transformed into a regional one.

Soon after the signature of the Bonn Convention, a regional association against the injections of chlorides called the Association de Défense contre les Injections de Saumures et de sauvegarde des ressources de la Haute-Alsace (ADIS) emerged in May 1978. Its well-organized protest strategies soon won the attention and support of most of the mayors in the Alsace region. Whether for truly environmental reasons or for political motives, the mayors indeed wished to protect their municipalities from groundwater pollution. The key role of this organization in the geographical extension of the protest movement is evident. In the beginning, only about twenty municipalities were concerned with the chloride issue; whereas after ADIS emerged, offering a structured protest group, more than one hundred and fifty municipalities banded together for the cause.

The FSM's second geographical transition, from regional to national, was then managed by a single person who made the issue a political and national affair. This political entrepreneur was one of the leading members of ADIS and a French Member of Parliament (MP). By voicing local concern in parliament—a national arena—this key actor alerted the entire French political class to the local injection problem. His political mediation was particularly successful as it garnered support from all major political groups in just days. Even the center-right party (then in power) soon joined the club in opposition to the injections. What had been a local environmental issue thus became a major national debate. The chloride issue made several appearances on the front pages of all major French newspapers and was featured on the televised evening news.

As these descriptions demonstrate, the power bases and extension mode of the two NSMs (French and Dutch) were quite different. The French Social Movement developed along a geographical line, growing out of a popularly supported local issue, then reaching the regional level, and finally, through politics, the national level. The DSM grew along a social and professional line: first, farmers and waterworks people constituted the core of the movement; then ecologists became involved; and finally, with the help of the media, it swayed public opinion. In spite of these differences, the DSM and the FSM did share four common features. First, both fulfilled the four criteria characteristic of social movements outlined earlier.[7] Second, in spite of differences in their initial support bases and evolution mode, their aggregation processes followed the same path:

- The actors most affected by environmental damage protested and formed the core of the emerging social movement (Dutch farmers and water workers, Alsacian communities)
- Other actors, not directly affected, yet concerned by the adverse effects of the problem, joined the emerging movement as the core group spread word of the situation (French and Dutch environmentalists, Alsacian local elected officials)
- Using news media, the movements were backed by broader support groups and eventually by general public opinion
- Protests become so strong and the pressure so intense, that the cause was taken up by political parties and, eventually, by national governments

Another common feature that the two movements shared is that both NSMs evolved dialectically: the FSM largely evolved in response to the DSM, and vice versa. The last and most important common feature is that in both cases, NSM segments managed to put the transborder chloride issue on their respective national agendas through joint and complementary actions, and from there onto the international agenda.

This shows how important social actors, individually as well as collectively, may be in solving transborder environmental problems. One of the hypotheses of this study is thus affirmed: interactions between different social actors must be taken into account as much as individual strategies, as group dynamics can tremendously influence transborder environmental cases. It should also be recognized that social actors may involve themselves at the very beginning of critical situations, not merely in managing them later.

Most of the literature on transborder environmental issues is concerned with the final stage of transborder pollution problems—management. Whether these analyses focus on state-related entities or on civil society, their basic assumption is the same: actors play a significant role at the denouement of the problem. For instance, studies that focus on states concentrate on regime theories to explain the management rationales at work (Young 1997; Bernauer 1995, 1997). Their purpose is to understand how governments and/or administrations get together to manage the pollution problem, and which financial and/or legal agreements they employ to solve it. Analyses of the Rhine chloride pollution problem have typically followed that trend, examining the international management aspects of the situation. Bernauer, for instance, "focuses on three types of phenomena: the existence or nonexistence of international river management institutions (IRMIs) and their geographical distribution; the features and functions of international river management; and the performance of institutions designed to manage international rivers" (1997: 158). Studies that focus on strategies used by civil society usually examine "civil management" issues as well, concentrating on governance schemes to discover why and how nonstate actors behave to solve transborder environmental crises. Using this perspective, many case studies try to see how NGOs improve bilateral cooperation by creating "diplomatic niches" (Manno 1994), how citizen groups from different countries get together to solve common problems, or how private companies cooperate to improve environmental conditions (Hocking 1993). In the chloride case, Bernauer and Moser found that to avoid further transborder troubles "many ... big chemical companies [on the Rhine] ... are no longer passive and reluctant targets of environmental regulations ... [It] appears that they have increasingly cut back on their emissions in anticipation of future legislation" (1996: 407).

These analytical perspectives are absolutely crucial to understanding social dynamics. However, because they are predominant and focus on the sole management part of the story, they might lead to the impression that actors, and particularly nonstate actors, merely assume management functions. By doing so, they might gloss over the fact that social actors may, in some cases, be involved as well at prior stages (such as agenda setting) or in "negative management" activities (such as blocking solutions to transborder pollution issues). A thorough comprehension of the role of actors, and social actors in particular, in transborder pollution problems therefore requires a look "upstream," that is, at the dynamics at work at the very beginning of the decision-making process.

The chloride issue shows that many nonstate actors were involved as early as the agenda-setting stage. By definition, social movements emerge to denounce events that seem unfair. Their purpose is not to settle, but to identify a problem and draw political attention to it. Thus, social movements, and most of the social segments they are composed of, typically intervene at the agenda-setting phase of the problem, as stated in the definition. In addition to this early involvement in the policy-making process, social actors may intervene to block rather than facilitate management of the problem. In the case of the Rhine, the French and Dutch social movements built and used powerful and efficient blocking strategies to dominate the Franco-Dutch diplomatic agenda, as the 1979 diplomatic crisis demonstrates.

The reasons for the 1979 crisis lay in the escalating opposition of the two social movements' claims. To understand the increasing tension between the two countries, one must look back to the events of 1976. That year, the French government agreed to slow down the salt dumping when it signed the Bonn Convention. However, domestic protests against the Bonn Convention became so strong that in September 1977, the French government was forced to pull back from enacting a decree for its ratification. It was defeated by its own majority. The Dutch government, the Dutch people, and concerned organizations were disappointed by this first withdrawal.

A year later, the French government made a new attempt to fulfill the agreement, but had to step back once again. The decree for ratification was sent back to the Senate for further study—a typical way of delaying sensitive issues—causing tensions to rise in Holland. Meanwhile, the leading Alsacian Member of Parliament, whose "environmental" activism was mentioned previously, edited and distributed to the congress a new report that underlined the dangers of injecting the salt in the subsoil. This caused the government's third defeat, as it tried to present the decree for ratification of the Bonn Convention to the parliament on December 5, 1979. Seeing that the convention had no chance of being ratified, the French government removed the project from the parliamentary agenda, signifying its defeat.

The Dutch government had long been patient with these numerous delays. Public frustration and anger had been growing since 1972 and, by 1979, political tension in Holland had become so intense that this last diplomatic "betrayal" was deemed unacceptable by the Dutch people. As a result, the Hague recalled its ambassador from Paris, thereby putting a hold on Dutch-French relations "for an undetermined period of time," according to official explanations. This decision was a direct consequence of pressure exerted on the Dutch government by various segments of the social movement, such as lobby and interest groups (farmers and water workers), ecologists (the Reinwater Foundation), the media, and judging by newspaper headlines and polls, a broad section of the Dutch public. Since it coincided with a crucial period for European unification (several new countries joined the European Community in 1979 and the European Parliament was just born), this was considered a very serious crisis in European diplomatic history. Indeed, such a diplomatic clash had not occurred in Europe since World War II. This event affirms the importance of social movements in transborder issues and stresses both their agenda-setting and blocking capacities. In the chloride case, both capacities seemed to result from their strategic ability to use the political and symbolic dimensions of borders. Can borders, then, still be considered to have merely a structural role in the emergence and development of transborder environmental issues?

Reconsidering Borders

With regard to transborder environmental issues, and especially water pollution issues, boundaries are traditionally interpreted in two rather contradictory ways. First, they are perceived as being "permissive" factors, facilitating the emergence of environmental problems. Second, they are perceived as being "complication" factors, impeding resolution of transborder problems. If, as will be seen, the chloride issue corroborates these two aspects of borders, it also puts forward a third way to comprehend them in the context of transborder pollution issues, namely as strategic factors for social actors.

Beginning with the "permissive" function of borders, it is generally thought that "human consumption of scarce resources, such as water, often produces negative externalities [8] [and that] such externalities are particularly likely to occur in the case of shared natural resources" (Bernauer 1997: 161). A boundary—that is, a delimitation between national jurisdictions—may be an incentive to pollute, as the polluter may not be liable for externalities that occur across the border. In cases of river pollution, the border's causal role in pollution cases is obvious: as long as an industry can get rid of unwanted by-products by dumping them into a river without having to pay the price of environmental externalities, it is rational for it to do so. The border is thus a clear permissive factor for international river pollution, increasing the likelihood of "the tragedy of the commons" (Badie and Smouts 1994; Le Prestre 1997). This may result in "the collapse of fisheries, the collapse of irrigated agriculture along transboundary rivers, or a shortage of drinking water" (Bernauer 1997: 162).

This is precisely what happened in the chloride case. Given its proximity to the Rhine, dumping salt waste into the river was the most rational thing for the MDPA to do since it was less costly than any other waste management technique available, all the more since the MDPA was not legally liable for the pollution in Holland (at least not when they began the dumping). In the absence of any legally binding authority, the environmental price of the pollution was thus solely borne by the victims of the pollution. Hence it is true that "like rivers, externalities often flow in one direction: from upstream downward" (Bernauer 1997: 162). In a national context, it is likely that the legislator, in response to the victims' outcries, would have enacted remedial policies, either by creating financial incentives or by enforcing preventive or curative laws. In this international context, and in the name of sovereignty,[9] the French government decided not to rule against the polluter, so the usual principle ("the polluter pays") did not apply. The border could almost be seen here as a legal incentive for firms to keep on being "free-riders."[10]

This encourages the idea that borders are not only permissive factors, but also causal factors of transborder river pollution. Most analysts actually see borders as engendering conflict: "externalities and the associated problems of overuse of freshwater are often major sources of conflict among riparian countries" (Bernauer 1997: 162). Some actually claim that the chances for a transborder environmental conflict to arise "are more severe if: (1) the quantity and quality of water available to the riparians is low, and no other sources are available at acceptable cost; (2) the entitlements of the riparians are ill-defined, not defined, or contested; and (3) externalities and their impact are clearly discernible and direct" (Bernauer 1997: 162). Each of these points is corroborated by the chloride issue.[11]

Still, other studies highlight the fact that border regions are peripheral and, as such, are not given the necessary attention by governmental authorities, encouraging environmental negligence. Some scholars also stress the fact that transborder pollution might be a consequence of intensive cross-border production, trade, and subsequent settlement (as in *maquiladora* [assembly plant] case studies along the U.S.-Mexican border). Although these two points are relevant to many cases of pollution, they are not in the chloride case for two reasons. First, the Rhine is not itself a territorial border between France and the Netherlands.[12] Rather, it is a geographical link between two nonadjacent territorial entities. Thus the "peripheral" and "contiguity" implications of borders are irrelevant. Second, Holland and France are not of symmetrical status, so that the latter argument loses its validity.

Borders can also be complicating factors that impede the resolution of the pollution issue at stake. Generally, cooperation between sovereign actors who represent antagonistic national interests proves to be more complex than cooperation between "internal" actors who, although they may not agree, are subject to a common authority in the end. Collaboration between internal forces therefore usually succeeds, one way or another, whereas, as Bernauer underlines, "the international nature of freshwater problems, and consequently, the need for international cooperation, often introduces additional difficulties" (1997: 157).

Such cooperative difficulties recurrently transpired in the chloride case. The best example of this is the international negotiations that were held to finance the salt evacuation once it had been decided that the French would inject it. As the French government agreed to reduce salt discharges into the Rhine, it asked for financial contributions from all other riparian states since France was only one of the saline polluters. Germany and France agreed to pay 30 percent each, Switzerland assumed 6 percent, and Holland the remaining 34 percent of the cost. Although this financial scheme was set in 1972 and approved by the parties in 1976, it took many years before common financing procedures were worked out. Some governments refused to pay before seeing that France was really beginning the injection program, and the French did not want to start the actual evacuation before money was made available. By delaying the evacuation of salt, the joint-financing program harmed the effective management of the pollution problem more than it helped. The MDPA continued discharging chlorides at the same high rate for years, arguing that it was justified in doing so since an international agreement could not be reached. When examining the function of the border, the aim of most authors (Bernauer and Moser 1996) is understandably to examine how national governments, local administrations, and even civil society (NGOs, interest groups, and companies) try to overcome the obstacle of the border by creating bilateral institutions or informal governance systems.

In addition to these analyses, another aspect of borders should be considered. While borders increase the chances that an environmental problem will emerge (permissive function) and decrease the likelihood that it will be resolved (complication function), they also might interfere with environmental issues due to the strategic function that actors give to them. This function confers upon borders a very different role in transborder pollution issues for at least two reasons. First, that role is continuous and not punctual, coming into play for the whole duration of the issue (from emergence to resolution). This differs from the permissive role of borders, which comes into play only at the emergence of the problem, and from its blocking role, which occurs only during the resolution phase. Second, this function confers an instrumental (versus a structural) function to borders. From this perspective, social actors have a proactive, not a reactive, relation to the border, using them rather than being subjected to them.

Social movements are not supposed to interact with borders. Instead, they are assumed to act only internally, leaving advocacy of their interests at the international level solely to the state. Most authors believe that "to make contact, Social Movements and world politics require some kind of mediating agent … [and therefore] the State has to mediate with other States" (Walker 1994: 670). However, in some cases, social movements may act by themselves in "world politics," using borders to build up their own "diplomatic" strategies. This process is quite evidently at work in the chloride case.

To begin to analyze this phenomenon, one must start with social actors' perception of borders. Advancing the hypothesis that NSMs "use" borders as strategic tools first implies that at least some of their segments are aware of their political meanings and strategic usefulness. As explained previously, a social movement is by definition an actor that is not border, but issue, related. Traditionally, it organizes its advocacy to fit the problem, regardless of where it lies. Logically, in the case of a transborder environmental problem, the emergence of a social movement should be structured around the environmental issue, not along the border. In the chloride case, however, two different environmental problems were put forward by opposing social movements: pollution caused by salt discharges (for the Dutch), and pollution caused by salt injections (for the French). This contradicts the idea that social actors are not concerned with borders. In any given transborder issue, these actors cannot help but acknowledge the existence of borders as at the core of the conflict. Still, one could argue that "national" social movements act within the boundaries of their own nations, using their government as an intermediary at the international level. If that were the case, they could be said to be border bound in their emergence, and border blind as far as strategy building is concerned. However, this theoretical statement proves wrong in the chloride case.

In this case study, social movements wielded international rationales and perpetrated both direct and indirect international actions, often using the border as an asset to build their "diplomatic" strategies. The Dutch and French social movements' segments actually built three types of "diplomacies": international, symbolic, and transnational. For the sake of clarification, "international" diplomacies mean any NSM strategy targeting state-related entities, such as foreign states or intergovernmental organizations (IGOs). According to international law, these strategies are deviant since the only "normal" dialogue partner for a state on the international level is another state (or IGO). "Symbolic" diplomacies refer to those social actors' discourses that use frontiers in such a way that they parody state diplomacy. "Transnational" diplomacies mean any NSM strategy that targets other social foreign actors.

Numerous international strategies were at work in the chloride case. Many segments of the French Social Movement, for instance, established contact with Dutch or European officials between 1972 and 1984. During this time span, the FSM did not want the chlorides to be injected into the French subsoil, whereas the French government wished to go forth with the injections to be in compliance with its international agreements with Holland. Because they were ignored on the French side and excluded from the international decision-making process related to this topic, some segments of the FSM decided to "go international" themselves. Their objective was thereby to present their position directly to their opponents and to European Community (EC) decision makers. Three main types of these "international paradiplomacies" were actually involved.

First, "direct dialogue" procedures were invented. In 1984, the ADIS extended an "official" invitation to several Dutch ministers "for them to realize the environmental disaster that injections would cause to the Alsacian environment" (L'Alsace 1981). The Dutch ministers attended, and returned the invitation six months later, inviting "an Alsacian delegation, composed of union-representatives, Alsacian ecologists and mayors, so that they could realize the damages caused to the Dutch by the salt emanating from the MDPA" (L'Alsace 1982). An official dialogue was thus established between the Dutch government and a panel of the most powerful representatives of the FSM. That dialogue was solely based on the initiative of one segment of the French Social Movement. The French government, supposedly the official intermediary between the two actors, was thereby bypassed (and quite displeased) by the FSM's "direct" diplomacy.

The second international paradiplomatic strategy invented by NSMs is that of recourse to "third parties." Several attempts were made by segments of both the Dutch and French NSMs to use international institutions to contact officials from third-party countries (in this case, Germany or Switzerland) in order to gain their support. The Council of Europe, the European Commission, and the European Parliament were all used for this purpose. The Dutch IAWR, for example, opposed dumping and favored injections. To advocate its position, it lobbied German delegations in most European institutions to draw their attention to the potential adverse effect of chlorides on German waterworks. This "linkage" strategy hoped to convince the German delegation to intervene in favor of the Dutch in further international negotiations. Similarly on the French side, delegates from ADIS often tried to lobby official delegations at international meetings to interfere with official discourse. Their purpose was to gain support by providing third-party delegations with alternative sources of information that stressed the environmental damage linked with injections.

The third type of international paradiplomatic strategy that occurred in the chloride case resembles "good offices" procedures, as defined by international law (Nguyen Quoc Dinh, Dailler, and Pellet 1994). In 1980, for instance, an Alsacian interest group called Communauté d'Intérêts Moyenne Alsace-Breslau (CIMAB) contacted the Ecumenical Council to learn what could be done to plead their cause at the international level. As a result, a Franco-German Christian delegation was sent to talk to the Dutch delegation to the International Commission for the Protection of the Rhine (ICPR). Similarly, on October 23, 1982, at the request of several Alsacian interest groups, the International Ecumenical Secretariat delegation to the Council of Europe went to Germany to alert its government to the environmental dangers of chloride injections in the Alsace region. Here again, a linkage strategy was attempted, as the delegation stressed the risks that injections would mean for the German environment. On a much smaller scale, both the 1980 and 1982 strategies are reminiscent of the "good offices" provided by the Vatican in conflict prevention.

These three types of NSM strategies bring forth the idea that sometimes NSMs "behave like states" to advocate their causes on the international scene. Indeed, they mimic "direct diplomacy" strategies, use "mediation," and appeal to "good offices" arbitration. As a matter of fact, all of these strategies are described by international law as being the typical means used by states to prevent (or solve) conflicts. This leads to the conclusion that when NSM segments want to overcome a conflict, they may have the same relationship to the border as states. That, in turn, means two things: that they may have the same perception of borders as states, and that they may employ similar strategies to work around them.

Either notion contradicts the idea that social actors, and informal social movements specifically, do not to deal with borders because they cannot take them into account. As seen earlier, NSMs, in spite of their informal, noninstitutionalized, nonborder-bound nature, are not border blind. On the contrary, they seem to be "border conscious," even "border-oriented," since some of their segments integrate borders into their action strategy.

Some "symbolic" diplomatic strategies used by NSMs further corroborate this idea. For instance, several NSM segments have made explicit references to international law and war, two themes that are typically attributed to states. By doing so, they sought to make borders the central issue in their advocacy campaigns. Using the symbolic rhetoric of war, the Alsacian ADIS organized a resistance movement against the Dutch "enemy." To lay a symbolic siege against Dutch "aggression," ADIS members took possession of a bunker located on the Maginot line, the most famous French line of defense against Germany during World War I. Even today, the French refer to the symbol of the Maginot line as the last barrier against foreign invasion. This warlike occupation lasted 286 consecutive days, 24 hours a day. It was supported by most other segments of the movement, who referred to it as a very successful action.[13] This symbolic action became extremely popular in the region, especially with the press; the opponents' actions were often given front-page coverage, incorporating pictures of the bunker.[14] National media soon took it up, and even the international press became interested—at least two articles appeared in the *New York Times*. By using the war rhetoric, the ADIS clearly inscribed the FSM's action within state boundaries, using the border to stress the nationalistic dimension of their protest. The symbolism was well rendered in newspapers, as articles referred more and more frequently to the "salt war" (*la guerre du sel*). It is clear from this example that several segments of the French Social Movement were not only conscious of the symbolic power of the border, but manipulated it very effectively.

The Dutch Social Movement (DSM) on the "other side" also used the symbolism of the border, albeit in the context of international law. The Reinwater Foundation created an International Water Court to judge chloride polluters in the same manner that an international court of justice would. The court had no actual legal power, so its judgments remained merely symbolic. Yet, it used real lawyers, real judges, and powerful infrastructures, including television transmission systems and computer facilities. The enterprise had a great influence on the media and, thus, on public opinion—partly because the event was well orchestrated and tailor-made for mass media consumption. Another reason for its success was the emotional charge linked with the event. The "trial" lasted several weeks and interest from the Dutch public rose with the cumulating evidence of French responsibility. Again the border was used consciously, this time by the DSM.

On yet another level, the Rhine case study shows that both NSMs had "transnational" diplomacies whose targets were foreign social actors. These transnational undertakings included boycotts. The Reinwater Foundation threatened that if Alsacian farmers and wine producers kept up their opposition to the salt injections, they would urge the Dutch people to stop purchasing Alsacian products. Although the final economic effect on Alsacian exports was not impressive, the effect of this maneuver on French public opinion was considerable. It had an even greater effect on Dutch public opinion: polls showed that a majority of the Dutch people was ready to support the boycott. Even the Dutch government encouraged this transnational boycott, albeit in a more subtle and indirect manner. The Hague eventually threatened to try the trick at the international level—to boycott French goods and upcoming armament imports in particular. The mimetic effect in this case was unusual, as governments imitated the NSM strategies.

Another example of transnational diplomacies can be found in the publicity strategies instigated by the main protagonists. For instance, the Dutch IAWR published information booklets about the adverse environmental and economic effects of chloride pollution.[15] These brochures, published in French, German, and English, were propaganda aimed at shaping public opinion in the entire Rhine region. They almost always pointed to the MDPA as being solely responsible for the saline pollution, even though the MDPA was actually responsible for only 40 percent of it. This strategy worked well, at least internally. Dutch history and geography books incorporated the IAWR information, stating that "the MDPA was the principal polluter of the Rhine," making France Holland's biggest environmental enemy. The MDPA counterattacked with publications that accused the IAWR of disseminating false information. These new brochures, translated into the same three languages, were distributed to the same targets—schools, municipalities, and the media—for "debriefing" purposes. As the March 2, 1982 issue of *L'Alsace* stated, "*la guerre des brochures*" (the brochure war) was launched in the transnational world.

Yet another example of transnational diplomacy is to be found in the MDPA's linkage strategy. Although a state-owned company, the MDPA instigated its strategy without the knowledge of the French government. In 1984, the MDPA faced a troublesome situation: while the French government, under increasing international pressure, requested that test drillings be made, increasingly violent local Alsacian opposition hindered the drilling. The situation seemed desperate for the MDPA. A solution was conceived by an MDPA engineer. He suggested that the injections be made, not at the locations initially planned, but a few meters from the German border. Moreover, the drilling would not be done vertically, but diagonally, so that the 5,906-foot (1,800-meter) deep injections would end up in German subsoil. This plan was thought to change Germany's position on the injections. The sites chosen by the French engineer for the diagonal injections were very sensitive (and sensible) locations: they were to be made right next to German thermal sources. Saline pollution of the subsoil aquifer there would have ruined the entire region's economy. This linkage strategy worked out well for the MDPA, as it caused the German government to drastically change its position in international negotiations. Bonn suddenly asked Paris to stop, or at least to alter, the injection program.

This plan would never have worked if local social actors had not pursued the linkage strategy at the microlevel. Given their very public position, the state-owned MDPA could not admit publicly that they were trying to blackmail the Germans with such an enterprise. To threaten the Germans, they needed the mediation of French social actors, who had no political liability. This mediation was actually quite easy to provoke. As they moved the injection site, the MDPA knew that protests would move along with the problem. French mayors, ecologists, and the media did indeed spontaneously organize protests. To give more weight to their claims, the protesters informed their German counterparts of the kinds of environmental threats they would face if the injections were done in the border region—and it worked.

These examples show that social segments, in the form of firms, environmentalists, politicians, or other local actors, are well aware of the political dimension of the border, and that they know how to use it as a strategic resource to achieve their ambitions—in international as well as symbolic and transnational ways. Three conclusions about the role of borders in transborder environmental issues can thus be made at this point. First, borders play not only structural roles (permissive and blocking) in the emergence and resolution phases of an environmental problem, but also conjunctive and strategic roles throughout the policy-making process—from agenda setting to resolution. This "strategic" dimension depends both on the actors' perception of the advantages associated with using the border, and on the actors' skills and resources. Second, social actors—although informal and not border bound—are not border blind, but border conscious, and even potentially border-oriented, for they reify the border to achieve their goals in many ways. Third, the concept of "paradiplomacy" suggested by Ganster and others (1997) should be amended. It was proposed to explain subnational foreign policy strategies in transborder issues. The starting point of this concept was the finding that:

> … regions are emerging from the paternalistic control of the state, defining their own policy interests and, more and more, engaging in their own form of foreign policy by establishing transboundary problem-solving dialogues … Subnational paradiplomacy, the generally informal avenue through which regions articulate and promote their interests internationally, has thus begun to take root in transboundary situations (Duchacek 1986). This allows border regions not only to establish an international local-government dialogue but also to promote transboundary problem-solving mechanisms that serve basic regional needs (Ganster et al. 1997: 7).

The concept of "subnational diplomacy" needs be widened to include all social actors' "diplomatic" strategies, while dissociating the notion of subnational diplomacy from that of subnational paradiplomacy. While subnational public actors build paradiplomacies in border regions, private actors may also have foreign policy ambitions regarding transborder environmental issues. Therefore, perhaps the notion of "subnational diplomacy" should be reserved for public subnational actors, such as local authorities (e.g., states), while the concept of "subnational paradiplomacy" should be reserved for private actors (such as NGOs, interest groups, social movements, and so on). The challenge, then, is to see what kinds of relationships paradiplomacies may have with official diplomacies, both in legitimacy and efficiency. Ganster and others also raised the problem of the paradoxical relation between subnational diplomacy and state diplomacy:

> While locally driven transboundary and interregional cooperation can help nations link up, the supporting role of central governments should not be underestimated. This, at the same time, represents a basic contradiction: nation states have, as yet, not been able to not devise administrative and legal mechanisms for dealing with subnational foreign policy … The apparent contradiction between intensifying subnational paradiplomacy and the persistence of national authority—a paradox of state power—is central to the issue of transboundary cooperation. No viable alternatives to the nation state as an organizer of political, social, and economic life exist. What is required, then, is a reconciliation of national-sovereignty concerns and national-policy prerogatives with the desire and need of subnational governments to conduct their

own brand of foreign policy. For this reason, utilitarian concepts, based on arguments of administrative efficiency, environmental protection and the promotion of citizen's welfare have frequently been employed to legitimize attempts to institutionalize transboundary cooperation (1997: 9–10).

If this legitimization through regimes and/or institutionalization is effective for reconciling national and subnational diplomacies, it is unlikely that it will reconcile diplomacies and paradiplomacies because in many cases the two work toward divergent goals. As shown earlier, paradiplomatic strategies often emerge when social actors disapprove of the direction taken by official diplomacies. Paradiplomacies are then put in place to bypass or overcome official diplomacies. The two diplomacies, however, are not always opposed; in some cases, paradiplomacies are intended to reinforce official positions. In the chloride case, this often proved true on the Dutch side, as Dutch official positions backed up (and were also supported by) the DSM's own strategies. For example, the symbolic International Water Court, with its impressive logistics, was only rendered possible by significant (yet confidential) funding from the Dutch government. How, then, can the relationship between the two often contradictory, but sometimes complementary, diplomatic rationales be described? Is there a generic rule to understand this relationship? Does it have an influence on the efficiency of paradiplomacies?

From the chloride case study, it appears that the relationship between the two types of diplomacies depends on two main factors: (1) whether the social movement segments tend toward international or transnational strategies; and (2) whether they are supported by or opposed to their home state. By crossing these two parameters, the following four standard situations can be identified:

In the first of the four situations outlined in Table 2, the relationship between the two diplomacies is conflictual. This was typical of many segments of the FSM (see earlier discussions of the French "direct" diplomacy, "good-offices," and "third-party mediation"). However, the official diplomacy was not seriously threatened by the FSM's paradiplomacy. It seems that at the international level, where states predominate, paradiplomacy is most often not a serious rival to state diplomacy. In the second case, it is assumed that paradiplomacies may be efficient if they manage to capture the media's attention. In that case, paradiplomacy may be a serious threat to the credibility of official diplomacy. In the third case, the "diplomatic" capacity of the NSM is likely to be efficient, as it is backed by its own state's official diplomacy. This support gives social actors the means to access (and eventually convince) many official dialogue partners, such as IGOs or other delegations. The only drawback for social movements' paradiplomacy in this case is that both its political and strategic autonomy are reduced. Obtaining official support and funding is likely to push many segments to obey official recommendations and follow governmental strategies. In the fourth situation, official diplomacy and paradiplomacy complement each other. Paradiplomatic strategies are likely to have the best chance of success in this configuration, as they benefit from both official support and strategic autonomy.

Table 2. Relationships between Official Diplomacies and Paradiplomacies

	Type of Paradiplomacy	
Relationship between official diplomacy and paradiplomacy	International	Transnational
Conflictual	1. Confrontational	2. Short-circuit
Consensual	3. Substitution	4. Complementarity

Yet again, political autonomy may be reduced. Thus, in some cases, borders may have very complex (and potentially contradictory) effects on transborder environmental issues. Borders not only create structural conditions that abet and perpetuate environmental harm in transborder regions, but they may also be used by social actors in diplomatic strategy building.

One could wonder why social actors are so ingenious and inventive in dealing with these transborder environmental issues. In existing analyses, the nature of the social actors' environmental motivations has not really been questioned. Throughout this case study though, it became clear that social actors were working only sometimes to defend their environment. Just how "green" were the French and the Dutch social movements? To determine why the movements mounted these paradiplomacies, the true nature of so-called "environmental" claims must be examined.

Reconsidering the Environment

On the international level, ecological justifications have always been put forward by all categories of opponents. But the environmental arguments did not stand. Every one, in fact, had its real motivations on the one hand, and its ecological pretexts on the other (Schreiber 1996).

Henri Schreiber, former head of the MDPA Department for Environmental Affairs, made this declaration regarding the abuse of "environmental justifications." Given his professional position, the assertion could be suspected of being biased. However, a thorough analysis of the "environmental" motivations involved in the chloride issue shows that Schreiber was right in many respects. Although some of the subnational actors truly had environmental motivations, for most of the leaders of the two social movements, the issues at stake were everything but environmental. Nonetheless, all actors used environmental "referentials" to maximize their negotiation power (Jobert and Müller 1984). Labeling the issues as "environmental" was perceived as a rallying cry, and was often used to mask unrelated political rationales. In some cases, the environment was also used to disguise economic and/or social rationales. These devious uses of environmental claims can best be revealed by deconstructing certain events in the chloride case.

The archetype of political misuse of environmental arguments in the chloride issue took place on May 29, 1979, during a parliamentary session of the Council of Europe that was specifically dedicated to the issue of chloride pollution in the Rhine River. Due to social and political pressures, the French government had by then already withdrawn the decree for ratification of the Bonn Convention twice from the agenda (in 1977 and 1978). To alleviate the political tensions between France and the Netherlands, the Council of Europe decided to examine the case. Most national, subnational, and international representatives interested in the issue were present at this session—from French mayors to Dutch environmentalists—as every group involved in the conflict sent delegates to Strasbourg. However, their motivations were not driven solely by environmental rationales. Some of the subnational delegates had very clear political reasons for being there.

It should be stressed that attending the session was an excellent opportunity for public and private subnational actors to gain political power for several reasons. First, it was a useful way for these actors to become known to the "outside" world—that is, by subnational or national delegates from other countries who were also involved in the issue. Second, and perhaps more importantly, the session was an excellent opportunity for subnational actors to establish contact with the "inside" world—that is, with other subnational actors or national delegates (ministers, heads of administrative departments, and so on). Third, the session provided a prime means for subnational actors to get publicity from international media, since more than thirty journalists from several countries attended the session. Indubitably, going "green" at this occasion was an excellent way for any subnational social actor to target a broad audience, which, in turn, was an effective means of gaining power.

One of the leading members of the French ADIS, who happened to be a member of the French parliament, understood this opportunity allowed for a large political audience. He did not, however, use it to defend the Alsacian environment against the salt injections. Instead, he took the opportunity to launch a political attack against the French government. For French politicians, the whole chloride issue was first and foremost a way to challenge the government; their eventual aim was to force the leading political party to resign, or at least to face a significant political defeat. That is why, paradoxically, the French ADIS delegate defended the Dutch stance against the French government's position. The attack was so aggressive that a Dutch diplomat stood up to publicly defended the French government. The media turned France's internal dissension into an international affair. By doing so, they further weakened the French government, which was precisely the MP's objective. He admitted in a March 1996 interview that by intervening in this session he had "hoped to destabilize the government. The fact that the attack was done publicly at the international level, in front of international opinion, was done on purpose, and was supposed to help discredit the government both internally and internationally." Another French politician who attended the Council of Europe session further confirmed that, in this case, "... the international context was far from being neutral. It gave more weight to everybody's claims, for the audience was larger." The MP thus managed to transfer the battle line from the French/Dutch conflict to the French government/French parliament conflict. It is clear from this example that, at least for some actors, the environment was not a primary concern in the chloride debate. Their concerns were political, and the chloride issue was a pretext to express their dissatisfaction with the government's administration. The international audience served as a means to voice and amplify the conflict.

This phenomenon actually recalls the "two-level-game" played by states (Putnam 1993).[16] Indeed, this example clearly shows how and why subnational actors may use environmental arguments on the international level to achieve political goals on the internal level. Social actors, as states, may have two sets of goals, one internal and another external. In their case, however, the principle is inverted. Subnational actors use the pressure potential they gain on the international scene to increase their pressure potential on the national level, whereas states have the opposite attitude. Meanwhile, they use the protest capacity they build up on an internal basis to access the international scene.

Further down the green line, other "environmental" arguments served economic interests in the chloride case. One French union representative who participated in the same session of the Council of Europe confirmed that his group "took advantage of the international dimension of the conflict ... To us, the environment was not really the matter, but protesting against the injections was an opportunity to voice our ambitions, which were to save jobs in the region by creating a salt mine." As long as environmental concerns promoted their economic interests, most Alsacian union representatives and politicians actually supported the fight against the injections, using pro-environment rhetoric. However, as soon as the two interests diverged, these actors returned to their initial positions and became once again environmentally indifferent. When the idea of a salt mine arose in the late-1970s, Alsacian politicians suddenly cast off their "green" agendas to promote the development of a huge salt facility that would have been a disaster for the Alsatian environment they had so strongly defended for many years. At the same time, the European "salt cartel" (comprising German, French, and Dutch companies), silent until then on this issue, suddenly joined the social protest for "environmental" reasons. It aided the launch of "green" national press campaigns against the creation of an Alsatian salt mine. In truth, however, the cartel was opposed to any new competitor entering the salt market. Clearly, environmental arguments were used in this case to mask economic ones.

Economic rationales were even more compelling to the Dutch. Dutch farmers openly asserted that their interests were primarily economic, and that public support was easier to get when protests were led under environmental auspices. Another indication of the economics underlying Dutch environmental claims was the type of legal arguments used in the several lawsuits that waterworks people, farmers, and horticulturists filed against MDPA. These arguments were exclusively economic, focusing on Dutch losses due to saline pollution. Yet in interviews, the victims usually pointed to environmental damage first, and mentioned economic losses second.

This is another case of using the environment as a banner to gain popular support through the media. Some scholars who focus on public policy analyses call this a "referential-building" process (Jobert and Müller 1984). The principle is simple: social actors whose only clout lies in their protest capacity try to gain support from other social actors (including media and public opinion) in order to increase their pressure potential. To garner the broadest possible support for their cause, they tend to use the most appealing slogan they can muster. The slogan may or may not be a true reflection of their real concerns. The goal is to choose the right catchword, the argument most likely to make people feel concerned for the issue and lend support to the cause. It so happens in the chloride case that environmental slogans were often chosen for their ability to structure protest.

In the end, there is even cause to wonder whether environmental concerns mattered to anyone in the chloride affair. Indeed, two more issues call further into question the authenticity of the "green" aspect of the subnational actors' claims. The first is that the entire Alsacian protest against injections was organized along false environmental arguments. The ADIS protested the injections on the grounds that they would pollute Europe's biggest subsoil potable aquifer, the Grande Oolithe. This argument was actually an obfuscation. The injections were certainly to be made in a subsoil layer, but into a nonpotable aquifer layer 5,906 feet (1,800 meters) below the surface. The real potable aquifer layer lies only 164 feet (50 meters) below the surface, and is separated from the target layer by 5,741 feet (1,750 meters) of solid, waterproof limestone. There was, therefore, almost no risk of contamination. Several ecologists and various local political protagonists were aware of this difference between the two aquifer layers; however, they still decided to fight to "Save the Oolithe," because they knew that under this banner they could gather much support from the local population—and it worked. The same actors (ADIS members, ecologists, and politicians) even tried to "sell" the Oolithe argument during the May 1979 Council of Europe session. However, the attempt failed since the attendees with technical counter-expertise reports at their disposal caught on to the swindle.

A second issue that further questions the authenticity of environmental claims is that the international solution reached in 1986 satisfied most of the protagonists who had been fighting "for the environment" in spite of the fact that this was actually the worst possible solution for the environment. It consisted of an agreement to stack the salt discharge in Alsace on top of a mere plastic cover. This solution was a real threat to the potable aquifer, as percolation risks were considerable. Saline leakage was very likely to occur and pollute the potable water that was only 164 feet (50 meters) below the stacks. Although the risks were real for both the French and the German environments, not a single opponent showed up at public inquiries to protest the solution. Environmental concerns seemed to have faded away. In addition to questioning the "environmental honesty" of the movement's leaders, one might also question the degree of public concern. It is as if the entire protest movement—the press, public opinion, and other groups participating in the FSM—were only temporarily interested in the quality of their environment. As long as it was a "hot" political issue, the environment was of real concern. The final outcome of the issue shows how low environmental concerns truly weighed on the scale.

By no means does this suggest that none of the protagonists' environmental motives were sincere. At some point, both the Alsacian and the Dutch public opinion, several ecologists, and perhaps the media truly fought for environmental rationales. However, these genuine environmental concerns remained limited both in scope and time, lasting only as long as they were driven by political leaders or the media. Many of the social movements' leaders were dishonest and used the environment as a political vector to gain audience and power to achieve other unrelated goals.

The three main points underlined here—the social nature of the actors, the strategic role of borders, and the questionable integrity of environmental claims—could be specific to the Rhine case, as most other studies on transborder environmental issues do not mention them. However, it may be that other cases present certain similarities to the Rhine case. In order to ascertain the situation and eventually develop some theoretical conclusions from these observations, more attention should be given to social actors, and particularly to emergent informal social groups (such as social movements) in further analyses of transborder environmental issues. Attention to these actors should help determine the factors involved in the emergence, development, and management of transborder environmental affairs with more accuracy.

Endnotes

1. See Scott 1989, 1993; Hansen 1992; Martínez 1986; Strassoldo and Delli Zotti 1982; and Anderson 1982.

2. Bernauer and Moser describe municipalities as "nonstate actors"; in this paper, however, municipalities are defined as state-related entities. Although they are not direct representatives of the state, municipalities are endowed with some of the regalian attributes of a state. They have both administrative and public functions, differentiating them from civil society and/or private entities, such as NGOs, interest groups, and so on, which are classified here as nonstate actors.

3. In addition, epistemological criticisms could be made about these theoretical attempts to transpose the NSM theory at the international level (see Finger and Princen 1994).

4. German mines discharge 298 pounds (135 kilograms) per second and Swiss mines 44 pounds (20 kilograms) per second.

5. The Reinwater Foundation was mentioned four times more often than French environmental NGOs in the international press. Even French newspapers published articles on the Dutch NGO, as did other international newspapers (including the *New York Times*). Globally, public opinion favored the Dutch cause over the French.

6. In 1979, for instance, a poll conducted for the Reinwater Foundation by an independent institute shows that a majority of Dutch citizens declared hostility toward the French in general, and to Alsatians in particular.

7. The four criteria read as follows:

- "They consist of informal interaction networks." It has been seen that the two sides were loosely connected. If highly structured actors (e.g., NGOs) intervened, then more informal actors (e.g., public opinion) also provided support. All such entities were loosely connected by informal information and communications, such as informal meetings or common undertakings. But alliances shift according to changing interests. French unions, for instance, first supported the FSM, then stopped supporting the fight against injections and abandoned environmental rhetoric as soon as the creation of a saline came into consideration.

- "They share common beliefs; and a common definition of the problem." The broad support gathered on the one hand by the ADIS "resistance" movement, and on the other hand by the symbolic water tribunal, show that the problem was perceived in common terms on both sides of the border.

- "Their action is based on protest; they emerge to denounce events that seem unfair or that they disagree with." Examples throughout this section show that the FSM was created to protest injections and, as discussed later, to work against the French government. Similarly, the DSM was created to fight saline pollution and French attitudes.

- "Their action largely occurs outside institutions." Segments of the FSM and the DSM used lobbying strategies, but many of their actions occurred outside usual formal negotiation arenas. They protested each others' positions by using the media to draw attention to spectacular noninstitutional negotiation events.

8. That is, costs that one actor imposes upon other actors.

9. Compare with the Harmon doctrine, which avers the unlimited sovereignty of riparian countries over their natural resources (Bernauer 1997: 164).

10. In fact, legal recourse remained unavailable to Dutch victims until an international jurisdiction, the European Court of Justice, was apprised of the case. It finally established the right of victims to take legal action against any European Union polluter in either the polluting or the polluted country (Romy 1990).

11. The first point is undoubtedly true for the Dutch, as they rely on the Rhine for 70 percent of their drinking and irrigation water. This means that they have almost no alternative to the Rhine since all other accessible water sources (such as the North Sea) are salty. The second point is also verified, as the environmental claims made by the different riparian states have been going on for many decades with no tangible results. The efforts of cooperating institutions only began to show effective results in the late 1970s. The salt issue was particularly hard to settle, in spite of much institutional discussion. The third point is corroborated by the chloride issue, since the MDPA was the most important and most visible point source of salt pollution. Its harmful effects on the Dutch environment were obvious and quantifiable, regardless of what other polluters contributed. The MDPA was thus a perfect target for Dutch claims. The case study matches the three analytical points, demonstrating that the border might indeed have been a "maximal" exacerbation factor in the chloride conflict.

12. There is no geographic borderline between France and Holland, but the Rhine connects the two countries, with France upstream and Holland downstream. Pollution caused by one country that affects another may thus be understood as "transborder" pollu-

tion, even if the "border" is more over time than over space, allowing the case of the Rhine to fit into this study.

13. Author's impression from semi-directive interviews.

14. Including significant regional newspapers such as *Les Dernières Nouvelles d'Alsace*, *L'Alsace*, and *Le Quotidien du Maire*.

15. The first booklet, titled "Salty Water, Rusty Pipes," was published by IAWR in 1982.

16. This well-known theoretical concept stresses the bargaining strategy used concomitantly by governments at the national and international levels. Its underlying principle is that, in order to gain latitude in one arena while bargaining in the other, governments alternately stress the national and international pressures they face.

References

L'Alsace. 1981. "L'association de défense contre les injections de saumures se mobilise." (17 October).

L'Alsace. 1982. "En Hollande: une délégation haut-rhinoise en position d'accusée." (17 April).

Anderson, Malcom. 1982. "The Political Problems of Frontier Regions." *West European Politics* 5 (4).

Anderson, Malcolm. 1997. "The Political Science of Frontiers." Pp. 27–46 in *Borders and Border Regions in Europe and North America*, Paul Ganster, Alan Sweedler, James Scott, and Wolf-Dieter Eberwein, eds. San Diego: Institute for Regional Studies of the Californias and San Diego State University Press.

Atkey, Ronald. 1970. "The Role of the Provinces in International Affairs." *International Journal* 26.

Becker, Mimi Larsen. 1993. "The International Joint Commission and Public Participation: Past Experiences, Present Challenges, Future Tasks." *Natural Resources Journal* 33 (Winter/Spring): 235.

Bernauer, Thomas. 1995. "The International Financing of Environmental Protection: Lessons from Efforts to Protect the River Rhine against Chloride Pollution." *Environmental Politics* 4 (3): 369–90.

Bernauer, Thomas. 1997. "Managing International Rivers." Pp. 155–96 in *Global Governance: Drawing Insights from the Environmental Experience,* Oran Young, ed. Cambridge: MIT Press.

Bernauer, Thomas, and Peter Moser. 1996. "Reducing Pollution of the River Rhine: The Influence of International Cooperation." *Journal of Environment and Development* 5 (4): 389–415.

Cooper, Andrew Fenton. 1986. "Subnational Activity and Foreign Economic Policy Making in Canada and the United States: Perspectives on Agriculture." *International Journal* 41 (3).

Diani, Mario. 1992. "The Concept of Social Movement." *The Sociological Review* (March): 1–25.

Duchacek, Ivo D. 1986. *The Territorial Dimension of Politics: Within, Among and Across Nations.* Boulder: Westview Press.

Duchacek, Ivo D. 1988. "Multicommunal and Bicommunal Politics and Their International Relations." In *Perforated Sovereignties and International Relations,* Ivo Duchacek, Daniel Latouche, and Garth Stevenson, eds. New York: Greenwood Press.

Duchacek, Ivo D. 1990. "Perforated Sovereignties: Towards a Typology of New Actors in International Relations." Pp. 1–33 in *Federalism and International Relations*, Hans Michelmann and Panayotis Soldatos, eds. Oxford: Clarendon Press.

Dymant, David. 1990. "Substate Paradiplomacy. The International Activities of Nonsovereign Governments: The Case of Ontario." Paper presented at the Conference of the Canadian Political Science Association, May, University of Victoria, British Columbia, Canada.

Evans, P.B., R.D. Putnam, and H.K. Jacobson. 1993. *Double-Edged Diplomacy. International Bargaining and Domestic Politics*. Los Angeles: University of California Press.

L'Express. 1983. "Pour une poignée de sel." (21 October).

Ganster, Paul, Alan Sweedler, James Scott, and Wolf-Dieter Eberwein, eds. 1997. *Borders and Border Regions in Europe and North America.* San Diego: Institute for Regional Studies of the Californias and San Diego State University Press.

Hocking, Brian. 1993. *Localizing Foreign Policy.* New York: St. Martin's Press.

Iglesias, Maria Teresa Ponte. 1995. "Les accords conclus par les autorités locales de différents Etats sur l'utilisation des eaux frontalières dans le cadre de la coopération transfrontalière." *Revue Suisse de droit international et de droit européen* 2: 103–34.

Jobert, Michel, and Pierre Müller. 1984. *Les politiques publiques.* Paris: Presses Univeritaires de France.

Klandermans, Bert, and J. Craig Jenkins. 1995. *The Politics of Social Protest: Comparative Perspectives on States and Social Movements.* Minneapolis: University of Minnesota Press.

Lemarquand, David. 1993. "The International Joint Commission and Changing Canada-U.S. Boundary Relations." *Natural Resources Journal* 33 (1): 59–92.

Le Prestre, Philippe. 1997. *Ecopolitique internationale.* Montreal: Guérin Universitaire.

Manno, Jack P. 1994. "Advocacy and Diplomacy: NGOs and the Great Lakes Water Quality Agreement." Pp. 69–120 in *Environmental NGOs in World Politics: Linking the Local and the Global,* Thomas Princen and Matthias Finger, eds. New York: Routledge.

Martínez, Oscar. 1986. *Across Boundaries: Transborder Interaction in Comparative Perspective.* El Paso: Texas Western Press and the Center for Inter-American and Border Studies.

Melucci, Alberto. 1989. *Nomads of the Present: Social Movements and Individual Needs in Contemporary Society.* Philadelphia: Temple University Press.

Nerfin, Marc. 1986. "Neither Prince nor Merchant: An Introduction to the Third System." *IFDA* 56: 3–29.

Nguyen Quoc Dinh, Patrick Dailler, and Alain Pellet. 1994. *Droit international public.* Paris: LGDJ.

Princen, Thomas, and Matthias Finger, eds. 1994. *Environmental NGOs in World Politics: Linking the Local and the Global.* New York: Routledge.

Putnam, R.D. 1993. "Diplomacy and Domestic Politics: The Logic of Two-Level-Games." In *Double-Edged Diplomacy. International Bargaining and Domestic Politics,* P.B. Evans, R.D. Putnam, and H.K. Jacobson, eds. Los Angeles: University of California Press.

Romy, Isabelle. 1990. *Les pollutions transfrontières des eaux: l'exemple du Rhin. Moyens d'action des lésés.* Lausanne: Payot.

Rosenau, James N. 1980. *The Scientific Study of Foreign Policy.* London: Pinter.

Schreiber, Henri. 1996. Interview with author. Paris, France (March).

Scott, James. 1989. "Transborder Cooperation, Regional Initiatives, and Sovereignty Conflict in the Upper Rhine Valley." *Publius: The Journal of Federalism* 19 (1): 139–56.

Scott, James. 1993. "The Institutionalization of Transboundary Cooperation in Europe: Recent Developments on the Dutch-German Border." *Journal of Borderlands Studies* 8 (1).

Scott, James. 1997. "Dutch-German Euroregions: A Model for Transboundary Cooperation?" Pp. 107–140 in *Borders and Border Regions in Europe and North America,* Paul Ganster, Alan Sweedler, James Scott, and Wolf-Dieter Eberwein, eds. San Diego: Institute for Regional Studies of the Californias and San Diego State University Press.

Smouts, Marie-Claude, and Bertrand Badie. 1994. *Le retournement du monde.* Paris: Presses de la Fondation Nationale des Sciences Politiques.

Strassoldo, Raimondo, and Giovanni Delli Zotti. 1982. *Cooperation and Conflict in Border Areas.* Milan: F. Angeli.

Tilly, Charles, Marco Giugni, and Doug McAdam, eds. 1999. *How Social Movements Matter.* Minneapolis: University of Minnesota Press.

Touraine, François Dubet, and Lichel Wieworka. 1984. *Le mouvement ouvrier.* Paris: Fayard.

Walker, R.B.J. 1988. *One World, Many Worlds: Struggle for a Just World Peace.* Boulder: Lynne Rienner Publishers.

Walker, R.B.J. 1994. "Social Movements/World Politics." *Millenium* 23 (3): 669–700.

Young, Oran, ed. 1997. *Global Governance: Drawing Insights from the Environmental Experience.* Cambridge: MIT Press.

Environmental Problems in the Seven Hungarian Border Regions

Imre Nagy[*]

Abstract

Hungary shares its border with seven different countries: Slovakia, Ukraine, Romania, Slovenia, Croatia, Yugoslavia, and Austria. The environmental problems that Hungary faces today are the result of a combination of geographical, political, and historical factors, and are not limited to national boundaries. As pollutants ignore boundaries traveling through the air or water, transborder problems may arise as pollutants leave one country and enter another. In addition, the changing political climate since the fall of communism and the development of new relationships in Central-Eastern Europe have affected the treatment of these issues. It appears that in most cases, cross-border cooperation for environmental management is being supported by new international organizations and agreements, although initiatives at the local level are lacking.

Introduction

Since the advent of the European Union (EU), a strengthening economic and social cohesion has made cross-border collaboration a supported and inevitable step toward harmonic development of the EU as a whole. However, differences in the level of development of individual regions are key concerns and the efforts made to decrease these asymmetries are important.[1]

The elimination of single-pole centralized economic and social control mechanisms has resulted in transitions in the political and economic life of Central-Eastern Europe. These transitions have brought about changes in cross-border cooperation, border traffic, and transborder environmental protection and management.

---

* Nagy is Senior Research Fellow at the Hungarian Academy of Sciences, Alföld Institute at Békéscsaba.

The quality of the environment and how available natural resources are used in border regions deserve attention, partly because of the special circumstances that surround border regions. These regions are atypical in terms of the spread of pollutants and have a significant influence not only on contiguous areas, but on the environments of whole countries. The goal of this study, then, is to understand how these buffer zones operate in their own countries and how they are affected by the new political circumstances in Central-Eastern Europe as a whole with the expanding market economy. This research effort outlines desirable opportunities for collaboration in environmental policy and nature conservancy. This study is initial research on this issue, presenting cardinal transborder problems, the present state of solutions to those problems, and issues of development.

Particular emphasis must be placed on potential environmental border programs that can be implemented with the full support of the countries involved based on common interests that unite nations. Such common interests include values already found in border regions, including sustainable uses of border rivers and protection of their water quality as well as the protection of both cityscapes and natural beauty.

In Hungary, environmental policy pays special attention to the problems of border regions and, therefore, to the mechanisms necessary for environmental management. In most Hungarian border districts, active cross-border cooperation is being organized and enjoys considerable support from the EU.

General Geographical and Historical Factors behind Hungary's Emerging Environmental Problems

Economic structure, geography, and urbanization are the main reasons for environmental damage in Hungary. Some environmental troubles decreased after the economic restructuring in the early 1990s. For example, the restructuring of heavy industry decreased pollutant emissions. In the agricultural sector, declining use of fertilizers and pesticides lowered pollutant levels. These economic changes also caused new environmental problems, such as uncontrolled influx of hazardous wastes from abroad and increased air pollution caused by growing border traffic and congestion. Such phenomena also occurred in neighboring countries, resulting in new border environmental hazards.

Geography also contributes to Hungary's environmental woes. Its location in the Carpathian Basin means that 94 percent of its surface waters come from outside its borders, carrying imported pollutants. Likewise, prevailing northwestern winds determine both the influx and outflow of air pollutants.

As a consequence of Hungary's historically changing borders, several towns now lie outside the country, but near present-day borders, including Bratislava, Košice, Oradea, Arad, Subotica, and Osijek. Following a period of industrial development, these towns became either sources of pollution or the recipients of pollutants carried from Hungary.

The valuable forests, groves, and protected natural areas that cover a large part of the border regions are also of concern. Their protection and proper management has important environmental implications for the border regions and the country.

Current Politics and Economics as Factors in the Environmental State of Border Regions

With the collapse of the Council for Mutual Economic Assistance (COMECON) and the Warsaw Treaty Organization in 1991, the political network that previously defined interstate relations ceased to exist. This has led to more open discourse about conflicts that formerly could not be discussed.

The seven Hungarian border areas changed significantly after the Central-Eastern European upheavals. Following the breakup of Czechoslovakia, the borderland adjacent to Hungary was inherited by Slovakia. This region's greatest environmental problems are caused by the hydroelectric station and reservoir on the Danube River. Also at this time, the old Hungarian-Russian (Soviet) border became the new Hungarian-Ukrainian border. The Hungarian-Romanian border remains intact and, following political changes in Romania, opportunities for cooperation, especially in water management, now exist. After the disintegration of the Soviet Socialist Republic of Yugoslavia, its single Hungarian border became three new international borders: Hungary-Yugoslavia, Hungary-Croatia, and Hungary-Slovenia. The Hungarian-Austrian border, which used to be a stark segment of the Iron Curtain separating Eastern from Western Europe, is now the site of some of the most fruitful cooperative efforts across borders.

Regional economic asymmetries are related to the changes that have taken place. Economic asymmetries in the border zones were contributed to by an increase in poverty due to both international and civil wars; economic recession brought about by the peripheral location of some neighboring states, such as Ukraine and Romania; and differences of living standards across borders, including food prices.

Changes in the region's borders that, in effect, parallel the political changes have resulted in new situations in environmental management. Negotiations began with Romania for water management and use, but there seem to be emerging conflicts with Croatia regarding the hydroelectric plant on the Dráva River. Ecotourism is being developed along the Austrian border with a resultant drastic increase in traffic and air pollution in border settlements. One of the most striking consequences of the changes in traffic volume in Central-Eastern Europe is the dramatic increase in waiting times at some border crossings. This is partly due to deficiencies in the physical capacities of border crossings, but also to the very slow operation of frontier guards and customs units that continue to follow the bureaucratic practices developed to cope with the comparatively limited traffic and restrictive function of the borders in previous decades.

Borderlands Environmental Policy: Regulatory Institutions, Laws, and Programs to Promote Development

The Ministry of Environment and Nature Protection officially controls Hungarian environmental policy through the Environmental Inspectorates[2] and Water Management Directorates. Unfortunately, the former only have limited jurisdiction. Other important organs involved in environmental policy are the National Public Health and Sanitary Services (concerned with public hygiene problems), the Plant and Animal Hygiene Stations, and the Directorates of the National Parks, which operates as a regional authority for nature conservation.

Supervision of the environment and monitoring environmental data in border regions are done by the following:

- West Transdanubian Environmental Inspectorate and Water Management Directorate
- North Hungarian Environmental Inspectorate and Water Management Directorate
- Upper Tisza Region Environmental Inspectorate and Water Management Directorate
- Körös Region Environmental Inspectorate and Water Management Directorate
- Lower Tisza Region Environmental Inspectorate and Water Management Directorate
- Lower Danube Valley Environmental Inspectorate and Water Management Directorate
- South Transdanubian Environmental Inspectorate and Water Management Directorate

The environmental problems in these border regions cannot be solved by central bodies alone; they must also be addressed systematically by local governments and cooperative alliances with local governments across borders. There have been only a few cross-border alliances since the mid-1990s, which have concentrated mainly along the western borders. Such regional associations and solutions are supported by the EU and are already able to show some positive results on environmental issues.

Responsibilities of local governments are to be defined more precisely as EU involvement and regulation is developed. Local governments do not presently have full authority to regulate environmental matters or to solve environmental problems, but some are capable of overseeing problems of air pollution from vehicular and industrial emissions and other sources, drinking water quality and supply, canals and sewage treatment, and treatment of solid waste. Some small settlements are threatened by poor waste and sewage deposition because they are hampered by limited budgets.

As early as the 1980s, transborder pollutants received considerable international attention. Research on the organizational and legal aspects of preventing cross-border air pollution was taken into consideration as COMECON was being framed. The 1979 Geneva Convention, the 1984 Hungarian-Austrian convention on environmental policy, and the 1978 agreement between Hungary and Yugoslavia on the ordering of national borders were followed by Hungary's participation in new agreements after 1990, including:

- The 1995 ratification of the VOC (volatile organic compounds) minutes on the regulation of volatile organic air pollutants and their flow across borders
- The 1996 signing of the new minutes on the protection and use of cross-border rivers and international lakes
- The 1997 ratification of the "Espoo" Convention on the examination of cross-border environmental effects
- Preparation of monitoring guidelines for border waters (in which Hungary led the Working Group for laboratory accreditation)
- The action program for sustainable transportation elaborated by the European Economic Committee (EGB)
- Important roles in implementing the Danube Basin environmental program and the Strategic Programme on the Danube

Regulation of border water management issues is done by bilateral interstate agreements. These agreements oblige upstream states to guarantee a minimum volume of river flow across borders for downstream states.

As the EU expanded east, it became necessary to support not only internal borders, but also those border regions adjacent to the EU. The INTERREG (International Regions) II program, under the Poland-Hungary Aid for the Reconstruction of the Economy (PHARE) program, launched the EU Cross-Border Cooperation (PHARE CBC) subprogram, a significant landmark of Hungary's involvement in such programs. In 1996, a Program Management Office was set up by the Ministry of Environment and Regional Development, which, within the framework of INTERREG II-PHARE CBC, works toward implementing Hungarian-Austrian, Hungarian-Austrian-Slovakian, and Austrian-Slovenian programs. The Program Management Office also oversees the implementation of a Hungarian-Romanian program as a model of PHARE country cooperation, as well as the preparation of a Hungarian-Slovakian program. The Hungarian-Austrian border region has produced more of such cooperative activities than any other Hungarian border area. Significant programs are being developed and carried out there, which will be discussed later in this paper.

Environmental nongovernmental organizations usually deal with protecting the ecosystems of lakes and rivers. They fight to protect these natural resources with limited financial means and strong public concern. In southern Hungary, the Tisza and Settlements organization coordinates local communities' cooperation with the Yugoslavian Community of the Tisza Region Settlements to actively protect the river and keep an eye on developments along its banks. Similarly, the "White Club" along the Hungarian-Romanian border and the Richard Chornai ecological organization in Yugoslavia promote joint manage-

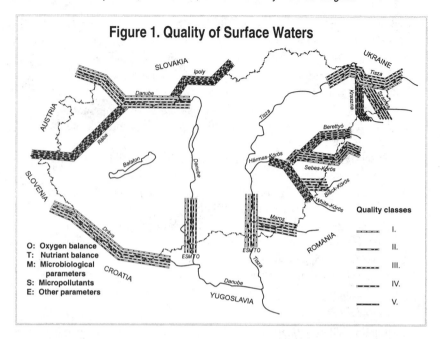

Figure 1. Quality of Surface Waters

O: Oxygen balance
T: Nutriant balance
M: Microbiological
   parameters
S: Micropollutants
E: Other parameters

Quality classes

I.
II.
III.
IV.
V.

ment and active preservation of protected areas on the Hungarian-Yugoslavian border.

Environmental Problems in the Border Regions

The Hungarian-Slovakian Border Area

The Hungarian-Slovakian border is the longest of Hungary's international borders, stretching from east to west. Its natural boundaries are the Danube and Ipoly rivers. Hungary is exposed to pollutants from Slovakia via prevailing northwest winds and both Hungarian and Slovakian industries contribute to the serious pollution of the region. On the Hungarian side of the border (along the Danube River), an alum earth factory, along with a cement factory, paper mill, coal mines, and the chemical industry, burden the region with their outputs. Although pollutant levels are far lower than they were in the 1960s and 1970s, problems created by heavy industry persist. The Slovakian side of the border contributes to regional pollution with its chemical industry, paper manufacturing (Šturovo), and heavy industry (Košice). The greatest challenge this region faces is that posed by the Gabcikovo-Nagymaros Barrage System, launched by joint effort between the two countries. Construction was finally stopped because of a number of existing and potential political problems surrounding the project (see Figure 1).

River water quality is determined by levels of nitrates, organic pollutants, and orthophosphates. When the Danube River enters Hungary, its water quality is poor due to emissions from the Bratislava sewage treatment plant, which releases an annual output of 26.1 million cubic yards (20 million cubic meters) of inadequately treated sewage—and partially to Viennese sewage. This pollution is aggravated by the lack of a regional sewage conveyance system. In Slovakia, the Danube contains a limited amount of organic materials, the levels of dissolved oxygen remain stable, and nitrite-nitrogen and orthophosphates are only minor pollutants. Occasionally, high coliform figures indicate major bacteriological pollution and, at times, concentrations of chrome, zinc, and cadmium exceed the limits set for heavy metals. Specific industrial pollution can also be high at times, including tan resin and viscose from plants in Komárom County.

The Ipoly River is moderately polluted when it enters Hungary. Concentrations of ammonium-nitrogen, nitrite-nitrogen, and the forms of phosphorous are high, while its bacteriological concentration varies. On its way along the border, Ipoly water quality improves due in part to natural cleaning processes.

The Sajó, Hernád, and Bodrog rivers enter Hungary with considerable levels of bacteriological pollution that worsen as they pass through Hungary, especially in the cases of the Sajó and the Hernád. The Hernád's high levels of fecal coliform and fecal streptococcus are troublesome. Zinc and aluminium levels are also fairly high in both the Hernád and the Bodrog rivers (see Figure 1).

Three main factors contribute to air pollution along the Hungary-Slovakia border: large-scale industry, increasing road traffic in the vicinity of Budapest, and pollutants from Bratislava plants (200,000 tons of sulphur dioxide per year). The pollutants from Bratislava are diluted during transport through the atmosphere, but because of the proximity of the town, pollution levels are high. Be-

Table 1. The Bacteriological Pollution of the Danube River and Its Tributaries along the Borders

River	Place of Sampling (Border Section)	Coliform Number i/ml	
		Average	p90%
Danube	Rajka (Hungary-Slovakia)	116	122
Mosoni-Danube	Mecsér (Hungary-Slovakia)	22	49
Danube	Szob (Hungary-Slovakia)	177	510
Ipoly	Ipolytarnóc (Hungary-Slovakia)	182	288
Ipoly	Balassagyarmat (Hungary-Slovakia)	-	-
Rába	Szentgotthárd (Hungary-Austria)	78	156
Rába	Győr (Hungary-Austria)	33	58
Lajta-főág	Hegyeshalom (Hungary-Austria)	90	157
Pinka	Felsőcsatár (Hungary-Austria)	-	-
Danube	Hercegszántó (Hungary-Yugoslavia)	299	570

Source: Ministry of Environment and Regional Development 1996.

cause large, state-supported heavy industrial plants have been closed down elsewhere, the sulphur dioxide concentration along this border is now the highest in Hungary. This region also suffers from Hungary's worst air pollution caused by particulates, a permanent presence that has been measured in excess of acceptable levels since 1991. The Central Environmental Fund recognized the problem and contributed 1 billion Hungarian forints (about US$3.5 million) to air quality protection, resulting in a significant decrease in the amount of settling dust in the Komárom industrial region (see Figure 2).

Emissions of nitrogen oxides from industrial sources have decreased and traffic is now the main source of these pollutants, especially in towns with heavy border traffic. Ozone levels are four to six times higher than the permissible limit. Now that heavy industrial plants all over the country are beginning to switch from coal to gas heating, they produce significantly lower emissions than before (see Figure 3).

Table 2. Industrial Plants Producing Hazardous Wastes in the Different Border Sections

Names of Industrial Objects	Settlements	Border Section
Richter Gedeon Pharmaceutical Co.	Dorog	Hungary-Slovakia
Flying ash deposit	Dorog	Hungary-Slovakia
Waste incinerator	Dorog	Hungary-Slovakia
Hungarian Viscose Factory	Nyergesújfalu	Hungary-Slovakia
Pest and Nógrád County Livestock Trading and Meat Processing Co.	Balassagyarmat	Hungary-Slovakia
Animal products and protein processing plant	Györ	Hungary-Slovakia
Railway Carriage plant of the RABA Factory	Györ	Hungary-Slovakia
Slaughterhouse	Sopron	Hungary-Austria
Kühne Agricultural Machinery Factory	Mosonmagyaróvár	Hungary-Austria
Vas County Meat Processing Company	Szombathely	Hungary-Austria
BPW-RABA Ltd.	Szombathely	Hungary-Austria
RABA Chassis Factory	Szombathely	Hungary-Austria
BPW-RABA Ltd.	Szombathely	Hungary-Austria
RABA Chassis Factory	Szombathely	Hungary-Austria
Airport Plant of the RABA Company of Györ	Györ	Hungary-Slovakia
Pannonglobus Trading and Servicing Ltd.	Györ	Hungary-Slovakia

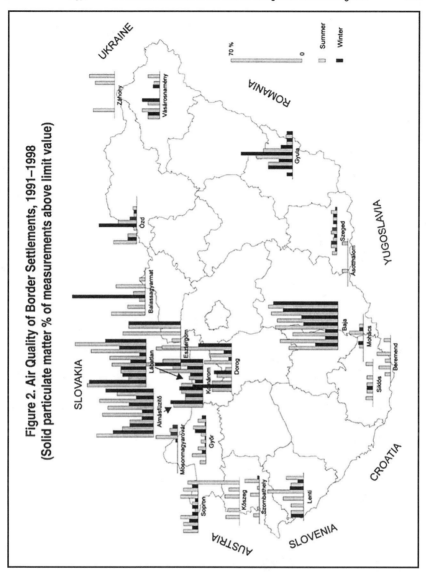

Figure 2. Air Quality of Border Settlements, 1991–1998
(Solid particulate matter % of measurements above limit value)

The Mochovce Nuclear Power Plant began operations in August 1998, despite community and international protest, representing a potential environmental threat to the Hungarian-Slovakian border area. The Slovakian plant's inadequate safety measures and design sparked fears of local environmental deterioration and possibly another Chernobyl-type disaster. Thus, the environmental integrity of the neighboring Hungarian border town of Mohi is at risk.

The region boasts several protected natural areas, including Aggtelek National Park, a transborder area of the caves of Aggtelek and Slovakian Karst that was included on the World Heritage list in 1995. The Protected Area of Fossils and the Landscape Protection Areas of Szigetköz, Gerecse, Pilis, Karancs-

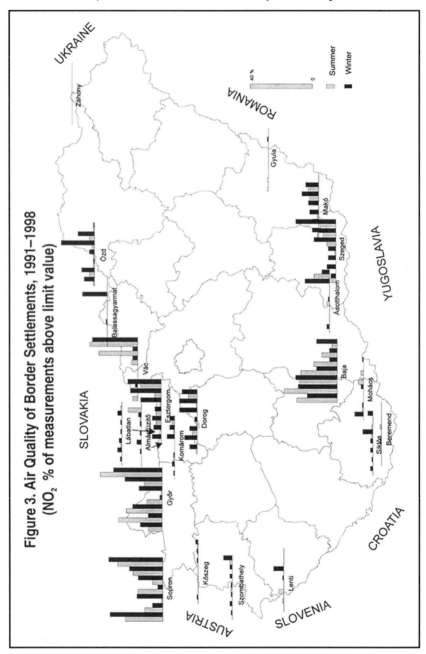

Medves, the Tarna Area, and Zemplén are also important. Several Slovakian protected areas are contiguous to Hungarian ones, such as the protected areas of the Karancs and Latorca. PHARE CBC support has made a significant contribution to the protection of the Karst water table of this border region. Since changes were made in the Slovakian government in 1998, prospects are brighter for closer and less problematic cooperation in solving environmental problems due to reduced international tensions.

The Hungarian-Ukrainian Border Area

The greatest environmental problems along the Hungarian-Ukrainian border are caused by flooding of the Tisza River and its tributaries. Large-scale, wasteful deforestation in the Carpathian Mountains (Romania and Ukraine) may be responsible for the catastrophic floods in the fall of 1998 that seriously impacted Hungarian, Slovakian, and Sub-Carpathian settlements.

Water quality in the Upper Tisza near the mouth of the Szamos River is good, by European standards, because industrial production and emissions of industrial wastes have been suspended in the Sub-Carpathian region. Some sewage is released into the Tisza, which adds bacteriological pollutants. The Kraszna and the Szamos rivers, out of Romania, are in much worse condition.

Other significant pollutants could affect this border region, including heavy metals from North Transylvania and waste salt from the Aknaszlatina salt mine on the Romanian-Ukrainian border (in spite of its polluting effects, the salt mine maintains its attraction through health tourism as a spa). The encroachments of

Table 3. The Bacteriological Pollution of the Tisza and Its Tributaries in the Border Areas

River	Place of Sampling (Border Section)	Coliform Number i/ml	
		Average	p90%
Tisza	Tiszabecs (Hungary-Ukraine)	56	86
Tisza	Záhony (Hungary-Ukraine)	46	77
Szamos	Csenger (Hungary-Romania)	365	744
Kraszna	Mérk (Hungary-Romania)	1,180	2,178
Ér-chanel	Pocsaj (Hungary-Romania)	19	40
Berettyó	Pocsaj (Hungary-Romania)	187	274
Sebes Körös	Körösszakál (Hungary-Romania)	314	1,011
White Körös	Gyulavári (Hungary-Romania)	47	120
Black Körös	Sarkad (Hungary-Romania)	48	96
Maros	Nagylak (Hungary-Romania)	499	875
Maros	Makó (Hungary-Romania)	273	1,100
Tisza	Tiszasziget (Hungary-Yugoslavia)	195	254

Source: Ministry of Environment and Regional Development 1996.

tourism on the precious natural areas of Sub-Carpathia, including the Nagydobrony Protected Area, have already disturbed aquatic bird life. Tourism poses many such potential problems along the Tisza because there is so little infrastructure to accommodate it. The gold mines of Muzsaj in the Sub-Carpathia are not currently productive, but if operations were to begin again, they might also yield serious pollutants that would adversely affect Hungary.

Záhony-Chop is an important railway and border crossing, yeilding the largest transfer and storage center in Europe. This station used to handle 50 percent of the total goods transported to Western Europe from the former Soviet Union (now Russia and Ukraine). This volume has since dropped to 20 percent of former levels. Hazardous wastes (fluid gas, oil products, fertilizers, chemicals, and war materials for Soviet troops) have polluted the soil at this station to a depth of 6.6 to 16.4 feet (two to five meters). Immediate collaboration is needed to eliminate this Russian (Soviet) soil pollution. As evidenced by the high levels of

Table 4. Nitrites (NO_3 mg/l) in the Danube, Tisza, and Maros Rivers, 1968–1991

	Danube		Tisza		Maros
	Rajka (Slovakian Border)	Hercegszántó Bezdán (Yugoslavian Border)	Záhony (Ukrainian Border)	Tiszasziget (Yugoslavian Border)	Romanian Border
1940	1.0				
1950	2.0				
1968	6.58	7.17	1.51	8.46	6.76
1991	10.36	10.87	4.56	10.53	16.73

Source: Ministry of Environment and Regional Development 1996.

particulates in Záhony, traffic jams at this border crossing, particularly caused by commercial vehicles, produces long lines and delays as well as air pollution from engine emissions.

Recent flooding on the Ukrainian side of the border has pointed to the need for Hungarian-Slovakian-Ukrainian collaboration to solve developmental problems and better manage the environment in this three-border region. River transportation, developed with EU support, could alleviate some problems and could be the impetus for a joint project with Slovakia to construct a port.

The Hungarian-Romanian Border Area

The Szamos River in the north and the Körös and Maros rivers to the south cross the Hungarian-Romanian border and are the most conspicuous carriers of pollutants from Romania. The water quality of the Szamos River is judged by volume of organic matter, nitrogen and phosphorous levels, dissolved iron and manganese, and its bacteriological count. Aluminum, zinc, cadmium, and copper concentrations are only occasionally significant (see Figure 1). The Kraszna River reaches Hungary with high concentrations of pollutants. It is heavily burdened with organic matter (which leads to low oxygen content), a high bacteriological count, as well as high concentrations of organic nutrients and ammonia. The water quality of the Berettyó River varies. It contains considerable fecal coliform and fecal streptococcus, as well as by-products of oil production.

The Romanian city of Oradea lies only 4.3 miles (seven kilometers) from the border with Hungary and has a population of 150,000. Heavy and light industry often operate with outdated technology and heavily pollute the Sebes-Körös, where chances for self-purification through natural processes are limited. The chemical industry in Oradea produces strong pesticides and related chemicals, and the furniture manufacturing and aluminium industries are also significant polluters. Sewage from a nearby pig farm (10,000 animals) also spills into border rivers. At the upper end of the Sebes-Körös River there is a cement factory and a white clay mine that also generate pollution.

The water quality of White and Black Körös rivers has improved since the change in government due to a decline in industrial production, and therefore pollution, rather than improved environmental management. Bacteriological pollution is still present in both Körös rivers, caused by the lack of a sewage collector system in Szalonta and the amount of sewage and manure that flow from pig farms and poultry processing plants in Szalonta. These increase the nitrite burden of the White Körös.

The Maros River, which enters Hungary at the southern end of the border, carries nitrites and fecal pollutants. The alluvial cone of the Maros, close to the Romanian border, provides drinking water that meets government standards for more than twenty communities. Seventy percent of the Maros's water comes from the Carpathian Mountains in Romania. This river is only partially protected and potential pollutants along its course—both in Romania and Hungary—could seriously endanger this vulnerable water supply. In fact, it has recently been discovered that a large-scale underground flow of pollutants is making its way toward this aquifer from the fertilizer plant in the Romanian town of Arad. In 1997, the threat to the aquifer of this pollution source was clearly established and both countries agreed to collaborate to solve the problem. Under the aegis of the Hungarian-Romanian Joint Committee of Water Management Technology, negotiations are taking place that will result in an international project proposal.

Important natural areas along this portion of the border are the protected areas of Szatmár-Bereg, the Bátorliget Meadows, the Bátorliget Marshlands, the Fényi Woods, and the Hajdúság region.

The Hungarian-Yugoslavian Border Area

At one time, this was the longest of Hungary's international borders; it is now only one-third of its original length and only the Vojvodina area is contiguous with Hungary. Situated between the Danube and Tisza rivers, the land here is mostly sandy and alkaline, and has not been farmed intensively. Ecotourism could thrive here if Yugoslavian and Hungarian protected areas along the flood plains of the rivers were integrated and jointly managed. However, the rivers that cross the northern borders of Yugoslavia are polluted, threatening the pristine nature of the region.

Just south of the Hungarian-Yugoslavian border, the water quality of the Danube is poor since the river leaves Hungary more polluted than when it entered. The biological oxygen demand (BOD) and the chemical oxygen demand (COD) figures are higher (five milligrams per liter at Hercegszántó) than at the northern border (two milligrams per liter at Rajka), although lower than at Budapest (six milligrams per liter). The coliform count is also highest here compared to other sections of the river.

Pesticide levels in this area were measured regularly during a six-year period in the 1970s. At Bezdán, the monitoring site measured a high concentration of DDT (LC50).[3] Other pesticides, such as Lindan, Aldrin, dieldrin, and heptachlor, were measured at approximately the permissible limits. Concentrations of heavy metals were found to be within acceptable limits.

Figures for dissolved oxygen in this section of the Danube are satisfactory, although indicators show the BOD to be high. Phenol and ammonia levels also indicate degradation.

Tisza River water quality is determined by several factors: the volume of bacteria and inorganic and organic matter from the untreated sewage it carries from Szeged (where there is no sewage treatment plant); the river dam constructed in the Yugoslavian section; and the Maros River, which introduces pollutants from Romania. The quality of the Tisza south of the Hungarian-Yugoslavian border (at Martonos) is a little better than it is farther north. There is a slight increase in dissolved oxygen and an improvement in BOD^5. The ammonia content, however, many times exceeds the maximum permissible concentration. Petroleum pollutants and decaying fish are frequently present. Permanent fecal pollution is indicated by the number of *bacilli coli* (probably over 24,000 cm^3) and frequent readings of Clostridium perfrigans. The Tisza has DDT (LC^{50}) levels twice as high as at Martonos. Other pesticides register within tolerable limits, but heavy metals (such as lead, nickel, cadmium, copper, and zinc) measured at Kanizsa are above acceptable limits. Fish also show heavy metal concentrations that periodically exceed permissible limits (see Figure 1).

Another small part of the Szabadka-Horgos sandy area (10,949 acres/4,431 hectares) lies near the Hungarian-Yugoslavian border. It has a remarkable landscape and valuable flora and fauna. The scenic Palics-Ludas regional park comprises the territory surrounding Palics and Ludas Lakes. Tourists enjoy Lake

Palics as a recreation area, while the Lake Ludas district is categorized as a park because of its flora and fauna. The Szelevény Forest, which has recently been declared a protected area, sits between the Hungarian-Yugoslavian border and the newly constructed Beograd state motorway. The sandy areas on the other side of the border have been recommended for protection and this forest could be an ideal adjunct as it would significantly expand the possibilities for ecotourism in the region.

Since 1982, nearly twenty-four thousand acres (ten thousand hectares) of forest on the flood and alluvial plains of the Danube have been protected and named the Upper Danube Region. Until 1991, this area was combined with the Kopács Fields,[4] which belonged to the then Croatian Socialist Republic. The ecological balance of the Upper Danube Region was disrupted by the civil war between the Serbs and the Croats that was fought nearby. The forest of large oaks *(Quercus robur, var. tardissima)*, oaks and hornbeams *(Carpinus betulus)*, oak and elm *(Ulmus effuza)*, and oak and black poplar *(Populus nigra)* was protected here. Cross-border collaboration and bilateral development programs might open up access to this national park for ecotourism.

Table 5. Categories of Protected Areas in the Hungarian-Yugoslavian Border Zone

Type of Protected Area	Number	Hectares/Acres
National Park	1	25,393 / 62,746
Regional Parks	8	28,375 / 70,114
Special Nature Reserves	1	29,352 / 72,528
Reserves for Scientific Purposes	4	1,815 / 4,484
Strictly Protected Areas	25	17,827 / 44,050
Groves, Lookout Towers	3	511 / 1,262
Total	42	103,273 / 255,187

Source: Priroda Vojvodine 1980.

Joint efforts are also needed to solve the water problems of the sandy area. Measures are needed to halt the lowering of the water level, alleviate borderland sewage problems, and deal with arsenic in the water table.

Since many towns are located very close to the border, monitoring emissions from their chemical plants is necessary to manage regional transborder air quality. For example, smoke from the fertilizer plant near Szabadka is intermittently dangerous. Air pollution is also caused by the endless lines of vehicles waiting to cross the border; most arrive from the Hungarian-Austrian border and travel toward the Balkans. This traffic has been alleviated by Turkish and Greek guest workers who use the border crossing on the Romanian side during holidays, but the Yugoslavian situation remains difficult since heavy traffic congestion may occur at border crossings at any time, causing large-scale air and soil pollution through runoff and point-source pollution that particularly affect Yugoslavian border settlements.

The Hungarian-Croatian Border Area

The Hungarian Danube-Dráva National Park runs the entire length of the 204-mile (329-kilometer) long Hungarian-Croatian border. There is some conflict between Croatia and Hungary over the construction of a Croatian hydroelectric plant in this region. For environmental reasons, the Hungarians blocked Croatian plans to build a river dam and creation of the Danube-Dráva National Park was raised by the Croatians as an issue.

The daily peaks of water consumption for hydroelectric and other uses produces large ebbs and tides twice per day in the Dráva River, causing a 3–5-foot (1–1.5-meter) flood wave. This effect would be increased by a new hydroelectric plant at Djurdjevac, which would jeopardize both terrestrial and aquatic ecosystems at the Danube-Dráva National Park and the future of local water sources. In the vicinity of the artificial reservoir, the level of subsoil water would probably rise, triggering a chain of environmental events. In nearby areas, the usually dry depressions would be turned into lakes and soils would in time turn into marsh and flood lands due to larger volumes of water. Such events would also change land cultivation, wetlands would evolve at higher elevations (to the detriment of meadow and pasture), and tilled lands would give way to meadow and pasture. It should be noted that Croatians are not united in the support of the hydroelectric plant. Croatia probably does not suffer from a shortage of energy and environmental groups have protested the construction of the dam by the "water management lobby."

The Dráva River, the boundary and hydrological backbone of the Danube-Dráva National Park, shows an increase in fecal coliform count at Drávaszabolcs. The Mura River in its upper reaches also shows an increase in the fecal coliform count.

The Rinya Stream, which flows into the Dráva River, is periodically polluted, as indicated by the fluctuating levels of organic matter and phosphoric forms. Pécs Brook, which carries sewage from the city of Pécs, is constantly and heavily polluted, as the river's low water output prevents its dilution. The lack of dissolved oxygen; a high volume of petroleum products, detergents, and bacteriological pollution; and high concentrations of heavy metals (especially mercury) are all dangers to the Dráva River ecosystems.

Top priorities should concern the elimination of arsenic from drinking water and protection of the water tables and surface water quality. The Croatian Physical Plan also urges the construction of sewage treatment plants in those border towns that currently dump sewage into border rivers. These include Varazdin, Cakovec, Koprivnica, Valpovo, Borovo, Vukovar, Virovitica, and Osijek.

Regional air quality is also at risk. The Beremend cement factory, only a few kilometers from populated areas along the Croatian border, is a source of dangerous air pollution that is exacerbated by prevailing northwest winds. In addition, heavy traffic causes unacceptable pollutant levels in the Barcs and Drávaszabolcs regions.

The Hungarian-Slovenian Border Area

Hungary shares its shortest border with Slovenia. Until recently, there was not even a direct railway connection between the two countries. After Slovenia gained independence and underwent major governmental changes in 1991, cross-border cooperation and new linkages began to develop rapidly. The Õrség and Szent György Valley Protected Areas extend into the borderlands in many places, increasing the ecological importance of the border zone. Only the problems caused by road traffic are significant and, although the Lenti region is one of the cleanest areas of Hungary, the amount of particulate matter frequently exceeds recommended limits. Those border settlements with twin-city connections are setting goals for joint environmental projects.

The Hungarian-Austrian Border Area

This border district can be considered Hungary's most advanced as far as environmental protection and development of collaborative programs are concerned. The two states have cooperated to develop their local economies, tourism, and trade, and have emphasized environmental management. Formerly a closed and prohibited zone, this area began to demonstrate the first signs of international cooperation after 1990 on Fertõ Lake (Neusiedler See), situated on the border and a favorite recreation area of the Viennese. A joint Hungarian-Austrian national park was established and was awarded the title "National Park of Europe" in 1993. Its calm and unspoiled natural environment and the subalpine and Pannonian climate make the area ideal for tourism.

Levels of cooperation between the two countries were demonstrated by the creation of the Borderside Regional Council and the Hungarian-Austrian Regional and Physical Planning Committee, made possible by local governments that also operate environmental and conservation working groups.

Water quality along this border is an important issue and water pollution is largely cyclical. The Gyöngyös Stream, which flows into Hungary from Austria, is polluted by sewage. The Rèpce is also heavily polluted by sewage and has a permanently high nitrite concentration. Heavy pollution in the Pinka Stream is infrequent, caused by periodic flooding. The Rába River usually arrives at the border carrying coliform bacteria and a high biological oxygen demand. Water output determines the volume of organic matter, nitrite-nitrogen, and phosphates.

Aside from this relatively low and periodic river pollution, this region is cleaner than others. Wide forest belts stretch across the Austrian border and the extensive Fertõ-Hanság National Park and Kõszeg and Õrség Protected Areas stretch into the border region. Austrians along this border are engaged primarily in greenhouse gardening, viticulture, and animal husbandry, reducing levels of serious environmental pollutants.

Conflicts do arise at times concerning private enterprise. In several cases, Austrian entrepreneurial ventures have released hazardous wastes into the Jánossomorja and Szentgotthárd rivers. Wastes have also been released into the Hungarian-Yugoslavian border region. In addition, Austrian pesticide use on their Hungarian land is uncontrolled, a problem recognized by local producers and municipalities. In general, however, cooperation toward environmental management is strong.

The Jánossomorja solid waste disposal site is run by three municipalities and serves 63 communities. It is up-to-date and compatible with EU standards. Settled on a mineral-foil bed, it produces biogases and is equipped with a complete infrastructure. This disposal site plays an important role in protecting natural resources in the northeastern part of Hungary (Szigetköz and Hanság). Its operation is supported by a grant from PHARE CBC.

In accordance with the principles of the Local Agenda, there is a push for the construction of regional sewage treatment plants along this border. In Vas County, plans have been drawn for sewage treatment plants that could handle all of its current needs, as well as future demand.

Although a much-needed binational sewage treatment plant for Gyõr-Moson-Sopron County has not yet been realized,[5] Szentpéterfa has built a joint sewage treatment plant with the neighboring Austrian village of Moschendorf. This is one of the best examples of the practical application of EU guidelines and transborder cooperation.

Of the 46 applications supported by the 1996–1998 PHARE CBC-INTERREG program in Gyõr-Moson-Sopron County (US$3 million), nine directly related to environmental development (total expenditure US$800,000) and another eight applications had indirect environmental relevance. A new Hungarian-Austrian collaborative program now supports the discovery and use of renewable energy sources (solar and biomass energy). A program has also been launched to develop rural and environmental tourism in Vas County. On both sides of the border, serious and effective development objectives have been set to improve the quality of the rivers, subsoil waters, meadows, and the soil.

Conclusion

Changing boundaries and relationships within Hungary's seven border regions have meant new challenges and opportunities for transborder cooperation regarding environmental issues. All of Hungary's border regions have valuable natural resources and populations that need protection, including various protected areas, water sources, agricultural zones, and so on. This need is currently being responded to by national and international entities and, in some regions, local entities have also begun to participate. The potential for these local entities to further enhance their cooperative mechanisms or create new ones has been strengthened by the changing political climate, which promotes cooperation and open borders.

The Iron Curtain, which harshly divided such border regions as Hungary-Austria, has come down and border regions are increasingly encouraged to create linkages and cooperate in the face of European integration. The expanding market economy creates incentives for neighbors to work with their asymmetries and share their comparative advantages to gain economically. The new political climate, typified by the expansion of the European Union, provides both political and economic incentive to cooperate across boundaries in the form of PHARE programs.

As this essay has demonstrated, all of Hungary's border regions are in need of improved environmental management at all levels. The increasing openness to cooperation that changes within Europe have spurred are a positive step in this direction, allowing efforts that would have never been able to take place under previous political and economic conditions.

Endnotes

1. The EU developed measures aimed at the social and economic development of less-developed regions, particularly EU border regions receiving structural funds. One project based on these financial resources is the INTERREG (International Regions) program, designed to assist cross-border cooperation, economic development of border regions, and optimal use of the opportunities presented by European integration.

2. This body oversees the definition, control, and evaluation of the limit values of air quality protection and regulations concerning local resources, traffic emissions, deposition of hazardous industrial waste, and the quality of surface waters.

3. LC^{50} is a lethal concentration of the micro-pollutant that kills European species of fish within 24 hours.

4. The Kopács Fields are rich in bird life. Rare and protected birds in this area include the osprey (*Haliatus albicilla*) and the black stork (*Ciconia nigra*).

5. Since acquisition of administrative authority involves dealing with excessive bureaucracy, the Austrian town of Hatturn was unwilling to wait any longer and built its own sewage treatment plant.

References

Central Statistical Office. 1998. *County Statistical Annuals 1991–1997*. Budapest: Central Statistical Office.

Csapó, T. 1996. "Cross-Border Cooperation in Vas County with Special Regard to the PHARE CBC-Interreg Program." Pp. 367–77 in *This Side of the Border and Across from Here*, A. Pál and A.G. Szónokyné, eds. Szeged: JATE University.

Gyuricza L. 1996 "The Physical Geography of Drávamente Area." Pp. 288–98 in *This Side of the Border and Across from Here*, A. Pál and A.G. Szónokyné, eds. Szeged: JATE University.

Hajdú, Z. 1996. "Dilemmas of the Cross-Border Co-operation in the Hungarian-Croatian Border Region." Pp. 306–12 in *This Side of the Border and Across from Here*, A. Pál and A.G. Szónokyné, eds. Szeged: JATE University.

Institute za Poljoprivredu Zemun. 1996. "Findings of the Survey of the Heavy Metal Content of the Bottom Ooze of the Tisza River, MK za Pracenje Stanja Reke Tise." Belgrade, Yugoslavia. Unpublished.

Ministry of Environment and Regional Planning. 1996. *The Quality of Our Waters 1995.* Budapest: Ministry of Environment and Regional Planning.

Ministry of Environment and Regional Planning. 1998. *Environmental Analysis of Hungarian Counties 1994–1998.* Budapest: Ministry of Environment and Regional Planning.

Nagy, I. 1999. "A Few Remarks on the Survey of the State of Environment in the Northeastern Border Region of Hungary." Pp. 172–203 in *The Present State of the Counties in the Northeast of the Great Plain: The Chances of Catching Up.* Debrecen: Centre for Regional Studies, Hungarian Academy of Sciences.

Nagy, I. 2000a. "Environmental Issues and Possibilities of the Cross-border Co-operation in the Field of Environmental Management in the Hungarian–Romanian Border Area." Pp: 141–46 in *Proceedings of the Seventh Symposium on Analytical and Environmental Problems*, Z. Galbács, ed. Szeged: SZAB.

Nagy, I. 2000b. "Environmental Issues in the Southern Border of the Great Hungarian Plain with Special Regards of the Cross-border Co-operation in the Field of Environmental Management." Pp. 411–28 in *Spatial Structure and Processes of Hungary at the Millennium*, Gy. Horváth and J. Rechnitzer, eds. Pécs: Centre for Regional Studies, Hungarian Academy of Sciences.

Rechnitzer, J. 1997. *Austrian-Hungarian Cross-Border Co-operations.* Györ: Centre for Regional Studies, Hungarian Academy of Sciences.

Upper Tisza Region Water Management Directorate. 1999. *Developing Program of Water Managment of Szabolcs-Szatmár-Bereg County.* Nyíregyháza: Upper Tisza Region Water Management Directorate.

Vargha, J. ed. 1997. "The Hague Decision." *Enciklopédia Kiadó*: 287.

Socioeconomic Processes in the Hungarian-Yugoslavian-Romanian Border Zone: Approaches to the Danube-Tisza-Maros-Körös (DTMK) Euroregion

Ágnes Pál[*]

Abstract

European regionalism is creating new challenges and opportunities to Central-Eastern European nations as they hope to integrate with Europe. Local governments are faced with new roles and responsibilities as the decentralization process transpires and the creation of cross-border regions introduces new relationships to the scene. This essay looks at this process in the Hungarian-Yugoslavian-Romanian border region and the Danube-Tisza-Maros-Körös (DTMK) Euroregion more specifically in an effort to understand the effects of various economic, political, and social changes on levels of cross-border cooperation and region building.

Introduction

Central-Eastern European countries that wish to integrate with Europe are finding new perspectives and opportunities presented by the spread of European regionalism. The new spatial evolution that crosses and transcends borders can be seen as a special case in the emergence of a new kind of European region. Central Europe is increasingly becoming a "Europe of Regions" (Töth 1996). Making national borders permeable is a priority at both regional and national levels. Adjacent regions and settlements near borders need assistance in forging regional

---

* Pál is in the Department of Geography at Juhasz Gyula Teachers' Training College in Szeged, Hungary. This research was supported by the OKTK Fund No. A/1411/III.b./ 98.

and local relationships and networks, as nations have demonstrated an inability to settle the majority of problems in border zones at the macrolevel (Tiner 1995).

Research on border regions has recently attracted a great deal of attention. For almost a decade and a half, Hungarian researchers have studied the economic, social, and environmental developments of border settlements along with new forms of spatial arrangement and the operational mechanisms of spatial structure. Their research has yielded significant results, especially for the Southern Great Plain region and the Hungarian-Yugoslavian-Romanian border zone. This dynamic research on Hungary's borders encompasses 74 Hungarian, 44 Romanian, and 23 Yugoslavian settlements. Their inclusion was intended to describe the economic structure of this particular border zone and to introduce and reassess the processes of cooperation (albeit without aiming at insight into all these processes). The spread of the European market economy has not only changed the regional economy from a state-controlled, closed system to an open system, but it has reshaped opportunities for cooperation as well.

European Interregional Cooperation

Traditional resources for growth are becoming exhausted in the northwest European economic grouping (based on metropolises and their agglomerations). In Alpine regions, new growth factors, such as high technology industries, play a dominant role and traditional organizations and settlements do not obstruct the introduction of new structures.

The Region in the Transforming Spatial Structure of Central Europe

Based on printed data, the areas that have been studied may illustrate potential growth. The first such area covers from the south of England, through Randstad in Holland, the Rhine-Main-Rhine-Neckar zone, and into Northern Italy (see Figure 1). The literature refers to this area as the "two bananas" due to its shape. It is organized around large cities, including London, Frankfurt, Stuttgart, Munich, and Milan. It also includes industrial regions such as Manchester-Liverpool and the Ruhr region.

Each unit of the Northwest European Greater Region is part of a Common Market country. A chief factor in the development of the units was that the regional centers (Brussels, The Hague, London, and Paris) are also member-country capitals and are home to major European organizations and institutions such as the European Union, the Council of Europe, and the European Bank of Redistribution and Development. In the recent past, the components of the emerging Central European regional system belonged to different political and military defense blocs. Even today, they belong to a variety of international economic associations.

Western socioeconomic practices are now being adopted in Eastern Europe. Thus, three "bananas" can now be drawn on the map of Europe (see Figure 2), including the "sun belt" in eastern Spain, stretching toward Eastern Europe. Green

Figure 1. The Economic Regions of the European Union

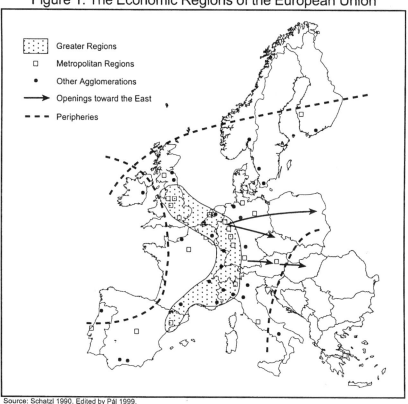

Source: Schatzl 1990. Edited by Pál 1999.

and orange bananas have been added to the original blue banana. In the late 1980s, spatial models and, most importantly, the famous "blue banana" concept were introduced by the French researcher, Roger Brunet (1989). His concept was further supported by Bernhard Butzin (1992) of Germany and Grzegorz Gorzelak (1996) of Poland, who promoted the green and the orange banana concepts along with that of the so-called Central European boomerang.

These researchers found a zone in the map of the Europe that resembled a banana. The "blue banana" included the most developed cities of Western Europe, while the green and orange bananas covered the Eastern European economic poles. This division also meant that after World War II, the socioeconomic development of the eastern half of Europe was inevitable. It was impossible to transfer the impact of the economic-developmental processes characteristic of the "blue banana" to the zones in the east. This failure can be explained by time as well as economic factors. In addition to temporal and developmental differences, it is important to see that while the settlements within the blue banana have been linked to one another with multiple ties, those in the east have tended to reach out toward the west: Prague has always been linked to Berlin, Bratislava to Vienna, and Budapest to Munich and/or Vienna. During the last century, these

Figure 2. European Territorial Model

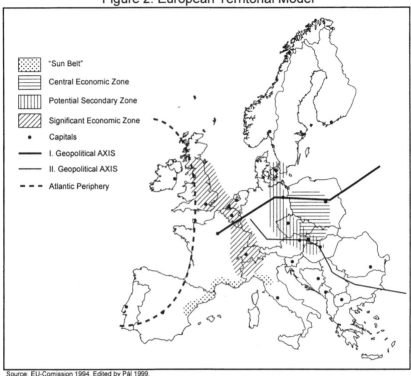

Source: EU-Comission 1994. Edited by Pál 1999.

latter cities functioned as the easternmost garrisons of Western European capitalist development.

Following the fall of the Iron Curtain and the establishment of market economy, the cities of Central and Eastern Europe acquired some of their former functions by reopening their former eastern and western corridors. Gorzelak also emphasized the most sensitive issue of the regional reshaping of Central and Eastern Europe—border regions.

The border regions taking shape in the Carpathian basin are being investigated both by Hungarian specialists and those from neighboring countries (see Figure 3). Such social and economic analyses may lay foundations for establishing a more homogenous economic region than before.

Characteristics of the Danube-Tisza-Maros-Körös (DTMK) Border Zone and Its Development into a Region

Factors such as geographical location and local statistical data are given for each region. Values that result from specific conditions fluctuate both in space and time and depend on the society in which they occur. As such, valuations of such factors can be made using external and internal mutual relationships (see

Figure 3. The Hypothetical Border Zone Regions in the Carpathian Basin

Source: Toth 1995. Edited by Pál 1999.

Figure 4. The Danube-Tisza-Maros-Körös Euroregion

Source: H. Rieser 1998. Edited by Pál 1999.

Figure 5. The Study Settlements in the Southern Great Plain Area

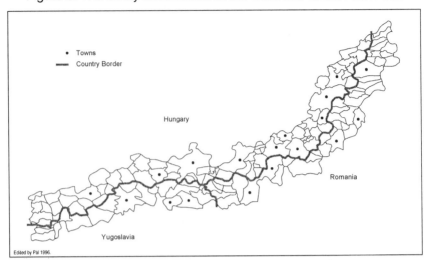

Figure 4). The border zones were determined by studying areas of interchange as defined by transportation patterns. The region on the other side of the national border was also identified by using transportational-geographic data.

A Historical Overview: The Relationship between Ethnic Groups as a Basis for Border Zone Cooperation

History and relationships among ethnic groups are important grounds for border zone cooperation. Arbitrary borders have little to do with the historical past and do not reflect ethnic or ethnographic realities (see Figure 5). In the Carpathian region, artificial borderlines caused the heaviest impact on ethnic groups in the Hungarian Plains. The mismatch between borderlines and the ethnic composition of the population has nearly always been to Hungary's disadvantage, particularly to those living in the southern region of Vajdaság.

The Population of the Border Region

More than 700,000 people live in the 141 settlements in the Danube-Tisza-Maros-Körös border region, as seen in Table 1. The number of settlements and inhabitants on the Hungarian side of the border is larger than on the Yugoslavian side. The number of settlements is relatively high on the Romanian side of the border, but the number of inhabitants is much lower.

Border zone settlements are typically characterized by the decrease of population. If the rate of decrease is examined more closely, a slowing down or stagnation can be observed, especially on the Hungarian side of the border. This is due to external and internal migration processes. With regard to the breakdown by age in the border region, the rate of senior citizens has increased over the years. This aging process in the border region is due to slow down to some ex-

Table 1. Characteristics of Border Zone Settlements under Investigation, 1992

| Country | Border Zone | | % of Towns | | Number and % of Population | | | |
	Number of Towns	Total Number of Settle-ments	Country	Border Zone	Town Popula-tion	%	Total Popula-tion of Settle-ments	%
Hungary	9	74	52.9	52.1	288,121	58.1	420,223	58.9
Yugo-slavia	3	23	17.1	16.9	146,149	29.5	187,691	26.3
Romania	5	44	29.4	31.0	61,209	12.4	105,777	14.8
Total	17	141	99.4	100.0	495,479	100.0	713,691	100.0

Table 2. Foreign Citizens in Szeged by Country of Origin

| | 1980–1988 | | | | 1988–1994 | | | |
| | Number | | Percent | | Number | | Percent | |
Country	A	B	A	B	A	B	A	B
Romania	86	31	4.8	5.1	3,618	2,246	37.3	28.0
Yugoslavia	103	90	5.7	14.7	435	4,195	45.0	52.2
Other	1,604	490	89.5	80.2	1,719	1,591	17.7	20.2
Total	1,793	611	100.0	100.0	9,687	8,032	100.0	100.4

Source: Szónokyné 1997.
A = number of people crossing the border
B = with residence permit

tent. The capability of border region settlements to retain population can be increased by planned cooperative efforts.

It cannot be stated that living in a border region is directly related to the increase in unemployment, although it does have indirect effects. Unemployment rates on both sides of the border are very high due to negative changes in the Hungarian economic structure, the Yugoslavian civil war's effect on the economy, and the underdevelopment of the Yugoslavian and Romanian economies.

Political and Economic Emigration

Large-scale migration to Hungary was sparked both by the change of its political system and the unsuccessful attempts to change the political systems in neighboring countries. The border region was affected by such movements, which can be exemplified by the case of Szeged. The *en masse* migration of Romanian residents to Szeged has been persistent since 1988. From 1988 to 1990 and on, a large number of refugees from the Yugoslavian civil war also arrived in Szeged.

In the first two years, the majority of immigrants were young men who wanted to escape military service. Since 1993, however, nearly as many women as men have moved to the town (mainly Hungarians from Vojvodina). The political motivation of emigration was replaced by an economic one, as the new immigrants wanted to save their capital. There was also great interest in getting involved in new business ventures (Szónokyné 1997).

Economic, Trade, Educational, and Tourist Relations

Recent and historical events, such as the economic incapacity of socialist systems and the Yugoslavian oil embargo (and later its lifting), have resulted in the launch of numerous regional programs and resultant economic changes. Measurable economic changes in rural areas have tended to be negative as the labor force shifted from a grey economy to a black market economy and later became largely unemployed. This dislocation caused by the economic transition from the old to the new system provided the opportunity for greatly increased criminal activity.

Trade and tourism between Yugoslavia and Hungary, which flourished during the period of great political changes in Hungary (1991–2000), broke down with the increasing political and economic tensions and the outbreak of the civil war in 1992.

Agriculture is the region's traditional employer. Animal husbandry (cattle, pigs, and poultry) and plant cultivation (wheat, corn, rye, vegetables, herbs, and fruits) play an important role in nearly every family's life. Agriculture has adjusted to accommodate changing political and market conditions as new products and production areas have emerged.

Local Industry and Its Organizations: New Entrepreneurial Forms

One radical change for the region, compared to development trends in previous decades, is the emergence of a significant service industry. This is an outgrowth of the industrial plants put in place under the socialist regime (with their low concentration, productivity, and efficiency). These range from heavy (oil) and light industries (textiles, hemp processing, manufacturing of shoe-uppers) to food processing (sugar and meat), packaging, and milling. These kinds of industries are usually present in the border zone settlements that were included in the Hungarian survey.

Entrepreneurship and the Effects of Privatization

Private enterprise is a new development in the region. As far back as the summer of 1988, several companies were established by multinational corporations using foreign (Italian, German, English, U.S., Canadian) capital to pursue industrial activities (see Table 2).

Based on the studies, the Great Plains area and the Hungarian-Yugoslavian-Romanian region in particular do not appear to have been favored by foreign investors. The major capital importers to the region as a whole have been German, Austrian, Swiss, French, English, Lichtensteiner, and Ukrainian (from the former Soviet Union). German capital dominates foreign investment, making up 24 percent of the total. Inevitably, Austrian investors have preferred the counties of northern Transdanubia. German capital has been more evenly distributed and its presence is felt by entrepeneurs in the border zone counties of Bács-Kiskun and Csongrád. Swiss and French capital is strong in centers near the southern and eastern national borders.

Possibilities for Developments in Trade Relations

Trade, research, development, and innovation play a most important role in shaping a region. Yugoslavia's failure to bring about changes in its social system and Hungary's relative success in doing so have led to thriving commerce in border zone settlements. In the first years of the new system, Western goods were distributed quickly and reached border zone markets right away. The imposition of the anti-Yugoslavian oil embargo in 1991 and border-crossing fees, however, caused a sharp decline in border crossings for the purpose of shopping and tourism. Black market trade fell as a result, but resurged when the embargo was lifted as more retailers tried to smuggle goods to avoid the duties.

In the post-embargo years, full-value trading and the renewal of old trading and commercial partnerships have generally increased. The creation of a duty-free zone is still pending, but the foundations for trade relations have been laid. Trade relations continually improve and the number of new businesses grows steadily. At present, agricultural goods dominate trade, but a growing number of trading businesses for other products have also begun to operate in the region. Changes can be seen on both sides of the border in both retail trade and ownership.

The Importance of "Shopping" Tourism and Ecotourism

The development of tourism has great potential for expansion. Given peaceful and more balanced economic cooperation, ecotourism and spa-related tourism typical of the Great Plains area could draw huge numbers of people to the region. Various forms of water activities and related ecotourism along the Danube and Tisza rivers could also be developed. Another potentially worthwhile project might be linking the nature conservation areas on the Yugoslavian and Hungarian sides of the border into a single system for ecotourism.

On the Economic Future of Border Zones

The prolonged Yugoslavian war has caused considerable damage to Hungarian export and import activities and has adversely affected Hungarian tourism and international transit routes to the Balkans. To improve the present situation, the most immediate aims are to improve relations between the countries, establish new border crossing points, and increase the capacity of existing crossings. Mass transportation and bus routes in both countries will also need to be coordinated at border crossing points.

Infrastructural Development

In the counties of Csongrád, Bács-Kiskun, and Békés, economists recommend the following developmental strategies:

- Developments initiated by the Yugoslavs that are advantageous for Hungary; that is, programs that contribute to improved bilateral relations and to furthering the development of border zone settlements, emphasizing disadvantaged neighborhoods
- Restructuring of traffic and transportation routes through reconstruction of the pre-Trianon railway lines and development of the existing line
- Building a logistical center in the city of Baja that would contribute to improvements achieved in trade and transportation in the southern border region
- Preventing stagnation and pollution of border zone rivers and waters is a necessary environmental task. A development plan will be crafted so that the partners may work together to develop the economies, social aspects, and infrastructure improvements in their region.

Conclusion

Border regions have special developmental problems as well as special potential. The development of settlements on both sides of this border is the link that most closely connects neighbors. Economic cooperation, joint projects by local governments and chambers of commerce, cooperation in environmental protection and regional water management (which has been a cooperative effort for some time), and a large number of other interactions are all issues of primary importance. To achieve their goals, the region's leaders must secure adequate financial support.

Various action plans have already been launched to promote the development of relations across the international boundary within the border zones. The most important of these is the Poland-Hungary Aid for the Reconstruction of the Economies Cross-Border Cooperation (PHARE CBC) project that aims to promote Hungarian-Austrian and Hungarian-Romanian relations (see Figure 6). The Hungarian-Yugoslavian border zone, however, did not receive this support due to political instability in the region. Changes in Yugoslavia's economic and

Figure 6. Regional Cooperation Extending beyond Hungary's Borders

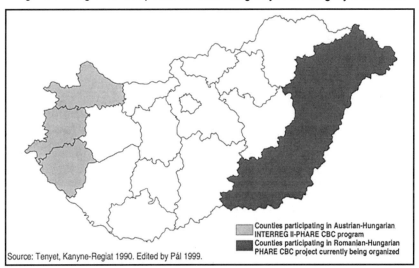

Counties participating in Austrian-Hungarian INTERREG II-PHARE CBC program
Counties participating in Romanian-Hungarian PHARE CBC project currently being organized

Source: Tenyet, Kanyne-Regiat 1990. Edited by Pál 1999.

political systems and Hungary's admission to the EU would qualify its border region for PHARE CBC support. Hungarian-Yugoslavian economic relations since the 1990s in terms of cooperation in the food industry (sugar, dairy, meat processing, plant breeding, and seed production) have become more efficient. The strengthening of cross-border economic relations was facilitated by the establishment of foundations for the development of enterprises, the closer cooperation between companies and chambers of commerce, as well as the organization of trade fairs, exhibitions, and business meetings. Examples of successful cooperation include the areas of trade, lumber, and the food, furniture, and textile industries.

Romanian-Hungarian economic relations are quite different due to organizational and legal differences, as well as the income disparities between the two countries. The region's economic relations with Romania are industrial, commercial, and agricultural in nature. Recent developments within the Danube-Tisza-Maros-Körös Euroregion include the identification of priorities and responsibilities according to the following: Yugoslavia was slated to be responsible for environmental and regional development, Hungary is to monitor developments in information and communication, and Romania is to coordinate industrial development.

References

Cséfalvay, Z. 1999. *Helyünk a Nap alatt.* Budapest: Kairosz Kiadó.

Enyedi, Gy. 1996. *Regionális folyamatok Magyarországon.* Budapest: Hirscher Rezsö, Szociálpolitikai Egyesület.

Golobics, P. 1996. "A határmenti térségek városainak szerepe az interregionális együttmûködésben Magyarországon." Pp. 224–30 in *Határon innen–határon túl,* A. Pál and G. Szónokyné, eds. Szeged: Szeged University.

Kereszty, A., ed. 1998. *Tények Könyve, Régiók.* Budapest: Greger-Delacroix.

Kovács, T. 1991. "A határmenti fekvés szerepe a falusi települések életében." *Tér és Társadalom* 4: 40–55.

Lengyel, I., I. Szabó, and Z. Végh. 1998. "Határtalan lehetöségek a magyar-román határon?" *Területi Statisztika* 1 (38): 154–74.

Mészáros, R. 1996. "Az európai regionalizmus néhány, számunkra is figyelemre érdemes eleme." Pp. 22–27 in *Határon innen–határon túl,* A. Pál and G. Szónokyné, eds. Szeged: Szeged University.

Nagy, I. 1996. *Environmental Aspects of the Urbanization Process in Agrarian Towns of the Great Hungarian Plain, RSS.* Prague: Central European University.

Pál, Á. 1996. "A dél-alföldi határmenti települések társadalom-gazdaságföldrajzi vizsgálata." Pp. 181–91 in *Határon innen–határon túl,* A. Pál and G. Szónokyné, eds. Szeged: Szeged University.

Pál, Á., and I. Nagy. 1998. "Socio-Economic Processes in the Hungarian-Yugoslavian Border Zone." Pp. 229–41 in *Curtains of Iron and Gold. Reconstructing Borders and Scales of Interaction,* Heikki Eskelinen, Ilkka Liikanen, and Jukka Oksa, eds. Aldershot: Ashgate.

Pál, V. 1997. "Az egészségügyi rendszer néhány földrajzi sajátossága a határmenti területeken." Pp. 52–53 in *Földrajz–hagyomány és jövő,* Nemerkényi, A., ed. Budapest: Hungarian Academy of Sciences Geographical Research Institute.

Rechnitzer, J. 1996. "Az osztrák-magyar határmenti térségek együttm–ködésének új dimenziói, egy potenciális eurorégió körvonalai." *Nyugat-Magyarországi Tudományos Intézet Közleményei* 33: 1–64.

Schatzl, L. 1993. *Wirtschaftsgeographie der Europaischen Gemeinschaft.* Töbingen: UTB.

Szónokyné, Ancsin G. 1997. "Külföldi bevándorlók és befektetők Szegeden." *Tér és Társadalom* 3: 143–56.

Tinner, T. 1995. "Határátlépõ nemzetközi személyforgalmunk néhány földrajzi jellemzõje." *Földrajzi Értesítõ* 3–4: 289–300.

Tóth, J. 1996. "A Kárpát-medence és a nemzetközi regionális együttm–ködés." *Határon innen–határon túl,* A. Pál and G. Szónokyné, eds. Szeged: Szeged University.

Cross-Border Development in Northern Ireland: A Focus for the Future

Derek Bond, Tom Frawley, and Charles Ferguson[*]

Abstract

The people of the Irish border region share common health needs alongside greater economic and social needs. They live in close proximity, share a common history, and often have cross-border family ties. As such, communities are increasingly recognizing their common problems on both sides of the border. More importantly, they are recognizing the need for collaborative attempts to find regional solutions that fit their historically and geographically specific needs. One such collaborative effort is Cooperation and Working Together (CAWT), a forum created for greater cross-border collaboration between health boards. This paper uses CAWT as the basis for an examination of the practical problems and policy issues of cross-border collaboration. The theory and practice of two CAWT projects—cross-border primary care and a childhood accident prevention project—are examined in detail. This study considers two major issues: (1) how experience gained through these CAWT programs might influence both the operation of institutions envisaged under the terms of the recent Northern Ireland peace agreement, and (2) how this experience might aid the further development of effective tools to evaluate cross-border policy. The paper concludes by placing the CAWT experience into a theoretical framework for cross-border development that attempts to widen some of the existing theoretical perspectives on cross-border development.

Introduction

For researchers involved in border issues, Ireland would appear to be an interesting and accessible laboratory; yet, the literature reveals few cases that use it to

---

* Bond and Ferguson are Senior Lecturers at the University of Ulster in Northern Ireland; Frawley is the Director General of CAWT (Cooperation and Working Together) and the Western Health and Social Services Board, also in Northern Ireland. The views expressed in this paper are those of the authors and do not represent the official views of CAWT or of any other organization.

develop or evaluate theories.[1] This paper considers some possible reasons why this might be the case. It also argues that Ireland needs a more radical and holistic approach to its border issues than that offered by the current trend toward multi-faceted and multidisciplinary methods. This argument is developed using the experiences with cross-border cooperation between health and social services providers within Ireland's two jurisdictions.

Ireland comprises two parts: the six counties of Northern Ireland (NI), which are part of the United Kingdom (UK) of Great Britain and Northern Ireland, and the 26 counties of the Republic of Ireland (RoI). The border between these segments is an internal border of the European Union (EU), and both segments are covered by relevant EU legislation. Ireland is viewed by the rest of Europe as being on the geographical periphery, and some of its border counties are viewed as being on the "periphery of the periphery." The border between Ireland's two jurisdictions may be viewed as under dispute, as recent troubles have attracted worldwide attention. The Good Friday Agreement was signed in 1998 and brought the possibility of accommodation between the different factions in Ireland. As a result, many now envisage the establishment of cross-border bodies (HMSO 1998). Such affiliations would not be new to Ireland. In recent years, as a result of EU monies, various bodies have been established primarily to deal with noncontentious subjects. One such coalition is Cooperation and Working Together (CAWT), a forum created for greater cross-border collaboration between health boards.

Following a brief introduction to the Irish border, this paper looks at some of the theoretical approaches being applied to the practical problems facing policymakers. It uses CAWT as an example, and particularly the theory and practice of two CAWT projects: cross-border primary care and a childhood accident prevention project. It considers how experience gained through these programs might influence both the operation of institutions envisaged under the terms of the Good Friday Agreement and the development of effective tools to evaluate policy. The paper concludes by putting the CAWT experience into a theoretical framework for cross-border development that may widen some existing perspectives.

Background

The historical and political background of the Irish border is complex. The historical span of the "Irish problem" has affected the current status of its border as outlined by Darby (1995):

> Since the twelfth century ... it is possible to discern significant shifts in the Irish problem. Until 1921, it was essentially an Irish-English problem and focused on Ireland's attempt to secure independence from Britain. From 1921 the emphasis shifted to relationships within the island of Ireland, between what later became the Republic of Ireland and Northern Ireland; this issue has somewhat revived since the signing of the Anglo-Irish agreement in 1985. Finally, since 1969, attention has focused on relationships between Catholics and Protestants within Northern Ireland.

Ireland's political and social history has been closely linked to its English neighbor. Centuries of conflict have arisen from this relationship, and the struggle for control is the hallmark of Irish history. Colonization, particularly during the plantation period when the Irish were dispossessed in favor of Protestant planters from Scotland and England, created not only a religious and cultural divide in Ireland, but also a legacy that survives to the present day in the collective conscience of the Catholic Irish.

From 1800 onward, Ireland was governed from London through a member of the cabinet known as the Irish Chief Secretary. Toward the end of the nineteenth century, a populist "home rule" movement took hold. This led eventually to the Home Rule Act of 1914, which was suspended by the advent of World War I. In 1916, a seemingly failed uprising led to an armed rebellion that finally resulted in the negotiated partitioning of Ireland by the Anglo-Irish Treaty in 1921. The treaty led to a civil war in Ireland that ended in 1922 with the Partition Treaty, established the Irish Free State (later called the Republic of Ireland), which consisted of 26 counties, and Northern Ireland, consisting of six counties. To the present day, this division has influenced the political, social, and economic landscape of the town jurisdictions and the British Isles.

For those of the Unionist tradition living in Northern Ireland, partition symbolized their British pride. For those of a nationalist persuasion, partition constituted a barrier to aspirations for a united Ireland. Relationships between the British and Irish governments have been dominated by a partitioned Ireland and the existence of the border has provided the backdrop for 30 years of violence in Northern Ireland.

Many have written about the history of the Irish border and its political implications, but few have concentrated on the socioeconomic issues that partition has created. The works that do exist tend to be descriptive rather than offering a theoretical analysis. This is perhaps unsurprising, for it is a complex border, and no single theoretical perspective can be applied to the study of borders. Much of the research on borders has been eclectic. Even a cursory glance at existing research literature reveals a diversity of standpoints based upon the focus of the given disciplines of scholars.

With such major changes in territorial alignment as those in Eastern Europe, scholars from different academic fields have found fresh interest in boundaries. A new, rich tapestry of border phenomena has emerged. For example, with the removal of some traditional borders has come a move toward integration within the EU. This move can be set against the emergence of new borders created by the breakup of the former Soviet Union. In the case of Ireland, the Good Friday Agreement has propelled cross-border collaboration to the forefront of the political agenda.

A key part of the Good Friday Agreement is the establishment of a North/South Ministerial Council charged with developing cross-border institutions.

Under a new British/Irish Agreement dealing with the totality of relationships and related legislation at Westminster and in the Oireachtas, a North/South Ministerial Council is to be established to bring together those with executive responsibilities in Northern Ireland and the Irish Government, to develop consultation, cooperation and action within the island of Ireland—including through implementation on an all-island and cross-border basis—on matters of mutual interest within the competence of the Administration, North and South (HMSO 1998).

The cross-border cooperation that is foreseen between the two jurisdictions has a wide scope, including agriculture, education, transportation, waterways, environment, social welfare, tourism, inland fisheries, aquaculture, health, urban and rural development, and EU programs. The advent of the Good Friday Agreement significantly changes state policy toward the border, ushering in a new, formalized "cross-border" policy devised through the joint regulation of a Ministerial Council. With its own civil service support in both jurisdictions, this new body will be instrumental and is likely to influence both the nature and extent of cross-border collaboration between the Republic of Ireland and Northern Ireland under the terms of the peace agreement.

With heightened interest in the Irish border, there is a need for a sound theoretical basis to better understand its complex dynamics. The view that border studies "can be brought together within a multidimensional, multidisciplinary framework for the future study of boundary phenomena" (Newman and Paasi 1998) is increasingly articulated. Borders are far more than simple definitions of geographical spaces. Recent literature on economic development in peripheral border regions highlights this, and many different theoretical viewpoints are represented by the concepts it introduces. These concepts include local milieu, network economy, distance work, pocket development, industrial clusters, and multihome based firms (Tykkläinen and Bond 1997).

Because so many different theoretical approaches are relevant to the study of the Irish border, a multifaceted, multidisciplinary approach that attempts to combine them is attractive. For example, the concept of "the social construction of reality" would seem apropos, since "even if [borders] are always more or less arbitrary lines between territorial entities, they may also have deep symbolic, cultural, historical and religious, often contested, meanings for social communities" (Tickner 1995). In geopolitical studies, the added dimension of power also plays a major role in understanding border issues.

The complexity of "development" in the Irish border region should be seen in the light of a range of factors, including:

- The interactions of the political boundary as an element of the cultural boundary
- The effect of the boundary upon the landscape and on economic activity
- The impact of the boundary on the attitudes of border inhabitants
- The effect of the boundary upon state policy

All of these factors distinguish the Irish border region, making it an ideal laboratory in which to develop a new multidisciplinary framework for studies of boundary phenomena. Such an approach is normally couched in the terminology of the positive, quantitative research paradigm. Attempts to apply this method have been only partially successful at best. Researchers tend to retreat, probably unintentionally, into their own disciplines.[2]

The relevance and limitations of this approach have been discussed in another study of the Finnish-Russian border (Bond and Tykkläinen 1996). One of the problems discussed therein was the lack of adequate data. Since both the UK and the RoI are members of the EU, it would seem reasonable to assume that data is readily available for the analysis of cross-border issues; however, this is not the case, despite increasing moves by Eurostat to coordinate data from member countries (Bond, Osborne, and Robinson 1994; Murphy 1998; Bond 1999). This lack of data could be beneficial in the Irish case, since the often-sterile macro approach to border analysis must be set aside without it. Microanalysis often leads to a more in-depth investigation of the issues because it uses both quantitative and qualitative criteria, and qualitative research on the Irish border would not run into common language problems (Saint-Germain 1995).

To understand how consideration of the Irish border might help in developing the relationship between theory and practice, Cooperation and Working Together (CAWT), a cross-border entity established in 1992, is used here as a case study. It will help illustrate some of the issues surrounding cross-border cooperation, as well as the difficulties in developing a multifaceted, multidisciplinary theoretical framework. Other institutional cross-border working arrangements made prior to the Good Friday Agreement in other sectors, notably transportation and tourism, might also be used for future studies.

The Practice of Cross-Border Cooperation

CAWT seeks to exploit opportunities for collaboration in both planning and providing health and social services across the Irish border. The agency facilitates joint cross-border projects and involves both the North Eastern and North Western Health Boards in the Republic of Ireland, and the Southern and Western Health and Social Services Boards in Northern Ireland.

There are approximately one million people living in the region served by CAWT. With the exception of the city of Derry in Northern Ireland, the area is mainly rural. The European Union defines the region as "Objective 1." Objective 1 regions are determined by the EU, on the basis of social and economic indicators, to require the greatest subvention in terms of EU grants and subsidies. Rural isolation, lack of adequate infrastructure, high unemployment, and an aging and declining population are some of the problems facing this region. The people of this border area suffered numerous atrocities during the past 30 years of dispute. They have been faced with restrictions on cross-border movement, the closure of many roads, and a strong military presence at checkpoints on main routes.

The people of the Irish border region share common health, economic, and social needs. They live in close proximity, share their history, and often have cross-border family ties. As such, communities are increasingly recognizing their common problems on both sides of the border. More importantly, they are also recognizing the need for collaborative attempts to find regional solutions that fit their historically and geographically specific needs.

While political differences do not rule out the possibility of collaboration in border regions, they do make for a difficult climate. The political framework provided by the Good Friday Agreement is a landmark in Irish history. It established the relationships between the two Irish jurisdictions and between Britain and Ireland. The new impetus toward cross-border institutions, based upon this more supportive political climate, augurs well for the further development and sustainability of all kinds of cross-border cooperative efforts. Of the proposed cross-border institutions to be created as a result of the agreement, health and social services are identified for continuing and heightened cooperation.

Although CAWT was established about eight years ago, before the fairly recent peace process achieved tangible political results, it has enjoyed sustained growth and change. Initially it concentrated on providing a means for individuals and groups to come together on a range of relevant regional issues. Most of CAWT's work has been organic, stemming from the involvement of community groups and their perceived needs as border communities. Participants were given the freedom and space to contribute to cooperative, and often highly innovative, cross-border ventures. Recently, CAWT has had to become more formalized to evaluate its impact on health care provision in order to justify continued support of the health boards. A major challenge for the future is to strike an appropriate balance between the need for "pioneering zeal" and the creation of formal structures and focused projects that will yield sustainability.

The range of CAWT projects is extensive (see Appendix 1), including collaborative work related to human resources, information technology, health promotion, social deprivation, acute hospital services, childhood accident prevention, and primary care. The practicalities of cross-border work are illustrated by an examination of the last two projects listed in Appendix 1—primary care and childhood accident prevention.

Primary care offers CAWT the opportunity to set in place long-term cross-border arrangements. As the first level of health care, it offers a potential environment for teamwork among professionals within and across professional and geographical boundaries. The main components of the primary care project are outlined in Table 1.

Expanding the primary care initiative entails selective inclusion of affiliated cross-border communities. The object is to engage communities in determining their priorities for health and social care. This work requires assessing needs based on a community development approach. CAWT aims to empower local border communities to enable them to define their priorities for health care provision. By doing so, its intention is to bolster the esteem of the communities con-

Table 1. Primary Care Project

Practice Organization

- Jointly establish core skills of practice management
- Train practice managers
- Personal development for administrative staff
- Promote solidarity among primary care team members
- Involve patients in primary care decisions

Services Development

- Role of nursing: skill mix, coordination of teams, joint training
- Develop protocols: asthma, diabetes
- Joint protocol training
- Share experiences with medical issues

Community Pharmacy

- Training on clinical issues
- Examine potential strategy for pharmacists' community role

Information Technology

- Assess need for computer skills; joint training
- Inventory information technology resources
- Assess utilization resources
- Develop email links
- Develop website
- Jointly develop and exploit information technology to further cross-border cooperation

Infrastructure

- Develop model primary care facility and apply knowledge gained from other CAWT projects

cerned and overcome the perceived social exclusion that exists in these communities. The goal is to meet needs and deliver services in ways tailored to particular border communities.

As part of its resolution to promote good health and social well-being, CAWT has undertaken a number of initiatives that target specific risk groups: drug education for children aged 11 to 13; assessment of men's mental health needs in rural areas, ages 15 to 30; and a community Childhood Accident Prevention Project (CAPP).

CAPP was established in 1995 and has sought to design and test a model for safety education for low-income families with children under the age of five. The project recruits and trains health workers from disadvantaged areas to work in their own neighborhoods.

CAPP has helped in the creation of safety clubs in all four health board areas. Initial evaluation of CAPP efforts is encouraging, as surveys show evidence of increased knowledge and changing attitudes and behavior. Surveys also show that parents feel a high level of satisfaction and enthusiasm for CAPP. This positive feedback makes it likely that the four health boards will incorporate CAPP into their mainstream programs, even when European funding ceases.

CAPP is a good testing ground for cross-border work. The project shows that diversity and community are reoccurring themes that make such initiatives both challenging and rewarding. Diversity, in this case, encompasses both urban and rural settings, as well as different cultures, legal systems, and health board structures. Even with these divisive factors, communities have been reinforced by the project, providing the basis for the networks and collaboration of a program that might not have yielded the same results if carried out by the health boards alone.

All of these positive factors provide momentum for CAWT; however, cross-border cooperation is certainly not without challenges. Northern Ireland and the Republic of Ireland often contend for the same inward investment opportunities from the EU in terms of grants or from foreign companies wishing to locate in Ireland, leading to a climate of intergovernmental competition. There are real differences in the social and economic systems of the two jurisdictions, including the way the public sector operates and is funded. Cultural differences, as well as different local political priorities and objectives, also get in the way when creating working arrangements between diverse organizations. The inevitable barriers created by different procedures and processes can make cooperation challenging. This is exemplified by CAWT's very limited progress in acute services.

Evaluation

Peripheral border regions are often dominated by a heavily subsidized and inefficient public sector that fails to provide the environment necessary for innovation and progress. The opposite appears to be true of CAWT. Several reasons for this exist. Health and social care issues generally transcend borders, which helps to explain the need for and relative success of CAWT. Based only upon humanitarian concern, CAWT offers the people it serves more benefits than could be achieved if the parties worked separately. The existence of CAWT hinges upon the growing acceptance by people with different cultures and religions of practical cooperation as they learn its benefits. Political support, in the form of funding from the European Union Peace and Reconciliation Fund, as well as matching funds from the Irish and British governments, is also generally recognized as vital to CAWT's survival. This amalgam of factors make CAWT a sustainable institution that can deliver benefits to its constituent cross-border population.

CAWT management is extremely aware of frequent comments made about the grant mentality that exists in Northern Ireland (Teague 1989). Seeking funding for its own sake is pure goal displacement. As a cross-border institution, CAWT is well placed to gain EU funding; however, its management does not see CAWT as a simple means of unlocking external funding. Rather, it has multiple objectives that involve the construction of social and health infrastructure to promote self-confidence and community development. For CAWT, cross-border cooperation is based upon the imperative to develop a common understanding of health and social care needs and to put in place sustainable infrastructure to benefit border communities long after any particular funding source has been exhausted.

Such a stance would seem to fit in well with current EU thinking, but it also emphasizes the problems with trying to move away from activity-based assessment to outcome-based measures. Given its stated aims, what criteria should be used to evaluate or assess CAWT? Has CAWT demonstrated the benefits—economically or socially—of cross-border cooperation? Is it possible to measure whether it has demonstrated, say, economic gains achieved through shared health and social care services, or social gains (particularly building social confidence and infrastructures) that enable isolated communities to be included in the greater world?

These questions are discussed here using CAPP as an example. CAWT directors argue that the project has produced a range of benefits, and the joint gains are evident. Through CAPP, workers have compiled important baseline information on accidents and safety, as well as demographic statistics on the populations involved. CAPP has also provided safety education that otherwise might not have been available. Part-time jobs for community project workers have increased. A new pool of trained and experienced lay people who can be employed to work on other health issues has been created. Perhaps CAPP's most significant outcome (which without CAWT would have probably never emerged) is that cross-border communities have had an opportunity to have a say in how problems of childhood safety are handled in their region. This is not a benefit that can be measured. Furthermore, CAPP's successes have not been uniform and no measurable pattern for success has emerged.

To examine CAWT's primary care project, a means must be devised by which to determine "need" and look at how this relates to cross-border issues. The failure of standard theory soon becomes apparent, as data are unavailable for comparable analyses, and if they were, there would no doubt be disagreements on their interpretation (Bond 1997). Needs assessment shows a fundamental difference between the analyses of borders in Europe and the United States due to fundamental differences in legislative and cultural attitudes toward data access. In Europe, data are only released if it is required, while in the United States, data are available unless a good reason can be shown that they should not (Bond, Elser, and Robinson 1996; Bond and Elser 1997). The lack of data in Europe has implications for the development of assessment techniques based on Geographic Information Systems (GIS) (Haslett 1991).

One interesting part of CAWT's primary care project is the development of its website to share information. Such a development shows that any theory must encompass the changing nature of peripherality. Given increasing economic globalization and the rapid development of production technology, telematics, and communications, peripherality based on physical distance may become more perceived than real.

CAWT appears to be generally successful; yet, using existing positivist theories, it is difficult to pinpoint why. It is even more difficult to use existing theories to explain why some projects have worked in some areas and not in others. Discussions with members of CAWT have raised issues that do not seem to fit neatly into any existing theory. In addition, much pertinent discussion has involved concepts (such as belief in self) that perhaps fit better into metaphysics. This may indicate that not only should a multifaceted, multidisciplinary approach include qualitative issues, but it should also be concerned with more than just the physical world.

Conclusions

Research about the Irish border has been limited, mainly atomistic, and lacking a multifaceted, multidisciplinary emphasis. Since cross-border cooperation under the Good Friday Agreement is envisaged as occupying a central role in accommodating differences in Ireland, there is a new imperative to ensure that theoretical issues surrounding cross-border development are handled in a more rigorous way. This is particularly important for policy evaluation. The evolving situation in Ireland offers a unique opportunity for testing policy initiatives and theories of cross-border development.

By briefly looking at the CAWT initiative, the inherent complexity of understanding cross-border initiatives becomes apparent. The benefits of shared health services seem obvious, largely politically neutral, and of humanitarian interest. However, the CAWT case study shows that there are still many barriers and difficulties in practicing cross-border cooperation.

Evaluation of CAWT would be limited if it relied purely on a positive, quantitative research paradigm. Not only would data collection prove difficult, given the organizational differences between health boards, but defining hard quantitative measures does not, in itself, constitute a fair reflection on CAWT's importance. Measurable outputs are important, but qualitative aspects—such as community involvement in the development of health care in a border region—are also important. Boosting self-confidence, reaching out to isolated border communities, and other qualitative aspects, are integral to the aspirations of CAWT; such objectives cannot be ignored in any evaluation of CAWT's worth. At this juncture, CAWT, in keeping with other cross-border initiatives, provides a "demonstration effect" of possibilities for mutual benefit, and can help allay the genuine fears that cross-border arrangements are threatening.

Endnotes

1. For a detailed listing of literature on the Irish border, see the CAIN website <http://cain.ulst.ac.uk>.

2. For examples, see the essay on the Finnish-Russian border in Kortelainen 1998.

References

Bond, Derek. 1997. "A Return to the Numbers Game." Report commissioned by the Southern Health and Social Services Board, Northern Ireland Regional Research Laboratory Report (NIRRL), no. 97/3. Belfast.

Bond, Derek. 1999. "Measuring Across-Borders." *IASSIST (International Association for Social Science Information Service and Technology) Quarterly*. Forthcoming.

Bond, Derek, and E. Elser. 1997. "Providing Access to Public Data during the Coming Decade." Paper presented at the IASSIST conference, 14–16 May, Odense, Denmark.

Bond, Derek, E. Elser, and G. Robinson. 1996. "The Changing Face of Europe: Problems of Obtaining Statistics." Paper presented at the IASSIST conference, 15–17 May, Minneapolis, Minnesota, USA.

Bond, Derek, R. Osborne, and G. Robinson. 1994. "Assessing Cross-Border Need." Report prepared for the Department of Health and Social Services and DH. Northern Ireland Regional Research Laboratory (NIRRL), No. 94/5. Belfast.

Bond, Derek, and M. Tykkläinen. 1996. "Northwest Russia: A Case Study in Pocket Development." *European Business Review* 96 (5): 54–60.

Darby, S. 1995. "Conflict in Northern Ireland: A Background Essay." In *Facets of the Conflict in Northern Ireland*, S. Dunne, ed. New York: St. Martin's Press.

Haslett, John 1991."Spatial Data Analysis—Challenges." *The Statistician* 41: 271–84.

Her Majesty's Stationary Office (HMSO). 1998. *Agreement Reached in the Multi-Party Negotiations*. Belfast: HMSO.

Kortelainen, J. 1998. *Crossing the Border: Development in Russian Karelia*. Joensuu: University of Joensuu.

Murphy, D. 1998. "Access to Anonymised Irish CSO Micro Data." Pp. 12–16 in *Research in Regional Statistics*, D. Bond, McCafferty, and M. Black, eds. Coleraine: University of Ulster.

Newman, D., and A. Paasi. 1998. "Fences and Neighbors in the Post-Modern World: Boundary Narratives in Political Geography." *Progress in Human Geography* 22 (2): 186–207.

Saint-Germain, Michelle A. 1995. "Similarities and Differences in Perceptions of Public Service among Public Administrators on the U.S.-Mexico Border." *Public Administration Review* 55 (6): 507–17.

Teague, P. 1989. "Economic Development in Northern Ireland: Has Pathfinder Lost Its Way?" *Regional Studies* 23 (February): 63–69.

Tickner, J.A. 1995. "Re-Visioning Security." In *International Relations Theory Today,* K. Booth and S. Smith, eds. Cambridge: Polity Press.

Tykkläinen, M., and D. Bond. 1997. "Borders as Opportunities in the Regional Development of Europe." Paper presented at the 37th European Congress of the Regional Science Association, 23–27 August, Rome, Italy.

Appendix 1. CAWT Projects, 1997–1998

- Reviewed drug compliance rates among the elderly
- Sponsored a mental health conference
- Studied cross-border recruitment and selection practices
- Conducted a feasibility study on developing a geographical information system for the border region
- Undertook a community Childhood Accident Prevention Project
- Developed primary health care in the border region
- Developed general practice services in the border region
- Identified common quality standards for general practice
- Reviewed learning disability and family care services

- Established guidelines for community pharmacists working with general practitioners
- Identified needed acute and public health services where collaboration is feasible

Appendix 2. A Vision for CAWT

CAWT is envisioned as a way to help improve the health and social well-being of the people it serves. To give life to this vision, CAWT must:

- Become an integral part of the strategy and service planning for the four CAWT health boards and their service providers
- Demonstrate measurable results
- Link with existing community development infrastructures and networks
- Contribute to local and regional community development
- Undertake health care needs assessment to identify and address border areas needs
- Develop its position as an advocate
- Ensure that its health and social services work recognizes no boundaries

To be recognized as an effective vehicle for cross-border cooperation, governments, health and social care staff, local politicians, and people of the north and south jurisdictions must recognize CAWT as being:

- Relevant to stakeholders
- Strategically significant
- Contributing to the individual agendas of stakeholders
- Effectively using expertise and resources

Project BORDER—Business Opportunities for Regional Development and Economic Regeneration: A Case Study in Developing an Irish Cross-Border Telematic Information Service[1]

Adrian Moore, Gerard Parr, and Sally Cook[*]

Abstract

In the context of European border regions, the Irish border corridor has suffered particularly severe economic and social deprivation, where problems of peripherality (both within national boundaries and Europe) have been exacerbated by the consequences of 30 years of politically motivated violence. It is imperative for the development of this region that the tendency toward economic isolation be addressed and effectively countered. The provision of advanced telecommunications technology is a key infrastructural requirement for the promotion of economic development by bringing information and services to businesses and individuals, thus enabling them to fulfill their competitive potential in a wider market. Funded by the Regional Development subprogram of the EU INTERREG (International Regions) II program, the University of Ulster (in Northern Ireland) and the Local Government Computer Services Board (in the Republic of Ireland) are developing a Geographic Information Systems-based teleservice to help promote the coordination and development of economic and

* Moore is Lecturer in Medical Geography and Geographic Information Systems in the School of Environmental Studies at the University of Ulster in Northern Ireland. Parr is Professor of Telecommunications and Distributed Systems in the School of Information Software Engineering at the University of Ulster. Cook is Lecturer in Geography in the School of Environmetnal Studies at the University of Ulster.

environmental opportunities throughout the entire border corridor. The system aims to offer a comprehensive description of the economic, social, and environmental characteristics of the region in an easily accessible and user-friendly way. This paper presents an overview of project BORDER from the conception of the idea in the early 1990s to the present. Consideration is given to the European/national strategic, technical, organizational, and everyday practical issues involved in developing and realizing this ambitious project.

Introduction

The development of modern society is increasingly facilitated by advanced communications technology and associated services, creating what is now known as the "information society." In such a society, information and knowledge are key strategic resources for economic development. The competitiveness of firms and the comparative advantages of regions increasingly depend on knowledge-based activities. Information and Communications Technologies (ICT) can underpin all sections of the service and production industries by overcoming the obstacles of distance and of political and administrative boundaries.

Telecommunications infrastructure is a primary means by which business and industry enhance their performance—especially between industrial sectors, suppliers and users, professional services, and consumers. Sectors most likely to benefit include the financial industry, government and professional services, distribution and retailing, publishing, printing, and light manufacturing (O'Siochru 1991).

Acquiring access to advanced telecommunications technology, therefore, is a key requirement for economic development. It can strengthen the economic and social cohesion of outlying areas by bringing information and services to businesses and individuals, enabling them to participate and compete in a wider market. It could be argued that a principal long-term benefit of diffusing telecommunications infrastructure is the equalizing effect of reducing the disadvantages of peripheral locations (Masser et al. 1992). For peripheral, economically disadvantaged areas, it could equally be argued that failure to introduce and make effective use of telecommunications infrastructure can only result in widening regional disparities, as core regions capitalize on the benefits of such services and further enhance their economic advantage.

In the context of European border regions, the Irish border corridor has suffered particularly severe economic and social deprivation. Its problems of peripherality (both within national boundaries and Europe) have been exacerbated by 30 years of politically motivated violence. It is imperative for the development of this region that the tendency toward economic isolation be recognized and effectively countered.

In Europe, recognition of the disadvantages of having wide economic regional disparities between and within member states led to a major policy initiative to redress the imbalance. A primary objective was to strengthen the competitiveness of the single European market in response to other growing continental markets. A central focus of the European Union (EU) Regional Development Policy (typified by the cross-border INTERREG programs) was to introduce structural changes in poorer, less favored regions, and to equitably provide access to advanced telecommunications services. Due to a lack of telecommunications infrastructure and services, it is difficult for less-favored regions to attract new industries, and for their indigenous industry to compete in core markets (O'Siochru 1991).

Although it was not the objective of EU policy to specifically tackle problems of regional inequalities, one of its core action programs was intended to establish telecommunications infrastructures and services in less favored regions. This was to be achieved primarily by two programs: Special Telecommunications Action for Regional Development (STAR), aimed at providing telecommunications infrastructure, and TELEMATIQUE, designed to promote uptake of telecommunication services.

By upgrading all 44 exchanges to digital switching, adopting optical fiber as the medium to cover the province, and providing fiber optic links to Great Britain and to the Republic of Ireland, the STAR program gave Northern Ireland one of the most advanced telecommunications infrastructures in the world. The Integrated Services Digital Network (ISDN) was also installed; this all-digital network can transmit and process every kind of communication—voice, data, text, and still and moving video images at speeds from 128K bits-2.4G bits. In 1992, these links were intended to open up a host of new opportunities for computer-based industries and to offer Northern Ireland's businesses a vital technological and marketing advantage in the single European market. At the same time, Telecom Eireann was also introducing new technology to its public network. The availability and interoperability of telecommunications services along the border region are now a reality.

The TELEMATIQUE program aimed at promoting uptake and development of new applications to take advantage of advanced telecommunications services in less favored regions. The purpose was to use an integrated European market to strengthen economic and social cohesion. While this program has achieved some measure of success in providing and promoting telematic services, in Ireland its success has been tempered by limited use of the facilities. In Northern Ireland, although 182 companies did secure support from the program, it has been suggested that the generally poor response to calls for proposals was partly a combination of lack of technological awareness, poor marketing, and distrust of the technology (Moore and Parr 1994). This pattern is not unique to Northern Ireland; it is also the case in other peripheral and less favored regions in Europe.

A number of preconditions that could facilitate sustainable and successful adoption of these technologies in less favored regions have been identified, including the development of a sufficiently broad client base to stimulate a cumulative self-sustained mechanism; clear identification of the usefulness of these technologies for business and other purposes; and proper integration and management of these technologies into established business and social structures.

Project BORDER aims to prepare its target area by providing the physical and organizational mechanisms to support entrepreneurial initiatives and to develop the business and economic potential of the border region.

Knowledge and information are basic to success in identifying and developing entrepreneurial and business potential; however, it can be difficult to assemble the required information. Fundamental stumbling blocks are availability, awareness, and accessibility of data. In a border zone, such problems are exacerbated by the difficulty of finding comparable data sources on similar spatial scales. These problems were made apparent by approaches made to the University of Ulster by a variety of groups, ranging from local governments to environmental protection agencies and community groups that requested advice on the availability of information on the economic, social, and environmental characteristics of their own local and neighboring cross-border areas. In a direct response to this growing number of requests, particularly the environmental and cross-border ones, the Schools of Environmental Studies and Information and Software Engineering at the University of Ulster collaborated with the Local Government Computer Services Board to develop the BORDER Telematic Information Service.

Developing the BORDER Concept

Following initial discussions about the potential for developing an information service for the Irish cross-border region, two challenges had to be met: (1) identification (through market research) of a real business and community need for such a service; and (2) how to finance the project's development. Only then could the aims and objectives of the project be formulated.

Market Research

Considerable time and money were spent conducting market research to help develop the BORDER concept. Rather than impose a top-down approach to decision making, its creators wanted to ensure that the project was appropriate to the border region and to its prospective users. To establish the level of local demand for the proposed service, and to more closely define the specific needs of potential users, the University of Ulster carried out extensive market research among organizations in business and commerce, local government, and the volunteer sector in the Irish border region. This entailed the employment of a full-time marketing researcher, attendance and presentations at conferences, formal and informal consultations with potential user groups and government departments, questionnaire surveys about user needs, the creation of a database of interested parties, and the organization of an all-day workshop for potential users (totaling an approximate UK£100,000, or US$150,263, investment over a two-year period).

Funding the Project

From the conception of the project, it was recognized that such a cross-border information service would be expensive to provide. Various options for funding were investigated early on, and the European Union INTERREG II program was thought to be the most appropriate option available at the time. The Ireland/ Northern Ireland INTERREG II program (1994–1999) is an EU Community Initiative designed to promote cross-border cooperation and to stimulate economic development in the region through grants to approved individuals, groups, and organizations. The program has a total budget of UK£207 million (US$311 million) available over the five-year period. Its principal objectives are to promote the creation and development of cross-border cooperation networks, and to help the region overcome those special development problems that arise from its relative isolation within the national economies and the European Union.

The program is managed by the two governments on a cross-border basis. Following discussions with relevant government officials, an application was submitted under the Regional Development subprogram, which is managed by the Department of Economic Development in Northern Ireland and the Department of Finance in the Republic of Ireland. Trying to match a particular proposal to specific funding bodies and programs, all with different aims and objectives, is a common problem. Fortunately, the general goals of the proposed project and those of the Regional Development subprogram were in accord. A crucial point in drawing up the proposal was to make sure the project met the qualification criteria of that particular measure, and that the objectives addressed pertinent issues. A phased approach was adopted, given the scale and time required to complete the project; the first phase was to last 18 months (for development), followed by a two-year main phase. The first phase would be funded under the INTERREG II program, and the second phase funded under the successor program.

The proposal was evaluated internally by the two government departments, then submitted for external technical review and economic appraisal before it was accepted for funding. The first phase of the project was funded under INTERREG II at a rate of 50 percent for commercial organizations and 75 percent for publicly funded bodies and nonprofit organizations.

Objectives and Perceived Benefits of Project BORDER

The principal objectives of BORDER are to:
* help realize the border corridor's full potential for economic development
* identify socioeconomic, infrastructural, and environmental resources and to conduct an audit of secondary (subsequently primary) data sources
* establish a Geographic Information Systems-based teleservice that will provide economic and environmental information to user groups in the border region using advanced telecommunications and database technology. This will facilitate higher levels of small- to medium-sized enterprises (SMEs) and small partnership business opportunities in the border corridor and beyond.

- promote the border corridor as an area for inward investment using advanced telematics technology
- foster more interaction between the two national governments about the physical environment, its protection, and its use in the border region
- facilitate more efficient and cost-effective integrated spatial planning
- advance the flow of information and ideas between groups and communities along the border corridor to enhance business opportunities in a manner compatible with protection of the local environment

Project BORDER coincides with the objectives of the INTERREG II program and specific objectives within the Regional Development subprogram, notably creation and development of cross-border networks and links for cooperation, trade, and economic development. Research established that there is a strong desire among border communities to develop cross-border linkages. Project BORDER will supply the means for such cross-border communication, and, by providing individuals and organizations with relevant information about other groups, companies, and markets, will aid development and exploitation of the economic potential of the entire border corridor. Spatially referenced information will be available on a comprehensive range of economic activities, including suppliers, producers, retailers, and wholesalers.

Development of Local Area and Community-Based (Cross-Border) Economic Action Plans

Market research revealed that the development of local area action plans is frequently thwarted by lack of cooperation and information, particularly in cross-border settings. By providing an apolitical, easily accessible, and comprehensive information system, regional community groups, chambers of commerce, local authorities, and other interested parties can come together and have equal access to information that may previously have been difficult to obtain for logistical reasons, or due to lack of knowledge or expertise. This information system's accessibility and availability will minimize the duplication of efforts by different groups, thus promoting efficient use of resources.

Promotion and Diversification of Local Economies

Project BORDER will help strengthen local economic activity by providing an information resource that can support development and increase the efficiency of existing enterprises. Partnership arrangements will be facilitated by the accessibility of information and networking, enabling joint marketing initiatives and joint business ventures, and allowing businesses to take better advantage of economies of scale.

Improvement of Internal and External Access

Interested parties will be able to use BORDER's facilities and information to more effectively form networks both within and beyond the border area. This will improve internal and external communication and boost inward investment. Facilities provided by the BORDER Telematic Information Service will give groups and organizations an opportunity to extend their contacts or sphere of influence farther afield than ever before. Border groups that wish to develop international connections might do so by creating Internet home pages. These groups could also use desktop conferencing applications over ISDN to help them develop "live" marketing or product distribution. Any group that wishes to develop international projects in business, culture, the environment, or tourism could use such techniques to ease the often difficult and time-consuming process of locating partners in other countries.

Improvement of Local Skills

Information Technology (IT) is increasingly prominent in the workplace, and those who lack basic technical skills are at a disadvantage in many occupations. The BORDER program's associated partner/demostrator sites (eight in the first phase) will have skilled on-site training staffs to help end-users learn the latest desktop multimedia and telecommunications technology and gain exposure to systems through formal courses and hands-on experience. These trained users will then be encouraged to pass their skills on to others.

Project Team

The schools of Environmental Studies and Information Software Engineering at the University of Ulster in Northern Ireland are the lead partners in the BORDER project. Joint partners in the Republic of Ireland are the Local Government Computer Services Board (a semipublic organization that provides IT solutions for local governments in the Republic) and Connect Ireland (an IT company in Dublin). Colin Stutt Consulting in Northern Ireland and Nexus Research in both the Republic of Ireland and Northern Ireland are associate consulting contractors. These organizations make up the Project Management Committee (PMC) and are responsible for all project activities. Specialist subgroups are organized within the PMC to tackle primary activities. There is a Technical Advisory Group comprised of key organizations on both sides of the border, such as census offices, Ordnance Survey, and telecom providers (BT and Telecom Eireann). Local User Group Committees are organized by Nexus Research and are made up of members from each of the eight associated partner sites. Each partner site receives all the necessary hardware and software for establishing a remote access site in a border location (four for each side of the border), including ISDN lines and line usage costs. A financial contribution is also made toward the salary and time of an employee to service the site and be available to the local community to give assistance and advice on how to use the service. Personnel at these sites are responsible for promoting the service in their local area, as well as helping to collate local data.

The Border Telematic Information Service

The Border Telematic Information Service is being realized through a combination of systems.

Enabling Technologies

The Internet is arguably the most important communications development since the original deployment of telephone networks in the second half of the nineteenth century. For the first time, there is a common platform for sharing information in any form (text, image, sound, and video), and for making it accessible to whole populations. This universal access is the great strength of the Internet and is the cause of its massive growth in recent years. However, this is only the beginning. In the next few years, Internet traffic is expected to overtake voice traffic in communications networks (see Figure 1). This is a revolutionary change and indicates that the Internet, while important now, will soon become even more so. The opportunities for BORDER, using the Internet as a delivery mechanism, are immense, and its strong "technology watch" aspect ensures "futureproofing" the service it will put in place. As network infrastructure and support services improve, BORDER will also be developed to take advantage of new systems.

The increasing use of digital technologies is bringing about a convergence of three industry sectors that have been quite distinct in the past. The IT industry has been based on digital technologies for some time (Analysys Consulting 1998b). Telecommunications has been moving toward digital technologies for the last 10 years, starting with its backbone networks, and now spreading to access networks. The implications of this convergence to BORDER are many, but the most important is that it may offer the means to seamlessly integrate interactive applications and visual content for distribution and access to a range of network services. Convergence is resulting in the interchangeability of content between these sectors. BORDER is designed to utilize all of these technologies.

Enabling Technologies: The Internet—Information Superhighway

In November 1998, Forrester Research, the Massachusetts-based market research firm, predicted that e-commerce sales could reach *US$2,300 billion* (more than 5% of all world sales) by 2003. Furthermore, Forrester forecast that even under the most adverse conditions, e-commerce sales will still exceed US$1,400 billion. There are endless possibilities for companies to reach global markets via the Internet, and these opportunities are as open to businesses and organizations in the border region of Ireland as to those in the United States. Using innovative techniques, BORDER will show users how to make the most of these opportunities.

Figure 1. Internet Traffic versus Voice Traffic

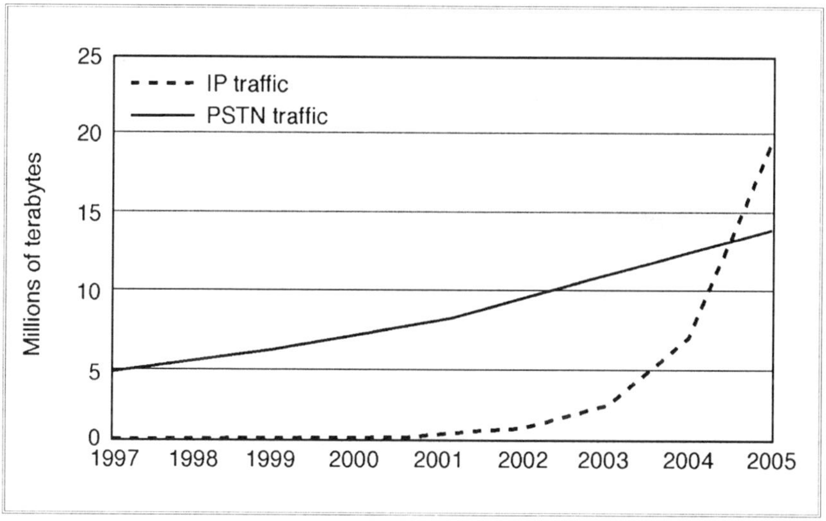

Source: Analysys Consulting 1998a.

Geographic Information Systems (GIS) and Distributed Systems

Before data can be accessed, a content preparation, presentation, and delivery facility must be established that allows data to be quickly and easily exchanged between computers and other intelligent processing devices. In most cases, when data are of the same type and from the same source, their manipulation is easily managed. However, integrating different classes of data that need to be merged or compared in order to address a particular set of spatial user queries may cause problems. Geographic Information Systems (GIS) technology can help solve such problems. Telecommunications technology now enables rapid access to and distribution of data and relevant manipulation tools. While the broad economic and social benefits of Geographic Information Systems have been identified, accepted, and widely exploited using desktop and intranet technologies, expanding GIS services and systems via telecommunications technologies is still a relatively new concept (Crowder 1996; VanBrakel and Pienaar 1997; Cole 1997; Heikkila 1998).

Today, a variety of proprietary GIS are widely used in stand-alone mode by government, business, and industry. But few systems or organizations have the potential to take advantage of the power of telecommunications to replicate the quality of service of a stand-alone GIS into a functional "Distributed GIS" (DGIS). The key value of developing DGIS is the resulting significant reduction in the costs of providing GIS services (hardware, software, liveware, and data) to the commercial sector, particularly to the hitherto untapped market of SMEs and community-based organizations.

Developing distributed client/server GIS requires sufficient networked telecommunication services. BORDER will employ a number of publicly available "transport" technologies that are widely provided both in the EU and globally. These will initially center around high-speed Internet access to BORDER servers, point-to-point (PTP) ISDN access for higher volume transactions, and additional desktop conferencing facilities. The choice of telecommunication transport services will be based on the volume of data required to satisfy client interaction with the BORDER server, and whether or not adequate network technology already exists at the client site.

BORDER Technical Architecture

The Project Management Team will collate and maintain a distributed multimedia database of spatially referenced data to which all associated partners will have access (conceptual user-group access is illustrated in Figure 2).

Figure 2. Conceptual Architecture of the BORDER System

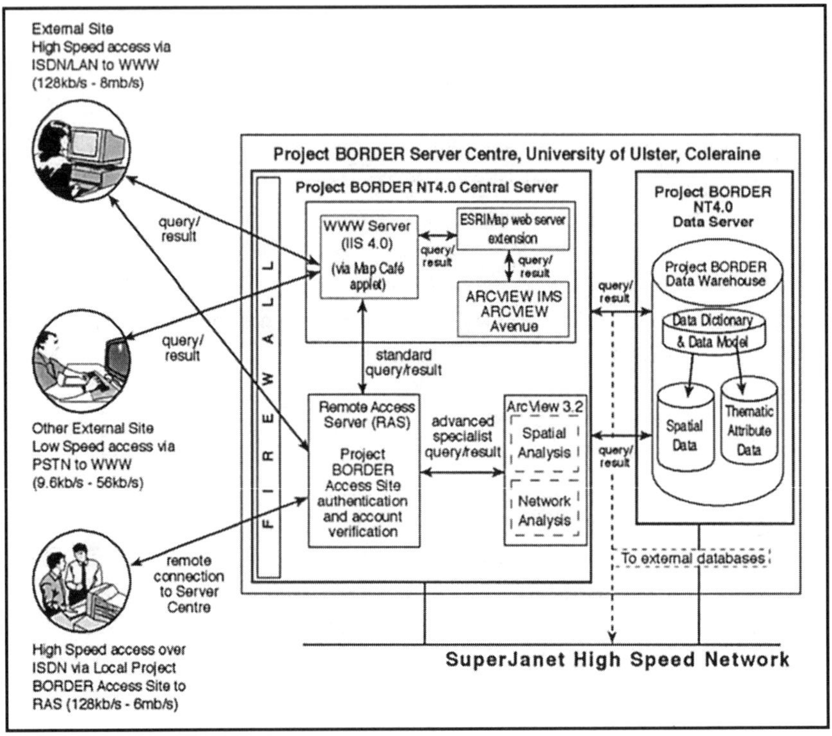

Advanced telecommunications facilities (the Euro-ISDN service) will support delivery software technology for client-server access. This will be realized at each site by a GIS compliant front end and associated software facilities provided by the latest desktop multimedia workstations. This will permit the retrieval, integration, and processing of a variety of spatial and aspatial datasets and related data in a user-friendly environment. Although there will initially be a central source for validation, entry, and maintenance of datasets, access sites are provided at eight strategic geographic locations throughout the border region (Figure 3).

As Figure 2 illustrates, access to BORDER servers is provided through a variety of means: over standard telephone lines via a modem from the home or office, via stand-alone multimedia using CD ROMs, or via point-to-point ISDN connections. There are also facilities for real-time desktop file exchange, shared whiteboard, remote applications sharing, and video conferencing over ISDN. These tools are being used for software development and testing, data feeds, and general project management. The central servers are currently located at and managed by the University of Ulster at Coleraine.

Experienced users can utilize the software at each BORDER Access Site to launch detailed spatial queries against the data. On-site technical support personnel will be trained in BORDER technology and will be aware of the systems and data available to address specific requests, allowing them to help inexperienced users gain access to the knowledge they need. In effect, BORDER Access Site personnel and equipment will be a local bureau service for all users. They will not only offer assistance with the technology and its use, but will also ensure that more detailed queries or data requirements are fed back to the main BORDER central control at the university for subsequent processing.

Currently, the GIS Engine is provided by MapInfo's MapXtreme 2.0 environment and is further enhanced by the BORDER software development team to

Figure 3. Geographical Coverage of BORDER Access Sites

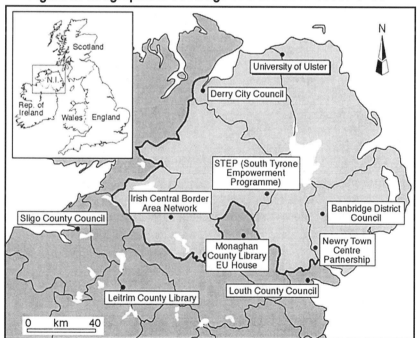

provide additional query processing capability. Various telecommunications services (such as Public Switch Telephone Network–PSTN, ISDN, Switched Multi-Megabit Data Service–SMDS, and Novell Local Area Network–LAN) are being examined to ensure that performance aspects of the service are met. For complex queries unavailable on the Internet service, additional functions such as network analysis are provided at the University of Ulster BORDER Office using ESRI software products. Such queries are received via email or through remote BORDER Access Site operatives. They are then analyzed, processed, and relevant resultant data are returned to the user by hardcopy and/or electronically.

Data Issues

The first phase of the project (June 1998-August 1999) used secondary data that already existed. The procedure for data procurement consists of secondary data audits at the federal (University of Ulster and Local Government Computer Services Board) and local (Nexus and border site representatives) levels. A meta-database is being compiled to detail data sources organized under the following main headings: Economic Activity, Social Infrastructure, Environment, and Tourism. Data are then selectively collected, depending on usefulness, form, nature, and ownership status.

With the availability of computer-based information over networks, to charge fees or not for information has become a significant problem in recent years (Crowder 1996). Certain data ownership issues have arisen with the introduction of distributed GIS, including data security, copyright, data standards, and who pays for data (users or local authorities). BORDER personnel are investigating the situation.

Data may come free of charge or may be purchased or leased from the owning organization. BORDER has a substantial budget for purchasing data. In certain circumstances, special permission and royalty agreements are needed before information can be put out on the Internet. In addition to royalties, BORDER is being offered as a test bed for organizations interested in pursuing the Internet as a route to doing business in the future.

Data integrity and security are serious issues, especially for commercially purchased or leased data from sources such as the Census and Ordnance Survey. Such issues must be accommodated in the technical architecture and delivery mechanisms of the service. For example, since BORDER needs to provide adequate security mechanisms to prevent unauthorized access to data and potential corruption of data structures and items, it has adopted a thin client/thick server architecture (hence the use of the MapXtreme internet GIS software as opposed to, say, Activemaps). Using such a system allows certain controls on the server side over how information can be accessed, distributed, and viewed. With census data, for example, users are denied access to certain types of raw count data at the most detailed level of spatial aggregation (for reasons of commercial sensitivity and data protection legislation), but are allowed to classify such variables by quartiles, quintiles, natural breaks, or standard deviations.

The question of charging for information has been factored into the development phase of the project. However, it is being investigated with respect to the long-term viability of the system. Once BORDER becomes commercial, it is possible that a charging system could be put into operation, perhaps along the lines of a Chip Secure Electronic Transaction (C-SET), an electronic dedicated charge card. The C-SET initiative is an Information Society Initiatives in support of Standardization (ISIS) project. Other methods include "pay-per-hit," "pay-per-theme," or just having "credits" allocated per user group.

Given the fact that this is a cross-border project and that information is thus procured in two countries from a variety of different sources, data comparability is a main issue for all types of map and thematic data. Census data are a classic example (Waters 1995). The census information gathered every 10 years in both Northern Ireland and the Republic of Ireland, while generally similar in content, does vary quite considerably in both the specifics of the questions included in each census and in the size of the geographical areas for which the data is publicly released (Cook et al. 1999; Waters 1995). BORDER addresses this problem by providing a data-dictionary to explain how each item of information was collected, its ownership, accuracy, date created, and most recent update. It is hoped that this will allow clients to make informed decisions before they undertake data comparisons between different regions.

Part of the data audit process and user needs studies are tailored to identify what users would like and which of these data or information do or do not already exist. These studies will develop data issues and strategies for the second phase of the project. It is envisaged that a substantial component of Phase II will involve collection and generation of primary data in addition to procurement of secondary data.

Conclusion

At the end of 1998, all project management structures were in place, and demonstrator sites have been selected and equipped. Preliminary data audits for Northern Ireland and the Republic of Ireland have been conducted, and local audits have been undertaken by demonstrator site representatives. A number of base datasets have been purchased, leased, or agreed upon, and the BORDER interactive query interface is being designed. The server and GIS software (MapXtreme) have been installed and tested. An alpha version of the system was released for internal (including demonstrator sites) testing and validation by February 1999. A BORDER website is functional <www.border.ulst.ac.uk>.

Prospects for future developments of the system are good, especially with the advent of the current peace process in Northern Ireland and the establishment of new cross-border government bodies. Plans for a follow-up funding program to INTERREG II are being developed. It is envisaged that BORDER serve as an "anchor initiative"—a base to support further program development and the realization of strategic objectives.

Endnote

1. The authors wish to acknowledge the financial support they received from the European Commission's INTERREG II program as managed by the DETINI (Belfast) and DOF (Dublin). They thank Howard Keery, Sean O'Sullivan, Stephen McAlister, Nigel McDowell, Kilian McDaid, and Mark Millar for all of their assistance. The authors also appreciate the information they referenced from report No. 98328, supplied by Analysys Consulting.

References

Analysys Consulting. 1998a. *Enabling Technologies*. Company technical report.

Analysys Consulting. 1998b. *Development of a Telecomms Strategy for Northern Ireland*. Telecomms Strategy Working Group, Northern Ireland Growth Challenge.

Capello, R. 1994. *Spatial Economic Analysis of Telecommunications Network Externalities*. Aldershot: Avebury.

Cole, S. 1997. "Futures in Global Space." *Futures* 29 (4–5): 393–418.

Cook, S., A.J. Moore, and M.A. Poole. 1999. "Methodological Issues in a Cross-Border Investigation of Poverty in Ireland." Pp. 75–94 in *Poor People, Poor Places: A Geography of Poverty and Deprivation in Ireland*, D.G. Pringle, J. Walsh, and M. Hennessy, eds. Dublin: Oak Tree Press.

Crowder, J. 1996. "Mapping the Information Superhighway." Pp. 110–13 in *The AGI Source Book for GIS*, D. Green, D. Rix, and C. Corbin, eds. London: Taylor & Francis.

Heikkila, E.J. 1998. "GIS is Dead; Long Live GIS!" *Journal of the American Planning Association* 64 (3): 350–60.

Masser, I., O. Sviden, and M. Wegener. 1992. *The Geography of Europe's Futures*. London: Belhaven Press.

Moore, A.J., and G.P. Parr. 1994. "The Implementation of European Union Advanced Telecommunications Programs in the Less Favored Regions of Europe: The Case of Northern Ireland." Paper presented at the Regional Science Association Conference, September, Trinity College, Dublin, Ireland.

O'Siochru, S. 1991. *Europe Connected Disconnected? Broadband Networks in Less Developed Regions*. Madrid: FUNDESCO.

VanBrakel, P.A., and M. Pienaar. 1997. "Geographical Information Systems: How a World Wide Web Presence Can Improve their Availability." *Electronic Library* 15 (2): 109–16.

Waters, R. 1995. "Data Sources and their Availability for Business Users Across Europe." In *GIS for Business and Service Planning*, P. Longley and G. Clarke, eds. Cambridge: GeoInformation International.

V
The Baltic Sea Region: Politics, Environment, and Transboundary Resource Management

Frontiers and Lines on Estonian Mental Maps

Eiki Berg[*]

Abstract

In recent years, geopolitical theories have been pushed aside as scholars and politicians have related them to greater power politics or legitimizing aggression in the global arena, forgetting that smaller states may also draw inspiration from geographical and historical realities in their sociospatial constructions. In this essay, reflections on the different spatial levels provide a vantage point for understanding the constructed visions of the state and the surrounding world. In the process, imaginative maps are created based on experiences and discourses pertaining to Estonia. Different discourses and geopolitical visions are mapped out, although none of them play a predominant role in making scholars think of Estonia in a similar manner.

Introduction

Geopolitical theories have often been dismissed as nationalistic visions, self-deceiving myths, or simple expressions of capricious human will. These theories have been related to attempts to legitimize realist thinking in international relations, power politics, and rivalry, often forgetting that small states in the throes of rethinking their national identity may draw inspiration from geographical and historical realities. This argument emphasizes the basic goals of every state: to delimit its territory and to separate what is "ours" from "theirs." Thus, the demarcation of boundaries is fundamental to the spatial organization of people and social groups.

The following analytical framework is derived from critical geopolitics—a culturally and politically varied way of describing, representing, and writing about both geography and international politics (see Ó Tuathail, Dalby, and Routledge 1998; Ó Tuathail and Dalby 1998). The factors that produce this perspective are multiple and pervasive. They are found at high (a national security memorandum or a foreign policy doctrine) and low levels (the headline of a tabloid newspaper or political cartoons), and are both visual (the images that move

---

* Berg is head of the Political Science Department at Tartu University.

states to act, such as perceived threats to the national interests) and discursive (such as speeches that justify military actions).

Critical geopolitics bears witness to the diversity of people and places as well as the ways that identity is formed and space is constructed out of many entities. It particularly focuses on boundary-drawing practices and behaviors that characterize the everyday life of states. Both the material borders that draw the limits of a state and the conceptual borders that designate boundaries between a state's internal security and an external anarchy are objects of investigation (Ó Tuathail and Dalby 1998). These practices include the definition of the "outside" of a state as well as the construction of "inside" and "outside" boundaries, "here" and "there," and "domestic" and "foreign."

Estonia provides the opportunity to test the process in which experience and discourse combine to create imaginative maps. Reflections on different spatial levels provide a vantage point for understanding constructed visions of the state and the surrounding world. The purpose of this essay is to shed light on what the Estonian nation and state mean to those living within its borders and on its frontiers.[1] Because geopolitics envelops more than just mapped boundaries, this study focuses particularly on maps of meaning—boundaries that are socially constructed and therefore studied as social frames instead of material barriers. It analyzes various lines of separation and cohesive frontiers on a number of different scales (national, local, and regional), stressing boundary-drawing practices.

State Level I: The Meaning of the "New" Estonia

The foundation and specification of the state as a national community are geopolitical acts. They involve making one national identity out of many, establishing a boundary with the outside, and converting diverse places into a unitary internal space. It also involves forging scattered and heterogeneous histories into a single, transcendent, and providential record (Dijkink 1996). These practices of nationhood involve the projection of envisioned community, the homogenization of nation-space, and the re-creation of a pedagogical history. The geopolitical imagination works to project a visual order for space (usually in the form of cartographic surveys and national atlases) across an uneven and broken landscape that is divided into territories by lines that delimit administrative provinces and an official interior and exterior. It is also at work in the founding of communities and the renegotiation of boundaries for citizenship and identification. It may raise such questions as: What, in reality, is the state called the Republic of Estonia? Is Estonia the new state (founded in 1991) or a reestablished one of the past (1918–1940)? What is the size and nature of the state?

An Old Nation-State

Foundations for the current Estonian state were laid between 1991 and 1994. The right-of-center political elite that came to power during those years declared the previous 50 years of Soviet annexation and occupation illegal and contrary to the will of the indigenous population. In this sense, the Estonian political elite chose a restitutionist interpretation of independence. This included the adoption—in spirit, though not in form—of much of the old 1922 constitution, along with claiming rights to some 772 square miles (2,000 square kilometers) of territory that had belonged to Estonia before World War II but was annexed by Stalin in 1945. The first paragraph of the 1992 constitution states that, "Estonia is an independent and sovereign democratic republic wherein the supreme power of the state is held by the people." Its legal interpretation has determined that all decisions regarding constitutional order are to be made by the citizens of Estonia, excluding about five hundred thousand Soviet-era immigrants in a population of 1.5 million.

Other constitutional provisions from 1992 established Estonian as the official state language, guaranteed Estonian citizenship based only on the rule of *jus sanguis,*[2] and limited public service jobs to Estonian citizens (Lauristin and Vihalemm 1997). Legislators tried to combine liberal principles of individual freedom and rights for all inhabitants of Estonia with guarantees for the development of Estonian national identity, language, and culture under the protection of the Estonian nation-state. It was essential that Estonia prove that it did not gain independence for the first time as one of the 15 Soviet successor states, but rather restored its statehood after a 50-year illegal occupation. Its recuperation of statehood resulted in its enlargement by 772 square miles (2,000 square kilometers), and its depopulation by half a million people (illegal Soviet-era residents) both in rhetoric and on paper. History and geography lessons, school atlases and maps, foreign policy rhetoric, and even weather forecasts depicted this constructed reality rather well. It became a state with certain territories that no Estonian could enter without crossing the demarcation line because they remained under the control of Russian Federation,[3] and where some 30 percent of the population had only resident alien status.[4] Officially, the reestablished Republic of Estonia was an old nation-state with only a 10 percent minority population whose minority rights were covered by the reinstated, yet stillborn, Cultural Autonomy Law (1993).

A New Multicultural State

A few days before the eightieth anniversary of Estonia, a number of people expressed doubt concerning the appropriateness of celebrating the birthday of the First Republic, which existed in the interwar period. Although there are important historical and legal linkages between the two periods—the relationship between grandparents, parents, and children, for example—a nation-state (its territory and population structure) and nation-time (the late 1930s and late 1990s) are not the same in comparative perspective. During the late 1980s, there already existed a countervision within the Estonian national independence movement of a new multicultural state to be formed gradually by taking over and restructuring the existing organs of state power, seceding from the Soviet Union, and proclaiming a new Estonian Republic. Following this logic, Estonia and the Russian Federation (then both subjects of the Soviet Union) signed a treaty in

1991 wherein the current border was mutually acknowledged. At about the same time, many moderate Estonian nationalists envisioned a multicultural Second Republic—one that would automatically guarantee citizenship to all Soviet-era immigrants who applied. Taking a liberal Western stance, they advocated a state with multiple, complementary identities and full political participation for all Russian-speakers. This may stem from the fact that Estonians were too small a majority to build a monolingual and monocultural nation-state. In 1991, Rein Taagepera envisioned an Estonia in which a majority of non-Estonians would become bilingual Estonian citizens and would proudly represent Estonia abroad. At the same time, Estonians would accept the Russian minority to the point that a native Russian-speaking prime minister who was fluent in Estonian would be nothing out-of-the-ordinary (Heidmets 1998: 250).

An Ethnic State with a Divided Society

According to Lauristin and Vihalemm (1997), asymmetrical national perspectives, such as those found between a small nation and its big neighbor, are the main obstacles to mutual recognition and trust between Estonians and local Russians. Estonians and non-Estonians have lived primarily separate lives, having experienced separate media channels and cultural systems, and little interaction or development of a common community. Estonians have felt that since most Russians came to Estonia as a result of the Soviet occupation, the large Russian population is alien and therefore not Estonia's responsibility. Russian-Estonians have tended to live in close-knit communities—attending their own schools, conversing exclusively in Russian, and maintaining little or no contact with the indigenous population. According to Ruutsoo (1996), the central impulse for constructing Estonian statehood was based upon anti-Russian and anti-immigrant sentiment. The Estonian understanding of nationhood has thus been ethnocentric and differentialist. According to this perspective, nationhood was an ethnocultural, not political, fact.

The current Estonian state has promoted two central government policies that call for cultural standardization and ethnopolitics via ethnic domination and assimilation of the minority group. Their goal is to give privileged status to the Estonian language and set in motion a cultural standardization of people and regions. Nation building is made more complicated given that state and nation are not synonymous in the Estonian context. In reality, the Estonian state is much larger than the Estonian nation and the latter comprises an ethnic connotation, distinguishing Estonian nationhood by those who speak Estonian, share Estonian cultural traditions, and have Estonian ancestors. Estonians do not regard Russian-speaking immigrants and noncitizens as members of the titular nation. Therefore, Estonia today resembles more of an ethnic state with a divided society than an integrated entity of a putative nation-state. Such is the outcome of conflicting geopolitical visions in a constructed reality.

State Level II: The Meaning of Borders

Borders and their meanings are historically contingent since they are part of the production and institutionalization of territories and territoriality. Territoriality is established by the popular acceptance of space being classified as "ours" and "theirs," and by the division of "us" and "them" (Agnew 1994). Even if borders are more or less arbitrary lines between territorial entities, they may also carry deep symbolic, cultural, historical (and often contested) meanings for social communities (Newman and Paasi 1998). Controversies about boundary demarcation arise when top priority is given to satisfying national interests at the expense of all other interests and needs. The role of the border and possible disputes over it may therefore be viewed differently at national and local levels (Paasi 1995). The location of a border may be of major importance to the states involved, but of minor importance to the people and places located in its immediate vicinity. Boundaries are sometimes considered barriers to local communities and exist only for the sake of political centers. They may ruin an already-existing settlement system and disturb regular local needs such as social contacts or religious ties. Thus, people living in border areas often develop regional identities and may look at the boundary from a cooperative rather than antagonistic perspective. These perceptions raise questions such as: How do political leaders explain existing borders and justify territorial claims? Do local people perceive borders as separation lines or as contact zones?

Material and Symbolic Limits of State Continuity and Sovereignty

Conflict along the border between Estonia and Russia arose immediately after Estonia reestablished its independence in 1991. At that time, Estonia asserted that its statehood was based on the 1920 Tartu Peace Treaty in which Soviet Russia recognized Estonia's independence.[5] The treaty also precisely delineated the border between the two countries. In 1944, however, Stalin annexed about seven hundred and seventy square miles (two thousand square kilometers) of Estonian territory to the Russian Soviet Federal Socialist Republic. In many respects, these annexed territories were not very valuable, but for Estonians they were important symbols of state continuity and sovereignty.[6] Official Estonian policy (1991–1994) called for the complete restoration of Estonian independence, including restoration of the border outlined in the Tartu Peace Treaty. Although there were reasonable legal arguments to back this up, simply raising the issue led the rest of the world to interpret the Estonian standpoint as merely a territorial claim against the Russian Federation. In December 1994, Estonia gave up its claim on the eastern territories and in November 1996, Estonia agreed not to demand recognition of the Tartu Peace Treaty as the legal basis for mutual agreement in future treaties with Russia. What is still missing, however, is a new border treaty between these two neighboring countries, which is difficult to explain. Although Estonia has removed all barriers to signing the border treaty, it has not met similar willingness from the Russians—most likely due to political disorder in Moscow.

A Contact Zone

The Estonian-Russian border became an ideological platform for conservative-nationalist parties in Estonia (such as "Pro Patria") and many ex-residents of the "lost territories." The closing of the border affected mostly those who had moved from villages to towns and were interested in preserving their "childhood playground" as a unified territorial unit. These people seemed largely connected to the disputed territory by their memories. In reality, the majority of them live in Tallinn and Tartu, not in the border zone. As a result, the desire to restore historical territories appears to increase with distance from the border area, whereas the issue has not been as urgent for borderland villagers (Berg 1997). For these residents, it is a source of everyday challenges. Their remote villages usually lack regular bus connections to other population centers and the nearest public services often remain on the other side of the border. Such problems are most visible in cases where villages and farmsteads are separated by the borderline, or when a church is located on one side of the border while a substantial part of its congregation lives on the other. Neither national interests nor "big politics" are important to many locals. Many would even agree to keep the border open to free crossings, as in earlier times.

Regional Level I: The Meaning of Geographical Location

The concept of boundary is also often used in a metaphorical sense (Jauhiainen 1998). Borders designate an inside and an outside. They can be crossed, but do not guarantee safety from foreign threats (Jaanus 1997). They are fragile, moveable, permeable, transgressable, and invadable. The questions that these constructs raise in Estonia include: How do Estonians perceive their country's geographical position? Is it considered a challenge or an opportunity?

Estonians have been invaded countless times: by neighboring countries; by a variety of languages and religions; and now by commercialism, pollution, and the electronic highway (Jaanus 1997). Estonia's position between Germany, Scandinavia, and Russia creates an ambiguous situation concerning regional identity. Identification with the Baltic Sea Region is more solidly recognized among Estonia's northern European neighbors than by more distant European metropolises. The continuing debate about European borders and the enlargement of the European Union (EU) and the North Atlantic Treaty Organization (NATO) is perceived in Estonia not only in terms of its own security and future economic prosperity, but also as a crucial determinant of its status in the European family of nations.

Estonia is often perceived as a frontier state—the last outpost of Western civilization (Lauristin et al. 1997). Estonia can also be seen, however, as one of the many world gateways: embryonic states in transitional zones that facilitate contact and exchange among different geopolitical realms (Cohen 1991). Gateway states are optimally situated to serve their neighbors' needs in specialized manufacturing, trade, tourism, and financial services, thus stimulating global economic, social, and political interaction as they benefit from Western capital, equipment, credits, and managerial and technical know-how. They are completely open to economic forces from both the East and the West. The gateway's promise is to facilitate the transfer of economic innovation from West to East and, ultimately, from East to West. It will accelerate the evolution of borders from zones of conflict to zones of accommodation.

A Frontier State

Centeno and Rands (1996) have identified a new international division line that begins in northern Estonia and continues in a generally southwestern direction, dividing Poland, Hungary, and the Czech and Slovak Republics from other countries to the East. These countries have succeeded in creating viable market economies and democracies (in contrast to those whose political and economic future remains unclear). In the context of Samuel Huntington's (1996) theory of cultural divisions in the post-Cold War world, some Estonian scholars have tried to argue that from a cultural point of view, the Baltic countries, along with Finland and the Visegrad countries, represent the last outpost of the West-European Roman (Catholic and Protestant) cultural tradition on the border of the Slavic Byzantine (Orthodox) world (Lauristin et al. 1997). These scholars also argue that Estonians have always identified themselves with the West—to the point that other Soviet nations regarded the Baltic countries as the "Soviet West" (Lauristin and Vihalemm 1993). Thus, Estonia's location along the border of Western civilization has been significant; it has determined Estonia's distant and proximate friends and enemies in the past, and is now the impetus for the national liberation movement to separate Estonia from the East and return to Europe. Integration with the EU and NATO is seen as an essential prerequisite for guaranteeing sovereignty in the geopolitically sensitive Baltic region and for a reliable defense against an unpredictable and potentially aggressive Russia. Estonian President Lennart Meri (1996) has made it his task to prove to the world that Europe will become integrated and safe only when the independence of Estonia and the other Baltic states is preserved. This vision for Estonia is most likely tied to North Atlantic security—that heavily militarized bridgehead in the new containment strategy herein Cold War-era communist Russia is replaced by post-Cold War uncertainty, insecurity, and political turbulence in the East.

A Gateway State

Because Estonia is located next to Scandinavia, it possesses dual business potential for transit and other types of trade: first, as an intermediary servicing of North-South traffic in goods and passengers (since Finland serves as a transit connection with Central Europe); and second, as an East-West connection servicing goods and passenger flows between the whole of Western Europe and

Figure 1. The Eastern Boundary of Western Civilization

Western Christianity circa 1500	Orthodox Christianity and Islam

SWEDEN

FINLAND

ESTONIA

RUSSIA

LATVIA

LITHUANIA

Baltic Sea

BELARUS

POLAND

CZECH REP.

UKRAINE

SLOVAKIA

AUSTRIA

MOLDOVA

HUNGARY

SLOVENIA

CROATIA

ROMANIA

BOSNIA

SERBIA

BULGARIA

Black Sea

MONTE-NEGRO

MACEDONIA

ITALY

ALBANIA

GREECE

TURKEY

Mediterranean Sea

Source: Huntington 1996.   0 ⊏⊐ 200
Miles

Russia. To a lesser extent, it may also encompass transit trade from the Far East through Russia (Terk 1995). According to this model, Estonia and Russia are seen as partners whose mutual interests are channeled via trade flows through Estonian ports. Estonia serves as both a European gateway to Russia's raw materials and the West's gateway to the wide Russian market. Estonians may benefit from their knowledge of the Russian language and former contacts there. This model tries to accommodate mutual interests and play upon comparative advantages. People who support the gateway vision are convinced that Estonia's future as an independent and economically prosperous state is more guaranteed if Estonia is opened toward both the East and the West (Eesti 2010 1998). Statements such as, "Europe has no geographical borders," "Europe is not a geographical concept," or "the character of Europe is real, it is indivisible," depict Estonia's gateway position in a zone of cohesion (Meri 1996).

Regional Level II: Estonian Sociospatial Consciousness

Ideologies are significant in that states are governed and held together by certain widely shared systems of belief. At their most elementary level, ideological systems provide support for the power structures within a state and its society. Boundaries form one part of the discursive landscape of social power, control, and governance that extends itself into the whole society and is produced and reproduced by various social and cultural practices (Newman and Paasi 1998). In this discursive landscape, a boundary plays a dual role, reflecting both collective and individual consciousness. Geographic and historical education in the school system fosters that sociospatial consciousness, makes space incontestable and exclusive, and defines friendly and hostile neighbors. Foreign policy is also a boundary-producing phenomenon in this view because nation-states need foreign policy to define "us" and "them" (Dijkink 1996). Consequently, national identity is continually rewritten on the basis of external events and foreign politics. It does not mechanically respond to real threats, but to constructed dangers. Boundaries assume considerable significance because they are simultaneously zones of uncertainty and security. In the Estonian context, questions that arise include: How can the Estonian sociospatial consciousness be characterized? How are neighboring places and peoples perceived by Estonians?

Distant and Proximate Places

In one of his 1992 speeches, President Lennart Meri called on his compatriots to become Europeans while preserving their Estonian roots (Meri 1996). For those who doubted the wisdom of his words, he found a reasonable explanation, stating that "we have always considered ourselves Europeans and Estonia as a state in Europe."

As mentioned previously, the Estonian "mental window" has been more open to the North and West than to the East. This is not surprising, given the fact that the Nordic peoples (Finns in particular) have traditionally had good relations with Estonians due to similar cultural and historical roots. In fact, the Baltic Sea Region is taught in Estonian high school geography lessons (Rummo 1993). Estonia, Finland, and Sweden are studied the most profoundly, while the other Baltic countries and Russia's Kaliningrad and Leningrad oblasts are studied the least. Russia's Pskov oblast, to the southeast of Estonia and now partly occupying the disputed eastern territories, has been left out of the Baltic Sea Region. The first Estonian school atlas since the reestablishment of Estonia (published in 1995) greatly depicted Finland and the Scandinavian region, while it excluded a large-scale map of Estonia and completely ignored the East.

Since 1995, a group of Estonian educational researchers has administered a geography test to high school students. In addition to the students' knowledge of other countries, the test also asked about the conceptual divisions between familiar and unfamiliar places, proximate and distant regions, the mythical East and West, and the North and South. The students divided Europe into more familiar and proximate "Europe-Proper," and less familiar, more distant "Also-Europe." "Europe-Proper" consisted of the Nordic countries, the Baltic states, France, Germany, the United Kingdom, Italy, Spain, and Poland. "Also-Europe" consisted of Portugal, Ireland, the Benelux countries, the Czech Republic, Hungary, Russia, and the Balkan countries. Unexpectedly, the countries of the former Soviet Union (excluding Russia) were seldom regarded as belonging to Europe, and all Eastern states were categorized as strange and unfamiliar (Palang, Vessin, and Liiber 1996). The students' responses were similar to the familiar comparisons of Australia being closer to Britain than to Indonesia and Russia being more distant to Romania than France.

Neighbors: Friendly or Hostile?

During the postwar years, Finland sustained hopes for an independent Republic of Estonia and kept the Estonians' vision of what their country might have been had they stood up to the Russians as the Finns had alive (Ruutsoo 1995). In the process of recognizing, developing, and protecting their cultural identity, the Estonians have received the most help and support from the Finns. Finland has also been of great help in surmounting Estonia's economic and social underdevelopment, and is clearly a dominant influence on Estonia's economy and culture. Estonia considers itself close to all of the Nordic countries. Such an emotional unity among the Baltic countries could be based on the fear of a common external danger (Vihalemm 1997).

Estonian-Russian relations have been cool for the past several years. In 1992, most Estonian parliamentarians considered Russia to be the most hostile state to Estonia (Zhuryari 1994). Indeed, the Baltic region has been in Russia's economic and military-strategic interest for centuries. Today, an additional factor complicates the situation: the many residents of Estonia who are ethnically connected to Russia. Russia's threats to intervene militarily to protect its "mistreated" compatriots have been taken very seriously in Estonia. It is likely that Estonian attitudes toward Russia and Russians are influenced by their ongoing geopolitical insecurity. This security threat, combined with past experience, leaves little space for trust or willingness to cooperate. In the opinion of many Western foreign policy analysts (Goble 1997), Russia's military doctrines, which include Estonia in the sphere of Moscow's vital political, military, and economic interests, are antagonistic. As demonstrated in the rhetoric of Estonian foreign policy and mass media, both an unpredictable and unstable Russia, as well as the "fifth column" within the frontier, are clearly perceived as threats.

Conclusions

This paper gives only a brief overview of the frontiers and borderlines found on Estonian mental maps. These lines and frontiers—some visible and many invisible—that separate "us" from "them" must be deconstructed to both deter potential conflicts and foster future cooperation. Mapping offered by the critical geopolitical discourse has proved difficult due to the variety of views and their conflicting natures. Only those real constructions and boundary drawings that seem most important have been considered here. Based upon the author's observations and critical analysis, there is no consensus regarding the meaning of a "new" Estonia or her regional identity. Both visions—the old nation state as the last frontier of Western civilization and the new multinational state as a gateway—are equally valid, but not equally useful. The model of Estonia as a Western-oriented ethnic state housing a divided society is a product of overlapping constructed and real boundaries, thus constituting a conflicting and contradictory vision. People living within the Estonian border region do not necessarily perceive the official state boundary as a separation line, nor as determined by categories posited by government officials. It is difficult to predict changes in the Estonian sociospatial consciousness or to foresee a large-scale cooperative effort emerging across the de facto Estonian-Russian borderline. For the moment, there are still more barriers than gateways on Estonian mental maps.

Endnotes

1. Traditional political geography makes a distinction between the notions of border and frontier (Parker and Dikshit 1997). Borders are perceived as no more than lines that separate sovereign territories, while frontiers constitute the area near a border whose internal development is affected by the existence of the line.

2. According to *jus sanguis* principle, citizenship is automatically guaranteed only to those who can prove their descendence from another citizen.

3. A visa regime has been in effect along the Estonian-Russian border since July 1992.

4. While the citizenship policy was generally argued on purely legal grounds, it was, in effect, an ethnic issue (Pettai 1996). In 1991, the restored body of citizens was 90 percent Estonian. Noncitizens were almost exclusively Russian-speakers.

5. This was later written into Estonia's constitution in 1992.

6. In his book, *Eesti-Vene piir* (The Estonian-Russian Border), Edgar Mattisen (1993) claims that the border (drawn according to the Tartu Peace Treaty) was determined on the basis of strategic calculation, as it was controlled by the Estonian army at the time. However, during the 1920s and 1930s, Estonian authorities began to officially emphasize the historical and ethnic aspects of the territories east of the Narva River (inhabited, for instance, by other Finno-Ugric tribes) and the southwest area of Setumaa (inhabited by the Setu ethnic group).

References

Agnew, John. 1994. "Boundary." In *The Dictionary of Human Geography,* R. Johnston, D. Gregory, and D. Smith, eds. Oxford: Blackwell.

Berg, Eiki, ed. 1997. *Common Borders, Shared Problems*. Tallinn: Akadeemia Trükk.

Centeno, M., and T. Rands. 1996. "The World They Have Lost: An Assessment of Change in Eastern Europe." *Social Research* 63 (2): 369–401.

Cohen, Saul. 1991. "Global Geopolitical Change in the Post-Cold War Era." *Annals of the Association of American Geographers* 81 (4): 551–80.

Dijkink, Gertjan. 1996. *National Identity and Geopolitical Visions: Maps of Pride and Pain*. London: Routledge.

Eesti 2010. 1998. (28 December) http://www.e2010.ee/.

Goble, Paul. 1997. "Primakov Offers Carrots and Sticks." *The Baltic Times* (6–12 March).

Heidmets, Mati. 1998. "Options for Estonia in 1998." In *Russian Minority and Challenges for Estonia*, M. Heidmets, ed. Tallinn Pedagogical University Press.

Huntington, Samuel. 1996. *The Clash of Civilizations and the Remaking of the World Order*. New York: Simon & Schuster.

Jaanus, Maire. 1997. "Estonia's Time and Monumental Time." *Journal of Baltic Studies* 28 (2): 125–52.

Jauhiainen, Jussi. 1998. "Estonia—Transition of Borders/Transgression of Boundaries." Paper presented at the 18th meeting of the Nordic Critical Geography, 24–27 September, Holbaek, Denmark.

Kooliatlas. 1995. Helsinki: Otava.

Lauristin, Marju, and Peeter Vihalemm. 1993. "The Baltics: West of the East, East of the West." In *Towards a Civic Society. The Baltic Media's Long Road to Freedom*, S. Hoyer, E. Lauk, and P. Vihalemm, eds. Tartu: Baltic Association for Media Research, Nota Baltica Ltd.

Lauristin, Marju, and Rein Vihalemm. 1997. "Recent Historical Developments in Estonia: Three Stages of Transition (1987–1997)." In *Return to the Western World: Cultural and Political Perspectives on the Estonian Post-Communist Transition*, Marju Lauristin, Peeter Vihalemm, K.E. Rosengren, and L. Weibull, eds. Tartu: Tartu University Press.

Lauristin, Marju, Peeter Vihalemm, K.E. Rosengren, and L. Weibull, eds. 1997. *Return to the Western World: Cultural and Political Perspectives on the Estonian Post-Communist Transition*. Tartu: Tartu University Press.

Mattisen, Edgar. 1993. *Estonian-Russian Border*. Tallinn: Ilo.

Meri, Lennart. 1996. *Presidential Addresses*. Tartu: Akadeemia Trükk.

Newman, David, and Anssi Paasi. 1998. "Fences and Neighbors in the Postmodern World: Boundary Narratives in Political Geography." *Progress in Human Geography* 22 (2): 186–207.

Ó Tuathail, Gearóid, and Simon Dalby, eds. 1998. *Rethinking Geopolitics*. New York: Routledge.

Ó Tuathail, Gearóid, Simon Dalby, and Paul Routledge, eds. 1998. *The Geopolitics Reader*. New York: Routledge.

Paasi, Anssi. 1995. "Constructing Territories, Boundaries and Regional Identities." In *Contested Territory. Border Disputes at the Edge of the Former Soviet Empire*, T. Forsberg, ed. Aldershot: Edward Elgar.

Palang, Hannes, Urmas Vessin, and Ülle Liiber. 1996. "Imagination of Europe among Estonian School Children." *Akadeemia* 2: 240–66).

Parker, Geoffrey, and Ramesh Dutta Dikshit. 1997. "Boundary Studies in Political Geography: Focus on the Changing Boundaries of Europe." In *Developments in Political Geography: A Century of Progress*, Ramesh Dutta Dikshit, ed. Thousand Oaks: Sage Publications.

Pettai, Vello. 1996. "The Situation of Ethnic Minorities in Estonia." In *Ethnic Minority Rights in Central Eastern Europe*, M. Opalski and P. Dutkiewicz, eds. Ottawa: Canadian Human Rights Foundation Forum Eastern Europe.

Rummo, T. 1993. *Geography of Baltic Sea Region for Step 9*. Tallinn: Avita.

Ruutsoo, Rein. 1995. "The Perception of Historical Identity and the Restoration of Estonian National Independence." *Nationalities Papers* 23 (1): 167–79.

Ruutsoo, Rein. 1996. "Constituting of Political Nation of Estonian Republic." *Revue Baltique* 7: 19–35.

Terk, Erik. 1995. "A Changing Economy in a Changing Society." *Nationalities Papers* 23 (1): 103–17.

Vihalemm, Peeter. 1997. "Changing National Spaces in the Baltic Area." In *Return to the Western World: Cultural and Political Perspectives on the Estonian Post-Communist Transition*. Marju Lauristin, Peeter Vihalemm, K.E. Rosengren, and L. Weibull, eds. Tartu: Tartu University Press.

Zhuryari, O. 1994. "The Baltic Countries and Russia (1990–1993): Doomed to Good-Neighborliness?" In *The Foreign Policies of the Baltic Countries: Basic Issues*, P. Joenniemi and J. Prikulis, eds. Riga: Center for Baltic-Nordic History and Political Studies.

Environmental Campaigns and Political Mobilization in the Northwestern Border Areas of the Former Soviet Union

Ilkka Liikanen[*]

Abstract

Environmental movements played a major role in the social and political mobilizations that shook Central and Eastern Europe in the late 1980s. Even within the Soviet Union, and particularly in union republics and various autonomous regions, public demonstrations that were formerly strictly controlled by the regime were launched under slogans of environmental protection. Environmental movements were important in at least two ways. First, they reintroduced the repertoire of collective action that had been suppressed by the communist regime, playing a crucial role in transforming the political arena. Second, new environmental movements coupled questions about land and nature with those about territory and identity—and ultimately, boundaries. Rhetoric about native lands or national landscapes, sometimes called "eco-nationalism," involved nationally or ethnically based claims on land that contested the structure and/or borders of the Soviet state. This chapter studies the foundations of the concept of "eco-nationalism" and presents brief case studies of environmental campaigns in the northwestern border areas of the former Soviet Union; specifically, the Union Republic of Estonia and the Autonomous Republic of Karelia. These case studies examine the effect of environmental movements on the mobilization of political opposition and the Popular Front Movement in particular. The recent social scientific debate on the constitution of mental and political boundaries is discussed and commented on from this perspective.

* Liikanen is Researcher at the Karelian Institute at the University of Joensuu, Finland.

Eco-Nationalism?

> In the case of the Soviet anti-nuclear movement, the power of the movement emerged from the fact that the nuclear threat could be easily translated into a symbol of the domination of one ethnic or political group over another. The poorly constructed and operated nuclear power stations were obvious symbols of Moscow's disregard for the welfare of its member nations. They represented the unequal relationship between Russians and other ethnic groups, and between the central Soviet authorities and republic and regional leaders. In this case, national inequalities and environmental complaints became synonymous (Dawson 1996: 162–63).

In her study on antinuclear activism and national identity in Russia, Lithuania, and the Ukraine, Dawson makes an important observation about the close relationship between environmental campaigns and national movements in late Soviet-era society. In the preface to her book, Dawson states that she was astonished by the revelation in her research of an unanticipated link between antinuclear activism and nationalism rather than the mere provision of a window into the rebirth of civil society. She was startled to learn that movements against nuclear power often represented popular demands for national sovereignty and regional self-determination rather than merely reflecting strongly held environmental principles (Dawson 1996: ix–x).

The evidence Dawson presents in support of her argument is quite convincing, especially in the case of the former Soviet Republics. She breaks down the mobilization process into chronologically accurate periods and helps to explain vital interconnections made during the course of events she studied. She states that environmental campaigns were almost nonexistent in the Soviet Union prior to 1985. It was the coincidence of Mikhail Gorbachev's reform program and the horrific accident at the Chernobyl nuclear power station that provided both opportunity and impetus for the first antinuclear environmental campaigns as well as other types of grassroots movements. These same antinuclear and environmental campaigns that had paved the way for more open political mobilization faded away at almost the same time that ethnically based movements stormed into the political arena. "Rather than forming the basis for a powerful anti-nuclear movement, which would fight for the closure of the more than forty nuclear reactors still operating on Soviet soil, public activism on this issue proved unexpectedly short-lived. The movements burst forth in the early period of *perestroika*, then faded away, leaving little evidence of their previous existence" (Dawson 1996: 3).

An analysis of resources and opportunities for collective action under Soviet conditions convincingly supports Dawson's main argument. It is evident that the Communist Party had monopolized resources needed to mobilize people. During *perestroika*, however, uneven and constantly changing access to key resources created a situation in which "movement surrogacy" might emerge. According to Dawson, it was not uncommon for radical actors to hide behind surrogate causes that targeted audiences similar to their true ones during the initial period of *perestroika*, arguing that in some parts of the former USSR "the anti-nuclear movement was little more than a surrogate for hidden nationalist demands" (Dawson 1996: 6–7). Nonetheless, the starting points of Dawson's analysis may be contested in at least two ways: (1) If movements in the republics were largely surrogates for hidden nationalist claims, what fueled them inside the Russian Federation? Consequently, (2) if, in the case of the Russian Federation, there were other reasons for mobilization, what role did these other factors play in the republics and what was their relation to the challenge of new nationalistic feelings?

Although Dawson does not raise these questions outright, she does address them in the text. She elaborates on the theme of the relationship between movement activism and political (national) identification, stating that in mobilizing against Moscow's decisions regarding nuclear power, movement participants could explore not only their attitudes toward the environment, but their own roles as members of a political community as well. Participation in this kind of unprecedented independent activism let people test and confirm their belief that citizens should have a greater role in political decision making. Dawson concludes that while movement participants largely agreed on the need to shift power from state to society, it was often much more difficult to reach a consensus on the nature of the political community and its membership: What political community did they identify with? The USSR? Their republic? Their territory or oblast? Who were the members of that community? Was membership limited to a particular ethnic group, or open to all residents of the region? In essence, the question was: who are "we"? (Dawson 1996: 168–69).

This question of political community and identification brings Dawson very near the ongoing discussions within border studies about social or political construction of identity (see Paasi 1996; Brubaker 1996). Such theories of political identification might provide a mediating link for defining the relationship between environmental movements and the rise of nationalism inside the former Soviet Union. Unfortunately, Dawson does not use this opportunity when interpreting the significance of antinuclear campaigns to popular mobilization. Her conclusions simply restate the basic twofold picture of her premise: in the republics, antinuclear campaigns led to more advanced, conscious nationalistic mobilization; in the Russian Federation, environmental campaigns led more to confusion and inaction than to rooted forms of mobilization. As for political identity, she concludes that the intellectual elite in Armenia and Lithuania possessed a clear sense of national identity early on and acted as movement entrepreneurs in mobilizing society on the nationalist platform. This was not the case, however, in the Ukraine, the national oblasts, or in most of the Russian Federation, where "both the intellectual elites and the mass of society found themselves confused about their primary political identification" (Dawson 1996: 171).

At first glance, these conclusions seem to apply to the case studies of environmental movements in Estonia and Karelia during the late Soviet period (examined later in this essay). In the Union Republic of Estonia, which was historically independent before the Soviet occupation of 1940, environmental movements were followed by broader nationalistic mobilization (Ruutsoo 1996). In the Autonomous Republic of Karelia, which administratively was part of the Russian Federation, the wave of environmentalism passed without major organizational repercussions (Tsygankov 1995). On the whole, however, the notion of "eco-nationalism" is too vague to satisfactorily explain the course of the mobilization process. It can be contested both in terms of movement theory, by questioning the degree to which a concept of "civil society" that relates the environmental movements in the Soviet Union to the "new social movements" in the West is applicable, and of nationalism theory, by contesting the way that nationality is taken as a self-evident basis for political identity and political community.

More precise guidelines for analyzing social movements, nationalism, and the construction of identity under late Soviet conditions are examined in the following brief reviews of recent discussions in these fields. Based on these reviews, this study elaborates an alternative view of the role that environmental movements had in combining questions of land and nature with those of territory and identity and, ultimately, mental and political boundaries. While it seems clear that rhetoric concerning native land or national landscapes involved nationally and ethnically based claims on land and contested the structure and/or borders of the Soviet state, it is not evident that this can be seen as the only function of the environmental movements. It can be argued that in Estonia and the Karelian Republic, the main role of the movements was connected to the rebirth of popular politics and that the degree to which they contested previous mental and physical borders can be considered first against broader change in political culture.

Civil Society and the State

Dawson's astonishment over the fact that environmental activism was linked to the rise of nationalism rather than an indication of the rebirth of civil society is tied to a basic debate within Western theories of social movement about the relationship between civil society and the state. Conceptual limitations can be traced back to fundamental discord between Anglo-Saxon and German traditions of political thinking and their ability to depict contemporary social and political change in Eastern Europe.

In 1989, Arato published a fierce polemic against John Keane and his use of the concept of civil society in his analysis of "Soviet type societies" in *Praxis International*. The controversy had many theoretical, historical, and political aspects. In more than one sense, the debate culminated in Arato's criticism of the way Keane "insists on operating with a two-part state and civil society framework" (Arato 1989: 141; compare with Keane 1988). According to Arato, the demarcation between state and civil society came from the English liberal tradition and stood open to neoconservative use. Arato himself spoke for a "three-part model" that separated state, civil society, and economy. Instead of a dichotomous juxtaposition of state and civil society, Arato wanted to focus on mediation between the three spheres. According to Arato, conceptualizing politics as mediation between state and society would allow the problem to be scrutinized within a "program of radical but self-limiting democracy" (1989: 141–44).

In their ambitious book, *Civil Society and Political Theory,* Cohen and Arato have further developed this argument. They explore the roots of the concept of civil society, particularly within the German (Hegelian) tradition, and argue strongly for its importance in the construction of modern political theory. Without identifying with the normative side of their political theory, it is easy to accept their criticism of the bipolar state vs. society demarcations that are typical of so-called theories of new social movements (Cohen and Arato 1992: 33, 43–47, 69–82; Arato 1990: 31–36).

In the 1980s, it was common within Western social thinking to differentiate between traditional social movements, seen as part of the prevailing system (the state), and new social movements, seen as representations of genuine voluntary association (civil society). These theories (adopted, for example, by the "fundamentalists" of the Green movement) guided Western study of civil society to so-called alternative movements, especially to peace, women's, and environmental movements. According to later critical appraisals, such perspectives led to a restricted view of politics and political organization (Cohen and Arato 1992: 468–74, 510–23).

These perspectives are also discernible in Russian discussions of civil society. The development of civil society has often been evaluated by the rise and fall of "new social movements" (see *Neformaly Rossii*; compare with Hosking, Aves, and Duncan 1992). The notion of civil society in Russia (in contrast to the West) became important in common political language and, curiously enough, to ideologists with various, even antagonistic, political ambitions. During the late Soviet period, political actors—from reform-minded communists to market-oriented liberals and grassroots activists—all found it convenient to define state and society in an antagonistic relationship and to attack the communist *apparatsniki* (officials of the state and party machinery) in the name of society (Brovkin 1990; Kagarlitski 1992; Krasin 1993).

In the late 1980s, expectations held that the Russian social arena would be taken over by "new social movements"; instead, it is occupied today by rather traditional organizations, including nationalistic and religious movements. Consequently, Russian politicians and researchers have largely given up on the concept of *gransdankoe obstsestvo* (civil society). Those members of the intellectual elite who were the most devoted activists in the new social movements feel betrayed and many have totally abandoned politics, which they now consider a playground for populists and marionettes (Stranius 1996). Many of the researchers who enthusiastically studied emerging new social movements at the beginning of the decade have become more and more convinced that these movements are marginally significant as indicators of Russian political culture (Temkina 1997: 29–53; compare with Alapuro 1993). Instead of applying Western models, new Russian studies have examined micro-level preconditions for the development of civil society (Ledeneva 1998) or have tried to develop adequate "Russian" concepts to depict the relationship between society and state under post-Soviet conditions (Volkov 1996).

Dawson's conclusions obviously reflect a pattern similar to the Russian studies. In spite of her narrow concept of civil society, Dawson's notion of the importance of political (national) identification can be used as a step toward overcoming the state/society dichotomy and as a starting point for studying the role of nationalism in the forming postcommunist political culture.

Nationalism and Modern Political Culture

Dawson's concept of "eco-nationalism" is important because it captures the relationships between civic organizations, nationalism, and politics in postcommunist societies. Unfortunately, she does not outline "nationalism" in sufficient depth to include the peculiar conditions of the Soviet successor states. Following the pattern of sociological modernization theory, she at first quite openly disapproves of nationalism as something archaic and backward and does not see it as part of emerging civil society in her theoretical frame, contradicting her use of it as a natural, given part of political identification in a similar pattern as classical nationalistic historiography when analyzing the developments in the Soviet republics. She understands ethnicity and ethnic identification in terms of organic historical continuity without looking at the complicated interconnections between ethnicity, nation building, and mass politics.

In recent social scientific literature, the traditional nationalist view that nationalism and nation-states are natural products of history has been seriously challenged by the idea that nation-states are not some form of organic entities, but that states were made and nations built during a specific period beginning in the seventeenth century (classic examples of this argument include Gellner 1964; Hobsbawm 1972; and Tilly 1975). Illuminating studies convincingly depict the conscious role of nation-minded elites in creating nations in different ethnic and geographical settings (Anderson 1983; Hobsbawm and Ranger 1983). In recent years, however, the so-called new cultural approach has pushed theories of nation building to the limit. The adherents to postmodernism tend to interpret national identities as purely cultural or symbolic practices that are either institutionalized from above or freely defined by individuals. Questions of nationality have been separated from their "ethnic origins" (Smith 1986), on the one hand, and the "social construction of nationalism" (Paasi 1996) on the other.

Similarly, mainstream Western sociology, inspired by Hans Kohn's classical formulations of differing patterns of Eastern and Western nationalism, often views post-Soviet nationalistic organizations as a premodern "Eastern" tradition. According to Kohn, Western nationalism had at its heart a rational adaption of common laws and patterns of voluntary civic association that were independent of the state and the domination of traditional collective bonds. He categorized Eastern nationalism as a mystified, often authoritarian form of ideology employed by populist intellectuals (Kohn 1945; compare with Kukathas, Lovell, and Maley 1991).

In the discussions triggered by the 200th anniversary of the French Revolution, this mode of thinking was seriously challenged by a notion of the common roots of national movements, modern civil society, and mass politics. These themes were especially intertwined in discussions of Francois Furet's interpretations of the revolution (Furet and Ozouf 1989). According to Furet, the most important changes brought about by the revolution occurred not at the level of social relations, but in political culture, as both the language and the arena of politics were redefined. In the first phase, when "the people" were proclaimed the supreme power instead of the king, power became symbolic and politics turned into a continuous ideological and symbolic battle for the right to represent the nation and the "will of the people." During the second phase, fulfilling the "will of the people" was connected to the new idea of voluntary association and became a driving force for popular political mobilization and the birth of a democratic political culture (Furet 1981: 53–72).

Other scholars have also emphasized the significance of the concept of nation and the theory of the sovereignty of the people as the nucleus of the revolution. They have, however, given primary importance to structural changes in society, and especially to new forms of organization and channels of public discussion that fed political conflict over representing "the will of the people." Hunt (1984) has emphasized that most of all, the French Revolution represented the birth of a new political culture—the formation of a new sphere of political activity between the state and emerging civil society.

Compared to revolutionary France, national movements in the Central and Eastern European empires and their successor states have played an even more crucial role in shaping the boundaries of politics. In the nineteenth century, as the basic driving forces of mass mobilization, national movements entrenched themselves in the new political arena forming between the state and civil society (Dann 1978). At the same time, by adopting as their slogan, "implementing the will of the people," Central and Eastern European national movements had a significant effect on the creation of a new political language. In the case of Finland, national movements were key actors in creating the new political arena in which state power was made legitimate and a continuous ideological and symbolic battle was fought over the right to represent the "will of the people." The making of the Finnish people was not only an ethnic demarcation between "us" and "them," but also a political act that constituted and identified a political community, its borders, and those who hold power (Hroch 1968; Liikanen 1999: 360–62). Contrary to standard notions of European development, nationalistic agitation and populist mass politics in Finland did not counter the development of modern civil society and politics; rather, they became the basis for such development (Liikanen 1995: 321–32).

Geoffrey Hosking (1998) has argued that Russia is currently going through the process of nation building for the first time. This argument severely challenges the validity of the study of late Soviet social and political mobilization in terms of the "new social movements." From this point of departure, national movements cannot simply be labeled "archaic" forces fighting modernization and Western "civic" values (Hosking 1998: 482–86). The following case studies employ a new perspective on national mobilization as one root in the formation of a new political community. In the following, it is suggested that this view helps to formulate a more structured view of the role of "eco-nationalism" in the breakdown of the Soviet Union and in the creation of postcommunist political culture.

Environmental Awakening and Political Mobilization in Estonia and Karelia

As early as the spring of 1987, one year before major antinuclear demonstrations took place in other parts of the Soviet Union, an Estonian campaign was initiated against planned phosphorite mines and industrial plants near Estonia's northeastern border with the Russian Federation. The campaign, which began under an ecological banner, soon became an openly political operation and resulted in the first overtly critical mass actions against the government. After two protest meetings in April 1987, students in the old university town of Tartu shocked the establishment by participating in the May Day demonstration with their own signs criticizing the mine project and attacking both Moscow's central government and Estonian communist leadership.

The environmental campaign in Estonia had a political agenda from the outset. During the postwar period, large-scale industrial projects in Estonia had always been accompanied by a wave of new Russian immigrants. By the 1980s, the Russian share of the population in Estonia had grown to almost 50 percent. According to opponents, the proposed mines and industrial plants would have brought another 30,000 Russian immigrants to Estonia, making the Slavic population a majority (Lauristin, Vihalemm, and Ruutsoo 1989; Raun 1987: 219–20).

This political aspect made the situation extremely sensitive. The Communist Party reacted immediately to the demonstrations, demanding that those guilty of protesting be punished. This aroused resistance at the university and among intellectuals, transforming the issue into a debate over limits of civic action and freedom of speech under the new conditions of *glasnost* (openness) and *perestroika* (restructuring). Journalists and leading public figures also added their voices to the criticism and, for the first time, the press criticized the government and the Communist Party.

The Phosphorite War, as the Estonians refer to the event, reintroduced the model and language of street demonstrations to Estonian political culture and created local and national contact networks. These later laid the foundation for more organized forms of opposition. Environmental activism did not die completely in Estonia, as in many of the cases Dawson refers to. Rather, it remained in the shadows of other forms of action. On the anniversary of the Molotov-Ribbentrop Pact of 1939, which had sealed the annexation of Estonia to the Soviet Union, illegal mass demonstrations were used as political tools under openly national banners. In the fall of 1987, public meetings and media criticism continued amid discussions of a program for Estonian economic independence. Gradually, the pressure of public debate began to shake the old power structure and open up new opportunities for political action (Lauristin, Vihalemm, and Ruutsoo 1989).

Political links formed during Estonia's environmental movement did not lead directly to nationalistic mobilization as they did in Dawson's case study in Lithuania. The Popular Front Movement that emerged in Estonia during the spring of 1988 was rooted partly in the environmental mobilization of 1987. Some of its most prominent leaders, including Marju Lauristin and Edgar Savisaar, had participated in the phosphorite debate. The Popular Front, how-ever, was not part of an openly nationalistic program; its main goal was to broaden civic and political liberties and eventually lessen Moscow's hold on Es-tonian politics (Park 1995). The Greens and various environmental groupings continued to have a considerable influence inside the Popular Front. In contrast to Dawson's case studies, these heroes of the late Soviet period were not pushed aside until Estonian independence was achieved and more nationalistic and mar-ket-oriented politics came to the fore (compare with Lauristin and Vihalemm 1997).

Environmental activism also played a key role in the Karelian Republic, rein-troducing forms of collective action that had been strictly suppressed by the gov-ernment under communist rule. Activists from the environmental group "Priroda" (Nature) were the first to take to the streets with slogans criticizing the system. During the November Revolution celebrations in 1988, members of Priroda marched with their own signs, proclaiming that nature was the "property of the people" and that "technocratic madness" should be placed on trial by the "court" of *glasnost*. They even indirectly attacked the central government with their demand that the Minister of Forestry be sent from Moscow to the peripheral forestry plant of Segeza in the Karelian backwoods (Tsygankov 1991: 208).

Priroda was formed in the summer of 1988 by officials of the local branch of the communist youth organization, Komsomol. Thus, it operated if not exactly inside the Soviet system, at least on its periphery. Unlike other volunteer quasipolitical clubs established in 1988, Priroda was officially registered and au-thorized to operate as a nongovernmental organization in October 1988. This can be seen as a vital step toward the establishment of the openly political Karelian Popular Front in November 1988. It should be noted, however, that the Front could not register until March 1990.

Registration gave the Priroda group broader possibilities for action. During the fall of 1988, they organized a campaign against a planned biochemical fac-tory. They collected 6,405 signatures on a petition against the factory—in itself a striking achievement since the petition was the first of its kind. During 1988, the members of the group became more openly political. They participated in Green movement conferences and in founding the *Demokratitseskii Initsiativ* (Democratic Initiative). A Green action group was formed by the students of the Petrozavodsk State University and began to publish its own underground bulletin (*samizdat*) (Tsygankov 1991: 208–29). In December 1989, a public demonstration against a planned nuclear power station was organized in Petrozavodsk by the university's Green action group. The demonstration was the first of its kind, drawing more than one thousand people (*Karjalan Sanomat* 1989).

After the collapse of Soviet power, members of the Green movement again tried to actively mobilize people in political campaigns against the old communist power structure. In December 1991, the Greens organized a mass demonstration to demand the immediate resignation of the republic's leadership (*Karjalan Sanomat* 1991). In the elections that followed the formation of the new Russian Federation, the formerly communist president of the Karelian republic managed to hold onto his position until the summer of 1998. The Green movement proved unable to gather the necessary support to win seats in the Republic's parliament (Tsygankov 1998). The movement did not launch any major political force, either nationalist or federalist. Instead, the environmental movement's greatest influence was in reintroducing the repertoire of collective action, voluntary associations, and public demonstrations. Its activities did not lead to high governmental posts, but they had perhaps an even deeper significance. The environmental movement renewed the political system and introduced a new type of political culture.

Conclusions

The environmental movements that arose in late Soviet society played the role of an avant-garde in the breakthrough of voluntary association and mass mobilization. In many cases, they were predecessors to nationalistic movements and, particularly in the union republics, they participated or even started the process of redefining the mental borders of identification with a certain political community. By the time of the Soviet Union's collapse, the wave of mobilization had shifted from environmental movements to national or ethnic movements. From the perspective of identity construction, however, this shift cannot simply be presented as a return to lost collective identities. The redrawing of mental borders was just as much an outcome of forward-looking political identifications and the aspiration to constitute a political community in which challenging and overcoming the old power structures would be possible.

In the case of Estonia, environmental campaigns were not openly nationalistic. National sentiments were apparently involved, but it is impossible to say whether conscious "nationalistic movement entrepreneurs" and "hidden nationalistic goals" existed behind the movement (compare with Dawson 1996: 171). It seems more plausible to conclude that the aims of the movement evolved only gradually. In the end, it is clear that the environmental movement strengthened the formation of an Estonian political community that was defined in ethnic terms. The environmental movement affected Estonian nation building not so much because of preexisting "eco-nationalism," but because it introduced forms of collective action that advanced the rebirth of Estonian political community and broadened the civic and political rights of its members.

The significance of Karelian environmental movements in civic and political mobilization was quite different than in Estonia. In Karelia, the movements did not represent open nationalism and were not followed by general nationalistic mobilization. By challenging the power structure in the name of the people, however, they gave impetus to the newly emerging political culture. From the beginning, the Karelian movements were part of the ideological battle over political hegemony and of a new contest over who was entitled to represent the people. In both Estonia and Karelia, environmental movements did not directly indicate the buildup of "imagined communities." Rather, they were significant because they prepared the ground for new forms of organization and collective action, thus defining the boundaries of political communities anew.

References

Alapuro, R. 1993. "Civil Society in Russia?" In *The Future of the National State in Europe*, J. Iivonen, ed. Aldershot: Edgar Elgar.

Anderson, B. 1983. *Imagined Communities. Reflections on the Origin and Spread of Nationalism.* London: Verso.

Arato, A. 1989. "Civil Society, History and Socialism: Reply to John Keane." *Praxis International* 9: 133–51.

Arato, A. 1990. "Revolution, Civil Society and Democracy." *Praxis International* 10: 24–38.

Brovkin, V. 1990. "Revolution from Below: Informal Political Associations in Russia 1988–1989." *Soviet Studies* 42: 233–57.

Brubaker, R. 1996. *Nationalism Reframed: Nationhood and National Questions in the New Europe.* Cambridge: Cambridge University Press.

Cohen, J., and A. Arato. 1992. *Civil Society and Political Theory.* Cambridge: MIT Press.

Dann, O. 1978. "Nationalismus und sozialer Wandel in Deutschland 1806–1850." Pp. 70–95 in *Nationalismus und sozialer Wandel*, O. Dann, ed. Hamburg: Hoffmann und Campe.

Dawson, J. 1996. *Eco-Nationalism. Anti-Nuclear Activism and National Identity in Russia, Lithuania and Ukraine.* Durham and London: Duke University Press.

Furet, F. 1981. *Interpreting the French Revolution.* Cambridge: Cambridge University Press.

Furet, F., and M. Ozouf, eds. 1989. *The Transformation of Political Culture 1789–1848. The French Revolution and the Creation of Modern Political Culture, Vol. 3.* Oxford: Pergamon Press.

Gellner, E. 1964. *Thought and Change.* London: Weidenfeld and Nicolson.

Hobsbawm, E.J. 1972. "Some Reflections on Nationalism." Pp. 385–406 in *Imagination and Precision in the Social Sciences*, T.J. Nossiter, A.H. Hanson, and S. Rockan, eds. London: Faber and Faber.

Hobsbawm, E.J., and T. Ranger, eds. 1983. *The Invention of Tradition.* Cambridge: Cambridge University Press.

Hosking, G. 1998. *Russia: People and Empire 1552–1917.* London: Fontana Press.

Hosking, G., J. Aves, and P. Duncan. 1992. *The Road to Post-Communism. Independent Political Movements in the Soviet Union 1985–1991.* London: Pinter Publishers.

Hroch, M. 1968. *Die Vorkämpfer der nationalen Bewegung bei den kleinen Völkern Europas.* Prague: Acta Universitatis Carolinae Philosophica et Historica 24.

Hunt, L. 1984. *Politics, Culture and Class in the French Revolution.* London: Methuen and Co. Ltd.

Kagarlitski, B. 1992. *Hajonnut monoliitti.* Helsinki: Kustannus Oy Orient Express.

Karjalan Sanomat. 1989. "Ydinvoimalan vastainen mielenosoitus Petroskoissa." (13 December).

Karjalan Sanomat. 1991. "Vihreiden joukkokokous Petroskoissa vaati Karjalan johtoa jättämään eronpyynnön." (17 December).

Keane, J. 1988. *Democracy and Civil Society.* London: Verso.

Kohn, H. 1945. *The Idea of Nationalism: A Study in its Origins and Background.* New York: Macmillan Co.

Krasin, J. 1993. "The Long Road to Democracy and Civil Society." *Sociological Research* 32: 49–63.

Kukathas, C., D. Lovell, and W. Maley, eds. 1991. *The Transition from Socialism. State and Civil Society in the USSR.* Cheshire: Longman.

Lauristin, M., and P. Vihalemm, eds. 1997. *Return to the Western World. Cultural and Political Perspectives on the Estonian Post-Communist Transition.* Tartu: Tartu University Press.

Lauristin, M., P. Vihalemm, and R. Ruutsoo. 1989. *Viron vapauden tuulet.* Jyväskylä: Gummerus.

Ledeneva, A. 1998. *Russia's Economy of Favours. Blat, Networking and Informal Exchange.* Cambridge: Cambridge University Press.

Liikanen, I. 1995. "Fennomania ja kansa. Joukkojärjestäytymisen läpimurto ja Suomalaisen puolueen synty." *Historiallisia tutkimuksia,* No. 191. Jyväskylä: Suomen Historiallinen Seura.

Liikanen, I. 1999. "The Political Construction of Identity: Reframing Mental Borders in Russian Karelia." Pp. 357–73 in *Curtains of Iron and Gold. Reconstructing Borders and Scales of Interaction,* H. Eskelinen, I. Liikanen, and J. Oksa, eds. Aldershot: Ashgate.

Neformaly Rossii. "O neformal'nyh politizirovannyh dvilenijah i gruppah v RSFSR." Moskva: Molodaja Gvardija.

Paasi, A. 1996. *Territories, Boundaries and Consciousness: The Changing Geographies of the Finnish-Russian Border.* Chichester: John Wiley.

Park, A. 1995. "Turning-Points of Post-Communist Transition: Lessons from the Case of Estonia." *Proceedings of the Estonian Academy of Sciences* 44 (3): 323–32.

Raun, T. 1987. *Estonia and the Estonians.* Stanford: Hoover Institution Press.

Ruutsoo, R. 1996. "Formation of Civil Society Types and Organizational Capital of the Baltic Nations in the Framework of the Russian Empire." Pp. 101–108 in *Civil Society in the European North,* K. Heikkinen and E. Zdravomyslova, eds. St. Petersburg: Centre for Independent Social Research.

Smith, A. 1986. *The Ethnic Origins of Nations.* Oxford: Blackwell.

Stranius, P. 1996. "The Role and Drama of the Russian Intelligentsia." Pp. 150–55 in *Civil Society in the European North,* K. Heikkinen and E. Zdravomyslova, eds. St. Petersburg: Centre for Independent Social Research.

Temkina, A. 1997. *Russia in Transition: The Cases of New Collective Actors and New Collective Actions.* Helsinki: Kikimora Publications.

Tilly, C., ed. 1975. *The Formation of National States in Western Europe.* Princeton: Princeton University Press.

Tsygankov, A. 1991. *K grazhdanskomu obshtshestvu.* Petrozavodsk: Kareliya.

Tsygankov, A. 1995. "Nuutuneen riemun aika." *Carelia* 4: 86–94.

Tsygankov, A. 1998. *Prishestvye izbiratelya. Iz istorii vibornih kampaniy v Karelii 1989–1996.* Petrozavodsk: Kareliya.

Volkov, V. 1996. "Obshchestvennost: An Indigenous Concept of Civil Society. In *Civil Society in the European North,* K. Heikkinen and E. Zdravomyslova, eds. St. Petersburg: Centre for Independent Social Research.

Challenges to and Opportunities for Development of an Effective Transboundary Water Management Regime in the Lake Peipus Basin: The Estonian-Russian Border Area

Gulnara Roll and Robben Romano[*]

Abstract

The Lake Peipus water basin is the fourth largest lake basin in Europe and one of the major lake systems of the Baltic Sea water basin. It is also situated on the Estonian-Russian border. After the border regime between Estonia and Russia was reestablished in 1992, two international environmental regimes began to develop: one for the management of fish resources and another for water resource use and protection. The Lake Peipus fish management regime is linked to the signed Estonian-Russian Lake Peipus fisheries agreement and the work of the bilateral commission on fisheries management. The Lake Peipus international regime on protection and use of transboundary waters is based on the Estonian-Russian transboundary water agreement signed in 1997 in accordance with the United Nations Economic Commission for Europe (UN ECE) Convention on Transboundary Waters of 1992. This paper describes the history of the formation of the transboundary water management system in the Lake Peipus basin and discusses challenges to and opportunities for its effective implementa-

* Roll is Director and Romano is Management Advisor at the Center for Transboundary Cooperation in Tartu, Estonia.

tion. The roles of different participants and other factors, such as communication, in the formation and implementation of the transboundary water management regime are an important focus of this paper.

Introduction

Lake Peipus lies on the border between Russia and Estonia. It is Europe's fourth largest lake system and its largest transboundary lake. This borderline was reestablished at the beginning of the 1990s and now divides the lake surface into two almost equal parts. When the border was reestablished, the existing environmental management system for the lake basin was abandoned, disrupting contacts between experts and decision makers from the two countries who, during the existence of the Soviet Union, had worked together on environmental monitoring and management of the lake and its resources. A new international governance system was needed to manage water and other natural resources in the lake basin.

Meanwhile, only the Estonians continued to monitor the water quality of the lake and only the Russians continued to monitor the lake's fish. Political and economic conflicts between the Russian and Estonian governments as well as mass media propaganda against Russia in Estonia and against Estonia in Russia created distrust between people on either side of the border. Social and economic problems in both countries cut off financial resources to support transboundary cooperation. Since the early 1990s, the process of establishing a system for joint management of shared water resources has been slow and difficult. As relations between the two countries have improved, however, there have been more opportunities to establish transboundary cooperation in different fields and on different levels of governance—from local municipalities to ministries. The signing of a number of intergovernmental agreements and the establishment of intergovernmental commissions from 1994 to 1998 have formed a solid basis for further development of the legal and institutional framework for Estonian-Russian environmental cooperation, specifically for the development of the Lake Peipus international environmental management regime. ("Regime" here refers to manmade systems devised to deal with conflicts that arise from conflicting social and political actions and interests.)

Background

Lake Peipus is called "Peipsi" in Estonian and "Chudskoe" in Russian. It is the fourth largest lake in Europe (1,373 square miles/3,555 square kilometers) and one of the major lake systems of the Baltic Sea water basin. Its water system actually consists of three unequal parts: northern Lake Peipus (1,009 square miles/2,613 square kilometers, maximum depth 42.3 feet/12.9 meters, water level 98.5 feet/30.01 meters above sea level, water capacity 5.19 cubic miles/21.79 cubic kilometers); southern Lake Pskov (273 square miles/709 square kilometers, maximum depth 17.4 feet/5.3 meters, water capacity .17 cubic miles/2.68 cubic kilometers); and the narrow, strait-like Lake Lämmi, which connects the two larger lakes (91 square miles/236 square kilometers, maximum depth 50 feet/15.3 meters, water capacity .14 cubic miles/0.60 cubic kilometers). The lake basin, including the lake itself, covers 18,455 square miles (47,800 square kilometers) of territory in Russia, Estonia, and Latvia.

Ecological Conditions

Lake Peipus is a eutrophic and highly biologically productive lake. Eutrophication due to significant nutrient loads in Lake Peipus represents a major threat for the water quality of the lake, which is adversely affected by nutrient leakage from farming in the basin and discharge of wastewater from the two large towns of Tartu, Estonia, and Pskov, Russia. The lake basin as a whole is eutrophic, but northern Lake Peipus maintains some mesotrophic features, Lake Lämmi is slightly eutrophic, and Lake Pskov is fully eutrophic (Nõges, Nõges, and Jastremskij 1996). The ecological conditions of Lake Peipus have constantly deteriorated over the last half of the twentieth century, although the situation with pollution load dynamics has changed since the collapse of the Soviet Union. The economic recession that followed the collapse of Soviet Union as well as the increased wastewater treatment capacity of big settlements contributed to improved ecological conditions in the lake (Stålnacke et al. 2001). Overall reductions in nutrient load into the lake and improvement in the lake's ecological condition have resulted in its compliance with the conditions of the 1992 Helsinki Accord signed by both Estonia and Russia.

The lake's eutrophication, which is expected to increase in correlation with the economic recovery of the region, is heavily dependent on agriculture. Only 7 percent of the nitrogen load from Estonian rivers originates from wastewater (point pollution sources), half of the load comes from agriculture, and 22 percent originates from forests and other diffuse sources. Of the phosphorus load, 36 percent comes from point pollution sources and 38 percent from agriculture via the rivers from catchment areas (Stålnacke et al. 2001). A potential increase in the agricultural production in the future without improvement in agricultural practices could considerably affect the lake's potential to support important Baltic Sea area habitats for wildlife (especially birds) as a resource for commercial fisheries and water use by local communities, and as a focus for the development of tourism and recreation activities.

The main commercial fishes are lake smelt, perch, ruff, roach, bream, pike, vendace, and pikeperch. The stock of vendace has sharply decreased in the last years, while the amount of pikeperch has increased. Considering annual fish catches (9,000–12,000 tons/25–40 kilograms per hectare), Lake Peipus exceeds those of all large lakes in northern Europe (Nõges, Nõges, and Jastremskij 1996.) Ecological conditions of the lake for fish are different on either side of the border. On the deeper Russian side, hydrographic conditions and the less active fishing industry are more favorable for fish. The shallower waters of the Estonian side become hotter in summer and freeze more quickly in the winter. At the same time, commercial fishing on the Estonian side is more intensive.

The Border on Lake Peipus

The borderline was recently reestablished along the lake median line in accordance with the Tartu Peace Treaty that was signed in 1920 by Russia and then-independent Estonia. During those negotiations, discussions that attempted to define the land border were heated. For the northern and southern parts of the border zone, excluding the water border on the lake, the question of delineating the border was bound to strategic security considerations and the ethnic representation of Estonians or Russians living in the border area. By contrast, there were no arguments regarding delineation of the border on the lake; in fact, the agreed-upon line followed a historic border that existed during tsarist Russia between the administrative regions on either side of the lake. In 1944, after the Soviet Union occupied Estonia, the USSR Supreme Soviet adopted a decree that gave the most eastern areas of Estonian territory to the Pskov and Leningrad regions of the Russian Federation.

Border policy between Estonia and Russia was reestablished in 1992 and 1993 after Estonia's independent status had stabilized. Estonia unsuccessfully attempted to reclaim eastern lands that had been annexed in 1944; however, after several years of negotiations, the Estonian government acceded to changes in the location of its borderline with Russia. Reestablishing policy on Estonian-Russian border crossing, as well as communications across the border, became quite complicated and have dramatically affected the local population, whose social and economic relationships were unrestricted prior to the establishment of national boundaries. Obtaining a visa to cross the border in either direction is now both expensive and time consuming. Only those who live close to the borderline can cross to visit relatives, churches, and cemeteries on the other side of the border with "permission" rather than a visa, and even then only on major state and religious holidays. Even this relaxed control was a temporary arrangement as Estonia had to comply with requirements of the Schengen agreement to be eligible for accession to the European Union. This agreement, signed by 10 EU member states, provided for visa-based border crossing on external EU borders. As such, visa-based crossing was established on the Estonian-Russian border in September 2000.

In the early 1990s, multiple conflicts took place in the Estonian-Russian border zone, most of which were connected to illegal border crossings by way of the lake. Commercial fishing is more intensive in Estonia because fishermen can sell their catch on the Western European market, an outlet the Russians in the Pskov region of the southern part of the lake do not have. The ability to fish on only half the lake, however, is not profitable enough to sustain local fishermen. From 1993 to 1995, as border guards started to work on both sides of the lake border, many fishermen, mostly from the Estonian side, attempted to cross the mid-lake border illegally. Their boats were confiscated and they were forced to pay high fines. With time, the number of illegal border crossings has decreased considerably. However, sociological studies and interviews conducted by the Estonian non-profit Center for Transboundary Cooperation show that while current border-crossing policies remain in place—making it especially difficult for those living in rural areas of the border region—cases of illegal border crossing on the lake as well as on land will continue.

Estonian border policies are being strengthened. Estonia is among five countries being considered for membership in the next wave of EU enlargement. Continuing social and political instability in Russia is a major concern for its neighbor as well as for the whole of the EU and is additional motivation to strengthen border regulations on the future EU border. The important process of developing the legal and institutional basis for intergovernmental cooperation between Estonia and Russia that began in 1992 continues today.

Legal and Institutional Framework for Management of the Lake Peipus Basin

The Lake Peipus governance system as a network of legal agreements and institutions is very young. Even after the 1992 border policies were established, no intergovernmental agreements were signed between Estonia and Russia that would regulate transboundary cooperation in the economic, social, or environmental realms. After the political schism of the early 1990s (when Estonia and the two other Baltic states, Latvia and Lithuania, elected to secede from the Soviet Union), the political climate was unfavorable to cooperation. Distrust between people in Estonia and Russia was a serious impediment to developing cooperation among researchers and experts, even on a nonpolitical level. As the political atmosphere has improved, however, there have been more opportunities to establish transboundary networks in many fields and at different governmental levels—from local municipalities to ministries.

To regulate bilateral relations, the Estonian Republic and the Russian Federation have now signed one agreement on border crossing points at Estonian-Russian customs borders (July 1993) and another on the activities of border representatives (December 1996). In early 1998, an Estonian-Russian Intergovernmental Commission on Trade, Economy, Scientific, Technical, Social, Humanitarian and Cultural Cooperation was created at the highest level to address problems in all areas affected by bilateral relations. The commission today plays an important role in expanding the legal basis for bilateral cooperation and resolution of disputes in intergovernmental relations. On December 4, 1998, the first meeting took place between Estonian Prime Minister Mart Siimann and Russian Deputy Prime Minister Valentina Matvienko. They signed two agreements—one recognizing academic qualifications and another on cooperation to preserve cultural heritage. The parties indicated a readiness to sign four more intergovernmental agreements and one protocol. The issues covered in the agreements include: transport (international access for automobiles and air transportation), customs, and the return of Estonian nationals incarcerated in Russia and Russian nationals incarcerated in Estonia during Soviet times so that they may serve their sentences in their own countries. The principals also committed to preparing 15 more agreements of mutual interest are to be presented in the future. The protocol created working groups charged with preparing agreements between the two governments, including:

I. Trade, economic, and technical scientific cooperation
   a. General trade and economic relations
   b. Encouraging and securing mutual investments
   c. Eliminating and avoiding double taxing
   d. Cooperation and mutual assistance in fighting illegal financial operations and money laundering through legalization of incomes
   e. Agreement on cooperation in preventing industrial accidents and disasters and handling their consequences
   f. Cooperation in rescue operations in the Gulf of Finland and other common water bodies
   g. Cooperative use of sea transportation for trade
   h. Railway transportation
   i. Scientific and technical cooperation

II. Social and humanitarian cooperation
   a. Mutual travel for people living in border areas
   b. Agreement about cross-border cooperation between regional and local authorities
   c. Status of Russian national military and civil populations in Estonia and Estonian nationals living in Russia

III. Cultural cooperation
   a. Developing regulations for departments and branches of Russian higher education institutions in Estonia
   b. Agreement between the two countries on the exchange of students, lecturers, and researchers from higher institutions of learning

The legal basis for economic cooperation in the Estonian-Russian border zone is still developing rather slowly since negotiations for economic regulations are bound to additional political considerations—such as Estonia's intention to join NATO (unacceptable to Russia) and discussions of the rights of Russian-speaking ethnic minorities in Estonia. The intergovernmental commission can assist in promoting mutually beneficial economic relations between Russia and Estonia.

Since no conflicts between Estonia and Russia on the use of natural resources in the shared transboundary water basin, there was consensus among representatives of the two governments on the importance of coordinating activities for the protection and use of natural resources in the border area. As such, the legal and institutional basis for such use developed rather quickly. In the early 1990s, before the intergovernmental agreements were signed, researchers, students, and local government representatives communicated and cooperated informally on the issues of environmental protection of the lake and its watershed. The Center for Transboundary Cooperation/Lake Peipsi Project facilitated this cooperation by organizing joint conferences, studies, and publications. Environmental officials and specialists from the two countries conferred and discussed their positions on developing a legal basis for bilateral environmental cooperation.

An informal network was formed that joined officials in national fisheries boards and ministries from Estonia and Russia. As a result of their efforts, an intergovernmental Agreement on the Protection and Regulation of the Use of Fish Resources of Lake Peipsi, Lake Lämmi and Lake Pihkva was signed by the Estonian National Board of Fisheries and the Russian Federal Committee for Fish Resource Management on May 4, 1995 in Pskov. A joint commission was set up that consisted of a working group on technical questions, another on research, and scientists, officials, and fishermen. The Lake Peipsi Fishermen's Union represented the interests of Estonian fishermen in the commission.

The Estonian-Russian Fisheries Commission on Lakes Peipsi, Lämmi, and Pskov continues to regulate catches of commercially important fish species on the lake, especially pikeperch. Two main factors have caused ongoing tensions since 1993 between Estonian and Russian specialists and fishermen about the regulation of pikeperch catches. The first includes differences in data obtained on fish stock by Estonian and Russian ichthyologists, because researchers in the two countries use different equipment and methods of assessment. The other factor concerns the two countries' differing economic interests: Estonian fishermen are interested in the larger pikeperch and bream for the European market, while the Russian fish canning industry processes the smaller vendace for local consumption. The need to sustain sizeable populations of each type of fish without compromising the ability of the others to thrive has created conflicts and resulted in disputes over regulation in the past. From 1995 to 1998, the Estonian-Russian fisheries commission has successfully dealt with the conflict (Orgusaar 1996).

In August 1997, after three years of preparation, the two governments signed a bilateral agreement on protection and sustainable use of transboundary water bodies. The agreement was signed in accordance with the UN ECE Convention on Transboundary Waters (1992) and applies to transboundary waters of the Narva River watershed, including Lake Peipus. (The Narva River is the outlet from Lake Peipus to the Gulf of Finland.) This agreement is designed to regulate and protect transboundary water bodies and their ecosystems and established a Joint Commission on Transboundary Waters to coordinate its implementation. The commission's responsibilities include:

- Organization of the exchange of collected data in accordance with an agreed-upon monitoring program
- Definition of priorities and programs of scientific study on protection and sustainable use of transboundary waters
- Agreement on common indicators of quality for transboundary waters and methods of water testing and conducting analyses
- Coordination of work by competent agencies when an extraordinary situation occurs on transboundary waters

- Facilitation of cooperation between agencies of executive power, local governments, scientific and public interest organizations, as well as other institutions in the fields of sustainable development and protection of transboundary waters
- Assurance of publicity for discussions of use and protection of transboundary waters

The first official meeting of the commission took place on May 19, 1998. Four working groups were established under the commission: Water Economy, Water Protection, Monitoring and Research, and Cooperation with International and Non-Governmental Organizations and Local Authorities. Signing this bilateral agreement and establishing the commission on Lake Peipus offers the opportunity for all concerned to effectively implement environmental monitoring and research environmental programs and to prepare a comprehensive plan of action to protect resources of the Narva River, Lake Peipus, and their watershed areas.

The ways in which Estonia and Russia carry out their responsibilities on international agreements (such as the UN ECE Convention on Transboundary Watercourses and International Lakes) will affect implementation of the Lake Peipus international environmental management regime. Setting up another international instrument—the yet to be adopted European Community Water Framework Directive—will create a wider, all-European water management regime that will greatly influence transboundary water management in the Lake Peipus basin.

In February 1997, the European Commission adopted its proposal for a Water Framework Directive. In addition to thoroughly restructuring community water policy, this directive will also contribute to putting in place the Convention on the Protection and Use of Transboundary Watercourses and International Lakes. The framework directive covers both surface water and groundwater. Its purposes are to: prevent further deterioration and protect and enhance the status of aquatic ecosystems, promote sustainable water consumption based on long-term protection of available water resources, and help provide a supply of water in the qualities and quantities needed for sustainable use (Blöch 1998). The Water Framework Directive establishes River Basin Districts for river basins shared by EU member states, as well as for those shared by EU member states and relevant nonmember states. To execute the framework directive, Estonia—as an EU accession state—will need to establish the Narva River Basin District in the Russian Federation with relevant authorities and to comply with rigorous requirements for collecting, reporting, and disseminating information and activities that concern management of transboundary surface and underground waters.

By signing and establishing such intergovernmental agreements and commissions from 1994 to 1998, Estonia and Russia formed a solid basis for further developing a legal and institutional framework for environmental cooperation and carrying out specific bilateral cooperative programs. However, the absence of a border agreement between the two countries remains an impediment to organizing joint studies of the lake. Negotiations on this border agreement continued in 1998. In 1999, comprehensive work was conducted, but it was not well coordinated. Many agencies, environmental and otherwise, are working to develop environmental protection at different levels of governance in different states. Given the existing political, economic, and environmental contexts, it is difficult to forecast the results of these efforts over the next five to ten years in terms of the sustainable development of the lake and lake basin. Forecasting and long-term plans of action to promote sustainable development in the region are clearly needed.

Researchers use mathematical models to describe different factors that influence the use of natural resources of shared ecosystems such as shared lakes, rivers, and water basins. These models generally describe natural environmental processes in detail, although they have a limited ability to incorporate these with social or political processes within the same model, as social, political, and economic systems function on different principles than processes in the natural environment. It is therefore extremely difficult to formulate policy advice based on ecological modeling for strategies for sustainable use of resources. It seems that along with using mathematical models and indicators of the environmental state of the lake and its ecosystems, it is also necessary to apply a theory of international regimes. This would make it possible to organize large amounts of information about legal and institutional arrangements for cooperation in border areas, as well as formal and informal relations between stakeholders in relation to specific topics—such as management of shared water resources or protected areas. Such a system could allow for the development of strategies for effective management of resources and resolution of existing and potential conflicts.

International Regimes Theory

The theory of international regimes has been discussed by scholars of international relations since the mid-1970s. In 1983, Stephen D. Krasner's *International Regimes* was published, in which 14 distinguished U.S. scholars of international political economy discussed the concept of international regimes. In the preface, Krasner wrote that the book was a synthesis of major arguments in the study of international relations in the 1970s. During this period, the state-centric, realist approach came under attack from liberal scholars who emphasized the importance of transnational and transgovernmental actors in the international system. The arguments also reflected the 1970s shift of focus in the agendas of policy makers and experts in international relations from only "hard" security issues (that is, military conflicts) to include "soft" security issues (such as inter-ethnic and international economic conflicts).

The authors of the book agree on the definition of regimes as "sets of implicit or explicit principles, norms, rules and decision-making procedures around which actors' expectations converge in a given area of international relations." Principles are beliefs of fact, causation, and rectitude; norms are standards of behavior defined in terms of rights and obligations; rules are specific prescriptions or proscriptions for action; and decision-making procedures are prevailing practices for making and implementing collective choices. In his contribution, Ernst B. Haas (1993) draws this definition of regime from the Random House English Dictionary: "a ruling or prevailing system." According to Haas, "regimes are manmade arrangements (social institutions) for managing conflict in a setting of interdependence, where interdependence implies a network of non-random links among actors, links that are organized or structured."

Regimes do not arise by themselves; they are an outcome of basic causal variables—primarily powers and interests. States, international organizations, private organizations, and individuals are all actors in regimes, acting according to their own self-interest and interacting with each other regarding concrete issues or in geographical areas. Being interdependent, the actors themselves define the principles, norms, rules, and decision-making procedures they follow in their interactions with each other.

In *International Regimes*, scholars from both liberal and realist traditions present conflicting views on international regime theory. The influence of changes in the global community that took place in the 1990s, many of which could not have been anticipated by scholars in the early 1980s, can no longer be ignored. These include the influence of the development of worldwide electronic communication on global governance, the rise of civil society in previously oppressed areas, and the strong and continuing influence at the state, regional, and local levels of international organizations, nongovernmental organizations (NGOs), and governments. Such comprehensive and dynamic changes in the lives of different communities in different parts of the world can hardly be explained as outcomes of the interplay of state powers alone, as scholars of the realist tradition proposed.

The liberal perspective and the broader intellectual movement of "neoliberal institutionalism" (Young 1994) that has developed offer instruments to explain international regimes that are complex and differ from each other both geographically and according to issue; they may also help to develop recommendations for more effective international regimes. According to Young, "international regimes ... are specialized arrangements that pertain to well-defined activities, resources, or geographical areas ... Thus, we speak of the international regimes for whaling, the conservation of polar bears" as well as the management of Baltic Sea fisheries.

Regimes appear as a result of " ... a societal concern whenever the members of the group find that they are interdependent in the sense that the actions of each impinge on the welfare of others. Interdependence is likely to become a source of conflict when the efforts of individual members of the group to achieve their goals interfere with or impede the efforts of others to pursue their own ends. It will be seen as a basis for cooperation, on the other hand, when opportunities arise to enhance social welfare by taking steps to coordinate the actions of the individual members of the group" (Young 1994).

In the first instance, the rules of convention of regimes apply to the actions of states. Yet the parties actually engaging in the activities governed by regimes are frequently private entities, such as multinational corporations, banks, and fishing companies (Young 1989). Young warns that smoothly functioning international regimes are not easy to establish since rights are not always respected and even widely acknowledged rules are violated with some frequency. Among the actors involved in international environmental regimes, state governments are dominant. Different actors have different interests and play different roles in forming and implementing international regimes.

Implementing the Bilateral Transboundary Waters Regime: Problems and Opportunities

In the Estonian-Russian Lake Peipus basin, two environmental regimes are developing: one is for management of fish resources, the other for water use and protection. The fisheries management regime is linked to the Estonian-Russian Lake Peipus fisheries agreement and the work of the bilateral commission on fisheries management. Its main players are the Estonian and Russian state governments, fishermen, fish experts, and international organizations.

The Lake Peipus international regime on protection and use of transboundary waters is based on the Estonian-Russian transboundary water agreement that was signed in 1997 in accordance with the 1992 UN ECE Convention on Transboundary Waters. The agreement established working groups that incorporated representatives of the research and NGO communities in the area as well as regional governments. The Estonian-Russian transboundary waters commission is a leader in this transboundary water regime, but active involvement of local authorities and businesses will be needed to ensure the regime's long-term sustainability.

In addition to examining existing institutional arrangements for water protection and use in the Lake Peipus basin, it is important also to examine both the international water protection and management regime's effectiveness and its mechanisms for complying with established formal rules and procedures. Analyzing both of these aspects should lead to specific recommendations to help make the regime function more effectively.

A primary goal of the regime is to improve the quality of the lake environment, lessening pollution by decreasing eutrophication of its waters. The effectiveness of all of the regime's water protection and management efforts may be gauged using its ability to decrease the lake's eutrophication as a criterion.

The dominant players in the regime are the Estonian and Russian governments. International organizations—such as the UN Economic Commission for Europe, the Baltic Marine Environmental Protection Commission (HELCOM), and the United Nations Development Programme—along with governments of other interested countries (Latvia, the Nordic countries, and the EU) are involved in facilitating sustainable development and environmental cooperation in the Lake Peipus basin. Nongovernmental organizations—such as the Center for

Transboundary Cooperation, the Cross-Border Cooperation Council, the Estonian Sea Tourism Association, and regional development foundations on the Estonian side of the lake—act to develop communication and information exchanges across the border and between different levels of government in Russia and Estonia.[1]

It is important to note the differences between institutions and organizations as actors in the region. This paper uses the distinction defined by Young (1994): "Whereas institutions are sets of rules of the game or codes defining social practices, organizations are material entities possessing offices, personnel, budgets, equipment, and more often than not, legal personality. Put another away, organizations are actors in social practices. Institutions affect the behavior of these actors by defining social practices and spelling out codes of conduct appropriate to them, but they are not actors in their own rights."

Along with the national governments, NGOs, international governments in the Lake Peipus basin, state organizations, and regional authorities from other countries also played an important role in facilitating transboundary cooperation and developing the Lake Peipus water protection and management regime. The Swedish Environmental Protection Agency (SEPA) started an environmental monitoring project in the Lake Peipus Basin in 1995 that was aimed at assisting Estonia and Russia in the implementation of the UN ECE Convention on the Protection and Use of Transboundary Watercourses and International Lakes in the Lake Peipus basin and compliance with the obligations laid down in the convention. Implementation of the project in the region facilitated more frequent communication between actors involved in work in the lake basin, which created favorable conditions for the formation of the water protection international regime in the Lake Peipus basin.

The idea for the Russian-Estonian monitoring project came from Mäns Lönnroth, Chancellor of the Swedish Ministry of the Environment. According to Lönnroth (1997), when Estonia regained its independence in the early 1990s, there was no intergovernmental agreement between Estonia and Russia to regulate the use of natural resources in their border area. The political climate surrounding bilateral relations was quite complicated and it was very difficult to pursue joint environmental or other projects on the intergovernmental level. The aggravated political situation greatly affected international projects in many fields.

For this reason, the Swedish government proposed a cooperative project between three regions: Älvsborg (currently Västra Götaland) County in Sweden, the Pskov oblast (county) of the Russian Federation, and Tartu County in the Estonian Republic. In 1995, a pilot environmental project was launched as a part of the Environmental Monitoring Project on Lake Peipsi. Representatives of the Estonian nonprofit Center for Transboundary Cooperation/Lake Peipsi Project were involved in administrating and organizing communication between Swedish, Russian, and Estonian participants. In 1996, interregional cooperative agreements between the Älvsborg County administration and the Pskov oblast government, and between the Älvsborg County administration and Tartu County were signed. The Swedes allocated 2.5 million Swedish kronor (about US$450,000) for the project's first year. The project's main goal was to strengthen the capacity of regional authorities for environmental monitoring by working on both sides of the border in the Lake Peipus area. It also aimed to develop contacts between environmental experts on each side and establish an environmental network of experts to promote environmental protection and sustainable use of resources in the Lake Peipus water basin.

The first stage of the project was successful. On the Estonian side, most of the trilateral environmental monitoring project's objectives were fulfilled, while fewer were accomplished on the Russian side. Delays related to customs for equipment sent to Pskov from Sweden was the main impediment to Russia's project development and economic problems in Russia made it even more difficult for environmental authorities in Pskov to implement the project. The following are some of the obstacles that may affect implementation of the water protection and management regime.

Environmental Management Differences between Project Participants

One of the primary causes of the delays in setting up the SEPA project in Russia was a limited amount of resources that Russian regional environmental authorities had to work with and lack of institutional capacity due to constant changes in the Russian environmental management structures. With several structural changes in the Russian Federation's environmental management from 1994 to 2000, the division of responsibilities among federal institutions changed many times and is still not clear. Until 2000, three federal environmental agencies—the State Committee for Environmental Protection, the Committee for Hydrology and Meteorology (Hydromet), and the Ministry for Natural Resources (MNR)—were responsible for different aspects of environmental monitoring on transboundary waterways in Russia. Since they did not coordinate their activities on the local level where the actual work of water monitoring was done, they often duplicated one another's efforts. In addition, persistent economic problems and the recent dramatic disintegration of the national economy have had various negative effects on federal agencies and their local branches. Many agencies lacked the funds to implement their tasks, had limited ability to receive information about innovations in environmental management from other countries (since only one of the four involved environmental agencies in Pskov had computers and e-mail connections), some agency employees were not paid for several months, and many experts lost their jobs in 1998 when the Pskov Regional Environmental Protection Committee was instructed to reduce its staff by 40 percent due to budget cuts.

Most state institutions tend to preserve the conservative management style developed under the old bureaucracy. The Decree of the President of the Russian Federation of May 17, 2000, "On the structure of federal executive bodies," eliminated the Committee on Environmental Protection of Russian Federation and Federal Forestry Service of Russia and merged them into the structure of the Ministry of Natural Resources. This reduced duplication of responsibilities concerning water management and monitoring in Russia. The restructuring will continue in 2001 and as of late 2000, the new structure of the Ministry of Natural Resources and distribution of responsibilities between the MNR and Hydromet were unclear. Frequent restructuring of the water management system hampers development of the capacity of water management and environmental protection agencies in Russia. More stability is needed for developing an effective water management system.

In Estonia, environmental management has evolved to a great extent since 1991. Many current Estonian governmental systems did not exist under centralized Soviet policies. Others have been completely replaced to expunge Soviet-style influences. As a result, Estonian agencies have relatively simple procedures and do not duplicate efforts or responsibilities. They are largely decentralized and delegate responsibilities to lower levels of government or to the private sector as part of a democratic political process. There are two principle reasons for this new direction: (1) there was a need to break up the system inherited from the Soviet era for political reasons; and (2) institution building was done with funds and advice from Western European countries, especially from the Nordic countries. In the process of accession to the European Union, the Estonian government is making serious efforts to develop the institutional capacity of state agencies as it is advised by the European Commission in its annual report on Estonia's preparation for accession (European Commission 2000).

Differences in management styles are reflected in differences in management systems. The Swedish sponsors have a Western European/U.S. management style that is responsive and flexible. At the same time, the management of technical assistance programs to Eastern Europe are often centralized and bureaucratic, sometimes creating tensions in countries that receive the aid when such assistance cannot fulfill their needs. For example, when training programs or consulting services are offered in place of expected investments in environmental infrastructure.

These differing styles and expectations create difficulties in coordinating project activities and reporting. Each participating group plays according to its own rules, which differ significantly from one another. Often there is not enough communication between partners to enable them to understand these differences so that they could try to adjust their own approach in a way that would accommodate the needs of their partner. The inability of partners to adopt each other's rules creates a serious challenge to the long-term success of the project. Developing strategies to overcome these cultural institutional barriers to environmental cooperation has a growing importance with the ongoing expansion of international cooperation at different levels of governance in the Baltic Sea Region and the European Union.

Cultural Differences

The countries' different approaches to this project may be broadly characterized as "cultural." Without going into an extensive background of the area's history, it may be noted that Estonia and Russia's pasts have less in common than one might expect. Estonia is a very small country with a history of social and cultural links to the West—most notably Scandinavia and Germany. It has a small and independent population that is eager to "rejoin" the West after 50 years of Soviet domination. National policy since its second independence in 1991 has promoted privatization and entrepreneurship. These are values that were already present during the first period of Estonian independence from 1918 through the early 1940s. By contrast, Pskov is located at the extreme western periphery of Russia, a massive country with a heterogeneous population that retains some of the attitudes developed over the last two to three centuries regarding land ownership and other social issues—attitudes largely developed during unsettled times under autocratic political systems. All of these factors most likely contributed to the Estonian team's relative success compared to Russia's problems with implementation of the water management project.

Project Implementation Process

From 1996 to 1998, the organizers of the Lake Peipus monitoring project initially focused on supportive communication and information management activities in addition to the main activities of environmental monitoring. Tasks also included developing institutional capacity and regional level infrastructure for management, data handling, evaluation, and dissemination of information concerning the environmental state of the lake and its watershed. An Internet homepage was established, as were e-mail and Internet connections on the Russian side to create networks and facilitate the flow of information. Participants conducted trilateral meetings and seminars and visited one another's agencies and observed their differences.

Strengthening the region's ability to manage its environment, set priorities, and resolve problems will be important next steps; however, given the local social, economic, and political situations, it is unrealistic to suppose that such progress will be fast or easy. To promote international projects, more efforts must be made to coordinate activities and retrain the Russian federal environmental agencies in international project management. The Russians will also need improved access to computer and communications technologies. More active use of such technology and incorporation with the transboundary water management system of the EU environmental program, "Agenda 21," should make the Lake Peipus environmental regime function more effectively.

Even with the comparatively low level of performance on the eastern side of the border, it is hoped that personal contacts and informal communications between experts on both sides will motivate progress. Thus, maintaining old contacts between experts who worked together earlier and developing a transborder "epistemic community" may be crucial to the success of the environmental management regime in the Estonian-Russian border area.

Recommendations

Proposals for a better institutional framework for transboundary environmental cooperation in the Lake Peipus basin and sustainable management of its natural resources should be based on studies of regime effectiveness and existing mechanisms of compliance with established formal rules and procedures. A study of transboundary environmental risks (and perception of risks by local stakeholders as well as people involved in implementing the transboundary environmental management regimes) will also need to be explored in the framework of the referenced international research program.

To promote the effectiveness of the international Lake Peipus water management regime, it is necessary to:

- provide more resources and support in management and administration (retraining and information) on the Russian side
- create a mechanism for local-level coordination of activities for implementing the international regime
- continue developing cross-border communication networks
- support informal networks for cooperation between experts in Estonia and Russia and the promotion of private enterprise (commercial and noncommercial) involvement in environmental management in the border zone

Conclusions

The future of the Lake Peipus international environmental regime will depend on many factors. These include the involved experts, further development of the environmental management institutional system, signing of the border agreement between Russia and Estonia, and the general economic and social situation in Russia and Estonia. One important positive factor that will support the development of the environmental regime is the region's strong informal network of experts, NGOs, and local government representatives involved in environmental protection and sustainable development. Taking into account the dynamic changes in environmental management structures in both Russia and Estonia and the influence of the political and economic situations in these countries, it is important to continue to evaluate and recalculate the regime's implementation and assess its ongoing effectiveness.

Endnote

1. This paper has already discussed institutional arrangements, including the legal basis for cooperation and the role of the joint transboundary water commission. For a discussion of the role of international and nonprofit organizations, see Roll and Abercrombie 1997; Roll 1997.

References

Blöch, H. 1998. "The European Community Water Framework Directive in Management of Transboundary Waters in Europe." Pp. 25–31 in *Proceedings of the International Conference on Management of Transboundary Waters in Europe*. Tartu: Center for Transboundary Cooperation.

European Commission. 2000. *Regular Report from the Commission on Estonia's Progress towards Accession*. Brussels: European Commission.

Haas, Ernst B. 1993. "Words Can Hurt You; Or Who Said What to Whom about Regimes." Pp. 23–61 in *International Regimes*, Stephen D. Krasner, ed. Ithaca and London: Cornell University Press.

Krasner, Stephen D., ed. 1983. *International Regimes*. Ithaca and London: Cornell University Press.

Lönnroth, Mäns. 1997. Interview by Gulnara Roll and T. Maximova. December.

Nõges, P., T. Nõges, and V.V. Jastremskij. 1996. "Primary Production of Lake Peipsi/Pihkva." *Hydrobiologia 338: 77–89.*

Orgusaar, T. 1996. Presentation at a workshop on Lake Peipus environmental management, October, Tartu, Estonia.

Roll, Gulnara. 1997. "Implementation of Transboundary Environmental Risks Management Strategies in Border Areas of the Baltics and New Independent States." Pp. 462–63 in *Proceedings of the Annual Meeting of the Society for Risk Analysis—Europe: New Risk Frontiers*. Stockholm: The Center for Risk Research.

Roll, Gulnara, and C. Abercrombie. 1997. "The Lake Peipsi Watershed, an Evolving Environmental Regime: Outline for Negotiation and Implementation Using the Existing Regulations of Baltic Sea Institutions." Pp. 344–50 in *Proceedings of the Second International Lake Ladoga Symposium 1996*. Joensuu: University of Joensuu.

Stålnacke, P., Ü. Sults, A. Vasiliev, B. Skalalsky, A. Botina, G. Roll, K. Pachel, and T. Maltsman. 2001. "Nutrient Loads to Lake Peipsi. Environmental Monitoring of Lake Peipsi/Chudskoe 1998–99. Subproject Report Phase 2." *Jordforsk Report* 4 (1): 66.

Young, Oran R. 1989. *International Cooperation: Building Regimes for Natural Resources and the Environment*. Ithaca and London: Cornell University Press.

Young, Oran R. 1994. *International Governance. Protecting the Environment in a Stateless Society*. Ithaca and London: Cornell University Press.

A Russian Enclave within the European Union? Kaliningrad Reconsidered

Lyndelle D. Fairlie[*]

Abstract

When the European Union (EU) enlarges to include Poland and Lithuania, it will create a Russian enclave within the EU: the Kaliningrad oblast. When the Soviet Union dissolved, Kaliningrad became an exclave of Russia, separated by the newly independent states of Lithuania, Latvia, and Belarus. Kaliningrad's problems are often blamed on the problems of being an exclave, including residual "hard security" issues, exchange rate volatility, and other problems affecting Russia as a whole. This paper explores whether or not an analysis of the success of other oblasts has policy implications for Kaliningrad. Kathryn Stoner-Weiss tested various hypotheses in an attempt to explain the varying performances and successes of four other oblast governments. After eliminating the importance of many of the same variables that are thought to affect Kaliningrad, Stoner-Weiss concluded that the most important factor determining the success of oblast governments was the degree of concentration in their economies. The more concentrated the economy, the more successful the government's performance; the more dispersed the economy, the less successful the government's performance. If this analysis applies to Kaliningrad, it would suggest to Moscow and Brussels that optimal policies affecting Kaliningrad's government performance would include projects that promote a "company town" type of concentrated economy.

Introduction

The enlargement of the European Union to include Poland and the Baltic states in the future raises the questions of what policies the EU and its member states should implement to achieve maximum cross-border trade between an enlarging EU and the Soviet successor states, while at the same time minimizing illegal immigration, pollution, and crime. Two of the areas that will soon be in the spotlight in the Baltic region are the Polish and Lithuanian borders with Russia at

---

* Fairlie is Associate Professor of Political Science at San Diego State University.

Kaliningrad and the border between Russia and Estonia. During the Soviet period, Narva and Ivangorod were part of the same country and shared the same infrastructure. Today, Ivangorod remains Russian, while Narva is a border town in Estonia. Poland and Lithuania are EU associates preparing for membership, which would leave neighboring Kaliningrad as a Russian enclave within the enlarging EU. Thus, the path toward development for Kaliningrad is unclear.

The consideration of appropriate policies to be implemented by the EU and its member states is particularly appropriate while negotiations between the EU and Poland are in an early stage and EU arrangements with Lithuania are even more embryonic. Ironically, the EU seems not to notice the important changes taking place in Poland and Lithuania in preparation for their accession, an event that will undoubtedly affect Kaliningrad. Instead, a recent report from the Working Party on Eastern Europe and Central Asia (1998) states that "the Partnership and Cooperation Agreement (PCA), which entered into force in December, 1997, provides the overall framework for EU-Russian relations and the basis for EU's comprehensive policy toward Russia." In fact, problems that occurred along Kaliningrad's border with Poland in 1998 occurred not because of the PCA, but because of changes rooted in Polish accession.

When considering potential policies, the EU and its member states can draw upon prior experiences of both border areas as well as other Russian regions. In the Baltic area, such experiences include the Finnish-Russian and German-Polish borders. In its *Vision 2000* document, the EU specified that policies for the external boundaries of an enlarging EU would fall within the categories of already-established policy, such as TACIS[1] aid to Russia and Euroregions. Most TACIS programs in Kaliningrad ended in late 1998 when the TACIS budget was cut and Russia failed to rank Kaliningrad as one of its high priorities for TACIS funding. Within Russia, policymakers may learn from Kathryn Stoner-Weiss (1997), who analyzed the causes of varying levels of oblast government success in the Russian oblasts of Nizhny Novgorod, Tiumen, Yaroslavl, and Saratov.[2]

The U.S.-Mexican border might also provide a helpful model for the EU. This border could provide insights into what a border between an enlarging EU and Soviet successor states may look like if modernist Cold War residue were removed and only postmodernist issues were to prevail.[3] The U.S.-Mexican border is challenged by postmodern, "soft" security issues, such as the management of trade, pollution, crime, illegal immigration, and protection of cultural identity, rather than "hard" security issues associated with the Cold War.[4]

The underlying limitation of EU policy options (as conveyed to the author during 1997 interviews with commission officials in Brussels) lies in what the EU can and will do out of deference to Moscow. Basically, the EU considered Kaliningrad to be the responsibility of Moscow, not of Brussels. In 1998, there was some indication that the EU could take increased interest in Kaliningrad as it may become a Russian enclave within its borders. In addition, disruption along the Polish border at Kaliningrad in early 1998 indicated to Brussels that, at the

Figure 1. Kaliningrad

very least, Kaliningrad should be provided with more information about the implications of possible EU membership for Poland and Lithuania.

Comparing Kaliningrad with Other Russian Oblasts

The EU and its member states' objectives include maximizing the benefits of cross-border trade between EU and non-EU states while minimizing "soft" security risks in the form of illegal immigration, crime, and pollution from non-EU border states. "Soft" security risks will be less likely if the non-EU neighbor is developing into a stable democracy with a healthy economy. Extensive analysis has focused on international institutions such as the International Monetary Fund (IMF) and interactions between Moscow officials and foreign governments. Russian federalism is still being negotiated and decisions from Moscow remain of great importance for Kaliningrad.

Another consideration for Russia is what determines a healthy economy and the successful performance of an oblast government.[5] Such a determination could help Moscow, Kaliningrad, the EU, and its member states to choose policies that would have the most beneficial effect on their non-EU neighbor, Kaliningrad. From the EU's perspective, an important by-product of good policy would be minimal "soft" security risks.

In order to assess the relevance of the Stoner-Weiss analysis for Kaliningrad, it is useful to first note the variables that analysts have considered important in Kaliningrad and then compare Kaliningrad with Stoner-Weiss's comparison of the causes of varying levels of governmental success in four other Russian oblasts. The following factors were given as causes or potential causes of damage to Kaliningrad's economy in June 1998, possibly making it a more risky neighbor for the EU and revealing the relevance of the Stoner-Weiss analysis: (1) the governor's alleged lack of experience; (2) incidents of political violence involving critics of the governor; (3) the increasing number of strikes by public sector workers; (4) increasing incidence of AIDS and other diseases, as well as higher infant mortality; and (5) declining subsidies from Moscow. The Fitch report on the oblast economy foresees potential trouble arising from a possible increase in economic problems in rural areas as compared to the city of Kaliningrad (Fitch IBCA 1998). Many observers added Kaliningrad's 80 percent dependence on imported food as another factor. This would indicate potential instability after the crisis following the ruble devaluation in August 1998. Locals attributed this major dependence on imports to the oblast's exclave status, although Vladivostok is equally dependent on imported food.

In her analysis of the performances of oblast governments in Nizhny Novgorod, Tiumen, Yaroslavl, and Saratov, Stoner-Weiss used comparative political literature to test hypotheses about those variables that might explain the different levels of success among the four oblasts. She drew upon the works of Gurr and McClelland (1971), Eckstein (1971), and Putnam, Leonardi, and Nanetti (1993) for indicators of government performance, as well as her own survey research. Her 12 indicators of government performance included the following subjects: governor selection, quorum, percentage of time spent on organizational matters, information services, trade policy, regional economic development programs, educational reform policy, approval of leadership, alienation, satisfaction with performance in specific policy areas, faith in problem-solving abilities of the government and oblast, and pace of economic reform.

Stoner-Weiss did not find significant differences in oblast government success due to: (1) wealth; (2) development indicators such as infant mortality; (3) the qualifications of oblast *duma* (legislature) members; (4) traditional importance of the oblast to Moscow; (5) differences in attitudes toward the market economy; (6) rural/urban disparities; (7) varying levels of voter participation; or (8) newspaper readership or other indicators of civic community as drawn from Putnam, Leonardi, and Nanetti's assessment of regional governments in Italy (1993).[6]

Stoner-Weiss concluded that the different success levels of the four oblast governments she studied were due to the degree of concentration in the regional economy. The more the regional economy resembled a "company town," the more successful the oblast government was.[7] Likewise, the more dispersed the economy, the less successful the oblast government. Stoner-Weiss (1997) summarized her findings as follows:

> ... in regions where economies were concentrated, as in Nizhnii Novgorod and Tiumen, cooperative relations were established between organized economic interests and political actors. The embeddedness of social interactions in regions that resembled "company towns" focused regional interests and heightened the interdependence of economic and political actors as the destabilizing transitions to the market and democracy transpired. The concentration of the regional economy also narrowed the pool from which political elites were drawn such that horizontal (preexisting) professional networks further helped to sustain credible commitments and collective action between political and economic actors.
>
> The cooperation that arose from the concentration of the regional economy was such that the state included economic interests in the policy process, and economic interests gained material advantages from the state. In return, economic interests helped guarantee broad consensus on key issues and used their resources to promote government efficacy and legitimacy within civil society. These convergent interests therefore sustained consensus and higher government performance at least in the short term.

Described in this way, these interactions sound virtuous, appropriate, and efficient; however, when one reads the actual details of these interactions in Chapter 6 of the same work ("The Political Economy of Government Performance: Testing the Theory"), they resemble the interactions described by critics of U.S. government as conflicts of interest or even corruption.

Stoner-Weiss is aware of the potential negative consequences or normative implications of her findings. "These include the obvious concern that high degrees of elite consensus and collective action could as easily lead to oligarchy as to higher regional government performance. Responsiveness to emergent groups could decrease as elite relationships freeze" (Stoner-Weiss 1997). One might add that conflict of interest and corruption could become the cornerstones of government links to business.

It is possible that the research Stoner-Weiss conducted from 1990 to 1993 is less relevant now than at that time. Alexander Sergounin, a noted scholar of Russian regionalism, observed that many Russian regions are now more or less equal in their lack of prosperity. A colleague from the oil-rich region of Tiumen had summarized the problem to Sergounin by stating that it does not matter if you are located where the oil enters the pipeline; what matters is where it empties out—implying that Moscow was collecting oil revenues, not Tiumen (Sergounin 1999).

The Kaliningrad Economy

How much does the "exclave" factor matter? What lessons can be drawn for Kaliningrad from the Stoner-Weiss research? Skeptics might argue that this research is not of much use in analyzing Kaliningrad's case due to its exclave status. When making their case in Moscow, Kaliningraders argue that they deserve special privileges to compensate for the extra transportation and border-crossing costs incurred when conveying people and goods between Kaliningrad and mainland Russia.

Another argument that yields some credibility in distinguishing the exclave from mainland Russia is that Kaliningrad may be much more a part of a duality of modernist and postmodernist agendas than the four interior oblasts studied by Stoner-Weiss. Many Kaliningraders are completely unaware of the "hard" security debates that affect Kaliningrad due to jobs that are unrelated to the military or the atavistic remains of Cold War politics. When asked in 1998 about what role issues like the enlargement of the North Atlantic Treaty Organization (NATO) played in their lives, Kaliningraders seemed unaware of and uninterested in such subjects.

While they may be unaware of those issues on the political agenda left over from the Cold War, Kaliningraders are vulnerable to the will of distant politicians who try to play the Kaliningrad card in "high" politics by negotiating the size of its military in conferences dedicated to revising the Conventional Forces in Europe Treaty, linking Start-2 (Strategic Arms Reduction Talks) ratification to exclude the Baltic states in the expansion of NATO, and so on. Such moves can play a subtle role in affecting Russian and foreign perceptions of the oblast's stability and the decisions of foreign business and government on political risk insurance, export subsidies, investment commitments, and so on.

Although Kaliningrad is a unique case, many other Russian areas and Moscow politicians think it is at least as well-off as the rest of the country. Its problems are often regarded as less severe than those in other areas; therefore, although it is important to keep the exclave factor in mind, insights may be gained by comparing Kaliningrad with other oblasts.

An Overview of the Kaliningrad Economy

Most analyses show the Kaliningrad economy as dispersed rather than concentrated. Most industries that flourished during the Soviet period—such as fishing, fish processing, and industries related to the military-industrial complex, including ship building and repair—have severely declined in the post-Soviet period.

It was hoped that new industries would arise as a result of the Free Economic Zone and later the Special Economic Zone, which theoretically allowed foreigners to export to the Russian mainland after adding value to products in Kaliningrad without paying duties. Fledgling industries, such as furniture manufacture and apparel, are designed to capitalize on these aspects of the Special Economic Zone. Analysis by a TACIS team (Hanson and Sutherland 1998) found that businesses with a foreign partner with expertise, technology, and capital were headed for success, while those without foreign partners were in decline.[8]

Kaliningrad's economy also involves other sectors that are more difficult to ascertain. It is commonly alleged that amber is smuggled to Poland and Lithuania where jewelers add value before export. The import and export of automobiles was also a thriving business in Kaliningrad until the rouble devaluation in August 1998. Due to its exclave status, citizens of Kaliningrad were allowed to import a car duty-free for use in the oblast, but could not reexport it to mainland Russia where Russians pay high import duties on foreign cars. When the International Monetary Fund (IMF) increased pressure on Moscow authorities to increase revenue, Moscow began to reduce some of these benefits due to suspicions that some Kaliningraders were illegally selling cars to mainland Russians, enabling them to avoid paying the foreign car tax.

If such allegations of large-scale smuggling in the post-Soviet Kaliningrad economy have merit, Richard Friman's (1995) theoretical insight into the oblast economy may be especially useful. He found that the "gray economy" is most likely to flourish when two conditions are present: (1) good access to target, and (2) openness of the economy. From a "soft" security perspective, Kaliningrad has changed dramatically in the post-Soviet period in the direction suggested by Friman. In the Soviet period, Kaliningrad was closed and inaccessible even to many Russians. It primarily focused on fishing, amber, and the military. Today, it is surrounded by EU applicants. If the EU is the target as a source of cars that can be smuggled to Russia and a source of customers for amber, then Kaliningrad's "access to target" has improved dramatically in the post-Soviet period.

"Openness" has also been prevalent in the post-Soviet period. Since Kaliningrad and Lithuania were both part of the Soviet Union, there was no border or border infrastructure between them in early post-Soviet days. The border between Poland and Russia was closed with the exception of infrequent diplomatic travel because Poland was seen as a source of dangerous ideas that undermined communism, such as the wishes for democratic representation expressed by workers in the Solidarity trade union. In the post-Soviet period, new border crossings with Poland have been opened. Poland is now one of Kaliningrad's leading foreign trade partners, along with Lithuania and Germany. In 1997, Kaliningrad's "foreign trade with Germany, Poland and Lithuania amounted to around 60 percent of its total volume" (Prudnikov 1999). Thus, both access and openness have changed in Kaliningrad in the post-Soviet period. The region is moving closer to participation in the globalization process, European trade, and facing such postmodern problems as posing potential pollution, crime, disease, and illegal immigration risks to its neighbors.

EU Policies Affecting Kaliningrad

The EU aims to encourage the best aspects of cross-border trade while minimizing "soft" security risks. Its current policies affecting Kaliningrad include the TACIS aid program in Russia, Euroregions that span borders, and various policies from the EU's *acquis communautaire*,[9] which must be gradually adopted by Poland and Lithuania. In 1998, focus centered on the substantial disruption of cross-border trade between Poland and Kaliningrad, resulting from Poland's fledgling attempts to begin its adjustment to the requirements of the EU Amsterdam Treaty, which mandated that all applicant countries must adopt the Schengen *acquis*.

The Schengen standards are based on the idea that the EU's external borders must be tightly monitored to guard against illegal immigration if it is going to have a single market among its member states that includes the free movement of labor. Considering that the incumbent governments of most major EU countries are currently in the hands of left-of-center political parties, this policy is likely to continue to receive high priority. For example, after the Social Democratic Party (SPD) and its coalition partners won the 1998 election in Germany, analysts speculated that German policy would move toward spending more money on solving domestic unemployment problems in Germany and the EU than on enlarging the EU to include more countries.

If Poland joins the EU, its borders with Russia (at Kaliningrad), Belarus, and Ukraine will become external EU borders. In accordance with the Amsterdam Treaty, Poland began to implement restrictions at these borders in 1998, introducing requirements of more expensive documents to identify travelers from these border countries. These policies were introduced during a holiday period when cross-border traffic was particularly high. Cross-border trade was disrupted and affected travelers became angry and confused due to miscommunications about these requirements.

With time, changes in policy and procedures made it easier to obtain the required documents, reducing the bottlenecks in cross-border trade. The effects of disrupted trade were felt by Poland's neighbors as well as those in eastern Poland who were are already living below the standard enjoyed in western Poland. This disparity caused resentment when asked to sacrifice some of their trade with neighboring Soviet successor states to benefit their more prosperous countrymen at the instigation of Brussels.[10]

Since no one had informed Kaliningraders about the effect that the Amsterdam Treaty would have on them, the disruption of cross-border trade and travel was not understood. Following that experience, Kaliningraders wondered if they would be exposed to the same problems someday with their Lithuanian border. At present, Kaliningraders can go to Lithuania for 30 days without a visa, a privilege not extended to other Russians. However, Lithuania has cautioned that this policy may be modified as it adopts the EU's *acquis communautaire* in preparation for membership. The EU only allows visa-free travel where there is a readmission agreement, which Lithuania lacks with Russia. Readmission agreements allow illegal immigrants to be deported to the country from which they crossed the border. The EU will probably insist that Lithuania require visas from all Russians as long it lacks such an agreement with Russia. Another reason Lithuania might tighten its borders is the suspicion that Poland deports illegal immigrants from Lithuania, as well as Belarus and Ukraine, to Lithuania.

Unless new visa requirements are handled better than they have been at the Polish border, they will likely cause political incidents, disruption of traffic, and anxiety for Kaliningraders who already feel isolated from mainland Russia and increasingly so from Poland. If trouble sprouts in Lithuania as well, Kaliningrad could feel like an island. The changes in requirements, documents, and procedures may seem insignificant to foreigners, but they could assume a significant emotional importance to Kaliningraders. By restricting its borders, Lithuania would be unilaterally revoking the Protocol to the Interim Agreement on Mutual Trips of Citizens signed in 1995. Such an action could become especially sensitive since both parties trusted each other and committed to a signed agreement.

Although border policies related to Schengen received the most publicity in Kaliningrad in 1998, TACIS and Euroregion programs were also present. Kaliningrad joined the Baltic Euroregion in 1998 and the area around Gusev is reportedly planning to join the Niemen Euroregion, linking Poland, Belarus, Lithuania, and Kaliningrad. These Euroregion programs are still too new to be evaluated.

TACIS programs in Kaliningrad have included economic planning, infrastructure development, environment, health, post-privatization, and sector development projects for fishing and amber. This list implies that TACIS programs are contributing to the diversity of the Kaliningrad economy, not its concentration. Most TACIS programs were scheduled to end by the end of 1998, sparking a need for the EU and Russia to negotiate future programs. Bilateral programs between Kaliningrad and EU member states and their regions have also been implemented for a variety of projects.

EU Member State Policies Affecting Kaliningrad

The EU Commission has competence (known in the United States as "jurisdiction") over some policy areas, while others remain largely within the control of member states. For example, ports and immigration policy reflect the primacy of member states as policymakers. From a "soft" security perspective, one of the most interesting changes in the future may be related to immigration. "One well-placed Eurocrat reckons that the Union's coming attempts to harmonise external immigration policies could present 'the next big row after the euro'—and could delay the EU's enlargement" (*The Economist* 1998).

If EU member states use the Stoner-Weiss analysis as a guideline for their own national policy formation, they might choose policies that enhance the concentration of the Kaliningrad economy rather than its dispersion. Member states can be important actors in this process by creating policies to assist their own businesses in undertaking foreign trade and investment with political risk insurance or export aid. Technology transfer is also an important dimension in this effort.

Conclusion

Stoner-Weiss found that Nizhny Novgorod had the most concentrated oblast economy and the most successful oblast government. Saratov had the least concentrated economy and the least successful oblast government. Her characterizations of the two oblasts are noteworthy for this study because the description of Saratov is essentially identical to that discerned from two weeks of interviews with the author in Kaliningrad in June 1998. Stoner-Weiss summarizes her findings as follows:

> In Nizhnii Novgorod and Tiumen, the two highest performers in the study, political actors, when asked in interviews what they viewed as their most significant accomplishment in such turbulent times in Russia, almost invariably responded "consensus" or "stability." In Saratov, by contrast, government suffered deadlock and repeated conflict between the legislative and executive branches, within the legislature itself, and between the capital city government and the oblast. The Saratov newspapers were routinely filled with articles concerning the latest blowout between the governor and the head of the oblast legislature. These included systematic opposition to gubernatorial appointments to executive posts, and no less than three times in fourteen months, the threatened resignation of the chairman of the oblast soviet over various similar conflicts. Deputy interviews also revealed instability within the Saratov oblast soviet itself (Stoner-Weiss 1997: 164).

The situation Kaliningraders described in June 1998 closely matched that of Saratov. There were conflicts between the city and the oblast as well as between the governor and the oblast *duma*. Critics of Governor Gorbenko were trying to launch a referendum that would result in his removal. They recalled what they remembered as the halcyon days of the previous governor, Matochkin, commenting on his competence and good relations with Moscow. Critics of Gorbenko seemed to think that Kaliningrad would be headed in the right direction if only they had a more progressive governor.

This focus on the governor as the source of Kaliningrad's problems was puzzling. Regardless of the shortcomings or errors of the current governor, Kaliningrad's economy performed poorly even under Matochkin. During the Matochkin era, Kaliningraders were quick to blame Moscow for unexpectedly terminating their first Free Economic Zone, thereby discouraging foreign investment.

The Stoner-Weiss analysis lends credence to this idea that one must look beyond the current governor and perhaps even beyond Moscow's troubles, residual "hard" security issues from the Cold War, and the exclave factor to find the root of Kaliningrad's problems. Perhaps, in addition to these commonly noted problems, the extent of dispersion in the Kaliningrad economy needs to be examined when assessing development potential.

The Optimal Future for the Kaliningrad Economy

In the post-Soviet period, the Kaliningrad economy has become increasingly dispersed. Experts differ in their suggestions for future prospects. One suggestion is for Kaliningrad to become part of a Baltic growth triangle (Kivikari 1997). In such a relationship, Kaliningrad would provide low-cost labor while foreign partners provide other resources, becoming an industrial center reminiscent of the *maquiladoras* (assembly plants) along the U.S.-Mexican border.

Such a concentration of economic activity in one sector might provide the concentration needed for a level of success comparable to Nizhny Novgorod.

Other suggestions may restrict further diversification of the Kaliningrad economy. A large number of Kaliningrad's problems arise from its exclave status and related vulnerability to "hard" security Cold War risks (reminiscent of access to Berlin). One TACIS project that focuses on the economic future of Kaliningrad suggests that these problems could be minimized by concentrating on the computer software, air transportation, and telecommunications industries, developed along the lines of models provided by Ireland and India (Dewar n.d.). Such industries are not dependent on border crossings that would entail modernist Cold War problems that could be exacerbated if Lithuania introduces a visa requirement. As Kaliningrad learned early in 1998 with its experience at the Polish border, border formalities can imply high transaction costs.

From Stoner-Weiss's perspective, the prescription for further diversification of the Kaliningrad economy is a recipe for failure. Her research demonstrated that the success of an oblast government is much more likely if its economy is concentrated, not dispersed. Nonetheless, she thought that dispersed economies could gain from her research, stating that "one of the lessons of this study for regions with dispersed economies is that the way in which demands on their government resources are packaged may enable them to accomplish more. In the long-term, they may want to encourage the development of organized interest groups that might help give rise to an environment of political inclusion" (1977: 26).

The most immediate implications of the Stoner-Weiss analysis are that Moscow, Brussels, and EU member states should direct TACIS programs and Euroregions in the direction of concentrating rather than diversifying the Kaliningrad economy. Stoner-Weiss also suggests that "Western countries that have rational foreign policy interests in encouraging democratization and marketization in Russia should act as political entrepreneurs in assisting in the development of organized interest groups (including, for example, chambers of commerce) throughout Russia" (1997: 201).

Even if the Kaliningrad economy becomes more concentrated and the oblast government more successful, there is still the normative risk of too much of a good thing. Stoner-Weiss observes that concentration can also lead to oligarchy, retention of obsolete industries through large subsidies, and the danger of smothering the development of pluralism. The EU and its member states are particularly aware of these problems. Poland's efforts to adopt EU policies, leading to efficient industries, have been resisted by Polish labor in some sectors, such as mining, presenting just the sort of risks Stoner-Weiss envisions—the retention of obsolete industries with the aid of large subsidies.

For significant changes to occur in Kaliningrad, they must go beyond what was observed in Brussels in 1997. At that time, commission officials indicated that because the EU defers to Moscow, what the EU can and will do for Kaliningrad is very limited. Moscow appears increasingly weak and disinclined to produce consistent policies, leaving Russian regions to fend for themselves as they are constrained by its unwillingness to delegate the necessary authority that would give regions the flexibility they need.

Although many regions (including those studied by Stoner-Weiss) complain about Moscow, Stoner-Weiss has demonstrated that some oblast governments have been more successful than others. Those that have been successful make the best neighbors; thus, the incentive to try to instill success in those that have failed is favorable.

Endnotes

1. Technical Assistance to the Commonwealth of Independent States (TACIS) was the original name of the EU foreign aid program for the Soviet successor states.

2. This analysis primarily covers 1990 to 1993.

3. For a discussion of modern and postmodern policies in the Baltic area, see Joenniemi 1998. The author makes the point that Finland, Sweden, and the Baltic states have adopted postmodern policies on "soft" security issues such as the environment, human rights, and freedom of the press, while simultaneously retaining modernist approaches to "hard" security issues that arose during the Cold War.

4. See Drinan and Pfau (1997) for cultural identity issues along the U.S.-Mexican border.

5. Kaliningrad, containing the capital city of the same name, is an oblast. Its comparison with the Stoner-Weiss analysis of four other oblasts is therefore appropriate. Stoner-Weiss held institutions constant, comparing oblasts to each other rather than to republics. Future research may consider whether a comparison of Kaliningrad with four interior oblasts is appropriate and if oblasts on borders (and the more extreme case of Kaliningrad as an exclave of mainland Russia) are fundamentally different from interior oblasts, making their comparison useless.

6. Stoner-Weiss notes that in the context of Russian history, she did not expect to find the kind of civic community that can be found in Western democracies. Nonetheless, part of her research design involved testing Putnam, Leonardi, and Nanetti's hypotheses to ascertain whether or not a civic community was developing in any of the oblasts and how these variables might relate to the success of oblast governments.

7. In Chapter 4, "Who Governs Russia *Well*? Measuring Institutional Performance," Stoner-Weiss (1997) used indicators of performance of oblast governments drawn from Putnam, Leonardi and Nanetti's study (1993) of Italian regional governments, and the indicators used by Ted Robert Gurr and Muriel McClelland in their book, *Political Performance: A Twelve Nation Study* (1971).

8. When Stoner-Weiss analyzed the role of foreign interest in Nizhny Novgorod (1997: 141), she found that "area specialists might also argue that foreign interest in Nizhnii Novgorod increased regional governing capacities. This argument, however, mixes cause and effect. In interviews with the International Finance Corporation in Nizhnii Novgorod, officials explained that they selected Nizhnii Novgorod over other oblasts as a region in which to consult on privatization because the regional government appeared competent (and also because Nizhnii was relatively close to Moscow and was a large industrial center)."

9. The *acquis communautaire* is an accumulation of the EU's laws, policies, and judicial decisions.

10. The author appreciates this assessment from her colleague and co-author of another article, Dr. Cezar Ornatowski.

References

Dewar, Stephen (EU TACIS consultant). n.d. Interview with author.

Drinan, Patrick, and Michael Pfau. 1997. "The San Diego-Tijuana Border: Concrete Local Demarcation Line or Fuzzy Political Concept?" Paper presented at the Border Regions in Transition: The Finnish-Russian Border Region in a Comparative Perspective conference, June, Joensuu, Finland.

The Economist. 1998. "Good Fences." 349 (8099) (19 December):19–22.

Fitch IBCA. 1998. *Sub-National Report: Kaliningrad Oblast.* (30 July). London: Fitch IBCA.

Friman, H. Richard. 1995. "Just Passing Through: Transit States and the Dynamics of Illicit Transshipment." *Transnational Organized Crime* 1 (1).

Gurr, Robert, and Muriel McClelland. 1971. *Political Performance: A Twelve Nation Study.* Beverly Hills: Sage.

Hanson, Philip, and Douglas Sutherland. 1998. "Kaliningrad: ndustrial Sector Overview." *Tacis PROMETEE II* (January). Unpublished.

Joenniemi, Pertti. 1998. "Prologue: Toward Post-Modern Arms Control?" Pp. 27–36 in *Arms Control Around the Baltic Rim II*, Working paper No. 25 Pertti Joenniemi, ed. Copenhagen: Copenhagen Peace Research Institute.

Kaliningrad This Week. 1999. "Lithuanian Medics Visit Gusev." *Tacis PROMETEE II* (25–31 January).

Kivikari, Urpo. 1997. "The Application of Growth Triangles as a Means of Development for the Kaliningrad Region." In *The External Economic Relations of the Kaliningrad Region*, Urpo Kivikari, Maarit Lindstrom, Kari Liuhto, eds. Report for the EU TACIS program.

Prudnikov, Vladimir N. (Deputy Governor of Kaliningrad oblast). 1999. Speech to CBSS Committee of Senior Officials (February).

Putnam, Robert D., Robert Leonardi, and Raffaella Nanetti. 1993. *Making Democracy Work: Civic Traditions in Modern Italy.* Princeton: Princeton University Press.

Sergounin, Alexander (Professor of Political Science, University of Nizhny Novgorod, Russia). 1999. Conversation with author. San Diego, Cal. (January).

Stoner-Weiss, Kathryn. 1997. *Local Heroes: The Political Economy of Russian Regional Governance.* Princeton: Princeton University Press.

Tracevskis, Rokas M. 1998. "Western Europe Abolishes Baltic Visa Requirements." *The Baltic Times* (10–16 December).

Working Party on Eastern Europe and Central Asia. 1998. "Russia: Progress Made in Developing a Comprehensive EU Policy." Report to COREPER/Council (1 December).

Kaliningrad as a Discursive Battlefield

Pertti Joenniemi[*]

Abstract

The future of Kaliningrad is discussed within the context of a variety of frameworks that influence the way that this small enclave in the Baltic Sea Region is
conceptualized and comprehended. It is argued that the influence of a European
logic of governance is growing, whereas the more traditional (primitive and realist) logics are losing ground. Yet all three remain in the game, bringing about a
rather problematic situation. It remains difficult for the relevant partners to agree
upon how to tackle the "Kaliningrad question" due to a lack of a joint logic and
joint points of reference. The logic of governance allows Kaliningrad to be conceived both as Russian and European, or more broadly, as a juncture in a world of
networks. The enhancement of the logic of governance may win out in the long
run, but currently, Kaliningrad shows alarming signs of turning into a liability
rather than an asset; although it also seems to reveal unifying and bor-
der-breaking functions by bringing about dialogue between Russia and the European Union (EU).

A Mixture of Views

With the breakup of the Soviet Union, a distance of some four hundred kilometers (248 miles) emerged between the Kaliningrad oblast and mainland Russia.
The position of the oblast was profoundly destabilized. Suddenly, with the Soviet Union falling apart, the rather isolated, protective, and strongly de-
fense-oriented region found itself far more exposed to the challenges of
European integration than any other area of Russia. It became Russia's westernmost outpost and was surrounded, somewhat uncomfortably, by Poland and
Lithuania—both engaged in developing a deeper relationship with the European
Union.

Kaliningrad once functioned as a fortification guarding against unwarranted
external influence; it is now called upon to spearhead change. Having been

* Joenniemi is Senior Research Fellow and Program Director for Nordic-Baltic Studies
  at the Copenhagen Peace Research Institute (COPRI), Denmark.

firmly embedded in a Soviet-style vertical hierarchy, the region is now compelled to assume features of a horizontal polity. It is void of tradition in dealing with the European North, unlike other Russian regions such as St. Petersburg, Pskov, or even Novgorod, and has yet to find its place within a certain international division of labor. Kaliningrad is required to tune in to its newly cooperative setting, broken off from national continuity and the previous constellation of divisive borders. It is heavily influenced by the European Union, Germany, Poland, Lithuania, and Belarus; yet, it remains within the sphere of Russian thinking, policy, and practice. An entity that was once closed, protective, and unyielding to reform has been compelled to open up, reposition itself, and relate to an increasingly integrated environment.

Hence, it is no surprise that Kaliningrad has attracted attention over the years. This closed entity (even Soviet citizens were required to get permission to enter the area), with features of a terra incognita has become known as the "Kaliningrad question" (Kricius 1999). It has gained a reputation as a trouble-spot out of tune with its environment. But what is the "Kaliningrad question" really about? This is far from clear, since differing approaches and ways of comprehending political space tend to provide different answers.

Kaliningrad is now at a crossroad regarding these different interpretations, and there appears to be a broad diversity of views concerning the issues at stake. Thus, both in analysis and practice, the region must cope with different political "languages" and logic that do not easily translate one to the other. Kaliningrad will need to deal with the return of some affective and nostalgic issues—here interpreted as representing primitive logic—and cope with various issues that pertain to so-called realism and the calculation of "national interests," as represented above all by Russia's central authorities. The oblast operates at the watershed between the integrated and unintegrated, making it necessary for it to adapt to a European logic of governance.

Primitive logic tends to be rather affective, nostalgic about the past, and ideological in content. Views on amity and enmity are not based on reasoning or the analysis of issues, but on convictions and interpretations of history. The revision of borders is seen as a key task in the organization of the political landscape so that it matches conceptualizations about right and wrong. Cooperation across previous divides is regarded as overly risky, and there is very little room for compromise with zero-sum perceptions of security.

The logic underpinning realist views is also premised on risk, but within limits set by calculations and interests. Deliberate efforts are made to stay aloof of any affective and explicitly ideological content. Policies are not made on the basis of preconceived convictions about friends and foes or prior experiences, nor are they settled by symbolic, moral, or ethical considerations. Instead, they hinge on the analysis of issues and rationalization of interests at stake.

Both the primitive and realist logics attach much importance to security and borders, whereas the logic of governance is more relaxed about these issues. It favors joint problem solving and transforms the meaning of security by moving away from narrow self-interest and zero-sum calculations. Security is seen as a relevant concern, but it is not emphasized as in the context of the two other logics. With security being relativized and borders becoming increasingly flexible, different projects, including those that cross borders, become possible. More space becomes available for debordering and crossing borders.

The goal of this study is to grasp some essential aspects of the "Kaliningrad question" by using this trilogy of logics. It is claimed that instead of a single argument—or a set of arguments confined to one particular logic—a variety of logics is at play. Each tends to provide its own answers. A mixture of departures and a variety of views exist, and a shift may be discovered in their relationships and relative importance over time as they are socially constructed and therefore conducive to change. They may coexist, and to some extent support each other, but more often they clash and compete. In the case of Kaliningrad, the latter seems to hold true. Diversity seems to have increased rather than decreased, and there appears to be no single point where the various views, or logics, can coalescence and meet.

This is also why a constructivist approach appears to be particularly applicable in tackling the "Kaliningrad question." Moreover, it sheds some light on why the question appears to constitute a dilemma that is exceptionally difficult to place in perspective, cope with, or settle.

In Search of a Past

The demise of the Soviet Union in 1991 destabilized Kaliningrad and revealed the region's ambiguous history. A breach in realist discourse raised the prospect of the oblast becoming a politically disputed territory. Although the region is significant to present-day Russia, it has a rather weak anchorage in Russia's past. Despite the lack of previous ties, it was annexed by Russia in the aftermath of World War II—a move backed by the Potsdam allies.

The dissolution of the Soviet Union opened up prospects for the area's "real" past regarding territorial issues to reappear as Kaliningraders engaged in politicizing history and moralizing politics. The region's status was questioned during the first part of the 1990s in a number of ways. Efforts were made to settle the geographic discontinuity that had opened up by proposing solutions grounded in primitive logic. Russia was confronted with a variety of proposals and demands, including the establishment of Kaliningrad as an autonomous republic within the Russian Federation, the creation of a Russian-Polish-Lithuanian-German condominium, and the foundation of Kaliningrad as a fourth (independent) Baltic state. Depending on which period and aspect of history were emphasized, some called for its annexation by neighboring states. The slogan "Small Lithuania" was used to legitimate Kaliningrad's connection to Lithuania. There were also proposals for the "re-Germanization" of the region, as well as calls to incorporate it into Poland, either in part or as a whole (Wellmann 1996: 172–74; Oldberg 1998: 3–4).

This debate was further fueled by various proposals to "demilitarize" and "internationalize" Kaliningrad, denying Russia control of its westernmost part. The governments in Vilnius, Warsaw, and Berlin did not take part in the debate, but there was reason to suspect that the questioning of Kaliningrad's status was not altogether without official support. It soon became clear that the oblast could not return to any past status without creating serious friction between Russia and neighboring countries. Officially raising issues pertaining to the past would have been tantamount to challenging Russia's territorial integrity. It would also have undermined a number of European treaties based on territorial status quo and acceptance of the borders put in place as a result of World War II (unless changes were accepted by all participating parties).

The debate about territorial belonging (based primarily on primitive logic) was relatively short-lived and never gained much ground. Nevertheless, it spurred some emotional Russian reactions and Kaliningrad acquired a highly symbolic posture in Russian discourse. Reforms were delayed, including the setback of one land reform due to suspicions that foreign purchases would somehow return the land to foreigners (meaning Germans). The various challenges were interpreted as a blow to Russia's collective self-conscious (Wellmann 1996: 172) and purported to be deliberate efforts to add to the burden of post-Cold War loser and "victim" of the period. Depriving Russia of Kaliningrad would, according to some interpretations, push Russia out of Europe. It was seen as undermining Russian self-esteem and grandeur, and as depriving Russia of what it rightfully gained in compensation for the sufferings of the Soviet-Russian people during the war against Nazi Germany. Some local Kaliningrad scholars added fuel to the debate by claiming that the oblast's residents had the legal authority to decide the region's fate (Kricius 1999: 4).

The End of Nostalgia?

The outcome of World War II and the postwar period left a number of scars on the region. However, opinions based on primitive logic were not strong enough to exert major destabilizing political influence. Kaliningrad has not been at the center of territorial quarrels in any real sense, and as Alexander Sergounin (1997a) observed, such disputes have played a marginal role in the Baltic Sea Region in recent years. Tensions have flared and some issues still remain to be settled, but the outcomes of these disputes have not corresponded to the expectations that prevailed during the first half of the 1990s. It has been possible to cope with the problems and, in many cases, to settle them satisfactorily.

The disparity between fear and reality has been conspicuous, and it is striking that disputes have not emerged. As Forsberg (1998) remarks, the puzzle is not the existence of certain territorial issues, but rather their nonexistence. For reasons that become clear when trends around the Baltic rim are compared to other border areas of the former Soviet Union and the Balkans, Forsberg concludes that, despite various possible reasons for making territorial claims, the Baltic Sea Region has been relatively free of territorial conflict in recent years.

The Kaliningrad case appears to be largely in line with such a view. The region has not turned into a bone of contention as it was imagined in the early 1990s. The nostalgic currents of opinion that emerged in Germany, Lithuania, and Poland have not been sufficiently strong or persistent to impose the issue on official agendas. With the prevailing norm of status quo, the states of the region have adhered to their course and pursued rather cautious policies. Despite some internal pressure and normative arguments, they have refrained from advancing territorial claims. The enlargement of the North Atlantic Treaty Organization (NATO) has reinstalled the dominance of realist logic, while the enlargement of the EU has highlighted the significance of the logic of governance. The messages sent have conveyed that if a nation wants to join the EU, territorial issues should not be raised and quarrels of the past should cease; such conflict should end and efforts toward stability and cooperative security should abound. These messages have been powerful and their influence has been discernible in the debates surrounding Kaliningrad.

Those who advocate territorial adjustment have lost ground. Much bitterness about regional history remains, but its intensity has dissipated with more open discussion of the issue. The provocative statements of the early 1990s have by and large disappeared, and there is far less questioning of the oblast's position. The region's main problem is no longer demand for change, but lack of interest and a low level of awareness of its other problems. Sensitivities about symbolic ideas have also lessened. "Re-Germanization" no longer carries the frightening connotations it did a few years ago, and there is greater readiness to tackle other contentious historical legacies. Russian authorities increasingly treat Kaliningrad as a normal part of the country in such spheres as granting visas, allowing tourism, and inviting the presence of foreign firms.

Moreover, with the previously divisive border becoming more permeable, former residents have been able to visit the region. Some have chosen to engage in activities such as raising monuments or restoring important historical sites. Fewer confrontational situations and less emphasis on the specific location of frontiers provide more space for both official and unofficial cooperative approaches to relevant issues.

Recent discussion within Kaliningrad has been less geared toward foreign threats and dangers, and attitudes are changing. Anxieties have declined regarding restitution and demands for demilitarization that were advanced (compare with Pedersen 1998; Kricius 1999) in discussions in the early 1990s with Poland and Lithuania. Attention is now focused, with good reason, on current problems. Rather than disputing territorial control, new issues concern economic decline, social ills, poor public health, and criminal acts, including smuggling and abuse of the environment. In general, many of these problems are more pronounced in Kaliningrad than in Russia. The views connected to primitive logic are now marginal, although Kaliningrad's lack of an acknowledged past remains a serious handicap, preventing the development of a sound local or regional identity.

Security

During the Cold War, Kaliningrad functioned primarily as a garrison. It was a closed territory that served as a base for the Baltic Fleet and the Eleventh Guard Army. The region hosted prepositioned weapons (including nuclear warheads) and was to host a large number of troops in case of war. Western experts believed that, in the case of war, the mission of troops in Kaliningrad was to strike targets in Denmark and southern Norway. Assault troops were to land on the shores of Sweden and deny enemy air, ground, and sea access to Soviet targets in the Baltic Sea Region and western Russia (Nordberg 1994: 82–93; Pedersen 1998). With the collapse of the Warsaw Pact, many troops passed through Kaliningrad from their previous bases and were either decommissioned or stationed in mainland Russia.

Realist logic strongly colored post-Cold War and post-Soviet debates about Kaliningrad. The core issues involved were hard security, military balances, levels of preparedness, threat scenarios, and so on. Russian authorities worried about transit and the viability of their small exclave; westerners raised concerns about Kaliningrad's over-militarized character. Security was a preeminent concern for both Russia and neighboring countries. The debate roused suspicions and accusations of hostile intent on both sides. Poland and the Baltic countries interpreted the military presence in Kaliningrad as a reason to aspire to NATO membership. Russian officials feared that the oblast might then be surrounded by an unfriendly alliance. In their view, NATO's enlargement was not only detrimental to Kaliningrad, but by undermining their forward defense, a threat to Russian security as well.

After receiving a number of political and military concessions, Moscow tacitly accepted the enlargement of NATO. The charter signed in Paris in May 1997 legitimized both NATO's enlargement around the Baltic Rim and Poland's forthcoming membership. It also justified Russia's defenses in Kaliningrad, dismissing grounds for complaints that Russia's military presence was too strong in the region. The charter also set conditions under which settlements can be reached when disagreements arise.

Although the enlargement of NATO undoubtedly heightened tensions and pinpointed Kaliningrad as a trouble spot, it also helped tone down some local controversies. NATO has made it clear that it will not grant membership to applicant countries if they have open, unsettled quarrels with their neighbors. This condition probably defused some border disputes and took the wind out of proposals to rename, demilitarize, or internationalize Kaliningrad. A NATO-Russia Council was established and NATO pledged to avoid offensive moves such as the deployment of nuclear weapons or nonindigenous troops in the new members' territory. Although some details of enlargement might still cause friction, conflicts in Kaliningrad declined once NATO membership discussions became less heated.

Russian military leaders seem to have concluded that Kaliningrad simply cannot be defended and that only a small contingent of air, ground, and naval units need to be stationed there for air and sea surveillance and local defense (Kricius 1999: 8; Pedersen 1998: 116). Western experts increasingly categorize Kaliningrad as of little military value, excluding it from their calculations based on realist logic. Russian troops in Kaliningrad no longer have a strong purpose since Polish and Lithuanian debates with the Kaliningrad Special Military District (KOOR) were terminated. The Eleventh Guard Army has been largely dissolved, with only a few remnants attached to units in the St. Petersburg region.

Russia has cut its forces in both the Baltic Sea Region and in its northwestern areas by some 40 percent. Debate now focuses on arms control rather than military strength as Russia appears to be reasonably secure against annexation or takeover. The likelihood of a foreign power attempting to challenge Russia's sovereign control of Kaliningrad is rather low. Territorial issues and the preservation of strict, divisive borders have therefore become less pressing. This more relaxed atmosphere, combined with the cautious policies of relevant European states and open discussion, implies a basis for mutual trust between Russia and its Baltic Rim neighbors.

These circumstances may be conducive to negotiations and could yield a framework for tackling other issues pertaining to Kaliningrad as a military base. Included in the agreement between NATO and Russia is the idea that arms control and disarmament will be discussed during revision of the Treaty on Conventional Forces in Europe (CFE). Talks began in Vienna in January 1997 among CFE nations. With the block nature (NATO vs. the Warsaw Pact) of the treaty abolished and national ceilings agreed upon as a principle for departure, Kaliningrad will appear in a new light (compare with Lachowski 2000: 512). To assure Russia that NATO's enlargement will not lead to a buildup of western forces in the new NATO countries, territorial ceilings have been discussed. These same limitations could, however, apply equally to Kaliningrad.

An agreement on sufficiency could be important, although such a breakthrough appears unlikely. Instead of an implicit deal, general agreement on a framework for regulating Kaliningrad's security issues could be reached. Such a framework could provide Russia with guarantees of free land, sea, and air transit—provided that defense measures in Kaliningrad do not infringe upon the security interests of its neighbors. Proposals put forward in September 1997 by then-Prime Minister Chernomyrdin in Vilnius moved in this direction. He proposed that, as part of a broader package, a hotline be established between military headquarters in the Kaliningrad region and the Baltic countries, and that military exercises in Kaliningrad be restricted to defense.

Kaliningrad has become less pronounced as a garrison with Russia's financial difficulties, a general decline in military preparedness, and the shift of conflict to the south. It is not only viewed as an exposed frontier region within a centralized empire, but may also be comprehended as part of an archipelago, combining various cultures, lifestyles, and geopolitical orientations.

Debates over Kaliningrad's status have largely disappeared and have not become a point of friction between the Western powers and Russia, as was expected. There is still some concern regarding military capabilities and troops in the region, but many experts do not view the situation with alarm (Pedersen 1998: 111). Kaliningrad has become a regional concern in the Baltic Rim, and less a part of a general military setting. Many still consider Kaliningrad based on realist logic, but elements of cooperation—and in some cases, the wish to avoid the creation of new divisive lines and reduce existing ones—seem to have grown in importance. Realist logic has increasingly led to discussion and the tuning down of any contentious issues. Although it has successfully stood its ground against challenges posed by primitive logic, it has incorporated many arguments formerly held by the logic of governance. Russia has increasingly been conceived as a partner and the security landscape around the Baltic Rim no longer constitutes a clear-cut division of "us" and "them." Rather, it has become variegated by cooperative groupings on bilateral, trilateral, and multilateral levels (compare with van Ham 2000).

In Search of a Future

With political rivalry declining and past wrongdoings openly aired, it is now recognized that border areas, such as Kaliningrad, are not necessarily doomed to peripherality. Ideally, they could become sites for mediating political, economic, and cultural contacts. Frontiers are no longer hard-edged barriers; they have great potential as junctures conducive to cooperation.

Such governance-oriented perspectives give a different slant to the Kaliningrad debate. Kaliningrad's proximity to major European centers have led some to describe it as a "Luxembourg" (Dörrenbächer 1994), a "Switzerland of the Baltic" (Matochkin 1995: 8), or a "regional Hong Kong" (Galeotti 1993: 58). These visions would have the region utilize its location and prospects for European integration to become a benign force for itself and the broader politico-economic environment. Instead of remaining a detached fortress, it might develop into a link with considerable potential for interaction across previous boundaries. Liberated from the constraints of territorial logic, Kaliningrad could achieve openness, cooperation, growth, as well as peace and stability. Regional actors now view the problems to be rooted in the difficulties inherent to Russia and Kaliningrad, not in conflicts between states. There is a growing conviction that concerted efforts must be made by Russia as well as a number of other actors if the region is to have a chance to move toward sustainable development.

Richard Rosencrance (1996: 45) asserts that "[d]eveloped states are putting aside military, political and territorial ambitions as they struggle not for a cultural dominance but for a greater share of the world output." In this new, nonterritorial way of thinking, he states that there is an emancipation from land as the determinant of production and power. Traditional political and territorial logic is increasingly dominated by logic that views centrality versus marginality as the core issue.

This new way of thinking affects the discourse on Kaliningrad. It engenders less emphasis on territoriality and the fate of the region is no longer seen as fixed or predetermined. The deep split that divided Europe during the postwar period and pushed local and regional issues to the background has largely closed. Borderlines and other territorial delineations have become less strict, and shifting and overlapping patterns of cooperation are now possible. Kaliningrad—increasingly both inside and outside of the European Union—stands to gain from these changes because it is no longer peripheral, relegated as an outpost threatening otherness, or void of its own potential.

New Thinking

Altered thoughts about political space may open doors for Kaliningrad as it attempts to integrate with its surrounding region; however, local economic and social hardships and backlashes in Russian politics may pose severe barriers to this integration. The Special Economic Zone (SEZ) was part of a general policy whereby Moscow aimed to establish a testing ground to pave the way for market forces. The SEZ presupposes sound political relations with neighbors and the existence of open borders and considerable foreign involvement. Thus, its implementation in Kaliningrad has faced difficulties. The SEZ originated as part of an outreach strategy for constructing political space, but the idea never fully materialized. There has been much resistance in Russia to this kind of regional differentiation. In the current Russian climate, there is even resistance to institutions like the International Monetary Fund (IMF), which grants special tax schemes or other privileges to particular regions. There could be similar opposition to Russia joining the World Trade Organization (WTO). Any Kaliningrad-Moscow development plan that relies on opening up to the outside appears to face considerable difficulties.

Kaliningrad has a long way to go before it develops into a bridgehead of Russia's Europeanization process and achieves the distinct features of a regional entity. The new agenda focusing on European integration presents several challenges, although it de-emphasizes standardization and homogenization and shows more tolerance for deviation. Some Moscow-based analysts and politicians seriously wonder whether a poor, but traditional Kaliningrad may not be a better choice than a prosperous and integrated one (Dewar 1998: 2). The reshuffling of political space allows for a broad range of alternatives, once the influence of the logic of governance increases. The role and policies of various actors are not as firmly determined by their geographic location as they once were, and norms that determine value, meaning, and position are increasingly open to interpretation. The logic of governance encourages plurality, although the Russian attitude toward pluralistic thinking remains somewhat wary.

New and previously unexplored ideas (compare with Medvedev 1998) about the new European agenda can be easily interpreted as elements of a new and unwelcome ambiguity. They are perceived as conflictive with national security in terms of realist logic. Many fear that they severely challenge Russia's sovereignty and territorial integrity. In the early 1990s, as Russia faced potential disintegration, cross-border cooperation was a daring notion. Later, tense relations with Baltic countries and the question of NATO enlargement kept reform at bay. Fear has been expressed that integration-oriented policies could fuel separatism, making Western actors cautious to put forward proposals that may fuel feelings that the standing of the central authorities in Russia would be undermined. The adherence to realist logic has prevented the adoption of more flexible views. The military in particular viewed the new process-oriented visions with suspicion, although attitudes have become somewhat more forthcoming over time (compare with Lachowski 2000).

Kaliningrad itself has displayed a limited ability to respond to process-oriented challenges, which has been particularly evident in the late 1990s. It appears that Kaliningraders are unprepared to embrace new opportunities. The oblast has been unable to keep up with the pace of economic development in Russia and has been hard hit (in some ways harder than any other region) by economic hardships (Kivikari, Lindström, and Liuhto 1998: 65–66). The result has been one of widespread social misery. Having become dependent on its neighbors for raw materials and agricultural products, Kaliningrad suffers unduly from inflation and the declining value of the ruble. Its location has not turned out to be a liability in the way it was imagined; however, EU policies have often contributed to its hardships, rather than relieved them (Fairlie 1999: 309).

The Impact of the European Union

With the EU's stronger presence around the Baltic Rim, politics are unavoidably changing. Although unable to provide security in any "hard" sense, the EU has defused a number of conflicts and reduced Kaliningrad's vulnerability to securitization (Buzan and Wæver 1998).

A new agenda, founded on the logic of governance, is emerging. The importance of realist logic is diminishing, and primitive logic is considerably reduced. The EU's civil power brings to the fore various domestic and transnational concerns. It supports inclusive, integration-oriented logic, thus, beginning the breakdown of borders. Instruments such as structural funds (Technical Assistance for the Commonwealth of Independent States–TACIS, International Regions–INTERREG) spur on the formation of regions. As they compete for dynamic growth and participation in politics, regions become less linked to their nation-states. Local actors cooperate to speed the breakdown of traditional geographic borders.

By providing "soft" security measures (compare with Christiansen 1999: 195), the EU helps to remove both international and domestic sources of conflict. The EU also helps avert nonmilitary threats to human welfare and survival by working to raise the standard of living, encouraging economic cooperation, and reducing economic asymmetries between nearby actors. Actors become increasingly interdependent when they actively pursue prosperity together. Their awareness of common interests increases through cultural, educational, and social exchanges, as well as through improved intraregional and transregional transportation and communication links. Such "socializing" effects, along with the evolving habit of frequent border crossings, can be particularly helpful to ease tensions stemming from older concepts of "us" and "them."

With respect to boundary disputes, the EU pressures contentious parties to reach an accord. It perceives such disputes as anachronistic, or part of the traditional, territorially fixed agenda, and no longer relevant. Member states are expected to comply with and live up to the new post-territorial agenda. However, such pressure has also been felt by states wishing to join the EU. Candidates understand that if they wish to join, they must first adapt to the EU's rules. The effects of this requirement have been quite powerful, as evidenced by changes in Polish and Lithuanian policies vis-à-vis Kaliningrad.

Recently, the EU has actively endeavored to link the Baltic countries and Russia with Europe, as evidenced by the inclusion of Estonia and the other six countries eligible for membership. The EU commission is active in both the Council of the Baltic Sea States and the Barents Euro-Arctic Council, which are of significance to Kaliningrad as they spur a more pluralist political landscape. Such regional schemes may make the EU border more permeable, strengthen cooperation in northern Europe, and facilitate participation in the integration process.

Although there is still much room for change, the EU does ask its members to pursue active policies that transcend borders. The EU's stronger presence in northern Europe is certainly correlated with the recent inclusion of Finland and Sweden. However, it also reflects a growth of EU interests in the northeast—a stance that Finland in particular has aspired to support. On the basis of a Finnish initiative, the EU European Council approved a report on the "Northern Dimension." It was accepted in Vienna in December 1998, singling out Kaliningrad and thereby bolstering the oblast's position on the EU's agenda. This is also evidenced by Russia's proposition in the context of the Northern Dimension Initiative, that the European Union and Russia sign a special agreement on Kaliningrad.

Influencing the EU Agenda

The EU committed itself to establishing a substantial partnership with Russia at the Madrid European Council in 1995. Its goal was to promote principles of democracy and respect for human rights. The strategy was complemented by an Action Plan in 1996 that listed practical measures and activities for Russian democratic reforms and economic development. Cooperation in the realms of justice, domestic affairs, and foreign policy were singled out, as was European security. The Action Plan codified and registered the bilateral cooperative efforts of its members and Russia. Although there is no special mention of the Baltic Sea Region, the plan's objectives are certainly relevant to developments in northwestern Russia, including Kaliningrad (Möttölä 1998).

The EU Baltic Sea Region Initiative, a program prepared by the commission and published in May 1996, is another indication of a "soft" approach. (Compare with Christiansen 1999: 200). Using the magnetism of integration and based on

EU principles, the Baltic Round Table was created. The idea was presented to the European Council in June 1993 and implemented in 1993 and 1994. It was introduced in the context of the European Pact of Stability, also known as the Balladur Plan. The project addressed those Central and Eastern European countries that are considered possible future members of the EU. The prime participants in the Baltic Round Table were Estonia, Latvia, Lithuania, and Poland. They were asked to provide solutions to a variety of problems that could be regarded as more domestic than foreign and to tackle these issues by exercising domestic authority rather than pressuring any external country.

Discussion at the Baltic Round Table encompassed regional transborder cooperation, minorities, the environment, and cooperation in economic, cultural, and legal aspects. Participants were expected to be conciliatory, to settle open issues concerning borders, and to engage in positive relations with their neighbors. They were expected to demonstrate competence within a concentric setting, in which the European Union is the center. The central issue for these countries has not focused on sovereignty, but on a counteractive push into a peripheral position, while being surrounded by an increasingly cooperative Europe. The Organization for Security and Cooperation in Europe (OSCE) evaluated the results of various round tables, including the Baltic Round Table, and finally concluded and signed a pact that drew the results together. The Balladur Plan envisaged a list of incentives the EU might offer states that agreed to observe the principles adopted by the evaluating conference.

The EU's Enclave

The increased prominence of the logic of governance changes the European configuration toward a less bordered, more cooperative, and integration-oriented constellation. "Low" policies become dominant and Europe increasingly assumes the figure of concentric rings. Kaliningrad's location makes the oblast sensitive to such changes. It is increasingly perceived as the EU's "near abroad." The region is influenced by both Russian and European politics. Kaliningrad has been far more exposed to the consequences of European integration in recent years than any other Russian region, increasing its need for special attention and multilateral measures to cope with the challenges.

The finding of a proper and broadly accepted approach is far from easy. Both Russian and EU endeavors are needed to develop some overarching cooperative structures. A sufficiently stable economic and political environment is required to safeguard against further degeneration. Even more importantly, the main actors need a joint interpretative framework in order to be able to deal with the issues at stake. In some cases, such frameworks exist, but there is also room for false interpretations and profound misreadings. Pretending that Kaliningrad is an ordinary case to be settled by some pragmatic, down-to-earth approach will not do. The region remains an overlapping case nested in differing logics. A realist reading still has a certain standing, although the oblast has become heavily influenced by the logic of governance in the last few years by having turned into the EU's enclave to a considerable degree.

These changes will become even more pronounced once the current round of enlargement, with Lithuania and Poland as applicants found eligible for membership, is completed. With a Russian region more or less inside the European Union, the EU is in need of a more explicit policy. This, in turn, calls for a more nuanced policy vis-à-vis Russia. Russia must be lifted out of an analysis premised on what has generally been comprehended as realist logic (to the extent its own policies allows for it). Frameworks that pose East against West or operate in terms of either/or and inside/outside should be discarded and new ones that go beyond such exclusionary categories should be used.

The adoption of more inclusive approaches brings with it questions about Russia's position in terms of European integration. It is neither easy to depict Russia as a future member of the EU, nor can it be omitted and treated as a total outsider. A closer relationship is called for, but within limits. One possibility would be to integrate parts of Russia—such solutions based on differentiation already exist elsewhere with the Aaland Islands (part of Finland), outside the customs policies of the EU, and with Greenland and the Faroe Islands (parts of Denmark), outside the EU. Strategies along similar lines are also debated in the case of Norway (Jervell 1998). Such a diversified solution, if applied to Kaliningrad, would not contradict the logic of governance, although it would conflict with the realist or primitive logics. The logic of governance does not aspire to homogeneous spaces based on strict divisions into inside/outside, whereas the latter do. The logic of governance allows for a loosely connected and EU-related Kaliningrad in a postsovereign Russia, while the two latter ones shy away from such solutions.

On a more practical note, the EU is interested in being assured that Russia does not object to the EU being engaged in Kaliningrad. This allows Moscow to withhold its permission until some more extensive agreement has been reached that grants Russia a more central place in the European integration process. Russia's leadership has announced an interest in EU membership, but there has not been much willingness (or ability) to accept the logic that underlies the EU more broadly. In this context, Kaliningrad could become a bargaining card for Russia in its aspiration for centrality. Such a move could lock issues in a problematic way or bring about dialogue not only on Kaliningrad, but also on broader and more pressing issues.

Some basis for a dialogue is already there, as demonstrated by Russia's proposal for a special agreement with the Northern Dimension Initiative. Both Moscow and Brussels are concerned that the privileges granted to Kaliningrad will not be utilized for smuggling, drawing advantages by circumventing import-export quotas, falsifying certificates of origin, or misusing various regulations to advance free trade and integration around the Baltic Rim. Both are interested that Kaliningrad does not become a haven of corruption, crime, and anarchy. More urgently, the parties need to discuss the position of Kaliningrad in the visa regimes. Its position thus far has been rather flexible, as Kaliningraders have been able to travel rather freely to Lithuania and Poland.

In January 1998, however, Poland implemented stricter border control measures in order to keep records of individuals crossing its borders. With potential EU member countries being asked to tighten their borders and follow standardized policies, even Lithuania might find reason to reconsider its policy of allowing Kaliningraders to visit Lithuania for 30 days without a visa (whereas Russians from the mainland need visas). Discussion is required concerning proposals such as those aimed at making Kaliningrad a visa-free region for visitors staying in the oblast only, but not allowing them to travel to other parts of Russia; keeping the visa-free arrangements with Lithuania in place; and for similar arrangements to be considered with Estonia and Latvia (compare with Fairlie 1999). Already, the wider implementation of the Schengen regulations around the Baltic Rim requires considerable coordination. Polish restrictions indicate that becoming increasingly EU-relevant may also imply bordering, isolation, and limitations in the region's ability to link with its nearby environment.

The EU appears to opt for rather rigid borders between those who are "in" and those who are left "out." Hence, its negative effects seem to prevail in the case of Kaliningrad. The EU follows the logic of the third pillar, one premised on sovereignty and stateness. The strategy assumed is reductionist, endeavoring to downplay the multiplicity of the situation.

Russia's limited ability to comprehend and accept solutions based on the logic of governance may leave such a line as the only one available. However, pursuing such policies are bound to have depressive effects on Kaliningrad's economy and social development. The EU does not provide, in the case of Russia and Kaliningrad, for any illusions of membership or options spurring economic reforms. While its neighbors are rewarded for their active policies, no such message is targeted at Kaliningrad. Thus, while its neighbors can boast their successes, Kaliningrad has to deal with failure and an increasing gap in future expectations. It stands out as a depressed Russian enclave within a booming region. The instruments utilized by the EU in Kaliningrad consist mainly of various TACIS projects, whereas neighboring countries also benefit from PHARE (Poland-Hungary Aid for the Reconstruction of the Economy) and INTERREG programs as well as considerable funds facilitating and accelerating adjustment to membership. The oblast is pushed into a rather problematic situation, unable to link back to its past and equally unable to find the road to a positive future.

Conclusion

Given the enormity of Russia's legacy and the immensity of the problems left over from the previous period, Kaliningrad's road toward a link to Europe and greater autonomy is hardly going to be a smooth one. The options available to the region seem to be limited, and it would be overly optimistic to think differently. Considering the oblast's location, the burden of history, the asymmetries of the situation, its dependency on fluent transit, visa arrangements, customs procedures, and considerable dependency on hard currency and imports, there is not much ground for optimism. There appear to be relatively good reasons why Kaliningrad has been frequently depicted as severely hampering—potentially or actually—more general developments around the Baltic Rim. It does not just stand in the way of overcoming the post-Cold War division between East and West, leaving behind the position of a European semiperiphery. It also adds—within limits—credibility to a more general discourse on risk, conflicts, and the necessity to stay behind well-defined and strongly defended territorial borders. It tends to stay within the confines of realist logic and a mindframe that sets many limits for participation in the process of Europeanization, or to state it even more generally, in viewing Kaliningrad as a junction in an informational and administrative Russia.

A menu of options has grown in significance with the emergence of post-Cold War Europe. New choices are becoming available as the territorial determinants of social life and political processes become less strict. It appears that Kaliningrad's greatest asset consists of giving credibility to Russia as a European polity—a Russia of regions. From this perspective, the oblast constitutes a key site in the discourse on broader issues. It holds out what might be called security at an existential level. The region does so in forming an arena that allows Russia to express its identity in nonadversarial terms and reconcile its uniqueness in its membership in a broader European and international community.

Thus, distance (in terms of borderlines in a geographic and physical sense) is not the only issue at stake per se. Many political, cultural, and mental barriers must also be dealt with in securing a more favorable place for Kaliningrad in present-day Europe. It is a determinant of whether Russia and Europe stand apart or whether they will be able to assume a complementary relationship. Policies may be pursued to make it more difficult to push Russia into some eastern "otherness" in order to achieve a distinct and orderly presentation of Europe—one with clear-cut external borders and a firm understanding of where it ends. With the emergence of a more pluralistic and spatially less determined Europe, relevant actors are offered the option of capitalizing on the weakening of many of the previous restrictions that have pertained to Kaliningrad. The region is offered the option of turning into a simultaneously Russian and European entity.

Given the lack of a deeply rooted and broadly legitimate past, the region's future tends to be conceptualized in terms of what is already there. Images of a different, less isolationist future easily generate fears that Russia and the current inhabitants of Kaliningrad could lose what emerged with the outcome of World War II. Changes are resisted as there is very little, if anything, of their own that they can project into the future. Alternative paths are inevitably seen as backlashes, and there is hence little tolerance for plurality. Reactions tend to become defensive and amount to bordering rather than debordering. More generally, they support the prevailing realist logic, and sometimes even primitive logic, leaving little room for anything positive and creative.

Some of the issues surrounding Kaliningrad are quite sensitive, such as its German rather than Russian past. The resurfacing of these issues has created uncertainty and bad feelings. However, with the collapse of walls in Europe there is no other option than to face the past and open up to a different future. Russia's framework is unavoidably changing. In an atmosphere where security no longer constitutes a label that automatically triggers demands for extraordinary and protective countermeasures, even the symbolic and identity-related matters such as the name of the oblast can be discussed (signaling the power of the Soviet center to determine images of the periphery as Mikhail Kalinin, President of the Soviet Union, never visited the region). Identities and departures that rest on a nonadversarial relationship with neighbors can be searched for. Although no immediate and completely problem-free solutions appear to be at hand, the existence of some problems related to Kaliningrad's name can be recognized, legitimizing a search for ways to settle them. Kaliningrad does not have to be perceived as a traditional issue pertaining to distance, borders, and territoriality in general; it may also be seen as an opportunity and a spatial resource with European connotations.

Recent developments point in a variety of directions. New thinking remains too weak to yield decisive results, and its effects have been different from those expected. A certain localism is developing, mainly in the form of Kaliningrad as a pocket-like troublespot on the new European agenda—an entity that adjusts to its changing environment in a unwarranted and profoundly problematic fashion. Borderlines are too often delineated by negative differences—crime, smuggling, corruption, the gray economy, some low level violence, and so on. They serve the purpose of border drawing, as functions aspired toward in order to preserve sufficiently strong notions of a separate "self." The political landscape premised on realist logic has been blown open by various factors pertaining to integration and the "information age," to be followed by new closures in the form of localism and regionalism.

Kaliningrad may be understood as being part of such a pattern. Its degree of closure, however, cannot be perceived in solely a positive sense. Instead of linking to integration in a positive vein, Kaliningrad shows too many features of closing in and shielding itself off in a negative manner, showing signs of turning into a troublespot. One factor that contributes to its negative choices is the lack of any decisive pushes in a positive direction by the oblast's major actors. The stimulus and the resources required are not there; hence, Kaliningrad seems to be deprived of positive options when reacting to the new challenges. It is increasingly part of the new and an expression of its inner logic, but it has been forced to represent the logic of governance in an adverse manner and in terms of a protracted crisis. Such a pattern is not uncommon in more remote aspects of international relations, although it constitutes an unexpected reaction and case on the southern shores of the Baltic Sea and the EU's "near abroad."

References

Buzan, Barry, and Wæver, Ole. 1998. *Security. A New Framework of Analysis*. Boulder: Lynne Rienner.

Christiansen, Thomas, 1999. "Between 'In' and 'Out': EU Integration and Regional Policy-Making in North-Eastern Europe." Pp.193–208 in *The NEBI Yearbook 1999. North European and Baltic Sea Integration*, Lars Hedegaard and Bjarne Lindström, eds. Berlin: Springer Verlag International.

Dewar, Stephen. 1998. "Why Kaliningrad is 'Unique' in the Russian Federation." Paper presented at the IESW conference, 8–9 September, Kaliningrad.

Dörrenbächer, Helke. 1994. "Die Sonderwissenschaftszone Jantar von Kaliningrad (Königsberg). Bilanz und Perspektiven." *Arbeitspapiere zür Internationalen Politik* 81. Bonn: Europa Union Verlag.

Fairlie, Lyndelle D. 1998. "Kaliningrad: Visions of the Future." Pp. 169–214 in *Kaliningrad: The European Amber Region*, Pertti Joenniemi and Jan Prawitz, eds. Aldershot: Ashgate.

Fairlie, Lyndelle D. 1999. "Kaliningrad: Recent Changes in Russia's Exclave on the Baltic Sea." Pp. 293-313 in *The NEBI Yearbook 1999. North European and Baltic Sea Integration*, Lars Hedegaard and Bjarne Lindström, eds. Berlin: Springer Verlag International.

Forsberg, Tuomas, ed. 1995. *Contested Territory: Border Disputes at the Edge of the Former Soviet Empire*. Aldershot: Edward Elgar.

Forsberg, Tuomas. 1996. "Explaining Territorial Disputes: From Power Politics to Normative Reasons." *Journal of Peace Research* 33 (4): 433–49.

Forsberg, Tuomas. 1998. "Settled and Remaining Border Issues around the Baltic Sea." Pp. 437–48 in *The Yearbook on North European and Baltic Sea Integration 1998*, Lars Hedegaard and Bjarne Lindström, eds. Berlin: Springer Verlag International.

Galeotti, Mark. 1993. "Kaliningrad: A Fortress Without State." *IBRU Boundary and Security Bulletin* 1 (July): 56–59.

Jervell, Sverre. 1998. *Norge foran oppbruddet*. Oslo: Europaprogrammet.

Kivikari, Urpo, Maarit Lindström, and Kari Liuhto. 1998. "The External Economic Relations of the Kaliningrad Region." Discussion paper, series C/2. Turku: Business Research and Development Center, Turku School of Economics and Business Administration.

Kricius, Richard J. 1999. "U.S. Foreign Policy and the Kaliningrad Question." Working Paper No. 18. Copenhagen: Danish Institute of International Affairs.

Lachowski, Zdzislaw. 2000. "Security Dialogue in the Baltic Sea Area: An Overview." Pp. 314–34 in *The NEBI Yearbook 2000. North European and Baltic Sea Integration*, Lars Hedegaard and Bjarne Lindström, eds. Berlin: Springer Verlag International.

Matochkin, Yuri. 1994. "Kaliningrad und Europa." Pp. 9–15 in *Königsberg/Kaliningrad unter europäischen Perspektiven*, Ernst Müller-Hermann, ed. Bremen: Verlag H.M. Hauschild.

Medvedev, Sergei. 1998. "Peripheral Spaces, Global Players: Russia's Regions in a World of Global Networks." Paper presented at the AAASS Annual Meeting, 24–27 September, Boca Raton, Florida, USA.

Möttölä, Kari. 1998. "Security around the Baltic Rim: Concepts, Actors and Processes." Pp. 363–404 in *The Yearbook on North European and Baltic Sea Integration 1998*, Lars Hedegaard and Bjarne Lindström, eds. Berlin: Springer Verlag International.

Nordberg, Erkki. 1994. *The Baltic Republics: A Strategic Survey*. Helsinki: National Defense College.

Oldberg, Ingmar. 1998. "Kaliningrad: Problems and Prospects." Pp. 1–32 in *Kaliningrad: The European Amber Region*, Pertti Joenniemi and Jan Prawitz, eds. Aldershot: Ashgate.

Pedersen, Klaus Carsten. 1998. "Kaliningrad: Armed Forces and Missions." Pp. 107–17 in *Kaliningrad: The European Amber Region*, Pertti Joenniemi and Jan Prawitz, eds. Aldershot: Ashgate.

Rosencrance, Richard. 1996. "The Virtual State." *Foreign Affairs* 75 (July/August): 45–61.

Sergounin, Alexander. 1997a. "Post-Communist Security Thinking in Russia: Changing Paradigms." Working Paper No. 4. Copenhagen: Copenhagen Peace Research Institute.

Sergounin, Alexander. 1997b. "Factors of Russia's Regionalization: The Internal Dimension." Working Paper No. 20. Copenhagen: Copenhagen Peace Research Institute.

Van Ham, Peter. 2000. "U.S. Policy towards Northern Europe: Political and Security Aspects." Pp. 294–303 in *North European and Baltic Sea Integration,* Lars Hedegaard and Bjarne Lindström, eds. Berlin: Springer Verlag International.

Wellmann, Christian. 1996. "Russia's Kaliningrad Exclave at the Crossroads." *Cooperation and Conflict* 31 (2): 161–83.

VI
Finnish Borders and Russian Regionalization

Across the Northern Divide: Initiatives of Transborder Cooperation along the Finnish-Russian Border

Heikki Eskelinen[*]

Abstract

This study investigates the first steps toward interaction and cooperation in a peripheral area in Northern Europe that lies across the western border of the Karelian Republic (Russian Karelia) between Finland and the Russian Federation. This border region accounts for more than half of the Finnish-Russian border, which has been the only land border between the European Union and the Russian Federation since 1995. The analysis deals with both conscious policies to promote cross-border cooperation and spontaneous developments that work toward the same goal. Its primary focus is on the roles that actors play at different spatial levels in this process and the factors conditioning cross-border cooperative initiatives that work toward genuine transboundary regionalism.

The findings on these developments along the Finnish-Russian border are dichotomous. The whole cross-border cooperation regime has been turned upside down in the space of a decade, and the region, to an increasing degree, resembles a normal European border region. Even so, cross-border cooperative activities have not made a visible contribution to fulfilling the goals of socioeconomic development that are usually put forward as their primary motivation, and the prospects do not seem promising. In the long run, the fundamental question will concern the extent to which these peripheries are able to link their cooperative activities to structures and actions at different levels—from local to multinational.

---

* Eskelinen is Head of the Social Science Department at the Karelian Institute at the University of Joensuu, Finland.

Introduction

The complementarism of resources is an important precondition for successful cross-border cooperation. Such cooperation can be analyzed from a static and a dynamic perspective. The latter is essential to assessing long-term development as it posits whether geographically contiguous partners are able to jointly create competitive resources by means of cross-border activities. If so, the resulting functional interdependencies can lead to the formation of integrated transboundary structures.

The political and economic changes in Eastern Europe, along with the partial opening of the East/West divide, have permitted direct connections and cooperative relationships within border regions. Direct transboundary links that were illegal only a decade ago are now supported by specific programs. This clearly represents a dramatic change in which room for regionality has been created along a decidedly divisive border (Christiansen and Joenniemi 1999: 110). In fact, these developments have given rise to a kind of laboratory situation for the analysis of how cross-border links emerge, how cooperative practices are created, and the potential of regions that have been functionally separated for a long time.

Although every border region is unique, certain structural factors condition the development and patterns of cross-border interaction and cooperation. Along the East/West divide, these include economic potential, settlement patterns, infrastructure networks, historical and cultural links of neighboring regions (as well as the length of their separated development), and regional roles in the ongoing European Union (EU) integration process.

This paper investigates the first steps toward interaction and cooperation at a local and regional level between Finland and the Russian Federation, across the western border of the Karelian Republic (Russian Karelia). This region lies between two potentially major regions in Europe—the Baltic region and the Barents region (Figure 1). This analysis deals with both conscious policies to promote cross-border cooperation and spontaneous developments that work in the same direction. Its primary focus is on the roles that actors play at different spatial levels in this process. It also focuses on the key issues that condition the rocky road of cross-border cooperation initiatives that work toward genuine transboundary regionalism.

The border region under consideration here accounts for more than half of the Finnish-Russian border, which has comprised the only land border between the European Union and the Russian Federation since 1995. Thus, it is natural to use the experiences of EU internal and external borders as a point of reference when assessing the development of cross-border cooperative practices in this particular case.

The Border between the Baltic Sea and the Barents Sea

The Finnish-Russian border, which is more than 744 miles (1,200 kilometers) long, runs from the Baltic coast almost to the Barents Sea (Figure 1). The

Figure 1. The Finnish-Russian Border Area

border, which has shifted many times in the past, has historically been a battle-field between Eastern and Western cultures and politico-economical spheres of influence in northern Europe. Yet, it did not represent a categorical dividing line nor an effective barrier to interaction until after the October Revolution and Finland's independence in 1917 (Laine 1994; Paasi 1996).

The closed border had obvious negative repercussions for the development of adjacent regions. In Finland, the east suffered from a lack of contacts with its historic centers of gravity. This problem was accentuated as a consequence of World War II, when part of eastern Finland was annexed by the Soviet Union. The population of the ceded territory (more than four hundred thousand people) fled to Finland and were replaced by people from various parts of the Soviet Union. As a result, functional regions were split, important infrastructure networks were cut off, and the region on the eastern side of the border was effectively disconnected from its history. New circumstances have caused a realignment of Finnish-Russian relations, causing the potential Karelian border dispute to be a standing issue in Finnish public discussions in the 1990s.

Direct transborder interaction between individual partners was practically nonexistent during the Soviet era; exceptions were arranged and controlled in terms of bilateral agreements between the two countries (for an example, see Tikkanen and Käkönen 1997). Foreigners were only allowed to visit a few places on the eastern side of the border, where such activities were subordinate to security and military considerations. Crossing points for international passengers and goods were in the southern corner of the border area along the routes to St. Petersburg, by far the largest urban center in the border region.

Thus, the construction of direct links within the Finnish-Russian border region had to begin almost from scratch as these links gradually became possible during the last years of the Soviet Union's existence. There are several basic preconditions for developing cross-border cooperation, such as existing networks of infrastructure links, a sufficient supply of public and private services, and the compatibility of institutions (Van der Veen 1993). In the case of the Finnish-Russian border, the regions in eastern Finland and northwestern Russia are sparsely populated, and their cross-border infrastructure networks have not been developed. For many years, these regions have been peripheries in their own spacioeconomic systems and have followed very different development trajectories since the October Revolution. In addition, the introduction of what could be called a European cross-border cooperation regime is complicated by the fact that the Russian Federation will not become an EU member in the foreseeable future, eliminating the preintegration process that would strengthen links across the border. Therefore, preconditions for collaboration across the Finnish-Russian border are much more bleak than those for any EU internal border and most external borders.

Notwithstanding these severe constraints, interaction and cooperation across the Finnish-Russian border have emerged in many forms in the 1990s. Clearly, various actors in the border area have been sufficiently motivated to have created contacts for a number of purposes, including security, regional development, industrial competitiveness, cultural and humanitarian considerations, and so on. This pursuit of transboundary regionalism is linked to simultaneous changes in socioeconomic development doctrines and in relationships between central and regional levels of governance and administration on both sides of the border.

Toward Cooperative Practices: Policy Initiatives

The first wave of direct contacts between partners across the Finnish-Russian border emerged spontaneously as soon as Soviet travel restrictions were relaxed in the late 1980s. Individuals, civic associations, and local organizations (such as municipalities and schools in the Finnish border region) created links across the divide, and the central governments were forced to react to this grassroots activity as a *fait accompli*. To establish the rules of this new practice, the Russian and

Finnish governments signed treaties in 1992 concerning neighborhood relations, trade, and neighboring cooperation. The latter was the first treaty of its kind in Russia, and it implied that both Finland and the Russian Federation accepted the development of direct interaction and cooperation within border regions and, at least in principle, gave support to such a strategy. In this context, the most important political precondition for improving economic, cultural, and other connections across the border was Finland's decision not to advance territorial claims against the Russian Federation. This was also an important prerequisite for the country's membership in the European Union in 1995.

Before Finland attained EU membership, cross-border cooperation was primarily a matter between the two countries, on the one hand, and actors in the border regions themselves, on the other. In Finland, cross-border cooperation was placed on the policy-making agenda in two main contexts: as domestic regional policy and as cooperation.

Lines of Policy Action in Finland

As part of its anticipated, and later realized, membership in the European Union, domestic regional policies underwent a major upheaval in Finland in the 1990s (Eskelinen, Kokkonen, and Virkkala 1997). First, responsibility for regional development was transferred to regional councils, which are bottom-up organizations based on municipalities (in the past, this responsibility lay with top-down regional organizations of the central government). Second, regional development strategies were harmonized with EU program practices, including the promotion of border regional development. Since regional councils in Finland cannot levy taxes, however, they did not have of funding sources earmarked for the promotion of cross-border cooperation (before the 1996 implementation of EU INTERREG [International Regions] programs). From the very outset, regional councils and municipalities were active in organizing local initiatives and unofficial consultative bodies (between eastern Finland and the Republic of Karelia, for instance), which later proved to be of practical importance to the preparation of actual cooperative projects.

The state, for its part, has invested in the improvement of transport connections and border crossing facilities. The growth of trade flows between Finland and Russia (after the collapse of earlier bilateral trade in the early 1990s), along with regional transit traffic, have been the most important reasons for these measures. Upgraded interaction at local and regional levels between neighboring border regions can only be cited as a secondary motivation.

Neighboring cooperation with Russia (funded by the Finnish national budget) focuses on the Karelian Republic, the Murmansk and Leningrad regions, and the city of St. Petersburg (see Figure 1). Since 1996, the Ministry of Foreign Affairs has taken a more decisive role as coordinator of neighboring cooperation, and has emphasized linking such cooperation to the policies of various international organizations, particularly the European Union. Regional working groups, which include representatives from government ministries and regional organizations, are responsible for coordinating these measures.

According to the strategy revised in 1996, the ultimate goals of the Finnish neighboring cooperation policy are the reduction of environmental risks; the promotion of stability, security, and welfare; and the improvement of preconditions for economic cooperation. In practice, various environmental and educational projects have been the most important instruments for achieving these goals in neighboring Russian regions. Finland allocated approximately FIM510 million (US$77.8 million), excluding loan guarantees, of national budget funding to neighboring cooperation with Russia from 1990 to 1997 (Ulkoasiainministeriö 1998). Russian Karelia received more than one-fourth of this funding, and was also the recipient of funding from several multiregional measures.

From the Finnish national perspective, neighboring cooperation has been primarily motivated by threats—both in its traditional military sense and in terms of issues concerning the environment, crime, and migration. This activity has faced problems similar to those encountered by recipient and donor countries in development aid programs. A weak commitment from Russian partners has been a problem in some cases, and expectations have been contradictory. In this sense, this process is similar to EU TACIS (Technical Assistance for the Commonwealth of Independent States) programs,[1] in which the West focuses on technical assistance, while the East calls for direct investments. Such contradictions are not limited to the implementation of projects in Russia; they are also evident in the allocation of funding in Finland. The declared target of state-funded neighboring cooperation is large projects in certain priority areas, which conflicts with local needs and plans as smaller local and regional partners are easily sidelined.

Toward the West on the Fringe of the Russian Federation

In recent years, developments in the Russian Federation have accentuated the roles of regions (*oblast, respublika, krays okrug*) as political and economic actors. This tendency has received special attention in border areas, including Finland's four neighbors (St. Petersburg, Leningrad, Russian Karelia, and Murmansk).

In contrast to many of Russia's fringe areas, those bordering Finland have not attempted to sever their ties with the Federation; rather, they have tried to utilize their geographical position to initiate direct ties with foreign countries, especially with neighboring regions (Bradshaw and Lynn 1996). Russian Karelia is an example of a region attempting to redefine and reconstruct itself as a type of national unit within the Russian Federation. This form of regionalization derives from Russian Karelia's institutional position in the Soviet ethno-federalist system, where there was a link between a titular group (in this case, the Karelians) and its administrative territory (until 1991, the Karelian Autonomous Socialist Soviet Republic), even if the actual role of the minority was politically and culturally marginal (Lynn and Fryer 1998). The development of direct economic and political links with foreign countries—with Finland and its border regions in particular—has been an important instrument in this nation- or region-building process. For the same reasons, the Republic of Karelia is also a member of the Barents Euro-Arctic Region (Bröms, Eriksson, and Svensson 1994). However, an important obstacle to implementing various activities in this multinational and multiregional setting is the fact that the bulk of neighboring eastern Finland has been excluded from Barents cooperation efforts.

Legislative changes in the Russian Federation have served as the necessary preconditions for Russian Karelia to create direct links with foreign countries. Many of these links have been based on case-specific agreements between the republic and the federation and, thus, have contributed to the increasing variation of the regulations concerning foreign firms and other organizations in Russia. However, the effect of these changes has remained limited due to the unclear division of power and responsibility between the republic and the federation, as well as the fact that some privileges were rescinded in 1995 (Eskelinen, Haapanen, and Izotov 1997). In addition to legislative changes, direct links have been supported by the opening of crossing points for international traffic without case-specific authorization. This occurred on the western border of the Karelian Republic in Vartius in 1991 and in Niirala in 1993 (see Figure 1). The findings on whether Russian Karelia has managed to utilize its border location are briefly surveyed later in this paper.

A New Partner: The European Union

Cross-border cooperation is not a new phenomenon. Many European border regions have been involved for decades in various forms of local cooperative arrangements and joint paradiplomatic activities; only since the 1980s have these activities been streamlined to fit the European Union regime. A common characteristic of organized cross-border activity has been tension between the domain and authority of different actors. The established realms of "high (foreign) politics" and "low (local) politics" are challenged by cross-border cooperation. Although the EU cross-border cooperation regime was originally designed for internal borders between member states, more recently it has also been applied, with some adjustments, to the Union's external borders (Scott 1999).

Motives for cross-border cooperation along the external borders of the European Union, as well as its targets and arrangements, differ from those along its internal borders. One major difference stems from the fact that cooperation across external borders has, in several cases (including that of Finland and Russia), implications for international relations. This is especially true in the case of multinational regions of cooperation such as the Barents and Baltic regions in northern Europe, where actors on different (transnational, interregional, and so forth) spatial scales are involved.

The INTERREG initiative is the European Union's most concrete instrument for supporting cross-border cooperation. It was introduced to the Finnish-Russian border in late 1996 when the first projects were funded (Segercrantz et al. 1998). Until 1999, cross-border cooperation along this border was organized by three programs: Southeast Finland (toward St. Petersburg and the Leningrad region); Karelia (the Republic of Karelia); and Barents (the Murmansk region).

These three programs (which received a total of ECU 33.9 million, or US$30.7 million, from the European Union between 1996 and 1999) have introduced a new phase of cooperation along the Finnish-Russian border. First, they emphasize regional actors, as regional councils have been given responsibility for the administrative tasks of the programs. In the Karelian program, for instance, three regional councils (North Karelia, Kainuu, and Northern Ostrobothnia) share this responsibility. This institutional solution has created a new cooperative region in Finland, defined on the basis of neighborhood as the Republic of Karelia borders these three regions (see shaded area in Figure 1). Second, INTERREG funding, although the use of it is limited to the European Union (in this case, Finland), has provided additional resources for cross-border initiatives. In fact, it can be regarded as a policy innovation in Finland because no corresponding funding mechanism has been developed for domestic regional policies or neighboring cooperation. In addition, the administrative requirements of the INTERREG program have already contributed to the careful establishment of policy priorities. Third, the need to create procedures for reconciling different programs has become a more acute policy concern. Currently, the European Union has no mechanism to secure links between the INTERREG and TACIS Cross Border Cooperation (CBC) projects, which are under way on both sides of the border.

The tension between central governments and regions when implementing INTERREG projects, and the technical problems of cross-border programs (such as between INTERREG and TACIS) have contributed to the fact that the regional councils in the Karelia INTERREG region and the Republic of Karelia have launched preparations for a Euregio (Cronberg and Sljamin 1999). They seek to create an integrated system of decision making and administration to promote cross-border cooperation. This is a very ambitious goal that, when in practice, will put EU policies toward both external borders and Russia to the test.

Overall, the INTERREG program has paved the way for regional cross-border cooperation activities that were previously dominated by the state. The financial competency of regional councils is still limited, however, as they struggle to wrest funding from the state and their member municipalities. INTERREG program management—not unlike the whole EU structural policy administration—seems to have become an arena of "contested governance" (Lloyd and Meegan 1996), with vertical competition among the European Union, the state, and regions, as well as horizontal competition between local actors, and specifically between ministries.

Trends, Repercussions, and Prospects of Cross-Border Flows

Cross-border cooperation is usually promoted on functional grounds because it is based on the challenges and opportunities faced by its partners. The results of collaboration are conditioned by the character of functional links and by their potential: complementary assets tend to contribute to interdependencies, whereas regions with completely different resource bases and competing goals find it difficult to initiate successful cooperation. The development of cooperative practices depends on relations among local, national, and multinational cooperative arrangements. Cross-border initiatives can be used to extend the scope of decision making at the regional and local levels (Keating 1998).

As noted earlier, development of cross-border cooperation programs across the Finnish-Russian border has been intertwined with tendencies toward regionalization on both sides of the border. The implementation of cross-border initiatives would not have been possible without the active involvement of regional and local partners. However, in the final analysis, cooperation programs and other cross-border initiatives must be evaluated on the basis of the dynamics of actual exchanges and their contribution to socioeconomic development in a broader sense. In the following, cross-border transportation and economic relations are surveyed and evaluated with regard to their implications for regional development.

Transportation

Passenger traffic between eastern Finland and Russian Karelia has increased rapidly in the 1990s. In addition to the permanent international crossing points (Niirala in the southern part of the region, Vartius in the north, see Figure 1), temporary ones are also used for special purposes, such as the import of timber. Approximately eight hundred thousand people used these crossing points in 1997, accounting for about one-fifth of the passenger traffic between Finland and Russia (Table 1).

These figures are small in comparison to more densely populated areas, but they are not negligible from a regional perspective. Since the EU-induced changes in the customs regulations of 1995, the total number of annual border crossings has been similar to the size of the population of eastern Finland. Understandably, the bulk of traffic between Finland and Russia flows through the southern crossing points toward St. Petersburg, Moscow, and other core regions of Russia. These border crossing points handled almost 80 percent of passenger traffic, and more than 80 percent of goods traffic by road in 1995. With regard to transit traffic, the portion handled by the Leningrad region is even more pronounced, as more than 98 percent of total transit traveled by road and 85 percent by railway in 1995. The dominant position of southeastern Finland and the Leningrad region as the main route to Russia is also reflected in the selection of targets for transportation infrastructure investments: the most important project for

Table 1. Passenger Traffic between Eastern Finland and the Karelian Republic from 1990 to 1997, and Goods Traffic from 1994 to 1995

	Niirala	Vartius	Finnish-Russian Border (Total)
Passenger Traffic (All border crossings, 1,000 persons)			
1990	75	16	962
1991	105	32	1,328
1992	149	62	1,309
1993	191	84	1,631
1994	202	98	2,026
1995	442	181	3,714
1996	504	195	4,017
1997	493	209	4,084
Goods Traffic by Road and by Rail (1,000 tons)			
Export[1] 1994	79	7	2,129
Export[1] 1995	108	4	2,519
Import[2] 1994	2,298	1,490	9,200
Import[2] 1995	3,236	1,839	14,019
Transit 1994	862	24	7,081
Transit 1995	569	35	5,031

[1] Exported from Finland.
[2] Imported into Finland.
Source: Statistics of Frontier Guards of Southeast Finland, North Karelia, Kainuu, and Lapland; Statistics of Finland's National Board of Customs and Ministry of Transport 1996.

upgrading the Russian connection is the Turku-Helsinki-St. Petersburg highway along the northern coast of the Gulf of Finland.

Trade and Direct Investments

For Russian Karelia, the foremost issue of cross-border cooperation in the years since the collapse of the Soviet Union is the development of trade and investment flows with foreign countries, especially with neighboring regions.

Clearly, trade volumes have increased. Russian Karelia's exports outside the Commonwealth of Independent States (CIS) totaled US$24 million in 1991 and

US$505 million in 1997. Growth in imports has been less significant, as imports amounted to US$144 million in 1997. Finland is the Karelian Republic's most important trading partner. In 1997, it absorbed about 31 percent of its exports and was the source of about 21 percent of its imports. The European Union (including Finland) made up 76 percent of Russian Karelian exports and sourced 59 percent of its imports (Goskomstat Respubliki Karelija 1998).

As for foreign direct investments, a total of 427 joint ventures (or firms with 100% foreign ownership) were registered in the Karelian Republic between 1990 and 1997. Of these firms, less than one-third could be considered operative by the end of 1997. Although the relative share of foreign economic activity is slightly higher on average in the Karelian Republic than in the Russian Federation, in terms of the number of firms, the typical foreign investment is very small; therefore, the volume of investments per capita is not higher in the Karelian Republic than in Russia as a whole. The small number of investments made in Russian Karelia can be explained by the fact that most of these investments (about 60%) have been made by small firms and individual businesspeople from neighboring Finland.

Although these figures demonstrate that the process of opening to the West has affected the border region indisputably, a closer look indicates that the positive expectations for cross-border exchanges in the early 1990s have thus far proved to be overblown visions in crisis-stricken Russian Karelia. First, exports consist of only a few staple commodities, such as timber. Three-digit growth figures should be looked at alongside a very low starting level. Second, although most foreign firms have imported new technology and upgraded the skills of employees to utilize it, the diffusion process has proceeded slowly; spill-over and spin-off firms have remained almost nonexistent; and contrary to the targets of official policies, the overmanning of enterprises is bound to lead to redundancies in nearly all investments. Third, the total absence of foreign investors in the paper and pulp industries, which form the backbone of the Russian Karelian economy, is the most explicit manifestation of the failure thus far of the internationalization strategy.

Expectations for increased cross-border exchanges in eastern Finland have also been slow to materialize. Due to the size difference of the two regional economies, the Karelian Republic cannot be an important trading partner for eastern Finland at present; thus, its role in the Finnish export-led growth strategy has remained minimal in the 1990s. The share of the entire Russian Federation in the imports of the easternmost region of Finland (northern Karelia) is only FIM100 million, or US$15.3 million (about 2.5–3%). Nevertheless, the geographical proximity of Russian Karelia is reflected by some small-scale transborder economic relations. Some companies in eastern Finland have subcontracted assembly work to Russian Karelia or have participated in investments in tourism. Overall, it has been estimated that the economic significance of passenger traffic, tourism, and services with the Russian neighboring regions is of the same limited magnitude for eastern Finland as the trade of goods (Eskelinen, Haapanen, and Izotov 1997).

Adaptation to Openness

Positive visions of cross-border interaction entail a transnational region in which the resources of the neighboring countries and regions are intertwined to permit the functional integration of economic and other activities and contribute to the creation of new resources and competitive advantages. This depends on the competitiveness and learning capacity of firms, public organizations, and other relevant actors.

In practice, the legacy of peripherality implies that border regions might not be capable of forming a transnational region, but they are capable of remaining passive corridors. Although transportation routes may run through them, the border regions are not capable of serving as seedbeds for interrelated economic activities. A third potential path of development asserts that in some isolated border regions, the prospects offered by more openness may not imply growth in any competitive economic activities, even transport. Therefore, cross-border links remain occasional and unimportant, and frontier regions may be utilized for quite different purposes; they might, for instance, be defined as protected natural areas. All three of these prospective paths have received attention in the blueprints for cross-border cooperation between Russian Karelia and eastern Finland.

These empirical observations of transport and trade flows illustrate very clearly that a lack of resources on both sides of the border and functional differences between the two partners set severe constraints on the formation of integrated cross-border structures along the Finnish-Karelian border.

On the Finnish side of the border, infrastructure facilities are up to date, and an increasing number of economic activities are being linked to global product competition (Maskell et al. 1998). Due to changing competitive conditions,[2] sectors that once gained their competitive edge from low-cost labor (such as the clothing industry) have already lost their importance in Finland and demand for subcontracting based on cheap labor remains limited. Moreover, new technology sectors do not find competitive resources in the Karelian Republic (Eskelinen, Haapanen, and Druzhinin 1999).

There is one important exception to the aforementioned limited joint interests and complementaries: forest-based industries. The operational environment of these is different from that of other industrial sectors. To a significant degree, the capacity of pulp and paper industries in eastern Finland has relied on imports of timber from Russia (Niemeläinen and Vanharanta 1996). This raises a serious challenge for the forest industries in Russian Karelia because increased exports of raw material tend to raise the price of timber and make technologically backward combines even less competitive. Yet companies involved with forestry on both sides of the border have common interests; in particular, they need to keep foreign customers convinced that forests are maintained on an ecologically sustainable basis. This challenge, which probably tests the learning capacities of the two partners, does not involve solely reforestation, but the protection of biodiversity as well (Lehtinen 1994). If a shared strategy for action can be found, the next task would be to find investors to help modernize forest-based industries in the Karelian Republic. These investments would not stop imports of raw materials to Finland, but they would contribute to increased political and social legitimacy for forestry businesses in Russian Karelia.

At present, a more stable pattern of daily cross-border connections has emerged only in the vicinity of the international crossing points, Niirala and Vartius. The prospects for these emerging mini-scale transnational regions will depend on the roles of these border crossings in international transportation networks leading to and from Russia. The construction and competitiveness of transportation corridors along the Finnish-Russian border are evaluated in connection with the development of links between northwestern Russia and Western Europe. Demand by international traffic must be warranted in advance to justify the large investments required, which can only be done for a few routes. However, each locale would also need satisfactory infrastructure links across the border to establish day-to-day cooperative practices. From an international perspective, the potentially most important railway route from the Karelian Republic runs from Russia's northern resource regions, through the Vartius crossing point (see Figure 1), toward the harbors on the northern coast of the Gulf of Bothnia on the Baltic.

In the long run, the formation of corridor and local transnational regions will be reflected in the settlement pattern of the border regions. The repercussions of spacioeconomic developments along the Finnish-Russian border seem bipartite. On the one hand, new cross-border connections expand the sphere of influence of some centers on the western side of the border and can, thus, temporarily support their traditional roles in the division of labor (based on raw material supplies and, to some extent, low labor costs). On the other hand, centers on the eastern side of the border should be able to initiate their transformation into nodal centers by forging contacts with different business partners in an international economy (Eskelinen and Snickars 1995). Clearly, resources for development of this kind are more abundant in St. Petersburg than in Russian Karelia.

Conclusions

The Finnish-Russian border is still carefully guarded as it was during the Soviet era and a visa is needed to cross it. However, the institutions and practices of interaction and cooperation between border regions have changed dramatically. The process of shifting toward proximity-based relations between actors in the border regions was initiated at the grassroots level in the late 1980s. In addition, its political framework was established in bilateral agreements between the two governments in 1992. Since 1995, the European Union has also become involved in promoting cross-border connections. At the regional level, actors have developed informal information exchanges between neighbors as they seek a joint political strategy to create integrated administrative structures that span the border.

The evolution of cross-border cooperative practices and policies is intertwined with the processes of regionalization in several ways. Regional actors must either gain, or be entrusted with, the decision-making capacities required for building external links with foreign partners. The aims of cross-border cooperation, however, are to compensate for the negative influences of borders and, in the end, to develop functional transboundary regions. In the case of Finland and Karelia, high levels of asymmetry account for the evolution of distinct regionalization processes related to cross-border cooperation.

To escape the economic crisis within the federation, Russian border regions have tried to create direct links with foreign partners as the Federation's capacity to control regional decision making and redistribute resources to them has largely waned. In the case of the Karelian Republic, for instance, the search for a kind of "national sovereignty" (in its Russian meaning) can be interpreted as a continuation of its earlier role as an administrative region nominally devoted to an ethnic minority. In practice, the vague nature of relations between the Russian Federation and the Karelian Republic throughout the 1990s has been a serious impediment to the formulation of any coherent policy to utilize cross-border linkages to assuage the economic crisis.

In Finland, partial regionalization of domestic policy institutions was a precondition for EU membership. The INTERREG program has served as a step toward this since it is administrated by regional councils (even though national government ministries have the final say in decisions regarding additional domestic funding). Currently, the regional councils of the Karelia INTERREG region in Finland and the Karelian Republic in the Russian Federation aim to establish cross-border cooperation on a permanent basis. This Euregio strategy attempts to fill the empty space between the two major prospective transnational regions in northern Europe—the Baltic region and the Barents region. Yet, whatever the merits of the Euregio Karelia strategy, there is no guarantee that the territory will evolve into a functional region. Even its identification as a region is an ambitious goal. One major obstacle is simply that the prospective Karelia Euregio is very large and its subregions have differing functional links and interests. With the possible exception of the forest sector, the complementary resources necessary for increased cross-border interaction are hard to find.

Developments along the Finnish-Russian border are paradoxical. The entire cross-border cooperation regime has been turned upside down in the space of a decade, and the region (to an increasing degree) resembles a normal European border region. Even so, cross-border cooperative activities have not made a visible contribution to fulfilling the goals of socioeconomic development usually put forward as their primary motivation and the prospects do not seem promising. In the long run, the fundamental question will concern the extent to which these peripheries are able to link their cooperative activities to structures and actions at different levels, from local to multinational.

Endnotes

1. The European Union's TACIS program provides grant financing for the 12 countries of the former Soviet Union (excluding the Baltic states) and Mongolia. It is the largest development program of its kind operating in the region, and has launched more than three thousand projects worth over ECU 3,290 million (US$2,986 million) since its inception in 1991.

2. In the Nordic peripheries (eastern Finland being a typical example), the key challenge has been accessibility: distances imply real costs and, thus, undermine competitiveness. Nowadays, the economic legacy of peripherality makes itself known, to an increasing degree, in the structural characteristics of the operational environment (Eskelinen and Snickars 1995).

References

Bradshaw, M.J., and N.J. Lynn. 1996. "The Russian Far East: Russia's Wild East." PSBF Briefing, No. 9 (November). London: The Royal Institute of International Affairs.

Bröms, Peter, Johan Eriksson, and Bo Svensson. 1994. *Reconstructing Survival: Evolving Perspectives on Euro-Arctic Politics*. Stockholm: Fritzes.

Christiansen, Thomas, and Pertti Joenniemi. 1999. "Politics on the Edge: On the Restructuring of Borders in the North of Europe." Pp. 89–115 in *Curtains of Iron and Gold: Reconstructing Borders and Scales of Interaction*, Heikki Eskelinen, Ilkka Liikanen, and Jukka Oksa, eds. Aldershot: Ashgate.

Cronberg, Tarja, and Valeri Sljamin. 1999. "Euregio Karelia—A Model for Cooperation at the EU External Borders." In *Crossing Borders in the Northern Dimension*. Oulu: Interreg II Karelia Programme.

Eskelinen, Heikki, Elisa Haapanen, and Pavel Druzhinin. 1999. "Where Russia Meets the EU: Across the Divide in the Karelian Borderlands." Pp. 329–46 in *Curtains of Iron and Gold: Reconstructing Borders and Scales of Interaction*, Heikki Eskelinen, Ilkka Liikanen, and Jukka Oksa, eds. Aldershot: Ashgate.

Eskelinen, Heikki, Elisa Haapanen, and Aleksander Izotov. 1997. *The Emergence of Foreign Economic Activity in Russian Karelia*. Joensuu: Karelian Institute, University of Joensuu.

Eskelinen, Heikki, Merja Kokkonen, and Seija Virkkala. 1997. "Appraisal of the Finnish Objective 2 Program: Reflections on the EU Approach to Regional Policy." *Regional Studies* 31 (2): 167–72.

Eskelinen, Heikki, Jukka Oksa, and Daniel Austin, eds. *Russian Karelia in Search of a New Role*. Joensuu: Karelian Institute, University of Joensuu.

Eskelinen, Heikki, and F. Snickars, eds. 1995. *Competitive European Peripheries*. Berlin: Springer Verlag.

Finland's National Board of Customs and Ministry of Transport. 1996. Unpublished statistics.

Frontier Guards of Southeast Finland, North Karelia, Kainuu and Lapland. 1996. Unpublished statistics.

Goskomstat Respubliki Karelija. 1998. *Statisticheskii bjulleten, No.1, No. 2*. Petrozavodsk.

Keating, Michael. 1998. *The New Regionalism in Western Europe. Territorial Restructuring and Political Change*. Cheltenham and Northampton: Edward Elgar.

Laine, Antti. 1994. "Karelia between Two Socio-Cultural Systems." In *Russian Karelia in Search of a New Role*, Heikki Eskelinen, Jukka Oksa, and Daniel Austin, eds. Joensuu: Karelian Institute, University of Joensuu.

Lehtinen, Ari. 1994. "Neocolonialism in the Viena Karelia." In *Russian Karelia in Search of a New Role*, Heikki Eskelinen, Jukka Oksa, and Daniel Austin, eds. Joensuu: Karelian Institute, University of Joensuu.

Lloyd, Peter, and Richard Meegan. 1996. "Contested Governance: European Exposure in the English Regions." *European Planning Studies* 4 (1): 75–98.

Lynn, Nicholas J., and Paul Fryer. 1998. "National-Territorial Change in the Republics of the Russian North." *Political Geography* 17 (5): 567–88.

Maskell, Peter, Heikki Eskelinen, Ingjaldur Hannibalsson, Anders Malmberg, and Eirik Vatne. 1998. *Competitiveness, Localised Learning and Regional Development. Specialisation and Prosperity in Small Open Economies*. London: Routledge.

Niemeläinen, Heikki, and Hannu Vanharanta. 1996. *Investment Opportunities for Forest Product Industries in North Karelia*. Joensuu: Department of Economics, University of Joensuu.

Paasi, Anssi. 1996. *Territories, Boundaries and Consciousness: The Changing Geography of the Finnish-Russian Boundary*. Chichester: Wiley & Sons.

Scott, James Wesley. 1999. "Evolving Regimes for Local Transboundary Cooperation. The German-Polish Experience." Pp. 179–93 in *Curtains of Iron and Gold: Reconstructing Borders and Scales of Interaction*, Heikki Eskelinen, Ilkka Liikanen, and Jukka Oksa, eds. Aldershot: Ashgate.

Segercrantz, Vladimir, Merja Kokkonen, Heikki Eskelinen, Kari Mäkelä, and Tönis Segercrantz. 1998. *INTERREG II A Karjala-, Kaakkois-Suomi ja Etelä-Suomen rannikkoseutu–ohjelmien väliarviointi. Väliarvioinnin loppuraportti*. VTT Yhdyskuntatekniikka. Tutkimusraportti 442. Espoo: Technical Research Centre of Finland.

Tikkanen, Veikko, and Jyrki Käkönen. 1997. "The Evolution of Cooperation in the Kuhmo-Kostamuksha Region of the Finnish-Russian Border." In *Borders and Border Regions in Europe and North America*, Paul Ganster, Alan Sweedler, James Scott, and Wolf-Dieter Eberwein, eds. San Diego: Institute for Regional Studies of the Californias and San Diego State University Press.

Ulkoasiainministeriö. 1998. *Tausta-aineistoa lähialueyhteistyöstä vuodelta 1997 ja 1998. Kauppapoliittinen osasto, Keski-ja Itä-Euroopan toimintaohjelmat*. KPO-23.6.4. Helsinki: Ministry of Foreign Affairs.

Van der Veen, Anne. 1993. "Theory and Practice of Cross-Border Co-Operation of Local Governments: The Case of Euregio between Germany and the Netherlands." In *Regional Networks, Border Regions and European Integration*, R. Cappelin, and P.W.J. Batey, eds. London: Pion.

National Divisions and Borderland Youth

Pirjo Jukarainen[*]

Abstract

Nationalist thinking is not dead in contemporary Europe, especially among its evermore globally conscious youth. Their nationalism is as much the carrying over of traditional thinking as it is reflective of everyday politics. Young people are not just passive carriers of traditions, nor are they radical reformists. Their nationalism has elements that are partially rooted in tradition (socially learned) and partially new (stemming from their everyday experiences).

This essay shows just how significant national boundaries are to the youth living in the Finnish-Russian and Finnish-Swedish borderlands. National boundaries remain significant as state borders are opened and even abolished, as demonstrated by the Finnish-Swedish border. These results are based on a comparative study conducted by the author. The research material used for this study consists of short essays and answers to a questionnaire produced by young people (ages 12 to 16) living in the historic borderlands known as Karelia (*Karjala*) and the Tornio River Valley (*Tornionlaakso/Tornedalen*). It reveals that nationalist thinking manifests itself in many ways among borderland youth. Central elements of their nationalism were clear linguistic divisions, fixed "self-other" differentiations, selective migratory orientation patterns, and hostile threat perceptions.

Introduction

This paper examines the cultural and national attitudes of young people living in two different border regions: the Finnish-Russian Karelia borderland and the Finnish-Swedish Tornio River Valley. The analysis is based on the author's survey of young people (ages 12 to 16) who live close to these national borders.

At first glance, it might seem that Finland's eastern and western borders are absolute antipodes: the western borderland exudes peace and harmony and the other still resembles an Iron Curtain. The Finnish-Swedish borderlands (like the Swedish-Norwegian) are often cited as examples of soft, invisible borders; areas

---

* Jukarainen is Researcher at the Tampere Peace Research Institute, Finland.

with an inner Nordic sense of togetherness. When examined from a sociocultural perspective, however, Finland's eastern and western border regions share many similarities. In the spatial and cultural views of young residents, both eastern and western national borders are culturally demarcating and limiting. On the western border, there is a sense of "Finns versus Swedes," in which Finnish youth, in particular, set themselves in opposition to their neighbors. In the east, the border is more sharply demarcated, with one interesting difference. Along the Finnish-Swedish border, both countries' young people have similar attitudes toward the culture and nation across the boundary. Finnish and Russian youth, however, have very different attitudes toward one another. Finns want to more or less close the border to prevent Russians from entering their hometowns, while Russians want to keep the border open to guarantee at least their own opportunities to cross the boundary. Interestingly, young Finns are more reserved and suspicious about cross-border activity in both the east and the west. The Finnish youth puts up a severe national-cultural barrier that is not easy to break through.

The Tornio River Valley

Although Finland's western border has been open for most of its history, a peculiar type of national-cultural divide exists between young Finns and Swedes. One teacher from the Finnish-Swedish twin-city of Tornio-Haparanda aptly stated that every cross-border cooperative activity is hindered by an underlying spirit of national battle (*maaotteluhenki*). National interests too often take precedence over regional or local needs. Despite Nordic harmony (the Finnish-Swedish border has been named by the media the most peaceful border in Europe) and border permeability, the last 200 years of national politics have created nationalist and separatist consciousnesses in its youth. Given these mental and national borders, it seems inevitable that there will be serious barriers to cross-border cooperation and the development of border region identities in the near future.

Tornio-Haparanda

The Tornio-Haparanda area was composed of a single town (Tornio) until 1809, when the border was established between Sweden and Russia and Finland was incorporated into Russia. Tornio had been an important northern trading center since the Middle Ages and in order to guarantee the continuation of trade and communication, it was deemed necessary to build another town (Haparanda) on the Swedish side of the new border. Haparanda achieved city status in 1842. After Finland's independence in 1917, and even more so after Finland and Sweden joined the European Union (EU) in 1995, the two towns managed to overcome administrative barriers in many fields of activity. Today, administratively and logistically, they are run more like one city than two. One of their cooperative organizations or forums is called "Provincia Bothniensis" (northern province). The twin-city (also called a "Eurocity") has about thirty-five thousand inhabitants, two-thirds of whom live on the so-called Finnish side.

Interviews and information from this area were collected primarily from a "cross-border school" (really a language school) where the classes are a mixture of pupils from both sides of the border. The respondents had daily contact with young people of another nationality and were being educated to be bilingual and bicultural. Nonetheless, they had not lost their national identities, although their nationalism was strangely ambiguous. The majority of the students were unable (or unwilling) to define what kind of fundamental differences there are between Finns and Swedes. Often, the differences they recognized were practical variations rather than fundamental cultural issues: some goods were said to be cheaper, better, or more easily available across the border; there is a one-hour time difference; or the other side was said to have a better public swimming pool, a taller city hall, more or better shops or cycling routes, and so on. The few who were able to define cultural and national differences spoke about the "others" in a negative fashion and used a variety of social and national stereotypes. They described the "other" as being worse than them in some ways and grouped them together by making generalizations: "they" were said to be snobbish, dumb, lazy, poorly dressed, proud, always complaining, too loud, badly behaved, and so on.

This attitude prevailed on both sides of the border. Both young Finns (from Tornio) and young Swedes (from Haparanda) found far more to complain about than to cherish in their neighbors. Only one minor difference was revealed, as there seemed to be a bit of jealousy underlying the remarks the Finnish youth made when criticizing their Swedish neighbors. They mentioned with some envy that the Swedes were more extroverted, better ice hockey players, or better musicians. The Swedes showed no signs of jealousy. In fact, three students from Swedish Haparanda, aged 15 to 16, sarcastically wished a "happy return to the Finnish side" to those Finns that complained about Swedish society, but lived in Haparanda nonetheless. These young Swedes had enough self-esteem to defend their own side of the border; they had pride in their homeland and wanted the Finns to know it.

The nationalist attitudes of these young people seem mild and ambiguous, but they were clearly there. They were not grounded in any deep or fundamental ethnic antagonism, but in a more postmodern cultural differentiation, contextually sensitive and complex rather than strong, deterministic, or coherent. This nationalistic ambiguity is best illustrated by the young people's general attitudes toward the border and their descriptions of their own everyday lives close to the border. They took the openness of the border for granted and liked the flexibility and ease they are accustomed to when crossing the border. At the same time, however, they saw many things through a "national lens." They talked about national points of interest and advantages, never forgetting their own nationalities. Their "sides" were central elements of their spatial "mind maps," even though most crossed the border weekly, almost without noticing.

From an administrative and logistical standpoint, the students viewed the border more positively than negatively. The majority on both sides of the border considered the current openness of the border either good or satisfactory. Some even appreciated it for introducing positive multiplicity and variety into the local milieu. In this respect, it could be said that they had a sense of borderlander mentality as far as everyday life was concerned. The border was there to be crossed and benefitted from; it was not thought of as a hindrance.

> A good thing about living near the border is that if one does not find nice clothes at home, one just has to cycle over [the border bridge] and see if one finds something over there. And then if one goes out, then it is good that they are so close to each other. It is good to go to Tornio if there are only a few people around in Haparanda.
> —Girl, age 16, Haparanda

> Border traffic should increase because Finnish people buy things from Sweden.
> —Boy, age 13, Haparanda

> Just now it is good that Haparanda lies close to the border. This way one has more opportunities.
> —Girl, age 15, Haparanda

The uncontrollable aspects of the border worried some students. Pollution from traffic, drug imports, and the transport of other illegal goods were named as reasons that border crossings should diminish. Their feelings about other, more social aspects, however, were mixed. They expressed patriotism in conjunction with a notion that the border would naturally continue to be open; they assumed that the border would always remain open in the future, but nevertheless wished to preserve and protect their own nations and nationalities.

> It can be very tough to live here on the border, especially when Finland wins the ice hockey games. But if the winner is Sweden, it is pretty cool.
> —Girl, age 16, Haparanda

> I don't care whether the border traffic increases or diminishes, as long as the Swedes stay on their side.
> —Boy, age 13, Tornio

> I think that Haparanda is getting bigger with inhabitants from Finland crossing over ... on the other hand, I hope that Haparanda stays Swedish.
> —Boy, age 13, Haparanda

Some young people worried about cultural segregation, but generally, they took the cultural/national borders for granted. They, too, felt that there were two sides, two nations.

> It is bad when, for example, Sweden and Finland meet in a hockey game. Then it becomes almost a competition between us [Haparanda and Tornio].
> —Girl, age 13, Haparanda

I don't know whether the border traffic should increase or diminish, since there
are Swedes in Tornio and Finns in Haparanda anyway.
—Girl, age 13, Haparanda

It is good that there is traffic. From both sides. There is nothing strange in that.
—Girl, age 15, Tornio

Isn't it beneficial for Finland and Sweden if there is more traffic crossing the
border?
—Boy, age 15, Tornio

Finnish Pello and Swedish Pello

Although they bear the same name and society and culture cross the border
over the delineating Tornio River, the two Pellos have no established twin-city
practices as Haparanda and Tornio do. The population is much larger on the
Finnish side than on the Swedish side. The Finnish municipality of Pello has approximately five thousand six hundred inhabitants, half of whom live in the city
itself. Its tiny neighbor, Swedish Pello, is a village of 498 people.

Young people's opinions in this region were very similar to those expressed
in Tornio-Haparanda as far as national differences were concerned. Most young
people described "us" and "them" in quite similar terms, but still found the identifying terms "Finnish" and "Swedish" natural and legitimate. One difference
became evident when students from Finnish Pello were interviewed. They were
rather disinterested in contacting their Swedish neighbors or finding out more
about their everyday lives. Of those interviewed, 26 percent (11 of 42) held negative attitudes toward the Swedes and Sweden in general, 45 percent (19 of 42)
showed no interest in their neighbors whatsoever, and only 29 percent (12 of 42)
expressed any kind of interest—some even thought that increased social communication would be beneficial for both sides. This should not be taken to mean
that the students never cross the border; quite the contrary, in fact. Even those
with the most negative attitudes said that they visited the other side at least once a
month. The reasons for doing so, however, were pragmatic: for cheaper candy,
better skiing and skateboarding, and so on. Only three of the respondents from
the Finnish side mentioned relatives or friends on the other side as reasons for
crossing the border.

Finnish-Russian Karelia

The Karelian situation was studied by conducting two local case analyses:
one with a pair of cities, Russian Vyborg (population 80,000) and Finnish
Lappeenranta (population 57,000); and another with a pair of towns, Russian
Haapalampi (approximate population 2,000), and Finnish Tohmajärvi (population 5,700). All lie close to the border established by the Soviet Union and Finland in 1944. The contemporary population of both Vyborg and Haapalampi is
mostly Russian speaking, as its predecessors were from different areas of the for-

mer Soviet Union. The original Karelians, literally a borderland population between the so-called Western and Eastern spheres of influence, are now a tiny minority (approximately 10 percent of the total population). Most of the Karelian population in the south was evacuated to Finland after the final peace treaty in 1944 and extensive practices of Sovietization (in the USSR) and Finlandization (in Finland) took place in Karelia. As a result, Karelian culture, including the language, slowly lost its importance.

The nationalistic attitudes of the youth living along this eastern border were quite similar to those held by their western counterparts. One major difference was that the Russians expressed a great deal of curiosity about and willingness to cross into Finland. Their interest, however, was connected to Russian patriotism in Vyborg and to feelings of regional belonging in Haapalampi. Young people from Vyborg wanted to cross the border for social and economic reasons, while remaining culturally and linguistically Russian. Those from Haapalampi were even more open to cross-border activities, but still wished to retain and protect their Karelian regional culture. The young Finns in the area were more distrustful and reserved about cross-border activities, making openly protectionist statements. Many had little or no respect for Russians, wanted more extensive border controls, or were even willing to change the location of the border. The following examples show the strong national-political opinions expressed by young people on both sides of the Finnish-Russian border.

The Finns

The Finnish-Russian border shouldn't stay the same as it is now. It should go far forward into Russia because Russia is many times bigger than Finland has ever been ... Finland can never give up to Russia. If that would happen, Russia would run the whole country, and at least the food economy would go bankrupt. Russians should stay on their side of the border and they should live as they can on their own. They have no reason to come here.
—Boy, age 13, Lappeenranta

This is just that kind of border town [marginalized] and you are not able to make yourself known that much here—in order to become famous, for instance. Maybe it is the castle that I like the most here, although the Russians will probably take it over sooner or later, as they have taken our jobs already.
—Girl, age 14, Lappeenranta

I kind of hope that Karelia will be taken back, as I think its natural resources would benefit Finland. If this does not happen, I think the border will remain the same as it is now. Good luck to efforts to buy Karelia back.
—Girl, age 15, Lappeenranta

I will never learn the Russian language, even if I have to die.
—Boy, age 13, Tohmajärvi

It really bothers me that the Russians' tactic is to buy weapons with all their money, then they ask for food supplies from other countries, and if the others won't give them, then they conquer that country.
—Boy, age 13, Tohmajärvi

The border traffic should diminish since there are now almost more Russians than Finns here.
—Girl, age 14, Tohmajärvi

The Russians

I believe in the rebirth of our home district, and it means that in the year 2020 everything will be well. In the twenty-first century, people of many nationalities will live here, but everybody will speak Russian ... I think that if I went abroad I would not be able to live there. Russian people are different. We have a different soul and a different humor. When I went to Finland, I met a Russian lady there; I was so happy when I understood that I could live here and still be in Russia.
—Girl, age 15, Vyborg

[In the year 2020] people here will speak Russian. In Russia everybody has to speak the same language, and no one can prohibit that.
—Girl, age 16, Vyborg

In the future, I think the border with Finland will be open. In my opinion, people will then speak Russian, and only Russian, here. Living in the neighborhood with Finland is no excuse for the Finnish language to invade our home.
—Boy, age 15, Vyborg

Tohmajärvi and Haapalampi

In the Russian village of Haapalampi in the Karelian Republic, young people enthusiastically described the beauty of their immediate surroundings and the nearby natural features of Karelia. Almost all of them showed personal affection for the rich flora and fauna of their area. Their positive praise of their homeland was overwhelming. It seemed that the young people from Haapalampi wanted to prove to this Finnish researcher that Karelia (their Karelia) was doing just fine.[1] The majority supported an increase in border crossings, stating idealistically that people should live peacefully, get to know each other, and be friends. Only four of 43 surveys turned in by respondents showed negative attitudes towards the "other side." Indeed, many even said they "love" the Finnish language and expected to use it a lot in the future, either at work, with their friends, or even with new relatives. For the most part, they saw Finland positively as a nation (one 15-year-old boy mistook Finland for a city), admiring its beauty and cleanliness.

I study Finnish because I live in Karelia, next to Finland, and here the Finnish language is more popular. It will be easier to find a job and get a profession.
—Girl, age 15, Haapalampi

> I study the Finnish language because lots of Finns visit us and Finland lies next to our country ... I would like it if Russians would learn Finnish and we would visit them more often and be in contact with them, and they visit us. Let them spend their vacation here, and ours there.
> —Girl, age 14, Haapalampi

> I decided by myself to study the Finnish language because I wanted to know more about life there on the other side of the border. I wonder why it is so clean there. No garbage anywhere, pure paradise.
> —Boy, age 13, Haapalampi

In the small municipality of Tohmajärvi in the Finnish province of North Karelia, ideas about the border and those who live on the "other side" were quite different. Young people found a great deal to criticize in Russian society. They wondered, for instance, how Russian houses could be so dilapidated, why the roads are so poor, the economic system so wrought, and people's salaries unpredictable. To them, Russia means the nearby Karelian Republic, which some of them had firsthand experience with and knowledge about. Still, they talked about Russia and Russians in general terms, not about Karelia or Karelians. This was an interesting contrast to their Russian counterparts' strong sense of their own regional Karelian identity. The young people from the Finnish town of Tohmajärvi did not acknowledge or endorse this regional identity.

Very few of those from Tohmajärvi found anything negative to say about Russians themselves. One girl stated that she does not trust Russians; others used the pejorative wartime name "ryssä"[2] for Russians. Almost all critiques and complaints focused on the Russian social and political system, not the Russian culture or people. In fact, some expressed a sort of pity and sympathy for the Russians, laying the blame on an abstract system rather than on individual persons.

Finnish Lappeenranta and Russian Vyborg

In this area, cultural differences were quite clear between Russians and Finns. The students on both sides were very attached to their cities. They described and analyzed the current and future development of their cities in a national framework, not a regional one. The "border region" of Karelia was hardly mentioned at all. Many young people from Russian Vyborg were more interested in learning Central European languages than Finnish.

> I think Finland may have lots of very interesting things, but not as much as Russia and the former Soviet Union. I think this because Finland has been part of Russia, and has been very influenced by it.
> —Boy, age 15, Vyborg (never been to Finland)

> I study English, German, and I started (but didn't continue) to learn Finnish. Language is a tool for communicating with people from other countries. English

is an international language. I will need English in my work and then I will be able to read English literature.
—Girl, age 15, Vyborg (visited Finland once)

Attitudes toward the border varied greatly on both sides. The majority of young people interviewed in Vyborg saw the increase in border crossings as useful and fruitful. Finns were once again more negative and skeptical about cross-border connections and the majority was against an increase in border traffic.

The Russians

In my opinion, border crossings should increase. From the Russian side it [the ability to cross] is a kind of sign of welfare. On the Finnish side, it is more a matter of tourist curiosity and economic benefit. It also helps communications between Russia and Finland.
—Boy, age 15, Vyborg

Border crossings should increase because Russia needs cooperation with Finland in many areas.
—Boy, age 16, Vyborg

To me, borders are not needed at all. Although a border is financially profitable (collecting money), it is not needed in this century. Borders bring only problems.
—Girl, age 16, Vyborg

I think border crossings should diminish as this would ease and hasten the crossing procedure because there would be less crowds. A border, however, cannot be invisible. It is a difficult question and Russia now has too many problems to fully open the border.
—Girl, age 16, Vyborg

[Ironically] Border crossings should increase as everybody should see the huge and almighty Finland.
—Boy, age 15, Vyborg

The Finns

Border crossings should decrease because horrible, rattling cars cross from Russia.
—Boy, age 13, Lappeenranta

Border crossings should be reduced a bit, and control of drug smuggling should be strengthened.
—Boy, age 13, Lappeenranta

There should be more frequent border crossings, especially when seen from an administrative perspective, so that the customs practices would be better organized. It is not fun to sit in a car for a couple of hours just for nothing.
—Boy, age 13, Lappeenranta

Border traffic should increase, as it would just bring more money to Finland.
—Boy, age 14, Lappeenranta

At the moment, one-third of all people in Lappeenranta are Russian, at least almost. The good thing is that they bring lots of money here, but there are bad sides as well. For example, in the hardware store, they serve Russians first. It is the priority and not in the service of us locals. Of course they want to create a good image of us, but in my logic it is inconsistent. In my opinion, there should be fewer Russians in Lappeenranta.
—Girl, age 15, Lappeenranta

Russians should come less to Finland and Finns should go more to Russia, as the Russians are not needed here stealing all kinds of stuff and driving like crazy, but Finns should go to Russia and bring CDs, spirits, and tobacco from there.
—Boy, age 15, Lappeenranta

Conclusions

Nationalist attitudes are certainly evident among young people living close to the Finnish-Swedish border, despite efforts to obliterate boundaries in the area. Even those who showed the most positive attitudes toward the culture and society across the border used nationalist terms (Finland, Sweden, Finnish, Swedish, and so on) and did not speak of a common borderland, such as the Tornio River Valley.

We should appreciate Swedish people and Sweden more, likewise the Swedes should appreciate Finland and Finnish people. We are similar and equal (although Finns are better in ice hockey).
—Girl, age 13, Finnish Pello

Language is traditionally one of the most (if not the most) important issues in modern nations and the concept of nationalism. The youth in the Tornio-Haparanda borderlands, however, regarded language in a very postmodern manner. These young people presumed (and even hoped) that the two sides to the border would remain in the future and that both sides would be bi- or multilingual, without clear linguistic divisions.

In Tornio, both Finnish and Swedish are—will be—spoken, since here we "live on the border."
—Boy, age 15, Tornio

The youth of Pello, however, seemed more reserved about being bilingual. The following statement crystalizes this attitude:

In Sweden, they speak some Finnish, but in Finland people hardly speak Swedish at all. In the year 2020 people might speak Swedish here in [Finnish] Pello.

—Girl, age 13, Pello

It is interesting that not one young person mentioned the existing borderlands language of the Tornio River Valley, meän kieli ("our language"), which is a kind of creole hybrid of Finnish and Swedish. Even more strange is that even those few who used this borderlands language when answering the questionnaire did not mention it as a future language of the area, but spoke about national ones instead.

On the Karelian border, most young Russians (both from Vyborg and Haapalampi) were proud of their language and wanted to protect it, although they were also very interested in learning other languages—mostly English, but also German, French, and even Finnish. This great interest is understandable. For a long time it was not possible for many Soviet citizens to learn foreign languages. Even now, there are problems finding fully qualified language teachers and learning opportunities.

Most Finns had a rather passive attitude toward learning other languages. Their most common answer to why they studied a particular language was that it was required by their school. To them, learning languages was an unavoidable task somewhat taken for granted.

In general, the national-cultural divide between Finns and Russians was most evident in the way the young people felt about so-called security issues. (Security issues here are understood broadly as anything based on perceptions of threat.) In Russian Haapalampi, in the Karelian Republic, main security issues involved environmental problems, forest industries in particular. The "other side" was heavily blamed for environmental contamination or devastation. The environment was, above all, perceived as national property to be protected from influences from across the border.

> In my mind, the border should not be crossed so often and we should have less tourists. In Karelia—my home country—we cut our forests and then send them to you, to Finland. There you grow your own trees and have beautiful forests. But now we have only empty places, we do not have full forests. You cannot walk anywhere and hear the birds sing.
> —Boy, age 15, Haapalampi

> There is plenty of forest in Karelia. Forests are very beautiful, but now lots of wood is taken away from Karelia. Why does everybody like our nature, our forests, and yet destroy them? Why does one appreciate only the riches one owns him or herself? Why aren't the other's riches appreciated?
> —Girl, age 15, Haapalampi

On the Finnish side, and especially in Lappeenranta, young people felt that the main security problem was illegal traffic in the form of smuggling, drug dealing, and criminals crossing the border. In Vyborg, the students were more concerned with their cultural (mostly linguistic) unity and survival. They were proud of their Russian culture and language and wanted to protect them from external invasions.

It really bothers me that in their own country Finns are very well behaved and obedient, but if they come to Russia they show all the signs of an uncivilized people. This hurts us deeply.
—Girl, age 15, Vyborg

Our two nations (Russia and Finland) should help each other ... But borders should never be "invisible," because of our centuries-old regional independence. Cultural development should not be united because it is important for every nation to keep up its own traditions. Mutual cultural relations should develop harmoniously, without national conflicts. The language should not be common because two cultures should not be mixed together.
—Girl, age 15, Vyborg

Finns are an interesting people, but they lack the kind of soulfulness, ingenuity, and resourcefulness that we Russians or their neighbors the Swedes have (I know from personal experience as I have been both to Finland and Sweden). But we have lots to learn from the Finns. Sometimes I am disturbed by misunderstandings due to our psychological differences.
—Boy, age 15, Vyborg

I believe that in the year 2020 Russian people will still live here and they will speak Russian. Rude and drunk Finns will finally feel ashamed of themselves and will respect both us (the whole of Russia) and me personally, as I will stay and live here also in the year 2020.
—Boy, age 15, Vyborg

Endnotes

1. In Karelia, words have many meanings, depending on who is speaking. Some Finns use the term, "lost Karelia" or "Russian Karelia," when referring to the ceded and evacuated areas now belonging to the Russian Federation, including areas that have never been under Finnish rule. The Karelian Republic excludes areas of the administrative region of Leningrad (Leningradskaja oblast) in the south, which Finns consider to belong to Karelia.

2. During World War II, the derogatory term, "ryssä," was commonly used by Finns to refer to the Russian enemy. Today, it has a more explicitly negative and racist connotation.

Russia's Regionalization in the Context of the Financial/Political Crisis

Alexander A. Sergounin[*]

Abstract

This study deals with the impacts of Russia's financial and political crises on the process of regionalization. Legal, economic, social, and political implications of the crises are examined and different levels of regionalization are studied, including bilateral, subregional, and transregional cooperation. The institutional framework of regionalization is also analyzed. Four main scenarios for the future of Russian federalism are suggested: asymmetric federalism; the establishment of a unified state; transforming the federation into a confederation; and disintegration, either partial or complete. It is concluded that the model of asymmetric federalism is more feasible than the other scenarios.

Introduction

This paper examines the various factors that contribute to Russia's regionalization as well as the implications of such a development. It looks at the legal, economic, social, political, and institutional aspects of the effects that the ongoing financial and political crises have had on relations between members of the Russian Federation, as well as between Moscow and the peripheral territories. This study also looks at the challenges and opportunities that arise from regionalization.

Factors of Regionalization

Russian and Western literature give a simplistic explanation of Russia's regionalization. According to some analysts, the economic crisis of 1998 led to Moscow's inability to control regions and, thus, encouraged the creeping process of autonomization. The country's regionalization, however, started much earlier than August 17, 1998, when the economic troubles began. The crisis was

* Sergounin is Professor of Political Science and International Relations at the Nizhny Novgorod Linguistic University, Russia.

a catalyst to, rather than a cause of, regionalization. A number of fundamental factors prompted region making in post-Communist Russia.

Lack of a Proper Legal Basis

A federation can be based on either constitutional or contractual principles. A constitution defines the prerogatives of the federal center and the members of a federation (for example, the United States or Germany). Within a contractual federation, the center and surrounding regions may sign bilateral or multilateral treaties (the Soviet Union was created in this way). These two principles were combined when post-Communist Russian federalism was put in place.

President Boris Yeltsin initially favored the contractual principle, so three federative agreements were signed in 1992. The December 1993 Constitution of the Russian Federation, however, made it clear that the constitutional principle was preferred. Nevertheless, in 1994, under pressure from the local elite, Moscow resumed signing agreements with regions and concluded with a set of bilateral treaties with seven republics (the first with Tatarstan). By late 1998, a total of 47 such treaties had been signed.

The treaties are relatively general documents that describe the nature of the division of power and shared powers. Each treaty differs slightly from the others, although they contain some common elements. They are accompanied by a series of agreements that can be signed any time after the conclusion of the treaties. The agreements are far more detailed than the treaties and, as such, are rather different for each region depending on specific policy concerns and resource endowments. Ekaterinburg, for example, signed 18 agreements in addition to its original treaty, ranging from the region's investment policy and use of natural resources to health and cultural policies. In contrast, Kaliningrad signed only three agreements: one on education and science, another on cultural questions, and the third on maintaining law and order in the region (Stoner-Weiss 1998: 22). Regions may also propose additional agreements. Many agreements were for a set period (two to five years) and terms allow for cancellation by either party prior to the expiration of the agreement. If no such notice is provided, the agreements are automatically renewed for an additional two to five years.

On March 12, 1996, President Yeltsin tried to compromise between the constitutional and contractual principles by issuing Decree Number 370. The decree stipulated that the treaties and accompanying agreements are not to violate the Russian Constitution, but must respect its supremacy. They can neither change the status of a federation member nor add to or change what is enumerated in those articles of the constitution that assign federal and joint authority (Articles 71 and 72, respectively).

However, a number of the treaties and agreements either contradict the constitution or go beyond what it had envisioned. Areas that in the constitution are ascribed exclusively to the federal center (Article 71) appear as areas of joint jurisdiction in many documents. For example, the treaties with Bashkortostan, Kabardino-Balkariya, North Ossetiya, and Tatarstan grant these republics the right to defend state and territorial integrity, and Ekaterinburg and Udmurtiya gained authority over the function of their defense industry. In some treaties, members of the federation have the authority to establish relations and conduct agreements with foreign states. In some treaties, areas identified by federal law as spheres of joint authority appear as the exclusive jurisdiction of regions, including civil rights protection and control over local precious metals and stones.

The Russian Constitution is vague about areas of joint authority. Rather than taking the lead in defining and limiting what regions are allowed to do, Moscow has either taken a wait-and-see attitude, or simply reacted to regional demands. For example, there is no federal law about private ownership of farmland, prompting some members of the federation (the Saratov, Novgorod, and other regions) to pass legislation of their own. The 1994 treaty with Tatarstan and accompanying agreements codified what was already in place in areas such as need-based social assistance programs, foreign trade, and external ties. In accordance with the 1996 Ekaterinburg treaty, the region has the right to establish its own civil service and internal legal regulation of joint regional and central jurisdiction, and even to suspend the normative acts of federal ministries and agencies.

As a result of historical traditions and the confusion of the constitutional and contractual principles, members of the Russian Federation have different powers and precedence. The federation consists of 89 federative units: 21 national republics; six provinces (*krai*); 49 regions (*oblast*); one autonomous region (*avtonomnaya oblast*); and 10 autonomous districts (*okrug*). This has led to Russia's so-called asymmetric federalism and its contradictory implications. On the one hand, it can appease local elites and prevent separatist tendencies (at least temporarily). On the other hand, asymmetric federalism is only a partial solution to numerous problems faced by the Russian political leadership and regions themselves. Moreover, growing dissimilarities between members of the federation are a permanent source of interregional rivalry and political instability, making asymmetric federalism fragile and vulnerable.

It should be noted that Russia's asymmetric federalism creates a favorable environment for further regionalization. Both gradual devolution of power from the center to members of the federation and interregional competition are conducive to region making. Regional leaders use the lack of clarity in federal law to carve out their own policies and, thus, become more independent of Moscow.

Historical Legacies

A typical Russian region is not an incidental or mechanical combination of proximate territorial units. At one time, regions were the end products of long-term economic, social, and political developments. However, these were not necessarily organic, and some regions were formed on an artificial basis. This was particularly true during the Soviet period, when some completely different ethnic and religious groups were grouped together merely because of administrative considerations. Nonetheless, the legacy of the Soviet command administrative system (especially in the realm of economics) should be taken into account to understand both the sources of and current trends in Russia's regionalization.

There were 11 economic zones in the Russian Socialist Federative Soviet Republic (RSFSR): the Northwestern, Northern, Central, Central-Black-Earth, Volgo-Vyatsky, Volga, North Caucasian, Ural, West Siberian, East Siberian, and Far Eastern zones (Lappo 1983). Interestingly, the country's regionalization pattern follows nearly the same lines; the economic interregional associations that emerged in the late Soviet and post-Communist periods almost coincide with these 11 zones. In the context of the recent crisis, an idea was put forth in the *Rossiyskaya Gazeta* (1998d) to enlarge Russian regions and form approximately twelve mega-regions ("economic conglomerates" according to Russian Prime Minister Yevgeny Primakov) to replace the 89 members of the federation (Herd 1998: 16). Spatial characteristics of the proposed mega-regions and the ex-Soviet economic zones had much in common.

Decentralization as a Result of Democratization

The Soviet political and administrative systems were also highly centralized. Along with the administrative structures Soviet control over regions was maintained through the Communist Party, *Komsomol* (the Young Communist League), labor unions, and other public associations. With the disbanding of the command economy and the gradual rise of the market economy, devolution of power from the center took place as private interests grew. The introduction of representative government and the election of governors in the federation also contributed to further decentralization. It became difficult for Moscow to remove or discipline regional elected leaders and bodies since they had a popular mandate and were accountable to their constituencies, not Moscow. Moscow, for example, failed to remove Yevgeny Nazdratenko, a self-willed governor of the Primorsky Krai maritime province who conducted somewhat independent policies on taxation, social assistance programs, energy supplies, foreign economic relations, demarcation of the Sino-Russian border, and more.

Lack of a Strong Party System

Political parties have many important functions: articulating, aggregating, and representing different social interests; producing political ideologies; recruiting elites and political leaders; organizing and serving election systems; executing political control over bureaucracy; providing feedback within the political system; and so on. In a stable federal state, parties overlook the equally important integrative function by serving as instruments of political representation for regions and as central officials that control local officials. Political parties are important ties that bind federal states together.

However, post-Communist Russia lacks a strong party system at the regional level. Only the Communist Party, the Liberal Democratic Party (led by Vladimir Zhirinovskiy), and perhaps the Yabloko (Apple) Party have somewhat developed organizational structures, mainly in the biggest cities (such as St. Petersburg, Nizhny Novgorod, Ekaterinburg, Samara, and others). Other parties have little institutional presence outside of Moscow. Few regional leaders have clear party affiliations. Most prefer to be elected on a nonpartisan basis and to build their own political coalitions. All attempts by Moscow-based political leaders to create either a pro-presidential or pro-governmental party in the regions (such as Chernomyrdin's Our Home Russia or Luzhkov's Fatherland) seem unsuccessful. There is little evidence that the present Russian party system is capable of performing unifying functions, thus hindering the development of a well-integrated Russian state.

Under these circumstances, interest groups try to replace parties—although they are incapable of taking over all party functions within the political system. Some political organizations that call themselves parties are in fact vehicles for group interests rather than real political parties. The State Duma, the lower chamber of the Russian Parliament, is surrounded by a network of lobbyist structures. The Council of the Federation, the upper chamber of parliament consisting of local officials, is a sort of forum for representing regional lobbies that fight each other for federal subsidies. Such interest groups play a contradictory role within a federal state. Some groups (such as oil and gas lobbies, the so-called financial-industrial groups, and so on) have a strong self-interest in Russia being a strong federative state. But many pressure groups have only parochial, regional-oriented interests that are not conducive to the country's integration.

The Rise of Regional Elites

In Soviet times, regional leaders were an important source for the national elite. Both Gorbachev and Yeltsin, for example, were brought to the Olympus of political power from the periphery (from Stavropol and Sverdlovsk/Ekaterinburg, respectively). However, regional elites in the Soviet Union have never played an independent political role, and were always absolutely loyal to Moscow. In contrast to Soviet practices, post-Communist regional leaders tried to build political coalitions of their own and to be independent of Moscow. Regional elites became a driving force for regionalization, hoping to benefit from it.

As its resource base shrinks, the federal government becomes more dependent on regional elites. Remarkably, during the debates over Chernomyrdin's candidacy in September 1998, Yeltsin appealed to the Council of the Federation, where regional leaders sit, rather than to the State Duma. It is also interesting that when there was a possibility of dissolving the Duma, had Chernomyrdin been rejected a third time, the majority of Russian senators promised to support Yeltsin. Primakov meets with governors regularly to persuade them that he needs their support and advice.

Moscow not only acknowledges the growing role of local leaders but also tries to cooperate with them and—in a typically Soviet way—to bring them to the capital to introduce "fresh blood" into the federal elite. For example, in spring of 1997, Yeltsin invited a number of popular regional reformers (Boris Nemtsov, Sergei Kirienko, Oleg Sysuev) to take up key ministerial positions in the Chernomyrdin cabinet. After Chernomyrdin's resignation in March 1998, Kirienko became a prime minister. Later, Primakov appointed Vadim Gustov, former governor of the Leningrad Region, to be his deputy. By employing regional leaders for federal jobs, Moscow tries both to capitalize on their political authority and to neutralize potential rivals in the periphery.

The Crisis of the Old Model of Federalism

Prior to the economic crunch of 1998, regionalism was mainly understood as Moscow's policy toward members of the Russian Federation based on redistribution of resources via the federal budget and subsidies (so-called budgetary federalism). However, this top-down method of state intervention in the regions proved inefficient in light of the systemic crisis in Russia.

Since the federal government failed to collect taxes and help regions through federal subsidies, many subjects of the federation realized that they must rely upon their own resources. Moscow is now perceived by regions as unnecessary, a redundant structure that consumes resources rather than provides them.

Regions that are rich in natural resources and are therefore potentially important contributors to the federal budget, are particularly discontented with the central tax policy. Under current legislation, state and private companies that harvest natural resources must pay taxes at the place of their registration rather than in the region where they operate. Since such companies are mostly registered in Moscow, money never reaches local budgets. The regions—via lobbyists in the State Duma and the Council of the Federation—have from time to time initiated bills aimed at changing tax legislation. So far, they have not succeeded. The old model of federalism no longer works. This is a powerful incentive for Russia's further regionalization.

Global Dynamics

Globalization and regionalization are two sides of the same coin, and newly coined words (such as glocalization and fragmegration) are used to denote this complex phenomenon. The entire world faces processes such as the erosion of the nation-state and national sovereignty and the shift of power from the national level toward supranational and regional institutions. Russia is a part of these global dynamics and cannot ignore the rules. Russia is affected by regionalization in Europe (EU enlargement, Baltic and Nordic subregional cooperation), Eurasia (the Commonwealth of Independent States–CIS), and Asia Pacific (Asia-Pacific Economic Cooperation–APEC). Moscow is trying to adapt to new realities, as is evident by its conclusion of an agreement on strategic partnership with the EU; its participation in the activities of various subregional organizations, such as the Council of the Baltic Sea States (CBSS), the Barents Euro-Arctic Council (BEAC), and the Black Sea Economic Cooperation regime; and its attempts to exercise economic and political leadership in the CIS. Russia also joined the Association of South East Asian Nations (ASEAN) Regional Forum in 1996 as a full-fledged member and the APEC in 1998.

Many foreign countries and international organizations prefer to deal with Russian regions rather than with Moscow. They regard regionalization as both a means to bypass the Moscow bureaucracy and as a good solution to many Russian problems. For example, the EU established a special INTERREG (International Regions) program to promote cooperation within European border regions, including Russia. The Technical Assistance for the Commonwealth of Independent States (TACIS) program, another EU initiative, is also designed to stimulate transborder cooperation and strengthen local government in Russia. Western foundations and organizations that specialize in programs that support education and research have also emphasized regional priorities. In the late 1990s, for instance, the Nordic Council of Ministers and the British Council launched special fellowship programs for the Russian Northwest. In 1998, the Soros Foundation started the Mega-Project, aimed at supporting and developing peripheral Russian universities. Despite its territorial dispute with Russia and lack of a peace treaty, Japan cooperates with Russian regions such as the Kurile Islands, Sakhalin, the Maritime Province, and so on in terms of trade, culture, and environmental protection.

All of these factors encourage Russian regionalization. All are long-standing and therefore likely to affect Russian regional dynamics in the foreseeable future. Along with these factors that cause regionalization, there are tendencies that serve as catalysts to decentralization. The crisis of 1998 is one of them. As Herd noted, some peculiarities of present-day Russian political life—such as the type of presidency, the character of the president, the way he exercises power, and the stress of the 2000 presidential election—tend to destabilize center-periphery relations and contribute to the devolution of power from federal government to regions (1998: 3).

Regionalization is a contradictory process that presents a federative state with both challenges and opportunities. Whether Russia will be able to cope with the challenges and opportunities is a fundamental question.

The Challenges of Regionalization

Economic Disintegration

Decentralization may lead to the disintegration of the single Russian economic and financial system and disrupt the traditional system of division of labor between and within regions. For example, in the post-Soviet period, the Cherepovets Metallurgical Combine, which traditionally provided central Russia with steel and rolled iron, decided to forge links with the northwest (including the Nordic countries) since these new partners were more reliable and profitable than the old ones. This created many problems for traditional customers: Vladimir Pugin, Director General of the Nizhny Novgorod Automobile Plant, had to make a special trip to Cherepovets in February 1999 to persuade local managers to provide his enterprise with necessary products and to secure good relations for the future. The Kaliningrad, Leningrad, and Murmansk regions, as well as Karelia, are more integrated economically with Baltic and Nordic economies than with Moscow or, say, the Urals. Another example can be found in the Russian Far East's dependency on trade with China, Japan, and South Korea rather than on other parts of Russia.

The 1998 crisis intensified fragmentation of Russian economics and finances. Many Russian regions established quotas on some exports or imports and erected customs checkpoints along their borders. In October 1998, the *Rossiyskaya Gazeta* (1998a) reported that the Volgograd regional government's decree (Number 469) prohibiting the exportation of food supplies from the region led to conflict with local farmers who tried to sell their products in the neighboring Voronezh region where prices were better. Some governors established monopolies by prohibiting the importation of vodka from other regions or by introducing complex certification procedures for rivals. Interestingly, they undertook such measures under the pretext of fighting bootleg vodka and organized crime. Some cash-poor regions had to issue coupons, local securities, and so on to pay salaries and keep local financial systems afloat. Some members of the Russian Federation started gold reserves of their own to protect themselves from federal instability.

This regionalization of the economy and of autarchic tendencies renders the Russian Federation more fragile and less cohesive, and inevitably leads to disparities between regions and encourages unhealthy competition between them.

Degradation of the Party System

Regionalization undermines the social base for national parties. As a result, it makes it impossible to establish a strong national party system, which could be a pillar of an efficient federation. Instead, the rise of regional parties and increasing pressure on federal bodies from interest groups is predictable. As elections in early 1999 demonstrated in St. Petersburg, regional parties and coalitions can be more successful than national-level organizations. Here, the Boldyrev regional bloc (Boldyrev was one of the founding fathers of the Yabloko party) easily beat the Yabloko candidates in the race for the local legislative assembly.

The ability of regional parties and lobbies to organize local politics, represent regional interests in Moscow, and serve as liaisons between the center and the periphery are unquestionable. Their integrative capabilities, however, are much weaker than those of political parties. Moreover, regional blocs and lobbies are more susceptible to corruption and pork barrel politics, and are less accountable to the public than national parties.

Regionalization of Armed Forces and Security Services

The growing dependence of the so-called power structures on local authorities is one of the negative and dangerous implications of regionalization. Many military commanders struggle with lack of funds and shortages of food, energy, and accommodations, and are forced to seek assistance from local governments. The *Rossiyskaya Gazeta* (1998d) reported that the Baltic Sea Fleet owed 75.5 million rubles (at the time US$5 million) to the Kaliningrad region for food supplies. As a result, Kaliningrad bakeries (to which the fleet owed 5 million rubles, about US$331,125) refused to continue providing the Navy with bread on credit. In 1997–1998, local energy companies cut power to the Pacific Fleet's land facilities several times (even to early warning systems and hospitals) for unpaid debts. To help the military and secure social stability, some regional and local governments provide federal troops with basic provisions from regional budgets. Governor Nazdratenko paid overdue wages to the Pacific Fleet out of regional budgets in return for promises that only those officers born in the region would serve in the fleet. Moscow's ITAR-TASS News Agency (1998) reported that Krasnoyarsk Governor Aleksandr Lebed reached an agreement with the leadership of the Siberian Military District on the use of local funds to supply federal military units with basic provisions.

Some recent trends in force structure and deployment will facilitate the army's regionalization. According to the Russian concept of military reform, commanders of military districts should cooperate with regional leaders. Local politicians even have some decision-making power in areas such as mobilization capacities, supplying federal troops with basic provisions, and determining where conscripts must serve. One Defense Ministry document, *Argumenty i Fakty* (1997: 48), suggested that regional collegiate bodies should be created comprising heads of local governments and the commanders of military districts and other troops, military formations, and agencies. These collective bodies would enable civilian officials and heads of civilian services to participate in operations commands in both the center and the regions.

New types of relationships between local military commanders and politicians emerged in post-Communist Russia. Some are based on dependency, others are more like alliances. In either case, they break traditional loyalty to federal security structures and make them more fragmented and less manageable. As post-Soviet developments in the Caucasian region demonstrated, in the case of political instability or civil or ethnic war, regional military commanders can be easily transformed into local warlords who supply the warring parties with arms and implement the famous imperialist principle of "divide and conquer." Moreover, questions inevitably arise about the reliability of centralized control over the nuclear weapons that are scattered around Russia.

Other security structures (such as the Ministry of Interior forces, the Federal Security Service [FSS], tax police, local police, among others) are even more susceptible to regionalization than the armed forces. On one hand, they were always more dependent on local authorities for basic provisions than the military. On the other, regional elites traditionally regarded them as a valuable asset in building a power base, dividing their interest in cooperating with local organs of the militia or the KGB/FSS (Komitet Gosudarstvennoi Bezopaznosti/Federal Security Service). In fact, since the late Soviet period, many security services have been well integrated into regional power structures. However, it took some time to replace old party heads with new regional elites. For example, on his way to power in the Nizhny Novgorod region, Boris Nemtsov portrayed himself as a person persecuted by the KGB and police. However, when he became head of the regional administration after the aborted coup in August 1991, he suddenly forgot about his conflicts with security services and used them extensively against his political rivals (such as Andrei Klimentyev).

The union of security services and local elites used to be detrimental to democracy in a region. Local politicians used power structures to consolidate their positions rather than to fight organized crime or to secure democratic reforms. For example, Murtaza Rakhimov, President of Bashkortostan, urged the local FSS station to gather sensitive information and discredit his rivals during the presidential election of June 1998. The same "election technology" was then exported to Udmurtiya, where Dagestani leadership repeatedly used police force to put down ethnic and religious uprisings. Makhachkala's neglect of peaceful methods of conflict resolution almost brought Dagestan to the brink of civil war. Some regional leaders use security services not only against their domestic enemies but also to confront other regions. For example, both Ingushetiya and North Ossetia used police units to fight each other during their border conflicts. Local security services there were also involved in kidnappings, terrorist operations, and smuggling activities.

Moscow is unable to stop the regionalization of security services. Moreover, the federal center allows local elites to control such power structures in return for loyalty to Moscow. In February 1999, for instance, Moscow signed an agreement with Ingushetiya that subordinated the local police to President Ruslan Aushev and enabled the republic to form a militia "in accordance with local traditions and norms."

Separatism

For Moscow, the most unpleasant implication of regionalism is the separatist tendencies of various national republics. Chechnya is not alone in demonstrating secessionist sentiments from time to time. In the early 1990s, Bashkortostan and Tatarstan were suspected of leaning toward separatism. There was even a movement to create an independent Idel-Ural republic that would consist of the Muslim peoples of the Volga region. Indus Tagirov, Dean of History at Tatarstan's Kazan University, argued that "the idea of the Idel-Ural has now become a necessity." Fanil Fajzullin, Dean of Humanities at Ufa State Aviation and Technical University (Bashkortostan), admitted that "if the dictatorship in Moscow persists with its demands for a unitary state, centrifugal forces may triumph and a new federation may be formed in the region of Idel-Ural and in the North Caucasus." The Head of the Bashkir Cultural Society, Robert Sultanov, agreed that "if the Russian Federation disintegrated ... [Bashkortostan and Tatarstan] would become the subjects of a new confederation, while retaining their independence" (Petersen 1996: 137).

The troubled Russian Far East has repeatedly discussed independent development. In 1994, Viktor Ishayev, head of the administration of Khabarovsk Province, said that the Russian government "has done all it could to sever the Far East from Russia." The workers of the Khrustalny tin extracting company, who had not been paid for several months, wrote in their declaration: "The government and the president don't pay any attention to our troubles. We have concluded that they have given up on us. Therefore we must also give them up and form our own republic with an independent government. There is no other way to survive" (Matveyeva 1994: 13).

Secessionist movements exist in the republics of Karelia, Kaliningrad, and North Caucasus as well, but do not press for immediate independence. To date, Chechnya is the only breakaway republic.

The Opportunities of Regionalization

Many analysts focus only on the dark side of Russian regionalization. In addition to the negative implications outlined previously, regionalization brings with it a number of positive changes. First and foremost, regionalization encourages further democratization of the Russian administrative system. An enterprise no longer needs Moscow's approval to change its products. A university professor does not have to ask the ministry's permission to publish a textbook or monograph, as in the past. The introduction of representative government, multiparty systems, independent mass media, and free elections to the regions draws millions of people into political life and make democratic reforms irreversible.

Second, regionalization opens the way to new forms of federalism in Russia. Contrary to the old top-down model, a new bottom-up interpretation of regionalism as a basic characteristic of civil society is gradually taking root. Interestingly, with the "help" of the 1998 crisis, many Russians discovered that civil society really exists (albeit in an embryonic form), and that it is much more reliable than the state, which failed to live up to its commitments and once again deceived its citizens. The crisis stimulated individuals, groups, and organizations to form a system of horizontal networks and connections that serves as a basis for civil society. Subregional, interregional, and transregional cooperation can all be considered a part of this endeavor.

Third, the division of labor within a region and cooperation with other Russian and foreign regions help federation members to survive the period of transition. Division of labor and cooperation are particularly important in remote and border regions. From 1992 to 1994, the Russian Far East managed to cope with its shortage of foodstuffs and other consumer goods thanks to barter trade with China (Portyakov 1996: 80). In the fall of 1998, Poland and Lithuania provided Kaliningrad with humanitarian assistance. Japan also launched a similar program for the Kuriles with food and energy supplies (*Rossiyskaya Gazeta* 1998c).

Fourth, the devolution of power forced members of the Russian Federation to become international actors. Between 1991 and 1995, Russian regions signed more than three hundred agreements with foreign countries on trade, economics, and humanitarian cooperation (Matvienko 1996: 91–92). This has helped to undermine Moscow's monopoly on foreign relations and to turn diplomacy away from "Grand Policy" issues and toward the pressing needs of the Russian periphery. Moscow can no longer make decisions about the international status of the regions without consulting them. With the assistance of the Russian Foreign Ministry, the local governments of Kaliningrad, Karelia, and St. Petersburg actively participated in negotiating and concluding a number of agreements on cross-border and transregional cooperation with EU member states and Baltic and Nordic countries. These resulted in fundamental institutional changes, such as the Foreign Ministry's establishment of a special unit on interregional affairs, and the ministry's establishment of new offices in regions engaged in intensive international economic and cultural cooperation as an adjunct to the national republics that traditionally had foreign offices.

Fifth, regionalization can help Russia come to terms with its neighboring countries. Kaliningrad's close cooperation with Lithuania, Poland, and Germany, for instance, prevented a rise in those countries' territorial claims and soothed their concerns about what they considered excessive militarization of the region. Cooperation between Finland and Karelia has eased tensions about the Karelia issue.[1] Cross-border cooperation between the Kuriles, Sakhalin, and Japan paved the way for quiet Russian-Japanese dialogue on disputed questions.

Finally, regionalization has been a major reason for Russia opening up to international cooperation and joining the worldwide trend toward intensive transregional cooperation. Regionalization thus has a very important civilizing function, preventing Russia from becoming isolated and helping build bridges between different cultures.

There are three main levels of regional cooperation in Russia. The first level is bilateral cooperation between members of the federation in areas ranging from economics and the environment to culture and even security. Such cooperation is developed both in neighboring regions (e.g., Karelia and the Murmansk region) and regions with no common borders that share common interests (e.g., the Nizhny Novgorod and Krasnodar regions, or the Komi Republic and Karelia). Such bilateral cooperation used to be institutionalized in agreements between local governments and/or individual companies, enterprises, universities, NGOs, and so on. This level is basic to other forms of regionalism.

The second level is subregional cooperation. There are several subregional associations or blocs in Russia, such as the Northwest Association, the Greater Volga Association, the Chernozem Association, the Ural Association, the Siberian Accords Association, and others, all of which deal primarily with economic and social issues. The members of these associations meet several times each year to discuss common interests that need attention, such as transportation, communication, food and fuel supplies, and joint projects. Regional blocs are seen by some analysts as tools in the struggle for regional domination (Goerter-Groenvik 1998: 96). For example, the Northwest Association is considered to be within the "sphere of influence" of St. Petersburg, and the Urals Association is dominated by Ekaterinburg. The members of regional blocs understand that these organizations are useful in managing regions that have common economic, social, environmental, and cultural problems. It is not surprising that after the crisis of 1998 many regional blocs intensified their activities (*Rossiyskaya Gazeta* 1998c).

The third level of regionalism is international cooperation, which includes cross-border (cooperative projects between neighboring regions) and transregional (collaboration with and within multilateral organizations) cooperation. A number of Russian and Chinese regions, for example, have developed close economic relations. In fact, the southern part of the Russian Far East and China's Dongbei Province have formed an interdependent and complementary economic body (Kerr 1996: 934–39).

In the northwestern Russian regions, cooperation with Nordic countries is important. Finland and Karelia traditionally cooperate in such areas as economics, transportation, communication, tourism, ecology, and culture. Even during the Soviet period, cooperation prevailed over confrontation. A number of joint projects implemented in Karelia were unique in Soviet relations with the West, including the establishment in the 1970s of a large-scale ore processing enterprise in the border city of Kostomuksha. In the post-Soviet period, Finnish-Karelian economic and cultural cooperation has continued. In Karelia, 56 percent of joint ventures were established with Finnish participation. A special agreement between Russia and Finland gave the Kostomuksha free economic zone (FEZ) international status. A report issued by the Ministry of Foreign Relations of the Republic of Karelia (1998) states that the geographical location of the republic (on the border of Russia and the EU) and the historical specialization of the Karelian economy have made it one of the leading exporters among members of the Russian Federation; Karelia's share of exports exceeds 40 percent of the total volume of its output. The Finnish and Karelian economies are complementary, and an embryonic interdependence has been created.

Russia cooperates with the Nordic countries in other spheres as well. Finland and Karelia jointly monitor the Finnish-Russian border environment. Norway pledged NOK300 million (ECU37 million or US$33.4 million) to reduce transboundary pollution by modernizing the Pechenganikel metallurgical combine (Sawhill 1998: 66). Moscow has signed a number of promising agreements with Sweden and Norway on environmental issues, including the handling of nuclear wastes and nuclear safety. According to these projects, priority will be given to the following activities: the Nordic Environmental Finance Corporation's (NEFCO) removal of hazardous nuclear waste stored on board the vessel Lepse in Murmansk; the Arctic Military Environmental Cooperation's treatment of radioactive waste in Murmansk; joint Norwegian-Russian arrangements for environmental cooperation in dismantling nuclear submarines; and multilateral energy efficiency projects under the auspices of the Barents Council, IEA, ECE, and Energy Charter (*Rossiyskaya Gazeta* 1997).

Along with such bilateral activities, some multilateral institutions have involved themselves in regional work, including the Council of the Baltic Sea States (CBSS), the Barents/EuroArctic Council (BEAC), and APEC. The *Diplomaticheskiy Vestnik* (1996) ran a report about the Visby Summit where the

CBSS adopted an ambitious program aimed at regional cooperation in economics, trade, finance, transportation, communications, conversion of the Russian defense industry, ecology, border and customs control, fighting organized crime, and more.

The BEAC is also involved in economic cooperation, environment, regional infrastructure, science, technology, education, tourism, health care, culture, and indigenous peoples of the region. Two working groups established under the auspices of the BEAC—the Environment Task Force of the Barents Council and the Environment Committee of the Barents Regional Council—successfully identified ecological problems in the Barents Euro-Arctic Region (BEAR) and secured funds to implement joint projects (Ojala 1997: 154–55).

Nordic multilateral institutions also contribute to transregional cooperation around the Baltic Sea and in the Barents Euro-Arctic Region. In 1990, the Nordic Council of Ministers created the Nordic Environmental Finance Corporation (NEFCO), a risk capital institution with a total capitalization of ECU80 million (about US$72.3 million). The purpose of this corporation is to facilitate environmentally beneficial projects in the Baltic/Nordic region. In addition to the previously mentioned nuclear safety project in Murmansk, NEFCO invested ECU245,000 (US$221,559) in waste treatment and recycling projects in St. Petersburg, provided St. Petersburg's local government with a loan of ECU1.2 million (US$1.09 million) for municipal wastewater treatment, and took a loan of ECU1.8 million (US$1.6 million) to carry out a modernization program at the Kostamuksha iron pellet plant (Sawhill 1998: 66–67). In 1996, the Nordic Council established an environmental lending facility within the Nordic Investment Bank with an initial capitalization of ECU100 million (US$90.4 million). This facility aims to reduce transboundary pollution in the BEAR and Baltic Sea areas by providing long-term loans and loan guarantees for public and private projects.

The European Union is also an important player in transregional cooperation. As far as Russia is concerned, its two EU neighbors, Finland and Sweden, are especially important. Finland is particularly enthusiastic about the so-called "Northern Dimension" of EU policy. Using its expertise in Russian affairs, Helsinki hopes to serve as a bridge between the EU and Russia (Heininen 1998: 33–34, 37–38). To promote economic cooperation between EU and non-EU countries, Brussels has allocated resources for investments and projects through the INTERREG program. With INTERREG programs, Finland and Sweden may involve Norwegian and Russian regions if they suit their own border region plans and if these partners are able to provide 50 percent in matching funds. At present, the northern parts of Russia are involved in two of four INTERREG programs. INTERREG Barents includes Nordland, Troms, and Finnmark in Norway, Lapland in Finland, Nordbotten in Sweden, and the Murmansk oblast in Russia. The program's total budget is ECU36 million (US$32.6 million). INTERREG Karelen includes Finnish Karelia and the Karelian Republic in Russia, and wields a budget of approximately ECU32 million (US$29.9 million) (Rawlingson 1997: 139; Wiberg 1998: 57–58).

Another important venue for EU regional policy regarding Russia is TACIS, a special program for restructuring technical, administrative, and legislative infrastructure in the former Soviet Union. The program was launched in 1991 to involve ex-Soviet governments, companies, private bodies, and individuals with partners in EU member states. An annual TACIS cross-border cooperation program for projects along Russia's borders began in 1996 with a budget of ECU30 million (US$27.1 million) (Rawlingson 1997: 142). Combined with the International and Technical Assistance program (INTAS) and the Program of Inter-University Cooperation (TEMPUS) to support Russian universities and individual scholars, these EU programs could be very helpful to the development of Russian regionalism. In contrast with other foreign assistance programs, TACIS, INTAS, and TEMPUS are designed to be investments in the country's long-term future, rather than to achieve immediate, short-term results. In short, regionalism not only offers opportunities, but it has already borne fruit and attracted institutional support.

Conclusion: Scenarios for the Future of the Russian Federation

Given the hardships of the ongoing economic and political crises, many observers predict a gloomy future for the Russian Federation. Four main scenarios are put forth in the literature: (1) retaining the asymmetric federalism model; (2) establishing a unified state; (3) transforming the federation into a confederation; and (4) disintegration, partial or complete (Petrov 1998: 8; Herd 1998: 8–18).

The first option, based mainly on a continuation of the current situation, can include variations. For example, some Russian politicians and experts favor enlarging membership of the federation to the level of "economic conglomerates" to make it more manageable from Moscow. This idea, however, is recycled old thinking rather than a feasible plan for today's Russian Federation. According to the *Rossiyskaya Gazeta* (1998d), local leaders do not object to the idea of building regional economic blocs and subregional cooperation, but it is unlikely that they are ready to give up their sovereignty (even economic), which they only recently achieved. Regions are also skeptical about Moscow's ability to lead reform in the federation and to manage the proposed "economic conglomerates."

Transforming Russia into a unified state is a popular notion among Russian extremists like Vladimir Zhirinovskiy (the Liberal Democratic Party) or Aleksandr Barkashov (leader of the Russian pro-fascist party). The extremists maintain that all federative states based on ethnic or ethnic/territorial principles failed to produce a viable model of federalism. Some of them even collapsed (the USSR, Czechoslovakia, and Yugoslavia). They suggest that all national republics, autonomous districts, autonomous regions, and other members of the Russian Federation be eliminated, and that a purely administrative system be introduced. According to this school, such measures would make all separatist and secessionist claims illegitimate, thus stabilizing the country. This is radical thought and no serious Russian leader would dare to implement such a plan or be able to handle the reaction of regional leaders.

The transformation from a federation to a confederation is plausible in the context of further devolution of power in Russia. Russian liberals, national leaders, and some foreign observers favor a "Russia of regions," a "CIS-like Russia" where the center performs only a limited number of functions, such as defense, foreign relations, and national currency (Petrov 1998: 8). They believe that this scheme would render Russia less aggressive, more democratic, and more open to international cooperation. However, this vision is opposed by proponents of strong state power (*gosudarstvenniki* or *derzhavniki*) who insist that democracy and federalism are complementary rather than mutually exclusive. The *gosudarstvenniki* argue that a confederation is not the best instrument for reform in a period of crisis and turmoil (often referring to the example of the American Confederation set up after the War of Independence). They underline that in reality, such a confederation would quickly be dissolved and a conglomerate of appanages would emerge in Russian territory.

The fourth option, disintegration of the Russian Federation, is not excluded by either of Russia's main political groups. However, it is seen as either a worst-case scenario or a means of intellectually intimidating rivals rather than as a real option. Neither Russian nor foreign experts believe that disintegration will actually happen. Drawing on lessons learned from history, notably from the collapse of the Soviet Union, Hale identifies six important factors that determine an area's inclination to secede (1998: 1–2):

1. *Cultural distinctiveness* (language, ethnicity, religion, and so on). There are several republics in the Russian Federation with non-Christian religious traditions and low rates of linguistic assimilation, including Adygeya, Chechnya, Dagestan, Ingushetiya, Kabardino-Balkaria, Kalmykia, and Karachaevo-Cherkessia. Religious tradition has clearly helped Islamic Chechnya rally domestic support for its opposition to historically Christian Russian rule. Compared with the USSR, however, the Russian Federation is homogeneous in ethnic composition, language, and culture. Ethnic Russians make up 87 percent of the country's population.

2. *A history of independence.* The only member of the Russian Federation to have had an independent political existence in the twentieth century is Tuva, which joined the Soviet Union in 1944. Some parts of Karelia belonged to Finland prior to the Finnish-Soviet War of 1939–1940, but the republic has never been an independent state.

3. *Regional wealth and proximity to lucrative foreign markets.* Some national republics are rich in natural resources (Yakutia/Sakha, Komi), but are far from potential markets. Some Siberian oil and gas rich regions (e.g., the Irkutsk Region) are relatively close to China but do not want to be under its protection because of various historical, ethnic, and geopolitical considerations. There is close economic and cultural cooperation between Karelia and Finland, but Helsinki refrains from making territorial claims and does not encourage secessionist

forces in Karelia. Chechnya has rich oil resources, but Moscow is reluctant to re-store the local oil industry and provide Grozny with access to foreign markets.

4. *Violent oppression.* Contrary to a number of Soviet republics (Azerbaijan, Georgia, Latvia, and Lithuania), the only republic to suffer violent oppression from Russia has been Chechnya.

5. *A foreign border.* As Hale (1998) stresses, no ethnic region without a for-eign border has ever actually seceded. The national republics in the Russian Fed-eration with a foreign border are Buryatia, Chechnya, Dagestan, Gorno- Altai, Ingushetiya, Kabardino-Balkaria, Kalmykia, Karachaevo-Cherkessia, Karelia, Khakassia, North Ossetia, and Tuva.

6. *Full-fledged republican status.* Such status makes secessionist claims more legitimate and technically feasible. There are 21 national republics in the Russian Federation.

According to these indicators, Chechnya, with five of the six factors, is the only republic with enough impetus to secede (and did secede from Russia, *de facto*). A number of other republics have relatively high "secessionist potential," including Dagestan (four factors), Ingushetiya, Kabardino-Balkaria, Kalmykia, Karachaevo-Cherkessia, Karelia, and Tuva (all with three factors). Such poten-tial may increase if Moscow were to intervene militarily in Dagestan or Ingushetiya. Currently, the situation is under control, and only extreme traumas are likely to drive Russian republics to actually secede.

Other factors are also important to determine possible secessions. Hanson (1998: 24) states that during the Soviet collapse, the Russian Socialist Federative Soviet Republic (RSFSR), the largest constituent part of the USSR, seceded from the center. The Russian elite was the driving force behind the Soviet Un-ion's disintegration. Present-day Russian elites, with the exception of some na-tionalist leaders in the republics, do not favor such disintegration. Many regional leaders want more power, but object to dissolving the federation. According to the *Rossiyskaya Gazeta* (1998a), even Governor Nazdratenko of the maritime province, who Moscow portrayed as a separatist, favors a strong federative state. It is important to note that some authoritative regional leaders (Moscow Mayor Yuri Luzhkov, Krasnoyarsk Governor Aleksandr Lebed, Samara Governor Dmytri Ayatskov, Kursk Governor Aleksandr Rutskoi, and former Nizhny Novgorod Governor Boris Nemtsov, among others) have federal ambitions and do not view their regional office as a final destination, but as a bridge to a suc-cessful federal political career.

The international environment is also crucial to the success or failure of se-cessionist efforts. While the international community received the dissolution of the Soviet Union and Yugoslavia in a positive light, it is unlikely that Russia's neighbors would be pleased to see the emergence of several dozen newly inde-pendent states, all emanating instability, mass migration, and threats of nuclear proliferation.

In the end, a unitary state is not realistic. Confederation and disintegration are both unlikely and undesirable options. Despite its faults, asymmetric federalism is Russia's probable future, unless economic stagnation were to persist or Moscow were to use force to secure its grip on national republics. Regionalism will play an important role in defining Russia's future. Depending on political wisdom and the degree of democratic culture among Russia's political actors, regionalism can serve as a catalyst for either successful reforms or further disintegration.

Endnote

1. After the Soviet-Finnish War of 1939–1940, the Soviet Union annexed a part of Karelia that belonged to Finland. Although there is no territorial claim at the official level, some Finnish nationalistic groups claim Karelia back.

References

Diplomaticheskiy Vestnik. 1996. (8 May): 9–11.

Goerter-Groenvik, W.T. 1998. "History, Identity and the Barents Euro-Arctic Region: The Case of Arkhangelsk." Pp. 95–109 in *The Barents Region Revisited*, Geir Flikke, ed. Oslo: Norwegian Institute of International Affairs (NUPI).

Hale, Henry E. 1998. *Breaking Up is Hard to Do: Applying Lessons from Soviet Disintegration to the Russian Federation.* Cambridge: Davis Center for Russian Studies, Harvard University.

Hanson, Stephen. 1998. *Ideology, Interests, and Identity: Comparing Recession Crises in the USSR and Russia.* Cambridge: Davis Center for Russian Studies, Harvard University.

Heininen, Lassi. 1998. "Finland as a Northern Country in the New North Europe." Pp. 25–47 in *The New North of Europe: Perspectives on the Northern Dimension*, Lassi Heininen and Jyrki Käkönen, eds. Tampere: Tampere Peace Research Institute.

Herd, Graeme P. 1998. "Russian Federal Instability and Baltic-Nordic Security." Paper presented at the Baltic-Nordic Conference, 24–27 September, Vilnius, Lithuania.

ITAR-TASS News Agency. 1998. (28 July): 9A.

Kerr, David. 1996. "Opening and Closing the Sino-Russian Border: Trade, Regional Development and Political Interest in Northeast Asia." *Europe-Asia Studies* 6: 931–57.

Lappo, G.M., ed. 1983. *Sovetskiy Soyuz: Obshiy Obzor, Rossiyskaya Federatsiya (The Soviet Union: General Review, the Russian Federation).* Moscow: Mysl.

Matveyeva, Y. 1994. "Russia's Far East: Tired, Cold and Ready for Independence." *Moscow News* (30 September-6 October): 13.

Matvienko, Valentina. 1996. "The Center and the Regions in Foreign Policy." *International Affairs* (Moscow) 4: 88–97.

Ministry of Foreign Relations of the Republic of Karelia. 1998. *Republic of Karelia 2000.* Petrozavodsk: Ministry of Foreign Relations of the Republic of Karelia.

Ojala, O. 1997. "Environmental Actions in the Barents Region." Pp. 153–58 in *Europe's Northern Dimension: The BEAR Meets the South*, Lassi Heininen and Richard Langlais, eds. Rovaniemi: University of Lapland Press.

Petersen, P.A. 1996. "Russia's Volga Region: Bridgehead for Islamic Revolution or Source for an Indigenous Alternative Political Paradigm?" *European Security* 1: 113–40.

Petrov, Vladimir. 1998. "V Poiskakh Sotsialnogo Mira (In Search of a Social Accord)." *Nezavisimaya Gazeta* (Moscow) (1 December): 8.

Portyakov, Vladimir. 1996. "*Kitaytzy Idut? Migratzionnaya Situatziya na Dalnem Vostoke Rossii* (The Chinese are Coming? The Migration Processes in Russia's Far East)." *Mezhdunarodnaya Zhizn* (Moscow) 2: 80–84.

Rawlingson, F. 1997. "European Union Structural Fund Financing in the Barents Region and Coordination with Other Funding Sources." Pp. 137–45 in *Europe's Northern Dimension: The BEAR Meets the South*, Lassi Heininen and Richard Langlais, eds. Rovaniemi: University of Lapland Press.

Rossiyskaya Gazeta. 1997. (13 March): 3.

Rossiyskaya Gazeta. 1998a. (3 October): 3–4.

Rossiyskaya Gazeta. 1998b. (29 October): 1.

Rossiyskaya Gazeta. 1998c. (30 October): 2.

Rossiyskaya Gazeta. 1998d. (31 October): 3.

Sawhill, S.G. 1998. "The Influence of Multilateral Development Banks over Environmental Politics in the Barents Region." Pp. 63–75 in *The Barents Region Revisited*, Geir Flikke, ed. Oslo: Norwegian Institute of International Affairs (NUPI).

Stoner-Weiss, Kathryn. 1998. "Central Weakness and Provincial Autonomy: The Process of Devolution in Russia." Pp. 21–27 in *Program on New Approaches to Russian Security Policy Discussion*. Cambridge: Harvard University.

Wiberg, Ulf. 1998. "The Barents Euro-Arctic Region and European Spatial Planning for Sustainable Development." Pp. 53–62 in *The Barents Region Revisited*, Geir Flikke, ed. Oslo: Norwegian Institute of International Affairs (NUPI).

VII
Asian Borders: Development and Conflict

Developing Transborder Regions: Planned or Spontaneous? Cases from Asia

Chung-Tong Wu*

Abstract

Cross-border developments continue to receive attention in the policy realm among Asian nations. Although some Asian governments have made significant investments in selected cross-border regions over a number of years, the development impacts have so far been difficult to assess. Utilizing several Asian cases, this study compares those regions that have developed with significant government investments to those that have emerged with little or no public sector funding. Six major factors were found to make important contributions to the differences in the degree of development achieved. These factors include political acceptance and willingness to cooperate, economic complementarity, location and proximity, private sector interest, institutional framework, and cultural differences.

Introduction

Even in the context of a continuing Asian financial crisis, Asian governments continue to include cross-border developments in their agendas. For many Asian countries, cross-border developments present opportunities to link the nation with the global economy. In order to promote economic development, multilateral agencies such as the United Nations Development Program (UNDP) and the Asian Development Bank (ADB) remain strongly supportive of large-scale regional infrastructure projects like the Greater Mekong Subregion development scheme (GMS).

* Wu is Dean of the Faculty of the Built Environment at the University of New South Wales, Australia. He wishes to thank Chuthatip Maneepong for her assistance in obtaining data on Thai border towns. This essay is adapted from a paper presented at the United Nations Center for Regional Development in Nagoya, Japan, in November 1998.

In spite of large investments of time and resources, successful planned cross-border economic developments are still rare. The renowned Hong Kong-Shenzhen planned cross-border development is one of the few that China has successfully developed.[1] Nonetheless, a number of seemingly successful spontaneous developments have emerged in different parts of Asia. This paper examines several Asian cases to ascertain what sets them apart and attempts to draw policy lessons from them.

Cross-border developments in Asia are many and varied. This paper deliberately focuses upon those cases drawn from China, Thailand, and Vietnam that are territorially contiguous and involve at least one transitional economy. Comparisons with cases from other parts of the world are beyond the scope of this paper; however, where appropriate, examples from Eastern Europe that involve transitional economies will be cited.

The following section outlines key differences between cross-border developments and other types of regional development. Several Asian cases are then examined and the last section draws together policy issues.

Differences between Cross-Border and Other Types of Regional Development

Before delving into their differences, it is necessary to acknowledge at least four similarities among cross-border and other types of regional development: (1) the role of infrastructure; (2) the significance of transportation costs; (3) the importance of factor supplies; and (4) the crucial role of government in promoting development. The importance and availability of adequate infrastructure to promote development is undisputed. Remote locations incur additional transport costs that affect decisions about location and involve trade-offs with the availability of inexpensive labor and land. Furthermore, in conventional regional development literature, government intervention to assist the development of specific regions is often seen as critical to initiating development or encouraging a particular kind of development. These aspects are well represented in regional development literature, but several aspects of cross-border development either differ from other types of regional development or are not traditionally considered.

Several characteristics distinguish cross-border development from other types of regional development. To facilitate a discussion of policy implications, cross-border developments are contrasted with assumptions from major theoretical foundations of regional development—regional growth theory, location theory (Alonso 1975), Friedmann's (1965) original formulations, and Perroux's growth pole theory (Darwent 1969; Hermansen 1972).

The Immobility of Factors of Production

Conventional regional development theory is based on the assumption that there are no obstacles to the mobility of factors of production, whereas cross-border development is founded on the immobility of factors of production, at least in its first stages. The border is important as a barrier that immobilizes factors of production—in most cases, the movement of people—although this immobility becomes less important as the process of development moves from regional toward "transborder" development. Borders hinder the free flow of labor to maintain large differentials in wage costs between two territories. By demarcating territories and allowing control of investments, it also ensures that differences in land or rent prices are maintained.

Transaction Costs and Delays

Borders impose their own transaction costs in the form of delays caused by clearing customs, traffic congestion, and other bureaucratic impositions. Stryjakiewicz (1998) cites a Dutch report that estimated the cost of delays to truck traffic at the eastern European Union border at an additional cost of NLG900 (US$470) per trip due to prolonged waits to complete formalities. In the early 1990s, frustrations with similar delays led to a brief truck driver strike at the Hong Kong-Shenzhen border, where overly bureaucratic and complicated procedures contributed to delays. Part of those delays could have been caused by a sudden rise in traffic that the border crossing was never designed to accommodate. Even at the Hong Kong-Shenzhen border crossing at Luowo, which has been upgraded a number of times over the years by expanding its capacity and streamlining procedures with electronic scanning devices to cope with the large volume of daily passenger throughput, there are still significant delays at peak times (such as festivals or holidays), even with the best of goodwill and cooperation on both sides. Put simply, delays add to the cost of doing business. When delays represent extreme costs, they can deter foreign investment.

Transaction costs are not all caused by events at the border. Costs are also imposed by cultural differences in the ways business is conducted or by psychological barriers that prevent individuals from seeking employment or other opportunities across the border—even in regions where there are historically open borders, such as between the Netherlands and Germany. In his study of the Rijin-Waal region, van der Velde (1998) found that knowledge of a region's language and geography are important factors that influence cross-border job searches. Unfortunately, similar studies in Asia are not yet available.

Incompatible Economic Systems

Some of the more challenging cases of cross-border development occur at borders where a transitional economy and a market-oriented economy meet, such as the Hong Kong-Shenzhen, Thailand-China, or Thailand-Burma-Laos borders. Cross-border developments that involve two or more transitional economies at different stages of evolution tend to entail additional complications. Conventional theories of regional development assume that market economic systems are at work because they were all derived from examples in market economies.

In cases where the same transitional economies are undergoing political reforms, problems are compounded, thereby causing further complications.

Bertram (1998) refers to cases that involve both political and economic changes as "double transformations." There are at least two aspects of double transformations that are worthy of consideration. First, additional institutional learning must occur as an economy moves from one system to another. Second, there are problems associated with being a latecomer to industrialization. Most transitional economies, including China and much of Eastern Europe, have a long history of industrialization, but their accumulated industries are generally technologically obsolete and/or moribund due to inefficient management practices. They face economic, social, and political challenges that are difficult to disentangle. Cross-border developments under these conditions can neither afford to ignore the constellation of issues nor try to tackle them in isolation.

Institutional Issues

Institutional issues such as profit repatriation regulations, double taxation agreements, guarantees of exchange rates, and political institutions for joint actions are crucial to cross-border developments. In the Hong Kong-Shenzhen region, many of the factors that contributed to its decade-long delay in showing a solid outcome had to do with institutional problems. Investors were not confident about the Chinese government's intentions and few were experienced in dealing with its complicated bureaucracy. At the same time, Chinese officials were searching for ways to conduct business that were acceptable to foreign investors. The national government had to progressively liberalize its many restrictions—notably, controls over wages, employment conditions, and lease of land to non-Chinese citizens. China's experiences in the transition from a command economy to a more market-oriented economy are characteristic of the problems that transitional economies face and their concomitant institutional issues.

Proximity of Differences

The economic complementaries of two territories involved in cross-border development might best be understood as the proximity of differences. This is especially evident in cases of contiguous territories. Hong Kong-Shenzhen and Singapore-Johor are prime examples of the elements of complementarity and proximity at work. While the proximity aspect may not be as evident in some other cases, economic complementarity must be; otherwise there would be few incentives for cross-border development to proceed.

Conventional regional development theory includes discussions of growth pole development and its spillover effects. It is postulated that the growth pole draws investment and labor into itself as it develops, but in later stages leads to the decentralization of growth toward underdeveloped areas, some of which may be border regions (Darwent 1969). Cross-border development bypasses this scenario by attracting investments across the border to the region with the least expensive labor force and land. In a "normal" course of events, conventional theory expects the movement of low-cost labor toward the growth center during the first phase of development. Many would argue that the expected second phase of decentralization would not eventuate, except in cases where borders deter the movement of labor, thus forcing capital to move.

The Role of the Informal Sector

Conventional development theory is structured around industrialization. Many cross-border developments are, however, based on informal sector activities, including trade and small-scale industries. This is true in Thailand's developments with its neighbors and between China and Vietnam. Informal sector activities are particularly germane in cases of spontaneous development that evolve from trade. In strategies to stimulate cross-border development, few policy or theoretical considerations are given to the role of the informal sector.

Trade is usually the beginning of more complex cross-border relationships. Traders in the informal sector tend to be flexible and are often willing to take advantage of niches and small margins. They often provide affordable consumer goods or hard currency in exchange for agricultural produce or raw materials, making it possible for small entrepreneurs to accumulate and subsequently invest in larger trading operations or to diversify. Instead of implementing expensive and complex projects, governments should consider promoting development by supporting small-scale traders and providing infrastructure as needed. This approach could potentially take advantage of what the private sector identifies as opportunities and aid their evolution into more complex and larger developments.

Asian Case Studies

There are numerous ways to categorize cross-border developments in Asia. Elsewhere (Wu 1988a), they have been grouped under the categories of "infrastructure driven," "investment driven," and "policy driven" to highlight the fundamental factors that drive developments. Another approach is to examine their characteristics and how truly cross-border the developments are. Here they are distinguished simply by whether they are "planned" or "spontaneous." Those cross-border developments that have attracted projects or programs sponsored by government or multilateral agencies are considered to be "planned." Those that began without such sponsorship are considered "spontaneous." These are clearly simplifications, since in reality no development is ever without some form of government participation or scrutiny—be it either in the form of permission to change land use or regulations on activities carried out at a particular location or building. Permits and/or sanctions, however, are vastly different from situations in which government funds are employed to build infrastructure to encourage private sector investment and promote cross-border development.

Planned Cross-Border Developments

The Tumen River Development Zone

In the northeast of China, straddling Russia and North Korea, lies the Tumen River Development Zone. Promoted by the United Nations Development Program (UNDP) with the participation of China, North Korea, Russia, and Mongolia, and supported by Japan and South Korea, the region is renowned for its natural resources and deepwater seaports. Since 1991, the UNDP has skillfully stitched together a coalition of interests among the various nations, attracted international interest and investment, and maintained the project's momentum. The UNDP has invested significant resources in research and planning for the region. The project aims to develop a trinational zone that will become a major transportation hub, the strategic location for an industrial complex, and a dynamic urban region with a population of around ten million.

Participating nations, however, have responded differently to the project. Russia is suffering from "double transformation" and the North Korean regime seems willing to engage the rest of the world only on its own terms. In anticipation of an economic boom that has yet to materialize, the Yanbian region (in China) has made large investments in infrastructure, including a planned international airport on the Chinese side of the trinational border. A limited number of international investments (largely from South Korea) have been made in the city of Hunchun in the Yanbian district, but so far with limited results. The Tumen River Development Zone is a planned cross-border development project championed by an international agency. At least three key problems have emerged: (1) a lack of coherent common interest among participating nations; (2) a lack of obvious and direct economic complementarity; and (3) the burden of a centuries-old history of cultural, ethnic, and national conflict. These factors, along with the changing economic fortunes of some of the participating and supporting nations and the depressed international economic climate, have slowed the progress of this project.

Hong Kong-Shenzhen

The Hong Kong-Shenzhen border region has attracted a great deal of attention over the last decade, with much of the focus on the rapid development of Shenzhen itself and the whole of the Zhujiang Delta area. The Shenzhen SEZ development began in 1979, although it took nearly ten years before it started to blossom. Shenzhen's economic development is largely due to the economic transformation of Hong Kong and the symbiotic economic relationship that has emerged between its manufacturing sector and the new industries in Shenzhen.

The Hong Kong-Shenzhen case is a good illustration that top-down planning can lead to significant and lasting development, given the right conditions. The proximity of economic complementaries was the first prerequisite. A growth pole in need of economic transformation (Hong Kong) and the availability of a contiguous territory with inexpensive labor and land were also necessary conditions. Cultural affinity and language compatibility were additional favorable conditions. China's willingness to adopt some of the economic practices of a market economy as a transitional economy was also of great importance. At first, developments involved property development and labor-intensive manufacturing, but later shifted to more technology-based activities.

Even in this case, where economic results have been excellent and political issues have been resolved, there is still significant friction due to the lack of ap-

Table 1. Asian Case Studies

	Examples	Political Will	Factor Immobility	Transaction Costs	Institutional Issues	Transitional Economies	Complementarities	Informal Sector	Cultural Barriers
Planned	Tumen (China, North Korea, Russia, Mongolia)	Divergent	Important prerequisite	Extremely high due to remote location	Complex Many actors	Diversity of transitional economic experiences; double transformation in Russia	Not evident	Not considered part of the plan	Possible antipathy
	Hong Kong-Shenzhen	Strong and convergent	Guaranteed by China for 50 years	Incompatible bureaucracies	Diminishing, but still considered a problem	Moving closer	Proximity of growth pole	Not part of original plan	High cultural infinity
	Nong Khai (Thailand)	Divergent	Barriers imposed by bureaucracy	High	Many	Laos economy is in transition	Laos has cheap land and labor	Significant	Not a major issue
	Sadao (Thailand)		Advantages of lower wages compared with Malaysia	Not a major issue	Diminishing	Familiarities with transitional economic problems	Low cost products to low income population	Significant	Significant
Spontaneous	China-Vietnam (Dong Xing and Mong Cai)	Overlapping interests	Not an issue	Not a major issue yet	Cultural- and local-based institutions still pose problems	Two transitional economies at different stages of change	Both offering inexpensive land and labor	Significant	Historical enmity and suspicions still barriers

Figure 1. The Tumen River Development Zone

propriate institutions to deal with cross-border issues such as land development, environmental protection, and infrastructure planning. In these respects, the Hong Kong-Shenzhen development has much to learn from the rest of the world.

Thailand and Its Neighbors

Although Thailand is eager to develop its border regions with China, Burma, and Laos, it has no comprehensive cross-border development programs that involve its neighbors. Thailand is a willing and keen supporter of the Greater Mekong Subregion project (GMS) under the auspices of the Asian Development Bank (ADB), but Thai authorities have not made that project their own. Instead, various government agencies have implemented a variety of schemes, including the designation of several border towns (such as Nong Khai and Chon Mek in the northeast) to spearhead cross-border development. Completed projects include the establishment of special economic zones (SEZs), free trade zones, the preparation of master plans for tourism, and the development of physical plans for a variety of border towns. Nonetheless, investors have largely bypassed these locations. A prime example of this is Nong Khai on the Thai-Laos border. It is situated only 9.3 miles (15 kilometers) across the Mekong River from Vientiane, the capital of Laos. It also lies on the main north-south route that links Hanoi, Vietnam, to Bangkok via Vientiane and on the alternate north-south route to China's

Yunnan province. Nong Khai has long been a major regional center, designated as a key border town by the government in recognition of its historical importance. In addition, the "Friendship Bridge" was constructed between Nong Khai and Vientiane in 1996 with Australian funding and opened with much fanfare. Despite of all this attention, Nong Khai has been virtually ignored by investors.

Nong Khai has actually suffered since the Friendship Bridge was opened. The Laotian government was not willing to let vehicle traffic pass over the bridge. Customs and other officials on both sides of the border imposed detailed and rigid controls over goods and traffic crossing the border, hampering rather than facilitating cross-border trade. Incompatible political systems and institutional issues have combined to further hinder cross-border development. Economic downturns in Thailand since mid-1997 and the earlier, more severe economic downturn in Laos have constituted additional complications.

Spontaneous Cross-Border Developments

China and Vietnam

Developments in the border region of Guangxi (China) and Quang Ninh (Vietnam) provinces are of interest because this region is representative of trade-based border development. Vietnam is trying to reform its economic system and is interested in developing industrial zones to attract foreign investors. This same interest has been expressed by its Chinese neighbor, the Dong Xing township in Guangxi province. About half of Guangxi's border trade crosses the border at Dong Xing (China) and Mong Cai (Vietnam). Booming trade since 1990 has resulted in rapid economic changes in Dong Xing and its township. As a result, the area is slowly attracting the attention of foreign investors.

Figure 2. Hong Kong and Shenzhen

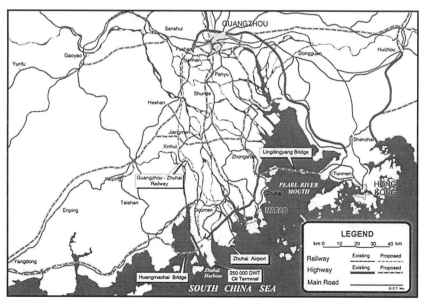

The Vietnamese town of Mong Cai and its province, Quang Ninh, are bene-fitting from renewed trade with China and are keen to exploit the possibilities of developing the border zone to attract foreign investment and Chinese tourists. Mong Cai is the center of a thriving market where a large variety of Chinese goods (mostly consumer electronics and clothing) are traded. Many traders from China cross into Mong Cai daily to do business in the market. Foreign investors seeking opportunities in tourism have also invested in a number of small hotels aimed at the Chinese market.

Figure 3. Thailand and Its Neighbors

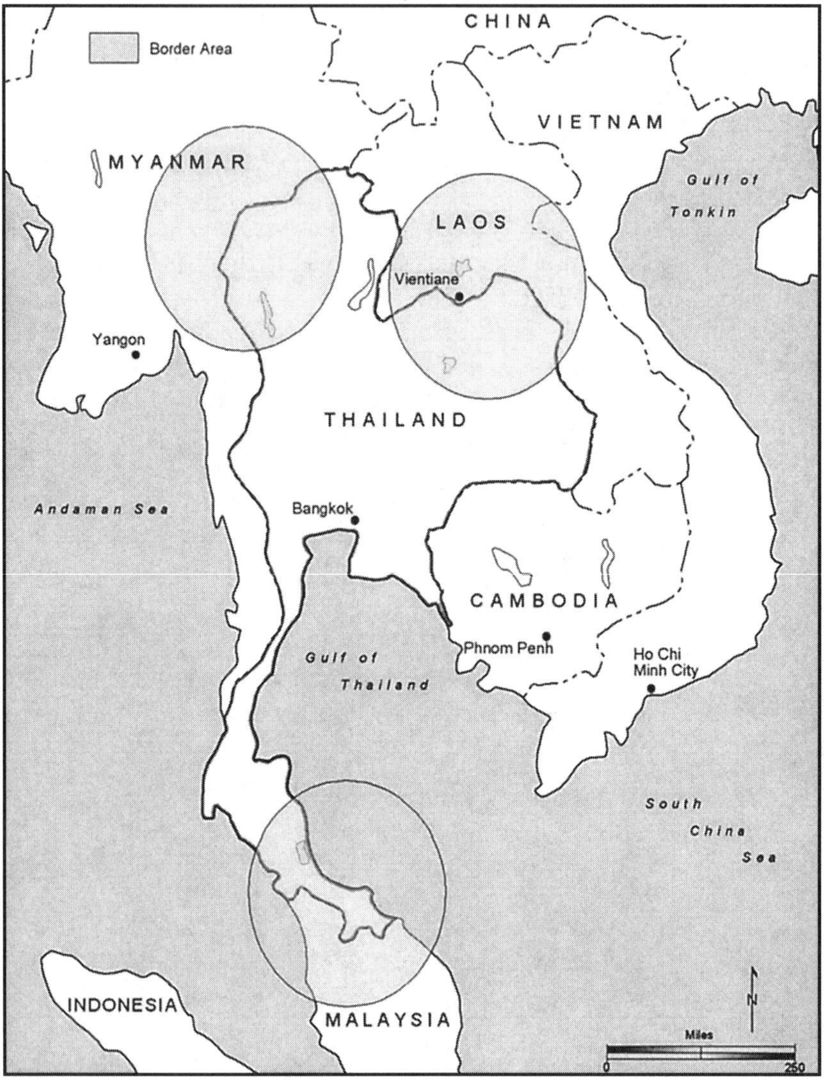

The Chinese and Vietnamese authorities both want to make the most of their locations and to develop industrial estates for foreign investors. The Guangxi government's plans are slightly more advanced than those of authorities in Quang Ninh, but their concepts are similar. Commercial and international business zones will be located in the border towns and adjacent to the border crossings to take advantage of the booming border trade. Immediately behind these will be locations for a variety of industrial developments known as export processing zones or industrial zones. Beyond these, plans call for a variety of residential and tourist facilities. Mong Cai is also considering the construction of an airport about sixteen miles (twenty-five kilometers) from the border. Major port facilities are also being planned by the Vietnamese in Cai Lan, 76.8 miles (124 kilometers) southwest of Mong Cai. Existing Chinese ports are located just east of Dong Xing at Fangcheng and Beihai. In addition, a strip of almost entirely new urban development is partly underway, stretching about twelve miles (twenty kilometers) from the Chinese border and another 9.9–12.4 miles (16–20 kilometers) on the Vietnamese side. This could develop into an urban belt up to 24.8 miles (40 kilometers) long along the Gulf of Tonkin.

Mong Cai and Dong Xing are good examples of spontaneous cross-border developments that were initiated by the informal sector and eventually gained official recognition and active promotion. Whether official support will flourish or not remains to be seen. Nevertheless, this example of government involvement illustrates that cross-border developments benefit from some degree of official sanction at different stages of development.

Figure 4. China-Vietnam Border Region

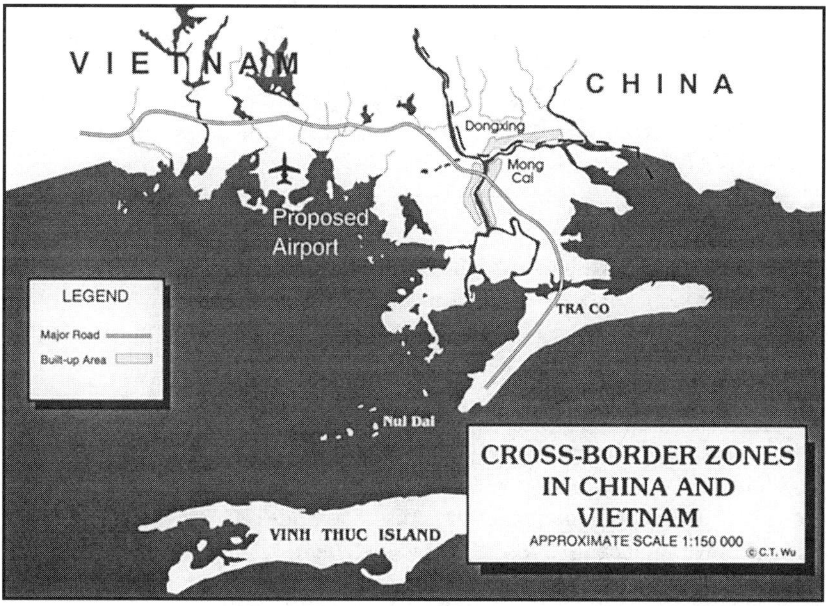

Southern Thailand-Sadao

About 50 percent of all Thai cross-border trade by land passes through the southern Thai border town of Sadao, near the Malaysian border. A number of factors contribute to Sadao's dominant position. It is located on the main road and rail links with Malaysia, which until 1997 was one of the fastest-growing Asian economies and had relatively high labor costs compared to Thailand. Due to its location on these key transportation routes, many tourists from Malaysia and Singapore must pass through Sadao to get to the tourist center of Hai Yai. Thai tourists also visit Sadao for duty-free goods from Malaysia.

The Thai government has recently recognized Sadao's significance. As part of its participation in the Indonesia-Malaysia-Thailand Growth Triangle (IMT-GT), the government has prepared a five-province Southern Thailand Development Master Plan. Projects have included the Inland Container Terminal at Sadao and a wholesale market at Sadao-Padang Besar. The terminal is now operational, but development of the wholesale market has suffered from downturns in the Malaysian economy and problems in finding a suitable location. This is due in part to bureaucratic disagreements between the Thai and Malaysian governments. While many of the slated development projects have received official sanctions from the Thai Board of Investors, resultant land encroachment and environmental pollution problems are severe.

Lessons

The examples cited above illustrate six key ingredients for the success of cross-border developments: (1) political acceptance and goodwill; (2) economic complementarity; (3) location; (4) private sector interest; (5) appropriate institutional frameworks; and (6) cultural factors.

Political Acceptance and Willingness to Cooperate

Cross-border development, be it planned or spontaneous, must have some level of political support. All six keys to success are dependent on political acceptance and the willingness of the countries involved to cooperate. The stumbling block to successful development is often unwillingness of the parties involved to cooperate to ensure the progress of cross-border development. Whether it is at the macro-level of goals and objectives, or at an operational level, such as the simplification of customs procedures or site selection for key developments, political will and willingness to cooperate must prevail. Tumen illustrates problems in reaching agreements on macro issues. Nong Khai illustrates problems in getting local bureaucracies to participate willingly. Sadao demonstrates that even where spontaneous development thrives, bureaucracies may become bottlenecks rather than facilitators.

Economic Complementarity

All of the case studies provided here illustrate that unless there are obvious economic benefits to be derived from cross-border development, little will occur. The powerful incentives provided by a neighboring growth pole to stimulate the cross-border development of Hong Kong-Shenzhen are prime examples of the requirements for success.

Cross-border developments will benefit both a growth pole in need of low-cost land and labor and its nearby territories. The border ensures that cost differences remain and that migration of labor is strictly controlled. Nonetheless, developments are unlikely to proceed without significant government facilitation or intervention to ensure sufficient safeguards for investments and repatriation of profits.

For collaboration to occur at the next stage, when further transborder developments are contemplated, there must be significant, realizable economic complementarities. The nature of the complementaries may have changed from one side supplying the other with inexpensive factors of production to both sides collaborating to exploit other opportunities, but real potential for deriving economic benefits must exist.

Location and Proximity

All forms of development depend on favorable locations; however, for cross-border developments, locations are strictly related to borders. Spontaneous developments illustrate this point. Sadao, Thailand, shows that location may help encourage spontaneous development. There are many other cases of cross-border developments driven by the private sector that illustrate their dependence on where private sector interests identify opportunities, even though these locations may not coincide with determinations by government officials. Nong Khai illustrates that location alone is insufficient to compensate for uncooperative bureaucracies. Not all locations are equally attractive to investors or may be affected by government actions. Even in cases where there are strict controls over locations for foreign investments, however, private sector interests are paramount.

The factors that influenced private sector interest in the Chinese special economic zones have to do with proximity, availability and ease of transport, and cooperation of government officials. In other words, economic complementarities, an institutional framework, and government intervention are all important, but location—or the proximity of complementaries—is equally important to stimulating and maintaining private sector interest.

Private Sector Interest

Few governments have the resources or the ideological inclination to pursue cross-border developments without first attracting significant private sector interest. Some governments, however, still believe that they know best when selecting locations for cross-border development. Cases where private sector interests led the way in promoting cross-border development illustrate that government involvement is not always necessary or desirable. Where trade is largely the basis for cross-border development, private sector interest almost always precedes government attention, which is certainly true in parts of China, Vietnam, and Thailand.

Because large, industry-based projects require major funding for infrastructure, government participation may be necessary. Even in such cases, unless significant private sector interests can be attracted, little develops—as the cases of Tumen and the early years of Shenzhen illustrate. However, private investors may have goals that conflict with public interests. One such area that consistently stands out is environmental protection. Government intervention is then necessary to provide a context and framework for dealing with conflicting interests.

Institutional Framework

An appropriate institutional framework is especially important when spontaneous developments become more formalized. The Sadao case clearly illustrates that an institutional framework helps development to progress smoothly. The transformation of spontaneous cross-border developments into more formal and planned ones may depend on an institutional framework to promote and protect investments or organizational collaboration. Institutional frameworks are especially important in dealing with environmental issues that often emerge. If projects with obvious economic benefits can run into problems, then projects such as environmental protection, which rarely receives high priority or financial support, can be expected to encounter even greater barriers without the backing of a strong institutional framework.

Cultural Differences

Time and again, studies have indicated that cross-border development involves the element of cultural empathy or the minimization of psychological and cognitive distance (van der Velde 1998; van Houtum 1997; Wilson 1998). Studies of the Netherlands and Germany, as well as other border regions, demonstrate that even if economic differences are minimal, cultural differences can serve as significant barriers. Individuals may not regard a cross-border region as distinct when searching for opportunities. Locally based cultural institutions can add undue costs to cross-border transactions by, for example, insisting on using business practices that are culturally specific and cumbersome, adding to delays and costs. Knowledge of the region's language and geography are important for labor markets. Even in the best of circumstances, where language and kinship links are numerous, cultural and institutional problems reflecting different economic and political experiences can become obstacles. Policies that focus only on economic aspects and assume that cross-border developments will proceed apace are likely to have only limited success. Programs that are sensitive to the cultural aspects of cross-border development and aim at minimizing potential conflicts must be part and parcel of a total policy package.

Endnote

1. In 1979, China designated four special economic zones (SEZs). Of these, Shenzhen and its neighbor Zhuhai (next to Macao, which was returned to China in December 1999), are the more developed.

References

Abonyi, G., and F.J. Pante. 1998. "Economic Cooperation in the Greater Mekong Subregion: The Challenge of Resource Mobilization." Pp. 327–72 in *Growth Triangles in Asia,* M. Thant, M. Tang, and H. Kakazu, eds. New York: Oxford University Press.

Alonso, William. 1975. "Industrial Location and Regional Policy in Economic Development." Pp. 66–96 in *Regional Policy: Readings in Theory and Applications*, John Friedmann and William Alonso, eds. Cambridge: MIT Press.

Bertram, H. 1998. "Double Transformation on the Eastern Border of the EU: The Case of the Euroregion Pro Europa Viadrina." *GeoJournal* 44 (3): 215–24.

Chan, R.C.K. 1998. "Cross-Border Regional Development in Southern China." *GeoJournal* 44 (3): 225–37.

China Academy of Urban Planning and Design. 1994. *Research into the Planning of Guangxi Border Towns*. Beijing: China Academy of Urban Planning and Design.

Cui, L., ed. 1994. *The Asia Pacific Era and the Development of the Tumen River Area*. Yanji: Yanbian University Press.

Darwent, D.F. 1969. "Growth Poles and Regional Centers in Regional Planning: A Review." *Environment and Planning I* 1: 5–31.

Downes, R. 1996. "Economic Transformation in Central and Eastern Europe: The Role of Regional Development." *European Planning Studies* 4 (2): 217–24.

Friedmann, J. 1965. *Regional Development Policy: A Case Study of Venezuela*. Cambridge: MIT Press.

Friedmann, J., E. McGlynn, et al. 1971. "Urbanization and National Development: A Comparative Analysis." *Revue Tiers-Monde* 12 (45).

Hermansen, Tormod. 1972. "Development Poles and Development Centers in National and Regional Development: Elements of a Theoretical Framework." Pp. 1–67 in *Growth Poles and Growth Centres in Regional Planning*, Antoni R. Kuklinski, ed. The Hague: Mouton.

Hinton, P. 1995. "Growth Triangles, Quadrangles and Circles: Interpreting some Macro-Models for Regional Trade." *Thai-Yunan Project Newsletter* (28 March): 3–8.

Hirokazu, S. 1998. "Tumen River Area Development Programme: North Korea and Multilateral Cooperation." Pp. 297–326 in *Growth Triangles in Asia*, M. Thant, M. Tang, and H. Kakazu, eds. New York: Oxford University Press.

Kim, K., and C.T. Wu. 1998. "Regional Planning's Last Hurrah: Tumen River Project." *GeoJournal* 44 (3): 239–47.

Kingdom of Thailand and Asian Development Bank. 1998a. *Border Towns Urban Development Project. Inception Report*. Bangkok: GIBB, Ltd. and PAL Consultants, Ltd.

Kingdom of Thailand and Asian Development Bank. 1998b. *Border Towns Urban Development Project. Interim Report*. Bangkok: GIBB, Ltd. and PAL Consultants, Ltd.

Lee, K.S. 1998. "The Role of the Border City Hunchun on the Tumen River, China." *GeoJournal* 44 (3): 249–57.

Lee, S.J., ed. 1994. *Tumen River Area Development Project: The Political Economy of Cooperation in Northeast Asia*. Seoul: Sejong Institute.

Leung, C.K., and C.T. Wu. 1995. "Innovation Environment, R&D Linkages and Technology Development in Hong Kong." *Regional Studies* 29 (6): 533–46.

Liew, P. W. 1992. *Reform and Openness in China and the Economic Development of the Pearl River Delta*. Hong Kong: Nanyang Commerce Bank.

No, K.Y. 1998. "Cross-Border Issues 'Need Policy Bureau Leadership.'" *South China Morning Post* (Hong Kong) (20 November).

Peng, J. 1993. "Guangxi: China's Southwestern Gateway to the Sea." *China Today* (April): 13–18.

People's Committee Quang Ninh Province. 1993. *A Brief Introduction to Quang Ninh Province*. Quang Ning: People's Committee Quang Ninh Province.

Perloff, H.S., and V.W. Dodd. 1963. *How a Region Grows: Area Development in the United States*. New York: Committee for Economic Development.

Stryjakiewicz, T. 1998. "The Changing Role of Border Zones in the Transforming Economies of East-Central Europe: The Case of Poland." *GeoJournal* 44 (3): 203–13.

Sung, Y.W., P.W. Liu, Y.C.R. Wong, and P.K. Law. 1995. *The Fifth Dragon: The Emergence of the Pearl River Delta.* Singapore: Addison-Wesley.

Tang, S.H. 1995. "The Economy." Pp. 117–50 in *From Colony to SAR: Hong Kong's Challenges Ahead,* J.Y. S. Cheng, and S. Lo, eds. Hong Kong: Chinese University of Hong Kong.

Tran, T.H. 1993. "Viewpoint and Oriented Objectives on Development Planning for Areas and Zones Given Priority to Receive Foreign Investment in Vietnam." Paper presented at the Conference on Infrastructure, Property Development and Construction, Ho Chi Minh City, Vietnam.

United Nations Development Program (UNDP). 1993. *A Regional Development Strategy for the Tumen River Economic Development Area and Northeast Asia.* New York: UNDP.

Van der Velde, M.R. 1998. *Labour Market in a Border Area.* Wien: European Regional Science Association 28th Congress.

Van Houtum, H. 1997. *The Development of Cross-Border Economic Relations.* Center for Economic Research, Tilberg University, Tilberg, The Netherlands.

Wen, L., ed. 1994. *The Developing National Model Autonomous Region—Yanbian.* Yanji: Yanbian Renmin Chubanshe.

Wilson, T.M., and H. Donnan, eds. 1998. *Border Identities: Nation and State at International Frontiers.* Cambridge: Cambridge University Press.

Wu, C.T. 1997. "Globalisation of the Chinese Countryside: International Capital and the Transformation of the Pearl River Delta." Pp. 57–82 in *Global-Local Relations in Pacific Rim Development,* P. Rimmer, ed. Sydney: Allen and Unwin.

Wu, C.T. 1998a. "Cross-Border Development in a Changing World: Redefining Regional Development Policies." Paper presented at the Global Forum on Regional Development Policy, 1–4 December, Nagoya, Japan.

Wu, C.T. 1998b. "Cross-Border Development in Asia and Europe." *GeoJournal* 44 (3): 189–201.

Wu, C.T., and D. Ip. 1985. "Forsaking the Iron Rice Bowl: Employment and Wages in China's Special Economic Zones." *Asian Journal of Public Administration* 7 (2): 216–42.

Common Pasts and Dividing Futures: A Critical Geopolitics of Indo-Pak Border(s)

Sanjay Chaturvedi[*]

Abstract

A critical geopolitics of the India-Pakistan border suggests that it is not just the most direct physical manifestation of "statehood" and sovereignty between two hostile South Asian neighbors. It is also manifested through the construction of symbolic/cultural boundaries between "us" and "them" in areas such as foreign policy, media discourses, and education systems. The territorial boundary provides the physical symbol or marker differentiating one geopolitical realm from another, but its construction occurs in sociocultural space. In this sense, the boundary can exist only as long as those that it binds continue to construct it. The goals of this essay are to: (1) deconstruct some of the boundary-producing discourses in India and Pakistan that lead to the geographies of rejection and exclusion, and (2) demonstrate that the worst victims of the "border wars" are their own citizens and border communities in particular.

Introduction

The cold war between the postcolonial, partitioned South Asian states of India and Pakistan continues to undermine both the sociocultural and political geographies of their border regions. Critical geohistorical and geopolitical views of the establishment, demarcation, and control of the "national" boundaries between India and Pakistan suggest how British imperial practices of constructing and mapping borders, coupled with the colonial "frontier" mentality, have been accepted rather uncritically by the political elite in both countries to disengage and secure the "national self" from the "neighboring other." Ironically, in the age of time-space compression, the twin-processes of globalization and fragmentation seem to have increased uncertainty in the power centers of both countries about "our place" and its markers.

* Chaturvedi is Reader in the Department of Political Science at the Centre for the Study of Geopolitics, Panjab University, Chandigarh, India.

The central argument of this essay is twofold. First, any worthwhile attempt to understand the dynamics of the India-Pakistan border should not be confined to the area adjacent to the physical dividing line. The concept of mental boundaries is equally important. It is invoked through a set of national symbols and institutions, legitimized by "reasons of the state," and sustained by (and in turn sustains) the politics of difference and exclusion. These invisible mental borders simultaneously construct "otherness" on either side and are constructed by it (Paasi 1998). In short, a critical geopolitics of Indo-Pak borders provides a reminder that this border is as much a metaphorical-symbolic phenomenon as it is a physical space.

Second, a critical geopolitics of the India-Pakistan borders reclaims the borderlands as homelands from strategic-military planners in both New Delhi and Islamabad. Central governments in both countries typically view borders as zones of conflict and exclusion, and deploy symbols and language that reinforce that imagery. While the centers of power typically think of their responsibility to border regions within the framework of national security, the local dynamics and preferences of the inhabitants of "broken villages"—who are exposed to the fear and danger associated with the border on a regular basis—are simply ignored. From yet another perspective, a critical geopolitics is concerned with "how power is embodied, encoded, represented, and manifested in state organs and institutions at various levels and guises in the borderlands and in the lives of those affected, in however small a manner, by their experience of or relationship to their nation's or their state's borders (Donnan and Wilson 1999: 63). In short, it underlines the need to humanize the borderlands.

This essay is divided into four sections. The first aims to provide the reader with a rather sketchy account of how critical geopolitical perspectives could provide valuable insights for analyzing the problematic relationship between state boundaries and the concepts of territorial sovereignty and national identity in the larger South Asian context. The next two sections offer a critique of some of the boundary-producing discourses in India and Pakistan in light of the persistent (and almost obsessive) concern of national institutions and intellectuals of statecraft with threats to "territorial integrity" and "national security." Finally, the last section examines state practices of securing the national borders and their implications for the communities, economies, and ecosystems in the border regions, particularly during war or conflict.

Critical Geopolitics, the Discourse of Territorial Sovereignty, and Morality of Borders in Postcolonial South Asia

Critical geopolitics has been described as the intellectual scrutiny of national and international politics of geographical knowledge (Dalby and Ó Tuathail 1996: 451–56). According to Ó Tuathail, "critical geopolitics … is a question not an answer, an approach not a theory, which opens up the messy problematic of geography/global politics to rigorous problematization and investigation"

(1994: 527). It is crucial to explore how geopolitical reasoning is integrated into political discourse to perpetuate, sustain, and justify social and political practices of dominance (see Dalby 1991). The texts of geopolitical discourse are rooted in power and knowledge, and help to sustain and legitimate certain interests, perspectives, and interpretations.

O'Tuathail points out that "it is along borders that one can best appreciate the acuteness of this perpetual struggle over space in global politics" (1996: 3). Or, as Donnan and Wilson put it, "boundaries may mark the extremities of state power, but this need not entail its weakening there ... While not everywhere the case, it is often precisely at borders that state power is most keenly marked and felt" (1999: 17). A critical geopolitics of Indo-Pak borders is, therefore, also the geopolitics of state power and practice.

The challenge to a critical geopolitical approach here is to understand how geographical knowledge of the border regions is transformed into the reductive geopolitical reasoning of the intellectuals of statecraft—that community of state bureaucrats, leaders, foreign-policy experts, and advisors who comment upon, influence, and conduct the activities of statecraft (O'Tuathail and Agnew 1992: 195). For example, how are various borderlands—homelands in their own right—reduced to the status of "security commodities" or zones of ambiguity, danger, or uncertainty that need to be controlled, managed, and mastered rather than understood in their complex totality?

Kim Rygiel's study of Turkey (1998) shows how the state constructs borders, both of national identity and territory, by using spatial strategies that homogenize identity and space. Waterman states that under the theory and practice of sovereignty, boundaries are perceived as demarcation lines to separate "us" from "them" and "citizen" from "alien" (1994: 32). One of the principal functions of the sovereign state, then, becomes not just organizing what goes on inside the state, but also controlling what crosses its borders. The power, therefore, to: (1) admit or exclude aliens; (2) regulate the movement of temporary desirables (those with passports); and (3) to keep out undesirables (through border fencing and patrols), is supposed to be inherent to sovereignty. Communities that are identified as coterminous with the *raison d'être* of state are made absolute, and individuals who (according to the same logic) do not qualify to be members are excluded and forgotten.

Mroz (1980) has argued that the typical response of unified state actors to challenges from within is to cope with external "threats" (real and/or imagined) by means of internal security. It is only by examining a state's perceived threats that the security practices of that state can be understood. Such practices may consist of defining security as "spatial exclusion," as was the case with U.S. policy toward the Soviets during the Cold War (see Frei 1986; Dalby 1990).

Eva convincingly argues (1994: 379) that the concept of frontier and boundary involves an attitude that is closely linked to feelings of security. In most cases, people are more willing to cooperate with each other as a nation only after they are made aware of their external borders. These, in turn, are based on perceptions of dangers built on fear or opposition to others. To minimize or escape the psychological stress of living under threat, a society may stereotype the "other" as constituting a collective threat. The "other" is labeled as the cause of the sense of vulnerability that is alleged to haunt and hurt the national consciousness of "self." However, when adversaries compete and collide—as in the case of the U.S. and the former Soviet Union during the Cold War—they apply different standards to evaluate their own actions and those of the rival (Frei 1986: 270).

Anssi Paasi, a Finnish geographer, has examined critically and at length the relationship between territory, boundaries, and the social construction of national identities (1996, 1999). He has meticulously studied the changing meanings of territoriality and state boundaries where nationalism and ethnoregionalism seem to be concomitantly giving rise to new boundaries and causing conflicts between social groups (reterritorialization). At the same time, the processes of globalization are compressing time and space, and reducing the effects of boundaries (deterritorialization). Contesting the perception that boundaries are merely fixed products of the modernist project, Paasi sees them as social processes. His insightful observation that the problematization of the links between state and nation must be a crucial part of any critical study of political boundaries is extremely relevant in the South Asian context.

The geohistories of the borders of what was to become known as South Asia were written by those who created them for their own power-political purposes. As a result, the maps that were drawn up by the imperial powers were both too static and too simple to capture the diversity and the dynamism of the borderlands. As Paula Banerjee points out, "based on these maps and with a mixture of territorialism, cartographic absoluteness, and frontierism the South Asian nation-states came into being, or to use a more current phraseology, were *constructed*" (1998: 11). The British imperialist, Lord Curzon, employed both strategic and geographic sense and set the stage for government, military, and secret service agents to appropriate border monopolies. The remarkable influence of Curzon's legacy can be gauged from the fact that South Asian states are still unable to escape the cartographic and political mind-set they inherited at the time of their independence. Fifty years later, governments continue to deny their own citizens access to maps of border areas, even outdated ones.

India's failure to emerge as a single independent nation was rooted in its inability to accommodate the politics of difference. The carving up of South Asia into modern nation-states through partitioned independence caused acute problems of population displacement and population movement. Nationalism in South Asia became reflexive. As Ranabir Samaddar puts it,

> India is nationalist with reference to Pakistan or Bangladesh and not so much with reference to the USA or the United Kingdom ... Reflexive nationalism in South Asia is a gross caricature of its predecessor, anti-colonial nationalism. It makes ethnic suppression and suffering in the wake of forced migration, tolerable to the ethics of a nation. And while political parties often give calls for sealing the

country's border to check migration, their "porous border" argument based on the fears of the native population, remains ignorant of the historically established patterns of the migration of people in South Asia. It is a phenomenon now laden and valorized with the history and politics of Partition (1998: 74–75).

Moreover, each of the South Asian states came to be labeled by the religio-cultural composition of its majority community (Muslim in Pakistan and Bangladesh, Hindu in India, and Buddhist in Sri Lanka). What inevitably followed was what Imtiaz Ahmed calls the "communalization of the frontiers ... each of which deludes itself of its increasingly religio-communal composition by blaming the other! The violent conflict in Kashmir and the illegal movement of people from Bangladesh, although qualitatively different in their compositions, provide evidence which are identical at each other's frontiers" (1997: 183).

Sacred Geography, Boundaries, and the Social Construction of Territorial Identities in India

Boundary-producing discourse in India is founded on geopolitical images of India's geographical-territorial realm, and is implicated in the puzzle of sovereignty, citizenship, and identity. In India, there are two principal geopolitical visions of national unity and national identity: "secular nationalism" (combining territory and culture) and "Hindu nationalism" (combining territory and religion) (Varshney 1993). For both, however, the defining principle of national identity is *territory*.

In the secular view, the territorial notion of India that has been emphasized for more than twenty-five hundred years is of a land stretching from the Himalayas in the north to *Kanya Kumari* (Cape Comorin) in the south, and from the Arabian Sea in the west to the Bay of Bengal in the east. What makes Indian civilization unique, according to this vision, are the virtues of syncretism, pluralism, and tolerance as reflected in the expression *Sarva Dharma Sambhava* (equal respect for all religions). Jawaharlal Nehru's, *The Discovery of India* (1946), is a good example of the secular nationalist construction of India's national identity. Nehru "discovers" India's unity in culture, not in religion. For him, the heroes of India's history subscribe to a variety of Indian faiths (Varshney 1993: 236).

In the Hindu nationalist geopolitical imagination, India is originally the land of Hindus—the only land that Hindus can call their own (Pattanaik 1998: 43–50). According to V.D. Savarkar, the ideological father of Hindu nationalism, "the ultimate criterion for being a Hindu was the definition of a 'holy land' (*pitrubhumi*), which is the geographical location of the sacred shrines and myths of one's religion" (cited in Hansen 1999: 78). In order to qualify as Hindu, a person or group must be part of three criteria: *territory* (between the Indus and the Seas), *genealogy* ("fatherland"), and *religion* ("holyland"). Hindus, Sikhs, Jains, and Buddhists were born in India and meet all three criteria. Christians and Muslims had potentially "extraterritorial loyalties" since their holy lands were outside the territory of India and, therefore, could not be counted as Hindus.

It is important to note that the boundaries of India suggested by secular nationalism coincide with the "sacred geography" of the Hindu nationalists' hallowed pilgrimage sites. As Varshney remarks:

> Since the territorial principle is drawn from a belief in ancient heritage, encapsulated in the notion of "sacred geography", and it also figures in both imaginations [secularist and nationalists] it has acquired political hegemony over time. It is the only thing common between the two competing nationalist imaginations. Therefore, just as America's most passionate political moment concerns freedom and equality, India's most explosive moments concern its "sacred geography", the 1947 partition being the most obvious example. Whenever the threat of another break-up, another "partition" looms large, the moment unleashes remarkable passions in politics (1993: 238).

Secular nationalists and Hindu nationalists share what Sankaran Krishna termed "cartographic anxiety," the anxiety surrounding questions of national identity and survival (1994: 508). Typical of a society that perceives itself as suspended forever between "former colony" and "not-yet-a-nation," such anxieties permeate everyday social, cultural, political, and administrative practices. Their most aggressive manifestation is the securing of the country's "vulnerable" borderlands.

Even a casual observer of contemporary India cannot fail to notice an increasing concern with threats to the unity and integrity of India, and infiltrations by shadowy "aliens" that are considered to be destabilizing and destroying the body as well as the soul of the Indian nation. According to Surinder Singh (1998), a retired inspector general of the Border Security Force,

> India has *live* borders touching Pakistan, China, Bagladesh and Myanmar. Borders with Nepal and Bhutan, sedate and quiet so far, are also showing convulsions. By reductionist logic, one can easily say that if India is today facing the danger of destabilization on account of infiltration of spies, saboteurs, communal agents, illegal Bangladeshi nationals and terrorists, *it is mainly due to our permeable borders*. Smuggling on land borders is rampant, though the bulk of it is carried out by sea and air. Pakistan has been singularly successful in aiding and abetting terrorism earlier in Punjab and now in J&K [Jammu and Kashmir] by pushing in terrorists, arms, ammunition and other sophisticated materials of violence and destruction. As *management of security of borders* of Punjab, Rajasthan and Gujrat was strengthened by resorting to improved manpower deployment and installation of technological devices, including fencing-cum-lighting, Pakistan redoubled its efforts to exploit the J&K area and other Indian borders touching Nepal, Bangladesh and Myanmar for its sinister designs (1998). (Emphasis added.)

As the physical preservation of national borders becomes synonymous with the very existence and survival of the state, the perceived indispensability for national unity of secure or inviolable borders diverts attention from the continued violence that produces and sustains the Indo-Pak border (Krishna 1994: 511). A classic example of how borders can lead to senseless, costly confrontation is found in the frozen wastes of the Siachen Glacier—a heavily glaciated terrain lying between the Great Karakoram Mountains and the Saltoro Range of the Himalayas at altitudes exceeding 19,685 feet (6,000 meters) above sea level. The conflict surrounding this "roof of the world" continues unabated despite colossal expenses in terms of skilled personnel and national exchequer, which India and Pakistan can ill-afford as developing countries.

Two-Nation Theory, National-Identity, and Security Discourse in Pakistan

In Pakistan, boundary-making rationales and related perceptions about security are deeply rooted in society's definition of threat and the way the sense of threat is coped with psychologically. The powerful political elite in Pakistan has been more successful in uniting the people on security matters than on any other issue, essentially because "the appeal to national security is related directly to the issue of protection against a dangerous enemy and involves the physical survival of one's family, friends and nation" (Withey and Katz 1965: 76). According to Saba Gul Khattak, an eminent Pakistani scholar,

> A large majority of Pakistanis live with the fear that Pakistan will disintegrate in the near future. This fear is the subject of many discussions centered around the question of the country's existence. It has been possible to produce such a mind-set because deterrence—the underlying philosophy of security in Pakistan—is based on fear of attack. The belief that India will attack, and that it is constantly scheming to undo Pakistan in order to incorporate that territory back into itself, has bred a deep distrust of India. *In Pakistan, as elsewhere, the narrative of security/insecurity has been constructed chronologically so as to lend it credence. This narrative constructs India as the enemy Other, making India central to the discourse* (1996: 344). (Emphasis added.)

Such thinking is cultivated and perpetuated by the educational system (Khattak 1996: 345–46). A critical look at Pakistani discussions about "national" security and integrity reveals that prestate Pakistani history has been systematically utilized and incorporated, with special attention given to the underlying geopolitical rationale of the two-nation theory. K.K. Aziz, a noted Pakistani historian, has shown how history in Pakistani schools and colleges has been reduced to the status of national mythology and further (ab)used as a vehicle for political indoctrination, and for constructing and nurturing an anti-India (anti-Hindu) mind-set. Aziz states:

> Either to rationalize the glorification of wars or for some other reason(s), the textbooks set out to create among the students a hatred for India and the Hindus, both in the historical context and as part of current politics. The most common methods to achieve this end are: to offer slanted descriptions of Hindu religion and culture, calling them "unclean" and "inferior"; to praise Muslim rule over the Hindus for having put an end to all "bad" Hindu religious beliefs and practices and thus eliminated classical Hinduism from India (both claims being false); to show that the Indian National Congress was purely a Hindu body ... This is done with a view to contrasting the alleged false colors and loyalty of the Congress with the purity and nationalistic spirit of the All India Muslim League; to assert

that the communal riots accompanying and following the partition of 1947 were initiated exclusively by the Hindus and Sikhs, and that the Muslims were at no place and time aggressors but merely helpless victims; to allot generous and undue space to a study of wars with India (1993: 193–94).

A recent rewriting of the history of the Indian subcontinent—allegedly covering prehistory to 1947—argues that the Indus region (Pakistan) has a primordial existence outside India with a centrifugal force of its own (Ahsan 1996). The essential purpose of this work, in the words of its author, is "to discover and define the Indus person, the Pakistani citizen." The history states that Pakistan is said to have existed "for almost five and half of the last six thousand years," and emphasizes that "Indus has seldom been a part of India." It therefore concludes that:

The essential differences between Indus and India are civilizational and cultural. These differences are deep-rooted, primordial and many. To restrict the differences merely to those of religion is to refuse to comprehend the issue. Fundamentalists on both sides are doing just that, and thereby exacerbating tensions and acrimony. Of the all-pervading differences, the religious difference is only one aspect but, as Iqbal and Jinnah implied, it is not the whole. If this were understood ... there would perhaps be less reason for conflict, and more peaceful co-existence between India and Pakistan. Pakistanis would be more confident of themselves. The Indians would also perhaps understand the irresistible centrifugal pull being exerted today by the Kashmiris who have, throughout history, formed an integral part of the Indus region (Ahsan 1996: 349).

The thesis that holds *The Indus Saga* together is that the creation of Pakistan was the culmination of the primordial division between the Indus region of the subcontinent to the west of the Gurdaspur-Kathiawar Salient and the remainder of India (see Figure 1). In drawing this too convenient cultural and geographical divide, Ahsan dismisses as myth the view of Indian oneness. The differences between Indus and India are depicted as "civilizational" and "cultural," and not merely religious. Material is then carefully selected from the Mohenjodaro era (2500–1500 BC) onward to support this ingenious refashioning of the Muslim League's historic two-nation thesis.

In addition to, and in conjunction with, these historical arguments, geography (or rather geohistory) also plays an important role in cultivating a sense of threat in Pakistan, particularly in legitimating the concept of spatial vulnerability. The militant anti-India and anti-Hindu rhetoric in Pakistan often compares the "smallness" of Pakistan's territory with the large space that India enjoys. Bitter memories of partition—and its devastating consequences, ranging from geographical, cultural, and social through economic and administrative—are also kept alive in one form or another. In the case of Pakistan, the partition of Punjab in August 1947 turned out to be politically far more significant than the partition of Bengal since it determined political attitudes toward India, the composition of the governing elite, and commitment to the "cause" of Kashmir.

Figure 1. The Historical Watershed

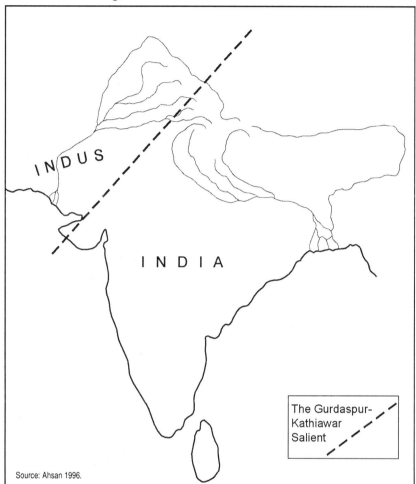

The Gurdaspur-
Kathiawar
Salient

Source: Ahsan 1996.

In less than five weeks in 1947, following no natural geographical features, Sir Cyril Radcliff drew up a complex boundary to divide a province of more than 36 million people (16 million Muslims, 15 million Hindus, and 5 million Sikhs, who, despite their religious differences, shared a common culture, language, and history), thousands of villages, towns, and cities, and a unified and integrated system of canals and communication networks (see Figure 2). There was almost no time to inspect the lands or the communities that this boundary would run through. Purewal (1997) has discussed at length the disruptive nature of the partition of Punjab and the long-term effects that partition-related migration has had on low-income (especially low-caste) groups who were uprooted from their native surroundings, livelihoods, and homes.

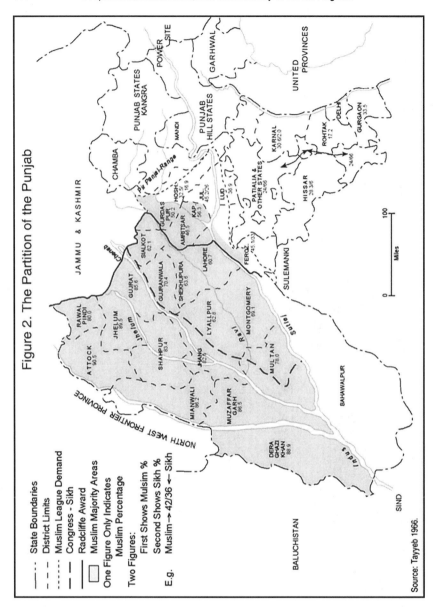

Figure 2. The Partition of the Punjab

"Secure" Borderlands and "Insecure" Communities on National Peripheries

On both sides of the India-Pakistan borders there are communities whose inhabitants' lives are abstracted, and in some cases even dehumanized, by concepts of citizenship, sovereignty, and territoriality. Such notions draw border people away from the border, toward the centers of power and culture within the state. Statecraft often glosses over the fact that borderlanders often migrate because of the cross-border pull of shared ethno-religious ties.

Evidence of restlessness in the borderlands is often a cause of serious worry to the ruling elite, but does not necessarily cause them to pay serious attention in the form of ecologically sustainable and socially just development. A large number of Indian and Pakistani border area communities remain physically and mentally isolated from the rest of their country. One Indian village, Kuria Beri, typifies a string of nearly sixty settlements that dot the almost inaccessible center of the Thar Desert in Rajasthan, bordering Pakistan, as it cries out for socioeconomic development. The sorry state of affairs in these villages is graphically described in the words of a keen press reporter from the area:

> Cut to reality: No electricity; no kerosene; only darkness and 15 families wading through it with just those pairs of tired eyes from the beginning of time. A pregnant woman with no hospital to go to, no medicines to take. A horde of generations far removed from the school black board. Young men out in the jungles grazing their cattle 12 days to a fortnight. Malaria, night-blindness, genetic disorders, malnutrition. And an accompanying graveyard bigger than the village itself … a Muslim village, it has nothing of its own, except for the ground below, the sky above and a shrinking cattle population. The food, as in *bajra*, comes from the Ramgarh *kasba* 43 km away. Mode of transport: human feet. Visits: once in six months, sometimes even longer (Rao 2000: 1).

Donnan and Wilson define alienated borderlands as those where routine cross-border exchange is prevented due to tensions and animosity between their respective states and/or border populations" (1999: 51). As long as the communities of such alienated borderlands in Rajasthan know that close to their homes India ends and Pakistan begins, that there is a fence that should not be crossed by either men or cattle, and that there are those on the other side who will give them incentive to spy or smuggle, life is considered more or less normal" and "under control" by the authorities.

Yet the inhabitants of such forgotten communities are never above suspicion. They are often alleged as long having been unwitting smugglers of inconsequential items or petty commodities like the *chappals* (sandals) needed by those on the other side of the border. According to official reports, "slowly these people were cultivated by Pakistan's ISI which became active in 1971. They used them as conduits of information and later also sneaked in arms and narcotics in their goods consignments" (Rao 2000). However, much to the relief of state agencies, "ever since the border fence came up, these so-called smugglers have been forced back to their cattle, except for a hardcore few who have spread a network of narcotics pushers" (Rao 2000).

The border region in the Indian Punjab is also being secured in response to the perceived designs of the hostile neighbor, and fenced to protect the nation and its inhabitants from perceived external threats. During the 1960s, industries were not established in the Indian Panjab because it was perceived to be a border state. During the 1980s, terrorism ensured that even traditional industries—such as hosiery and bicycle making—moved to neighboring Haryana. The apparent crux of the problem was that the nonagricultural sector, which could have absorbed a sizable percentage of the educated youth, has failed to take off (Arora 1998: 9). The border areas of this border state suffer the most due to lack of infrastructure development, tardy growth, and poor border roads. The problem of financially compensating the farmers whose land fell between the fence and the international border has not been resolved, nor have special budgetary allocations to border areas for implementing various social and community development programs.

In the partitioned Punjab, the international boundary between India and Pakistan is about 343 miles (553 kilometers) long, about 70 (113) of which are in river areas. Policing the international border (which is the central task of the Border Security Force–BSF) in this riverine belt is not easy, partly because the Ravi River enters Pakistan from India 13 times, and runs from Pakistan into India 12 times; and the Satluj River runs from India into Pakistan 11 times, and goes from Pakistan into India 10 times (see Figure 3). The roughly 279 miles (450 kilometers) of constructed fencing on the Indian side of the international boundary in Punjab was completed between 1988 and 1993.

Muthianwala, a village located on the bank of the Satluj River a couple of hundred meters from the international border, exemplifies the communities on both sides of the border in this region. It has a total population of about one thousand, of which about four hundred are eligible voters. Many of the two hundred or so youth of this village are unemployed. Among the 200 children studying in a Government Primary School (virtually run by BSF personnel since few are willing to teach in a border school), only 30 to 35 go on to the high school located about three miles (five kilometers) away in the village of Toot. Most are deprived of even basic health facilities since the nearest health center is also in Toot. As many as fifty Muthianwala families have land (for an approximate total of 300 acres) between the fence and the international border. The villagers seem to have reconciled themselves somehow to their existence as a border community, but the experience of having to carry identity cards while tilling their own land under the gaze of the BSF can be extremely alienating. Although a number of households have a television set, there is not a single telephone in the village. Moreover, the soil is such that even moderate showers create nearly impassable mud that renders Toot almost inaccessible. In a nutshell, this author found Muthianwala quite remote and marginal compared to either the rest of Punjab or to the country as a whole. It remains within what David Sibley describes as "zones of ambiguity," where danger and uncertainty prevail (1995: 32–33). For the people of this border region, their homelands are no more than "a zone of abjection, one which should be eliminated in order to reduce anxiety, but this is not always possible. Individuals lack the power to organize their world into crisp sets and so eliminate spaces of ambiguity" (Sibley 1995). Such communities have yet to gain control of even their day-to-day lives.

Figure 3. The Radcliffe Award—Punjab-Lahore-Amritsar-Gurdaspur
Districts: Communal Distribution

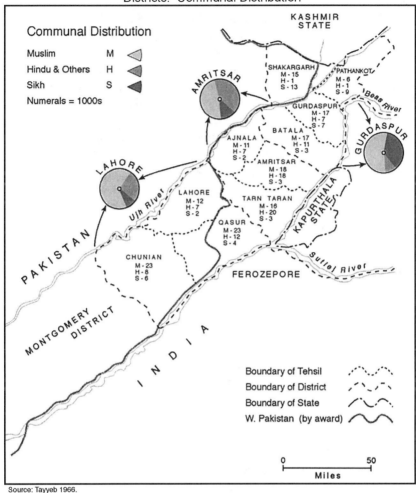

Source: Tayyeb 1966.

Epilogue: Enemies and the Border War at Kargil

Both India and Pakistan, as Sumantra Bose points out, "have chosen to make possession of Kashmir central to their respective national ideologies—secular nationalism in the case of India, and Muslim nationalism in the case of Pakistan" (1999: 1,523). The cartographic anxiety of two hostile neighbors reached its zenith during May 1999 in the Kargil conflict in Jammu and Kahsmir, the northernmost state of the Indian Union. It was exactly one year after India and Pakistan conducted nuclear tests, and in the wake of Indian Prime Minister Atal Bihari Vajpayee's symbolic ride to Pakistan (February 1999) on the first run of bus service between New Delhi and the Pakistani city of Lahore. Along a barren mountainous stretch of the 496-mile (800-kilometer) line of control, a localized war between the two countries erupted near the Indian town of Kargil on the disputed Kashmir border.

All histories of conflict are replete with enemies. But the Kargil conflict (or "war" as some prefer to call it) between India and Pakistan proved to be a mega-exercise for both countries in what Tidwell has termed "enmification" (1998). Even though the causes of conflict over Kashmir/Kargil are deeper than the drive to create enemies, examining the Kargil conflict from the perspective of "enmification" is illuminating. Although it was not the cause of the conflict, enmification certainly prolongs and perpetuates conflict. Its sudden and dramatic eruption, as in Kargil, not only forced boundary-crossing policies of civil societies to become defensive, it also injected a strong dose of emotion into the boundary-reinforcing geopolitical discourses of the ruling elite.

With much dramatic effect, the Kargil episode proved beyond a doubt that enmity, more often than not, is a dangerous and destructive force that is responsible for many tragedies. To quote Tidwell:

> An enemy is, in some ways, an opponent, but also much more. An enemy is a value-laden, emotionally charged entity, one that is the recipient of specific negative value connotations and meanings. Enmification is the process of creating negative value associations with an opponent ... Regardless of the source of enmity, however, it manifests itself in dividing the world up between "them" and "us" ... poor behaviour on the part of them is attributed to their character and personality, whereas the same behaviour engaged in by us is excused and explained by situational factors ... People forgive their own trespasses more readily than they forgive those who trespass against them. Not only do people forgive themselves, but also through the process ... of enmification engage in acts of incredible cruelty (1998: 127).

It is not surprising, then, that during the Kargil conflict, both sides of the line of control spewed out what the South Asia bureau chief of *The Washington Post*, Pamela Constable, rightly calls "competing versions of elusive truths" (1999). Indian authorities reported that the Pakistani fighters were committing gruesome atrocities in the heights. Even as vehemently contradictory reports of Indian troops committing similar acts came in, the authorities insisted that India treated the wounded and the dead from the opposing side with due respect and protocol.

According to a report in the June 5 issue of the New Delhi *Hindu*, the battle over the borders near Kargil left nearly 21,000 people homeless during May 1999 alone, turning Kargil and Drass into ghost towns. The Kargil conflict also affected border areas in Punjab. According to official estimates, 80 to 90 percent of the populations of the 166 villages along the border in Gurdaspur, Batala, Amritsar, Majitha, and Tarn Taran districts migrated to Punjab. On June 27, the New Delhi *Hindu* reported that about 1.80 *lakh* (180,000) of an approximately 3.35 *lakh* (335,000) population migrated after the troop buildup in the area. *Dawn*, the leading Pakistani daily from Karachi, reported on June 16 that 300,000 people were hit by cross-border shelling in the so-called *Azad* Kashmir, which India refers to as Pakistan Occupied Kashmir (POK). According to one estimate (Manchanda 1999: 23), over the past 10 years of insurgency in the Kashmir valley and the border hill districts that girdle the center of conflict, more than half a million people from both sides of the line of control have been displaced. According to the same source, the exodus includes 200,000 Kashmiri Hindu Pandits and 70,000 Kashmiri Muslims to India, and 120,000 Kashmiri Muslims to Pakistan. From Kargil and the border districts, some 35,000 people have been displaced in Pakistan, and 100,000 in India.

What clearly emerges from this account of shattered lives and homes is that the civilian populations of both India and Pakistan are suffering the most from the conflict in Kashmir. Since one of the primary weapons in this conflict is artillery fire, shelling aimed at villages does not discriminate between military and civilian targets. Many border villages are the only known and reachable targets. Whether intentionally or not, both sides are destroying civilian property and creating thousands of displaced people.

The escapees of the Kargil War may somehow survive, but for the thousands of displaced, can there ever be a return to the "homeland," a return to what one highly perceptive observer calls a "remembered society imbued in the ethos of Kashmiriyat, i.e., a common Muslim-Pandit identity built around a shared history, language and culture?" (Manchanda 1999: 23). For those concerned with mental boundaries and borders, it is of interest to note that in the past decade or so there has been a hardening of the Islamicization of a reconstructed Kashmiri identity. Manchanda goes on to say that "symbolic of the new Islamicised Kashmir is the fact that many more women are wearing burqua." Equally worrisome, says Manchanda, is that " ... a generation has grown up in the valley and camps, which has no memory beyond the bitterness of the Pandit-Muslim divide. School children have learnt to view the Hindu as 'the other.' 'Hindus, drink urine!' a student of the elite Burn Hall school said to me. In Poonch, a group of young schoolgirls I stopped to chat with, wanted, first of all to know, 'what is your religion?'"

Conclusions

This paper has attempted to examine boundary-producing discourses in India and Pakistan as integral parts of these states' geopolitical quest for secure and safe spaces. Internal and external threats are being used to raise basic existential issues that face India and Pakistan as states, and the peoples that make up their societies. This study looks at how India and Pakistan have become, in each other's geopolitical imaginations, dangerous and silent places outside familiar boundaries. Selective use of media representations of purity and defilement, plentifully evident during the Kargil War, further exaggerates the extent to which this opposition figures in state-centric geopolitical doctrines.

All over South Asia, sovereign states continue to construct their national identities and delineate borders through policies that are hostile to diversity. Border communities are rendered peripheral and marginal by the power centers' formal geopolitical reasoning, as geographical thinking and systems of power perceive border regions as zones of suspicion and uncertainty.

The complex interplay of space and politics and identities and ideologies continues to undermine attempts by boundary-producing policies to stake out territory and to secure Indo-Pak borders. So far, Indian and Pakistani efforts to completely demarcate borders, which includes India's fencing of its borderlands (with the exception of Jammu and Kashmir), may have yielded some results in tackling the problems of "clandestine" migration across the borders, and smuggling or trafficking arms, drugs, or insurgencies. However, such rigid demarcation also works against topography, economy, ecology, kinship networks, and other links in the region.

Ecologically sustainable, socially just, and gender sensitive development of Indo-Pak border regions demands, first and foremost, liberating South Asian borderlands from their imperial legacies. As O'Tuathail states, "critical geopolitics is one of the many cultures of resistance to Geography as imperial truth, state-capitalized knowledge, and military weapon. It is a small part of a much larger rainbow struggle to decolonize our inherited geographical imagination so that other geo-graphings and other worlds might be possible" (1996: 256). A "new" geopolitical imagination is called for in South Asia: a humane people-centric imagination that takes borderlands seriously as the setting for human life—in all its diversity—and necessitates an understanding of national and regional politics in terms of their impact on the material welfare, cultural identities, and basic human rights of borderlanders.

References

Ahmed, Imtiaz. 1997. "Maldevelopment, Environmental Insecurity and Militarism in South Asia." Pp. 171–200 in *Sustainable Development: Environmental Security, Disarmament and Development Interface in South Asia*, D.D. Khanna, ed. Delhi: Macmillan.

Ahsan, A. 1996. *The Indus Saga and the Making of Pakistan*. Karachi: Oxford University Press.

Ali, D., ed. 1999. *Invoking the Past: The Uses of History in South Asia*. Delhi: Oxford University Press.

Arora, K. 1998. "Unemployment Haunts Youth in Punjab." *The Tribune* (Chandigarh) (10 December): 9.

Aziz, K.K. 1993. *The Murder of History: A Critique of History Textbooks Used in Pakistan*. Lahore: Vanguard.

Banerjee, P. 1998. "To Re-Instate Historians in the History of Border." Paper presented at the Asian Geopolitics: Borders and Transborder Flows seminar, 23–24 March, New Delhi, India.

Barth, F. 1996. "Introduction." Pp. 1–3 in *Ethnic Groups and Boundaries: The Social Organization of Cultural Difference*, F. Barth, ed. Boston: Little, Brown & Company.

Behera, N.C. 1998. "Perpetuating the Divide: Political Abuses of History in South Asia." *Indian Journal of Secularism* 1 (4): 53–71.

Bhambhri, C.P. 1998. "BJP Agenda: Hidden or Real?" *The Pioneer* (New Delhi) (15 April).

Bose, Sumantra. 1997. "'Hindu Nationalism' and the Crisis of the Indian State: A Theoretical Perspective." Pp. 50–75 in *Nationalism, Democracy and Development: State and Politics in India*, S. Bose and A. Jalal, eds. Calcutta: Oxford University Press.

Bose, Sumantra. 1999. "Kashmir: Sources of Conflict, Dimensions of Peace." *Survival* 41 (3): 149–71.

Constable, Pamela. 1999. "Selective Truths." Pp. 35–61 in *Guns and Roses: Essays on the Kargil War*. New Delhi: Harpers Collins Publishers.

Dalby, S. 1990. "American Security Discourse: The Persistence of Geopolitics." *Political Geography Quarterly* 9 (2): 171–88.

Dalby, S. 1991. "Critical Geopolitics: Discourse, Difference and Dissent." *Environment and Planning. D: Society and Space* 9 (3): 261–83.

Dalby, S., and G. Ó Tuathail. 1996. "Editorial Introduction. The Critical Geopolitics Constellation: Problematizing Fusions of Geographical Knowledge and Power." *Political Geography* 15 (6/7): 451–56.

Dijkink, G. 1996. *National Identity and Geopolitical Visions: Maps of Pride and Pain*. London: Routledge.

Dixit, J.N. 1995. *Anatomy of a Flawed Inheritance: India-Pakistan Relations 1971–1994*. Delhi: Ajanta Publications.

Dixit, J.N. 1998. "Blasting a Straitjacket." *Outlook* (New Delhi) (1 June).

Dodds, K.J., and J.D. Sidaway. 1994. "Locating Critical Geopolitics." *Environment and Planning. D: Society and Space* 12: 515–24.

Donnan, H., and T.M. Wilson. 1999. *Borders: Frontiers of Identity, Nation and State*. Oxford: Berg.

Eva, F. 1994. "From Boundaries to Borderlands: New Horizons for Geopolitics." Pp. 372–80 in *Political Boundaries and Co-Existence*, H. Glausser, ed. Bern: Peter Lang.

Frei, F. 1986. *Perceived Images: U.S. and Soviet Assumptions and Perceptions in Disarmament*. New Jersey: Rowman and Allanheld.

Graham, B. 1993. *Hindu Nationalism and Indian Politics: The Origins and Development of the Bharatiya Jana Sangh*. Cambridge: Cambridge University Press.

Hansen, T.B. 1999. *The Saffron Wave: Democracy and Hindu Nationalism in Modern India*. Delhi: Oxford University Press.

Hasan, M. 1996. "The Myth of Unity: Colonial and National Narratives." Pp. 185–208 in *Making India Hindu: Religion, Community, and the Politics of Democracy in India*, D. Ludden, ed. Delhi: Oxford University Press.

Hodson, H.V. 1997. *The Great Divide: Britain-India-Pakistan*. Karachi: Oxford University Press.

Jain, S. 1998. "Pakistan's 'Cricket Match' Mindset." *The Pioneer* (New Delhi) (18 June): 8.

Kak, M.L. 1998. "Confidence Replaces Terror." *The Tribune* (Chandigarh) (2 December): 13.

Karlekar, H. 1998. "Are They Suffering from a Death Wish?" *The Pioneer* (New Delhi) (19 June): 8.

Katzenstein, M.F., U.S. Mehta, and U. Thakkar. 1998. "The Rebirth of Shiv Sena in Maharashtra: The Symbiosis of Discursive and Institutional Power. Pp. 215–38 in *Community Conflicts and the State in India*, A. Basu and A. Kohli, eds. Delhi: Oxford University Press.

Kaviraj, S. 1994. "Crisis of the Nation-State in India." *Political Studies* 42: 115–29.

Khattak, S.G. 1996. "Security Discourses and the State in Pakistan." *Alternatives, Journal of Social Transformation and Humane Governance* 21: 341–62.

Khilnani, S. 1998. *The Idea of India*. London: Penguin Books.

Kothari, R. 1998. *Communalism in Indian Politics*. Ahmedabad: Rainbow Publishers, Ltd.

Krishna, S. 1994. "Cartographic Anxiety: Mapping the Body Politic in India." *Alternatives, Journal of Social Transformation and Humane Governance* 19: 507–21.

Ludden, D., ed. 1996. *Making India Hindu: Religion, Community, and the Politics of Democracy in India*. Delhi: Oxford University Press.

Maheshwari, A. 1998. "The Face behind the Mask." *The Hindustan Times Sunday Magazine* (New Delhi) (8 August): 1.

Malik, Y.K., and Singh, Y.B. 1994. *Hindu Nationalists in India: The Rise of the Bharatiya Janata Party*. New Delhi: Vistaar Publications.

Manchanda, R. 1999. "Barricaded Kashmiri Pandits: Letting Go the Right to Return." *Refugee Watch* 7: 23–25.

Mroz, J.E. 1980. *Beyond Security: Private Perceptions among Arabs and Israelis*. New York: Pergamon.

Nandy, A., S. Trivedi, Mayaram, and A. Yagnik, eds. 1995. *Creating a Nationality: The Ramjanmbhumi Movement and the Fear of the Self*. Delhi: Oxford University Press.

Nehru, J. 1946. *The Discovery of India*, Reprint. Delhi: Jawaharlal Nehru Memorial Fund, Oxford University Press, 1981.

Ó Tuathail, G. 1994. "(Dis)placing Geopolitics: Writing on the Maps of Global Politics." *Environment and Planning. D: Society and Space* 12 (5): 525–46.

Ó Tuathail, G. 1996. *Critical Geopolitics: The Politics of Writing Global Space.* London: Routledge.

Ó Tuathail, G., and J. Agnew. 1992. "Geopolitics and Foreign Policy: Practical Geopolitical Reasoning in American Foreign Policy." *Political Geography* 11: 190–204.

Paasi, A. 1994. "The Changing of Boundaries: The Finnish-Russian Border as an Example." Pp. 103–11 in *Political Boundaries and Co-Existence*, H. Glausser, ed. Bern: Peter Lang.

Paasi, A. 1996. *Territories, Boundaries and Consciousness: The Changing Geographies of the Finnish-Russian Border*. Chichester: John Wiley & Sons.

Paasi, A. 1998. "Boundaries as Social Processes: Territoriality in the World of Flows." *Geopolitics* 3 (1): 69–88.

Paasi, A. 1999. "Nationalising Everyday Life: Individual and Collective Identities as Practice and Discourse." *Geography Research Forum* 19: 4–21.

Panikkar, K.N. 1998. "The Color of Education." *The Hindustan Times* (New Delhi) (31 October): 13.

Pasha, M.K. 1996. "Security as Hegemony." *Alternatives, Journal of Social Transformation and Humane Governance* 21 (3): 283–302.

Pattanaik, D.D. 1998. *Hindu Nationalism in India: Conceptual Foundation*. New Delhi: Deep & Deep Publications.

Purewal, N.K. 1997. "Displaced Communities: Some Impacts of Partition on Poor Communities." *International Journal of Punjab Studies* 4 (1): 129–45.

Rao, M. 2000. "Classic Case of Desertion." *The Pioneer* (New Delhi) (7 May): 1.

Rygiel, K. 1998. "Stabilizing Borders: The Geopolitics of National Identity Construction in Turkey." Pp. 106–30 in *Rethinking Geopolitics*, G. Ó Tuathail and S. Dalby, eds. London: Routledge.

Samaddar, R. 1997. "Understanding Migratory Flows in South Asia: A Humanitarian Agenda." Pp. 70–86 in *States, Citizens and Outsiders: The Uprooted Peoples of South Asia*, T.K. Bose and R. Manchanda, eds. Kathmandu: South Asia Forum for Human Rights.

Samaddar, R. 1998. *Marginal Nation: Transborder Migration from Bangladesh to West Bengal*. New Delhi: Sage.

Sibley, David. 1988. "The Purification of Space." *Environment and Planning. D: Society and Space* 6: 409–21.

Sibley, David. 1995. *Geographies of Exclusion: Society and Difference in the West*. London: Routledge.

Singh, S. 1998. "India's Security Concerns: Merger of Border Forces Needed." *The Tribune* (Chandigarh) (5 December).

Tai Yong, T. 1997. "Sir Cyril Goes to India: Partition, Boundary-Making and Disruptions in the Punjab." *International Journal of Punjab Studies* 4 (1): 1–19.

Tayyeb, A. 1966. *Pakistan: A Political Geography*. London: Oxford University Press.

Tidwell, A.C. 1998. *Conflict Resolved? A Critical Assessment of Conflict Resolution*. London: Pinter.

Varshney, A. 1993. "Contesting Meanings: India's National Identity, Hindu Nationalism, and the Politics of Anxiety." *Daedalus* 122 (3): 227–61.

Waseem, M. 1997. "Partition, Migration and Assimilation: A Comparative Study of Pakistani Punjab." *International Journal of Punjab Studies* 4 (1): 21–41.

Waterman, S. 1994. "Boundaries and the Changing World Political Order." Pp. 23–35 in *Global Boundaries, Vol. I of World Boundaries*, C.H. Schofield, ed. London: Routledge.

Withey, S., and D. Katz. 1965. "The Social Psychology of Human Conflict." Pp. 64–90 in *The Nature of Human Conflict*, E.B. McNeil, ed. Englewood Cliffs: Prentice Hall.

Index